Handbook of Leadership Theory and Practice

HANDBOOK OF LEADERSHIP THEORY AND PRACTICE

An HBS Centennial Colloquium on
Advancing Leadership

EDITED BY

Nitin Nohria
Rakesh Khurana

Harvard Business Press
BOSTON, MASSACHUSETTS

Library of Congress Cataloging-in-Publication Data

Handbook of leadership theory and practice / edited by Nitin Nohria & Rakesh Khurana.

   p. cm.

ISBN 978-1-4221-3879-3 (hardcover : alk. paper)

1. Leadership.　2. Executive ability.　3. International business enterprises.
I. Nohria, Nitin, 1962- II. Khurana, Rakesh, 1948-

HD57.7.H3564 2009

658.4'092—dc22

                    2009021185

We dedicate this book to Sumantra Ghoshal and Aage Sorensen, our dearest and most demanding intellectual mentors, whose untimely deaths we still mourn, yet whose inspiration still burns brightly in our hearts and minds.

Contents

Acknowledgments   xii

SECTION ONE

THE IMPACT OF LEADERSHIP: PERFORMANCE AND MEANING

Chapter 1

Advancing Leadership Theory and Practice

Nitin Nohria and Rakesh Khurana (Harvard Business School)

3

Chapter 2

When Does Leadership Matter? A Contingent Opportunities
View of CEO Leadership

Noam Wasserman, Bharat Anand, and Nitin Nohria (Harvard Business School)

27

Chapter 3

Revisiting the Meaning of Leadership

*Joel M. Podolny (Apple, Inc.), Rakesh Khurana (Harvard Business School), and
Marya L. Besharov (Cornell School of Industrial and Labor Relations)*

65

Chapter 4

What Is This Thing Called Leadership?

J. Richard Hackman (Harvard University)

107

SECTION TWO

The Theory of Leadership: Personal Attributes, Functions, and Relationships

Chapters that take stock of different disciplinary perspectives on leadership and articulate an agenda for future research

Chapter 5

Leadership Through an Organization Behavior Lens: A Look at the Last Half-Century of Research

Mary Ann Glynn and Rich DeJordy (Boston College)

119

Chapter 6

Psychological Perspectives on Leadership

Jennifer A. Chatman and Jessica A. Kennedy
(University of California, Berkeley)

159

Chapter 7

A Clinical Approach to the Dynamics of Leadership and Executive Transformation

Manfred Kets de Vries and Elisabet Engellau (INSEAD)

183

Chapter 8

Classical Sociological Approaches to the Study of Leadership

Mauro F. Guillén (Wharton School, University of Pennsylvania)

223

Chapter 9

Economists' Perspectives on Leadership

Patrick Bolton (Columbia University), Markus K. Brunnermeier
(Princeton University), and Laura Veldkamp
(New York University)

239

Chapter 10

An Economic Perspective on Leadership

Mark A. Zupan (University of Rochester)

265

Chapter 11

Leadership and History

Walter A. Friedman (Harvard Business School)

291

Chapter 12

Power and Leadership

Joseph S. Nye, Jr. (Harvard Kennedy School of Government)

305

SECTION THREE

THE VARIABILITY OF LEADERSHIP: WHAT'S CORE AND
CONTINGENT

*Chapters exploring similarities and differences in leadership across task,
culture, and identity*

Chapter 13

Leadership and Cultural Context: A Theoretical and Empirical
Examination Based on Project GLOBE

*Mansour Javidan (Thunderbird Business School), Peter W. Dorfman (New Mexico State
University), Jon Paul Howell (New Mexico State University), and Paul J. Hanges
(University of Maryland)*

335

Chapter 14

Women and Leadership: Defining the Challenges

Robin J. Ely (Harvard Business School) and Deborah L. Rhode (Stanford Law School)

377

Chapter 15

A Contingency Theory of Leadership

Jay Lorsch (Harvard Business School)

411

SECTION FOUR

THE PRACTICE OF LEADERSHIP: AGENCY AND CONSTRAINT

Chapters on the multiple facets of leadership practice

Chapter 16

What Is Leadership? The CEO's Role in Large, Complex Organizations

Michael E. Porter and Nitin Nohria (Harvard Business School)

433

Chapter 17

What Makes Teams of Leaders Leadable?

Ruth Wageman and J. Richard Hackman (Harvard University)

475

Chapter 18

Decision Making as Leadership Foundation

Michael Useem (Wharton School, University of Pennsylvania)

507

Chapter 19

Leading Change: Leadership, Organization, and Social Movements

Marshall Ganz (Harvard Kennedy School of Government)

527

Chapter 20

Leadership in a Globalizing World

Rosabeth Moss Kanter (Harvard Business School)

569

Chapter 21

Unlocking the Slices of Genius in Your Organization: Leading for Innovation

Linda A. Hill (Harvard Business School), Maurizio Travaglini (Architects of Group Genius), Greg Brandeau (Pixar Animation Studios), and Emily Stecker (Harvard Business School)

611

SECTION FIVE

THE DEVELOPMENT OF LEADERS: KNOWING, DOING, AND BEING

Chapters on the development of leaders

Chapter 22

Identity-Based Leader Development

*Herminia Ibarra (INSEAD), Scott Snook (Harvard Business School),
and Laura Guillén Ramo (INSEAD)*

657

Chapter 23

The Experience Conundrum

Morgan W. McCall, Jr. (University of Southern California)

679

Chapter 24

Leadership Development Interventions: Ensuring a Return on the Investment

Jay A. Conger (Claremont McKenna College)

709

Chapter 25

Pursuing Authentic Leadership Development

Bruce J. Avolio (University of Washington)

739

Chapter 26

Adult Development and Organizational Leadership

Robert Kegan and Lisa Lahey (Harvard Graduate School of Education)

769

Index   789

About the Contributors   807

About the Editors   821

ACKNOWLEDGMENTS

THIS VOLUME resulted from a colloquium that was organized as part of the centennial celebrations of Harvard Business School. The centennial provided an extraordinary opportunity for the school, and for us as faculty members, to take stock of our past and to imagine our future. It is in this crucible of reflection that we discovered how far leadership research now lagged the espoused mission of most business schools—to educate leaders—and how urgent the need was to spur scholarship on this topic. We thank Harvard Business School and the organizers of our centennial events for the opportunity and resources to organize this conference and publish this edited volume. Special thanks go to Dean Jay Light, who was a champion of this project from the very start; to John Quelch, who was the overseer of the entire centennial celebration; to Warren McFarlan, whose unflagging support and endless resourcefulness enabled us to stretch our imaginations and do things we would not otherwise have dreamt of; and to Srikant Datar, who as dean of the Division of Research provided generous intellectual and financial resources.

Within Harvard Business School, our conference was organized under the aegis of the Leadership Initiative, an interdisciplinary initiative whose purpose is to stimulate leadership research and teaching across the school. We are grateful to Linda Hill, the chair of the initiative, for partnering with us every step of the way and for helping us convene this conference and produce this volume. We are equally thankful to Tony Mayo, the Director of the Leadership Initiative, who is the prototype of the quiet leader—someone who leads without any need to be noticed, but without whom nothing would ever get done. We are just as thankful for the tireless behind the scenes support of the rest of the Leadership Initiative team, Letty Garcia and Amanda Pepper.

There aren't enough words or ways that we can thank Meg Gardner, our conference coordinator. But for her countless e-mails, phone calls, reminders, and follow-ups, we would never have been able to organize ourselves, let alone the conference. It was her endless patience and infinite persistence that also ensured that the people we invited attended, and those we asked to write papers for the conference and this volume turned them in on time. Meg was also our interface with the rest of the HBS centennial organization, who helped us in many visible and invisible ways. We are especially grateful to Eileen Keohane and Chris Ramsay and their team from Harvard's centennial planning committee.

The person whose generosity and creativity had the greatest impact on our colloquium was Maurizio Travaglini. He and his associates at Architects of Group Genius created a physical and intellectual space and a program that enabled all of us to have a dialogue on leadership that felt fresh and forward-looking. They were responsible for creating the spirit of the conference, and we will forever be grateful for that. They remind us that one of the most important leadership tasks is creating a space where good things can happen.

We are grateful to Deborah Blagg, Margaret Kelley, and especially Laura Singleton (who did the major share of this work) for preparing executive summaries of the articles in this book, which helped conference participants familiarize themselves with these ideas and participate in our discussions. Thanks in the same spirit are also due to Martha Spaulding from the *Harvard Business Review*, who helped write a great case that sparked a spirited discussion on the challenges of managing a diverse global leadership team, and to our colleague David Thomas, who led this case discussion with inimitable flair.

Organizing a conference and pulling together an edited volume is more work than we had imagined, and a lot of the unexpected burden fell on our assistants Debby Bell, Meredith Cook, and Clair Linzey, who bore it with good humor and grace. We are especially grateful to Clair for her tireless efforts in assembling the final volume to get it ready to send to our publishers, from working with authors to secure their permissions, to checking all the references and tables, to putting it all together in the right format and order.

Our editor at HBS Press, Melinda Merino, deserves a medal of honor for having the courage to pursue the publication of this book, which breaks so many of HBSP's norms. It is an edited volume, it is long, it is not aimed at a trade audience, and it is a big sprawling book on a big sprawling topic. Yet, Melinda always saw what we did—the need to promote serious scholarship on leadership and the possibility of this book to catalyze research in this important area. We are grateful for her support and her imagination, which will allow each of the chapters in this book to be available in electronic form, so that they can be ordered and assigned on an individual basis.

We owe a debt to our families, who patiently suffered our absence as we worked through the organization of this conference and the production of this edited volume.

We also want to thank Mike Jensen and Gregg Gordon, the founders of SSRN, who inspired and helped us launch the Leadership Research Network (LRN), an electronic journal that is part of the ever-expanding SSRN family. LRN will provide a place for leadership scholars to electronically publish both their work in progress and their published work, and help to disseminate it more quickly and broadly.

Last, but not least, we must thank the participants at our conference and the contributors to this volume. Leadership is a collective enterprise, and it is the joint effort and commitment of all who joined us and gave us their invaluable time and intellectual effort that has made this volume possible. Let's hope it fulfills our collective aspiration to stimulate new research in the field of leadership.

SECTION ONE

THE IMPACT OF LEADERSHIP

Performance and Meaning

I

ADVANCING LEADERSHIP THEORY AND PRACTICE

Nitin Nohria and Rakesh Khurana

THIS EDITED volume has one primary purpose—to stimulate serious scholarly research on leadership. At a time when societies around the world are crying out for more and better leadership, when our current leaders (especially in business, but also in government and other spheres of public life) have lost legitimacy, questions are being asked, sometimes angrily, of the institutions that school these leaders: What kinds of leaders are these institutions developing that have caused so much hardship for so many? Are these institutions developing leaders who have the competence and character necessary to lead the web of complex institutions that have become so vital to the collective health of modern societies? What is the vision or model of leadership that animates the curriculum and developmental models in these institutions? If there is such a model, does it need to be revisited, reexamined, and revised in light of the widespread failures in leadership? Do we really understand what it takes to develop better leaders? What advice can scholars give leaders who are entrusted with the challenges of leading organizations and ensuring their continued viability and prosperity?

Our view, as editors of this volume, is that the current state of scholarly research on leadership doesn't allow us to answer these questions with confidence. Indeed, despite leadership being central to the mission and purpose of most institutions of higher education, there is little serious scholarship and research on leadership in these same schools. This is not a tenable or desirable state of affairs. Institutions of higher education derive their legitimacy from their ability to produce knowledge and develop students who can apply that knowledge in a manner that benefits society. If society expects us to develop better knowledge about leadership and a better ability to develop leaders who will benefit society, we must meet that call or risk undermining our legitimacy (as business schools are now painfully experiencing). This edited volume tries to answer this call by encouraging serious research on leadership. It makes no pretense that we already have the answers to the questions that are being asked about leadership in the world today. Rather, it tries to reinvigorate research on leadership—in as broad a manner as possible, across a wide variety of disciplines—with the hope that we can stimulate new ideas and thinking about leadership, by the best scholars in our institutions, so that we can respond to society's urgent need for better leadership and, in turn, fulfill the espoused mission of our own institutions to develop better leaders who can serve society.

The Gap Between Purpose and Practice in Institutions That Aim to Develop Leaders

Many universities, especially in their graduate programs of business administration, law, education, public health, and public policy, claim that their mission is to educate leaders who will advance the well-being of society in their respective fields. For example, Harvard Business School's formal mission statement is "to educate leaders who make a difference in the world." Dartmouth's Tuck School of Business defines its primary educational goal as preparing "students for leadership positions in the world's foremost organizations." Stanford's business school aims to "develop innovative, principled, and insightful leaders who change the world," and MIT's Sloan School of Management aims to "develop principled, innovative leaders who improve the world."

There are some signs that the adoption of a new leadership mission is having some impact on the field. MIT's Sloan School of Management has developed a new framework built around four leadership capabilities, including sense-making, relating, visioning, and inventing (Ancona et al., 2007). The positive psychology perspective has also incorporated leadership as part of its teaching and research interests (see Ben-Shahar, 2008, as an example). Important research institutions, such as the Social Science Research Network, have introduced a Leadership Research Network as part of activities for collecting and diffusing working papers and teaching materials on leadership. Yet, the reality is still that research on leadership is at best at the periphery rather than the center of most schools that profess to educate the leaders of the future. There are many signs of this intellectual neglect: adjunct rather than tenure track faculty teach most leadership courses; there are few papers on leadership published in the most prominent academic journals; and there are virtually no doctoral courses on leadership.

How can we explain this disconnect between the mission and everyday practice? Perhaps it is because leadership is an elusive construct, riddled with so much ambiguity that it is hard to even define let alone study systematically. Perhaps it is because it is hard to get tenure pursuing research on such a difficult topic. Perhaps it is because it is hard to grasp leadership unless you have been a leader. Whatever the reason, research on leadership has languished in the academy.

Yet, the demand for insights about leadership has only increased over time, and has largely been met by popular writers. Most of the leadership best sellers have been written by consultants, journalists, and by business school academics who were either denied tenure or have broken ranks with their more traditional academic colleagues. Or they have been written by practicing leaders who have attained an iconic status and now want to share their wisdom, secure their legacies, or cash in on their success.

It is easy to enumerate the flaws of this genre of leadership literature: It seldom conforms to the norms of the scientific method; it employs casual and sometimes self-serving empirical evidence; it is rarely grounded in any well-established theoretical tradition. In short, it lacks intellectual rigor. However, in the absence of a credible alternate body of leadership research that is conducted with greater rigor while still being relevant and useful to practice, academics should not complain. We have what we deserve.

Yet, if we continue to allow the thinking on leadership to be framed, defined, and sustained by this popular tradition, we are open to various risks: Will students really take the mission statements of the universities they join seriously? Will they trust that these are the institutions where one can learn to develop one's leadership? Or will they view universities as places where one obtains credentials and connections, and some knowledge, but not lessons about leadership? Will leadership largely be seen as a means of getting ahead, of gaining power, rather than of being understood as a serious professional calling with social responsibilities?

Besides risking our mission being seen as hollow by our students, we risk our mission being seen as hollow by society. If we proclaim that our purpose is to develop leaders who can benefit society, we must dedicate our best minds to understanding what leadership means and how we can best develop leaders who can deliver on our promise to society.

To prevent our mission statements from becoming hollow advertising—or worse, corrupt advertising—we need to reinvigorate serious research and scholarship on leadership. We need to make it an intellectual activity undertaken by the best scholars in the mainstream of the academy. We need to mobilize not only the leading established scholars to refocus their energies toward this topic, but also the next generation of scholars by teaching PhD courses and encouraging dissertations that center on leadership.

The State of Research on Leadership

How does the scholar interested in pursuing research on leadership get started? It is a vast and sprawling field with no clear contours or boundaries, which has been pursued in fits and starts across different disciplines and intellectual traditions.

The colloquium "Leadership: Advancing an Intellectual Discipline" that we organized as part of the Harvard Business School centennial events was aimed at taking a step in this direction. We invited leading scholars from different disciplinary backgrounds to take stock of what we know about leadership and to set an agenda for future research. This volume is the compilation of the papers presented for the conference, supplemented with a few additional papers that help make this a more comprehensive volume on advancing leadership.

Our goal in this volume is to provide a variety of perspectives on different dimensions of leadership, and thereby to convey its multiple meanings, units of analysis, and complexity. The book is organized into sections covering many dimensions of leadership research, from how it has been developed in academic disciplines, to the contingencies that leadership research needs to address if it is to develop as a subject, to the practical and organizational challenges leaders face, to how leaders are developed. By including authors who typically reside in different disciplines, this volume tries to bridge the structural holes across these disciplines. The various sections in the volume also correspond to important questions that we believe need to be addressed if the field of leadership is to advance in organizational research.

Each section centers on one of a set of dualities that cut across the articles in the volume and seem to be at the heart of research on leadership: (1) the duality between the leader's role in producing superior *performance* or results and the leader's role in making *meaning*; (2) the duality between the leader as a special *person* (with a unique personality and character traits, emphasized by disciplines such as history, psychology, and psychoanalysis) and leadership as a *social role* (defined as an influence relationship between the leader and society, emphasized in fields such as sociology, political science, and economics); (3) the duality between leadership being *universal* (there's something in common that unites leaders across all situations and contexts) and leadership being *particular* (each person must lead differently depending on his or her own identity and that of the situation); (4) the duality between the leader's ability to exercise *agency* (the power, influence, will, and ability to do, to act, to change) and the leader's need to attend to *constraints* (such as the organization's history, myriad demands, and constituencies); and (5) the duality between thinking of leader development in terms that emphasize leaders' capacity for *thinking and doing* (which puts an emphasis on various competencies) to *becoming and being* (which puts an emphasis on an evolving identity).

In the remainder of this introduction, we develop these dualities in a bit more detail and show how the papers in each section inform these fundamental tensions in how we think about leadership. We also provide brief summaries of the individual chapters in each section, so that readers have a road map that can help them navigate the large number of papers in this volume. We start, though, with a brief history of leadership research in the field of organizational behavior, the tradition that we are both most familiar with, because it provides an example of the ebbs and flows in the study of leadership that may be instructive to scholars in other disciplines as well.

A Brief History of Leadership in Organizational Behavior

Early organization theorists who are regarded as the founders of the field, from Weber through Selznick, regarded the concept of leadership as worthy of serious intellectual inquiry. Weber (1946, 1964) developed his study of social change by describing the role of leaders who possess "a certain quality of an individual personality by virtue of which he is set apart from ordinary men" (1964:329) and, in part because of their unique individual capacities, are able to set up broad orientations, propound new norms, articulate new goals, establish organizational frameworks, and mobilize the resources necessary for all these purposes—actions that are fundamental to institution building in any social system.

Similarly, in his famous observation of organizations that are initially "expendable" "rational instruments" "engineered to do a job" that over time become transformed into institutions that are "infuse[d] with values beyond the technical requirements of the task at hand," Selznick (1984:7) argued that leadership—through its ability to create, mold, and embody "in thought and feeling and habit" the values of an organization—is the primary agent of this process.

These vital roles of leadership identified by the early intellectual giants of organizational behavior animated research on leadership in organization theory for a long time. However, for the past thirty years, the concept of leadership and its study have been subject to criticism and marginalization by the dominant organizational paradigms and perspectives (Rost, 1991).

One group of scholars has argued that the concept of leadership itself is too loosely defined and is ultimately an amalgam of behaviors and attributes that can be more tractably defined and linked to performance when they are analytically decoupled. Social scientists have long recognized a reflexive human tendency to explain organizational outcomes by privileging the role of leaders and neglecting situational factors (Pfeffer, 1981). This focus blinds us to the reality that many organizational events are not driven by individual actors, but are derived from and perhaps even determined by the organization's environment. In their classic study of 167 companies, Lieberson and O'Connor (1972) studied several internal and external factors affecting organizational performance, including the impact of macro-economic conditions (year), industry, company, and finally the organization's chief executive. While the impact of the chief executive varied by industry (from modest to meager), external factors such as the organization's industry and the organization's inherited characteristics were greater than any "leadership" effect. In a detailed examination of forty-six college and university presidents, Cohen and March (1974) concluded that leadership is principally mythological. Likening the role of an organization's leader to the driver of a skidding car, they write that there is little a leader can do to influence organizational outcomes, and "whether he is convicted of manslaughter or receives a medal for heroism [is] largely outside his control." Numerous empirical studies have since supported these early authors' basic conjecture that factors outside the control of any single individual primarily drive organizational performance (for a review of these studies, see Thomas, 1988).

More recent theoretical developments in organizational research have argued that the realm in which single individuals can impact organizational performance is so limited that there is essentially no reason to worry about whether there are any behaviors or attributes that are unique to leadership. Organizational performance, in other words, is an overdetermined variable. For example, resource dependence research (Pfeffer and Salancik, 1978; Pfeffer, 1997) argues that most organizational action can be understood not as an exercise of individual agency but as an organizational response to the demands of external actors upon which organizations depend for resources and support. In a related notion, the new institutional perspective (Powell and DiMaggio, 1991) on organizations highlights that these external actors impose very specific expectations on what the organization should be doing. These external expectations are so strong as to often provide a template of strategies and structures that an organization mimics because they are perceived as legitimate and appropriate. Related work in the social network literature, which often employs the imagery and concepts of resource dependence and/or new institutional theory, stresses the importance of interorganizational linkages on the flow of resources and legitimacy (Podolny, 2001). Finally and most forcefully, organizational ecology, which studies the entire population of an industry, finds that changes in organizational populations are largely driven through the processes of organizational founding and dissolution, rejecting any notion of any individual organization's ability (and by logical extension any leader's ability) to adapt to changing environments (Hannan and Freeman, 1989; Carroll and Hannan, 2000). In sum, the general thrust of this research is that because of constraints and forces that are beyond the control of any single individual, even those occupying leadership roles, there is not much of an effect of leadership on organizational performance. Stated in its harshest light: the dominant organizational scholarship of the past thirty years does not see a substantive role for leadership and hence, little need for leadership research.

Scholars who continued to emphasize that leadership is a vital force in organizational life, such as Bennis (1959), Kotter (1988), and others, had to do so in the context of this harsh dominant intellectual land-scape, in which leadership was seen as an insignificant factor in shaping important organizational outcomes. Not surprisingly, they were pushed to the margins of the field—and much of the most active thinking on leadership, as a result, began to occur outside the field.

If leadership is to return to the mainstream of research in organiza-tional behavior, one of the main questions that will need to be reestab-lished is the significance of leadership in organizational life. It is ironic that the significance of leadership to important organizational out-comes may need to be addressed in scholarly research at precisely the time when society at large is viewing the unprecedented organizational failures that have occurred as irrefutable evidence of leadership fail-ures. Yet, it is worth asking: Is the current outcry that holds leaders accountable for the mess in the global economy well placed or merely another vivid example of the "fundamental attribution error"—our reflexive tendency to hold individuals who may actually have had little real influence responsible for organizational outcomes?

The papers in the first section of this edited volume attempt to address this central question: Does leadership matter? And if so, in what way?

Section I. The Impact of Leadership: Performance and Meaning

Underlying most criticisms of the leadership concept is a common and fundamental assumption: that the significance of leadership for organi-zational life is best assessed by the direct impact of leadership on orga-nizational performance. Put more simply, if leadership does not directly impact or significantly impact organizational performance, then lead-ership does not matter to organizational life. These scholars implicitly conclude that social phenomena such as meaning, morality, or culture are of marginal concern because of their weak explanatory power with respect to economic outcomes. Indeed, certain organizational scholars argue that the primary concern of organizational theorists in business schools, where most organizational research is now done, should be aimed at improving organizational performance.

Linking leadership to organizational performance, and showing that it is at best a weak link, is the strategy used by the critics of leader-ship research. Trying to establish the strength of the performance rela-tionship is the common counterstrategy of leadership's strongest advocates (see, for example, books by Kotter [1988] and Bennis [2009], two of the most well-known leadership scholars). Titles such as *Leadership and Performance Beyond Expectations* (Bass, 1985) or *Improving Organizational Effectiveness Through Transformational Leadership* (Bass and Avolio, 1994) exemplify attempts to make the case for a strong link between leadership and performance.

The paper by Wasserman, Anand, and Nohria that follows this introduction in the first section of this volume tries to provide a more balanced assessment of the extent to which leadership can influence organizational performance. Replicating the variance partitioning methodology adopted by Lieberson and O'Connor to analyze the performance of public companies in the United States over a more recent twenty-year period, they conclude that although external forces such as industry structure and company history may indeed explain a greater fraction of the variance in company performance over time, the influence of leadership in absolute terms is also substantial—although it may vary across industries. Indeed, in some circumstances, changing a CEO may be a decision that can have the same significance as the board of directors of a company deciding to change the industry in which the company operates. Because leadership changes occur routinely and can be more readily influenced by boards of companies than the external context in which they operate, the role of leadership, and its impact on corporate performance, is significant and should be taken seriously.

The next paper in this section, by Podolny, Khurana, and Hill-Popper, contends that the study of leadership in organizational theory went awry when the concern with leadership became too tightly coupled to a concern with organizational performance. If one revisits the concerns of scholars such as Weber, Barnard, and Selznick, these scholars were not concerned with leadership because of the concept's ability to explain economic performance, but because of its importance for infusing purpose and meaning into the lives of individuals. Although concerns regarding economic performance are not irrelevant to these scholars' examination of leadership, they are not central. For these organizational scholars, the primary significance of leadership rests on its importance in stemming the loss of meaning that they and other social theorists—for example, Tonnies (1957), Durkheim (1947a, 1974b), and Coleman (1990)—ascribe to modernity. Accordingly, if we are to judge the importance of leadership to organizational life, we need to assess the importance of leadership in a broader way than it is currently treated in organizational scholarship. Applied to the current crisis of leadership, these scholars would argue that the failure of leadership we should be concerned about is not just the economic collapse of the firms they led, but the moral collapse of these firms, and the attendant confusion and loss of meaning they have engendered.

In an integrative essay that he wrote after attending the conference, which rounds out this section, Hackman argues that the role of leaders is best understood not in terms of their direct impact on organizational outcomes but through their indirect influence, which stems from their ability to shape key contextual features of an organization (such as its goals, incentives, culture, member composition, etc.). The ability to influence the context, which in turn influences the behavior of potentially everyone else in the organization, is, according to Hackman, the proper way to understand the role and impact of leaders.

Although they have very different points of departure and emphasis, we hope the four papers in the introductory section of this volume will convince readers that leadership is not a topic that needs urgent attention just because of the demand for more and better leadership that society is putting on the institutions of higher education to which we as scholars belong, but because leadership, contrary to the paradigms that have tended to be dominant in organization theory in recent years, does indeed have an important influence on organizational life— not just on an organization's performance, but perhaps even more importantly on the social nature and structure of organizations.

Section II. The Theory of Leadership: Personal Attributes, Functions, and Relationships

This section provides a broad review of the leadership research across eight major disciplines, including organization behavior, psychology, psychoanalysis, sociology, economics, history, and political science. We start by briefly introducing the papers in the section and then discuss another central tension in the research on leadership that cuts across these papers.

The first paper in this section, by Glynn and DeJordy, assesses leadership research in organizational behavior from the mid-twentieth century to the present. Their assessment of the published leadership research in the field's leading journals finds a "definitional quagmire" that stretches across approaches that have focused variously on the personality of the leader, the process of leadership, the impact of leadership, and leadership performance. They conclude with a series of suggestions that may lead to a more productive agenda for the field's future.

Focusing on leadership at the individual and group level, Chatman and Kennedy's chapter frames the psychological perspectives on leadership, with particular emphasis on research that identifies the important capabilities for successful leadership in organizations and at the group level. Chatman and Kennedy suggest three critical capabilities for organizational leadership that are distinct from the commonly cited personality or intelligence dimensions. These are a leader's diagnostic abilities, behavioral flexibility, and unambiguous signaling of intentions. At the team level of leadership, the authors describe three key tasks: convening the group and developing identification, coaching group members, and setting group norms.

In their chapter on clinical and psychoanalytic research, Kets de Vries and Engellau uncover the role of the unconscious intrapsychic dynamics that underlie leader behaviors. Drawing on clinical data and psychoanalytical concepts, the authors assert that leaders are what they are, and lead the way they lead, due to their early development, and that people in organizations are to be understood at their psychological and emotional levels—at their most basic human levels—to understand how to motivate them, reward them, and enable them to carry out the larger goals of the organization. They highlight the importance of three triangles—the mental life triangle, the conflict triangle, and the relationships triangle—that animate the clinical dynamics of human behavior and are essential to a deeper understanding of leadership.

Sociology, Guillén argues, has had an evolving model of leadership that originated with a focus on formal authority rooted in Max Weber's discussions of bureaucracy, then developed into a focus on value-imbued institutions associated with Selznick's institutional functionalism, followed by a critical-theory tradition concerned with the power and perpetuation of elites, and then to a contemporary emphasis on the social and relational elements for exercising power and influence.

Bolton, Brunnermeier, and Veldkamp discuss the role that leadership plays in economic approaches to the firm. They acknowledge that leadership has received somewhat limited attention in economics. They note that classical economics treats the firm as a "black box" production function and thus ignores any role for leadership in the firm. Building on the principal-agent framework, they introduce an economic model of leadership that specifies an organizational leader's challenge as credibly communicating a mission that enables coordinated actions by followers in the face of potential changes. First, the leader receives information about the environment and defines a mission statement, setting forth the vision component of leadership, and communicates it to followers. Next, followers, having their own information about the environment, each choose a course of action. After this, the leader gets new information about the environment, which is subsequently incorporated into a strategy for implementation. High payoffs result from a well-coordinated execution of strategy that is also well suited to the organizational context.

Starting from the classical prisoner's dilemma as a point of departure, Zupan argues that a leader's role, from an economic perspective, can be framed as moving people who are stuck in an inferior equilibrium of the game (a one-shot game) into a superior equilibrium (an indefinitely repeated game). Enabling members of the organization to move to this superior equilibrium requires the leader to focus on six essential tasks: vision, enrollment, commitment, integrity, communication, and authenticity.

Friedman asserts that history as a discipline delivers a valuable element of perspective to the study and teaching of leadership, through both building understanding of past situations and highlighting differences from or similarities to the present. Applying a comparative and historical lens should serve to advance understanding of both the evolution and dynamics of leadership. Friedman reviews the research of two historians, Fritz Redlich and Alfred Chandler, who respectively use history to illuminate the phenomenon of leadership, particularly the conception of leadership as a Schumpeterian "disruptive art."

In the final paper in the section, Nye, from a political science perspective, considers the relationship between power and leadership, which he sees as inextricably intertwined. He characterizes power as having both a hard form (coercive) and a soft form (attractive), with each being exercised to some degree by nearly every leader. An effective leader will combine both forms, resulting in what Nye terms "smart power." The right proportions will vary, as will the amounts of hard and soft power available, based on a leader's context. Leaders, followers, and the contexts in which they interact are three key components of the social and power dynamics that define a leadership role.

Together, these papers help illuminate another central tension in the research on leadership. For some scholars, the focus is on the special characteristics of the person that distinguishes him or her from others and makes that individual a leader. The idea that a leader is a distinctive person cuts across disciplines. It can be found in business history and economics (see chapter 11), where Schumpeter famously described the entrepreneur as a "rogue elephant" who has the courage and chutzpah to overturn the existing order. It can be found in sociology (see chapter 8), where Weber emphasized that one source of leaders' authority may lie in their "charisma"—a special, distinctive quality of an individual that sets them apart from ordinary people, causes them to be viewed as having exemplary or divine qualities, and thus enables them to be treated as leaders. Numerous other personality dimensions, special competencies, and character traits have been highlighted in the literature in psychology (see chapter 6). One of the early and enduring examples from psychology was the work of McClelland, who emphasized the importance of the achievement and socialized power motives in leaders. However, the list of leadership traits identified by psychologists has by now proliferated and is in need of a synthetic meta-analysis. The personal characteristics, such as narcissism and neuroticism, that animate the intrapersonal life of a leader have been the focus of the related discipline of psychoanalysis since Freud, although this perspective was brought into the leadership literature by scholars such as Bion, Zaleznick, and Maccoby (see chapter 7). A focus on the person can also be found in the literature in political science, although here the emphasis tends to be on how the leader exercises power or differences in leadership styles (see chapter 12). The source of these style differences in how leaders exercise power is often seen to reside in the leader's personality, worldview, or character. Inasmuch as organization behavior is an interdisciplinary field that draws on all these disciplines, there is a well-established strand of research in this field as well that focuses on the distinctive qualities of leaders (see chapter 5).

Another set of scholars in many of these disciplines believes that the search for the distinctive characteristics of leaders is misguided. They argue that what makes someone a leader is not that they have special or exemplary attributes relative to others, but that they are able to fulfill vital functions that help meet their followers' needs for meaning, social order, group identity, and goal accomplishment. By focusing on the relationship between the leader and his or her followers, this group of scholars argues that the proper emphasis in leadership research should be on the behaviors of leaders and how they address the essential needs of their followers in an organizational context (see chapter 8). One of the early and influential advocates of this perspective was Barnard (1968), who emphasized the leader's role in establishing a system of communications (purpose, objectives, information flows, and decision rights) that would secure the voluntary cooperation of the organization's members and ensure coordination across their efforts. In a related vein, Selznick (1984) emphasized the leader's role in creating meaning for the members of the organization and ensuring that the organization was institutionalized (i.e., developed a certain taken-for-grantedness that secured its ongoing viability). More recently (as Guillén discusses in chapter 8), the emphasis in sociology has shifted to the leader's position and role in a broader system of relationships (a relational network). The idea that leaders must mobilize support across different identity and interest groups because organizations inevitably sit at the intersection of multiple constituencies has a rich provenance in the political science literature as well (see chapter 12). Sociological and political perspectives on leadership also warn us against idealizing leaders. They remind us that leaders can be coercive and have a vested interest in preserving their dominance, both individually and as a class (a ruling elite or inner circle), relative to those they lead (see chapter 8).

Interestingly, economic perspectives on leadership share this focus on the functions and relations, rather than the attributes of the leader. Traditionally, the firm has been viewed as a black box and leadership has thus largely been ignored in the economic literature (except to some degree by economic historians). However, the principal-agent framework created the foundation for a growing economics literature on the role of leadership. This literature has tended to focus on the leader's role in allocating decision rights and structuring incentives (see, for example, the work of Jensen, 2003). However, economists (see chapters 9 and 10) have more recently begun to appreciate and formally model the leader's role in setting a vision, communicating a direction, empowering or delegating authority to others, ensuring execution, and modeling integrity (actions consistent with words).

Taken together, the papers in this section of the volume suggest that the tension between viewing the leader as someone with a special set of attributes or as someone who performs specific social functions or occupies a specific role or position in a system of social relationships can be found in most disciplines, although the emphasis varies across them. Rather than resolve this tension, we think it may be more productive for now to sustain it—and to encourage leadership research that advances our understanding of both the distinctive attributes of leaders and of their social functions and relationships.

Section III. The Variability of Leadership: What's Core and Contingent

This section is composed of three papers that center on another duality in the research on leadership. Most models of leadership posit attributes, functions, or relations that are core to leadership and are implicitly or explicitly universal (i.e., important and applicable in most situations). However, leadership scholars equally recognize that there is no universal model or one best way to lead and that leadership must be contingent on the specifics of any given situation. These contingency approaches highlight how leadership might vary across different kinds of situational variables (such as the nature of the firm, the culture in which it operates, or its strategic challenges). They also investigate how leadership might vary depending on the characteristics of the leader (his or her gender, race, nationality, or other background variables).

It is hard to argue against the proposition that effective leadership must to some extent be contingent on the situation and the person. However, there are clear trade-offs involved in moving to an entirely contingent model of leadership. First, it raises the question of the extent to which leadership can ever be a separate subject of inquiry apart from the situation. It is hard to imagine what leadership is if there isn't a core set of leadership functions or behaviors that cut across different situations and persons. Second, a contingent theory of leadership that is broad enough in scope to include virtually all situational factors makes integration and a middle-range theory substantially more difficult. If the list of contingencies becomes infinitely large, the concept of contingency also runs the risk of losing all meaning. A pragmatic approach for addressing this vexing dilemma, we believe, may lie in middle-range research that attempts to look both for what's core and what's contingent across a range of important situational and personal contingencies. The three papers in this section exemplify the middle-range approach we are advocating.

The first, by Javidan, Dorfman, Howell, and Hanges, examines a contingency that is a central challenge in a more global economic and organizational landscape—how much effective leadership varies across national and cultural boundaries. Importantly, they also ask the following question: What elements of leadership are core and more universal across these boundaries? The foundation of their approach is the notion that organizations and societies have implicit leadership theories, wherein beliefs about the attributes that define effective leadership are contained in distinctive cognitive structures, or schemas. The content of such schemas shapes perceptions by individuals regarding who is and who is not a leader. While schemas about leadership are shaped by an individual's early personal experiences with and observations of those acting as leaders, a shared schema may also develop within a cultural group and influence the most effective way to lead across these cultural groups.

Ely and Rhode look at leadership contingencies that stem not from the environment but from the identity of the leader. They explore perceptions of leadership effectiveness based on gender identity. The authors contend that female leaders must deal with ambivalent reactions rooted in gender stereotypes. Generally, the assertive, dominant behavior typical among leaders tends to be viewed as atypical and unattractive in women. Studies of attitudes toward women in traditionally male roles show that they effectively trade perceptions of competence for likability—the more successful they appear, the less affectively they are regarded. Such trends affect both organizational openness to female leaders and the conceptions women have about themselves as leaders.

Lorsch attempts to develop a middle-range theory of the situational contingencies that might be most significant for research on leadership. The leader's relationship with followers is central to Lorsch's analysis: followers' values and expectations must align with the goals set by the leader, communication between the parties must be strong, and the leader must draw effectively on power as a function of position (a directive approach) and on influence through perceived competence and charisma (a participative approach). The appropriate mix will depend on contingent factors as follows: (1) the leader's chosen goals and available sources of power and influence, (2) the followers' expectations, (3) the complexity of the organization, and (4) the certainty or uncertainty of the task.

Section IV. The Practice of Leadership: Agency and Constraint

In this section, our contributors focus on some of the most important practical problems facing leaders: how to cope with the complexity of the CEO's role, how to build effective senior leadership teams, how to lead in a more global environment, how to make critical leadership decisions, how to mobilize social movements that can address some of society's most pressing concerns, and how to lead to stimulate innovation. By showcasing empirically informed research by renowned scholars on these topics, this segment of the volume demonstrates that difficult problems of leadership in practice can be the object of research that is both rigorous and relevant.

Porter and Nohria present results from an in-depth study examining the CEO's role in large, complex organizations. They identify several core leadership functions that leaders must fulfill in any enterprise: direction, organization, selection, motivation, and implementation. Although these core functions have long been recognized as "what" leaders need to do, what is less well understood is "how" leaders can accomplish these objectives given the numerous constraints they experience, especially the limited time they can personally devote to the myriad issues with which they must deal. Their focus is to identify these constraints and illuminate how CEOs can best execute their roles within these constraints. They highlight the importance of indirect over direct means of influence and the allocation of personal presence as key levers in performing the CEO's job. They also underscore the importance of a CEO's personal legitimacy for effective leadership.

Wageman and Hackman also identify leadership as a matter of ensuring that certain necessary *functions*—establishing direction, creating structures and systems, engaging external resources—are fulfilled so that members can accomplish shared purposes. Yet, they note that many leaders and leadership teams have difficulty fulfilling these critical functions. Based on a study in two settings, they show that teams of leaders necessarily must contend with, and often fall victim to, four paradoxes that pervade their work. These are as follows: (1) Leader teams are composed of powerful people, yet they tend to be underdesigned, underled, and underresourced; (2) membership is important and coveted, but members often don't know who is on the team, and they don't really want to come to team meetings; (3) members are overloaded, but tend to waste enormous amounts of time in team meetings; and (4) authority dynamics pervade leadership teams and complicate team processes, but members won't talk about them.

Useem's chapter focuses on the decision-making function of leadership. He makes three arguments. First, Useem suggests that good and timely decisions should be considered a critical feature of organizational leadership. Second, leadership decision making is not a natural capacity, and because those in leadership positions tend to make predictable decision errors, such errors are also preventable. Third, the chapter suggests that by looking at how company leaders—in this case, company directors—actually make decisions, we can help resolve long-standing conceptual questions about how organizations operate.

Ganz describes how leadership in social movements is distinct from leadership in organizations. He finds that the role of leadership in social movements goes well beyond that of the stereotypical charismatic public personas with whom they are often identified. Identifying, recruiting, and developing leadership at all levels—helping others develop a personal story that connects and commits them to the movement—is a core element of effective social movements. This distributed leadership forges a community and mobilizes its resources, a primary source of a social movement's power.

Kanter asks the question, Is leadership different in a globalizing world than in other more geographically and institutionally bounded contexts? There is a great deal of continuity with enduring tasks performed by leaders. However, she also identifies three aspects of globalization—increased uncertainty, complexity, and diversity—that fundamentally reshape the work leaders must perform. Based on field observations of leaders in large global firms, she finds that three distinctive leadership tasks follow from these conditions: (1) institutional work to deal with uncertainty, (2) integrative work to deal with complexity, and (3) identity work to deal with diversity.

Hill, Travaglini, Brandeau, and Stecker provide field-generated insights on leaders of teams or organizations that have produced breakthrough innovations more than once, as well as on leaders who have managed to transform their teams into hotbeds of innovation work. They find that leading for innovation is about (1) creating a world to which people want to belong—one in which individuals are affirmed in their identity (unleashing their "slices of genius," or talents) and are able to be a part of and contribute to something larger than themselves (harnessing the diverse slices of genius to develop innovative solutions for a collective purpose); (2) developing the individual and collective capacity for co-design; and (3) a leadership style that is more akin to leading from behind than leading from the front.

Looking across the papers in this section, we observe another leadership duality. On the one hand the very word *leader* evokes an image of someone with an unusually high capacity for agency—someone who can organize, mobilize, and drive change. Yet, on the other hand, the reality that leaders must confront is that they must contend with all manner of constraints—the expectations of myriad constituencies, internal and external pressures, difficult followers, their own personal limitations, and the availability of necessary resources such as time, information, and money. The list could go on. Navigating this tension between agency and constraint—recognizing the limits to their power, yet finding a way of taking action—is at the heart of the practice of leadership, and must continue to be vigorously investigated in future research.

Section V. The Development of Leaders: Knowing, Doing, and Being

Ultimately, one of the most important reasons to study leadership is to enable the development of leaders. Yet, leadership scholars are still confronted by the age-old question: Are leaders born or made? Or, to put it differently: Is leadership innate or can leaders be developed? The authors of the papers in this section of the volume all come out on the side that leaders are made or developed, although they acknowledge that people may start with different levels of inherited or innate leadership capabilities. However, there are subtle differences across these papers that suggest another leadership duality.

Some scholars who study leadership development focus on what Snook and colleagues have called the "knowing" and "doing" dimensions of becoming a leader. Knowing highlights the cognitive capabilities, or the multiple intelligences, the leader requires (Gardner, 1993; Riggio et al., 2001)—analytical intelligence, practical intelligence, social intelligence, emotional intelligence, and contextual intelligence are among the most commonly cited. Doing emphasizes the behavioral or skills dimensions of becoming a leader—developing better problem solving, communication, conflict management, or adaptive skills, for example (Mumford et al., 2000). In contrast to knowing and doing, scholars who focus on "being" highlight that leadership is perhaps more importantly a matter of developing the identity of a leader—a self-concept that enables someone to think of himself or herself as a leader and to interact with the world from that identity or sense of being (see chapter 22).

Although their emphasis varies, leadership scholars recognize that knowing, doing, and being are all important to the development of leaders. The question then becomes, How do we help leaders develop along all these dimensions? The papers in this section, which are representative of the broader literature in the field, suggest that leaders develop (and can be helped to develop) in multiple ways. The most significant influence on a leader's development appears to be an individual's naturally occurring life experiences and what he or she learns from them. Bennis (2009), for example, has highlighted the profound importance of life's crucibles, or trying moments, in the development of leaders. Building on the importance of experience, McCall's chapter highlights how organizations can help the right people get the right experiences at the right time to accelerate their development as leaders. Career transitions, or moments when people enter new roles in their organization, across organizations, or across careers, are especially poignant moments in the development of leaders—fraught with both peril and possibility. Helping people navigate these transitions effectively is thus vital to developing leaders (see chapter 23).

The importance of experiences, events, and transitions does not imply that formal or structured leadership development programs, such as educational programs or other types of interventions, are not useful. Indeed, formal training can play an important role not only in the development of individual leaders, but also as an intervention to enhance the overall quality of leadership in an organization, such as increased alignment, goal congruence, and support for change initiatives (see chapter 24 by Conger).

Although none of the papers in this section focuses in depth on how role models, mentors, coaches, and other relationships can influence the development of leaders, the importance of these relationships cannot be overstated.

Finally, the willingness and capacity for individuals to be self-reflective, to be actively engaged in developing themselves as leaders, must also be recognized as crucial to the development of leaders. Indeed, developing this capacity for disciplined and honest self-reflection may be essential to becoming an authentic leader (see chapter 25 by Avolio).

Taken together, the papers in this section of the volume present a broad range of perspectives on the development of leaders, including the identity transformation involved in becoming a leader, how to develop leadership skills, the role of experience and formal programs in leader development, the development of more authentic leadership, and the potential of adults to keep growing and evolving as leaders. Brief summaries of the papers follow.

Ibarra, Snook, and Guillén Ramo argue that the development of leadership skills is inextricably integrated with the development of the person's self-concept or identity as a leader. In developing an identity-based model of leader development, they discuss the key transitions and experiences that shape leaders' careers, specifying processes and moderating conditions for identity transformation.

McCall's chapter takes stock of where we are today in our knowledge of the role of experience in developing leadership talent and suggests where we might go next in our quest for wisdom about this topic. Five leverage points available in organizations are described that can create a context supportive of learning from experience: identifying developmental experiences; identifying people with potential to develop as leaders; developing processes for getting the right experience at the right time; increasing the odds that learning will occur; and taking a career-long perspective with a focus on transitions. The paper concludes with some challenges for both practitioners and researchers if we are to advance our understanding of this complex process.

Conger reviews a half-century of formal leadership development approaches. He finds that formal leadership development initiatives can be organized into four general categories: (1) individual skill development, (2) socialization of the corporate vision and values, (3) strategic interventions that promote a major change throughout an organization, and (4) targeted action learning approaches to address organizational challenges and opportunities.

Avolio discusses what he considers to be the critical question in the science and practice of leadership: How do we accelerate the development of positive leadership for sustainable impact on individuals, groups, communities, and nations? The chapter surveys the research and intellectual history that has led to the current focus on authentic leadership development.

Finally, Kegan and Lahey apply adult development theories to the concept of leadership development. They argue that the field has overemphasized *leadership* and underemphasized *development*. Consequently, the underlying "operating system" necessary for effective leadership development—which sets the terms on mastery; which shapes our thinking, feeling, and social relating—is unaddressed. They argue that the processes of leadership development would be significantly enhanced if the concept were anchored in what we now know about fostering the development of the meaning-making self in adulthood.

We recognize that those reading this volume might be overwhelmed by the sheer immensity of the book. We hope the organization of this book into five sections that each centers on some of the key themes and tensions found in the leadership literature provides a useful lens on organizing this vast and sprawling field. Despite the scale and scope of this book, we don't pretend for a moment that it is comprehensive or covers all aspects of leadership. However, by providing a range of leadership writings grounded in different academic disciplines, the practice of leadership, and leader development, we believe this volume offers a useful starting point for scholars and teachers seeking to integrate leadership into their own research, practice, and teaching. Advancing the theory and practice of leadership is our primary goal. Admittedly, we also have loftier goals. We hope that this volume helps create a new future, that improving the research, practice, and teaching of leadership allows us to develop better leaders and a better world. The world is crying out for better leadership. We hope this volume improves the supply.

References

Ancona, Deborah, Thomas W. Malone, Wanda J. Orlikowski, and Peter M. Senge. "In Praise of the Incomplete Leader." *Harvard Business Review*, 2007.

Barnard, Chester. *The Functions of the Executive*. Cambridge, MA: Harvard University Press, 1968.

Bass, Bernard M. *Leadership and Performance Beyond Expectations*. New York: The Free Press, 1985.

Bass, Bernard M., and Bruce J. Avolio. *Improving Organizational Effectiveness Through Transformational Leadership*. Thousand Oaks, CA: Sage Publications, 1994.

Bennis, Warren G. "Leadership Theory and Administrative Behavior: The Problem of Authority." *Administrative Science Quarterly* 4 (1959): 259–301.

———. *On Becoming a Leader*. 4th ed. Philadelphia: Basic Books, 2009.

Ben-Shahar, Tal. *Happier: Can You Learn to Be Happy?* New York: McGraw-Hill Professional, 2008.

Carroll, Glenn R., and Michael T. Hannan. *The Demography of Corporations and Industries*. Princeton, NJ: Princeton University Press, 2000.

Cohen, Michael D., and James G. March. *Leadership and Ambiguity: The American College President*. New York: McGraw Hill, 1974.

Coleman, James S. *Foundations of Social Theory*. Cambridge, MA: Harvard University Press, 1990.

Durkheim, Émile. *The Division of Labor in Society*. Translated by George Simpson. Glencoe, IL: The Free Press, 1947a.

———. *The Elementary Forms of the Religious Life: A Study in Religious Sociology*. Translated by Joseph W. Swain. Glencoe, IL: The Free Press, 1947b.

Gardner, Howard E. *Frames of Mind: The Theory of Multiple Intelligences.* 10th ed. Philadelphia: Basic Books, 1993.

Hannan, Michael T., and John Freeman. *Organizational Ecology.* Cambridge, MA: Harvard University Press, 1989.

Jensen, Michael C. *A Theory of the Firm: Governance, Residual Claims, and Organizational Forms.* Cambridge, MA: Harvard University Press, 2003.

Kotter, John P. *The Leadership Factor.* New York: The Free Press, 1988.

Lieberson, Stanley, and James F. O'Connor. "Leadership and Organizational Performance: A Study of Large Corporations." *American Sociological Review* 37 (1972): 117–130.

Mumford, Michael D., Stephen J. Zaccaro, Mary Shane Connelly, and Michelle A. Marks. "Leadership Skills: Conclusions and Future Directions." *Leadership Quarterly* 11, no. 1 (2000): 155–170.

Pfeffer, Jeffrey. "Management as Symbolic Action: The Creation and Maintenance of Organizational Paradigms." *In Research in Organizational Behavior.* Vol. 3, edited by Barry M. Staw and Larry L. Cummings, 1–52. Greenwich, CT: JAI Press, 1981.

———. *New Directions for Organization Theory: Problems and Prospects.* New York: Oxford University Press, 1997.

Pfeffer, Jeffrey, and Gerald R. Salancik. *The External Control of Organizations.* New York: Harper & Row, 1978.

Podolny, Joel M. "Networks as the Pipes and Prisms of the Market." *American Journal of Sociology* 107, no. 1 (July 2001): 33–60.

Powell, Walter W., and Paul J. DiMaggio, eds. *The New Institutionalism in Organizational Analysis.* Chicago: University of Chicago Press, 1991.

Riggio, Ronald E., Susan E. Murphy, and Francis J. Pirozzolo, eds. *Multiple Intelligences and Leadership.* Mahwah, NJ: Laurence Erlbaum, 2001.

Rost, Joseph C. *Leadership for the Twenty-First Century.* New York: Praeger, 1991.

Selznick, Philip. *Leadership in Administration: A Sociological Interpretation.* Berkeley, CA: University of California Press, 1984.

Thomas, Alan Berkeley. "Does Leadership Make a Difference to Organizational Performance?" *Administrative Science Quarterly* 33 (1988): 388–400.

Tonnies, Ferdinand. *Community and Society.* Translated and edited by Charles P. Loomis. East Lansing, MI: Michigan State University Press, 1957.

Weber, Max. *From Max Weber: Essays in Sociology.* Edited by H.H. Gerth and C. Wright Mills. New York: Oxford University Press, 1946.

———. *The Theory of Social and Economic Organization.* Edited by Talcott Parsons. New York: The Free Press, 1964.

2

WHEN DOES LEADERSHIP MATTER?

A Contingent Opportunities View of CEO Leadership

Noam Wasserman, Bharat Anand, and Nitin Nohria

Introduction

Does it matter who the CEO of a firm is? This simple question has received rather different answers in the literature on leadership. "Conventional" management theorists, to use Thomas's (1988) term, posit that CEOs can have a significant influence on the performance of their companies. From their perch at the top of an organization, CEOs are able to actively direct which opportunities the firm will pursue (Barnard, 1938), and in turn shape the firm's strategy, structure, and culture. In contrast, more recently, other scholars—notably organizational ecology researchers—have argued that CEOs are so constrained by their environments that they have little ability to affect company performance. For instance, a company's culture, the structure of its industry, and its fixed assets are all inertial forces that reduce the CEO's ability to take actions that will impact the company (Hannan and Freeman, 1989).

This paper presents a "contingent opportunities" view of leadership that reconciles these divergent views and tests the resulting predictions in a large sample. The core difference in approach is that rather than frame the question of CEO impact in black-and-white terms ("Does leadership matter?") we ask instead "*When* does leadership matter?"

We depart from past approaches to understanding leadership in a few ways. Most past studies—including the theoretical papers described above and most of the major empirical studies of CEO leadership to date—do not examine the role of context on CEO impact. A notable exception is Lieberson and O'Connor's (1972) study nearly three decades ago that examines cross-industry variation in CEO impact.

Our theoretical framework builds on certain prior work that incorporates a contingent view of leadership, notably Hambrick and Finkelstein's (1987) theory of managerial discretion. However, our perspective differs from theirs in certain important ways. Most important, we differ from their core conclusion that CEO impact is greatest in situations characterized by *plentiful* opportunities. In particular, we posit (for reasons explained later) that where opportunities are *scarce*, CEOs have a larger impact on company performance, but that in settings where opportunities are plentiful, they have limited impact on company performance.

Our empirical strategy centers on a variance decomposition analysis of firm performance across forty-two industries. Among other things, our sample size is considerably larger than prior studies. Our results show that while on average there is a statistically significant effect of CEOs on firm performance, this effect varies markedly across industries. This effect is robust to different measures of firm performance, controls for firm size, and CEO tenures. Having established this basic tenet of the contingent opportunities view of CEO leadership, we then explore the factors that account for the differing effects that CEOs can have on their firms' performance, and test hypotheses regarding the drivers of CEO impact. We conclude by exploring certain interesting implications of our results for the governance of organizations, including, for example, the CEO search process and the structure of CEO compensation.

Leaders Versus Constraints

Studies of leadership differ, often greatly, in their assessment of the leader's impact on firm performance. Some scholars argue that leaders strongly impact performance while others note that leaders are inextricably bound by a variety of constraints (internal and external) so that their performance impact is not meaningful. For convenience we refer to these two perspectives as the "leadership" and the "constraints" views.[1]

The "Leadership School"

Studies of leadership describe how, by adapting their organizations' missions, strategies, structures, and cultures to their companies' environments, CEOs can have a substantial impact on company performance. For example, Child (1972) states that CEOs make material strategic choices that can influence firm performance. These strategic choices include "not only the establishment of structural forms but also the manipulation of environmental features and the choice of relevant performance standards" (Child, 1972:2). Similarly, others note how corporate leaders adapt organizational structures in response to technological and environmental changes (Lawrence and Lorsch, 1967; Woodward, 1965; Thompson, 1967).

An interesting line of questioning (and one that is closely related to our empirical inquiry) is to ask not only whether leaders can impact firm performance through their actions, but why they might differ in their actions. There are various reasons why this might be the case. The literature on leadership characterizes various sources of differences across leaders, highlighting, in turn, the role of ability, of beliefs (and vision), and of incentives. For example, Drucker (1954:1) notes the role of differences in ability across leaders: "in a competitive economy, above all, the quality and performance of the managers determine the success of a business, indeed they determine its survival." Ability might refer to, as well, the extent to which a leader can mobilize individuals and resources. For example, Barnard (1938) describes leaders as "formulating a collective purpose that binds organizational members." Similarly, Kotter (1996) characterizes how leaders can differ in their abilities as "change agents"—who not only develop a vision and strategy, but establish a sense of urgency, form "guiding coalitions," create short-term wins in order to build momentum, and institutionalize new approaches.

The role of vision has been described by various scholars and receives formal treatment in Rotemberg and Saloner (1998), who argue that a core task of CEO leadership is having the vision to make idiosyncratic choices. Those leaders who have such a vision—"a bias in favor of projects that are consistent with the CEO's view of the likely evolution of the industry"—can have a large impact on performance. Similarly, the role of incentives has received much attention in the work of Jensen and Meckling (1976) and others, who note the role of managers as active agents pursuing personal interests, with the result that a CEO's own interests can contribute significantly to variations in company performance.

Some scholars have also noted how a CEO's ability to impact performance depends on the circumstances under which he or she entered the position. While CEOs who come into a company after the forced turnover of their predecessors tend to improve company performance, CEOs usually hurt company performance in two cases: natural turnover followed by an outsider successor, and forced turnover followed by an insider successor (Khurana and Nohria, 1999). In addition, outsider CEOs have a higher likelihood of making significant changes to organizational strategy (Wiersema, 1992).

The "Constraints" View

Contrasting with this is a host of other studies that we refer to, collectively, as the "constraints" view of leadership. The difference in perspective of this work from that described above lies not necessarily in their views on whether or not leaders can influence firm performance, or the reasons for differences among leaders, but in their characterization of constraints that operate on them. Simply put, there are so many factors (both external and internal to the firm) that tie a CEO's hands in practice that the impact of leadership on performance ends up being limited. These studies highlight the role of inertia, of competition, of complexity (both environmental and cognitive), and politics.

Hannan and Freeman (1989) state that inertia prevents executives from changing strategy and structure quickly enough to react to changes in their environments. Sources of inertia include both *internal* factors, such as internal politics, existing control systems, previous investments in fixed assets, and organizational norms, and *external* factors, such as competitive pressures and barriers to exit and entry. In short, "[i]nertial pressures prevent most organizations from radically changing strategies and structures" (Hannan and Freeman, 1989:22). Therefore, they conclude, "individual managers do not matter much in accounting for variability in organizational properties" (Hannan and Freeman, 1989:43). Others state that existing power relationships will cause inertia when attitudes and behaviors become increasingly institutionalized

(Burkhardt, 1991). Culture researchers point out that the existence of subcultures and countercultures within an organization can inhibit a leader's efforts to change the organization (Martin, 1992). Even when managers can take actions to manage dependencies, such actions are never completely successful and end up producing new patterns of dependence and interdependence (Pfeffer and Salancik, 1978).

In addition, the confusion and complexity inherent in managerial decision making imposes cognitive, organizational, and political constraints on decision makers (March and Simon, 1958; Cyert and March, 1963; Simon, 1976). The impact that leaders can have is also limited by their own unreflective behaviors that reflect taken-for-granted institutionalized beliefs and practices (Powell and DiMaggio, 1991). Instead of having idiosyncratic views that shape their actions, Pfeffer (1977) states that career ladders and institutionally specified selection processes filter out idiosyncratic people, resulting in relative homogeneity across CEOs.

As a result, top-level leaders will not be able to have much impact on organizational performance for they are often rather severely constrained in their ability to make decisions or take actions that will affect firm performance.

Empirical Studies of CEOs

Existing theoretical work therefore presents a range of different perspectives not only on whether or not CEOs can influence performance, but also on the performance variation one might expect across CEOs. Most of the empirical work linking CEOs and firm performance studies this latter question.

There have been four notable empirical studies that employ a variance decomposition approach to studying "CEO effects" (Bowman and Helfat, 1997), starting with Lieberson and O'Connor (1972). In a study of 167 major public companies from 1946 to 1965, and using a sequential decomposition of variance in performance (discounting first the year effect, then industry, then company, and then leadership), they attribute this variance to each of the four factors. Their core finding is that performance differences across CEOs account for 14.5 percent of the total variance in profit margins, while "industry effects" have the biggest impact on profitability, explaining 28.5 percent of the variance.

Two follow-on studies (Weiner, 1978; Weiner and Mahoney, 1981) find, using different industry samples and different time periods, slightly different results. For example, Weiner (1978) uses a sample of

193 manufacturing companies over the period 1956 to 1974 and finds that the CEO effect accounts for 8.7 percent of the variance in performance. However, Weiner and Mahoney (1981) find that this effect (called "stewardship" in their paper) explains 12.8 percent of the variance in profitability, more in line with Lieberson and O'Connor's results. More recently, using a much smaller sample (12 U.K. retailing firms over the period 1965 to 1984), Thomas (1988) finds that the CEO effect explains only 5.7 percent of the variance in profitability.

Interestingly, the results in these studies have been argued to be consistent with different theoretical perspectives on leadership. For example, Lieberson and O'Connor conclude based on their results that "the leadership effect on company performance does matter" (Lieberson and O'Connor, 1972:123). They further note that when analyzing forward-lagged measures of performance (in order to account for the time lag between a CEO's actions and the resulting impact on profitability), the "leadership influence on profit margins (.32) exceeds that for either the industry (.273) or company (.222) effects." On the other hand, Pfeffer and Salancik present Lieberson and O'Connor's study as support for their "external control" perspective, noting that the study showed that "the magnitude of the administrative effect was dwarfed by the impact of the organization's industry and the stable characteristics of a given organization" (Pfeffer and Salancik, 1978:10).

Recently, Bertrand and Schoar (2003) employ a different approach to studying the impact of CEOs on firm performance. Their empirical strategy relies on movements of individuals across firms. Specifically, they estimate manager fixed effects for such individuals and study how the inclusion of these fixed effects increases the adjusted R^2 of firm performance regressions. In contrast to the variance decomposition approach that exploits performance variation across different CEOs of the same firm to reveal a "CEO effect," Bertrand and Schoar's identification strategy rests on performance differences for the same individual across firms. They find that including CEO fixed effects increases the R^2 of performance regressions by roughly 5 percent. Beyond establishing performance differences, they also provide strong evidence for how CEOs systematically differ in their decisions over a wide range of policy variables (notably R&D, acquisition and diversification decisions, dividend policy, interest coverage, and cost cutting policies), thereby establishing as a basic empirical fact that CEOs have different "styles."

A Contingent Opportunities View of Leadership

In this paper, we propose and validate a perspective that begins to reconcile these different perspectives. Our approach builds on a "largely speculative" paper by Hambrick and Finkelstein (1987), who start by noting that constraint—"the obverse of discretion"—can vary by organization. Top managers of some organizations have more discretion than do top managers of others, and discretion afforded a particular top manager can vary over time. Where CEO discretion is high, the CEO (an "Unconstrained Manager") can have influence, and where it is low, the CEO (a "Titular Figurehead") cannot exceed "his or her discretionary bounds" without losing influence. Hambrick and Finkelstein propose this theory of managerial discretion as "a bridge between points of debate by ecologists and strategic choice theorists" (Hambrick and Finkelstein, 1987:403). The concept that CEO impact varies given the nature of the situation is also similar to Fiedler's formulation of contingent leadership (Fiedler, 1965; Fiedler, 1967).

We build on this perspective to propose the following basic hypothesis concerning the role of leaders on firm performance:

Hypothesis 1: The CEO effect varies across industries.

This hypothesis extends earlier work by examining whether the CEO effect varies across contexts. Interestingly, in rejecting the role of context on CEO effects *a priori*, Thomas (1988) stated that "organizational constraints are constant across samples just as the constraints that are imposed on a racing driver by the characteristics of the car are the same regardless of whether it is raced against identical cars or very different ones" (Thomas, 1988:398).

In what follows, we flesh this view further by focusing on two dimensions that affect the level of CEO impact. The first class of drivers concerns the characteristics of a company's external task environment and the "opportunity set" it provides CEOs to act. The second class of drivers concerns the resources available to a CEO to act. The roles of scarce opportunities and of resource constraint or slack are described in detail next.

Scarce Opportunities and the External Task Environment
We start by noting that the set of opportunities available to CEOs and firms may differ greatly according to certain features of the external

environment. We draw heavily on Burt's (1980, 1992) work in focusing attention on two features in particular that drive structural autonomy: industry concentration and "exchange-constraint." These are related to other factors such as industry structure and competitive position that have received attention from strategy scholars.

According to Burt's (1992) theory of structural holes, industry A is dependent on industry B when it buys or sells a significant portion of its output to industry B. Furthermore, if there are only a few members of industry B, those members can coordinate their actions and thereby increase their power over industry A. In addition, when a firm engages in exchanges with actors who in turn exchange with each other, the focal firm's "power" is less than it would be if its exchange partners were not connected to each other. As a result, firms in industry A have a high level of discretion under any of the following conditions: industry A sells a small portion of its output to industry B, industry B has a lot of members, or industry A's exchange partners do not trade with each other.

According to Burt (1992), in industries with high exchange-constraint and concentration, the opportunities to act are scarce. In such industries, the ability of a CEO to take advantage or miss opportunities when they arise can end up having large performance consequences. The reason is that when opportunities are abundant, one would expect that a CEO who misses an opportunity can pursue another with relative ease. However, when opportunities are scarce, a missed opportunity is a lost opportunity. Conversely, CEOs who do exploit opportunities when they arise in these circumstances can end up differentiating their firms from the pack as well. In other words, the impact of CEOs on firm performance is likely to be greater.

This logic suggests that where opportunities are scarce, CEO effects should be high. In contrast, in situations where opportunities are abundant, CEO effects should be low.

As a concrete example of these ideas, it is useful to consider two industries—Communications Equipment (SIC 3660) and Meat Products (SIC 2010)—that differ in certain characteristics to see how these may affect CEO impact. Companies in the first industry design and manufacture telecommunications gear that they sell to communications-service providers. At key junctures, these service providers make huge investments in upgrading their networks, buying from the communications equipment industry large amounts of equipment to handle data networking, high-bandwidth transmission, and other critical components of their telecommunications infrastructures. During the period covered by our study, the communications equipment industry was characterized by higher-than-average industry concentration and very high exchange-constraint, leading us to predict that the CEO effect will be large here. In contrast, Meat Products was characterized by far-below-average measures for both factors.

When we examine the input/output (I/O) tables used by Burt for each of these industries as well, we find marked differences in their patterns of use of input commodities (which they have to buy from other industries) and in their sales of outputs to other industries. As shown in table 2-1, Meat Products (part of I/O industry number 14) buys 27 percent of its inputs from its main-input industry and 24 percent from its second biggest supplier industry. Both supplier industries are highly fragmented with relatively low levels of concentration. On the other hand, the Communications Equipment industry (part of I/O industry number 56) buys 40 percent of its main input from a single-input industry, which in turn is relatively concentrated.

While the contrast is less stark when it comes to output sales (table 2-2), we see a similar pattern. The Meat Products industry sells all but 0.3 percent of its output to a single I/O industry (eating and drinking places/retailers). That industry in turn has very low concentration, giving Meat Products many alternative customers for its products. The Communications Equipment industry, in contrast, sells almost 6 percent of its output to industries outside of its main buying

TABLE 2-1

Input/output table: Industry inputs for Meat Products and Communications Equipment

	Meat Products (from I/O industry #14)		Communications Equipment (from I/O industry #56)	
% bought from top 5 industries	60,821	26.97%	8,193	40.23%
	54,695	24.26%	1,970	9.67%
	22,262	9.87%	1,472	7.23%
	16,850	7.47%	1,418	6.96%
	8,683	3.85%	782	3.84%
Total use of commodities	225,473	100.00%	20,363	100.00%

TABLE 2-2

Input/output table: Industry outputs for Meat Products and Communications Equipment

Selling of outputs	Meat Products (from I/O industry #14)		Communications Equipment (from I/O industry #56)	
% sold to top 5 industries	325,129	99.74%	38,346	94.22%
	497	0.15%	1,140	2.80%
	136	0.04%	433	1.06%
	84	0.03%	273	0.67%
	39	0.01%	127	0.31%
Total output	325,972	100.00%	40,700	100.00%

industry, but the industry to which it sells 94 percent of its output is highly concentrated, making the opportunity to form supplier relationships even more scarce and critical.

Based on the earlier logic, when we combine the I/O exchange-constraints of these industries with data on the degree of industry concentration, our prediction is that the CEO effect in Meat Products is lower than the CEO effect in Communications Equipment.

The discussion above yields the following hypotheses that characterize the relation between industry concentration, exchange-constraint, and CEO effects.

> Hypothesis 2: Industries characterized by a high exchange-constraint will display higher CEO effects than industries with a low exchange-constraint.

> Hypothesis 3: Industries characterized by high firm concentration will display higher CEO effects than industries with low concentration.

In addition to concentration and exchange-constraint measures, we use industry growth rate as an additional measure that captures the scarcity or abundance of opportunity sets available to firms. CEOs in fast-growing industries should find it easier to locate opportunities—a "rising tide lifts all boats." For example, under these circumstances a company's CEO can freely choose "the clientele it shall serve" (Child, 1972), when and how to expand its productive capacity, and which research and development projects to pursue. In contrast, slow-growth industries are characterized by fewer opportunities, with the result that CEO actions can have greater impact on performance for the same reasons outlined earlier. This logic generates the following hypothesis:

> Hypothesis 4: High-growth industries will display lower CEO effects than industries with low levels of growth.

Resource Availability

In addition to the role of the opportunity set confronting firms examined above, the supply of resources will also affect the ability of CEOs to impact performance. Simply put, when opportunities present themselves, CEOs must possess the resources to pursue them. For instance, they must be able to make a critical acquisition when it presents itself, to invest money in developing a critical technology, or to roll out a large-scale marketing campaign at the right time. In general terms, this view of the effects of resource availability is similar to Hambrick and Finkelstein's (1987) "managerial discretion." In studying these issues, we consider two measures of resource availability that have received prior attention: firm leverage and slack.

According to the "control hypothesis" in the agency-theory literature, high leverage reduces the cash flow that a firm's CEO can direct toward investments or acquisitions, reducing his or her ability to affect company performance (Jensen, 1986). In addition, since high debt increases bankruptcy risk *ceteris paribus*, a firm's lenders are likely to conduct more stringent due diligence on a firm before they are willing to lend further, in turn reducing a CEO's impact. For both reasons, high leverage should constrain CEO actions.

> Hypothesis 5: Firms with high leverage will display lower CEO effects than those characterized by low levels of debt.

Counteracting the "handcuff of leverage" is the amount of slack at the CEO's disposal. Slack resources are those that the CEO can redirect relatively easily from low-opportunity areas toward higher-opportunity areas. For instance, the CEO might be able to take uncommitted marketing resources and invest them instead in further product development. It is worth noting that while there is disagreement in the literature about whether high slack helps or hurts an organization (Nohria and Gulati, 1997), there is perhaps greater consensus about the impact of slack on performance variability. On the one hand, high slack may result in managerial self-interest and waste, resulting in decreases in performance (Jensen and Meckling, 1976). On the other hand, slack implies that people or assets can be redeployed easily, providing CEOs with resources to manage conflicting demands from external groups that otherwise tie their hands (Galbraith, 1973).[2] These different perspectives suggest that high slack can result both in large negative or large positive changes in performance, implying a higher CEO effect.

> Hypothesis 6: Firms characterized by high levels of slack will display higher CEO effects than those characterized by low levels of slack.

Returning to our earlier industry examples, we can examine the role of resource availability as well. Meat Products is characterized by a higher-than-average ratio of debt-to-assets and slack—as measured by selling, general, and administrative (SG&A) costs as a percentage of sales—that is far below average. In contrast, in Communications Equipment, the level of debt has been about average while the level of slack resources has been above average. Therefore, we would predict that the CEO effect should be higher in Communications Equipment than in Meat Products.

The Contingent Opportunities Matrix

The matrix in table 2-3 summarizes the predictions of the contingent opportunities view of leadership described above. The matrix displays two dimensions that determine the magnitude of the CEO effect: scarcity of opportunities (which is a function of industry structure and growth), and resource availability (a function of leverage and slack). In "Impact" industries, where opportunities are scarce and the CEO has the resources needed to pursue the opportunities that arise, CEOs can have a large impact on company performance. At the other extreme, in "Impotent" industries, opportunities are rare and the CEO is resource constrained, so that his or her impact on company performance is lower. In between these cases are "Constrained" industries, where opportunities are scarce but resources to pursue them are not freely available, and "Munificent" industries, where resources are available but an abundant opportunity set implies that the CEO impact on performance will be moderate.[3]

TABLE 2-3

Matrix: The contingent opportunities view of leadership

		Scarcity of opportunities (industry concentration, exchange-constraint)	
		Low	High
Resource availability (low leverage, high slack)	Low	"Impotent" (Low CEO effect)	"Constraint" (Moderate CEO effect)
	High	"Munificent" (Moderate CEO effect)	"Impact" (High CEO effect)

Methods

Sample

Our sample consists of a hierarchical data set that tracks the performance of CEOs within companies over time. Our data include 531 companies from forty-two industries. Our selection criterion was to include all industries (classified as three-digit SIC) that had at least eight companies with Compustat data for the period 1979 to 1997. Forty-two industries fulfilled this criterion and were included in our data set. These industries included a wide variety of heavy manufacturing companies, service providers, and other businesses, and a mix of both small and large companies. Appendix 2-1 shows these forty-two industries.

Variables

DEPENDENT VARIABLE: FIRM PERFORMANCE

To test Hypothesis 1 and to estimate the CEO effects that are the basis for the subsequent cross-sectional regressions, we use two different measures of performance: return on assets (ROA), and Tobin's Q. ROA, measured as the ratio of operating income to total assets, is the measure of choice in prior work going back to Schmalansee (1985). However, as is well known, accounting-based measures such as ROA have certain shortcomings—they neglect the impact of inflation (Whittington, 1983) and risk (Schmalensee, 1981); they are sensitive to time lag considerations (for example, current ROA reflects investments that previous managers made in corporate assets [McGahan, 1998]);

and they do not include the value of intangible assets such as brand equity and technical competence (which, for some industries, comprise a significant fraction of asset bases). Therefore, following recent work such as McGahan (1998), we use Tobin's Q (the firm's market value divided by its book value) as a second measure of performance. A value of Tobin's Q greater than 1 reflects expectations that corporate actions will generate a greater return from the company's assets than if those assets were outside the firm. A value less than 1 reflects expectations that those assets could generate greater returns if they were deployed outside the firm. Notice that while accounting profit reflects a firm's *past* decisions, Tobin's Q reflects a firm's *prospects* for profitability (McGahan, 1998). As a result, Tobin's Q will incorporate more information about firm performance, for when they are making investment decisions, investors consider a wide range of company information not captured in ROA. Since this measure of performance is log-normally distributed, we use the natural logarithm of Tobin's Q as our dependent variable.

INDEPENDENT VARIABLES: YEAR, INDUSTRY, COMPANY, AND LEADER

Independent variables (for the analysis estimating the CEO effect) include time, industry, firm, and CEO dummies. *Year dummies* pick up variations in macroeconomic conditions, such as the state of the financial markets and the stage in the business cycle. *Industry dummies* (for each three-digit SIC code) pick up the effect of structural forces that are common to all firms in an industry, such as barriers to entry and exit, investments in fixed assets that are common to competitors, or technologically related switching costs. *Company or firm dummies* pick up the effect of differences in firm positioning relative to other firms in the same industry. Large firm effects imply large differences in average performance across firms in the same industry. Last, *CEO or leader dummies* pick up the variation in performance across CEOs within the same firm. If such effects are large, it implies that, after sweeping out the firm effect common to all CEOs of the same organization, there remain large differences in firm performance across the different CEOs. In other words, firm performance under each CEO differs consistently from the average performance across all the firm's CEOs.

In order to isolate the CEO effect, we gathered the names of the chief executive officer of each of our 531 companies across all 19 years in our sample, relying on annual reports and Dun & Bradstreet, Standard & Poor's, and Moody's publications. We attribute the performance in any given year to the CEO who was in place at the end of that year. Our data set included a total of 1,384 CEOs, for an average of 2.6 CEOs for each of our 531 companies. The average CEO tenure across the entire data set was 7.0 years, with a high of 10.1 years in SIC 6790 (Other Investing) and a low of 4.8 years in SIC 4810 (Telecommunications Services). Having 19 years of data in the data set allows us both to generate more intra-firm variation across CEOs and to reduce the problem of left and right truncation regarding CEO tenures.

Variables for Cross-Sectional Regressions

To test Hypotheses 2 through 6, we want to analyze the factors that affect the amount of CEO effect. To do this, we used the same forty-two industries as we used to test Hypothesis 1. The vector of CEO effects computed in our test of Hypothesis 1 was our dependent variable, and our independent variables were the factors hypothesized to have a large effect on CEO effect: industry structure and resource availability.

DEPENDENT VARIABLE: CEO EFFECT

To test these hypotheses, we wanted to analyze the factors that affect the level of CEO effect. Therefore, our dependent variable is the vector of CEO effects (shown in table 2-3) that we calculated while testing Hypothesis 1. Given Tobin's Q's explanatory superiority in our test of Hypothesis 1, for the remainder of our analyses, we used the CEO effects calculated in our Tobin's Q regressions.

INDEPENDENT VARIABLES: OPPORTUNITY SCARCITY AND RESOURCE AVAILABILITY

As described above, we posit that CEO effect will be affected by industry structure and dynamics, which drive the scarcity of opportunities, and by resource availability, which drives the CEO's ability to pursue opportunities. Therefore, to test these hypotheses, we modeled the drivers of CEO effect by using variables that dimensionalize industry and test the features of industries that are associated with leader effects.

We tested two central dimensions of industry structure: concentration ratios and exchange-constraint measures. For the first of these, Burt

(1982) used the input/output tables in the Department of Commerce's Survey of Current Business as measures of the structural relationships ("constraints") between industries. We therefore used the same constraints data as he used. While concentration data is not readily available, we obtained Burt's SIC-level four-firm concentration ratios on all of our industries. These ratios are both log-normally distributed. Therefore, we used the natural logarithms of these constraint and concentration ratios as our two external constraint measures. (Because the effect of concentration on the CEO effect is likely to depend on industry constraints, we introduced an interaction term that captures this nonlinear effect.) The midpoint of our data panel is 1987, so we used the 1987 benchmarks.

To test industry growth rate, our other indicator of opportunity scarcity, we computed each industry's average annual growth rate of sales revenue.

The resource availability factors that we tested were debt level, amount of slack, and cost structure. For debt level, we used Compustat data to compute the industry average ratio of total debt to firm assets. For slack, we used Compustat data to compute the industry average ratio of SG&A to net sales. For cost structure, we used Compustat data to compute the industry average ratio of cost of goods sold (COGS) to net sales.

We used industry-level averages for these regressions, for two main reasons. First, the Burt (1992) industry concentration and exchange-constraint numbers are at the industry level. Second, each company has, on average, only three CEOs across the nineteen years in the data set, giving us few data points with which to compute company-level CEO effects. Therefore, we wanted to use the industry-level CEO effects (where all industries had at least thirty CEOs across the nineteen years in our data set).

Approach

Hambrick and Finkelstein (1987:400) pose the problem of how to measure CEO discretion and impact. There are two common approaches to measurement in the literature: event study analysis and variance decomposition. Whereas the former are useful in studying the market reaction to discrete events (for example, the announcement of a new CEO, or the firing of an existing one), their main drawback is that they only incorporate market expectations of performance rather than actual performance. For this reason, we follow prior work looking at the CEO effect by relying on variance decomposition techniques.

Our approach to variance decomposition follows McGahan and Porter (1997), who in turn build on the work of Schmalensee (1985) and Rumelt (1991) to disaggregate firm performance into components associated with industry, company, and other effects. One advantage is that rather than simply indicate *whether* a specific factor is important, this approach helps answer *how important* each factor is. Schmalensee's (1985) influential paper relies on one year of data and disaggregates firm performance into industry and firm effects, with these two factors explaining about 20 percent of the variance in performance. McGahan and Porter (1997) exploit fourteen years of data (1981–1994) and conduct hierarchical OLS regressions.[4] The incremental R^2 obtained by adding each variable to the regression provides an indicator of how important each factor is in explaining firm performance. Under this approach they find that year, industry, and firm effects together explain about 52 percent of the variance in firm performance.

To study the role of CEOs, we extend McGahan and Porter's (1997) hierarchical regression approach to include CEO dummies after all the other factors have been included and use the incremental R^2 to measure the importance of each factor. Notice that this variance-partitioning procedure attributes shared variation to higher-level factors in the hierarchy; for example, the variance shared by Year and Industry is attributed to Year. To test whether the CEO effect varies by industry (Hypothesis 1), we run these regressions at the industry level.[5]

Results

Table 2-4 presents the results of our aggregate regressions. Regardless of the performance measure used (ROA or Tobin's Q), firm effects explain the largest share of performance variation across the entire sample. In both sets of regressions, the CEO effect is significant at the $p < .01$ level, and explains between 13 percent and 15 percent of the total variation. This basic finding is consistent with prior work, and serves as the basis of our subsequent analyses.

Tables 2-5 and 2-6 present the results of our industry-level analyses. The most important finding here is that, regardless of the performance measure used, the CEO effect exhibits large differences across industries. Using ROA as the dependent variable, the CEO effect varies from a low of 4.6 percent to a high of 41.0 percent. Using Tobin's Q as the dependent variable, the CEO effect varies from a low of 2.4 percent to a high of 22.8 percent. Industries that consistently display a large CEO

TABLE 2-4

Incremental explanatory power (incremental R^2) from adding each independent variable to the aggregate regression models

Independent variables	Model 1 (ROA)	Model 2 (Tobin's Q)
Year	0.026	0.052
Industry	0.063	0.155
Company	0.255	0.328
Leader	0.147	0.135
Total R^2	0.491	0.670
Number of observations	10,089	10,089

Note: Model 1 uses return on assets (ROA) as the dependent variable. Model 2 uses Tobin's Q as the dependent variable. Number of observations = 531 companies × 19 years = 10,089.

effect (i.e., are ranked in the top third regardless of performance measure used) include SIC 3560 (General Industrial Machinery), SIC 3620 (Electrical Industrial Apparatus), SIC 3820 (Measuring and Controlling Devices), SIC 3810 (Search, Detection, and Navigation Instruments and Equipment), SIC 4920 (Gas Production and Distribution), SIC 5060 (Wholesale Electrical Goods), SIC 6330 (Fire, Marine, and Casualty Insurance) and SIC 8710 (Engineering, Architectural, and Surveying Services). Industries that consistently display a low CEO effect (i.e., are ranked in the bottom third regardless of performance measure used) are SIC 2620 (Paper Mills), SIC 2840 (Cleaning Preparation and Toiletries), SIC 3710 (Motor Vehicles and Equipment), SIC 4810 (Telecommunications Services), SIC 6020 (Commercial Banks) and SIC 6790 (Investing). The correlation of CEO effects in the two tables is 0.21, and the rank order correlation of the industries in the two tables is 0.30.

Table 2-7 shows the correlation matrix for the independent variables that we used to test Hypotheses 2 through 6. Table 2-8 presents the results of this cross-regression.

Looking first at opportunity scarcity, both the measures of industry concentration and exchange-constraint are highly significant predictors ($p < .01$) of a CEO effect. Industry growth rate, an obverse indicator of opportunity scarcity, is significant at the $p < .05$ level. The empirical

TABLE 2-5

Incremental explanatory power (incremental R^2) from adding each variable to the regression model, using ROA as the dependent variable

SIC	Industry name	Year	Company	Leader
1310	Crude Petroleum and Natural Gas	18.3	22.7	12.2
1380	Oil and Gas Field Services	36.6	22.0	12.6
1530	Construction	19.2	7.7	9.7
2010	Meat Products	13.4	22.1	11.0
2620	Paper Mills	35.4	27.3	4.6
2830	Drugs	1.9	42.7	12.3
2840	Cleaning Preparations and Toiletries	4.7	37.2	5.8
2890	Chemical Products (Other)	4.6	64.9	8.1
2910	Petroleum Refining	22.9	13.3	18.9
3080	Plastic Products (Other)	6.2	42.0	12.6
3310	Blast Furnaces and Basic Steel Products	18.1	34.6	12.7
3440	Fabricated Structural Metal Products	12.9	29.9	11.4
3530	Construction and Related Machinery	30.4	18.8	7.6
3560	General Industrial Machinery	10.8	28.6	19.6
3570	Computer and Office Equipment	8.6	11.6	10.7
3620	Electrical Industrial Apparatus	13.3	30.0	22.3
3640	Electric Lighting and Wiring Equipment	9.7	27.8	10.8
3660	Communications Equipment	17.2	13.0	12.2
3670	Electronic Components and Accessories	8.8	23.4	14.8
3710	Motor Vehicles and Equipment	18.3	6.9	8.7
3720	Aircraft and Parts	12.5	7.2	13.5
3810	Search, Detection, Navigation, Guidance, Aeronautical and Nautical Systems Instruments and Equipment	16.1	12.3	24.2

(continued)

TABLE 2-5 *(continued)*

Incremental explanatory power (incremental R^2) from adding each variable to the regression model, using ROA as the dependent variable

SIC	Industry name	Year	Company	Leader
3820	Measuring and Controlling Devices	4.3	25.6	26.9
3840	Medical Instruments and Supplies	5.9	46.2	6.9
4810	Telecommunications Services	13.2	45.9	8.8
4910	Electric Power Generation, Transmission, or Distribution	13.8	14.7	12.7
4920	Gas Production and Distribution	6.0	53.0	19.5
4930	Combination Utility Services	13.3	33.4	12.9
4940	Water Supply	15.4	18.5	25.4
5060	Electrical Goods (Wholesale)	8.6	21.8	30.8
5310	Department Stores	12.9	29.9	18.6
5410	Grocery Stores	4.0	45.8	24.2
5810	Eating and Drinking Places	4.9	40.9	10.5
6020	Commercial Banks	18.8	16.0	10.5
6140	Personal Credit Institutions and Credit and Debit Cards	8.7	27.3	9.5
6310	Life Insurance	12.3	65.5	5.8
6330	Fire, Marine, and Casualty Insurance	5.7	11.0	17.5
6510	Real Estate Operators and Lessors	7.2	10.0	13.2
6790	Investing (Other)	15.5	19.0	7.8
7010	Hotels and Motels	6.0	28.2	41.0
7370	Computer Programming, Data Processing, Related Services	6.0	32.8	12.8
8710	Engineering, Architectural, and Surveying Services	8.5	16.9	14.8

proxies for resource availability are also both significant, with debt/assets significant at the $p < .01$ level and SG&A/sales significant at the $p < .05$ level. As a whole, the explanatory power of these covariates in the cross-sectional regression is high ($R^2 = 0.56$).

TABLE 2-6

Incremental explanatory power (incremental R^2) from adding each variable to the regression model, using Tobin's Q as the dependent variable

SIC	Industry name	Year	Company	Leader
1310	Crude Petroleum and Natural Gas	28.8	27.6	20.3
1380	Oil and Gas Field Services	29.0	21.1	10.7
1530	Construction	18.1	19.2	5.5
2010	Meat Products	23.9	47.7	2.4
2620	Paper Mills	30.4	45.0	8.2
2830	Drugs	16.1	35.5	15.4
2840	Cleaning Preparations and Toiletries	32.7	31.0	9.8
2890	Chemical Products (Other)	8.1	47.0	17.3
2910	Petroleum Refining	27.0	38.6	11.2
3080	Plastic Products (Other)	26.1	41.6	9.9
3310	Blast Furnaces and Basic Steel Products	26.4	38.2	10.2
3440	Fabricated Structural Metal Products	15.8	32.1	8.0
3530	Construction and Related Machinery	25.5	21.2	10.5
3560	General Industrial Machinery	7.7	42.8	17.7
3570	Computer and Office Equipment	24.3	22.9	17.7
3620	Electrical Industrial Apparatus	11.3	47.6	17.3
3640	Electric Lighting and Wiring Equipment	12.7	33.0	19.1
3660	Communications Equipment	13.9	25.3	22.0
3670	Electronic Components and Accessories	17.0	33.9	9.9
3710	Motor Vehicles and Equipment	44.0	21.5	6.0

(continued)

TABLE 2-6 *(continued)*

Incremental explanatory power (incremental R^2) from adding each variable to the regression model, using Tobin's Q as the dependent variable

SIC	Industry name	Year	Company	Leader
3720	Aircraft and Parts	15.5	48.2	7.9
3810	Search, Detection, Navigation, Guidance, Aeronautical, and Nautical Systems, Instruments, and Equipment	24.9	16.1	16.0
3820	Measuring and Controlling Devices	7.0	41.2	22.8
3840	Medical Instruments and Supplies	8.2	32.7	10.7
4810	Telecommunications Services	69.4	7.5	7.1
4910	Electric Power Generation, Transmission, or Distribution	65.3	12.4	7.1
4920	Gas Production and Distribution	38.2	24.8	21.1
4930	Combination Utility Services	39.5	37.0	5.9
4940	Water Supply	66.3	9.7	10.2
5060	Electrical Goods (Wholesale)	15.5	28.6	15.7
5310	Department Stores	25.9	50.9	13.3
5410	Grocery Stores	19.7	45.1	15.1
5810	Eating and Drinking Places	8.9	47.8	11.2
6020	Commercial Banks	59.3	17.8	8.3
6140	Personal Credit Institutions and Credit and Debit Cards	45.8	0.1	16.7
6310	Life Insurance	31.7	45.5	10.6
6330	Fire, Marine, and Casualty Insurance	7.6	36.5	21.2
6510	Real Estate Operators and Lessors	9.7	67.3	8.6
6790	Investing (Other)	15.1	51.7	4.5
7010	Hotels and Motels	10.8	61.5	3.5
7370	Computer Programming, Data Processing, Related Services	10.4	48.4	12.4
8710	Engineering, Architectural, and Surveying Services	6.0	44.2	15.5

TABLE 2-7

Correlation matrix for independent variables included in the regression model in table 2-8

	Concen-tration	Constraint	Interaction	Debt/ Assets	Sales growth	SG&A/ Sales
Concentration	1.0000					
Constraint	0.1725	1.0000				
Interaction	0.7630	0.7645	1.0000			
Debt/Assets	−0.1625	−0.0179	−0.1134	1.0000		
Sales growth	0.3981	−0.1024	0.1849	−0.1870	1.0000	
SG&A/Sales	0.4852	0.2436	0.4585	−0.2476	−0.1100	1.0000

Note: "Interaction" is interaction between Concentration and Constraint.

Discussion

CEO Effects

In our aggregate analyses, the CEO effect accounts for 14.7 percent of the variance in company performance when using ROA as the dependent variable, and for 13.5 percent of the variance when using Tobin's Q as the dependent variable. Both results are consistent with Lieberson and O'Connor's (1972) result of 14.5 percent on a much smaller sample. The CEO effect is strongly significant ($p < .01$). Furthermore, the unexplained variance in company performance declines notably (to less than 0.3) when a CEO effect is also included in the analysis, comparing favorably with past variance decomposition analyses (such as McGahan and Porter, 1997).

In subsequent analyses and discussion we focus on the Tobin's Q measure of performance, given its various advantages (including lower susceptibility to lags and incorporation of information regarding risk and intangible assets) over an accounting measure like ROA.

Interindustry CEO Effect Results

A core finding of our work is that CEOs have much greater impact in some industries than in others. In industries where time effects and firm effects are large, such as in SIC 4910 (Electric Power Generation, Transmission, or Distribution) where the two variables account for

TABLE 2-8

Contingent opportunities regression model, using Tobin's Q–based CEO effects from table 2-6 as the dependent variable

Independent variables	Model
Concentration	55.573***
	(17.361)
Constraint	61.791***
	(20.543)
Interaction of Concentration and Constraint	−18.563***
	(5.940)
Sales growth rate	−52.363***
	(22.793)
Debt/Assets	−12.192***
	(3.822)
SG&A/Sales	6.086**
	(2.977)
Constant	−158.933***
	(59.006)
R^2	0.5564
Number of observations	42

Note: Standard errors are in parentheses.
* $p < .10$
** $p < .05$
*** $p < .01$

78 percent of the variance in performance, CEOs take few actions that affect company performance. (Later in this paper, we explore reasons why this might be true.) In industries where the year and company effects are large, such as in SIC 3660 (Communications Equipment), where the two variables account for less than 40 percent of the variance in performance, CEOs have greater impact. This set of results not only contrasts with earlier work (that more or less neglects interindustry differences) but also contrasts with Thomas's racing-driver analogy— indeed, our findings suggest that CEOs *can* be faced with very different situations across different industries.

These results support Hypothesis 1, that CEO effect varies by industry. In some settings, CEO impact is large, while in other settings, CEOs have little impact.

It is worth reinforcing here that a large CEO effect need not imply a positive impact of CEOs on performance but rather, simply, that the variance in performance across CEOs is greater. Indeed, as noted by Thompson (1967), deviant discretion—discretion that is inappropriate to the specific situation—can be harmful. In other words, industries that exhibit CEO effects may include many CEOs whose actions *negatively* impact company performance. The disadvantages of high CEO discretion are also noted by Hambrick and Finkelstein, who state that "if we had to choose as a society between doing away with Figureheads or Unconstrained Managers, clearly it is the Figureheads we would keep" (Hambrick and Finkelstein, 1987:404).

Before proceeding, we examine whether our results could merely reflect small-sample biases. That is, CEO tenures last on average eight years, with a standard deviation of four years. This implies that, by sheer good luck, the tenure of some CEOs could coincide with a series of high-performance years. Similarly, other CEOs might have the misfortune of witnessing successive negative performance shocks during their tenure. Idiosyncratic shocks to performance would cancel out if there were enough observations on each CEO. However, because this is not the case, the concern is that the "CEO effect" might simply reflect the fact that some CEOs are just lucky, others not. We ran Monte Carlo simulations to get an estimate of how large this small-sample bias is. We randomly allocated performance data across all of the company-years within each of the forty-two industries and iteratively re-ran our variance-decomposition regressions as we had done with the actual performance data. The resulting CEO effect estimated in these simulations serves as a benchmark against which to evaluate our results.

In twelve industries, the CEO effect estimated from actual data was more than 5 percentage points (significant at the $p < .05$ level) greater than the (spurious) effect estimated from the simulated data, and in five industries it was more than 10 percentage points greater. At the same time, for a little more than half of the industries, the difference between the observed and spurious CEO effect was less than one percentage point. These results further reinforce our conclusion that while in some industries the CEO effect is large, in others it is negligible.

Figure 2-1 presents the estimates of the observed CEO effect (i.e., in the actual data) versus the effect arising from purely random processes in Monte Carlo simulations. The closer the observed CEO effects are to the 45° line, the harder it is to reject the hypothesis that

FIGURE 2-1

CEO results: Actual data versus Monte Carlo CEO results

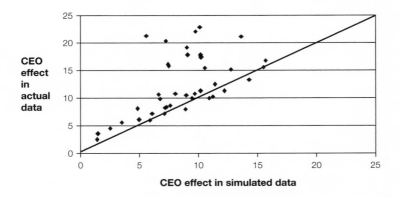

these effects are spurious. As shown in the figure, many industries are, indeed, close to this line—these industries also turn out to be the ones where CEOs are so constrained that they are predicted to have little effect on performance. However, as is also shown, there are several other industries where the observed CEO effect lies noticeably above the 45° line (and where the differences are statistically significant). In these industries, CEOs have a large impact on company performance.[6]

Before proceeding, it is worth noting a few caveats to our analysis that cause us to either overstate or understate the true magnitude of the "leadership effect." First, our CEO effect uses the CEO of the company to assess the impact of leadership on company performance. However, if a change in CEOs also signals a change in the broader management team (for example, if each CEO brings in a new CFO, COO, and CTO with him or her), then this effect would reflect too the broader impact that management teams have on company performance, rather than the impact of an individual. For this reason, the true CEO effect may be less than that estimated here. Second, our variance-decomposition models rely on contemporaneous performance measures rather than lags. However (and despite the associated advantages of the Tobin's Q measure), for many CEO decisions (such as major capital investments and attempts to change company culture) the impact of CEO actions may not be reflected for several years. For this reason, the true CEO effect may be greater than the effect estimated here. Third, because we only introduce CEO dummies in the regressions *after* accounting for all the other variables, our estimate of the actual magnitude of the CEO effect may be a conservative estimate of the true effect. As a result of all these limitations, while our findings of differences in the CEO effect across industries are unlikely to alter, the absolute magnitude of our estimates of the CEO effect must be interpreted with caution. Beyond this, as Hambrick and Finkelstein (1987:378–389) point out, in addition to the characteristics of the task environment and the characteristics of the internal organization (both of which we test here), the characteristics of the specific CEO are important determinants of a CEO effect. There are reasons to believe that differences in CEO characteristics may not play a large role. For instance, Pfeffer (1977) argues that CEOs are relatively homogeneous because career ladders filter out people with certain characteristics before they get to the CEO position. Despite this (and despite it being beyond the scope of this study to assess how individual characteristics affect the CEO's impact on company performance), this is a fruitful area of inquiry going forward.

Opportunity Scarcity and Resource Availability

Our results also show that the scarcity of opportunities and the availability of resources are both critical factors in determining how much impact a CEO can have on company performance. First, regarding opportunity scarcity, our results support the hypotheses (2 and 3) that an industry's level of exchange-constraint and concentration are critical indicators of CEO impact. In industries highly constrained by their external relationships, company leaders have fewer opportunities to act. Similarly, our results support Hypothesis 4, that in industries with low growth rates, the CEO effect is higher. Since opportunities are scarcer in low-growth industries, there is a premium on a CEO's ability to take advantage of every opportunity. In contrast, in industries where opportunities are plentiful, CEOs have less impact on company performance.

Second, with regard to internal firm characteristics, we find three significant factors. Our results confirm the hypothesis that high debt handcuffs a CEO, strongly supporting Hypothesis 5. When a company is obligated to pay out a large percentage of its free cash flow to its debt holders (or otherwise risk bankruptcy), CEOs have lower impact on company performance. In contrast, with lower debt, CEOs can deploy free cash flow to new investments or other activities that can alter company performance. Notice that lower constraints do not imply that average firm performance improves (indeed, as is familiar, agency problems can result in decreases in performance), but rather that the variation in performance is greater.

Our results also show support for Hypothesis 6. Low slack implies that CEOs do not have resources with which to pursue scarce opportunities, therefore reducing their impact on company performance. However, when slack is high, CEOs are more able to take advantage of opportunities or proactively pursue projects that may change company performance. Notice, again, that the CEOs need not improve performance on average when slack is high, but rather that the *variance* in performance is greater. For example, with high slack CEOs can better satisfy competing external demands that otherwise would constrain them. Alternatively, CEOs with high slack may also waste company assets at a faster rate, thereby having a big negative impact on company performance. In either case, slack is a key factor in CEO impact.

Robustness

We conclude with a brief discussion of robustness tests. In measuring the role of firm-specific constraints, one might argue that some of the independent variables are not entirely exogenous. For example, a firm's debt level or SG&A spending may reflect choices of the firm's CEO rather than constraints operating on him or her.[7] The econometric concern generated by this logic is that any relation between, for example, slack and a "CEO effect" cannot be causally attributed to the regressors but, rather, reflects the presence of some other unobserved factor. Further, the estimated correlation may merely reflect a mechanical relationship between the variables (for example, reduced SG&A implies lower costs and therefore higher performance) rather than any deep correlation. In our econometric implementation, the main reason to think this may not be of concern is that in measuring the role of constraints (through leverage or slack) we rely on industry-level measures (averaged across all firms in the industry) rather than firm-level ones. Furthermore, in our sample, the intra-industry differences in leverage and SG&A are much lower than the differences across industries, justifying the assumption that CEOs have at best partial control over these variables.

While most of the variables we test are well defined, the variable proxying for slack is not. SG&A is an imperfect indicator of slack because it includes many things, such as committed advertising expenditures, that are not slack resources redeployable by the CEO. In addition, the definition of SG&A may differ by industry; for example, some industries may include marketing expenses in SG&A, while others have a separate line for reporting marketing expenses and therefore don't include them in SG&A. While SG&A is the most appealing single measure of slack we have, there is room for further work in this area.

Last, we test for the robustness of our results to the inclusion of three other sets of performance drivers: firm size, CEO tenure, and intra-industry variance in Tobin's Q. To begin with, Thomas (1988) notes that company size should impact CEO performance since, for example, a CEO of a smaller company has more information about the entire workings of the company and is therefore in a better position to directly impact its performance. Second, regarding CEO tenure, CEOs are more likely to be fired when firm performance is low or when the change in firm performance is negative. This would overstate the CEO effects because of the following bias: CEOs who are fired are more likely, inter alia, to have experienced a decline in performance. In contrast, CEOs who are in office have not experienced poor performance yet. Right-censoring would therefore cause the mean performance to be lower for those CEOs whose tenures have ended and higher for those whose tenure has not.[8]

Last, an additional concern is that variance in Tobin's Q may reflect industry differences in the variance of performance rather than a CEO effect. In industries where performance swings wildly from year to year or from company to company, firm performance data exhibits a higher variance and we would expect to observe larger CEO effects. The observed CEO effects would then have little to do with scarcity of opportunities and resource availability, but merely reflect the underlying variance in performance.

We perform an auxiliary analysis that adds to our regression model three sets of variables: average firm assets in each year, CEO tenures, and variances in Tobin's Q for each of our forty-two industries. This regression is shown in table 2-9. Size, tenure, and variance in performance have no statistically significant impact on the CEO effect.

Conclusion

This paper examines the importance of CEOs to variations in performance of organizations. Using an augmented variance decomposition

TABLE 2-9

Sensitivity of the CEO effect to firm size, CEO tenures, and variance of performance, using Tobin's Q–based CEO effects from table 2-6

Independent variables	Model
Average assets	0.000
	(0.001)
Variance of Tobin's Q	0.880
	(0.597)
CEO tenure	−0.373
	(0.741)
Constant	13.424
	(5.716)
R^2	0.0732
Number of observations	42

Note: Standard errors are in parentheses.
* $p < .10$
** $p < .05$
*** $p < .01$

approach, we find, like prior work, that who the CEO of an organization is, matters. On average, variation in performance across CEOs explains about 14 percent of total variation in performance of firms. The main contribution of this paper is to explore the contexts in which CEOs matter. We find large and interesting differences across industries in how much of the variance in performance can be attributed to a CEO effect. For example, in Communications Equipment, the CEO effect accounts for 21 percent of the variance in company performance, while in Meat Products, the CEO accounts for only 2 percent of the variance. We benchmark our results against Monte Carlo simulations where a CEO effect arises even as a result of purely random processes and the cross-industry differences appear starker, with more than half of all industries showing an "adjusted CEO effect" of near-zero while other industries display a large and statistically significant CEO effect.

The "bottom line" of our results is that in a clear subset of industries, leadership matters a lot, whereas in other industries, it matters little. In other words, focusing on *the contexts where leadership matters* appears to be perhaps a more productive line of inquiry than simply asking *whether* leadership matters.

We further develop our contingent opportunities view of CEO leadership by exploring industry characteristics that might explain differences in the CEO effect. Building on Hambrick and Finkelstein's (1987) theory of discretion and on Burt's (1992) theory of structural holes, we examine how the CEO effect is related to the scarcity of opportunities in an industry and to available resources with which CEOs can pursue opportunities that present themselves. We show that exchange-constraint and industry concentration are significant factors in explaining CEO impact. In addition, the amount of resources available to pursue opportunities—proxied by the level of debt and the level of slack—also significantly affects CEO impact. CEOs in industries where organizations are characterized by low debt and high slack are better able to take advantage of opportunities.

Our findings have interesting positive and normative implications for CEO compensation and CEO succession that are worth exploring further. For example, it would be useful to examine whether pay-for-performance sensitivity of CEO compensation is lower in industries characterized by a low CEO effect than in industries characterized by a high CEO effect. Similarly, one might expect that the nature and intensity of the CEO search process should vary across industries depending on structural attributes like scarcity of opportunities, exchange constraint, and industry concentration. In addition, as suggested by Hambrick and Finkelstein (1987), the characteristics necessary to perform well in a constrained industry (as a Titular Figurehead) are probably very different from the characteristics necessary to perform well in an unconstrained industry (as an Unconstrained Manager).

An interesting corollary to our results concern contextual effects in stock market reactions to CEO turnover. For example, in industries with a high CEO effect, a firm's stock price should react more when there are changes in CEO, and conversely in industries where the CEO effect is low.

Beyond this, much work remains regarding the factors that affect the amount of impact that CEOs can have. One particular set of factors concern personal CEO characteristics (discussed in detail in Hambrick and Finkelstein, 1987) such as a leader's commitment, ability to deal with cognitive complexity, tolerance of ambiguity, ability to build a power base, and political acumen. Another area is the processes by which CEOs try to proactively increase their level of impact. Our findings suggest, again, that examining how these characteristics and processes vary with context is likely to be an important line of inquiry.

At a broader level, we feel that our results speak to a deep and long-lasting debate within the organizational literature around the relative importance of individual agency vis-à-vis social structure on human and organizational action. On the one hand, Durkheim argues that structural factors are "independent of the particular individual" and "exist outside of the consciousness of the individual" (Durkheim, 1982:45, 51). These factors, or "social facts," exert "external coercive power" (Durkheim, 1982:53) and hereby constrain the actions of actors. In the face of these structure factors, "the individual circumstances which may have played some part in producing the phenomenon cancel each other out and consequently do not contribute to determining the nature of the phenomenon" (Durkheim, 1982:55). On the other hand, agency-oriented scholars (e.g., Coleman, 1964; Homans, 1964) argue that individual actors create, adapt to, and change the rules of society. Instead of norms controlling people, "norms arise through the actions of men rationally calculating to further their own self interest" (Homans, 1964:813). Our results suggest that a contingency perspective that examines *when* agency or structure plays a greater role, respectively, may offer a productive reframing of this debate, in order to better understand the contexts in which leadership, agency, and structure influence organizations and the actors within them.

Appendix 2-1

List of Industries Included in the Data Set

SIC	Industry Name
1310	Crude Petroleum and Natural Gas
1380	Oil and Gas Field Services
1530	Construction
2010	Meat Products
2620	Paper Mills
2830	Drugs
2840	Cleaning Preparations and Toiletries
2890	Chemical Products (Other)
2910	Petroleum Refining
3080	Plastic Products (Other)
3310	Blast Furnaces and Basic Steel Products
3440	Fabricated Structural Metal Products
3530	Construction and Related Machinery
3560	General Industrial Machinery
3570	Computer and Office Equipment
3620	Electrical Industrial Apparatus
3640	Electric Lighting and Wiring Equipment
3660	Communications Equipment
3670	Electronic Components and Accessories
3710	Motor Vehicles and Equipment
3720	Aircraft and Parts
3810	Search, Detection, Navigation, Guidance, Aeronautical, and Nautical Systems
3820	Measuring and Controlling Devices
3840	Medical Instruments and Supplies
4810	Telecommunications Services

(continued)

List of Industries Included in the Data Set (*continued*)

SIC	Industry Name
4910	Electric Power Generation, Transmission, or Distribution
4920	Gas Production and Distribution
4930	Combination Utility Services
4940	Water Supply
5060	Electrical Goods (Wholesale)
5310	Department Stores
5410	Grocery Stores
5810	Eating and Drinking Places
6020	Commercial Banks
6140	Personal Credit Institutions and Credit and Debit Cards
6310	Life Insurance
6330	Fire, Marine, and Casualty Insurance
6510	Real Estate Operators (Except Developers) and Lessors
6790	Investing (Other)
7010	Hotels and Motels
7370	Computer Programming, Data Processing, and Other Computer Related Services
8710	Engineering, Architectural, and Surveying Services

References

Barnard, C. *The Functions of the Executive.* Cambridge, MA: Harvard University Press, 1938.

Bertrand, M., and A. Schoar. "Managing with Style: The Effect of Managers on Firm Policies." *Quarterly Journal of Economics*, vol. CXVIII (2003): 1169–1208.

Bowman, E.H., and C.E. Helfat. "Does Corporate Strategy Matter?" Working paper, Wharton School, University of Pennsylvania, 1997.

Burkhardt, M.E. "Institutionalization of Technological Change." Working paper, Wharton School, University of Pennsylvania, 1991.

Burt, R. "Autonomy in a Social Topology." *American Journal of Sociology* 85 (1980): 892–925.

———. *Toward a Structural Theory of Action.* New York: Academic Press, 1982.

———. *Structural Holes.* Cambridge, MA: Harvard University Press, 1992.

Child, J. "Organizational Structure, Environment and Performance: The Role of Strategic Choice." *Sociology* 6 (1972): 1–22.

Coleman, J.S. "Collective Decisions." *Sociological Inquiry* 34 (1964): 166–181.

Cyert, R.M., and J.G. March. *A Behavioral Theory of the Firm*. Englewood Cliffs, NJ: Prentice-Hall, 1963.

Drucker, P.F. *The Practice of Management*. New York: Harper & Row, 1954.

Durkheim, E. *The Rules of Sociological Method*. New York: The Free Press, 1982.

Fiedler, F.E. "Engineer the Job to Fit the Manager." *Harvard Business Review* 43, no. 5 (September–October 1965): 115–122.

———. *A Theory of Leadership Effectiveness*. New York: McGraw-Hill, 1967.

Galbraith, J.R. *Designing Complex Organizations*. Reading, MA: Addison-Wesley, 1973.

Hambrick, D.C., and S. Finkelstein. "Managerial Discretion: A Bridge Between Polar Views of Organizational Outcomes." *Research in Organizational Behavior* 9 (1987): 369–406.

Hannan, M.T., and J. Freeman. *Organizational Ecology*. Boston: Harvard University Press, 1989.

Homans, G.C. "Bringing Men Back In." *American Sociological Review* 29 (1964): 809–818.

Jensen, M.C. "Agency Costs of Free Cash Flow, Corporate Finance, and Takeovers." *American Economic Review* 76 (1986): 323–329.

Jensen, M.C., and W.H. Meckling. "Theory of the Firm: Managerial Behavior, Agency Costs, and Ownership Structure." *Journal of Financial Economics* 3 (1976): 305–360.

Khurana, R., and N. Nohria. "The Performance Consequences of CEO Turnover." Working paper, Harvard Business School, Boston, 1999.

Lawrence, P.R., and J.W. Lorsch. *Organization and Environment*. Boston: Harvard University Press, 1967.

Lieberson, S., and J. O'Connor. "Leadership and Organization Performance: A Study of Large Corporations." *American Sociological Review* 37 (1972): 117–130.

March, J.G., and H.A. Simon. *Organizations*. New York: Wiley, 1958.

Martin, J. *Cultures in Organizations: Three Perspectives*. New York: Oxford University Press, 1992.

McGahan, A.M. "The Performance of U.S. Corporations: 1981–1994." Manuscript, Harvard Business School, 1998.

McGahan, A.M., and M.E. Porter. "How Much Does Industry Matter, Really?" *Strategic Management Journal* 18 (1997): 15–30.

Nohria, N., and R. Gulati. "What Is the Optimum Amount of Organizational Slack?" *European Management Journal* 15 (1997): 603–611.

Pfeffer, J. "Towards an Examination of Stratification in Organizations." *Administrative Science Quarterly* 22 (1977): 553–567.

Pfeffer, J., and G.R. Salancik. *The External Control of Organizations: A Resource Dependency Perspective*. New York: Harper & Row, 1978.

Powell, W.W., and P.J. DiMaggio, eds. *The New Institutionalism in Organizational Analysis*. Chicago: University of Chicago Press, 1991.

Rotemberg, J.J., and G. Saloner. "Visionaries, Managers, and Strategic Direction." Working paper 98-118, Harvard Business School, 1998.

Rumelt, R.P. "How Much Does Industry Matter?" *Strategic Management Journal* 12 (1991): 167–185.

Schmalensee, R. "Do Markets Differ Much?" *American Economic Review* 75 (1985): 341–351.

———. "Risk and Return on Long Lived Tangible Assets." *Journal of Financial Economics* 9 (1981): 185–205.

Simon, H.A. *Administrative Behavior.* 3rd ed. New York: Macmillan, 1976.

Thomas, A.B. "Does Leadership Make a Difference to Organizational Performance?" *Administrative Science Quarterly* 33 (1988): 388–400.

Thompson, J.D. *Organizations in Action.* New York: McGraw-Hill, 1967.

Weiner, N. "Situational and Leadership Influence on Organization Performance." *Proceedings of the Academy of Management,* 1978, 230–234.

Weiner, N., and T.A. Mahoney. "A Model of Corporate Performance as a Function of Environmental, Organizational, and Leadership Influences." *Academy of Management Journal* 24 (1981): 453–470.

Whittington, G. *Inflation Accounting: An Introduction to the Debate.* Cambridge: Cambridge University Press, 1983.

Wiersema, M.F. "Strategic Consequences of Executive Succession Within Diversified Firms." *Journal of Management Studies* 29 (1992): 73–94.

Woodward, J. *Industrial Organization: Theory and Practice.* New York: Oxford University Press, 1965.

Notes

1. Interestingly, while the scholarship on leadership is vast, much less theoretical work has been done about the role of CEOs in particular. Most CEO studies are concerned with compensation or stratification issues rather than leadership per se. Therefore, in characterizing these different perspectives we draw heavily on the more general literature on leadership in what follows.

2. March and Simon (1958) also note that slack allows CEOs to take advantage of opportunities more easily. Similarly, Thompson (1967) notes that "the larger the fund of uncommitted capacities, the greater the organization's assurance of self-control in an uncertain future." Last, Pfeffer and Salancik (1978:275) note that slack resources enable organizations to create loosely coupled subunits that reduce the pressure from environmental constraints, "for without slack, subunits could not be loosely connected and could not respond to their immediate environments without affecting the entire system.

3. Worth noting is that some of our hypotheses conflict with predictions made by Hambrick and Finkelstein (1987). In particular, they posit that high constraint situations (such as in the Communications Equipment industry) will produce CEOs who are Titular Figureheads who have little impact on company performance.

4. In this approach they first include year dummies, then year and industry dummies, then year, industry, and firm dummies, in order to test the marginal importance of each.

5. In other words, for each industry, we sequentially apportion the variance in company performance to year, company, and CEO effects by calculating the incremental variance explained by adding each independent variable to the regression.

6. Notice that we can construct a crude measure of an "adjusted CEO effect" that subtracts the estimated spurious CEO effect from the observed one. The correlation between this measure and the observed CEO effects is 0.83.

7. More generally, in order to gain control over the resources their organizations need, managers can adapt or alter the constraints under which they work; alter their interdependencies through merger, diversification, or growth; negotiate the environment by forming associations and joint ventures and by creating interlocking directorships; and use political action to change the legality or legitimacy of its environment. As Pfeffer and Salancik (1978:18) note, "there are many possibilities for managerial action, even given the external constraint on most organizations. Constraints are not predestined and irreversible."

8. In other words, suppose the true performance of each CEO is equal. Right-censoring implies that we observe a CEO effect when there really isn't any.

3

REVISITING THE MEANING OF LEADERSHIP

Joel M. Podolny, Rakesh Khurana, and Marya L. Besharov

Introduction

Through the 1960s, leading organizational theorists regarded the concept of leadership to be worthy of serious intellectual inquiry. Scholars such as Weber, Barnard, and Selznick believed that one could not fully understand what those in organizations believe or how they behave without reference to the presence (or absence) of organizational leaders. Leaders are the source of institutionalized values which, in turn, condition the actions of organizational members. Yet, for at least the past thirty years, the concept of leadership has been subject to criticism and marginalization by the dominant organizational paradigms and perspectives.

These criticisms have largely followed two related lines. One is that leadership, as a concept, is too loosely defined and is ultimately an amalgamation of behaviors and attributes that can be more readily defined and linked to performance when they are analytically decoupled (Pfeffer, 1977; Kerr and Jermier, 1978; Meindl, Ehrlich, and

Author note: We wish to thank Rod Kramer, Mike Tushman, Barry Staw, and Jeff Pfeffer for helpful comments on an earlier version of this paper.

Dukerich, 1985; Hackman, 2002). While this particular criticism has been made forcefully by scholars who have sought to de-emphasize the leadership construct in the study of organizations, the criticism actually can be traced to advocates of the leadership construct in the 1960s and 1970s. Scholars such as Bennis (1959) and Stogdill (1974) bemoaned the lack of any agreement as to the defining elements of the leadership construct.

A second criticism, which has its origins in an influential study by Lieberson and O'Connor (1972), is that little variance in organizational performance can be systematically attributed to differences among individuals, and to the extent that differences in performance outcomes cannot be ascribed to individual differences, then leadership by definition cannot matter. Lieberson and O'Connor decomposed the over-time performance of 167 companies into the variance explained by macroeconomic conditions, industry, company, and finally the organization's chief executive. Although the impact of the chief executive varied by industry (from little to none), external factors such as the type of industry and the organization's inherited characteristics account for far more variance than any "leadership" effects.[1] Around the same time, Cohen and March (1974) conducted a detailed examination of forty-six college and university presidents and concluded that leadership is principally mythological. Likening the role of an organization's leader to the driver of a skidding car, they argue that there is little a leader can do to influence organizational outcomes, and "whether he is convicted of manslaughter or receives a medal for heroism [is] largely outside his control" (Cohen and March, 1974:203). Numerous empirical studies have since supported Cohen and March's basic conjecture that factors outside the control of any single individual drive organizational performance (for a review and critical assessment of these studies, see Thomas, 1988, especially pp. 388–395, and also Wasserman, Anand, and Nohria, 2001).

The conclusion that individuals have an extremely limited capacity to impact organizational performance became a pillar of the dominant macro-organizational paradigms that emerged in the 1970s. Resource dependence scholars (Pfeffer and Salancik, 1978; Pfeffer, 1987) have contended that organizational action can be understood not as an exercise of individual agency, but as a response to the demands of the external actors upon which the organization depends for resources and support. Sharing a similar theoretical premise, the new institutional perspective (Powell and DiMaggio, 1991) has maintained that external actors impose very specific expectations on what the organization should be doing. These external expectations can be so strong that they generate a template of strategies and structures that an organization mimics on the basis of presumed legitimacy (DiMaggio and Powell, 1983; Meyer and Rowan, 1977). Finally, organizational ecologists have argued that internal and external demands for accountability and reliability place tremendous constraints on the ability of individuals to direct organizational change so that the change improves the organization's fitness with its environment. Leaders can certainly make changes to the organization, but the combined effects of uncertainty and the constraints implied by the reliability and accountability demands mean that leadership has at most a tenuous impact on the success and failure of the organization (Hannan and Freeman, 1989; Carroll and Hannan, 2000).

Granted there is a micro-organizational literature on leadership that can be traced back to Bales and Slater's studies (Bales, 1950; Bales and Slater, 1955) of emergent leadership behavior within small teams. In contemporary micro-organizational scholarship, the perspective of this literature is reflected in Hackman's (2002) research and in Hambrick and Finkelstein's (1987) studies of top management teams, which do reveal the impact of leadership behavior on the performance of teams. Pfeffer and Davis-Blake (1986), to take another example, found that NBA teams improve their performance after hiring a new, experienced coach. However, such research does not challenge the conclusions of Lieberson and O'Connor or Cohen and March, who are clearly focused on the significance of leadership for performance outcomes at a macro level, where the leader's success is thought to depend on his or her ability to impact the behavior of individuals with whom the leader does not have an ongoing personal relationship. Moreover, we believe that it is safe to assert that in the popular imagination, instances of great leadership are at least thought to occur in social contexts that are on a larger scale than a team or group.

In fact, far from contradicting these two major critiques of the leadership construct, the micro-organizational behavior literature reinforces these critiques by offering a view of leadership as an attribution process (Calder, 1977; Pfeffer, 1977). Rather than leadership being a determinant of superior organizational performance, the level of organizational performance determines the perception of leadership

(Meindl, Ehrlich, and Dukerich, 1985). When individuals observe high-performance organizations, they assume that leadership must be present. In this sense, the belief in leadership is essentially one instantiation of the fundamental attribution error (Weber, Camerer, Rottenstreich, and Knez, 2001; Emrich, 1999).

Of these two major critiques of leadership, we believe that the second—that individuals can only have a limited impact on organizational performance—is a more serious challenge to the study of leadership than the first—that leadership is a poorly defined analytical construct. If the actions of individuals do not matter to organizational performance, then it necessarily follows that the actions of a leader cannot matter to organizational performance, regardless of whether a more adequate definition of leadership emerges from the field.

Having briefly reviewed these two critiques, we would now like to draw attention to a fundamental assumption that is common to both: if leadership does not directly impact organizational performance, then leadership does not matter to organizational life. In effect, the relevance of leadership as an organizational phenomenon is circumscribed by its direct impact on performance. Critics of leadership research are not the only ones who seem to assume that the importance of leadership should be couched in terms of its direct impact on performance. Such an assumption certainly resonates with much work in neo-classical economics, in which a social phenomenon's importance is judged by its impact on economic outcomes. This assumption also resonates with what many see as the mission of business schools—to develop leaders who should ultimately be judged on their ability to improve organizational performance (see Pfeffer and Fong, 2004). Even some of the strongest advocates of leadership as a construct take as a given that leadership is important because it is important to performance. Titles such as *Leadership and Performance Beyond Expectations* (Bass, 1985) or *The Leadership Factor* (Kotter, 1988) or *The Transformational Leader: The Key to Global Competitiveness* (Tichy and Devanna, 1986) exemplify attempts to make explicit links between leadership and performance. While there has been some work that moves beyond the impact of leadership on performance, it remains largely the case that a concern with leadership is inseparable from a concern with performance.

The central premise of this chapter is that the study of leadership within organizational theory went awry as this assumption seeped into the disciplinary concern with leadership. If one revisits the work of scholars such as Weber (1946, 1978), Barnard (1968), and Selznick (1984), it becomes clear that they were not concerned with leadership because of the concept's ability to explain economic performance. Instead, leadership was deemed important because of its capacity to infuse purpose and meaning into the lives of individuals. Although the issue of economic performance is not irrelevant to their examination of leadership, it remains of secondary importance. Accordingly, if we are to judge the importance of leadership to organizational life, we need to assess the importance of leadership in terms of its ability to infuse purpose and meaning into the organizational experience.

However, this observation begs several questions: (a) If the concept of leadership was initially couched in terms of its significance for meaning-making, why and when did the concept become decoupled from meaning-making? (b) How does one assess the extent to which a leader infuses action with meaning? (c) What is the connection between meaning-making capacity and economic performance? These questions are the central focus of this chapter. Before we address them, however, a review of the literature pertaining to the meaning-making capacity of leaders is in order.

Leadership as Meaning-Making

The preoccupation of classic social theorists with the meaning-making capacity of leaders can be traced to an even more fundamental concern with the uneasy relationship between the capitalist mode of exchange on the one hand, and the state of modern lived realities on the other. Early nineteenth-century scholars, while embracing modernity, also recognized its implications for the human spirit and creativity. They were troubled by the emerging tensions between traditional meaning-making institutions, such as religion, family, and community, and modern institutions, such as the bureaucratic organization and the market economy. Tonnies (1957) dichotomized the life of community (*Gemeinschaft*) and the transactional life of society (*Gesselschaft*); Durkheim (1947a) described the transition from mechanical to organic solidarity as a smooth, gradual process, but a discontinuous and potentially anomic process that disconnected individuals from the traditional institutions that infused value into their lives. Finally, Weber (1946, 1978) believed modernization implied an ever-increasing rationalization of all aspects of life, as the dry logic of bureaucratic institutions steadily replaced the meaning systems derived from the wonder and enchantment of religion, respect for tradition, or the awe of charisma (see especially Weber, 1946:137–143, 155; Weber, 1978:1121–1157). According to Weber, although it was true that the "ghost of dead religious beliefs" continued to animate industrial capitalism in the form of social habits like delayed gratification, thrift, and a sense of calling, modern society was rapidly constructing an "iron cage" of impersonal rationalism which would suffocate the human spirit and deprive human existence of meaning (Weber, 1992:181–182).

While the concern with the loss of meaning was common across these theorists, Weber stands out from the others in looking to "extraordinary," charismatic individuals as a counter to the inevitable decline in meaning. Durkheim (1947a), for example, looked to professional associations to provide individuals with a shared and common meaning; the problem, of course, was that there was little evidence that these professional associations could equal the meaning-making capacity of the more traditional institutions, such as family or religion. In contrast, Weber (1946) could point to extraordinary individuals who were able to bring an alignment between the actions that individuals undertook and the meaning that they sought (see pp. 245–252 on charismatic authority and pp. 79–80 on political leadership). For example, in his discussion of the emergence of ascetic Protestantism, Weber details how John Calvin led his parishioners to adopt new attitudes in which worldly activity took on a religious value; manual labor and the pursuit of profit through business enterprise became infused with meaning, and, as a by-product, traditional Christian suspicions toward wealth were reconciled with the requirements of capitalism (Weber, 1992).

Almost by definition, the phenomenon of charismatic leadership implies that followers come to perceive their actions as coupled to valued aspects of their lives. As Shils would later comment (1982:122):

> The charismatic quality of an individual as perceived by others, or himself, lies in what is thought to be his connection with (including possession by or embodiment of) some *very central* [italics added] feature of man's existence and the cosmos in which he lives. The centrality coupled with intensity, makes it extraordinary. The centrality is constituted by its formative power in initiating, creating,

governing, transforming, maintaining, or destroying what is vital in man's life.

The close relationship between charismatic leadership and meaning is rooted in the fact that both are concerned with the contribution to and reproduction of a social order that is inherently valued by the individual.

For Weber, charismatic leadership is essentially antithetical to organization and therefore an inevitable transitional phenomenon (1946:248–252). In order for the followers of a charismatic leader to feel that their actions have impact, the leader must organize those followers, and if this organization is to be effective, the leader will need to put in place structures and routines that necessarily imply the routinization of action. The meaning imbued in the original charismatic movement becomes embedded in the structures and practices of a rational, bureaucratic organization. Over time, Weber argued, routinization initiates a process that neutralizes and then finally obliterates the original values that led to the development of the organization in the first place (Weber, 1978:1121–1157).

Organizational scholars of the early to mid twentieth century, such as Barnard (1968), Roethlisberger (Roethlisberger and Dixon, 1939), Mayo (1960), and Homans (1950), questioned the inherent incompatibility between the development of organization and the infusion of values and purpose. The primary reason that these scholars did not see as strong a tension is that they did not see bureaucracy as having unquestionably superior organizational properties. They argued that the survival of an organization depends on the willingness and ability of its members to adjust in a coordinated fashion to any environmental change that threatens the existence of the organization. This desire and capacity to respond in a coordinated fashion cannot be induced by bureaucratic structures or strong economic incentives. Rather, it depends on the extent to which those in the organization internalize a common purpose and perceive the connection between their actions and the organization's ability to fulfill this common purpose.

In *The Functions of the Executive*, Barnard (1968) asserts that it is the role of the leader to create a common awareness of and belief in the organization's purpose, without which there would be insufficient effort to ensure the organization's survival. Barnard denied the adequacy of economic incentives for fostering a level of effort sufficient to ensure the long-term survival of the organization. "It seems to . . . be definitely a general fact that even in purely commercial organizations material incentives are so weak as to be almost negligible except when reinforced by other incentives" (1968:144). For Barnard, the survival of the organization rested on the executive's capability in establishing a common purpose as a basis for cooperation and creating a system for communicating that purpose.

Barnard thus offers a view of organization in which there is congruence between the creation of meaning and purpose, on the one hand, and efficient and effective organization, on the other. In establishing this congruence, Barnard seems to collapse the concepts of purpose and meaning, assuming that the former is tantamount to the latter. Such an assumption represents a departure from Weber. As just noted, for Weber, meaningful action is necessarily action that supports "vital" aspects of the individual's life. Such vitality need not necessarily be an aspect of organizational purpose; purpose can be experienced as an external constraint or force compelling the individual to make choices that the individual regards as inconsistent with his or her identity. The difference is perhaps best reflected in a vignette that Barnard offers about a telephone operator's adherence to the moral code of her organization (1968:269):

> I recall a telephone operator on duty at a lonely place from which she could see in the distance the house in which her mother lay bedridden. Her life was spent in taking care of her mother and in maintaining that home for her. To do so, she chose employment in that particular position, against other inclinations. Yet she stayed at her switchboard while she watched the house burn down . . . She showed extraordinary "moral courage" . . . in conforming to a code of her organization—the moral necessity of uninterrupted service.

The operator certainly feels the purpose of the organization in choosing to remain at her station, but it is hard to believe that the activity carries more meaning than saving the life of the loved one whose care provided the initial impetus for taking the job. As we shall discuss in more detail later in this chapter, one unfortunate consequence of confounding meaningful action and purpose-imbued action is that it leads scholars to assume that strong culture organizations are necessarily infused with meaning. As a number of ethnographic studies have shown, strong culture organizations can often be ones in which individuals have the greatest difficulty reconciling action with their own identity and, accordingly, find themselves engaging in action that they do not regard as meaningful (e.g., Kunda, 1992; Van Maanen, 1991; Martin, 1992; Weeks, 2004).

Selznick's work on organization and leadership echoes Barnard's, though Selznick's conception of meaning is closer to Weber's. Like Barnard, Selznick conceptualizes an organization as a cooperative system. Selznick describes the dual nature of organizations as both economic entities, with the goal of achieving technical efficiency vis-à-vis the process of production, and as "adaptive social structures" whose fundamental goal is organizational survival (Selznick, 1984). For Selznick, an organization is, at a minimum, "a lean, no-nonsense system of consciously co-ordinated activities. It refers to an *expendable tool*, a rational instrument engineered to do a job" (1984:5). However, an organization becomes an institution when it is "infuse[d] with values beyond the technical requirements of the task at hand" (Selznick, 1984:17). It is the role of leadership to turn an organization into an institution, by infusing the organization with values and creating a distinct organizational identity and sense of purpose that is in fact internalized by organizational members as meaningful.

Selznick identifies four key activities of leaders: definition of institutional mission and role; institutional embodiment of purpose; defense of institutional integrity; and the ordering of institutional conflict (1984:62–64). In each of these activities, balancing internal and external constraints is central.[2] To the degree that the leader successfully executes the four key activities, the subordinate's participation in organizational life gives rise to a distinctive set of valued commitments. The subordinate comes to regard his or her actions as meaningful in so far as those actions further the organizational purpose.

To summarize, Weber, Barnard, and Selznick were all concerned with leadership as a phenomenon because of the importance of leaders for creating meaning. There are, however, important differences between the three scholars. For Weber, leadership is almost necessarily a non-organizational phenomenon, since the rationalization implicit in organization undercuts meaning. For Barnard and Selznick, leadership is an organizational phenomenon, but Barnard does not distinguish between adherence to an organization's purpose and an alignment of purpose with the vital aspects of an individual's life. Later in this chapter, we shall return to some of these scholars' ideas, especially when we seek to develop more definitive conceptions of leadership and meaning for research going forward. For now, we simply wish to establish the existence of a "classic" tradition in which leadership is significant primarily because of its importance for meaning creation.

Decoupling the Joint Focus on Leadership and Meaning

Having underscored that leading organizational scholars identified leadership with meaning-making and having noted these and other scholars' concern with loss of meaning in modern organizations, we can now return to answering the first of the three questions posed in the introduction: if the concept of leadership was initially couched in terms of its significance for meaning-making, why and when did the concept become decoupled from meaning-making? Our answer is necessarily a speculative exercise in intellectual history. However, we believe that the reason for the departure can be traced to four particular developments in post–World War II organizational theory.

If, as social theorists since Weber have argued, a central tendency of modernity has been the extraction of meaning from action, and if this tendency has become manifest across organizations, then it should not be surprising that scholars should no longer see meaning-making as central to organizational life. The fact that meaningful action is less present in the typical organization does not necessarily imply that it is any less important to understand how meaning in organizations is created. However, it is easy to understand how interest in a phenomenon can wane when that phenomenon is not observed.

A second reason for the declining interest in the meaning-making capacity of leaders is that social processes involving meaning-making are difficult to quantify and operationalize. Since the early 1970s, organizational theory has increasingly concerned itself with phenomena that lend themselves to more straightforward quantification and statistical analysis (Sørensen, 1998). Against this backdrop, a phenomenon such as meaning-making seems less useful as an analytical construct than the more easily quantified indicators of performance. Put more crudely, return on investment (ROI) makes for a more tractable dependent variable than meaning.

A third and related reason for why organizational scholarship emphasizes the connection of leadership to economic performance over other more subjective variables such as meaning is the shift in the location of organizational research in universities. Today, most organizational research takes place in business schools (Pfeffer, 1997:13; Walsh, Weber, and Margolis, 2003:871). Since performance is arguably the central concern for business organizations in general, the desire to elucidate the causes of performance is very strong in the marketplace of ideas. Walsh, Weber, and Margolis (2003), for example, found that organizational research over the past decade has increasingly focused on economic performance (or some variant of it) as a dependent variable. In explaining this trend, we note that Pfeffer and Fong's (2004) comment about business school students applies equally well to faculty: business school faculty are social beings—they are subject to social influence, to learning from their environment about what is important, and to the frames provided by their organization (see also Salancik and Pfeffer, 1978 and Pfeffer 1997:14–16). Faculties have responded to messages about the importance of performance as a dependent variable and, as a result, their research emphasizes exactly what one might expect.

Changes in institutional theory represent a fourth cause of decoupling a focus on leadership from a focus on meaning. Of all the schools of organizational thought, the new institutional theory of organizations comes closest to being a perspective that puts meaning at the center of its conceptual framework. Like Selznick's early institutionalism, the new institutionalism focused attention on the link between organizational processes and how they came to be understood by organizational actors. However, perhaps as part of the general backlash against Parsonsian functionalism in the 1960s, new institutional theory supplanted the idea of meaning-making with the more cynical notion of myth creation (Meyer and Rowan, 1977). Those at the top of the organization did not facilitate an organization's survival by infusing it with a meaning that transcended short-term economic performance. Rather, they improved the prospects of long-term survival by engaging in symbolic behavior that buffered the organizational core. Whereas Selznick saw the displacement of an organization's formal goals by those which are more general and directed toward organizational survival as a natural part of institutionalization, new institutional theorists interpret this action as if it were an indication that an organization has sold out its goals in order to survive and/or grow.

A few examples of the way new institutional scholarship looks behind the "myths" of organizations might serve to clarify our argument. In his study of a California community college, Clark

(1960a, 1960b) showed that although most students saw the community college as continuing education preparing them for transferring to a four-year college, because of the students' marginal academic abilities much of the course work was in fact a repeat of the last two years of high school.[3] Neither the teachers nor the students overtly acknowledged that the community college course work was an attempt to supplement and draw attention away from failing high schools. In fact, much of the remedial nature of the community college was guaranteed and supported by a web of individuals and organizations in the community, including the teachers from the failing high schools who also worked at the community college. Clark's account suggests that community college merely served to shield students from the reality that their high schools had failed to adequately prepare them for college.

More recently, Dobbin and colleagues' research on equal opportunity and diversity programs suggests that these programs are decoupled from core organizational goals and routines; they serve a largely symbolic, not substantive, role. Studying the creation of equal opportunity offices and programs following the Civil Rights Act of 1964, Dobbin and Sutton (1998) find that adoption was driven not by what organizational leaders regarded as meaningful but rather by the activity of management specialists in response to new and highly ambiguous federal legislation. Once in place, the programs remained decoupled, symbolic entities that allow the organizational core to continue human resource management routines in an unchanged fashion. The shift in the rhetorics used to justify the programs is one sign of the symbolic role they played (Dobbin and Sutton, 1998; Kelly and Dobbin, 1998). Initially couched in terms of legal compliance, the programs were then justified based on efficiency rationales (Dobbin and Sutton, 1998). In a second rhetorical shift, antidiscrimination programs were reframed as diversity management programs (Kelly and Dobbin, 1998). Finally, examining the impact of diversity programs in changing the racial composition of management ranks, Dobbin and colleagues find that the programs' effectiveness is significantly greater among firms subject to federal affirmative action law, as compared to firms subject only to the more general equal opportunity law (Kalev, Dobbin, and Kelly, 2004). Absent regulatory force, the programs seem to have little impact on core organizational practices.

A similar interpretation is given to organizational attempts to provide members with a sense of broader purpose or to explicitly articulate organizational values. Khurana (2002), for example, sees this as part of a broader trend toward elevating business to an activity that transcends the profane task of money-making and infusing it with a moral dimension. Corporations' significance for their members, Khurana argues, "has become quasi-religious, as suggested by the importation of terms such as *mission* and *values* into the contemporary corporate lexicon" (Khurana, 2002:71). The implication is that the changes are more symbolic than real.

At the same time that some institutional theorists were reinterpreting meaning-making as myth creation, other institutional theorists were arguing that the meaningless pursuit of economic efficiency in the twentieth century had actually emerged as a culturally meaningful social end. Whereas Weber's Calvinists regarded the ascetic accumulation of capital as meaningful because it provided information as to whether they were predestined for heaven, those living in the twentieth century came to regard efficient economic organization as a valued end regardless of the output or purpose of the organization. Efficiency and rationalism are thus seen as part of a specific cultural system of measuring value (Smelser, 1995; Bell, 1976).

Roy (1997) and Marchand (1998), for example, argue that large corporations came to be accepted as legitimate not because they performed better than smaller firms, but because scale economies were rationalized as central to operating efficiency, and efficiency was simply a taken-for-granted social good. If the pursuit of efficiency is necessarily meaningful, then Selznick's (1984) distinction between routine administrative activities and the institutional function of leadership necessarily breaks down, because what is profitable becomes defined as vital and central to an individual's life. A focus on leadership and a focus on economic performance become inseparable.

As we see it, the problem with both trends in institutional theory is that they water down any distinction between meaningful and meaningless activity and, as a consequence, make "meaning creation" a meaningless notion. Meyer and Rowan (1977) provide no basis upon which to distinguish a meaningful purpose from a meaningless myth. Similarly, if practically any economic action can be rationalized as being in the pursuit of economic efficiency, and if economic efficiency is a valued end in itself, then any action can be understood as meaningful. Institutional theory assumes that the ritualistic and symbolic activity at, for example, a Mary Kay annual meeting is simply mythic activity designed to fool the legions of saleswomen that what they are doing is meaningful when in fact it is not; or, institutional theory assumes that the pervasiveness of the market culture ensures that an investment banker can find as much meaning in her work as a priest.[4] Both assumptions give rise to a vacuous notion of meaning. In order for individuals to find meaning, the possibility of meaningless activity must be present to them.

Of course, we cannot redress these turns in institutional theory unless we develop an operationalization of meaningful activity that does allow one to distinguish what is meaningful from what is not. That is, to the extent that one cannot assess the creation of meaning, then one is essentially replacing the difficult-to-operationalize construct of leadership with the difficult-to-operationalize construct of meaning-making. This leads us to the second question posed at the outset of this chapter: how does one assess the extent to which a leader infuses action with meaning?

To answer this second question, we need to realize three objectives. We need to offer a definition of meaningful action. We then need to provide an empirical methodology for ascertaining whether action in a particular context can be interpreted in a way that conforms to the conception of meaning. Finally, we need to specify the scope of leadership behaviors that are of at least potential relevance to the infusion of meaning.

Defining Meaningful Action in Organizations

Our earlier review of Weber, Barnard, and Selznick provides some indication as to how meaning might be defined; their work suggests that meaningful action is action that is internalized as having significance beyond mere technical efficiency—as being connected to vital aspects of one's life. However, unless the term "vital" is unpacked, it is not clear that the term has any greater analytical specificity than meaning.

We contend that there are two ways in which the vital aspects of one's life and hence meaning can be conceptualized. Each can be considered a component of a full conception of meaningful action in organizations. One component draws on German social theory and emphasizes that meaning is created when action is directed toward a broader ideal; the other component draws on French social theory and emphasizes the importance of relationships to meaning. Let us consider each component in turn.

The German conception of meaning originates with Hegel's (1952) concept of human action as oriented toward a *Geist* or ideal. Weber (1964) uses the term "substantive rationality" (*wertrational*) to describe this orientation and contrasts it with "formal rationality" (*zweckrational*).[5] Whereas action guided by formal rationality involves simple means-end calculations, action guided by substantive rationality implies that action originates from "a conscious belief in the absolute value of some ethical, aesthetic, religious, or other form of behavior, entirely for its own sake and independently of any prospects of external success" (Weber, 1964:115). In modern society, these aspects of life may be in tension with one other. The tension between substantive and formal rationality is most apparent when aspects of society that are considered sacred are profaned by equating their purported value with the price these products can command in the course of commercial exchange. Zelizer, for example, has described the tensions between the market for child labor and the substantive values of childhood as a sacred period in human life, as well as those between the market for life insurance and the normative resistance against such a product, resistance rooted in the notion of human life as sacrosanct and priceless (Zelizer, 1979, 1985). More recently, these tensions can be identified in efforts to establish commercial blood banks, the debate over public funding for stem cell research, and prohibitions against the sale of human organs (e.g., Healy, 2004).

The second component of meaningful action can be traced at least to Rousseau, who recognized the importance of social interconnectedness and communal relations in infusing our lived experience with meaning. In *The Social Contract and Discourses*, Rousseau writes (1993:142–143):

> [E]very man is virtuous when his particular will is in all things conformable to the general will, and we voluntarily will what is willed by those whom we love . . . [in this way,] they might at length come to identify themselves in some degree with this greater whole, to feel themselves members . . ., and to love it with that exquisite feeling which no isolated person has save for himself . . .

Rousseau, in effect, contends that the quest for meaning is attained through social communion, a process in which an individual realizes herself through achieving solidarity in transparent relationships with others. Durkheim has a similar understanding of the individual as finding meaning through his or her connections to others, though Durkheim (1947b) replaces Rousseau's conception of the "general will" with his own conception of the *conscience collective*. Prior to the secularization of modern life, religion played this meaning-making role by providing a set of "beliefs and practices which unite into a single moral community . . . all those who adhere to them" (Durkheim, 1947b:62). Absent collective life, the individual cannot distinguish between ends which are healthy and those which lead to anxiety and anomie. This standpoint is identical to that set out in Durkheim's discussions of the problem of modernity for human existence in both *Suicide* (1951) and *The Division of Labour* (1947a). In modern society, Durkheim saw organizational life replacing the traditional meaning-making role of religion. The rules of one's occupational role occupy the same imperative that religion once did. "They force the individual to act in view of ends which are not strictly his own, to make concessions, to consent to compromises, to take into account interests higher than his own. Consequently, even where society relies most completely upon the division of labor, it does not become a jumble of juxtaposed atoms, between which it can establish only external transient contacts. Rather the members are united by ties which extend deeper and far beyond the short moments during which the exchange is made. Each of the functions that they exercise is, in a fixed way, dependent upon others, and with them forms a solidary system." (Durkheim, 1947a:228).[6] As was the case for Rousseau, Durkheim proposes that for action to be meaningful, the enactment of values or purpose needs to occur in the context of community.

Though Selznick does not draw a direct connection between his conception of meaning and these two traditions, the emphases of both are implicit in the activities that Selznick associates with the institutional function of leadership. In discussing the definition of institutional mission and role, Selznick observes (1984:65):

> The institutional leader in his role as goal-setter must confront all of the classic questions that have plagued the study of human aspiration. When is an aim, such as "happiness," specific enough to be meaningful? What is the right role of reason, and of opportunism, in the choice of ends? How may immediate practical goals be joined to ultimate values?

The connection to the German conception of meaning should be apparent in the above quote. At the same time, the other three leadership functions—the institutional embodiment of purpose, the defense of institutional integrity, and the ordering of institutional conflict—represent important aspects of transforming the collection of individuals in the organization into a community that finds meaning in their continuing pursuit of common objectives. Selznick writes (1984:16):

> To the extent that they are natural communities, organizations have a history; and this history is compounded of discernible and repetitive modes of responding to internal and external pressures. As these responses crystallize into definitive patterns, a social structure emerges. The more fully developed its social structure, the more will the organization become valued for itself, not as a tool but as an institutional fulfillment of group integrity and aspiration.

In linking the fulfillment of group integrity and aspiration to the development of community and social structure, Selznick evokes the French conception of meaning.

To summarize, our definition of meaningful action within organization has two components. An action is meaningful when its undertaking (1) supports some ultimate end that the individual personally values and (2) affirms the individual's connection to the community of which he or she is a part.[7]

Operationalizing Meaningful Action in Organizations

While we can draw on the German and French traditions for a two-component definition of meaning, in order to provide a concept of leadership as meaning-making that is analytically tractable, we must move beyond a definition and consider the issue of operationalization. We noted earlier our belief that scholarship on leadership moved away from a concern with meaning creation at least in part because meaningful action is so difficult to operationalize.

One could even argue that a concern with meaning defies operationalization, at least in so far as the term *operationalization* implies the construction of variables that are amenable to conventional quantitative analysis. If one can only understand the meaning of action through the empathetic comprehension of intentionality and context (what Weber [1964] called *verstehen*), then any distillation of a social context into reified variables potentially interferes with that understanding. For example, given an objective of assessing the meaning of action, we would have to question the utility of any survey methodology in which participants are asked such questions as "Do you find your work meaningful?" or "Does your work make you happy?" The answers to such questions hardly seem to lend themselves to elucidating the meaning that Weber (1992) identified in *The Protestant Ethic* or Selznick (1952) uncovered in *The Organizational Weapon*, his study of the Bolshevik party's transformation from a voluntary organization to a "combat party."

Language as a Lens

We propose a methodology that does not rely on survey responses, but instead relies on the language that individuals employ for talking about work as an unobtrusive indicator of the meaning they derive from their experiences. Rather than focusing on *what* individuals say about work (e.g., "I am happy"), we draw on recent developments within the field of linguistics and contend that it makes more sense to focus on *how* individuals talk about their work. For example, consider the following two sentences that a worker might use to describe his experience of work:

1. We feel considerable pressure to perform when we are at work.

2. There is a lot of performance pressure for those who work here.

In terms of content, the two sentences express essentially identical content. Both reflect a sentiment of experienced performance pressure. However, there are differences in the pronoun references ("we" versus "those . . . here"). In comparison to the second sentence, the first sentence implies less distancing of the self from the others at work and less distancing of the self from the work experience. In the first sentence, the performance pressure is temporally bounded ("when we are at work"), whereas the second sentence does not imply a similar temporal bounding. More subtle, in the first sentence, there is a sense that the "we" exists before and after work; so while the performance pressure of work is temporally bounded, "we" is not. Finally, in the second sentence, performance pressure has become reified as a thing in the environment rather than a feeling that is "owned" by the participants.

While neither sentence allows us to conclusively assess the extent to which the experience of work is meaningful in the sense of being connected to ultimate ideals, the first sentence clearly reflects greater meaning in the sense that the individual is connected to others around him. Moreover, the fact that "performance pressure" has been reified in the second sentence is at least a clue that the pressure reflected in the second sentence is less likely to be connected to the self and therefore almost necessarily what the self values. So, while one cannot conclusively make an inference about which sentence is more indicative that the worker finds his work to be meaningful, we would assert that sentence 1 is at least suggestive of greater meaning than sentence 2, and to the extent that sentence 1 is situated among more sentences that were similarly suggestive of the meaningfulness of work, we could in fact draw stronger inferences.

We believe this focus on grammar as an indicator of meaning can be justified on two grounds. First, there is research on the relationship between language and health outcomes that has found that the content of what people say and write yields few significant relationships to a variety of mental and physical health indicators, but that *how* people speak and write is associated with the health outcomes of interest (e.g., Pennebaker, 2002; Campbell and Pennebaker, 2003; Pennebaker and Graybeal, 2001). Psychologists, in particular, have turned their attention to what linguists call "particles"—linking words such as articles, pronouns, prepositions, conjunctions, and auxiliary verbs. Pennebaker (2002), for example, finds that disproportionate use of the first-person singular pronoun "I" is associated with depression, whereas references to other people (e.g., by use of the first-person plural "we") are disproportionately absent among depressed individuals. In related studies, Campbell and Pennebaker (2003) find that flexibility in using pronouns (e.g., diversity in use of pronouns across a body of written narratives) is associated with positive health outcomes. Summarizing the results of this work, the authors conclude: "Changes in writing styles were consistently associated with better health, whereas similarity in the content of writing was unrelated to health outcome. Closer analyses of the factors that defined writing styles indicated that particles, and in particular pronouns, predicted the health changes. Individuals who altered their individual and social perspectives from day to day were the participants most likely to benefit from the disclosure exercise" (Campbell and Pennebaker, 2003:64). Obviously, mental health and meaning are not identical constructs, and because this psychological work does not focus on how an individual's conception of self is (or is not) grounded in the experience of work, there are limits as to how much one can directly infer from this research to date. At the same time, this research is important insofar as it provides some justification for making inferences about meaning based on how individuals express themselves rather than on simple extrapolation from the content of what is expressed.

Further justification for a focus on how an individual communicates rather than what he or she communicates comes from the field of linguistics itself. Scholars such as Halliday (1994; Halliday and Matthiessen, 1999) and Silverstein (2003) have increasingly turned their attention to understanding the connection between the language with which the individual describes his or her reality and the way in which that reality is experienced. Matthiessen and Halliday (1997) express the premise guiding the focus on language: "Language does not passively 'reflect' or 'construct' some pre-existing reality. Language constructs reality; or rather, we, as human beings, construct reality in language. We do this through the metafunctional interplay of action and reflection: language both enacts interpersonal relationships and construes human experience." The link between language and experience is not automatic. In construing experience through language we have a range of lexical and grammatical options on which we can draw, and the choice of one particular means of expressing our experience over another is the process by which we construe our reality in a particular way.

Further below, we shall consider some of the systematic grammatical rules uncovered by linguists that can be useful in making inferences about the extent to which an individual finds meaning in his or her actions. However, before doing so, we believe that a few examples can help to make the case for the focus on language as a lens to uncovering meaning. For the purpose of this illustration, we draw on a few interviews from Studs Terkel's *Working* (1972), a book in which individuals from a broad spectrum of occupations provide the author with their personal reflections on their work. Terkel opens the book with an interview of a steelworker who reflects on the difficulty of finding meaning in manual labor (1972:1–2):

> You can't take pride any more. You remember when a guy could point to a house he built, how many logs he stacked. He built it and he was proud of it. I don't really think that I could be proud if a contractor built a home for me. I would be tempted to get in there and kick the carpenter in the ass (laughs), and take the saw away from him. 'Cause I would have to be part of it, you know.

It's hard to take pride in a bridge you're never gonna cross in a door you're never going to open. You're mass producing things, and you never see the end result. (Muses) I worked for a trucker one time. And I got tiny satisfaction when I loaded the truck. At least, I could see the truck depart loaded. In a steel mill, forget it. You don't see where nothing goes.

It is interesting to attend to the shift in pronouns. While the steel worker uses "I" when talking about activities that did or would make him proud and provide him with satisfaction ("I would be tempted to kick the carpenter . . . I got tiny satisfaction when I loaded the truck"), he shifts to "you" when talking about what manual labor in a steel mill is like. ("You can't take pride any more . . . It's hard to take pride in a bridge you're never gonna cross . . . In a steel mill, forget it. You don't see where nothing goes.") Implicitly, there is less distance between the self and the activity when the activity is more meaningful. Reading through the full interview, moreover, it is noteworthy that the worker almost never refers to "we" when discussing work. There is no natural community of which he feels a part. In short, how the steelworker talks about work reveals as much about the distance of his self from his work and from others at work as does the content of what he says.

Terkel also interviews a prostitute, who reveals another type of linguistic distancing of self from work (1972:96):

You're expected to be well dressed, well made up, appear glad to see the man . . . There's a given way of dressing in that league—that's to dress well but not ostentatiously. You have to pass doormen, cab-drivers. You have to look as if you belong in those buildings on Park Avenue or Central Park West. You're expected not to look cheap, not to look hard . . .

Preparations are very elaborate. It has to do with beauty parlors and shopping for clothes and taking long baths and spending money on preserving the kind of front that gives you a respectable address . . .

As with the steelworker, the pronouns are an important part of the story. Though we have not included some references to "I" for the sake of space, it is clear that the prostitute describes much of her work in terms of what "you" need to do. However, beyond the pronoun references, there are two other features of the speech that stand out. In the first paragraph, most of the agency resides with the expectations of others. That is, "you have to" act a certain way because of what others expect. Perhaps even more notable is the reliance on gerund constructions ("shopping," "taking," "spending") as a way of objectifying her actions; the gerund constructions allow for the self to be completely removed from the speech.

By way of comparison, consider the following transcript of an interview with a jockey (Terkel, 1972:472–473):

> I have been having a little problem of weight the last three weeks. I've been retaining water which I usually do not do . . . I've learned to reduce from other riders who've been doing it some twenty-some years. They could lose seven pounds in three hours.
>
> Riding is very hazardous. We spend an average of two months out of work from injuries we sustain during the year. We suffer more death than probably any other sport . . .
>
> The most common accident is what we call clippin' another horse's heels. Your horse trips with the other horse's heels, and he'll automatically go down. What helps us is that the horse is moving at such momentum, he falls so quick, that we just sail out into the air.

In this interview, there is almost a continual alternation between "I," "they," "you," and "we." There are in fact no clear boundaries that are being drawn between the self and others. There is also little objectification of action through the nominalization of activities, implying a more direct involvement of the self in the activity.

Based on the excerpts above, we would conclude that the jockey finds more meaning in his actions than does the steelworker or the prostitute. We of course recognize that such a conclusion is far from systematic; however, this brief discussion of the excerpts should make clear how grammatical clues would provide the basis for a more systematic comparison.

Grammatical Indicators of Meaning

With these illustrations in mind, we turn now to a discussion of some of the grammatical distinctions uncovered by linguists that can provide clues to the way in which organizational experiences have meaning for those involved. We have defined meaningful action as involving two components: action that is directed toward a broader ideal and action that is pursued in relationship with other members of a community. Operationally, the first component can be measured in terms of the distance of self from action. To the extent that actions are experienced as something external, impersonal, or beyond one's control, the possibility for meaning is diminished. The second component can be measured in terms of distance of self from others. To the extent that action is experienced as an individual, rather than collectively shared, experience, the possibility for meaning is diminished.

Work by Halliday and his collaborators (Halliday, 1994; Halliday and Matthiessen, 1999) provides a basis for making inferences about the first component. Halliday treats the clause as the fundamental unit of meaning. It is the linguistic unit by which we impose order and pattern on the otherwise undifferentiated flow of experience. At the level of the clause, experience is construed through "processes"—verbal configurations that can be distinguished on the basis of the grammar. Each clause consists of the process itself, phenomena that play the role of participants in the process, and other phenomena that make up the circumstances of the process (Halliday and Matthiessen, 1999:512). For example, in the clause "The boy hit the ball over the fence," we have a process ("hit"), two participants ("the boy" and "the ball"), and a set of circumstantial conditions ("over the fence").

The three main types of process that Halliday identifies correspond to three distinct modes of construing experience.[8] *Material* processes are those of doing (to), happening, and creating. These processes take place in the external world (e.g., "I am building a new house"), although material processes can also involve metaphorical doings (e.g., "The manager dissolved the committee"). *Mental* processes are inner processes of sensing. Thinking, feeling, and seeing are the major subtypes. For example, the clause "She enjoys her job" would be classified as a mental process, as would the clause "I feel overwhelmed in my current role." Finally, *relational* processes involve classification and identification. They relate one component of experience to another in terms of identity, attributes, or circumstances, as in the clause "The company has 500 employees."

Importantly, it is features of the grammar that distinguish one type of process from another. For example, in distinguishing material from mental processes, Halliday notes that the unmarked (usual) form of the present tense for material processes is the present-in-present (e.g., "I am building," not "I build"), while the unmarked present tense for mental processes is the simple present (e.g., "I like," not "I am liking"). Moreover, one participant in a mental process must be a conscious being (or an inanimate object endowed with consciousness), while this is not a requirement for material processes. (For example, the material clause "The box fell off the shelf" has no conscious participant in it, but you would not say "The box felt sad" unless you were attributing consciousness to the box.) Our point here is not to elaborate the full set of grammatical rules for distinguishing one type of process from another (the details can be found in Halliday, 1994:106–175) but simply to point out that the basis for the distinction lies in the grammatical structures at the clause level.

How can the process types be used to identify the extent to which one is distancing oneself from one's actions? Relational processes, in which abstract relations are set up between experiences, can be understood as implying greater distance of self from experience than either material or mental processes. When we choose (consciously or not) to employ a relational construction to describe a particular experience, we are construing this experience in abstract, symbolic terms—classifying it, identifying it as belonging to a particular type, ascribing attributes to it, or specifying its circumstances—but we are not directly engaging in the experience itself. The count of relational clauses as a percentage of total clauses in narratives describing one's experience can therefore be taken as an indicator of distancing of self from action. The greater the count of relational clauses as a percentage of total clauses, the greater the distancing of self from action.

However, the simple prevalence of material and mental processes over relational processes does not in itself imply that the experience described in a narrative is meaningful. There is an important distinction to be made between material and mental processes. Although the distance between self and action and between self and others may be similar for mental and material processes, the use of mental processes suggests a different type of engagement with the experience—one that is cognitive or emotional in nature. The requirement that at least one participant in a mental process be a conscious being is one indicator of this difference. When we construe experience through a material process, we are making sense of it as an activity in which we may be involved as a participant, but when we construe the experience through a mental process, we are engaging with it on a deeper level. The percentage of mental clauses in a narrative is therefore an important second indicator of the extent to which the speaker or writer is deriving meaning from the experience.

Another feature of the grammar of clauses that is particularly useful to us is what Halliday terms "grammatical metaphor." When we think of metaphorical language, we tend to think of what linguists would term "lexical metaphor"—a figure of speech in which a word or phrase that literally denotes one thing is used in place of another, to suggest a similarity between the two. For example, "applauded loudly" could be expressed with the lexical metaphor "applauded thunderously." Grammatical metaphor involves a shift in the grammar rather than the lexis. For example, "applauded loudly" could be expressed with the grammatical metaphor "loud applause." The grammatical metaphor in this case involves a verbal process ("applauded loudly") being reconstrued as a nominal group ("loud applause"). Nominalization of a verbal group is in fact one of the most prevalent forms of grammatical metaphor, although Halliday elaborates a number of others (see Halliday and Matthiessen, 1999:246–248). The common feature across all types is the shift from one grammatical role to another.

The significance of grammatical metaphor for accessing meaning comes from the fact that the primary tendency in grammatical metaphor is what Halliday describes as "the drift towards 'thing'"—toward expressing circumstances, processes, and qualities as nominal groups (Halliday and Matthiessen, 1999:263). Nominal groups have the greatest potential for classification and elaboration, and the use of grammatical metaphor therefore tends to expand the options available for conveying information. But it also means that experience becomes construed as more abstract and remote. Instead of construing experience directly, as a process, the speaker or writer construes it remotely, as a piece of information. In this sense, the use of grammatical metaphor implies a depersonalization of experience and greater distance of one's self from one's actions. One cannot be a participant in a process once that process has been nominalized. (Although of course the object itself can become a participant in other processes; herein lies the source of the nominal group's potential for elaboration and classification.)

As Halliday acknowledges, "unpacking" a grammatical metaphor into its congruent (nonmetaphorical) form can be difficult, as there are often multiple possible congruent forms from which the metaphorical expression could have evolved. However, for our purposes, it is necessary only to recognize the instance of grammatical metaphor, not to unpack it to the precise congruent form intended by the speaker. To assess distance from experience, then, one can simply code nominal groups as either grammatical metaphors or congruent forms, and take the percentage of grammatical metaphor as an indicator of the distance of self from action.

The grammatical rules discussed so far have primarily emphasized the first component of meaning—the distance of one's self from one's actions. Analyzing the use of pronouns, as we did in the vignettes, provides some more indication of the first component of meaning, but even more important, it provides a means of getting at the second component of meaning—the distance of one's self from others. As noted above, psychologists are increasingly finding the relative prevalence of different pronouns to be indicators of mental states. While we draw on these findings, because our interest is in meaning in the context of organizational work, it would be important to also code whether use of a particular pronoun is embedded in a clause related to work.

Consider some of the implications that could be drawn from coding the degree to which an individual disproportionately relies on the first-person singular, first-person plural, and third-person plural when prompted to discuss work. Figure 3-1 depicts some possible combinations of pronoun use, where a letter signifies a comparatively heavy use of the pronoun-context combination in the particular cell. For example, A denotes a disproportionate use of first-person singular ("I," "me") for non-work-related clauses and a disproportionate use of third-person plural ("they," "them") for work-related clauses. This combination clearly suggests that the "self" is not identified with work or with coworkers. In contrast, the combination represented by B—a disproportionate use of the first-person singular and first-person plural in the work context—does indicate that the self is identified with both work and coworkers. The C combination would be expected from an individual who identifies with a natural community, but one that is not centered on work. The D combination denotes an individual who identifies with the people at work, but does not identify his or her self with the activities of work. One might expect this combination from an individual who is part of an organizational subgroup that does not value that company's collective goals. There are clearly other combinations; our purpose here is not to thoroughly review all possible

FIGURE 3-1

Some pronoun profiles

		First-person singular	First-person plural	Third-person plural	Other
Work clause	Yes	B	B, D	A, C	
	No	A, D	C		

A Self not identified with work or coworkers
B Self identified with work and coworkers
C Self not identified with coworkers, but with natural community outside of coworkers
D Self identified with coworkers, but self is apart from activity of work

combinations, only to show how the reliance on particles can be used as a basis for making inferences about the meaning that individuals derive from work.

Meaning and "Strong" Culture

For readers who may have residual questions or concerns about how our understanding of meaning relates to conceptions of strong culture organizations (e.g., O'Reilly and Chatman, 1996; Deal and Kennedy, 1982), this focus on operationalization should hopefully further clarify the distinction. Proponents of the strong culture concept often emphasize that a strong organizational culture is one in which all individuals espouse similar values (e.g., Kanter, 1983; Peters and Waterman, 1982). However, as work by Van Maanen (1991) and Kunda (1992) illustrates, this espousal may be induced by external constraint or implicit social threat, rather than by individuals' belief in the meaning of their action. In fact, Van Maanen and Kunda's work suggests that a strong culture can *undermine* the meaning that individuals derive from their actions and also create divisions within the organization, threatening any sense of natural community—for example, by imposing uniformity that is actually more aligned with the beliefs of one subgroup in the organization than others.

One might argue that strong culture organizations impose a uniform grammar in addition to a uniform content of beliefs, affecting how people express themselves as much as the content of what people express. Ultimately, this is an empirical question. Arguments about beliefs tend to emphasize the role of stories and rhetoric. Eccles and Nohria (1992), for example, describe the role of organizational rhetoric as sources of worker identity and cognitive categories enabling action. However, there is no work within the strong culture perspective that identifies "grammatical control" as an aspect of strong culture, and even if "grammatical control" were a part of an explicitly managed strong culture, we find it hard to believe that the controls would map onto the indicators of meaningful action that we have identified.

This observation that the grammar of speech is less amenable to strategic manipulation than is the content of speech gives rise to a final point. In emphasizing the importance of grammar as a property of language that provides insight into meaning, we do not wish to imply that content is irrelevant. We certainly expect that one could gain some insight into the consequences of leadership by looking, for example, at counts of positive and negative adjectives, references to an individual's group or organization, and even obvious allusions to meaning or significance. However, we are concerned that, like organizational mission statements that can be posted on a wall but not reflected in individual action, the content of speech is a frequent target of strategic manipulation and impression management. Therefore, at a minimum, we would hope that any focus on content would be complemented by a focus on grammar as a way to minimize the confounding effects of personal influence tactics and strategic behavior on the inferences that are drawn from what is said.

Identifying the Scope of Leadership Activities

Having provided some indication as to how meaningful action might be operationalized, we can now turn to the final issue relevant to answering the second question: how does one assess the extent to which a leader infuses action with meaning? This final issue involves defining the scope of activities with the potential to impact the meaning that individuals experience as part of an organization, and, within this, identifying those that can be effectively labeled as leadership activities. As Bresnen (1995) observes, the scope question is a vexing one for the leadership literature. On the one hand, there has been a tendency to identify leadership with any personality characteristics, behaviors, or actions that can significantly impact performance. Such an approach suffers from a naïve functionalism and gives rise to the view that leadership is nothing other than an attribution that is made when an organization experiences high performance. On the other hand, there are scholars (e.g., Bass, 1985; Bennis and Nanus, 1985; Rafferty and Griffin, 2004) who have sought to segment out those executive activities that can be labeled "transformational" rather than "transactional," where the former label refers to those activities that change beliefs and values and the latter refers to those activities that change behavior through either positive or negative inducements. The focus on transformational activities has, in turn, led scholars to follow the strong emphasis that Barnard (1968) placed on the communication acts of organizational leaders, reserving other decisions or choices for the label of "management." However, as Bresnen (1995) observes, scholars seem to have given communication acts a privileged status without any actual empirical backing that communication deserves this privileged status. Unless there is some empirical basis for establishing that communication is the most effective leadership tool, such a focus seems unjustifiably restricted.

In our view, this dilemma is a consequence of the trend in the literature that formed the point of departure for this chapter: the insistence that leadership behavior in economic organizations be tantamount to behavior that improves economic performance. Because of this coupling, the distinction between leadership behaviors and characteristics and management behaviors and characteristics becomes either blurred or arbitrary.

However, in so far as leadership is identified with meaning creation, one can then attach the label of leadership to those attributes or behaviors that provide meaning for another as long as those attributes or behaviors can be ascribed to an individual. What do we mean by attributes or behaviors "ascribed to an individual"? We use the phrase to refer to attributes or behaviors where an individual can be identified by the researcher as the agent behind those attributes or behaviors. Agency is, in effect, the inverse of Meyer and Rowan's (1977) notion of "taken-for-grantedness."[9] If an individual is seen as undertaking an action or cultivating an attribute that is not taken-for-granted, then the individual can be understood as the agent of that attribute or action. To the degree that the researcher can identify the individual as the agent or author of a particular action and to the degree that the action—either by itself or in combination with other actions on the part of the individual—creates meaning for others, the action could be characterized as an act of leadership.

In adopting the perspective of the researcher for the purpose of distinguishing agentic from taken-for-granted acts, we allow for the possibility that organizational members will not always be aware of actions that an individual undertakes to create meaning, and therefore also allow for the possibility that acts of leadership may not always be seen as such by organizational followers. The researcher, of course, confronts an empirical challenge in trying to define the scope of investigation for determining what is taken-for-granted and what is agentic, and in devising a method for objectively attributing an action to an individual. What is not taken-for-granted in a particular organization (e.g., casual dress on Friday) may be taken-for-granted in the broader context in which the organization finds itself, and it is incumbent upon the researcher to make this distinction. However, such empirical challenges seem essentially similar to those faced by institutional theorists and ecologists in adequately defining what is taken-for-granted.

An empirical agenda is thus opened up, in which everything from an individual's choice about task design to his or her communication acts are examined as *potential* determinants of the meaning that others derive from what they do. To be clear, we believe it is important to avoid the trap of leadership being an aggregate construct that can encompass all aspects of an executive's behavior—a trap to which we alluded at the outset of this chapter. Impact on meaning must be recognized as a scope-delimiting factor, separating out what is leadership from what is not. As this empirical agenda is followed up, certain actions may in fact acquire a privileged status as a more important determinant of meaning. But at the outset, we see no basis on which to privilege some actions over others. In particular, we suspect that an individual may have to engage in significant "transactional" behavior to order institutional conflict (one of the four categories of activity that Selznick [1984] identified with the leadership function), but if the ultimate outcome of that transactional behavior is the creation of a more natural community, then there is no reason that this transactional behavior should be seen as less germane to leadership.[10]

If a researcher were to privilege communication activities to a degree that implied the downplaying of organizational design as an aspect of leadership, the researcher would run the risk of overlooking how the features of the organization would have an impact on the way the communication is received. For example, the higher the pay disparity within an organization, the more difficult it will be for an individual to infuse meaning with a message of solidarity. The medium is very much a part of the message, and the organization is the medium.

We offer the typology in figure 3-2 as a way of clarifying our particular specification of attributes, acts, and behaviors with at least the potential to infuse meaning. To the extent that an executive's attributes or behaviors are taken-for-granted (as we have defined the term in this chapter), they are not the attributes, acts, or behaviors of leadership, regardless of their impact on meaning. Rather, it is those attributes, acts, and behaviors in the second column of the figure that are the potential "pool" from which leadership attributes, acts, and behaviors are drawn. Exactly which attributes, acts, and behaviors from the second column are most critical for meaning-making is, of course, an empirical question.

To summarize, our answer to the question of how one assesses the extent to which a leader infuses action with meaning has three parts. First, we offer a two-component definition of meaning, where one component refers to the tight connection between one's actions and one's ideals and the other component refers to a feeling of closeness to a natural community. We then argue that linguistic earmarks provide a way of rigorously operationalizing this definition. Finally, given the definition and operationalization of meaning and given the classical identification of leadership with meaning creation, we propose an empirical agenda in which researchers consider a broad range of actions that can impact meaning.

FIGURE 3-2

A typology of executive attributes, acts, and behaviors

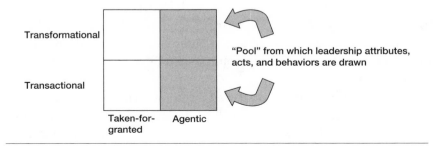

The Relationship Between Meaning-Making and Economic Performance

We have now made clear our position that many of the problems that have confounded the study of leadership can be addressed if a focus on leadership is decoupled from a focus on economic performance and instead coupled to a focus on meaning-making. However, because so much of the leadership literature currently focuses on the link between leadership and performance, this raises the third question articulated at the outset of the chapter: what is the connection between meaning-making capacity and economic performance?

We would like to offer two answers to this question. Our first answer is an admittedly defiant one: we don't much care what the relationship is. One of the most significant problems with the study of organizations is that the concern with economic outcomes has trumped the concern with other outcomes. Satisfaction, meaning, and social welfare all seem to be regarded as of secondary or mediating significance when compared to economic outcomes such as profitability or survival. In our earlier review of some of the classic scholarship on leadership, we noted that Weber's focus on leadership is at least partially attributable to his concern about the loss of meaning associated with modernity. This concern does not disappear with Weber or other theorists writing at the turn of the century. In *The Organization Man*, Whyte (1956) voices his concern that the modern corporation does not allow individuals to realize their own unique identity. In *The Asymmetric Society*, Coleman (1982) observes that "corporate persons" have as many legal rights as "natural persons," but corporate persons have more resources.

We agree with Selznick's observation that an obsession with the question of efficiency necessarily detracts from a focus on what is most important. As Selznick asks rhetorically, "Does a preoccupation with administrative efficiency lead us to the knottiest and most significant problems of leadership in large organizations?" (1984:2). The meaningfulness of action is an important enough outcome that one should not have to justify a focus on meaning by establishing a connection to economic performance.

Having offered this first answer, we know that it will be dissatisfying to many. Most obviously, it will be dissatisfying to those for whom the relationship between leadership and performance is of central significance. But even if one believes that meaning is the outcome of paramount interest, there are reasons why this first answer may not be satisfactory. A leader cannot continue to infuse meaning over time unless the organization can survive, and since survival depends on some minimum level of performance, a focus on meaning cannot be maintained to the complete exclusion of a focus on performance.

Our second answer to this question is therefore the following: there is some work that suggests a positive relationship between the meaningfulness of work and economic performance. For example, Hackman and Oldham's (1980) job characteristics theory specifies that, on average, people are more productive when they have a high degree of autonomy and can observe the consequences of their actions. Hackman and Oldham (1980) also find that autonomy and an ability to observe consequences are both positively related to the meaning that individuals derive from work, though they operationalize meaning with responses to direct questions about the meaningfulness of work and not with an operationalization like the one we have suggested above. Moreover, popular management texts (e.g., Collins and Porras, 1994) certainly leave the impression that the long-term prosperity of an organization is enhanced to the degree that the organization has a mission that is regarded as meaningful by the organization's members. However, we would like to see more compelling ways of assessing meaning before drawing definitive conclusions about the impact of meaning and economic performance.

Finally, as scholars explore the relationship between meaning and performance, they should not assume that causality flows entirely from the former to the latter. Just as it seems reasonable to assume that individuals could perform at a higher level when they derive more meaning from their work, so it seems reasonable to believe that a high level of economic performance could positively affect the meaning that individuals derive from their work. As Barnard observed, profitability does not define an organization's purpose; rather, it is an indicator of how well an organization is achieving its purpose (Barnard 1968:154, especially footnote 7). To the extent that a leader infuses meaning by enabling individuals to realize their ideals and values through organizational action, there will be comparatively little meaning that individuals can derive from association with a poorly performing organization. Put simply, if performing poorly is not much better than not performing at all, one would expect that the level of performance will place an upper bound on the meaning that can be created within an economic organization.

Conclusion

In this chapter, we have argued that leadership research went awry when the concept of leadership became decoupled from the notion of meaning and inextricably tied to a concern with performance. We considered some explanations for why this decoupling took place; there are several, but probably the most important is the lack of clear definition and operationalization of the meaning that individuals derive from work. Through some illustrations and through guidelines derived from the field of linguistics, we have provided some indications as to how the concept of meaning might be made analytically tractable. Finally, while we argued that a concern with meaning should not always be subordinated to a concern with economic outcomes, we acknowledged that it is important to understand the connection, especially given that the causality can flow in both directions.

By way of concluding, we would like to reference figure 3-3, which is intended to further clarify the view of leadership that we have put forth in this chapter. As we did in figure 3-2, we divide the attributes, acts, and behaviors of an executive into four categories by drawing on the distinctions of transactional versus transformational and agentic versus taken-for-granted. When we conceptualize leadership as meaning-making, we focus on how the attributes and actions that would be categorized as agentic impact on meaning (arrows 2 and 4), as

FIGURE 3-3

Conceptions of leadership and management

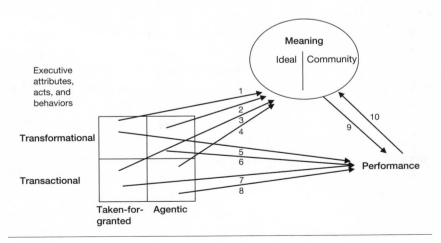

well as on the connection between meaning and performance (arrows 9 and 10). We reserve the term *management* for all of those executive attributes, acts, and behaviors that impact on performance without creating meaning (arrows 5, 6, 7, and 8). In contrast, the transformational view of leadership tends to emphasize those attributes and actions that would be reflected in arrows 1, 2, 5, 6, and 9—there is no distinction made between taken-for-granted and agentic behavior, and meaning is a relevant outcome only to the extent that it is linked to performance.

This framing creates the possibility for further research to form falsifiable tests of the different conceptions of leadership and the relative importance of leadership and management to economic performance. In terms of figure 3-3, this would involve testing the magnitude of the different arrows. For example, the strength of arrows 7 and 8 provides some indication of the importance of management as compared to leadership (defined either as transformational leadership or as meaning-making). The strength of the arrows leading to economic performance (arrows 5, 6, 7, and 8) as compared to those leading to meaning (arrows 1, 2, 3, and 4) would provide a test of our argument that meaning be considered as a key outcome. Finally, comparing the magnitude of arrows 1, 5, and 6 with that of arrows 4 and 10 would provide a test of the transformational concept of leadership as compared to our conception of leadership as meaning-making.

Figure 3-3 also suggests some related empirical questions. Separate from the relationship between leadership and management on the one hand and meaning and economic performance on the other, considering the relationship between taken-for-granted versus agentic behaviors and transformational versus transactional behaviors leads to a number of interesting research questions. For example, given that the process of institutionalization can be understood as a shift in actions and attributes from agentic to taken-for-granted status, one could be interested in the organizational dynamics underlying this shift. Does it also involve a shift in the nature of executive attributes and actions, from transformational to transactional? One could also be interested in the conditions under which action shifts from taken-for-granted to agentic. To what extent is this shift driven by environmental changes, for example, and to what extent is it driven by changes in individual actors within the organization (e.g., CEO and top management team turnover)?

Clearly there are still some thorny empirical issues that must be addressed before we can investigate such questions, but the empirical challenges should not mask the significance of the broader questions we have raised in this chapter. In asking whether leadership has an impact on performance that transcends the impact of management, we are essentially considering the extent to which agency has more impact when meaning creation is a central target of that agency. Even if we ultimately find that meaning creation does not have a significant impact on economic performance, we maintain that greater attention must be given to meaning as an outcome that is worthy of explanation. Meaning creation is an important phenomenon regardless of its relation to economic performance. Indeed, we can think of no other phenomenon that is more worthy of explanation.

References

Bales, Robert F. *Interaction Process Analysis: A Method for the Study of Small Groups.* Chicago: University of Chicago Press, 1950.

Bales, Robert F., and Philip E. Slater. "Role Differentiation in Small Decision-Making Groups." In *The Family, Socialization, and Interaction Processes*, edited by Talcott Parsons and Philip E. Slater, 259–306. Glencoe, IL: The Free Press, 1955.

Barnard, Chester. *The Functions of the Executive.* Cambridge: Harvard University Press, 1968.

Bass, Bernard M. *Leadership and Performance Beyond Expectations.* New York: The Free Press, 1985.

Bell, Daniel. *The Cultural Contradictions of Capitalism.* New York: Basic Books, 1976.

Bennis, Warren G. "Leadership Theory and Administrative Behavior: The Problem of Authority." *Administrative Science Quarterly* 4 (1959): 259–301.

Bennis, Warren G., and Burt Nanus. *Leaders: Strategies for Taking Charge.* New York: Harper & Row, 1985.

Bresnen, Michael J. "All Things to All People? Perceptions, Attributions, and Constructions of Leadership." *Leadership Quarterly* 6, no. 4 (1995): 495–513.

Brint, Steven, and Jerome Karabel. "Institutional Origins and Transformations: The Case of American Community Colleges." In *The New Institutionalism in Organizational Analysis*, edited by Walter W. Powell and Paul J. DiMaggio, 337–360. Chicago: University of Chicago Press, 1991.

Brinton, Mary C., and Victor Nee, eds. *The New Institutionalism in Sociology.* New York: Russell Sage Foundation, 1998.

Calder, Bobby J. "An Attribution Theory of Leadership." In *New Directions in Organizational Behavior*, edited by Barry M. Staw and Gerald R. Salancik, 179–204. Chicago: St. Claire, 1977.

Campbell, Sherlock R., and James W. Pennebaker. "The Secret Life of Pronouns: Flexibility in Writing Style and Physical Health." *Psychological Science* 14, no. 1 (2003): 60–65.

Carroll, Glenn R., and Michael T. Hannan. *The Demography of Corporations and Industries.* Princeton, NJ: Princeton University Press, 2000.

Clark, Burton R. "The 'Cooling-Out Function' in Higher Education." *American Journal of Sociology* 65 (1960a): 569–576.

———. *The Open-Door College: A Case Study.* New York: McGraw-Hill, 1960b.

Cohen, Michael D., and James G. March. *Leadership and Ambiguity: The American College President.* New York: McGraw-Hill, 1974.

Coleman, James S. *The Asymmetric Society.* Syracuse, NY: Syracuse University Press, 1982.

———. *Foundations of Social Theory.* Cambridge, MA: Harvard University Press, 1990.

Collins, James C., and Jerry I. Porras. *Built to Last: Successful Habits of Visionary Companies.* New York: HarperBusiness, 1994.

Deal, Terrence E., and Allan A. Kennedy. *Corporate Cultures: The Rites and Rituals of Corporate Life.* Reading, MA: Addison Wesley, 1982.

DiMaggio, Paul J., and Walter W. Powell. "The Iron Cage Revisited: Institutional Isomorphism and Collective Rationality in Organizational Fields." *American Sociological Review* 48 (1983): 147–160.

Dobbin, Frank, and John R. Sutton. "The Strength of a Weak State: The Rights Revolution and the Rise of Human Resources Management Divisions." *American Journal of Sociology* 104 (1998): 441–475.

Durkheim, Emile. *The Division of Labor in Society,* translated by George Simpson. Glencoe, IL: The Free Press, 1947a.

———. *The Elementary Forms of the Religious Life: A Study in Religious Sociology,* translated by Joseph W. Swain. Glencoe, IL: The Free Press, 1947b.

———. *Suicide: A Study in Sociology,* edited by George Simpson. Glencoe, IL: The Free Press, 1951.

Eccles, Robert G., and Nitin Nohria. *Beyond the Hype: Rediscovering the Essence of Management.* Boston: Harvard Business School Press, 1992.

Emrich, Cynthia G. "Context Effects in Leadership Perception." *Personality and Social Psychology Bulletin* 25, no. 8 (1999): 991–1006.

Flynn, Francis J., and Barry M. Staw. "Lend Me Your Wallets: The Effect of Charismatic Leadership on External Support for an Organization." *Strategic Management Journal* 25 (2004): 309–330.

Hackman, J. Richard. *Leading Teams: Setting the Stage for Great Performances.* Boston: Harvard Business School Press, 2002.

Hackman, J. Richard, and Greg R. Oldham *Work Redesign.* Reading, MA: Addison Wesley, 1980.

Halliday, M.A.K. *An Introduction to Functional Grammar.* 2nd ed. London: Hodder Arnold, 1994.

Halliday, M.A.K., and Christian M.I.M. Matthiessen. *Construing Experience Through Meaning: A Language-Based Approach to Cognition.* New York: Continuum, 1999.

Hambrick, Donald, and Sidney Finkelstein. "Managerial Discretion." In *Research in Organizational Behavior.* Vol. 9, edited by Larry L. Cummings and Barry M. Staw, 369–406. Greenwich, CT: JAI Press, 1987.

Hannan, Michael T., and John Freeman. *Organizational Ecology.* Cambridge, MA: Harvard University Press, 1989.

Healy, Kieran. "Sacred Markets and Secular Ritual in the Organ Transplant Industry." In *The Sociology of the Economy,* edited by Frank Dobbin, 308–331. New York: Russell Sage Foundation Press, 2004.

Hegel, Georg W.F. *The Philosophy of Right*, translated by T.M. Knox. New York: Oxford University Press, 1952.

Homans, George C. *The Human Group*. New York: Harcourt Brace, 1950.

House, Robert J., William D. Spangler, and James Woycke. "Personality and Charisma in the U.S. Presidency: A Psychological Theory of Leader Effectiveness." *Administrative Science Quarterly* 36, no. 3 (1991): 364–396.

Kalev, Alexandra, Frank Dobbin, and Erin Kelly. "Two to Tango: Affirmative Action, Diversity Programs and Women and African-Americans in Management." Working paper, Harvard University, 2004.

Kanter, Rosabeth Moss. *The Change Masters*. New York: Simon and Schuster, 1983.

Kelly, Erin, and Frank Dobbin. "How Affirmative Action Became Diversity Management." *American Behavioral Scientist* 41 (1998): 960–984.

Kerr, Stephen, and John M. Jermier. "Substitutes for Leadership: Their Meaning and Measurement." *Organizational Behavior and Human Performance* 22 (1978): 375–403.

Khurana, Rakesh. *Searching for a Corporate Savior: The Irrational Quest for Charismatic CEOs*. Princeton, NJ: Princeton University Press, 2002.

Kotter, John P. *The Leadership Factor*. New York: The Free Press, 1988.

Kunda, Gideon. *Engineering Culture: Control and Commitment in a High-Tech Corporation*. Philadelphia: Temple University Press, 1992.

Lieberson, Stanley, and James F. O'Connor. "Leadership and Organizational Performance: A Study of Large Corporations." *American Sociological Review* 37 (1972): 117–130.

Marchand, Roland. *Creating the Corporate Soul: The Rise of Public Relations and Corporate Imagery in American Big Business*. Berkeley, CA: University of California Press, 1998.

Martin, Joanne. *Cultures in Organizations: Three Perspectives*. New York: Oxford University Press, 1992.

Matthiessen, Christian M.I.M., and M.A.K. Halliday. "Systemic Functional Grammar: A First Step into the Theory." Working paper, Macquarie University, Australia, 1997.

Mayo, Elton. *The Human Problems of an Industrial Civilization*. New York: Viking Press, 1960.

Meindl, James R., Sanford B. Ehrlich, and Janet M. Dukerich. "The Romance of Leadership." *Administrative Science Quarterly* 30 (1985): 78–102.

Meyer, John W., and Brian Rowan. "Institutionalized Organizations: Formal Structure as Myth and Ceremony." *American Journal of Sociology* 83 (1977): 340–363.

O'Reilly, Charles A., III, and Jennifer A. Chatman. "Culture as Social Control: Corporations, Cults, and Commitment." In *Research in Organizational Behavior*. Vol. 18, edited by Barry M. Staw and Larry L. Cummings, 157–200. Greenwich, CT: JAI Press, 1996.

Pennebaker, James W. "What Our Words Can Say About Us: Toward a Broader Language Psychology." *Psychological Science Agenda* 15 (2002): 8–9.

Pennebaker, James W., and Anna Graybeal. "Patterns of Natural Language Use: Disclosure, Personality, and Social Integration." *Current Directions in Psychological Science* 10 (2001): 90–93.

Peters, Thomas J., and Robert H. Waterman. *In Search of Excellence*. New York: Harper & Row, 1982.

Pfeffer, Jeffrey. "The Ambiguity of Leadership." *Academy of Management Review* 2, no. 1 (1977): 104–112.

———. "Management as Symbolic Action: The Creation and Maintenance of Organizational Paradigms." In *Research in Organizational Behavior.* Vol. 3, edited by Barry M. Staw and Larry L. Cummings, 1–52. Greenwich, CT: JAI Press, 1981.

———. "A Resource Dependence Perspective on Intercorporate Relations." In *Intercorporate Relations: The Structural Analysis of Business,* edited by M.S. Mizruchi and M. Schwartz, 25–55. Cambridge, England: Cambridge University Press, 1987.

———. *New Directions for Organization Theory: Problems and Prospects.* New York: Oxford University Press, 1997.

Pfeffer, Jeffrey, and Allison Davis-Blake. "Administrative Succession and Organizational Performance: How Administrator Experience Mediates the Succession Effect." *Academy of Management Journal* 29 (1986): 72–83.

Pfeffer, Jeffrey, and Christina T. Fong. "The Business School 'Business': Some Lessons from the U.S. Experience." *Journal of Management Studies* 41, no. 8 (2004): 1501–1520.

Pfeffer, Jeffrey, and Gerald R. Salancik. *The External Control of Organizations.* New York: Harper & Row, 1978.

Powell, Walter W., and Paul J. DiMaggio, eds. *The New Institutionalism in Organizational Analysis.* Chicago: University of Chicago Press, 1991.

Rafferty, Alannah E., and Mark A. Griffin. "Dimensions of Transformational Leadership: Conceptual and Empirical Extensions." *Leadership Quarterly* 15 (2004): 329–354.

Roethlisberger, Fritz J., and William J. Dixon. *Management and the Worker.* Cambridge, MA: Harvard University Press, 1939.

Rousseau, Jean-Jacques. *The Social Contract and Discourses,* translated by G.D.H. Cole. London: Everyman, 1993.

Roy, William G. *Socializing Capital: The Rise of the Large Industrial Corporation in America.* Princeton, NJ: Princeton University Press, 1997.

Salancik, Gerald R., and Jeffrey Pfeffer. "A Social Information Processing Approach to Job Attitudes and Task Design." *Administrative Science Quarterly* 23 (1978): 224–253.

Selznick, Philip. *The Organizational Weapon: A Study of Bolshevik Strategy and Tactics.* Santa Monica, CA: The Rand Corporation, 1952.

———. *Leadership in Administration: A Sociological Interpretation.* Berkeley, CA: University of California Press, 1984.

Shils, Edward. *The Constitution of Society.* Chicago: University of Chicago Press, 1982.

Silverstein, Michael. "Indexical Order and the Dialectics of Sociolinguistic Life." *Language and Communication* 23 (2003): 193–229.

Smelser, Neil J. "Economic Rationality as a Religious System." In *Rethinking Materialism: Perspectives on the Spiritual Dimension of Economic Behavior,* edited by Robert Wuthnow, 73–92. Grand Rapids, MI: William B. Erdmans, 1995.

Sørensen, Aage B. "Theoretical Mechanisms and the Empirical Study of Social Processes." In *Social Mechanisms: An Analytical Approach to Social Theory,* edited by Peter Hedström and Richard Swedberg, 238–266. New York: Cambridge University Press, 1998.

Stogdill, Ralph M. *Handbook of Leadership: A Survey of Theory and Practice.* New York: The Free Press, 1974.

Swedberg, Richard. *Max Weber and the Idea of Economic Sociology.* Princeton, NJ: Princeton University Press, 1998.

Terkel, Studs. *Working.* New York: Random House, 1972.

Thomas, Alan Berkeley. "Does Leadership Make a Difference to Organizational Performance?" *Administrative Science Quarterly* 33 (1988): 388–400.

Tichy, Noel M., and Mary Anne Devanna. *The Transformational Leader: The Key to Global Competitiveness.* New York: Wiley, 1986.

Tonnies, Ferdinand. *Community and Society,* translated and edited by Charles P. Loomis. East Lansing, MI: Michigan State University Press, 1957.

Van Maanen, John. "The Smile Factory: Work at Disneyland." In *Reframing Organizational Culture,* edited by P. Frost et al., 58–76. Newbury Park, CA: Sage Publications, 1991.

Walsh, James P., Klaus Weber, and Joshua D. Margolis. "Social Issues and Management: Our Lost Cause Found." *Journal of Management* 29 (2003): 859–881.

Wasserman, Noam, Bharat Anand, and Nitin Nohria. "When Does Leadership Matter? The Contingent Opportunities View of CEO Leadership." Working paper 01-063, Harvard Business School, Boston, 2001.

Weber, Max. *From Max Weber: Essays in Sociology,* edited by H.H. Gerth and C. Wright Mills. New York: Oxford University Press, 1946.

———. *The Theory of Social and Economic Organization,* edited by Talcott Parsons. New York: The Free Press, 1947, 1964.

———. *Economy and Society: Volume Two,* edited by Claus Wittich and Guenther Roth. Berkeley: University of California Press, 1978.

———. *The Protestant Ethic and the Spirit of Capitalism.* New York: Routledge, 1992.

Weber, Roberto, Colin Camerer, Yuval Rottenstreich, and Marc Knez. "The Illusion of Leadership: Misattribution of Cause in Coordination Games." *Organization Science* 12, no. 5 (2001): 582–598.

Weeks, John. *Unpopular Culture: The Ritual of Complaint in a British Bank.* Chicago: University of Chicago Press, 2004.

Whyte, William H. *The Organization Man.* New York: Simon and Schuster, 1956.

Zelizer, Viviana A. *Morals and Markets: The Development of Life Insurance in the United States.* New York: Columbia University Press, 1979.

———. *Pricing the Priceless Child: The Changing Social Value of Children.* New York: Basic Books, 1985.

Notes

1. A few macro-level studies suggest that the impact of leadership on performance variation is greater than implied by the Lieberson and O'Connor study (e.g., House, Spangler, and Woycke, 1991), and there is evidence that the short-term price of a company's stock is influenced by the individual characteristics of the CEO (Flynn and Staw, 2004). Nonetheless, the evidence linking leadership attributes or behaviors to performance variation is thin, particularly in light of the popular belief in the importance of leadership to the performance of complex organizations.

2. The emphasis on external constraint is one way in which Selznick departs from Barnard. In his discussion of organizational mission, for example, Selznick

describes the role of a university president: "A university president may have to accept some unwelcome aspects of alumni influence; he would be a poor leader if he did so without knowing whether his dependency was truly part of the institution's character" (1984:70).

3. See also Brint and Karabel (1991) for a discussion of the transformation of community colleges.

4. While not firmly within the institutional theory paradigm, Pfeffer's (1981) view of management as symbolic action shares many similarities with the Meyer and Rowan (1977) interpretation of management behavior as myth-making.

5. Weber defined formal rationality as an orientation toward action in which "the end, the means, and the secondary results are all rationally taken into account and weighted" (Weber, 1964:117). The conception is closest to economic notions of action: independent agents consciously evaluating choices and making decisions based on optimizing the costs and benefits between a series of alternatives. Examples can be found in rational choice theories in sociology, economics, and political science (e.g., Coleman, 1990; Brinton and Nee, 1998; see also Swedberg, 1998, for an extended discussion of Weber's original concepts of formal and substantive rationality).

6. Later in his life, however, Durkheim expressed greater skepticism about the role of professional associations in providing this meaning, calling instead for a secular religion in the form of nationalism (Durkheim, 1947b).

7. This definition allows us to distinguish meaningful from meaningless action by specifying the *form* that meaningful action will take. The *content* of what is found meaningful—the valued end toward which action is directed—can vary considerably across individuals.

8. There are also three hybrid process types; these are elaborated in Halliday, 1994:106–175.

9. Given their analytical focus, Meyer and Rowan and those who have followed the neo-institutional tradition have generally conceived of "taken-for-grantedness" at the level of an institutional field. So, when a neo-institutional scholar writes about a taken-for-granted organizational form or taken-for-granted practice, she is usually assuming that the taken-for-granted status is common across the institutional field. For our purposes, the level of analysis that is most relevant is that which encompasses an individual actor and those whom the actor is trying to direct toward a particular goal. In this case, what is taken-for-granted may vary across organizations.

10. In defining leadership activities in this way, we also treat as an empirical question the relationship between leadership and formal position. Leadership activities are not necessarily performed only by an organization's formal head or senior team. We suspect, of course, that those individuals with greater formal authority will have more opportunities than other organizational members to engage in activities that have the potential to create meaning for a significant number of organizational participants. Conceptually, however, leadership is not restricted to the occupants of particular formal positions.

4

What Is This Thing Called Leadership?

J. Richard Hackman

After participating in two days of discussions about leadership, I am tempted to suggest in these closing comments that our focal concept is little more than a semantic inkblot, an ambiguous word onto which people project their personal fantasies, hopes, and anxieties about what it takes to make a difference. That would be more provocative than constructive, however, because there really *is* something there. The challenge is to find it, tame it, and set it off on a course that generates knowledge about leadership that is more robust, cumulative, and useful than what we collectively have produced so far. The papers and discussions at this conference offer a number of leads for doing just that. In these remarks, I raise six themes that emerged from our conference sessions, themes that strike me as having special promise for advancing our collective understanding of organizational leadership.

Domain

We have been mainly concerned at this conference with the leadership of *purposive social systems*, by which I mean sets of people who are identifiable as system members and who work interdependently to accomplish one or more collective objectives. Dyads, groups, and whole organizations all can fall within our domain if it is possible to distinguish members from nonmembers and if members coordinate their activities in pursuing some shared purpose. An evangelist without a flock or the writer of a political tract would fall outside our domain (no social system) until such time as the evangelist formed a congregation or the writer joined a political cell. Travelers waiting to board a plane also would be outside our domain (no shared purpose) until such time as, say, the flight is canceled and the travelers begin to discuss hiring a bus to get them to their destination.

The domain of purposive social systems may seem too restrictive for a robust analysis of leadership phenomena. The popular press, after all, frequently refers to the "leadership" that is provided by a charismatic orator, a clever financier, or even a brilliant scientist. That much inclusiveness would hobble scholarly work on the topic. Productive research and theory on any phenomenon, leadership included, requires finding the sweet spot on a continuum that ranges from narrow specificity (e.g., analysis of a particular kind of leader in particular circumstances at a particular historical time) to unbounded inclusiveness (e.g., anyone who makes any kind of a difference in any domain). Restricting our attention to the leadership of purposive social systems gives us a domain that is wide enough to be interesting, while protecting us from the impossibility of trying to herd a diverse set of incomparable phenomena into the same conceptual pen.

Criteria

Even if you accept the domain just described (and thereby implicitly agree to the restrictions on generalizability that come with any reduction in domain scope), there remains the question of what we actually mean when we talk about "good" or "effective" or "successful" leadership. In his remarks at this conference, Joel Podolny noted that we tend to focus on those leader behaviors that can be shown to foster successful organizational outcomes. We might learn more about leadership, he suggested, if we studied leadership *qua* leadership, decoupled from outcome indicators.

There is merit in what Joel suggested. Too often we thoughtlessly accept conventional system outcomes, such as productivity or profitability, as the ultimate criteria of leadership success and label leaders who were in place when the favorable outcomes appeared as "effective." But I do not want to give up so easily on leader-outcome links. Indeed, if we accept the view that leaders are those who make a difference, then it is incumbent upon us to answer the question "a difference in *what?*" The answer to that question is important, because it requires us to be explicit about the values that underlie our leadership research.

So perhaps what we need is not a decoupling of leadership from success, but instead an expansion of what we *mean* by success. Specifically, what if we viewed great leadership as that which enhances what I will call "system viability"? A viable social system, as I have argued elsewhere, has three attributes. First, those who are affected by the work of the system (for example, clients, collaborators, or other stakeholders) are reasonably satisfied, and perhaps even pleased by, what the system produces. Second, the system itself becomes more capable as a performing unit over time. And third, individual members derive at least as much personal learning and fulfillment as frustration and alienation from their work within the system.

System viability can be readily conceptualized, and can be measured (although sometimes with difficulty) at any level of analysis: a dyad, a group, an organization, or even a nation state can be assessed on these three dimensions. And, in this view, anything that fosters system viability is an act of leadership.

Functions

If we code leadership as any action that fosters system viability, then we are taking what is generally known as the *functional* approach to leadership. In this approach, anyone who helps get critical system functions accomplished, including members who hold no formal leadership role, is exercising leadership. No one person is solely responsible for accomplishing leadership work, nor is there any one best strategy or style for carrying it out.

A key feature of the functional approach is that one needs to know as much, or more, about the system being led as about the personal qualities of those who would lead it. There can be no useful theory of leadership, therefore, without an accompanying theory that specifies what is required for systems to achieve their main purposes. Ever since 1938, when Chester Barnard published his classic book *The Functions of the Executive*, scholars have sought to identify the functions that, when accomplished, contribute to the viability of organizational systems. My own work, which is mainly at the team level, has identified both some generic functions (for example, diagnosing team strengths and vulnerabilities, creating performance-enabling structures and systems, and helping team members find ways to exploit the positive features of their performance situation), as well as a number of more specific functions that have specifically to do with fostering and sustaining teamwork.

The functional approach nudges us away from the most extreme versions of both psychological and sociological thinking about leadership. Because members can use their own special skills and preferred styles to fulfill system functions, we are released from the psychologists' unending search for the traits of effective leaders. And because actions that fulfill critical system functions actually do affect system viability, we need not be too bothered by the claim of some sociologists that leaders are but pawns in a larger drama that is driven almost entirely by external forces.

In addition to his concern about the outcome focus of leadership research, Joel also was worried about the degree to which our concepts and theories resonate with the managers who we hope would be helped by our scholarly contributions. There are two contrasting ways to go wrong in bringing the fruits of our research to working leaders. The first—and I think this is the one that Joel was worried about—is to expect leaders to learn, and then to use, concepts and models that are abstract and far removed from their daily experiences. We would be asking them to think like a scholar rather than a manager, and then to do the translation from theory to practice on their own. We should not require leaders to do that, nor should we expect that they will be disposed to do so.

A second way to go wrong is to tell leaders exactly what they are most ready to hear. To illustrate, lay observers, including many working managers, tend to attribute to leaders causal responsibility for system outcomes that actually may be shaped by more powerful but less salient influences. This tendency is so strong that Ruth Wageman and I have given it a name: the Leader Attribution Error. To the extent that we focus our research and teaching on the personal attributes and behavioral styles of individuals who are widely viewed as great leaders (e.g., "Here is how Jack Welch did it, and if you use him as a model you can do it too") we perpetuate that attributional error. Leaders are likely to accept and affirm what we say, but they will not be challenged to consider alternative ways of thinking about leadership or to come up with alternative strategies for enacting their leadership roles.

The functional approach offers a third way, one that is neither so familiar and acceptable that it can be assimilated intact into leaders' existing cognitive structures, nor so discrepant from those structures that it will be ignored or dismissed out of hand. In the language of psychology, the functional approach prompts accommodation, a change in cognitive structure, rather than either assimilation or rejection. And, in my experience, leaders do resonate with research findings that identify those leadership functions that are most critical to system viability—and that prompt them to consider fresh strategies for getting those functions fulfilled.

Context

The context of leadership was the most frequently mentioned construct in the opening session of this conference—all speakers but one addressed it explicitly. Context is indeed a challenge: What are we to do about the radical differences in the context of leadership for, say, a Boy Scout troop, a senior leadership team, a professional string quartet, and a product development team in an industrial firm? Could it really be true that leadership operates the same way in these radically different contexts? Indeed, does leadership even *mean* the same thing across these contexts?

The two most common suggestions for dealing with contextual differences are to develop contingency theories that take account of context, and to develop mid-range theories that are tailored for certain contexts but that are not presumed or expected to apply to others. There are nontrivial difficulties with both of these approaches.

Contingency models identify those attributes of situations that moderate the impact of leader behaviors or styles on collective outcomes, thereby providing research-based guidance about how leaders ought to behave in various contexts. In some contexts, for example, a participative style may be called for, whereas in others a more directive style may work best. Contingency models necessarily become complex as research identifies more and more situational attributes that moderate the leader behavior–collective outcome relationship. And in that inevitability lies the rub: the more complete and complex a contingency model, the more it requires of leaders a level of on-line cognitive processing that can exceed human capabilities—especially when the stakes are high and the leader is under high cognitive load.

An alternative strategy for dealing with contextual differences would be to develop what Joe Nye described as "mid-range" leadership theories. That is, rather than have one general model of leadership that is riddled with contingent propositions, we could develop separate models for each type of context in which we have special interest. Each of those mid-range theories would be specifically tuned to the features of the context addressed. So we might have, for example, a separate leadership model for, say, volunteer organizations, another for small entrepreneurial businesses, and yet another for multinational conglomerates. Such models could indeed be more helpful to leaders in each of those contexts than any general model could ever be. But this approach strikes me as a bit inelegant from a scholarly perspective. Do we really want to have different theories of leadership even for contexts as different as public sector organizations versus businesses versus nonprofit organizations? Or for European versus Asian enterprises? Or for manufacturing versus service-providing firms? The list could get long and cumbersome.

Is there an alternative to contingency models and mid-range theories for dealing with the very real differences in leadership contexts? Might it be possible to develop models of system leadership in which leaders find themselves quite naturally and automatically taking appropriate account of the special opportunities and constraints of their context? I realize that this may sound like magic, so I hasten to say that I do not have such a model in mind. But behavioral models do exist in some domains that have exactly this property.

Consider, for example, transactions that take place within an economic system. It does not make much of a difference whether we are trading products, services, futures, or favors. Nor is it consequential where the exchanges happen—the basic laws of transaction economics apply in all cases so long as the overall economic system is appropriately structured. Or consider mechanism design theory, again from economics. This approach, as set forth by Eric Maskin and his colleagues, involves the design of rules that generate a desired collective outcome even though individual participants act solely on the basis of their personal interests.

These examples from economics have little direct relevance to leadership theory, and I have provided them only to show that when the right conditions are in place appropriate behavior can occur automatically, without continuous or effortful on-line management. But note well that such models require that certain structural conditions be in place—a systemic infrastructure if you will—if they are to work properly. It could be interesting to speculate about the structural features of social systems that would help leaders naturally and appropriately take the special features of their contexts into account as they carry out their leadership work. This line of thinking, in all likelihood, will take us nowhere. I have sketched it here in hopes that we can continue to generate alternatives, even seemingly radical ones, that offer the possibility of finding ways for dealing with leadership contexts that are both conceptually satisfying and of practical value to those who work within them.

Conditions

Earlier in these remarks I suggested that if we are to develop robust leadership models we will need to move beyond our human tendency to attribute system outcomes to the actions of individual leaders. There is another natural human tendency that, I believe, also is impeding our progress—namely, the disposition to rely on cause-effect models in leadership research, theory, and practice. We want to *make* the team perform superbly, the conference succeed, the organization achieve its purposes, the nation prosper. Let me suggest that traditional cause-effect thinking is not merely inappropriate for the analysis of social system leadership but that it actually impedes progress in our field. And let me also propose an alternative. Rather than try to identify the direct causes of what transpires in social systems, might we instead focus on identifying the structural conditions that, when in place, increase the likelihood (but do not guarantee) social system viability?

To think about the conditions within which systems chart their own courses is very different from conventional cause-effect models as well from the action strategies that derive from those models. To illustrate, let me draw on an analogy I have used before—namely, the two different strategies that can be used by a pilot in landing an aircraft. One strategy is to manage the system continuously in real time. The pilot actively flies the airplane down, continuously adjusting heading, sink rate, and airspeed with the objective of arriving at the runway threshold just above stall speed, ready to flare the aircraft and touch down smoothly. The alternative strategy is to get the aircraft stabilized on approach while still far from the field, making small corrections as needed to heading, power, or aircraft configuration to keep the plane "in the groove." It is well known among pilots that the safer strategy is the second one; indeed, when a pilot winds up in the first situation, the prudent action is to go around and try the approach again.

To be stabilized on approach is to have the basic conditions established such that the natural course of events leads to the desired outcome—in this case, a good landing. The same way of thinking applies in many other domains of human endeavor. Consider, for example, constantly tinkering with a nation's interest rates, money supply, and tax policies, versus getting fundamentally sound economic conditions in place and letting the economy run itself. Or micromanaging the development of a child, versus creating a good family context that promotes healthy but mostly autonomous development. Or trying to foster creativity by telling someone to "be creative" and giving that person lots of creativity instruction and exercises, versus providing a relaxing and resource-rich setting and letting the creative response appear when it will.

In all of these instances the better strategy is to devote the first and greater portion of one's energies to establishing conditions that lead naturally to the desired outcomes and the lesser portion to on-line process management. The same considerations apply to the design and leadership of social systems. Having the right conditions in place opens possibilities, allowing leaders to do their work in their own way given their particular systemic contexts, using their own special strengths and styles, and drawing on the full array of other resources that are available to them.

To illustrate, let me describe an instance in which a leader took the condition-creating approach in a highly improbable setting—a symphony orchestra concert hall. I had the opportunity to observe Russian conductor Yuri Temirkanov lead a major U.S. orchestra in a performance of a Mahler symphony—the kind of piece that can invite the grandest arm-waving, body-swaying gyrations. But not from Temirkanov. He cued the musicians to begin and then his hands went to his sides. The orchestra played, and he *listened*. When some adjustment or assistance was needed, he provided it—signaling players with his eyes or body, or guiding a transition with his arms and hands. But that was about the extent of it. He had prepared the orchestra well during rehearsals and all the right conditions were in place. Now, at the performance, when it counted most, he was managing at the margin.

As Temirkanov demonstrated, to focus on conditions rather than causes is to think differently about social systems, and to act differently when leading them.

It

Let me end my remarks with a mystery. We've all had the experience of seeing a master leader in action—someone who knows just what to do, how to do it, and precisely when to act to help a system achieve its purposes. We also have seen the opposite, individuals who have been carefully selected for leader roles, who have excelled in numerous leader development courses, and who have amassed considerable leadership experience—yet who somehow manage to do the wrong thing at the wrong time in the wrong way.

The same kind of thing is seen in the behavior of master teachers, psychotherapists, consultants, and others whose work requires them to intervene with people and systems. They somehow know just when to push and when to back off. When to focus on the individual and when to attend more to the social context. When to lighten up and when to tighten up. When to ask, when to suggest, and when to wait. These people operate at a level that extends far beyond whatever training they have had. Indeed, some masters seem able to do the right thing at the right time without having had any formal training at all.

Even more mysteriously, masters often are entirely at a loss when asked to explain why they did what they did at the time they did it. "I don't really know," they say. "I just felt that was the thing to do right then." The contrast with novices and experts could not be more apparent. Novices do not yet know what they should do or how to do it, so they have to rely on instructions from someone else. Experts know what they should do, and they can tell you exactly why that is the proper action to take in their present circumstances. But masters transcend rules, guidelines, and principles—and wind up doing things that in many cases are as unexpected as they are effective.

So what is the "it" that master leaders have that the rest of us do not? How did they get it? And what might we do to help others develop it? We know a few things that may help us start to answer these questions. We know from decades of research that it is something quite different from what we have measured in our search for the traits of effective leaders. We know from doctoral student Colin Fisher's research that it assuredly involves a finely honed sense of timing—knowing without deliberately thinking about it when to act and when to wait. I know from frustrating personal experience that we are unlikely to be able to train someone to become a master leader, not even when we use the best pedagogies currently available: master-level leadership is something more than the sum of one's accumulated knowledge and skill. And, finally, we know that merely putting a label on whatever it is that these leaders have (for example, calling it "social intelligence" or "charisma") does not help much in understanding what it is that these people have or how they got it.

It is going to take some ingenuity to understand "it," in part because people who have it are unable to explain what it is but also because they may be disinclined to tell us even if they could. I once asked someone who quite clearly had it if I could follow him around for a month or so over the summer to try to understand his superb capabilities. "No," he said. "That wouldn't be a good use of your time. And, besides, to do that would be *wrong*." He meant it. He knew he had something special, but he seemed fearful that if someone were to closely inspect and analyze whatever it was, he just might lose it.

My exchange with that individual has stayed with me a long time (I propositioned him back when I was just starting out as a researcher). And now doctoral student Sujin Jang is going to take another run at it—this time not by following a master around but by using some recently developed methodologies to see if, at the very least, we can reliably assess individual differences in the degree to which people have whatever "it" is. I hope that she succeeds, and that in these brief remarks I may have tempted a couple of others to join the hunt. Because if we could solve this mystery we would be able, at our next conference, to explore some fascinating frontiers of leadership thought and practice that lay just beyond our collective reach at this one.

SECTION TWO

THE THEORY OF LEADERSHIP

*Personal Attributes, Functions,
and Relationships*

5

LEADERSHIP THROUGH AN ORGANIZATION BEHAVIOR LENS

A Look at the Last Half-Century of Research

Mary Ann Glynn and Rich DeJordy

LEADERSHIP IS one of the most enduring—and elusive—constructs in the organizational behavior (OB) literature; as Bass (1990:3) puts it, leadership is "one of the world's oldest preoccupations." Articles on leadership appeared in the early pages of major organizational behavior journals in midcentury, including *Administrative Science Quarterly* and the *Journal of the Academy of Management*, which later evolved to become the *Academy of Management Journal*, and the *Academy of Management Review*. Today, interest in leadership research remains keen. The *Harvard Business Review* alone has published nearly 500 articles since 1923 that reference leadership in their abstracts. And yet, in spite of all of this inquiry and interest, there seems to be little consensus within OB concerning what leadership is, how it functions, and to what effect. Podolny, Khurana and Hill-Popper (2005) comment on this state of the field, decrying the trajectory that leadership research has taken:

> During the past 50 years, organizational scholarship on leadership has shifted from a focus on the significance of leadership for

Author note: We greatly appreciate the generous support of the Boston College Winston Center for Leadership and Ethics in enabling this research.

> meaning-making to the significance of leadership for economic performance. This shift has been problematic... (Podolny, Khurana, and Hill-Popper, 2005:1)

Heeding this observation, we take stock of leadership research in OB, reviewing both the theoretical models of leadership that have dominated organizational discourse, as well as empirical investigations. We map the historical trajectory of leadership theories in the OB domain and show how they tend to cluster around three primary models, focusing on: leadership traits, leadership behaviors, and leadership contingencies. We examine published empirical research over the last 50 years focusing explicitly on leadership in three of the major OB journals: *Administrative Science Quarterly*, *Academy of Management Journal*, and *Organization Science*. Although we find evidence of a prototype design in leadership research, there is no clearly dominant theoretical perspective on leadership. Finally, we conclude with a discussion and agenda for future leadership research using an OB perspective.

Historical Trajectory of OB Leadership Theories

As much as leadership has attracted great interest, it has also attracted vigorous debate, discussion, and contestation. There has been a proliferation of definitions, theories, and models within the OB literature, but little consensus among leadership theorists. As Bass (1990:37) observes, "there has been no shortage of modeling and theorizing about leadership. However, relatively few models and theories have dominated the research community, and many have been restatements of the obvious."

Leadership theories span levels of analysis, ranging from micro-level approaches that focus on the individual traits or behaviors of the leader to macro-level approaches that focus on leadership attributions, processes, and outcomes for a collective, an organization, or a nation-state. In any number of studies, leadership often becomes the proverbial "black box," a bundle of processes and mechanisms that function in a multiplicity of ways with both intended and unintended results. We try to lift the lid on this "black box" by reviewing the major theoretical perspectives in the OB literature, asking: What are the dominant trends in how leadership scholars have theorized and studied leadership over the years?

Leadership Defined

The leadership research in OB seems to be a definitional quagmire: "There are almost as many different definitions of leadership as there are persons who have attempted to define the concept" (Stogdill, 1974:259). Bass cuts through the bog with this integrative definition:

> Leadership is an interaction between two or more members of a group that often involves structuring or restructuring of the situation and the perceptions and expectations of the members. Leaders are agents of change—persons whose acts affect other people more than other people's acts affect them. Leadership occurs when one group member modifies the motivation or competencies of others in the group. (Bass, 1990:19–20)

OB researchers have defined leadership in a myriad of ways. Some definitions focus on the persona of the leader. Gardner (1995:6), for instance, asserts that leaders are those "who significantly influence the thoughts, behaviors, and/or feelings of others." Other scholars focus on the process or conduct of leadership, for example, "Leadership emphasizes the exercise of interpersonal influence and motivation to accomplish the mission" (Snook, 2002:31) or "as a process that occurs within the minds of individuals who live in a culture—a process that entails the capacities to create stories, to understand and evaluate these stories, and to appreciate the struggle among stories" (Gardner, 1995:22). Still other scholars define leadership in terms of its effects, that is, as "the act of making a difference" and evidenced "when the vision is strategic, the voice persuasive, the results tangible" (Useem, 1998:4). Focusing on leadership performance or effectiveness has been a resounding theme in the OB literature (Podolny, Khurana, and Hill-Popper, 2005). We review the relevant literature to map the theoretical and empirical trajectory of leadership research; we begin with the evolution of leadership theories.

Leadership Theorized

Over the last half-century of OB research, leadership has been theorized in a number of different ways but with a characteristic pattern:

> Leadership has been conceived as the focus of group processes, as a matter of personality, as a matter of inducing compliance, as the exercise of influence, as particular behaviors, as a form of persuasion,

as a power relation, as an instrument to achieve goals, as an effect of interaction, as a differentiated role, as initiation of structure, and as many combinations of these definitions. (Bass, 1990:11)

The theoretical trajectory of OB leadership research is historically patterned, developing within the broader theoretical milieu of its period as well as the needs and events of the times in which these models develop (Mayo and Nohria, 2005a, 2005b). Our brief overview of leadership theories in OB focuses on describing the dominant models chronologically; we find a general progression from leadership traits to behavioral styles, and finally, leadership contingencies as well as the dynamics of transformation, change, and networks.

Early History: The Search for Traits That Distinguish Leaders (From the Rest of Us)

Initially, leadership research was launched from a psychological perspective and with the overriding assumption that leaders were somehow different and in possession of special, unique, or extraordinary personality attributes, abilities, skills, or physical characteristics that others did not have (e.g., Stogdill, 1948). Leaders could seemingly accomplish what others could not: they could lead. Early scholarship was rooted in identifying this distinguishing set of traits. Stogdill (1974), for instance, identified these traits as critical to leadership: dependability, cooperativeness, assertiveness, dominance, high energy, self-confidence, stress tolerance, responsibility, achievement orientation, adaptability, cleverness, persuasiveness, organizational and speaking abilities, and social skills.

Trait theories are sometimes referred to as "Great Man" theories both because leadership was thought to be the province of males and because leadership had a mythical, heroic sense of destiny (with leaders assumed to be born, not made). However, the search for definitive and universal leadership traits met with only limited success; moreover, trait theories did little to explain why everyone who possessed these special attributes did not rise to become leaders. As a result, scholarly attention turned to other explanations, refocusing away from "who leaders are" (traits) to "what leaders do" (behaviors).

Emergence of Behavioral Theories of Leadership

Behavioral theories focus on a leader's style of action, typically categorized with regard to a *task orientation*, which emphasizes the achievement of work goals or objectives and organizing structures, rules, or designs; and *people orientation*, which emphasizes interpersonal relationships and consideration for followers. Like traits, behavioral styles are theorized to be stable properties of the individual leader and thus invariant to the particular organizational context or work situation.

This approach had its origins in the work of Lewin, Lippitt, and White (1939) who outlined three basic leadership styles: autocratic, democratic, and laissez-faire. About twenty years later, researchers at Michigan (e.g., Katz and Kahn, 1960) identified two basic leadership styles: production-oriented and employee-oriented. Working around the same time, Ohio State researchers provided a theoretical framework and operationalization that has endured; this work modeled the critical behavioral dimensions as *initiating structure*, whereby leaders define and organize work roles and design, as well as patterns of communication, and *consideration*, whereby leaders nurture warm, friendly working relationships and cultivate mutual trust and respect. Leadership style is assessed with a widely used scale, the Leader Behavior Description Questionnaire (LBDQ; originated by Stogdill, 1963).

Despite its early promise, the considerable body of behavioral research (like the trait studies that preceded it) found that a particular leadership style was not universally effective; a style that was effective in one setting was not always effective in a different setting. As well, behavioral theories tended to rely on abstracted concepts of behavioral types that were often difficult to identify (Yukl, 1989). And so leadership scholars began searching for more situationally specific theories of leadership.

CONTINGENCY THEORIES OF LEADERSHIP

In contrast to trait and behavioral theories, contingency theories explicitly assume that leadership can vary across situations and that there may not be a universally effective way to lead; different contexts may call for different kinds of leadership. Leaders are assumed to have a repertoire of leadership attributes and behavioral styles from which they can draw, adapting these as needed to the demands of the specific task situation or the particular followers they lead. Contingency theories focus on aspects of context, such as favorableness of the environment for the leader (Fiedler, 1964), the relative complexity of the task and expertise of followers (Vroom and Yetten, 1973), and the dyadic relationship between leaders and followers (Graen, Liden, and Hoel, 1982). Early iterations of contingency theories focused primarily on the immediate situation, narrowly defined as the organizational context and employees who were often subordinate to the leader's authority.

Fiedler's (1964) contingency theory leveraged the insights of behaviorists to propose that the effectiveness of a leader's style (broadly construed as task versus people orientation) depended upon the favorableness of the situation, assessed by the Least Preferred Coworker (LPC) Scale. This is a projection technique asking leaders to think about the type of person with whom they would work the least well. Leadership effectiveness was predicated upon the fit between the leader's preferred orientation and the receptivity of followers to this orientation. Scholars elaborating Fiedler's contingency theory saw the leadership role as important in directing employees' attention and efforts toward work goals and in articulating the paths by which to achieve them. This path-goal theory of leadership delineates four basic styles—directive, supportive, participative, or achievement-oriented—which are deployed as they fit the work environment and followers' needs (House, 1971). Vroom and his colleagues (e.g., Vroom and Yetton, 1973; Vroom and Jago, 1988) proposed a normative model of contingency theory such that leaders' type of participation (e.g., autocratic, democratic, or consultative) in decision making should fit the situation.

Contingency theories of leadership usefully contextualized leadership and modeled it as more supple, adaptive, and situationally flexible than trait or behavioral theories. However, contingency theories were not without their limitations. In particular, the contexts examined were fairly local and narrow, focusing on a leader's particular work situation or immediate subordinates. Additionally, contingency models tended to be highly complex and often difficult to apply. How leadership processes may be contingent on broader aspects of organizational and institutional environments, including societal norms, cultural sensibilities, cross-national variations, and demographic differences, remains largely unspecified.

LEADERSHIP THEORIES OF CHANGE, INFLUENCE, AND CHARISMA

In recent years, several variations of leadership theories have taken root in the OB literature. In important ways, a number of these build on and extend the earlier advances of trait, behavioral, and contingency theories. Generally, these newer models treat leadership as a change process and the leader as a primary catalyst of change. Bass (1985), for instance, theorized that leadership change may be either *transformational*, inspiring and exciting followers to high levels of performance through visionary leadership or, by contrast, *transactional*, that is, more instrumental, using rewards or punishments to motivate subordinate efforts.

Focusing on leaders in the context of their followers, Leader-Member Exchange theory (LMX) emphasizes the relational bases and influence tactics that leaders use and how they vary vis-à-vis followers: when followers are similar to leaders, LMX predicts that leaders will give them more responsibility, attention, and rewards, but when followers are different, leaders will tend to give them less attention, managing by relying more on formal rules and structures (e.g., Graen, Liden, and Hoel, 1982). Thus, leaders' personal and behavioral styles are theorized to be more supple and situationally adaptive, and, when leadership is appropriate to the contingencies of a situation, effectiveness and intended change are more likely to result. As Mayo and Nohria (2005a:45) explain: "Without an ability to read and adapt to changing business conditions, personality and skill are but temporal strengths."

In a formulation which redounds to trait, behavioral, and transformational approaches, interest has resurged in leadership *charisma*, that is, the power of a leader's personal abilities and talents to influence followers in profound, extraordinary, and transformative ways (e.g., Conger and Kanungo, 1987). The authority and influence of charismatic leadership flow from their unique attributes and ability to envision new possibilities and thus interject values ("substantive rationality") into those economic organizations that tend to be dominated by technical efficiency ("formal rationality") (Weber, 1978). Charismatic leaders infuse work and organizations with meaning and a value-driven mission (e.g., Glynn and Dowd, 2008) in ways described by early institutionalists (e.g., Selznick, 1957); moreover, the charismatic authority of leadership became an increasingly sought-after commodity as the institutional environment of business changed in the 1980s (Khurana, 2002). Beyond theories of charisma, new advancements in leadership theories relate to network structure (e.g., Kilduff and Krackhardt, 2008; Sparrowe and Liden, 2005), emotional intelligence (Goleman, 1995) and positive organizing processes (Cameron and Lavine, 2006; Cameron, 2008).

Overall, the theoretical trajectory of leadership seems propelled by increasing attribution of agency to leaders, moving from "who they are" to "what they do" to "when they do what." In the following section, we track research related to this evolution by examining empirical work on leadership published in three major organizational behavior journals.

A Brief Survey of Empirical Research on Leadership

We surveyed empirical studies of leadership published in three prominent OB journals: *Administrative Science Quarterly* (ASQ), *Academy of Management Journal* (AMJ), and *Organization Science* (OS). We chose these three journals because all speak to a broad community of OB scholars (e.g., Palmer, 2006); all occupy prominent, historical roles in the field of OB, thus affording a long time horizon (ASQ began publishing in 1956; AMJ in 1963, and OS in 1990); and all have published empirical research on leadership.

We examined the abstracts of these journal publications with regard to the study's theoretical framework (discussed earlier), research context, methods and data analyses, and modeling of antecedents, outcomes, and processes of leadership. As well, we tracked how empirical studies in these OB journals reflected Podolny, Khurana, and Hill-Popper's (2005:5) observation that organizational scholarship on leadership has shifted away from a focus on meaning-making, that is, leaders' "ability to infuse purpose and meaning into organizational experience," and toward a focus on economic performance. In addition, we investigated how a number of other features of leadership research resemble trends previously observed in organizational scholarship. We compare trends in leadership studies to trends observed in ASQ over the last half-century, including its predominance of quantitative empirical methods (over qualitative), prevalence of "macro" (over "micro") approaches, and a North American parochialism (Palmer, 2006), as well as the use of theory to provide explanations (of processes and mechanisms) or to predict outcomes (including effectiveness and performance) (Davis and Marquis, 2005).

Methods

We selected all abstracts from ASQ, AMJ, and OS that referenced the terms *leader, leaders,* or *leadership* in either the abstract or the title.

This generated our initial sample of 319 abstracts (ASQ = 98, AMJ = 181, OS = 40). Both authors reviewed all abstracts and eliminated 168 of these because they either were not empirical or not reflective of an OB perspective, focusing instead on corporate, strategic, or competitive behaviors such as "market leadership" or "[corporate] leaders in innovation." This yielded a final set of 151 abstracts, which are listed in appendix 5-1.

We used an iterative process to develop our coding scheme, moving between the published abstracts and the theorization of leadership (reviewed previously). First, the two authors separately coded 5 percent of the articles to generate initial ideas for a codebook. We then compared each others' coding ideas in light of various theories of leadership; this resulted in a refined set of codes, which we then applied to another round of coding and subsequently reviewed. This process resulted in a final set of thirty-one codes, broken down into nine major categories (in alphabetical order): (1) context (geographic location of study: U.S., non-U.S., comparative, or not specified), (2) domain of theory (micro or macro), (3) level of analysis (individual, group, organization, organizational field/society, or multilevel), (4) leadership variable (leadership modeled as independent variable, dependent variable, or both, as in mediating models), (5) methods (quantitative, qualitative, or meta-analytic), (6) model (process/explanatory or variance/predictive), (7) research context (lab or field), (8) theoretical focus (behavioral, contingency, dyadic/relational, trait, or the meaning of leadership), and (9) additional topics (leadership and change, diversity, networks, performance, strategic, or top management team/CEO). We present our complete codebook, including code descriptions, frequencies, and exemplars, in table 5-1.

Coding was performed using EZ-Text (Carey, Wenzel, Reilly, Sheridan, and Steinberg, 1998) which facilitates coding defined units (in this case abstracts) with a predefined codebook as well as conducting interrater reliability analysis. Using EZ-Text, the two authors independently coded 10 percent of the abstracts in two iterations; we met after each iteration to refine and clarify the subtleties of each code. We then coded all the abstracts. Interrater reliability ratings were calculated, and we found that kappa scores ranged from 0.582 to 1.000, with an average of 0.758, and percent agreements ranged from 80.13 percent to 100 percent, with an average of 93.55 percent. Only two codes had kappa values lower than 0.6: LOA_SUP (supraorganizational level of analysis)

TABLE 5-1

Codebook with examples and frequencies

Area	Code and frequency	Description	Exemplars
Context	CXT_USA 15 (10%)	The research setting was entirely within the United States.	"[S]urveyed management teams in 102 hotel properties in the United States . . ." [A129]
	CXT_FOR 12 (8%)	The research setting was entirely within a single country outside the United States.	"Using a sample of 499 supervisor-subordinate dyads collected in China in two studies, we found . . ." [A150]
	CXT_GBL 0 (0%)	The research setting explicitly included contexts across multiple countries.	None available, but, conceptually, the GLOBE studies and other cross-national studies of leadership would meet this criterion.
	CXT_NS 123 (81%)	No specific information about the national/geographic research context available from abstract.	N/A. Absence of any of the above led to this code.
Domain	D_MICRO 121 (80%)	Focus of research was on micro organizational theory. Issues of motivation, cognition, etc.	"We propose that transformational leadership is associated with the way followers view their jobs." [A106]
	D_MACRO 31 (21%)	Focus of research on macro organizational theory including issues relating to structural, organizational, or supraorganizational contexts.	"[T]he immigration of leaders possessing different skills, understandings, assumptions, and values can promote change within institutionalized organizations and fields." [A079]
Level of analysis	LOA_IND 94 (62%)	Level of analysis is the individual.	"[I]nvestigated how the leadership behavior of a large number of supervisors, as measured by consideration and initiating structure scales, was related to their subordinates reported burnout." [A117]
	LOA_GRP 18 (12%)	Level of analysis is the group.	"[L]iterature on the effects of group size and spatial arrangements upon group decision making performance, member satisfaction, member consensus, and leadership emergence." [A021]
	LOA_ORG 17 (11%)	Level of analysis is the organization.	"This paper focuses on how cultural leadership that innovates, by either creating or changing organizational cultures, is likely to differ from that which maintains organizational cultures." [A136]

Area	Code and frequency	Description	Exemplars
	LOA_SUP 4 (3%)	Level of analysis is organizational field or society.	"[C]oncepts of leadership in Greek literature prior to the fourth century B.C., including the Homeric tradition and the tradition of the fifth century Athens." [A112]
	LOA_MUL 18 (12%)	Study explicitly spans levels of analysis.	"We hypothesized that organizational culture moderates the relationship between justice perceptions and leader-member exchange (LMX)." [A037]
Leadership variable	LDR_IV 114 (75%)	Leadership is independent variable.	"We argue that team information acquisition mediates the effect of the relationship of team locus-of-control composition and leadership structure on team financial performance in a decision-making context." [A015]
	LDR_DV 44 (29%)	Leadership is dependent variable.	"Perceived similarity significantly predicted LMX quality." [A036]
Methods	M_QUANT 128 (85%)	Study employs quantitative methods.	"Sampling three industries to enhance generalizability, we found that board vigilance was positively associated with CEO duality." [A040]
	M_QUAL 22 (15%)	Study employs qualitative methods.	"The article discusses the managerial style and effective communication of Sir Winston Spencer Churchill . . . particularly on the language used by Churchill in his speeches," [A137]
	M_META 3 (2%)	Study is a meta-analysis.	"A meta-analysis of 37 studies of teams in natural contexts suggests that . . ." [A005]
Model	MDL_P 24 (26%)	Study offers a process model.	"Content analyses of the data produced a process model showing that effective external leaders . . ." [A030]
	MDL_V 127 (84%)	Study offers a variance model.	"LMX and mentoring each also accounted for meaningful incremental variance over the other with respect to rated performance, salary progress, and promotion rate. Implications are briefly discussed." [A113]

(continued)

TABLE 5-1 (continued)

Codebook with examples and frequencies

Area	Code and frequency	Description	Exemplars
Research context	RC_LAB 20 (13%)	Study was performed in a lab or simulated.	"We manipulated transformational and transactional leadership styles." [A072]
	RC_FLD 128 (85%)	Study was performed in the field.	"A field study of 84 registered nurses and their supervisors revealed that . . ." [A105]
Theory	T_BEHAV 67 (44%)	Employed a behavioral theory of leadership. This included references to the "leadership grid," concerns for production and people, and initiating and consideration structures.	"[I]nvestigated how the leadership behavior of a large number of supervisors, as measured by consideration and initiating structure scales, was related to their subordinates' reported burnout." [A117]
	T_CONTIG 41 (27%)	Employed a contingency theory of leadership. References to path-goal theory, Fiedler's contingency model or its components, the situated model of leadership, etc.	"[C]areers of successful military leaders were analyzed to determine if successful military leadership could be predicted by Fiedler's contingency model." [A138]
	T_DYAD 27 (18%)	Employed a dyadic theory of leadership. Primarily used for LMX, but also any explicit reference to "leader-follower," although "supervisor/ subordinate without reference to leadership was not included.	"We developed a model in which leader-member exchange mediated between perceived transformational leadership behaviors and followers' task performance and organizational citizenship behaviors." [A063]
	T_TRAIT 26 (17%)	Employed a trait-based theory of leadership. Major traits that affected leadership or responses to leadership included self-confidence, charisma, gender, and race.	"This study on the exercise of influence examines selected relationships among leader characteristics." [A097]
	T_MEAN 17 (11%)	Theorized about the meaning of leadership.	"[C]oncepts of leadership in Greek literature prior to the fourth century B.C., including the Homeric tradition." [A015]

Area	Code and frequency	Description	Exemplars
Additional topics	X_CHNG 23 (15%)	Investigated the interaction of leadership and change. Change included organizational or individual change and references to "transformational leadership."	"The model focuses on the relationship between a dying organization and its members and on how leaders help orchestrate changes in the socially defined reality that members share about the organization's viability." [A132]
	X_DVRST 17 (11%)	Investigated the interaction of leadership and attributes of diversity (e.g., gender, race). Nationality only if raised as an issue beyond the national context captured above.	"[W]e explored dynamics and dilemmas associated with women leading a women's group based on feminist principles." [A007]
	X_NETW 5 (3%)	Investigated the relationship between leadership and social networks. Included references to network concepts (e.g., brokerage) and patterns of informal relationships or other relational structures.	"This article discusses the integration of leader-member exchange (LMX) and social network perspectives in organizations and the development and testing of a model of the relational antecedents of members influence." [A127]
	X_PERF 71 (47%)	Investigated the relationships between leadership and performance (of individual, group, organization, or leadership effectiveness).	"This paper evaluates research on the impact of chief executive officers on corporate performance, taking Lieberson and O'Connor's path breaking study as its starting point." [A135]
	X_STRAT 4 (3%)	Investigated the relationship between leadership and strategy.	"In this article, the authors draw on five case studies in health care organizations to develop a process theory of strategic change in pluralistic settings characterized by diffuse power and divergent objectives." [A025]
	X_TMT 14 (9%)	Investigated the relationship between leadership and the top management team. Key terms included "CEO," "Executives," and "Top Management Team."	"The authors also hypothesized that the relationship between CEO leadership attributes and performance depends on perceived environmental uncertainty, as reported by immediate CEO subordinates." [A144]

at 0.587 and T_BEHAV (behavioral theory) at 0.582. While LOA_SUP had over 97 percent agreement but very low frequency (affecting its kappa calculation), T_BEHAV only had 80 percent agreement. This was primarily due to differences between the coders in the application of the code, with one taking an expansive view and the other a narrower view. We reviewed our coding and met to agree upon formal criteria for the application of the code; then we easily resolved outstanding conflicts. Thus, reliability analysis indicates that both coders generally agreed on the application of the codes; we reviewed any coding differences and then finalized the codes for each article. We used these codes to perform our analyses.

Findings

The frequency of leadership publications over time is illustrated in figure 5-1, which shows the number of publications by year, from 1957 to 2007. From the figure, it is evident that publications peaked in the mid-1970s and then fell off sharply in the early 1980s, with a resurgence of publications in the last three years (2005–2007). Although it is hard to tell whether this resurgence is simply part of the normal cycle of publication (also evident in the early 1990s and at the turn of the century), it clearly speaks to the persistence of the construct as a matter of scholarly inquiry for OB researchers. This pattern and resurgence is all the more noteworthy when we take into account that two dedicated journals, *Leadership Quarterly* and the *Journal of Leadership and Organization Studies* (nee *Journal of Leadership Studies*) began publishing in 1990 and 1998, respectively.

To better understand the extent to which empirical work tracked the theoretical trajectory described previously, we examined the overall prevalence of each of the five theoretical perspectives we coded (behavioral, contingency, dyadic, trait, and meaning-based theories) and charted their use over time. Not unexpectedly, behavioral theories were the most often cited, appearing in nearly half (44 percent) of the abstracts, followed by contingency (27 percent), dyadic (18 percent), trait (17 percent) and meaning-based perspectives (11 percent). The observation of Podolny, Khurana, and Hill-Popper (2005) still rings true: there seems to be a relative dearth in studying leadership meaning-making (which represents only a subset of the meaning-based perspectives); this contrasts significantly with leadership performance, which appears in nearly half of the studies (47 percent).

FIGURE 5-1

Empirical leadership studies published by year: ASQ, AMJ, OS

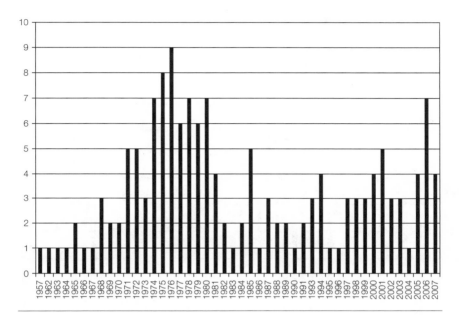

Figure 5-2, which displays the prevalence of these theories over time, indicates that while behavioral and contingency theories framed the bulk of empirical work until the mid-1980s, there has not been a dominant theoretical perspective since. There is no evidence of cumulative theory-building occurring within leadership research. Instead, the field of leadership in OB seems to be what Pfeffer (1993, 1995) describes as "low paradigm," that is, "characterized by the proliferation of multiple theoretical orientations that tend to examine different research questions with different research methods and come to different conclusions about the nature, causes, and consequences of organizational behavior" (Palmer, 2006:543). Although we do not take a normative stand in the debate as to whether scholarship within a field advances via paradigmatic homogeneity (e.g., Pfeffer, 1993, 1995) or paradigmatic heterogeneity (e.g., Perrow, 1994; Cannella and Paetzold, 1994; Van Maanen, 1995), our findings suggest that empirical research on leadership is characteristic of the latter. While this may reflect the developmental stage of the field, it also suggests that the persistent heterogeneity of theories in empirical leadership research may undermine

FIGURE 5-2

Theoretical perspectives used in empirical research on leadership by year

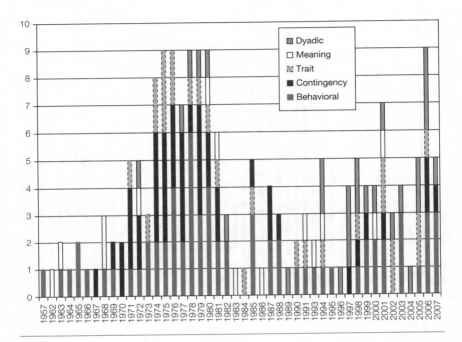

our ability to develop cumulative knowledge that builds on itself (Palmer, 2006). On the other hand, this same persistence stands as a testament to the utility and resonance of OB leadership theories first presented twenty to thirty years ago.

To test if Palmer's characterization of the paradigmatic heterogeneity of the organization studies field applies to leadership studies, we used network analysis to investigate patterns among the codes to see if particular methods were tied to particular theories. We first loaded the data into UCINET (Borgatti, Everett, and Freeman, 2002) and correlated the codes based on their presence or absence across the 151 cases (published abstracts). In order to ease interpretation, we viewed the correlation matrix as a network (DeJordy, Borgatti, Halgin, and Roussin, 2007) using NetDraw (Borgatti, 2002). Figure 5-3 is a visualization of the network. In this figure, each of the codes is represented by a circle, and a line (or edge) exists between two codes if the correlation between them is greater than 0.35. We chose this level because it both represents a moderate level of correlation and because it best captures the underlying structure of the correlation matrix (DeJordy et al., 2007), determined by examining the data iteratively.

To simplify the graph, any code with no correlations greater than 0.35 was removed. What can be seen is that there are some moderately strong correlations among the codes. For instance, the group of connected codes (a *component* in network terms) in the upper left corner of figure 5-3 (LOA_IND; D_MICRO; MDL_V, M_QUANT) reveals the following research pattern: a micro perspective, at the individual level of analysis, that investigates a variance model, typically with quantitative research methods. Although the pattern is perhaps not surprising, it does demonstrate how succinctly the network diagram

FIGURE 5-3

Network structure of correlations of codes assigned to articles

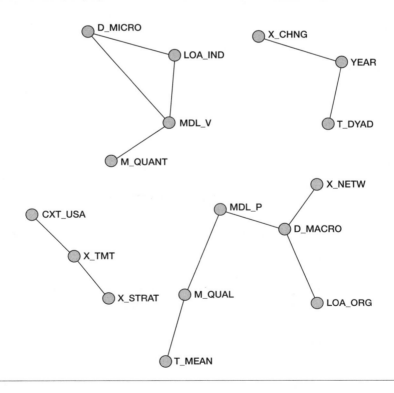

conveys the pattern. On the other hand, the component in the upper right corner of figure 5-3 (T_DYAD, YEAR, X_CHNG) indicates a moderate correlation between year and both change and dyadic theories, suggesting that leadership research using these constructs has become more prevalent over the years; the lack of a line between change and dyadic makes it clear they are not correlated with each other. Further, leadership research on top management teams characteristically tends to be conducted in the United States and to investigate strategic issues (see the bottom left component: X_TMT, CXT_USA, X_STRAT). Finally, we find that leadership research at the macro level tends to focus on the organizational level of analysis, examining network structures and process models, which, in turn, are associated with qualitative methods, themselves associated with meaning-based perspective on leadership (see bottom right component in figure 5-3). These four components represent a very rudimentary breakdown of some of the trends in leadership research.

We observe that we find a tight and coherent coupling among several research design elements. The pattern is not unexpected: level of analysis and micro/macro domain, model (process or variance), and methods (qualitative or quantitative), as well as contextual (U.S.—TMT—strategy) and temporal variations. However, the only theory that appears in this correlational analysis is dyadic theory, which is simply associated with "year," a likely result of this theory's later emergence in the field. That there is not a noticeable association between particular theories and particular methods suggests considerable variations in leadership research.

Since this is a network of correlations, it takes into account patterns of nonoccurrence as well as occurrence. Given that some codes are applied more (or less) frequently, correlations may overly reflect patterns of nonoccurrence. To address this, we looked at patterns of co-occurrence only. First, we removed the nondichotomous variables (year and journal) from the original data and then performed a cross-product on that matrix. This yielded a code-by-code matrix where cell X_{ij} contained the number of times code i and code j were both assigned to the same abstract, and the diagonal recorded the number of times each code was assigned overall. We normalized this matrix between 0 and 1 by dividing each cell by the number of cases (151), so each cell now had the percentage of cases for which the codes co-occurred.

We again visualized this as a network, filtering at co-occurrences in at least 35 percent of the abstracts and eliminating those codes that did not co-occur at least 35 percent of the time with at least one other code. The result is presented in figure 5-4.

Figure 5-4 depicts a single component with more codes than any grouping in figure 5-3 and relatively high density (0.92). In this figure, we have also sized each node proportional to its frequency of use. Thus, you can see that, of these codes, T_BEHAV is the least commonly assigned code, corresponding to its frequency of 45 percent, X_PERF is next at 47 percent, all the way up to RC_FLD, which is the most common at almost 85 percent. From both their size and the fact that they are connected to fewer other codes, we can see that both T_BEHAV and X_PERF are not as embedded in this network as the other nodes. Nonetheless, as a technique for data reduction, we have trimmed thirty-one codes down to nine, which all co-occur with at

FIGURE 5-4

Code co-occurrence in over 35 percent of articles

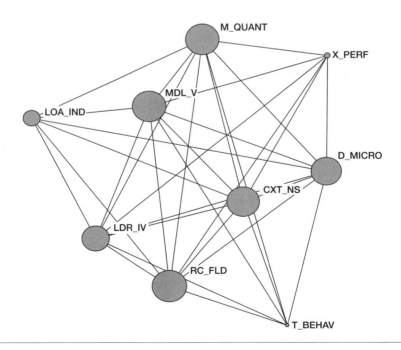

least six of the others in at least 35 percent of the cases studied. This represents the best approximation of the prototypical empirical study of leadership in these three journals: a field study, whose geographic context is not specified, that focuses on the micro, individual level using quantitative methods to test a variance model, in which leadership behavior predicts performance.

To illustrate, we present two abstracts describing different leadership studies coded with exactly this set of codes.

> The article presents information on a study which investigated how the leadership behavior of a large number of supervisors, as measured by consideration and initiating structure scales, was related to their subordinates' reported burnout. Details related to the study's methods and results for hierarchical regression analysis of burnout are presented. The author provides an analysis of variance for subordinate burnout. A discussion is presented about the effects of leadership on employee morale and work environment. [Seltzer and Numerof, 1988; A117]

> Recent research in the area of leadership seems to point to the existence of four basic dimensions of leadership: support, interaction facilitation, goal emphasis, and work facilitation. Data from a recent study of 40 agencies of one of the leading life insurance companies are used to evaluate the impact of both supervisory and peer leadership upon outcomes of satisfaction and factorial performance measures. Results from the study suggest that this conceptual model is useful and that leadership's relation to organizational outcomes may best be studied when both leadership and effectiveness are multidimensional. Both peer and supervisory leadership measures relate to outcomes. In most instances, the ability to predict is enhanced by taking simultaneous account of certain nonleadership variables. [Bowers and Seashore, 1966; A016]

Interestingly, although these articles were published more than twenty years apart, they are remarkably similar in the conceptualization and investigation of leadership. And, although it is useful to look at these as archetypes of leadership research, it is important to note that no article that has appeared in the last twenty years in these three OB journals has had exactly this pattern of codes, although many have very similar patterns that differ by only one or two codes. However, we can use this "prototype" as a template to identify the variations in leadership research.

A research approach that contrasts starkly with this prototype is one investigating the meaning of leadership. Although these studies appear infrequently, they do reveal the cultural-cognitive underpinnings of leadership as these two studies show, even though they span nearly a quarter-century:

> To explore the social construction of the concept of leadership, we studied the rise and fall of Donald Burr and People Express, one of the most celebrated sagas of business management and entrepreneurial spirit of the last decade. We examined the image of Donald Burr projected for readers by the popular press throughout the changing fortunes of People Express. Content analyses of image descriptions and metaphors revealed that the image of Burr was reconstructed so as to account for the dramatic performance failure of the company, but in a way that also maintained consistency with previous constructions. Various forces that converge to affect image reconstructions are considered, and the implications for understanding press organizations, organizations in general, and leadership are discussed. [Chao and Meindl, 1991; A018]

> The article discusses the concepts of leadership in Greek literature prior to the fourth century B.C., including the Homeric tradition and the tradition of the fifth century Athens. Legal authority does not convey the right to give arbitrary commands and demand implicit obedience. The Greek concept of honor did not admit the propriety of feigning false humility. Of the four leadership qualities, valor and craft are always compared. The Homeric and Athenian traditions are notorious for their extreme emphasis on the dignity and independence of the individual. [Sarachek, 1968; A112]

Finally, we summarize our stock-taking of the empirical research on leadership with figure 5-5, which presents the network display of each of the 151 abstracts (the small circles without labels) with a line extending to any codes assigned to it. Here, the nine most "central" codes are forced to the center of the diagram because they connect to the most articles (DeJordy et al., 2007); again, these are the nine codes that construct our prototypical article. However, figure 5-5 also reveals the least-used codes, which are placed on the periphery (DeJordy et al., 2007). The periphery is populated by the theoretical codes other than behavioral (i.e., trait, contingency; dyadic, and meaning-making), along with a number of empirical characteristics, such as macro-level or

FIGURE 5-5

Links between articles (circles) and codes (squares)

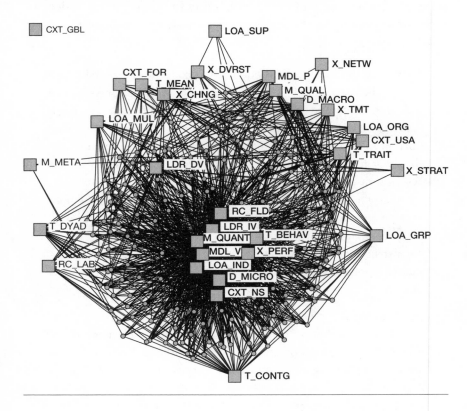

multiple levels of analyses, laboratory settings, process (or explanatory) models, network approaches, and the study of leadership. This figure also makes it clear that no articles were assigned the code that indicates comparative, cross-national leadership studies (CXT_GBL). Despite considerable interest in issues of globalization, we did not find even a single article that used a cross-cultural research setting for leadership research in these three journals. Also evident in this figure is the peripheral nature of two other codes: meta-analysis (M_META) and the use of the supraorganizational level of analysis (LOA_SUP), such as nation-states, country/industry cultures, or institutional environments. These less frequent empirical approaches to studying leadership represent potentially fertile areas for future research; we discuss these possibilities next.

From the Last Half-Century to the Next:
A Research Agenda

Twenty years ago, in the introduction to his review of leadership theory and research, Yukl (1989:251) wrote, "The field of leadership is presently in a state of ferment and confusion." We find this to be just as true today.

Our review of the last half-century of theoretical and empirical work on leadership revealed its resiliency but also its heterogeneity. Although there seems to be a straightforward progression of theoretical perspectives on leadership, from traits to behaviors to contingencies, such a progression was not evident in the 151 empirical studies published in *Administrative Science Quarterly*, the *Academy of Management Journal*, and *Organization Science*. Like organization studies more generally (e.g., Palmer, 2006; Pfeffer, 1993, 1995), leadership research seems resistant to the cumulative theory-building that occurs in other social sciences such as economics. This is evident in our finding that there is no dominant theoretical approach or research paradigm; rather, there has been a proliferation of approaches, with some receiving more attention than others. For example, our work affirms Podolny, Khuran, and Hill-Popper's (2005) observation that leadership research has gravitated toward the prediction of performance, to the apparent neglect of other, less tangible aspects of leadership.

Jim March (quoted in Augier, 2004:173) reminds us that "Leadership involves plumbing as well as poetry"; leadership *research*, however, seems to emphasize plumbing over poetry, at least when published in these three general-purpose OB journals. Poetry involves inspiration and values—when leaders create meaning, purpose, and mission beyond the work at hand—while plumbing involves mechanics—what leaders do in order to be effective. Our findings indicate that leadership research tends to investigate the plumbing, the systems and apparatus—of leaders' individual traits, skills, behaviors, styles, and adaptations—for high performance. Although this is a necessary aspect of leadership, the emphasis has been problematic, as it seems to have been purchased at the expense of other theorizations of leadership. Podolny, Khurana, and Hill-Popper (2005:1) point out the need for inquiry in this direction: "[I]f we are to judge the importance of leadership to organizational life, we need to assess the importance of leadership in terms of its ability to infuse purpose and meaning into the organizational experience." We agree.

Our findings indicate that understanding how leadership infuses meaning, values, and purpose is an underdeveloped area of leadership research but, we suggest, a potentially rich and fruitful area of inquiry. To advance research in organization studies more generally, Weick (1996:301) encourages scholars to "drop your tools": "To drop one's tools is simultaneously to accept mutation and to modernize remembered values or to believe the past as well as doubt it." The "complex simultaneity" that Weick observes implies that we might do well to hold on to some theoretical tools tightly while, at the same time, loosening our grip on others. We use Weick's advice to outline suggestions for an agenda for future research. From the simultaneous holding and loosening of our theoretical grips on different sets of tools, two research paths emerge: cumulative theory-building within the current domain of leadership scholarship (i.e., hanging on to the theoretical tools we have), and integrative theory-building across domains of scholarship (i.e., loosening our grip so that we can pick up other tools). We explore these two paths and their implications for building an agenda for future research.

Cumulative Theory-Building Within the Current Leadership Paradigm

Within each of the three foundational leadership paradigms—trait-based, behavioral, and contingency—there has been cumulative theory-building. However, the cumulative process does not seem to extend beyond each parochial level of theoretical specification. At the more general level of theorization, it is not in evidence. Our review of empirical studies leaves us with an image that is the perceptual inverse of an Impressionist painting. Up close, within a particular theoretical perspective, we see coherence, unity, and knowledge accumulation. Stepping back from the microdots of individual theories, however, the image is more confused and jumbled; there is little integration of the microdots to create a more holistic theory of leadership. And, although such theoretical variety has its benefits, it also has its limitations. We address the latter and consider how cumulative theory-building within the current heterogeneous leadership paradigm might proceed. Without suggesting that we need to embrace one dominant paradigm for leadership research, we offer some thoughts on how, for instance, we might integrate across existing theoretical divides within OB research on leadership.

First, our "prototype" of the classic empirical study—a quantitative design focusing on leadership behavior at the micro level to predict performance—might usefully be elaborated. For instance, examining individual leadership with qualitative inquiry and an explanatory, process model might uncover some of the dynamics of value infusion and meaning-making in organizations. Some research has used this approach to reveal nuanced aspects of leadership, such as the potency of charismatic authority (Khurana, 2002), how leaders infuse money with meaning (Biggart, 1989), and emotive leadership (Glynn and Dowd, 2008). Such a research strategy would begin to answer calls for understanding leadership dynamics that yield insights on affecting meaning and values, in addition to profit and performance.

Second, leadership scholars might consider switching gears from theory-driven to problem-driven inquiry. As Davis and Marquis (2005) have observed, many of our organizational theories, developed in the 1970s and 1980s, no longer fit the times; the same can be said of leadership theories. Davis and Marquis (2005) urge theorists to redirect their attention to problems, issues, and events that arise in the real world and that potentially complicate our theorization. In recent years, there has been no shortage of provocative leadership events; these range from the rise of CEOs as cultural icons like Oprah Winfrey (Illouz, 2003) or Martha Stewart (Glynn and Dowd, 2008), as well as the downfall of criminal CEOs like Dennis Kozlowski of Tyco (Gaile and Bopst, 2006) and Kenneth Lay and Jeffrey Skilling of Enron (Allio, 2007). Not all CEOs are enshrined as venerable role models or saviors (Khurana, 2002); rather, "[l]eaders are like the rest of us: trustworthy and deceitful, cowardly and brave, greedy and generous. To assume that all good leaders are good people is to be willfully blind to the reality of the human condition" (Kellerman, 2004:2). Studying leaders in the full richness of their traits, behaviors, and contexts might elaborate current theories and extend their reach. Investigating "extreme cases" such as these headline-grabbing CEOs can deepen existing theory (Eisenhardt, 1989).

Finally, understanding how leadership dynamics are embedded in multiple and complex contexts would usefully extend contingency theory. Generally, leadership studies have focused on fairly local contexts, to the neglect of more supraorganizational or global environments (see figure 5-5), but there are notable exceptions (see, for instance, the work done on the Global Leadership and Organizational Behavior Effectiveness "GLOBE"; e.g., Javidan, Dorfman, De Leque, and House, 2006). Incorporating considerations of the broader cultural context in which leaders operate (e.g., Biggart, 1989; Glynn and Dowd, 2008; Illouz, 2003), particularly at more macro levels, would build on theories of leadership-in-situ. Larger social, historical, or institutional settings could offer a broader view of the contingencies leaders face. For instance, the institutional environment delineates field-level dynamics that arise from corporate and social infrastructure, governmental-political forces, and cultural-cognitive factors (Scott, 2001). These forces shape the taken-for-granted scripts and schemas that often unconsciously inform our interpretation of behaviors as legitimate forms of and objects of leadership, or not.

These three examples suggest there is ample opportunity to leverage the heterogeneity of existing perspectives, theories, and methods to reinforce work in the existing leadership paradigm. Using theory elaboration, leadership scholars may be able to hold tightly onto, and reconcile, seemingly different yet alternatively compelling theoretical perspectives. However, by loosening our grip on these, we may also make room for additional perspectives that can extend leadership research into new domains, as outlined in the following section.

THEORY-BUILDING TO EXTEND THE LEADERSHIP PARADIGM

Leadership is a construct that lies at the crossroads of micro and macro theorizing. To date, however, researchers have tended to rely more on psychological theories that emphasize the individual and less on the more macro-level theories that might situate leadership. For instance, sociology can furnish explanations of context and collectives; political science can inform the critical leadership dynamics of power and influence; and anthropology can illuminate the cultural and societal milieu that embeds leadership. Here, we focus on one possibility: institutional theory.

Institutional theory offers a prevalent sociological perspective on organization theory that might offer novel insights into leadership research. While research under the umbrella of institutional theory also comprises a variety of perspectives, common to all of them is the existence of persistent and resilient patterns of social interaction (Hughes, 1936; Scott, 2001). Marrying institutional theory with leadership would adopt the perspective that, since organizations exist in an institutional context, and organizational behavior is enacted within these organizations and their context, leaders might explicitly engage this context and the institutions which comprise it in a number of ways.

Research emerging from this perspective might examine how leaders manipulate this context, focusing on the leadership (rather than institutional) processes that enable institutional change (e.g., Suddaby and Greenwood, 2005), infuse values into the institutions (e.g., Selznick, 1957), and align and legitimate social arrangements to societal values (e.g., Elsbach and Sutton, 1992).

Another stream might evolve around the role of leader in sense-giving and sense-breaking within the organization (DeJordy, 2007; Gioia and Chittipeddi, 1991; Weick, 1993). When and how leaders translate the institutional context for their followers could explain elusive phenomena like the manner in which organizations adapt (or not) to institutional change (e.g., Fox-Wolfgramm, Boal, and Hunt, 1998), or how they handle organizational decline and death (Sutton, 1987). Investigating the role of leaders in translating the institutional context might also help uncover when (and how) institutions serve as sources of cognitive constraint (DiMaggio and Powell, 1991) or when they can help prime, trigger, and edit the sense-making process (Weber and Glynn, 2006).

While there is no shortage of opportunity within the existing boundaries of leadership research, these examples illustrate just how fertile the domain really is. So, we conclude our stock-taking of leadership research affirming the wisdom in Weick's (1996:301) observation that taking stock is "a complex mixture of appreciation, wariness, anticipation, regret, and pride, all fused into thoughts of renewal." We have tried to capture both the contributions and limitations of the first half-century of leadership research from an OB perspective as well as the exciting potential which lies before us; we eagerly await what is to come in the next half-century.

Appendix 5-1

Leadership Abstracts of Empirical Studies in ASQ, AMJ, and OS

A001   Adams, J., Rice, R. W. & Instone, D. 1984. Follower attitudes toward women and judgments concerning performance by female and male leaders. *AMJ*. 27:636.

A002   Agle, B. R., Nagarajan, N. J., Sonnenfeld, J. A. & Srinivasan, D. 2006. Does CEO charisma matter? An empirical analysis of the relationships among organizational performance, environmental uncertainty, and top management team perceptions of CEO charisma. *AMJ*. 49:161.

A003   Anderson, C. R. & Schneier, C. E. 1978. Locus of control, leader behavior and leader performance among management students. *AMJ*. 21:690.

A004   Avolio, B. J., Howell, J. M. & Sosik, J. J. 1999. A funny thing happened on the way to the bottom line: Humor as a moderator of leadership style effects. *AMJ*. 42:219.

A005   Balkundi, P. & Harrison, D. A. 2006. Ties, leaders, & time in teams: Strong inference about network structures effect on team viability and performance. *AMJ*. 49:49.

A006   Bartol, K. 1974. Male versus female leaders: The effects of leader need for dominance on follower satisfaction. *AMJ*. 17:225.

A007   Bartunek, J. M., Walsh, K. & Lacey, C. A. 2000. Dynamics and dilemmas of women leading women. *OrgSci*. 11:589.

A008   Bauer, T. N. & Green, S. G. 1996. Development of a leader-member exchange: A longitudinal test. *AMJ*. 39:1538.

A009   Baumgartel, H. 1957. Leadership style as a variable in research administration. *ASQ*. 2:344.

A010   Bernardin, H. J. & Alvares, K. M. 1976. The managerial grid as a predictor of conflict resolution method and managerial effectiveness. *ASQ*. 21:84.

A011   Binning, J. F., Zaba, A. J. & Whattam, J. C. 1985. Explaining the biasing effects of performance cues in terms of cognitive categorization. *AMJ*. 29:521.

A012   Blanchard, K. H. 1967. College Boards of Trustees: A need for directive leadership. *AMJ*. 10:409.

A013   Bono, J. E. & Judge, T. A. 2003. Self-concordance at work: Toward understanding the motivational effects of transformational leaders. *AMJ*. 46:554.

A014   Bons, P. M. & Fiedler, F. E. 1976. Changes in organizational leadership and the behavior of relationship- and task-motivated leaders. *ASQ*. 21:453.

A015   Boone, C., Van Iffen, W. & Van Witteloostuijn, A. 2005. Team locus-of-control composition, leadership structure, information acquisition, and financial performance: A business simulation study. *AMJ*. 48:889.

Leadership Abstracts of Empirical Studies in ASQ, AMJ, and OS

A016   Bowers, D. G. & Seashore, S. E. 1966. Predicting organizational effectiveness with a four-factor theory of leadership. *ASQ*. 11:238.

A017   Carson, J. B., Tesluk, P. E. & Marrone, J. A. 2007. Shared leadership in teams: An investigation of antecedent conditions and performance. *AMJ*. 50:1217.

A018   Chao, C. C. & Meindl, J. R. 1991. The construction of leadership images in the popular press: The case of Donald Burr and People Express. *ASQ*. 36:521.

A019   Colella, A. & Varma, A. 2001. The impact of subordinate disability on leader-member exchange relationships. *2001*. 44:304.

A020   Coltrin, S. & Glueck, W. F. 1977. The effect of leadership roles on the satisfaction and productivity of university research professors. *AMJ*. 20:101.

A021   Cummings, L. L., Huber, G. P. & Arendt, E. 1974. Effects of size and spatial arrangements on group decision making. *AMJ*. 17:460.

A022   Cummings, L. L. & Schmidt, S. M. 1972. Managerial attitudes of Greeks: The roles of culture and industrialization. *ASQ*. 17:265.

A023   Delbecq, A. L. 1964. Managerial leadership styles in problem-solving conferences. *AMJ*. 7:255.

A024   Delbecq, A. L. & Kaplan, S. J. 1968. The myth of the indigenous community leader. *AMJ*. 11:11.

A025   Denis, J.-L., Lamothe, L. & Langley, A. 2001. The dynamics of collective leadership and strategic change in pluralistic organizations. *AMJ*. 44:809.

A026   Denison, D. R., Hooijberg, R. & Quinn, R. E. 1995. Paradox and performance: Toward a theory of behavioral complexity in managerial leadership. *OrgSci*. 6:524.

A027   Detert, J. R. & Burris, E. R. 2007. Leadership behavior and employee voice: Is the door really open? *AMJ*. 50:869.

A028   Dobbins, G. H. 1985. Effects of gender on leaders responses to poor performers: An attributional interpretation. *AMJ*. 28:587.

A029   Downey, H. K., Sheridan, J. E. & Slocum Jr., J. W. 1975. Analysis of relationships among leader behavior, subordinate job performance and satisfaction: A path-goal approach. *AMJ*. 18:253.

A030   Druskat, V. U. & Wheeler, J. V. 2003. Managing from the boundary: The effective leadership of self-managing work teams. *AMJ*. 46:435.

A031   Duncan, W. J. & Roberts, C. D. 1972. An analysis of choice consistency and perceptual uniformity in a paramilitary organization. *AMJ*. 15:33.

A032   Durand, D. E. & Nord, W. R. 1976. Perceived leader behavior as a function of personality characteristics of supervisors and subordinates. *AMJ*. 19:427.

(continued)

Leadership Abstracts of Empirical Studies in ASQ, AMJ, and OS (*continued*)

A033	Dvir, T., Eden, D., Avolio, B. J. & Shamir, B. 2002. Impact of transformational leadership on follower development & performance: A field experiment. *AMJ*. 45:735.
A034	Egri, C. P. & Herman, S. 2000. Leadership in the North American environmental sector: Values, leadership styes, and contexts of environmental leaders and their organizations. *AMJ*. 43:571.
A035	Emrich, C. D., Brower, H. H., Feldman, J. M. & Garland, H. 2001. Images in words: Presidential rhetoric, charisma, and greatness. *ASQ*. 46:527.
A036	Engle, E. M. & Lord, R. G. 1997. Implicit theories, self-schemas, and leader-member exchange. *AMJ*. 40:988.
A037	Erdogan, B., Liden, R. C. & Kraimer, M. L. 2006. Justice and leader-member exchange: The moderating role of organizational culture. *AMJ*. 49:395.
A038	Eulau, H. 1962. Bases of authority in legislative bodies: A comparative analysis. *ASQ*. 7:309.
A039	Fiedler, F. E. 1972. The effects of leadership training and experience: A contingency model interpretation. *ASQ*. 17:453.
A040	Finkelstein, S. & Daveni, R. A. 1994. CEO duality as a double-edged sword: How boards of directors balance entrenchment avoidance and unity of command. *AMJ*. 37:1079.
A041	Fleming, L. & Waguespack, D. 2007. Brokerage, boundary spanning, and leadership in open innovation communities. *OrgSci*. 18:165.
A042	Ford, J. D. 1981. Departmental context and formal structure as constraints on leader behavior. *AMJ*. 1981:274.
A043	Franklin, J. L. 1975. Relations among four social-psychology aspects of organizations. *ASQ*. 20:422.
A044	Galaskiewicz, J. & Shatin, D. 1981. Leadership and networking among neighborhood human services organizations. *ASQ*. 26:434.
A045	Green, S. G., Nebeker, D. M. & Boni, M. A. 1976. Personality and situational effects on leader behavior. *AMJ*. 19:184.
A046	Greene, C. N. 1979. Questions of causation in the path-goal theory of leadership. *AMJ*. 22:22.
A047	Griffin, R. W. 1980. Relationships among individual, task design, and leader behavior variables. *AMJ*. 23:665.
A048	Hammer, T. H. 1978. Relationships between local union characteristics and work behavior and attitudes. *AMJ*. 21:560.
A049	Helmich, D. L. 1975. Corporate succession: An examination. *AMJ*. 18:429.
A050	Helmich, D. L. & Erzen, P. E. 1975. Leadership style and leader needs. *AMJ*. 18:397.

Leadership Abstracts of Empirical Studies in ASQ, AMJ, and OS

A051	Heneman, R. L., Greenberger, D. B. & Anonyou, C. 1989. Attributions and exchanges: The effects of interpersonal factors on the diagnosis of employee performance. *AMJ*. 32:466.
A052	Herold, D. M. 1977. Two-way influence processes in leader-follower dyads. *AMJ*. 20:224.
A053	Hill, W. A. 1969. The validation and extension of Fiedler's theory of leadership effectiveness. *AMJ*. 12:33.
A054	Hill, W. A. & Fox, W. M. 1973. Black and White marine squad leaders perceptions of racially mixed squads. *AMJ*. 16:680.
A055	Hill, W. A. & Ruhe, J. A. 1974. Attitudes and behaviors of black and white supervisors in problem solving groups. *AMJ*. 17:563.
A056	Hills, R. J. 1963. The representative function: Neglected dimension of leadership behavior. *ASQ*. 8:83.
A057	Hoppe, M. W. 1970. Leadership style and effectiveness of department chairmen in business administration. *AMJ*. 13:301.
A058	House, R. J. 1971. A path goal theory of leadership effectiveness. *ASQ*. 16:321.
A059	House, R. J., Filley, A. C. & Kerr, S. 1971. Relation of leader consideration and initiating structure to R and D subordinate satisfaction. *ASQ*. 16:19.
A060	Hovey, D. E. 1974. The low-powered leader confronts a mess problem: A test of Fiedler's theory. *AMJ*. 17:358.
A061	Howell, J. M. & Higgins, C. A. 1990. Champions of technology innovation. *ASQ*. 35:317.
A062	Howell, J. P. & Dorfman, P. W. 1981. Substitutes for leadership: Test of a construct. *AMJ*. 24:714.
A063	Hui, W., Law, K. S., Hackett, R. D., Duanxu, W. & Chen, Z. X. 2005. Leader-member exchange as a mediator of the relationship between transformational leadership and follower's performance and organizational citizenship behavior. *AMJ*. 2005:420.
A064	Hunt, J. G. 1971. Leadership-style effects at two managerial levels in a simulated organization. *ASQ*. 16:476.
A065	Hunt, J. G., Osborn, R. N. & Larson, L. L. 1975. Upper level technical orientation and first level leadership within a noncontingency and contingency framework. *AMJ*. 18:476.
A066	Huxham, C. & Vangen, S. 2000. Leadership in the shaping & implementation of collaboration agendas: How things happen in a (not quite) joined up world. *AMJ*. 43:1159.
A067	Jago, A. G. & Vroom, V. H. 1978. Predicting leader behavior from a measure of behavioral intent. *AMJ*. 21:715.

(continued)

Leadership Abstracts of Empirical Studies in ASQ, AMJ, and OS (*continued*)

A068	Jago, A. G. & Vroom, V. H. 1980. An evaluation of two alternatives to the Vroom/Yetton normative model. *AMJ*. 23:347.
A069	Janssen, O. & Van Yperen, N. W. 2004. Employees' goal-orientations, the quality of leader-member exchange, and the outcomes of job performance and job satisfaction. *AMJ*. 47:368.
A070	Jermier, J. M. & Berkes, L. J. 1979. Leader behavior in a police command bureaucracy: A closer look at the quasi-military model. *ASQ*. 24:1.
A071	Jones, H. R. & Johnson, M. 1972. LPC as a modifier of leader-follower relationships. *AMJ*. 15:185.
A072	Jung, D. I. & Avolio, B. J. 1999. Effects of leadership style and followers cultural orientation on performance in group and individual task conditions. *AMJ*. 42:208.
A073	Kavanagh, M. J. 1972. Leadership behavior as a function of subordinate competence and task complexity. *ASQ*. 17:591.
A074	Keller, R. T. & Szilagyu, A. D. 1976. Employee reactions to leader reward behavior. *AMJ*. 19:619.
A075	Kent, R. L. & Moss, S. E. 1994. Effects of sex and gender role on leader emergence. *AMJ*. 37:1335.
A076	Kirkman, B. L. & Rosen, B. 1999. Beyond self-management: Antecedents and consequences of team empowerment. *AMJ*. 42:58.
A077	Klein, H. J. & Kim, J. S. 1998. A field study of the influence of situational constraints, leader-member exchange, and goal commitment on performance. *AMJ*. 41:88.
A078	Klein, K. J., Ziegert, J. C., Knight, A. P. & Yan, X. 2006. Dynamic Delegation: Shared, hierarchical, & deindividualized leadership in extreme action teams. *ASQ*. 51:590.
A079	Kraatz, M. S. & Moore, J. H. 2002. Executive migration and institutional change. *AMJ*. 45:120.
A080	Larson, L. L., Hunt, J. G. & Osborn, R. N. 1976. The great hi-hi leader behavior myth: A lesson from Occam's Razor. *AMJ*. 19:628.
A081	Larson, L. L. & Rowland, K. M. 1974. Leadership style and cognitive complexity. *AMJ*. 17:37.
A082	Leister, A., Borden, D. & Fiedler, F. E. 1977. Validation of contingency model leadership training: Leader match. *AMJ*. 20:464.
A083	Lester, S. W., Meglino, B. M. & Korsgaard, M. A. 2002. The antecedents and consequences of group potency: A longitudinal investigation of newly formed work groups. *AMJ*. 45:352.
A084	Liden, R. C. & Graen, G. 1980. Generalizability of the vertical dyad linkage model of leadership. *AMJ*. 23:451.

Leadership Abstracts of Empirical Studies in ASQ, AMJ, and OS

A085	Lord, R. G. 1977. Functional leadership behavior: Measurement and relation to social power and leadership perceptions. *ASQ*. 22:114.
A086	Lowing, A., Hrapchak, W. & Kavanagh, M. J. 1969. Consideration and initiating structure: An experimental investigation of leadership traits. *ASQ*. 14:238.
A087	Luckham, A. R. 1971. Institutional transfer and breakdown in a new nation: The Nigerian military. *ASQ*. 16:387.
A088	Luecke, D. S. 1973. The professional as organizational leader. *ASQ*. 18:86.
A089	Manz, C. C. & Sims Jr., H. P. 1987. Leading workers to lead themselves: The external leadership of self-managing work teams. *ASQ*. 1987:106.
A090	Masterson, S. S., Lewis, K., Goldman, B. M. & Taylor, M. S. 2000. Integrating justice and social exchange: The differing effects of fair procedures and treatment on work relationships. *AMJ*. 43:738.
A091	Meindl, J. R. & Ehrlich, S. B. 1987. The romance of leadership and the evaluation of organizational performance. *AMJ*. 30:91.
A092	Meindl, J. R., Ehrlich, S. B. & Dukerich, J. M. 1985. The romance of leadership. *ASQ*. 30:78.
A093	Miles, R. H. & Petty, M. M. 1977. Leader effectiveness in small bureaucracies. *AMJ*. 20:238.
A094	Miller, D. 1993. Some organizational consequences of CEO succession. *AMJ*. 36:644.
A095	Misumi, J. & Peterson, M. F. 1985. The performance-maintenance (PM) theory of leadership: Review of a japanese research program. *ASQ*. 30:198.
A096	Morgan, R. B. 1993. Self- and co-worker perceptions of ethics and their relationships to leadership and salary. *AMJ*. 36:200.
A097	Mowday, R. T. 1979. Leader characteristics, self-confidence, and methods of upwards influence in organizational decision situations. *AMJ*. 22:709.
A098	Mullen, J. H. 1965. Differential leadership modes and productivity in a large organization. *AMJ*. 8:107.
A099	Nebeker, D. M. 1975. Situational favorability and perceived environmental uncertainty: An integrative approach. *ASQ*. 20:281.
A100	Niehoff, B. P. & Moorman, R. H. 1993. Justice as mediator of the relationship between methods of monitoring and organizational citizen behavior. *AMJ*. 36:527.
A101	Nystrom, P. C. 1978. Managers and the hi-hi leader myth. *AMJ*. 21:325.

(continued)

Leadership Abstracts of Empirical Studies in ASQ, AMJ, and OS (*continued*)

A102	Osborn, R. N. & Vicars, W. M. 1976. Sex stereotypes: An artifact in leader behavior and subordinate satisfaction analysis. *AMJ*. 19:439.
A103	Penley, L. E. & Hawkins, B. 1985. Studying interpersonal communication in organizations: A leadership application. *AMJ*. 28:309.
A104	Petty, M. M. & Bruning, N. S. 1980. A comparison of the relationships between subordinates perceptions of supervisory behavior and measures of subordinates job satisfaction for male and female leaders. *AMJ*. 23:717.
A105	Phillips, A. S. & Bedeian, A. G. 1994. Leader-follower exchange quality: The role of personal and interpersonal attributes. *AMJ*. 37:990.
A106	Piccolo, R. F. & Colquitt, J. A. 2006. Transformational leadership and job behaviors: The mediating role of core job characteristics. *AMJ*. 49:327.
A107	Podsakoff, P. M., Todor, W. M. & Skov, R. 1982. Effects of leader contingent and noncontingent reward and punishment behaviors on subordinate performance and satisfaction. *AMJ*. 25:810.
A108	Roberts, K., Miles, R. E. & Blankenship, L. V. 1968. Organizational leadership satisfaction and productivity: A comparative analysis. *AMJ*. 11:401.
A109	Rossel, R. D. 1970. Instrumental and expressive leadership in complex organizations. *ASQ*. 15:306.
A110	Rossel, R. D. 1971. Required labor commitment, organizational adaptation, and leadership orientation. *ASQ*. 16:316.
A111	Rubin, R. S., Munz, D. C. & Bommer, W. H. 2005. Leading from within: The effects of emotion recognition and personality on transformational leadership behavior. *AMJ*. 48:845.
A112	Sarachek, B. 1968. Greek concepts of leadership. *AMJ*. 11:39.
A113	Scandura, T. A. & Schrisheim, C. A. 1994. Leader-member exchange and supervisor career mentoring as complementary constructs in leadership. *AMJ*. 37:1588.
A114	Schriesheim, C. A. 1979. The similarity of individual directed and group directed leader behavior descriptions. *AMJ*. 22:345.
A115	Schriesheim, C. A., Neider, L. L. & Scandura, T. A. 1998. Delegation and leader-member exchange: Main effects, moderators, and measurement issues. *AMJ*. 41:298.
A116	Schriesheim, C. A. & Von Clinow, M. A. 1977. The path-goal theory of leadership: A theoretical and empirical analysis. *AMJ*. 20:398.
A117	Seltzer, J. & Numerof, R. E. 1988. Supervisory leadership and subordinate burnout. *AMJ*. 31:439.
A118	Sgro, J. A., Worchel, P., Pence, E. C. & Orban, J. A. 1980. Perceived leader behavior as a function of the leaders interpersonal trust orientation. *AMJ*. 23:161.

Leadership Abstracts of Empirical Studies in ASQ, AMJ, and OS

A119	Shamir, B., Zakay, E., Breinin, E. & Popper, M. 1998. Correlates of charismatic leader behavior in military units: Subordinates attitudes, unit characteristics, and superiors appraisals of leader performance. *AMJ*. 41:387.
A120	Sheridan, J. E. & Vredenburgh, D. J. 1978. Predicting leadership behavior in a hospital organization. *AMJ*. 21:679.
A121	Sheridan, J. E. & Vredenburgh, D. J. 1979. Structural model of leadership influence in a hospital organization. *AMJ*. 22:6.
A122	Shin, S. J. & Zhou, J. 2003. Transformational leadership, conservation, and creativity: Evidence from Korea. *AMJ*. 46:703.
A123	Siegel, J. P. 1973. Machiavellianism, MBAs and Managers: Leadership correlates and socialization effects. *AMJ*. 16:404.
A124	Singleton, T. M. 1978. Managerial motivation development: A study of college student leaders. *AMJ*. 21:493.
A125	Smith, J. E., Carson, K. P. & Alexander, R. A. 1984. Leadership: It can make a difference. *AMJ*. 27:765.
A126	Smith, K. K. & Simmons, V. M. 1983. A Rumpelstiltskin organization: Metaphors on metaphors in field research. *ASQ*. 28:377.
A127	Sparrowe, R. T. & Liden, R. C. 2005. Two routes to influence: Integrating leader-member exchange and social network perspectives. *ASQ*. 50:505.
A128	Sparrowe, R. T., Soetjipto, B. W. & Kraimer, M. L. 2006. Do leaders' influence tactics relate to members' helping behavior? It depends on the quality of the relationship. *AMJ*. 49:1194.
A129	Srivastava, A. 2006. Empowering leadership in management teams: Effects on knowledge sharing, efficacy, and performance. *AMJ*. 49:1239.
A130	Steger, J. A., Kelley, W. B., Chouintere, G. & Goldenbaum, A. 1975. A forced choice version of the MSCS and how it discriminates campus leaders and nonleaders. *AMJ*. 18:453.
A131	Stinson, J. E. & Johnson, T. W. 1975. The path-goal theory of leadership: A partial test and suggested refinement. *AMJ*. 18:242.
A132	Sutton, R. I. 1987. The process of organizational death: Disbanding and reconnecting. *ASQ*. 32:542.
A133	Szilagyu, A. D. & Keller, R. T. 1976. A comparative investigation of the supervisory behavior description questionnaire (SBDQ) and the revised leader behavior description questionnaire (LBDQ-FORM XII). *AMJ*. 19:642.
A134	Szilagyu, A. D. & Sims Jr., H. P. 1974. An exploration of the path-goal theory of leadership in a health care environment. *AMJ*. 17:622.

(continued)

Leadership Abstracts of Empirical Studies in ASQ, AMJ, and OS (*continued*)

A135	Thomas, A. B. 1988. Does leadership make a difference to organizational performance? *ASQ*. 33:388.
A136	Trice, H. M. & Beyer, J. M. 1991. Cultural leadership in organizations. *OrgSci*. 2:149.
A137	Urwick, L. 1965. Leadership and language. *AMJ*. 8:146.
A138	Utecht, R. E. & Heier, W. D. 1976. The contingency model and successful military leadership. *AMJ*. 19:606.
A139	Valenzi, E. & Dessler, G. 1978. Relationships of leader behavior, subordinate role ambiguity, and subordinate job satisfaction. *AMJ*. 21:671.
A140	Vardi, Y., Shirom, A. & Jacobson, D. 1980. A study on the leadership beliefs of israeli managers. *AMJ*. 23:367.
A141	Vecchio, R. P. 1979. A dyadic interpretation of the contingency model of leadership effectiveness. *AMJ*. 22:590.
A142	Vecchio, R. P. 1985. Predicting employee turnover from leader-member exchange: A failure to replicate. *AMJ*. 28:478.
A143	Wageman, R. 2001. How leaders foster self-managing team effectiveness: Design choices versus hands-on coaching. *OrgSci*. 12:559.
A144	Waldman, D. A., Ramirez, G. G., House, R. J. & Puranam, P. 2001. Does leadership matter? CEO leadership attributes and profitability under conditions of perceived environmental uncertainty. *AMJ*. 44:134.
A145	Watson, K. M. 1982. An analysis of communication patterns: A method for discriminating leader and subordinate roles. *AMJ*. 25:107.
A146	Wayne, S. J., Shore, L. M. & Liden, R. C. 1997. Perceived organizational support and leader-member exchange: A social exchange perspective. *AMJ*. 40:82.
A147	Wearing, A. J. & Bishop, D. W. 1974. The Fiedler contingency model and the functioning of military squads. *AMJ*. 17:450.
A148	Weed, S. E. & Mitchell, T. R. 1980. The role of environmental and behavioral uncertainty as a mediator of situation-performance relationships. *AMJ*. 23:38.
A149	Weiner, N. & Mahoney, T. A. 1981. A model of corporate performance as a function of environmental, organizational, and leadership influences. *AMJ*. 24:453.
A150	Wing, L., Huang, X. & Snape, E. 2007. Feedback-seeking behavior and leader-member exchange: Do supervisor-attributed motives matter? *AMJ*. 50:348.
A151	Yammarino, F. J., Dubinsky, A. J., Comer, L. B. & Jolson, M. A. 1997. Women and transformational and contingent reward leadership: A multiple-levels-of-analysis perspective. *AMJ*. 40:205.

References

Allio, R. "Bad Leaders: How They Get That Way and What to Do About It." *Strategy & Leadership* 35, no. 3 (2007): 12.

Augier, M. "James March on Education, Leadership, and Don Quixote: Introduction and Interview." *Academy of Management Learning and Education* 3 (2004): 169–177.

Bass, B.M. *Leadership and Performance Beyond Expectations.* New York: Free Press, 1985.

———. *Bass & Stogdill's Handbook of Leadership: Theory, Research, and Managerial Applications.* 3rd ed. New York: The Free Press, 1990.

Biggart, N.W. *Charismatic Capitalism: Direct Selling Organizations in America.* Chicago: University of Chicago Press, 1989.

Borgatti, S.P. *NetDraw: Graph Visualization Software.* Harvard, MA: Analytic Technologies, 2002.

Borgatti, S.P., M.G. Everett, and L.C. Freeman. *UCINET for Windows: Software for Social Network Analysis.* Harvard, MA: Analytic Technologies, 2002.

Cameron, K. *Positive Leadership: Strategies for Extraordinary Performance.* San Francisco: Berrett-Koehler Publishers, 2008.

Cameron, K., and M. Lavine. *Making the Impossible Possible.* San Francisco: Berrett-Koehler Publishers, 2006.

Cannella, A.A., and R.L. Paetzold. "Pfeffer's Barriers to the Advance of Organizational Science: A Rejoinder." *Academy of Management Review* 19 (1994): 331–341.

Carey, J.W., P.H. Wenzel, C. Reilly, J. Sheridan, and J.M. Steinberg. "CDC EZ-Text: Software for Management and Analysis of Semistructured Qualitative Data Sets." *Cultural Anthropology Methods* 10, no. 1 (1998): 7.

Conger, J.A., and R.N. Kanungo. "Toward a Behavior Theory of Charismatic Leadership in Organizational Settings." *Academy of Management Review* 12 (1987): 637–647.

Davis, G.F., and C. Marquis. "Prospects for Organization Theory in the Early Twenty-First Century: Institutional Fields and Mechanisms." *Organization Science* 16, no. 4 (2005): 332–343.

DeJordy, R. "Institutional Leadership: Agency and Sense-Giving at the Institutional Level." Presentation at the Academy of Management Meeting, Philadelphia, PA, 2007.

DeJordy, R., S.P. Borgatti, C. Roussin, and D.S. Halgin. "Visualizing Proximity Data." *Field Methods* 19, no. 3 (2007): 25.

DiMaggio, P., and W.W. Powell. "Introduction." In *The New Institutionalism in Organizational Analysis,* edited by P.J. DiMaggio and W.W. Powell, 1–38. Chicago: University of Chicago Press, 1991.

Eisenhardt, K. "Building Theories from Case Study Research." *Academy of Management Review* 14 (1989): 532–550.

Elsbach, K., and R. Sutton. "Acquiring Legitimacy Through Illegitimate Means: A Marriage of Institutional and Impression Management Theories." *Academy of Management Journal* 35 (1992): 699.

Fiedler, F.E. *A Theory of Leader Effectiveness.* New York: McGraw-Hill, 1964.

Fox-Wolfgramm, S.J., K.B. Boal, and J.G. Hunt. "Organizational Adaptation to Institutional Change: A Comparative Study of First-Order Change in Prospector and Defender Banks." *Administrative Science Quarterly* 43, no. 1 (1998): 87–126.

Gaile, P., and C. Bopst. "Machiavelli and Modern Business: Realist Thought in Contemporary Corporate Leadership Manuals." *Journal of Business Ethics* 65 (2006): 235.

Gardner, H. *Leading Minds: An Anatomy of Leadership.* New York: Basic, 1995.

Gioia, D., and K. Chittipeddi. "Sensemaking and Sensegiving in Strategic Change Initiation." *Strategic Management Journal* 12 (1991): 433.

Glynn, M.A., and T. Dowd. "Charisma (Un)Bound: Emotive Leadership in *Martha Stewart Living* Magazine, 1990–2004." *Journal of Applied Behavioral Science* 44 (2008): 71–93.

Goleman, D. *Emotional Intelligence.* New York: Bantam Books, 1995.

Graen, G., R. Liden, and W. Hoel. "Role of Leadership in the Employee Withdrawal Process." *Journal of Applied Psychology* 67 (1982): 868–872.

House, R.J. "A Path-Goal Theory of Leader Effectiveness." *Administrative Science Quarterly* 16 (1971): 321–338.

Hughes, E.C. "The Ecological Aspect of Institutions." *American Sociological Review* 1 (1936): 180.

Illouz, E. *Oprah Winfrey and the Glamour of Misery: An Essay on Popular Culture.* New York: Columbia University Press, 2003.

Javidan, M., P.W. Dorfman, M.S. De Leque, and R. House. "In the Eye of the Beholder: Cross-cultural Lessons in Leadership from Project GLOBE." *Academy of Management Perspectives* 20, no. 1 (2006): 67.

Katz, D. and R.L. Kahn. "Leadership Practices in Relation to Productivity and Morale." D. Cartwright and Z. Zander (eds.) *Group Dynamics.* Evanston, IL: Harper and Row, 554–570, 1960.

Kellerman, B. "Leadership: Warts and All." *Harvard Business Review* 82, no. 1 (January 2004): 40–45.

Khurana, R. *Searching for a Corporate Savior: The Irrational Quest for Charismatic CEOs.* Princeton, NJ: Princeton University Press, 2002.

Kilduff, M. and D. Krackhardt. *Interpersonal Networks in Organizations: Cognition, Personality, Dynamics, and Culture.* New York: Cambridge University Press, 2008.

Lewin, K., R. Lippitt, and R.K. White. "Patterns of Aggressive Behavior in Experimentally Created 'Social Climates.'" *Journal of Social Psychology* 10 (1939): 271–299.

Mayo, A., and N. Nohria. "Zeitgeist Leadership." *Harvard Business Review* 83, no. 10 (October 2005a): 45–60.

———. *In Their Time: The Greatest Business Leaders of the 20th Century.* Boston: Harvard Business School Press, 2005b.

Palmer, D. "Taking Stock of the Criteria We Use to Evaluate One Another's Work: ASQ 50 Years Out." *Administrative Science Quarterly* 51 (2006): 535–559.

Perrow, C. "Pfeffer Slips!" *Academy of Management Review* 19 (1994): 191–194.

Pfeffer, J. "Barriers to the Advance of Organization Science: Paradigm Development as a Dependent Variable." *Academy of Management Review* 18 (1993): 599–620.

———. "Mortality, Reproducibility, and the Persistence of Styles of Theory." *Organization Science* 6 (1995): 681–686.

Podolny, J., R. Khurana, and M. Hill-Popper. "Revising the Meaning of Leadership." *Research in Organizational Behavior* 26 (2005): 1–36.

Scott, W.R. *Institutions and Organizations*. 2nd ed. Thousand Oaks, CA: Sage Publications, 2001.

Selznick, P. *Leadership in Administration*. Berkeley, CA: University of California Press, 1957.

Snook, S. *Friendly Fire: The Accidental Shootdown of U.S. Black Hawks over Northern Iraq*. Paperback ed. Princeton, NJ: Princeton University Press, 2002.

Sparrowe, R., and R.C. Liden. "Two Routes to Influence: Integrating Leader-Member Exchange and Social Network Perspectives." *Administrative Science Quarterly* 50 (2005): 505–535.

Stogdill, R.M. "Personal Factors Associated with Leadership: A Survey of the Literature." *Journal of Psychology* 25 (1948): 35–71.

———. *Manual for the Leader Behavior Description Questionnaire—Form XII*. Columbus, OH: Bureau of Business Research, Ohio State University, 1963.

———. *Handbook of Leadership: A Survey of the Literature*. New York: The Free Press, 1974.

Suddaby, R., and R. Greenwood. "Rhetorical Strategies of Legitimacy." *Administrative Science Quarterly* 50, no. 1 (2005): 35–57.

Sutton, R. "The Process of Organizational Death: Disbanding and Reconnecting." *Administrative Science Quarterly* 32 (1987): 542.

Useem, M. *The Leadership Moment*. New York: Three Rivers Books, 1998.

Van Maanen, J. "Style as Theory." *Organization Science* 6 (1995): 133–143.

Vroom, V.H., and A.G. Jago. *The New Leadership: Managing Participation in Organizations*. Englewood Cliffs, NJ: Prentice-Hall, 1988.

Vroom, V.H., and P.W. Yetton. *Leadership and Decision Making*. Pittsburgh: University of Pittsburgh Press, 1973.

Weber, K., and M.A. Glynn. "Making Sense with Institutions: Context, Thought, and Action in Karl Weick's Theory." *Organization Studies* 27 (2006): 1639–1660.

Weber, M. *Economy and Society: An Outline of Interpretive Sociology*, edited by Guenther Roth and Claus Wittich. Berkeley, CA: University of California Press, 1978.

Weick, K. "The Collapse of Sensemaking in Organizations: The Mann Gulch Disaster." *Administrative Science Quarterly* 38 (1993): 628–652.

———. "Drop Your Tools: An Allegory for Organizational Studies." *Administrative Science Quarterly* 41 (1996): 301–313.

Yukl, G. "Managerial Leadership: A Review of Theory and Research." *Journal of Management* 15 (1989): 2

6

PSYCHOLOGICAL PERSPECTIVES ON LEADERSHIP

Jennifer A. Chatman and Jessica A. Kennedy

LEADERSHIP HAS been a central but sometimes controversial topic in organizational research (e.g., Chemers, 2000; Hogan, Curphy, and Hogan, 1994; House and Aditya, 1997; Judge and Piccolo, 2004; Khurana, 2002; Meindl, 1990). For example, reflecting a macro-OB perspective, Podolny, Khurana, and Hill-Popper observed that "for at least the past thirty years, the concept of leadership has been subject to criticism and marginalization by the dominant organizational paradigms and perspectives" (2005:1). Part of this skepticism has resulted from questions about the definition of the construct as well as whether leadership has discernible effects on individual behavior and organizational outcomes (e.g., Hannan and Freeman, 1984; Pfeffer, 1977). Proponents argue that leaders, by their very roles, are responsible for making decisions that help their organizations adapt and succeed in competitive environments (e.g., Bass, 1991; Waldman and Yammarino, 1999). In contrast, those who view organizations as heavily constrained claim that leadership is largely irrelevant and, at best, a social construction (e.g., Hannan and Freeman, 1989; Meindl, 1990).

While provocative, the assertion that leaders in organizations do not play a distinct role in influencing groups and individuals to achieve organizational goals is not supported by the empirical evidence; leaders often have a substantial impact on performance (e.g., Barrick, Day,

159

Lord, and Alexander, 1991; Bass, Avolio, Jung, and Berson, 2003; Bertrand and Schoar, 2003; Judge and Piccolo, 2004; Judge, Piccolo, and Ilies, 2004; Koene, Vogelaar, and Soeters, 2002). Even senior executives who are neither founders nor in the top jobs (e.g., CEOs) can have an inordinate influence on organizations (e.g., Miller and Droge, 1986). Less clear, however, are the capabilities required and circumstances under which leaders can affect individual behavior and organizational performance (c.f. Hambrick, Finklestein, and Mooney, 2005).

Numerous definitions of leadership exist. We adopt one that Vroom and Jago (2007:18) recently proposed in which leadership is "a process of motivating people to work together collaboratively to accomplish great things," with "great things" defined in the minds of the leader and followers. Our goal in this paper is to take stock of psychological approaches to leadership, focusing on how leaders develop capabilities and interact with smaller work groups and larger organizations. We do this by considering various perspectives on leaders, identifying what they need to do as individuals to garner followers, how they can best inspire small groups, and finally, how leaders capture an entire organization's attention and cultivate intense commitment among members to realize organizational goals. Since understanding the effects of leadership on organizational performance may require examining multiple levels of leadership simultaneously (Hunter, Bedell-Avers, and Mumford, 2007), we scan the relevant levels of analysis to gather a comprehensive psychological picture of when and why leaders influence others. We also consider the extent to which continuity across levels of leadership is important for individual and organizational effectiveness.

We begin with two assumptions. First, through the history of leadership research, many have considered leaders to be born rather than made. Despite recognizing that situations affect individuals, their research primarily suggests that it is something about a person that determines whether she will be an extraordinary leader (e.g., House, 1977, 1988; Judge, Bono, Ilies, and Gerhardt, 2002). Instead, our view is that leadership is about what people do, not who they are and, as such, leadership is inherently developmental. Our second assumption is that leadership is a paradox in that the most effective leaders are likely those who are self-aware, calculated, and interpersonally adept, but ultimately dispensable. That is, a leader's role in a team or organization is to set the context for others to be successful. Indeed, our "acid test" of effective leadership is how well the team does when the leader is not present, and whether the leader has helped members internalize organizational objectives so that they can make judgment calls and trade-offs that are organizationally aligned on their own.

Developing as a Leader

We suggest that three capabilities are critical for leaders, but these are not the most obvious traits. The obvious traits such as confidence, dominance, assertiveness, or intelligence have not, as it turns out, shown the level of predictive validity that one would hope for (e.g., Ames and Flynn, 2007; Fiedler, 1995; Judge, Colbert, and Ilies, 2004; Zaccaro, 2007). Rather, we suggest three subtle but likely more powerful qualities that transcend particular individual differences and behaviors. They are a leader's diagnostic capabilities, the breadth and flexibility of his behavioral repertoire, and his understanding of the leadership paradox. We discuss each below.

Leaders as Astute Diagnosticians

Leadership is a diagnostic activity requiring a person to ask, in each situation, "What is the maximum and unique value that a leader could bring to this situation?" The obvious value of this insight is best reflected in the enormous industry that has emerged around this theme, including the most popular of these, the Situational Leadership Model (e.g., Hersey, Blanchard, and Natemeyer, 1979). Such approaches emphasize the importance of accurately understanding various situations and how leader demands vary within them. Interestingly, the concept of situational leadership has been difficult to pin down empirically (see Graeff, 1983, and Vecchio, 1987, for critical discussions), despite its popularity among practitioners.

The more recent focus on a number of related but more tractable constructs, such as self-monitoring and emotional intelligence, represents attempts to address a person's diagnostic capacity by highlighting the importance of accurately assessing the social and emotional cues in a situation. For example, those who are high on self-monitoring perceive the needs of the group and pattern their own behavior accordingly (e.g., Ellis, 1988; Zaccaro, Foti, and Kenny, 1991). Though there are popularized versions such as the "primal leadership" model (e.g., Goleman, Boyatzis, and McKee, 2004), there are also a number of scholarly treatments, with corresponding empirical evidence, pointing to the importance of emotional intelligence for effective leadership (e.g., Wolff, Pescosolido, and Druskat, 2002; Wong and Law, 2002). In particular, emotionally intelligent people are more accurate in appraising emotions, they use emotion to enhance cognitive processes and decision making, and they are generally more adept at managing their emotions (e.g., George, 2000). We turn next to the closely related, but distinct, concept of behavioral flexibility.

Flexible and Self-Aware Behavioral Repertoire

Once a leader has accurately diagnosed a situation, she needs to have a broad and flexible behavioral repertoire to respond appropriately across a wide array of complex situations (Zaccaro, Gilbert, Thor, and Mumford, 1991; Hooijberg, 1996). People often react to different situations using a narrow band of behavior, or their dominant responses, particularly under stressful conditions (e.g., Bargh and Chartrand, 1999; Gioia and Poole, 1984; Staw, Sandelands, and Dutton, 1981). This uniformity may be appropriate and desirable in specialist roles, but can be limiting for people attempting to influence and compel others across the variety of situations that leaders face.

Hall, Workman, and Marchioro (2002) found that leaders who were more behaviorally flexible—those high on self-monitoring, self-reported behavioral capabilities, and androgyny—were viewed as more effective by their followers. Other researchers have identified related personal qualities, such as adaptability and openness, as important for leaders (e.g., Howard and Bray, 1988; Miller and Toulouse, 1986; Mumford and Connelly, 1991). These perspectives suggest that flexibility emerges from a constellation of cognitive, social, and dispositional qualities, though each type of flexibility is considered independent. For example, integrative complexity (e.g., Tetlock, 1983) allows a leader to develop the elaborate cognitive responses that are required in complex dynamic environments, whereas behavioral flexibility reflects the ability to translate thought and reflection into appropriate action across a diverse array of organizational situations (Zaccaro, 2001). Boal and Whitehead (1992) described individuals who are high on both integrative complexity and behavioral flexibility as being "informed flexible" since they have a wide array of both cognitive maps and behavioral responses.

In addition to developing a broad and flexible behavioral repertoire, leaders need to display their intentions unambiguously. Accuracy in behavioral signaling arises from self-awareness and cross-situational consistency (e.g., Kenny, Mohr, and Levesque, 2001). Personality psychologists have suggested that behavior can be more "observable" based on the extent to which an act is given the same meaning by two (or more) perceivers (Gosling, John, Craik, and Robins, 1998; Kenny, 1994). Highly observable acts tend to require less inference to judge their occurrence and meaning than do less observable acts. Thus, the more observable an act is, the more likely those observing the behavior will attach the same meaning to it. Conversely, observers will be more likely to disagree about the meaning of a less observable act, which will require a great deal of inference about the target's internal thoughts and feelings. To the extent that leadership in organizations is associated with hierarchical authority, ambiguity in a leader's behavior can have negative consequences for followers' motivation and performance (e.g., Meindl, 1990), particularly when the behavior appears hypocritical (e.g., Cha and Edmondson, 2006).

Putting together the importance of consistency and behavioral flexibility, a significant challenge for leaders is to be perceived as consistent while engaging flexibly in a wide array of behavioral responses. The very behavioral flexibility that is critical for leading across diverse situations can be perceived instead as behavioral inconsistency, unreliability, or even labeled as erratic by followers. How might leaders manage this balance? Given the premium placed on appearing consistent (Chatman, Bell, and Staw, 1986; Ross and Staw, 1993), effective leaders need to figure out how to maintain a level of decisiveness even when the social cues do not point clearly to an appropriate response. One way that leaders may become viewed as reliable by followers is by adhering consistently to their values, specifically in their commitment to the greater good—that is, to organizational objectives (e.g., Bass, 1990; Mannix and Neale, 2005). A second way is to ensure that followers are convinced of a leader's commitment to *their* success (not just to her own), as well as how their success and the leaders' are intertwined (e.g., House, 1996). We elaborate on both of these issues in the following section on groups and teams.

Understanding the Leadership Paradox

In addition to the complementary capabilities of diagnosing situations and responding flexibly to them, leaders also need to embrace the paradox of leadership: that their success is unequivocally derived through others. This is likely to be particularly challenging for leaders in organizational settings with typical hierarchical structures. In these settings, leaders have arrived in their position by virtue of their exceptional individual contributions, which are typically based on a strong achievement orientation (e.g., McClelland, 1985). Yet, leading others requires recognizing that their main role is to set the context for others to do excellent work (e.g., Goleman, 2000). Attempting to be singularly heroic limits leaders because the scope of most serious leadership roles is simply too wide and too diverse to be capably performed by a solitary person (Spreier, Fontaine, and Malloy, 2006). Thus, the behavior that delivered a leader into the role, in most cases, differs notably from the outlook and set of behaviors necessary to perform effectively within it.

Some who aspire to leadership roles may be high in the need for power rather than the need for achievement (e.g., McClelland and Burnham, 2003; Kotter, 1977). The challenge for those high in the need for power may be to develop an accurate understanding about their status in a group. Research in psychology has shown that those who more accurately perceive their own status, and especially those who avoid erring on the side of overestimating it, are more likely to be influential (Anderson, Srivastava, Beer, Spataro, and Chatman, 2006; Judge, LePine, and Rich, 2006). Thus, high achievers may be deficient in hubris, whereas the high power individuals may be deficient in humility.

Leading Work Groups and Teams

Insight into leadership effectiveness can, of course, also derive from understanding leaders' impact on others. Managers are responsible for a variety of organizational tasks (e.g., Mintzberg, 1971). Debates over the distinction between leaders and managers notwithstanding (Bass, 1990), we believe that three of the most critical tasks for team leaders are convening task groups, coaching group members, and setting group norms. We consider how leaders affect people's understanding about their own relation to the team, how leaders support members along the way, and which norms may be usefully cultivated in small groups.

Creating Strong Identification with the Group and Verifying Members

Social identity theory refers to the process by which people define their self-concept in terms of their membership in various social groups (e.g., Hogg and Terry, 2000; Markus and Cross, 1990). A salient social category functions psychologically to influence a person's perception, behavior, and how others treat him (Turner et al., 1987). To the extent that a particular in-group membership is salient, one's perceived similarity to others in the in-group is increased (Brewer, 1979). Increasing the salience of in-group membership causes a depersonalization of the self, defined as perceiving oneself as an interchangeable exemplar of the social category (Turner, 1985:99). Members of a salient in-group are more likely to cooperate with in-group members, compete against out-groups, and focus on achieving the group's goals (e.g., Chatman and Flynn, 2001).

Research has shown that members who identify strongly with their organization and its values perform more effectively than those who do not (e.g., Chatman, Polzer, Barsade, and Neale, 1998; O'Reilly and Chatman, 1996; Jehn, Northcraft, and Neale, 1999). Higher group identification is associated with a stronger effect of norms on individuals' behavioral intentions (Terry and Hogg, 1996), improved motivation and task performance (Van Knippenberg, 2000), reduced conflict and bias toward minority group members (Gaertner et al., 1993), and more cooperative behavior, particularly when people perceive that they have significant discretion over their behavior (Dukerich, Golden, and Shortell, 2002). Identification is also associated with organizational citizenship behavior (Dutton, Dukerich, and Harquail, 1994) and compassion (Dutton, Worline, Frost, and Lilius, 2006). Many of these improvements in functioning persist even in the presence of forces that potentially alienate people from their group, such as demographic diversity (e.g., Ely and Thomas, 2001; Lau and Murnighan, 1998). These groups often suffer from lower productivity and less cohesion than do more homogenous groups, but leaders can change this by encouraging people to recognize their common commitments rather than dwelling on their individual differences. Indeed, when an organizational culture emphasizes employees' shared fate (Dovidio, Gaertner, and Validzic, 1998)—the fact that they're all going to succeed or fail together as a group—diverse teams of employees are more productive and creative than are homogenous teams (Chatman et al., 1998).

Shared fate and identification with the group improve performance by satisfying the self-enhancement motive, the basis of social identity theory. But research suggests that other key motives are also in play in group and organizational settings. For example, researchers have found that increasing interpersonal congruence, or the extent to which team members see one another as each sees himself, makes even highly diverse groups effective (Swann, Milton, and Polzer, 2000). Members are also motivated by belonging, or a person's desire to feel close and accepted by others (Baumeister and Leary, 1995), and feeling distinctive, or the desire to establish and maintain a sense of differentiation from others (Vignoles, Chryssochoou, and Breakwell, 2000). Thus, a challenge to leaders is to determine when each of these motives is relevant and to help members satisfy them (Ormiston and Wong, 2008).

Coaching Members and Publicizing Their Strengths

Coaching members is important and consequential. Fortunately, a comprehensive theory of team coaching has been elegantly articulated by Hackman and Wageman (2005). We will not attempt to summarize their theory here, except to mention that for such coaching to result in performance gains, leaders must focus their coaching on task-relevant issues and time the type of coaching they offer with the somewhat predictable phases of team evolution (e.g., provide motivational coaching at the beginning, strategic coaching at the midpoint).

Researchers have also focused on leaders' role in increasing teams' external visibility within organizations, which improves their long-run performance (e.g., Ancona and Caldwell, 1992). We focus here on the importance of publicizing members' strengths *within* the group. This has become increasingly important as work groups have become more diverse (e.g., Mannix and Neale, 2005). In particular, if someone is a member of a group that has historically been underrepresented in a workplace—whether it is women, African Americans, or another group—coworkers will expect that person to perform poorly on tasks that have not typically been performed by members of his or her group. This is true no matter how skilled the person actually is at that task (Chatman, Boisner, Spataro, Anderson, and Berdahl, 2008).

These expectations, unfortunately, are often self-fulfilling (e.g., Steele, Spencer, and Aronson, 2002). One way to avoid this bias and the resulting performance decrement is for the person to advertise his or her own talents. Indeed, research shows that minority members who are more extraverted are less likely to be discriminated against (Flynn, Chatman, and Spataro, 2001). But, placing responsibility on the minority member can be daunting. An effective alternative is for a leader to explicitly articulate the minority member's task-relevant capabilities, especially when the person joins a new work group (Flynn et al., 2001; Ibarra, 1992). Research suggests that this sponsorship has a strong and positive impact—not just on the focal person's performance, but on the performance of the entire group. This may be because the employee receives a confidence boost, and the rest of the group is relieved of the discouraging notion that they will have to "carry" a poor performer (Chatman et al., 2008).

Setting Group Norms

Researchers have long recognized that a key role for leaders in groups is to set and monitor group norms. Group norms, defined as legitimate, shared standards against which the appropriateness of behavior can be evaluated (Birenbaum and Sagarin, 1976), influence how group members perceive and interact with one another. Norms represent regular behavior patterns that are relatively stable and expected by group members (Bettenhausen and Murnighan, 1991:21). Though the list of possible work group norms is long and leaders are responsible for determining which norms fit the task at hand, a few norms transcend specific tasks and likely apply generally to work groups. We discuss two of these below.

Promoting Cooperation

An organization relies on members to cooperate with one another in accomplishing goals to enhance its very survival (Simon, 1976). Leaders are responsible for creating norms that support such cooperation, which otherwise may not emerge. Research has shown numerous constraints on cooperation within organizations, including people's focus on their own self-interest (e.g., Frank, Gilovich, and Regan, 1993) and promotion and reward systems (e.g., Petersen, 1992). Interestingly, even a group's composition can reduce members' propensity to cooperate. Research has shown, for example, that demographically diverse teams are less likely to develop cooperative norms than are homogeneous groups, but that cooperative norms mediate the negative relationship between heterogeneity and cooperation (Chatman and Flynn, 2001). Thus, leaders need to figure out how to instill cooperative norms in groups particularly when groups are made up of diverse members.

Leaders can enhance cooperation within work groups by increasing the extent to which members view one another as part of their in-group. Teams that emphasize collectivism—that is, shared objectives, interchangeable interests, and commonalities among members—are more likely to view organizational membership as a salient identity than teams in which individualistic norms are salient (Chatman et al., 1998). Further, leaders can instill collectivistic norms through their own actions. For example, they can decide to reward and celebrate success accomplished by teams rather than individuals. By doing this, they can change reward structures to make cooperating more appealing and defection (through individualism or competition) less attractive (e.g., Petersen, 1992). They can also frame and interpret success in terms of the collective and explicitly share credit for organizational outcomes (e.g., Goncalo, 2004; Flynn and Chatman, 2001; Wageman, 1995). Cooperation can be reinforced by making the future more salient than the present and allowing members to use the threat of retaliation to reduce defection. This is consistent with research showing that longer time horizons, specifically manifested in lower employee turnover, contribute to cooperative decision making (e.g., Mannix and Loewenstein, 1994). Cooperative orientations can also be enhanced by teaching people values, facts, and skills that will promote cooperation, such as the importance of reciprocity and how to recognize social norms (e.g., Cialdini, 2001).

Endorsing Political Correctness (Sometimes)

In the context of increasingly diverse work groups, leaders need to consider norms relevant to interpersonal understanding and sensitivity. Research has examined how people react to political correctness, which can be defined as censoring language that might be offensive to members of other demographic groups (e.g., Norton, Vandelo, and Darley, 2004). Many leaders are understandably reluctant to advocate political correctness in the workplace, assuming that it stifles the free exchange of ideas (Norton et al., 2006). But one study showed some benefits (Goncalo, Chatman, and Duguid, 2008). Teams were either encouraged or discouraged from using politically correct language in their discussions. The teams were then observed in terms of how they performed on a creativity task. In more homogenous teams, political correctness noticeably constrained creativity. But in more diverse teams, encouraging political correctness actually boosted creativity while also promoting sensitivity to members' differences. Though people are often anxious about cross-group interactions, political correctness provided clear ground rules for their conversations, helping to promote feelings of comfort and trust and enabling team members to focus their attention more completely on the creative task at hand.

Leading Organizations

At the organizational level, leaders serve as embodiments of the organizations they create and lead. Though the list of requirements is long, three specific domains may be among their highest priorities. First, leaders need to develop an intentional model of organizing, especially when starting an organization. Second, they need to cultivate a strong, strategically relevant, and adaptable culture that helps to ensure that people execute their strategy. Third, they need to send a clear and consistent signal to followers across the organization. We discuss each of these below.

Starting Off Right: Developing an Intentional Model of Organizing

Researchers have been particularly interested in prominent organization figures, such as founders and CEOs, and how they might affect organizational structures and processes. In a longitudinal study of high-technology start-up firms, Baron and Hannan (2002) showed that a founder's "blueprint" for her organization, her mental model of how the organization would "look and feel," had a pervasive and long-lasting influence over how the organization developed, who was hired, and how effectively it executed its stated strategy (see also Baron, Burton, and Hannan, 1999). Founding blueprints tended to be extremely robust, often lasting through all stages of organizational growth and decline. Further, attempted changes in organizational blueprints were highly destabilizing to young technology start-ups, causing employee turnover, reducing bottom-line financial performance, and even threatening the firm's survival. The concept of a blueprint reflects a founder's fundamental values and mental models regarding organizational membership, including how employees are selected, the basis of their attachment, and how their efforts are coordinated and controlled. Interestingly, the most successful blueprint in terms of survival, profitability and, for small start-ups, time to IPO (initial public offering) and initial stock price, was the "strong commitment" model of organizing, in which employees were deeply attached to the organization.

Similarly, Schein (1983) argued that the founder plays an instrumental role in creating organizational culture by rigorously screening employees to identify those who support his ideals and values. Once selected, founders continue to socialize their employees into their way of thinking, and serve as a role model, encouraging employees to internalize these values. Schein's research implies that employee fit is particularly important during periods of organizational creation and change, and it is during these periods that those who hold and promote the founder's values will have greater impact on the organization than during stable periods. Taken together, these perspectives suggest those leaders who are intentional about developing and maintaining a strong culture will be more able to influence members to achieve key objectives from the organization's inception. Thus, we discuss below the importance of using culture as a leadership tool, not just in the beginning, but throughout an organization's evolution.

Using Culture as a Leadership Tool

Perhaps one of the most significant leadership roles is that of developing and managing organizational culture, as culture can determine whether or not an organization is able to deliver on its strategic promises. Culture is most closely related to organizational performance when three criteria are met (Chatman and Cha, 2003; Kotter and Heskett, 2002). First, the culture should be strategically relevant, meaning the behaviors that are emphasized and rewarded are actually the ones necessary to accomplish pressing and relevant organizational objectives. Second, the culture should be strong, meaning that people both agree about what is important and care (e.g., O'Reilly, 1989). Third, one core value needs to focus on innovation and adaptation and change if the organization is to sustain high levels of performance over time (Sorensen, 2002).

From a psychological perspective, how can leaders incite members to agree with and care intensely about organizational objectives? They can do so by increasing members' openness to organizational influence, which may include both unfreezing members' prior beliefs and influencing subsequent beliefs and behaviors through shared expectations of valued others (e.g., O'Reilly and Chatman, 1996). A variety of psychological mechanisms can then be used to clarify expectations and create a similar construal of organizational norms among members. When people are unsure of themselves and their own judgment, or when the situation is unclear or ambiguous, they are most likely to look to and consider other people's actions as appropriate, specified in the well-documented social comparison process (e.g., Banaji and Prentice, 1994). Leaders can also make particular information salient. Leaders often forcefully interpret events and behaviors, calling attention to important norms for internal and external followers (e.g., Flynn and Staw, 2006; Staw, McKechnie, and Puffer, 1983).

Consistent Signaling

Leaders have been characterized as signal generators who embody organizations (e.g., Tushman and O'Reilly, 1996). The visibility of their actions and blurring of their identity with the organization suggests that consistency in signaling is critical. We discuss two types: consistency in words and actions and across hierarchical levels.

CONSISTENCY IN WORDS AND ACTIONS

Because leaders can influence employees' fate, employees attend vigilantly to leaders' behavior, even to the rather mundane aspects such as what leaders spend time on, put on their calendar, ask and fail to ask, follow up on, and celebrate (Pfeffer, 1992). These behaviors provide employees with evidence about what counts and what behaviors are likely to be rewarded or punished. They convey much more to employees about priorities than do printed vision statements and formal policies. Once leaders embark on the path to using culture as an influence tool, it is critical that they regularly review their own behavior to understand the signals they are sending to members.

Ironically, leading through culture can set leaders up to be vulnerable to a series of psychological processes labeled the hypocrisy-attribution dynamic (Cha and Edmondson, 2006). Cultural values are powerful because they inspire people by appealing to high ideals (Walton, 1980) and clarify expectations by making salient the consistency between these values and each member's own behavior (Rokeach, 1973). But, just as emphasizing cultural values inherently alerts us to our own behavior, it makes others' behavior salient too, giving us high standards for judging them as well. We then become particularly attentive to possible violations, especially by leaders who are salient based on their relative power over our fate at work. When we detect potential inconsistencies between stated values and observed actions, it activates our deep cognitive tendency to judge others harshly.

Leaders who emphasize cultural values should expect employees to interpret those values by adding their own layers of meaning to them.

Over time, an event inevitably occurs that puts a leader at risk of being viewed as acting inconsistently with the values he has espoused. When leaders behave in ways that appear to violate espoused organizational values, employees, driven by the actor-observer bias (Jones and Nisbett, 1971), or people's tendency to explain their own behavior generously (viewing good outcomes as caused by their enduring dispositional attributes and bad outcomes as caused by situational influences) and to explain others' behavior harshly (attributing good outcomes to situational influences and bad outcomes to others' enduring dispositional traits), conclude that the leader is personally failing to "walk the talk." In short, organization members perceive hypocrisy and replace their hard-won commitment with performance-threatening cynicism. To avoid this undermining dynamic, leaders need to uphold their commitment to their culture even in the most trying times (e.g., Chatman and Cha, 2004).

CONSISTENCY ACROSS ORGANIZATIONAL LEVELS

In addition to behavioral consistency, signals are clearer when leaders within organizations are aligned with one another. In large organizations, it may be the aggregate effect of leaders at different hierarchical levels that helps or hinders the implementation of strategy and thereby affects organizational performance. While most previous studies of leadership have focused on the effectiveness of a single person (e.g., the CEO, a general manager, or a supervisor), alignment among leaders at different levels in an organization has long been acknowledged (Hunt, 1991). For example, Berson and Avolio (2004) argue that the actions of upper-level leaders influence the ways lower-level leaders translate and disseminate information about a new strategy. One of the critical ways leaders influence organizational and group performance is by providing a compelling direction (Hackman and Wageman, 2005). The lack of a clear, consistent message across levels of the leadership may provide mixed signals about the importance of an initiative and lead to a lack of focus (Cha and Edmondson, 2006; Osborn, Hunt, and Jauch, 2002).

But, *how* aggregate leadership influences organizational performance is not straightforward. For instance, a powerful senior leader may compensate for less effective leaders at lower levels. Alternatively, a less effective but highly aligned set of leaders across levels may successfully implement change. Or, an effective set of subordinate managers who do not support a strategic initiative may block change.

Regardless of the effects of an individual leader, alignment or misalignment of leaders across hierarchical levels may enhance or detract from the successful implementation of a strategic initiative. One study showed that leadership at one level compensated for or undermined the effects of leadership at another (O'Reilly, Caldwell, Chatman, Lapiz, and Self, 2008). Said differently, senior leaders' ability to implement a strategic initiative may depend critically on the alignment of organizational leaders across hierarchical levels.

Conclusion

The preponderance of empirical evidence over the past twenty years certainly shows that leadership matters; the important but harder-to-answer question is which capabilities are important. In this paper we have focused on various psychological bases for leader influence. Our (albeit incomplete) summary demonstrates just how much insight psychological research provides into how leaders influence followers in large and small groups. Still some say that research on leadership needs to move beyond the "tentative and exploratory stage" of simply looking for associations between leadership traits and performance outcomes and begin to focus on how these effects occur (Wasserman, Nohria, and Anand, 2001:26). Phills (2005) highlights the importance of examining the processes through which leaders affect behavioral change and, drawing from the medical sciences, suggests the need for researchers to examine "mechanisms of action," or the processes through which leaders affect organizational performance.

As Meindl and his colleagues demonstrated, there may be a tendency for observers to overattribute responsibility for outcomes to a leader (e.g., Chen and Meindl, 1991; Meindl and Ehrlich, 1987). However, to an important degree, leadership is a perceptual phenomenon, with followers observing the words and actions of their superiors and making inferences about their superiors' motives (Epitropaki and Martin, 2004; Lord, 1985; Pfeffer, 1981). Even if implicit leadership theories affect perceptual measures of leadership effectiveness, there is evidence that these ratings converge with objective measures of performance (Judge et al., 2002; Hogan et al., 1994). Recognizing this, Podolny, Khurana, and Hill-Popper (2005:47) argued that leadership is explicitly about those words and actions that create meaning for employees. The same "objective" leader actions can, therefore, result in different "subjective" interpretations and substantive variations in performance.

We identified a few developmental capabilities, including diagnostic abilities and behavioral range and flexibility, but we are also acutely aware that much of leadership is about constructing meaning for others, and, as a result, the exact path to becoming an influential leader is difficult to specify. Leadership is not amenable to easy formulas and is likely to continue to stimulate confusion, stereotypic behavior, and possibly imitation of behavior in the wrong context or of behavior uncorrelated with any real measure of performance. We are convinced, however, that leaders who understand the value of behavioral flexibility, managing meaning, and setting the context for others are likely to be influential. On the other hand, the simultaneous and opposing requirements of some hubris and substantial humility may explain why leadership is illusive for so many.

References

Ames, D.R., and F.J. Flynn. "What Breaks a Leader: The Curvilinear Relation Between Assertiveness and Leadership." *Journal of Personality and Social Psychology* 92, no. 2 (2007): 307–324.

Ancona, D.G., and D.F. Caldwell. "Bridging the Boundary: External Activity and Performance in Organizational Teams." *Administrative Science Quarterly* 37, no. 4 (1992): 634–665.

Anderson, C., S. Srivastava, J. Beer, S. Spataro, and J. Chatman. "Knowing Your Place: Self-Perceptions of Status in Social Groups." *Journal of Personality and Social Psychology* 91, no. 6 (2006): 1094–1110.

Banaji, M.R., and D.A. Prentice. "The Self in Social Contexts." *Annual Review of Psychology* 45 (1994): 297–332.

Bargh, J.A., and T.L. Chartrand. "The Unbearable Automaticity of Being." *American Psychologist* 54, no. 7 (1999): 462–479.

Baron, J.N., M.D. Burton, and M.T. Hannan. "Engineering Bureaucracy: The Genesis of Formal Policies, Positions, and Structures in High-Technology Firms." *Journal of Law, Economics, and Organization* 15, no. 1 (1999): 1–41.

Baron, J., and M. Hannan. "Organizational Blueprints for Success in High-Tech Start-ups: Lessons from the Stanford Project on Emerging Companies." *California Management Review* 44 (2002): 8–36.

Barrick, M.R., D.V. Day, R.G. Lord, and R.A. Alexander. "Assessing the Utility of Executive Leadership." *Leadership Quarterly* 2, no. 1 (1991): 9–22.

Bass, B.M. "From Transactional to Transformational Leadership: Learning to Share the Vision." *Organizational Dynamics* 18, no. 3 (1990): 19–31.

———. *Bass and Stogdill's Handbook of Leadership: Theory, Research and Managerial Applications*. New York: The Free Press, 1991.

Bass, B.M., B.J. Avolio, D.I. Jung, and Y. Berson. "Predicting Unit Performance by Assessing Transformational and Transactional Leadership." *Journal of Applied Psychology* 88, no. 2 (2003): 207–218.

Baumeister, R., and M. Leary. "The Need to Belong: Desire for Interpersonal Attachments as a Fundamental Human Motivation." *Psychological Bulletin* 117, no. 3 (1995): 497–529.

Berson, Y., and B.J. Avolio. "Transformational Leadership and the Dissemination of Organizational Goals: A Case Study of a Telecommunication Firm." *Leadership Quarterly* 15, no. 5 (2004): 625–646.

Bertrand, M., and A. Schoar. "Managing with Style: The Effect of Managers on Firm Policies." *Quarterly Journal of Economics* 118, no. 4 (2003): 1169–1208.

Bettenhausen, K.L., and J.K. Murnighan. "The Development of an Intragroup Norm and the Effects of Interpersonal and Structural Challenges." *Administrative Science Quarterly* 36, no. 1 (1991): 20–35.

Birenbaum, A., and E. Sagarin. *Norms and Human Behavior.* New York: Praeger Publishers, 1976.

Boal, K.B., and C.J. Whithead. "A Critique and Extension of the Stratified System Theory Perspective." In *Strategic Leadership: A Multi-organizational Perspective,* edited by R.L. Phillips and J.G. Hunt. Westport, CT: Quorum Books, 1992.

Brewer, M.B. "In-Group Bias in the Minimal Intergroup Situation: A Cognitive-Motivational Analysis." *Psychological Bulletin* 86, no. 2 (1979): 307–324.

Cha, S.E., and A.C. Edmondson. "When Values Backfire: Leadership, Attribution, and Disenchantment in a Values-Driven Organization." *Leadership Quarterly* 17, no. 1 (2006): 57–78.

Chatman, J., N. Bell, and B. Staw. "The Managed Thought: The Role of Self-Justification and Impression Management in Organizational Settings." In *The Thinking Organization: Dynamics of Social Cognition,* edited by D. Gioia and H. Sims. San Francisco: Jossey-Bass, 1986.

Chatman, J., A. Boisner, S. Spataro, C. Anderson, and J. Berdahl. "Being Distinctive Versus Being Conspicuous: The Effects of Numeric Status and Sex-Stereotyped Tasks of Individual Performance in Groups." *Organizational Behavior and Human Decision Processes* 107, no. 2 (2008): 141–160.

Chatman, J., and S. Cha. "Leading by Leveraging Culture." *California Management Review* 45, no. 4 (2003): 20–34.

Chatman, J., and F. Flynn. "The Influence of Demographic Composition on the Emergence and Consequences of Cooperative Norms in Groups." *Academy of Management Journal* 44, no. 5 (2001): 956–974.

Chatman, J., J. Polzer, S. Barsade, and M. Neale. "Being Different Yet Feeling Similar: The Influence of Demographic Composition and Organizational Culture on Work Processes and Outcomes." *Administrative Science Quarterly* 43, no. 4 (1998): 749–780.

Chemers, M.M. "Leadership Research and Theory: A Functional Integration." *Group Dynamics: Theory, Research and Practice* 4, no. 1 (2000): 27–43.

Chen, C.C., and J.R. Meindl. "The Construction of Leadership Images in the Popular Press: The Case of Donald Burr and People Express." *Administrative Science Quarterly* 36, no. 4 (1991): 521–551.

Cialdini, R.B. *Influence: The Psychology of Persuasion*. 4th ed. Boston: Allyn and Bacon, 2001.

Dovidio, J., S. Gaertner, and A. Validzic. "Intergroup Bias: Status, Differentiation, and a Common In-Group Identity." *Journal of Personality and Social Psychology* 75, no. 1 (1998): 109–120.

Dukerich, J., B. Golden, and S. Shortell. "Beauty Is in the Eye of the Beholder: The Impact of Organizational Identification, Identity, and Image on the Cooperative Behaviors of Physicians." *Administrative Science Quarterly* 47, no. 3 (2002): 507–533.

Dutton, J., J. Dukerich, and C. Harquail. "Organizational Images and Member Identification." *Administrative Science Quarterly* 39, no. 2 (1994): 239–263.

Dutton, J., M. Worline, P. Frost, and J. Lilius. "Explaining Compassion Organizing." *Administrative Science Quarterly* 51, no. 1 (2006): 59–96.

Ellis, R.J. "Self-Monitoring and Leadership Emergence in Groups." *Personality and Social Psychology Bulletin* 14, no. 4 (1988): 681–693.

Ely, R.J. and D.A. Thomas. "Cultural Diversity at Work: The Effects of Diversity Perspectives on Work Group Processes and Outcomes." *Administrative Science Quarterly* 46, no. 2 (2001): 229–273.

Epitropaki, O., and R. Martin. "Implicit Leadership Theories in Applied Settings: Factor Structure, Generalizability, and Stability Over Time." *Journal of Applied Psychology* 89, no. 2 (2004): 293–310.

Fiedler, F.E. "Cognitive Resources and Leadership Performance." *Applied Psychology* 44, no. 1 (1995): 5–28.

Flynn, F., and J. Chatman. "Strong Cultures and Innovation: Oxymoron or Opportunity?" In *International Handbook of Organizational Culture and Climate*, edited by S. Cartwright et al. Sussex: John Wiley and Sons, 2001.

Flynn, F.J., J.A. Chatman, and S.A. Spataro. "Getting to Know You: The Influence of Personality on the Impression Formation and Performance of Demographically Different People in Organizations." *Administrative Science Quarterly* 46, no. 3 (2001): 414–442.

Flynn, F.J., and B.M. Staw. "Lend Me Your Wallets: The Effect of Charismatic Leadership on External Support for an Organization." *Strategic Management Journal* 25, no. 4 (2006): 309–330.

Frank, R.H., T. Gilovich, and D.T. Regan. "Does Studying Economics Inhibit Cooperation?" *Journal of Economic Perspectives* 7, no. 2 (1993): 159–171.

Gaertner, S., J. Dovidio, P. Anastasio, B. Bachman, and M. Rust. "The Common Ingroup Identity Model: Recategorization and the Reduction of Intergroup Bias." *European Review of Social Psychology* 4, no. 1 (1993): 1–26.

George, J.M. "Emotions and Leadership: The Role of Emotional Intelligence." *Human Relations* 53, no. 8 (2000): 1027–1055.

Gioia, D., and P.P. Poole. "Scripts in Organizational Behavior." *Academy of Management Review* 9, no. 3 (1984): 449–459.

Goleman, D. "Leadership That Gets Results." *Harvard Business Review* 78, no. 2 (March–April 2000): 78–90.

Goleman, D., R. Boyatzis, and A. McKee. *Primal Leadership: Learning to Lead with Emotional Intelligence*. Cambridge, MA: Harvard Business School Press, 2004.

Goncalo, J.A. "Past Success and Convergent Thinking in Groups: The Role of Group-Focused Attributions." *European Journal of Social Psychology* 34, no. 2 (2004): 385–395.

Goncalo, J., J. Chatman, and M. Duguid. "Political Correctness and Creativity in Mixed and Same Sex Groups." Working paper, Cornell University, 2008.

Gosling, S.D., O.E. John, K.H. Craik, and R.W. Robins. "Do People Know How They Behave? Self-Reported Act Frequencies Compared with On-line Codings by Observers." *Journal of Personality and Social Psychology* 74, no. 5 (1998): 1337–1349.

Graeff, C.A. "The Situational Leadership Theory: A Critical View." *Academy of Management Review* 8, no. 2 (1983): 285–291.

Hackman, J.R., and R. Wageman. "A Theory of Team Coaching." *Academy of Management Review* 30, no. 2 (2005): 269–287.

Hall, R.J., J.W. Workman, and C.A. Marchioro. "Sex, Task, and Behavioral Flexibility Effects on Leadership Perceptions." *Organizational Behavior and Human Decision Processes* 74, no. 1 (2002): 1–32.

Hambrick, D., S. Finkelstein, and A. Mooney. "Executive Job Demands: New Insights for Explaining Strategic Decisions and Leader Behaviors." *Academy of Management Review* 30, no. 3 (2005): 472–491.

Hannan, M.T., and J. Freeman. "Structural Inertia and Organizational Change." *American Sociological Review* 49, no. 2 (1984): 149–164.

———. *Organizational Ecology.* Cambridge, MA: Harvard University Press, 1989.

Hersey, P., K.H. Blanchard, and W.E. Natemeyer. "Situational Leadership, Perception, and the Impact of Power." *Group and Organization Management* 4, no. 4 (1979): 418–428.

Hogan, R., G.J. Curphy, and J. Hogan. "What We Know About Leadership." *American Psychologist* 49, no. 6 (1994): 493–504.

Hogg, M.A., and Deborah J. Terry. "Social Identity and Self-Categorization Processes in Organizational Contexts." *Academy of Management Review* 25, no. 1 (2000): 121–140.

Hooijberg, R. "A Multidirectional Approach Toward Leadership: An Extension of the Concept of Behavioral Complexity." *Human Relations* 49, no. 7 (1996): 917–946.

House, R.J. "A 1976 Theory of Charismatic Leadership." In *Leadership: The Cutting Edge*, edited by J.G. Hunt and L.L. Larson. Carbondale: Southern Illinois University Press, 1977.

———. "Power and Personality in Organizations." *Research in Organizational Behavior* 10 (1988): 305–357.

———. "Path-Goal Theory of Leadership: Lessons, Legacy, and a Reformulated Theory." *Leadership Quarterly* 7, no. 3 (1996): 323–352.

House, R.J., and R.N. Aditya. "The Social Scientific Study of Leadership: Quo Vadis?" *Journal of Management* 23, no. 3 (1997): 409–473.

Howard, A., and D. Bray. *Managerial Lives in Transition: Advancing Age and Changing Times.* New York: Guilford Press, 1988.

Hunt, J.G. *Leadership: A New Synthesis.* Newbury Park, CA: Sage Publications, 1991.

Hunter, S.T., K.E. Bedell-Avers, and M.D. Mumford. "The Typical Leadership Study: Assumptions, Implications, and Potential Remedies." *Leadership Quarterly* 18, no. 5 (2007): 435–446.

Ibarra, H. "Homophily and Differential Returns: Sex Differences in Network Structure and Access in an Advertising Firm." *Administrative Science Quarterly* 37, no. 3 (1992): 422–447.

Jehn, K., G. Northcraft, and M. Neale. "Why Differences Make a Difference: A Field Study of Diversity, Conflict and Performance in Work Groups." *Administrative Science Quarterly* 44, no. 4 (1999): 741–763.

Jones, E.E., and R.E. Nisbett. *The Actor and the Observer: Divergent Perceptions of the Causes of Behavior.* Morristown, NJ: General Learning Press, 1971.

Judge, T.A., J.E. Bono, R. Ilies, and M.W. Gerhardt. "Personality and Leadership: A Qualitative and Quantitative Review." *Journal of Applied Psychology* 87, no. 4 (2002): 765–780.

Judge, T.A., A.E. Colbert, and R. Ilies. "Intelligence and Leadership: A Quantitative Review and Test of Theoretical Propositions." *Journal of Applied Psychology* 89, no. 3 (2004): 542–552.

Judge, T.A., J.A. LePine, and B.L. Rich. "Loving Yourself Abundantly: Relationship of the Narcissistic Personality to Self- and Other Perceptions of Workplace Deviance, Leadership, and Task and Contextual Performance." *Journal of Applied Psychology* 91, no. 4 (2006): 762–776.

Judge, T.A., and R.F. Piccolo. "Transformational and Transactional Leadership: A Meta-analytic Test of Their Relative Validity." *Journal of Applied Psychology* 89, no. 5 (2004): 755–768.

Judge, T.A., R.F. Piccolo, and R. Ilies. "The Forgotten Ones? The Validity of Consideration and Initiating Structure in Leadership Research." *Journal of Applied Psychology* 89, no. 1 (2004): 36–51.

Kenny, D.A. *Interpersonal Perception: A Social Relations Analysis.* New York: Guilford Press, 1994.

Kenny, D.A., C.D. Mohr, and M.J. Levesque. "A Social Relations Variance Partitioning of Dyadic Behavior." *Psychological Bulletin* 127, no. 1 (2001): 128–141.

Khurana, R. *Searching for a Corporate Savior: The Irrational Quest for Charismatic CEOs.* Princeton, NJ: Princeton University Press, 2002.

Koene, B.A., A.L. Vogelaar, and J.L. Soeters. "Leadership Effects on Organizational Climate and Financial Performance: Local Leadership Effects in Chain Organizations." *Leadership Quarterly* 13, no. 3 (2002): 193–215.

Kotter, J.P. "Power, Dependence, and Effective Management." *Harvard Business Review* 55, no. 4 (1977): 125–136.

Kotter, J.P, and J.L. Heskett. *Corporate Culture and Performance.* New York: Free Press, 2002.

Lau, D., and J.K. Murnighan. "Demographic Diversity and Faultlines: The Compositional Dynamics of Organizational Groups." *Academy of Management Review* 23, no. 2 (1998): 325–340.

Lord, R.G. "An Information Processing Approach to Social Perceptions, Leadership and Behavioral Measurement in Organizations." *Research in Organizational Behavior* 7 (1985): 87–128.

Mannix, E., and G. Loewenstein. "The Effects of Interfirm Mobility and Individual Versus Group Decision Making on Managerial Time Horizons." *Organizational Behavior and Human Decision Processes* 59, no. 3 (1994): 371–390.

Mannix, E., and M.A. Neale. "What Differences Make a Difference? The Promise and Reality of Diverse Teams in Organizations." *Psychological Science in the Public Interest* 6, no. 2 (2005): 31–55.

Markus, H., and S. Cross. "The Interpersonal Self." In *Handbook of Personality: Theory and Research*, edited by L.A. Pervin. New York: Guilford Press, 1990.

McClelland, D.C. "How Motives, Skills, and Values Determine What People Do." *American Psychologist* 40, no. 7 (1985): 812–825.

McClelland, D.C., and D.H. Burnham. "Power Is the Great Motivator." *Harvard Business Review* 81, no. 1 (2003): 117–126.

Meindl, J.R. "On Leadership: An Alternative to the Conventional Wisdom." *Research in Organizational Behavior* 12 (1990): 159–203.

Meindl, J.R., and S.B. Ehrlich. "The Romance of Leadership and the Evaluation of Organizational Performance." *Academy of Management Journal* 30, no. 1 (1987): 91–109.

Miller, D., and C. Droge. "Psychological and Traditional Determinants of Structure." *Administrative Science Quarterly* 31, no. 4 (1986): 539–560.

Miller, D., and J.M. Toulouse. "Chief Executive Personality and Corporate Strategy and Structure in Small Firms." *Management Science* 32, no. 11 (1986): 1389–1409.

Mintzberg, H. "Managerial Work: Analysis from Observation." *Management Science* 18, no. 2 (1971): 97–110.

Mumford, M.D., and M.S. Connelly. "Leaders as Creators: Leader Performance and Problem Solving in Ill-Defined Domains." *Leadership Quarterly* 2, no. 4 (1991): 289–316.

Norton, M.I., S.R. Sommers, E.P. Apfelbaum, N. Pura, and D. Ariely. "Color Blindness and Interracial Interaction: Playing the Political Correctness Game." *Psychological Science* 17, no. 11 (2006): 949–953.

Norton, M.I., J.A. Vandelo, and J.M. Darley. "Casuistry and Social Category Bias." *Journal of Personality and Social Psychology* 87, no. 6 (2004): 817–831.

O'Reilly, C.A. "Corporations, Culture, and Commitment: Motivation and Social Control in Organizations. *California Management Review* 3, no. 1 (1989): 9–25.

O'Reilly, C., D. Caldwell, J. Chatman, M. Lapiz, and W. Self. "How Leadership Matters: The Effects of Leadership Alignment on Strategic Execution." Working paper, Stanford University, 2008.

O'Reilly, C., and J. Chatman. "Culture as Social Control: Corporations, Cults and Commitment." In *Research in Organizational Behavior*. Vol. 18, edited by B. Staw and L. Cummings, 157–200. Greenwich, CT: JAI Press, 1996.

Ormiston, M., and E. Wong. "The Role of Identity Motives in Similar and Diverse Groups." In *Research on Managing Groups and Teams: Diversity and Groups*. Vol. 11, edited by M.A. Neale and E.A. Mannix (Series eds.), and K. Phillips (Vol. ed.). Emerald Group Publishing Limited, 2008.

Osborn, R., J.G. Hunt, and L. Jauch. "Toward a Contextual Theory of Leadership." *Leadership Quarterly* 13, no. 6 (2002): 797–837.

Petersen, T. "Individual, Collective, and Systems Rationality in Work Groups: Dilemmas and Market-Type Solutions." *American Journal of Sociology* 98, no. 3 (1992): 469–510.

Pfeffer, J. "The Ambiguity of Leadership." *Academy of Management Review* 2, no. 1 (1977): 104–112.

———. "Management as Symbolic Action: The Creation and Maintenance of Organizational Paradigms." *Research in Organizational Behavior* 3 (1981): 1–52.

———. *Managing with Power: Politics and Influence in Organizations.* Boston: Harvard Business School Press, 1992.

Phills, J.A. "Leadership Matters—or Does It?" *Leader to Leader* 36 (2005): 46–52.

Podolny, J.M., R. Khurana, and M. Hill-Popper. "Revisiting the Meaning of Leadership." *Research in Organizational Behavior* 26 (2005): 1–36.

Rokeach, M. *The Nature of Human Values.* New York: John Wiley, 1973.

Ross, J., and B.M. Staw. "Organizational Escalation and Exit: Lessons from the Shoreham Nuclear Power Plant." *Academy of Management Journal* 36, no. 4 (1993): 701–732.

Schein, E.H. "The Role of the Founder in Creating Organization Culture." *Organizational Dynamics* 12, no. 1 (1983): 13–28.

Simon, H.A. *Administrative Behavior: A Study of Decision-Making Processes in Administrative Organization.* New York: The Free Press, 1976.

Sorenson, J.B. The Strength of Corporate Culture and the Reliability of Firm Performance. *Administrative Science Quarterly* 47, no. 1 (2002): 70–91.

Spreier, S., M. Fontaine, and R. Malloy. "Leadership Run Amok: The Destructive Potential of Overachievers." *Harvard Business Review* 84, no. 6 (June 2006), 72–82.

Staw, B.M., L.E. Sandelands, and Dutton, J.E. "Threat Rigidity Effects in Organizational Behavior: A Multilevel Analysis." *Administrative Science Quarterly* 26, no. 4 (1981): 501–524.

Staw, B.M., P.I. McKechnie, and S.M. Puffer. "The Justification of Organizational Performance." *Administrative Science Quarterly* 28, no. 4 (1983): 582–600.

Steele, C.M., S.J. Spencer, and J. Aronson. "Contending with Group Image: The Psychology of Stereotype and Social Identity Threat." In *Advances in Experimental Social Psychology.* Vol. 34, edited by M.P. Zanna, 379–440. New York: Academic Press, 2002.

Swann, M., L. Milton, and J. Polzer. "Should We Create a Niche or Fall in Line? Identity Negotiation and Small Group Effectiveness." *Journal of Personality and Social Psychology* 79, no. 2 (2000): 238–250.

Terry, D.J., and M.A. Hogg. "Group Norms and the Attitude-Behavior Relationship: A Role for Group Identification." *Personality and Social Psychology Bulletin* 22, no. 8 (1996): 776–793.

Tetlock, P.E. "Accountability and Complexity of Thought." *Journal of Personality and Social Psychology* 45, no. 1 (1983): 74–83.

Turner, J.C. "Social Categorization and the Self-Concept: A Social Cognitive Theory of Group Behavior." In *Advances in Group Processes.* Vol. 2, edited by E.J. Lawler, 77–122. Greenwich, CT: JAI Press, 1985.

Turner, J.C., M.A. Hogg, P.J. Oakes, S.D. Reicher, and M.S. Wetherell. *Rediscovering the Social Group: A Self-Categorization Theory.* Oxford, England: Blackwell, 1987.

Tushman, M., and C.A. O'Reilly. "Ambidextrous Organizations: Managing Evolutionary and Revolutionary Change." *California Management Review* 38, no. 4 (1996): 8–27.

Van Knippenberg, D. "Work Motivation and Performance: A Social Identity Perspective." *Applied Psychology* 49, no. 3 (2000): 357–371.

Vecchio, R.P. "Situational Leadership Theory: An Examination of a Prescriptive Theory." *Journal of Applied Psychology* 72, no. 33 (1987): 444–451.

Vignoles, V., X. Chryssochoou, and G. Breakwell. "The Distinctiveness Principle: Identity, Meaning, and the Bounds of Cultural Relativity." *Personality and Social Psychology Review* 4, no. 4 (2000): 337–354.

Vroom, V.H., and H.G. Jago. "The Role of the Situation in Leadership." *American Psychologist* 62, no. 1 (2007): 17–24.

Wageman, R. "Interdependence and Group Effectiveness." *Administrative Science Quarterly* 40, no. 1 (1995): 145–180.

Waldman, D.A., and F.J. Yammarino. "CEO Charismatic Leadership: Levels-of-Management and Levels-of-Analysis Effects." *Academy of Management Review* 24, no. 2 (1999): 266–285.

Walton, R.E. "Establishing and Maintaining High Commitment Work Systems." In *The Organization Life Cycle: Issues in the Creation, Transformation and Decline of Organizations*, edited by J. Kimberly and R. Miles. Chicago: University of Chicago Press, 1980.

Wasserman, N., N. Nohria, and B. Anand. "When Does Leadership Matter? The Contingent Opportunities View of CEO Leadership." Working paper 01-063, Harvard Business School, Boston, 2001.

Wolff, S.B., A.T. Pescosolido, and V.U. Druskat. "Emotional Intelligence as the Basis of Leadership Emergence in Self-Managing Teams." *Leadership Quarterly* 13, no. 5 (2002): 505–522.

Wong, C.S., and K.S. Law. "The Effects of Leader and Follower Emotional Intelligence on Performance and Attitude: An Exploratory Study." *Leadership Quarterly* 13, no. 3 (2002): 243–247.

Zaccaro, S.J. "Organizational Leadership and Social Intelligence." In *Multiple Intelligences and Leadership*, edited by R.E. Riggio, S.E. Murphy, and F.J. Pirozzolo. New York: Lawrence Erlbaum Associates, 2001.

———. "Trait-Based Perspectives on Leadership." *American Psychologist* 62, no. 1 (2007): 6–16.

Zaccaro, S.J., R.J. Foti, and D.A. Kenny. "Self-Monitoring and Trait-Based Variance in Leadership: An Investigation of Leader Flexibility." *Journal of Applied Psychology* 76, no. 2 (1991): 308–315.

Zaccaro, S.J., J.A. Gilbert, K.K. Thor, and M.D. Mumford. "Leadership and Social Intelligence: Linking Social Perspectives and Behavioral Flexibility to Leader Effectiveness." *Leadership Quarterly* 2, no. 4 (1991): 317–342.

7

A Clinical Approach to the Dynamics of Leadership and Executive Transformation

Manfred Kets de Vries and Elisabet Engellau

We know what we are, but know not what we may be.
—William Shakespeare

What progress we are making. In the Middle Ages they would have burned me. Now they are content with burning my books.
—Sigmund Freud

Your vision will become clear only when you look into your heart . . . Who looks outside, dreams. Who looks inside, awakens.
—Carl Jung

You cannot discover new oceans unless you have the courage to lose sight of the shore.
—Andre Gide

Invited paper for Harvard Business School 100th Anniversary. To be presented at the colloquium "Leadership: Advancing an Intellectual Discipline." Manfred Kets de Vries is the Raoul de Vitry d'Avaucourt Clinical Professor in Leadership Development, INSEAD, France, Singapore, and Abu Dhabi, and Director of INSEAD's Global Leadership Center. Elisabet Engellau is an Adjunct Clinical Professor in Management, INSEAD, France, Singapore, and Abu Dhabi, and Program Director of INSEAD's Global Leadership Center.

Introduction

There is a story about a thief and a rich man who were traveling together on a train. The thief, of course, was following the rich man precisely because of his wealth. Whenever the rich man went to the bathroom, or went to buy food when the train stopped, the thief would rifle through the compartment they shared. At every stop he looked somewhere new. "Maybe in the overhead locker," "Maybe in his overcoat," he thought, and continued searching. Eventually, as the train began to slow and their journey drew to an end, exasperated by his failure, the thief confessed to his fellow traveler, "Do you know, I'm a thief, and I have been trying all the time we have been traveling together to get your money—but you have outwitted me." The rich man went over to the thief's bed, bent down, and began pulling his money out from underneath it. "I hid it here," the rich man said, "because I knew that the last place you would look for it was underneath your bed."

Like the thief in this story, many management scholars studying the behavior of people in organizations not only don't know where to look, but often don't know how. Far too often they miss things that are hidden in plain view. Their inability to see affects their understanding of what really happens in organizations. They seem to subscribe to the myth that it is only the conscious—what we see and know—that matters. That myth is grounded in concepts of organizational behavior based on assumptions about human beings made by (at worst) economists or (at best) behavioral psychologists. The spirit of the economic machine seems to be alive and well and thriving in organizations. Although the existing repertoire of "rational" concepts has proved to be inadequate time and again, the myth of rationality, the need to maintain an illusion of control, persists—whereas in fact the most important things in life are invisible.

Consequently, far too often, organizational behavior concepts used to describe processes such as individual motivation, leadership, interpersonal relationships, collusive behavior, group and intergroup processes, corporate culture, organizational structure, individual and organizational change, and transformation are based on behaviorist models, with an occasional dose of humanistic psychology thrown into the equation for good measure. This approach (where the irrepressible ghost of the advocate of scientific management, Frederick Taylor, is still hovering about) has its merits but is not sufficient to untangle the knotty problems we encounter in organizations. It sets the stage for a rather two-dimensional way of looking at the world of work. Far too many executives (and scholars of management) hold on to the belief that behavior in organizations concerns only conscious, mechanistic, predictable, easy-to-understand phenomena. The more elusive processes that take place in organizations—phenomena that deserve rich description—are conveniently ignored.

That the organizational man or woman is not just a conscious, highly focused maximizing machine of pleasures and pains, but also a person subject to many (often contradictory) wishes, fantasies, conflicts, defensive behavior, and anxieties—some conscious, others beyond consciousness —is not a popular perspective. Neither is the idea that concepts taken from such fields as psychoanalysis, psychodynamic psychotherapy, clinical psychology, and dynamic psychiatry might have a place in the world of work. Such concepts are generally rejected out of hand on the grounds that they are too individually based, too focused on abnormal behavior, and (in the case of the psychoanalytic method of investigation) too reliant on self-reported case studies (creating problems of verification).

Valid as some of these criticisms may be, the fact remains that any meaningful explanation of humanity requires different means of verification. In spite of what philosophers of science like to say about this subject, no causal claim in clinical psychology (or history and economics, for that matter) can be verified in the same way as can be done in empirical sciences such as experimental physics or astronomy. When we enter the realm of someone's inner world—seeking to understand that individual's desires, hopes, and fears—efforts at falsification (in an attempt to discover an observed exception to science's postulated rules) become a moot point (Popper, 2002). Even en masse, people are subject to different laws than can be tested in experimental physics. In addition, like it or not, abnormal behavior is more "normal" than most people are prepared to admit. All of us have a neurotic side. Mental health and illness are not dichotomous phenomena but opposing positions on a continuum. Moreover, whether a person is labeled normal or abnormal, the same psychological processes apply.

Given these observations, business scholars and leaders need to revisit the following questions: Is the typical executive really a logical, dependable human being? Is management really a rational task performed by rational people according to sensible organizational objectives? Given the plethora of highly destructive actions taken by business and political leaders, we shouldn't even have to ask. It should be clear that many of these incomprehensible activities ("incomprehensible" from a rational point of view, that is) signal that what really goes on in organizations takes place in the intrapsychic and interpersonal world of the key players, below the surface of day-to-day behaviors. That underlying mental activity and behavior needs to be understood in terms of conflicts, defensive behaviors, and emotions. In that respect, the human mind should be looked at as a dark sea swarming with strange forms of life, most of them unconscious and not illuminated. Unless we can understand how the motives that issue from this obscurity are generated, we can hardly hope to foresee or control them.

It is something of a paradox that, while at a conscious level we might deny the presence of unconscious processes, at the level of behavior and action we live out such processes each day of our lives. Although we base business strategies on theoretical models derived from the "rational economic man," we count on real people (with all their conscious and unconscious quirks) to make and implement decisions. Even the most successful organizational leaders are prone to highly irrational behavior, a reality that we ignore at our peril—the global financial meltdown of 2008 being a prime example.

In the case of many knotty organizational situations, a more clinical orientation can go a long way toward bringing clarity and providing solutions. And no body of knowledge has made a more sustained and successful attempt to deal with the meaning of human events than psychoanalytic psychology. The psychoanalytic method of investigation, which observes people longitudinally, offers an important window into the operation of the mind, identifying meaning in the most personal, emotional experiences. Its method of drawing inferences about meaning out of otherwise incomprehensible phenomena can be highly illuminating. By making sense out of executives' deeper wishes and fantasies, and showing how these affect their behavior in the world of work, a psychoanalytically informed investigation can be highly effective in discovering how people and the organizations they work in *really* function. Far too many well-intentioned and well-thought-out plans derail daily in workplaces around the world because of out-of-awareness forces that influence behavior.

The Freud Conundrum

Although a growing group of management scholars are coming to realize that they need to pay attention to weaker, below-the-surface signals in organizational systems, that trend is belied by frequent articles in popular journals asking whether Freud is dead. People who pose that question are not only typically unaware of the extent to which Freud's *Weltanschauung* has been embraced by popular culture, but also they are unaware of more recent developments in the theory and the practice of psychoanalysis. They usually attack Freudian views of the early twentieth century, forgetting that psychoanalytic theory and psychodynamic therapy have continued to evolve since that time. Psychoanalytic theory and technique have become increasingly sophisticated, incorporating the findings from domains such as dynamic psychiatry, developmental psychology, ethology, anthropology, neuroscience, cognitive theory, family systems theory, and individual and group psychotherapy. To condemn present-day psychoanalytic theory as outdated is like attacking modern physics because Newton did not understand Einstein's theory of relativity. Although quite a few aspects of Freud's theories are no longer valid in light of new information about the workings of the mind, fundamental components of psychoanalytic theory and technique have been scientifically and empirically tested and verified, specifically as they relate to cognitive and emotional processes (Barron and Eagle, 1992; Westen 1998). As disappointing as this fact may be to some of his present-day attackers, many of Freud's ideas have retained their relevance.

A broad integrative, clinically oriented, psychodynamic perspective that draws upon psychoanalytic concepts and techniques (as well as other disciplines) has much to contribute to our understanding of organizations, the practice of management and the hidden dynamics in the world of work (Czander, 1993; DeBoard, 1978; Gabriel, 1999; Kets de Vries and Miller, 1984; Kets de Vries, 1984, 1989, 1991, 1994, 2001, 2006a; Kets de Vries et al., 2007a, 2007b; Levinson, 1972, 2002; Zaleznik, 1966; Zaleznik and Kets de Vries, 1985). Advocates of the psychodynamic approach recognize the limits of rationality and reject a purely economist, behaviorist view of organizations. Behavioral and statistical data-gathering experiments can make only a partial contribution to the understanding of complex organizational phenomena, though advocates of management as a natural science would like to believe differently. An additional dimension of analysis will greatly advance the understanding of the vicissitudes of organizational behavior and the people working in the system. In other words, without a clinical lens we would never know that when we think a thing, the thing we think is not the thing we think, but only the thing that makes us think we think the thing we think.

The Clinical Paradigm

Although our brains are genetically hardwired with certain instinctual behavior patterns, that wiring is not irrevocably fixed. Over the crucial first months and years of our life (and in later years, though to a lesser extent) rewiring occurs in response to developmental factors to which we are exposed. The interface of our motivational needs with environmental factors (especially human factors, in the form of caretakers, siblings, teachers, and other important figures) defines our essential uniqueness. Together, these elements draft the scripts for our inner theater. For each one of us, they determine our character and contribute to our mental life triangle—a tightly interlocked frame of cognition, affect, and behavior.

Motivational Need Systems

To understand the human being in all its complexity, we have to start with motivational need systems, the operational code that drives personality. Each of these need systems is operational in every person beginning at infancy and continuing throughout the life cycle, altered by the forces of age, learning, and maturation. The importance that any one of the need systems has for an individual is determined by three regulating forces: innate and learned response patterns, the role of significant caretakers, and the extent to which the individual attempts to recreate positive emotional states experienced in infancy and childhood. As these forces and need systems interact during maturation, mental schemas emerge—"templates" in the unconscious. These schemas create symbolic model scenes (what we call "scripts" in a person's inner theater) that regulate fantasy and influence behavior (Erikson, 1963; Emde, 1981; Kagan and Moss, 1983; McDougall, 1985, 1989; Lichtenberg, 1991; Lichtenberg and Schonbar, 1992).

Some of these motivational need systems are more basic than others. At the most fundamental level is the system that regulates a person's physiological needs—that is, needs for food, water, elimination, sleep, and breathing. Another system handles an individual's needs for sensual enjoyment and (later) sexual excitement, while still another deals with the need to respond to certain situations through antagonism and with-drawal (fight-flight). Although these primary need systems impact the work situation to some extent, two other, higher-level systems are of particular interest for life in organizations: the attachment/affiliation need system and the exploration/assertion need system.

Taking the attachment/affiliation motivational need system, we find that there is an innately unfolding experience of human related-ness among humans (Spitz, 1965; Bowlby, 1969; Mahler, Pine et al., 1975; Winnicott, 1975). Humankind's essential *humanness* is found in seeking relationships with other people, in being part of something. That need for attachment involves the process of engagement with other human beings, the universal experience of wanting to be close to others. It also involves the pleasure of sharing and affirmation. When the human need for intimate engagement is extrapolated to groups, the desire to enjoy intimacy can be described as a need for affiliation. Both attachment and affiliation serve an emotional balancing role by con-firming an individual's self-worth and contributing to his or her sense of self-esteem.

The need for exploration/assertion also has a lot to do with who a person becomes and how that person sees him- or herself. The need for exploration—closely associated with cognition and learning—affects a person's ability to play and to work. This need is manifested soon after birth: observation of infants has shown that novelty, as well as the discovery of the effects of certain actions, causes a prolonged state of attentive arousal in them. Similar reactions to opportunities for explo-ration continue into adulthood. Closely tied to the need for exploration is the need for self-assertion, the need to be able to choose what one will do. Playful exploration and manipulation of the environment in response to exploratory-assertive motivation produces a sense of effectiveness and competency, of self-efficacy, autonomy, initiative, and industry (White, 1959; Bandura, 1997). Because striving, competing, and seek-ing mastery are fundamental characteristics of the human personality, exercising assertiveness—following our preferences, acting in a deter-mined manner—serves as a form of affirmation.

As noted above, each motivational system is either strengthened or loses power in reaction to innate and learned response patterns, the developmental impact of caretakers, and the ability to recreate previous emotional states. Through the nature-nurture interface, these highly complex motivational systems eventually determine the unique "internal theater" of the individual—the stage on which the major themes that define the person are played out. These motivational systems are the *rational* forces that lie behind behaviors and actions that are perceived to be *irrational*. The clinical paradigm looks beyond a person's irrational activities and attempts to acknowledge, decipher, and offer tips for mastering these forms of irrationality. The clinical approach to organizational assessment and consultation helps executives and consultants become organizational "detectives."

The Rationale Behind Irrationality

The "prototype" or "script" of self, others, and events that each one of us carries within us is put into motion by the aforementioned motivational needs systems. These scripts influence how we act and react in our daily lives, whether at home, at play, or at work (George, 1969; McDougall, 1985). We bring to every experience a style of interacting, now scripted for us, initially learned in childhood. In other words, how we related to and interacted with parents and other close caregivers during the early years affects how we relate to others—especially authority figures—in adulthood.

In the course of these maturation processes, we all develop particular themes in our inner theater—themes that reflect the preeminence of certain inner wishes that contribute to our unique personality style. These "core conflictual relationship themes" (CCRT) translate into consistent patterns by which we relate to others (Luborsky and Crits-Cristoph, 1990). Put another way, these basic desires shape our life scripts, which in turn shape our relationships with others, determining the way we believe others will react to us and the way we react to others. People's lives may be colored by the desire to be loved, for example, or the wish to be understood, or to be noticed, or to be free from conflict, or to be independent, or to help—or even to fail, or to hurt others.

When we go to work, we take these fundamental desires—our core conflictual relationship themes—into the context of our workplace. We project our desires on others and, based on those desires, rightly or wrongly anticipate how others will react to us; then we react not to their *actual* reactions but to their *perceived* reactions. Who among us doesn't know a leader who is the epitome of conflict avoidance, tyrannical behavior, micromanagement, or manic behavior? That dominant style, whatever it may be, derives from the leader's core conflictual relationship theme. So potent is a person's driving theme that a leader's subordinates are often drawn into collusive practices and play along, turning the leader's expectations into self-fulfilling prophecies. Unfortunately, the life scripts drawn up in childhood on the basis of our core conflictual relationship themes often become ineffective in adult situations. They create a dizzying merry-go-round that can take us into a self-destructive cycle of repetition.

The Importance of Unconscious Processes

As mentioned earlier, Sigmund Freud explored the importance of the human unconscious—that part of our being which, hidden from rational thought, affects and interprets our conscious reality. We are not always aware of what we are doing (even aside from the issue of *why* we are doing it). As we suggested—like it or not—most of our behavior originates outside consciousness. We all have our blind spots. In addition, we all have a shadow side—a side that we don't know (or even don't *want* to know) (Jung, 1973). Freud was not the first person to emphasize the role of the unconscious; many poets and philosophers explored that territory before him. He was the first, however, to build a psychological theory around the concept.

Because the key drivers in the unconscious are in our personal, repressed, infantile history, we usually deny or are simply unaware of the impact and importance of the unconscious. It is not pleasant to admit that we are sometimes prisoners of our own unconscious mind (contrary to our cherished illusion that we are in control of our lives). And yet accepting the presence of the cognitive and affective unconscious can be liberating, because it helps us to understand why we do the things we do, make the decisions we do, and attract the responses we do from the environment. Once we become aware of how and why we operate, we are in a much better position to decide whether we want to do what we have always done or pursue a course that is more appropriate to our current life situation and stage of development.

Prisoners of the Past

As was noted in the discussion of motivational need systems, there is strong continuity between childhood and adult behavior. As the saying goes, "Scratch a man or woman and you will find a child." This does not mean that we cannot change as adults; it simply means that by the time we reach the age of thirty, a considerable part of our personality has been formed (McCrae and Costa, 1990; Heatherton and Weinberger, 1994). And unless we recognize the extent to which our present is determined by our past, it is quite likely that we will repeatedly make the same mistakes. Organizations the world over are full of leaders who are unable to recognize repetitive behavioral patterns that have become dysfunctional. They are stuck in a vicious, self-destructive circle and don't even know it—much less know how to get out of it. The clinical paradigm can help such people recognize their strengths and weaknesses, understand the causes of their resistance to change, and recognize where and how they can become more effective. In other words, it can offer choice.

The Psychodynamics of Leadership

Recognizing the role that psychodynamic processes play in organizational life also leads to greater insight about leadership. Understanding humankind's complex nature leads to a more realistic understanding of why leaders act the way they do. Anyone wanting to create or manage an effective organization needs to understand the dynamics of leadership and the intricacies of superior-subordinate relationships.

The study of leadership is difficult because (as one wit said) leadership is like pornography: hard to define, but easy to recognize. At its heart, however, leadership is about human behavior. It revolves around the highly complex interplay between leaders and followers, all put into a particular situational context. Leadership is about understanding the way people and organizations behave, about creating and strengthening relationships, about building commitment, about establishing a group identity, and about adapting behavior to increase effectiveness. It is also about creating meaning. True leaders are merchants of hope, speaking to the collective imagination of their followers, co-opting them to join them in a great adventure. Great leaders inspire people to move beyond personal, egoistic motives—to transcend themselves, as it were—and as a result they get the best out of their people. In short, exemplary leadership makes a positive difference, whatever the context (Burns, 1978; Bass, 1985; Bennis and Nanus, 1986; Kets de Vries, 1994, 2006a; Pfeffer, 1998; Stogdill, 1974).

Contrary to the writings of various management theorists who attribute all variations in leadership effectiveness to environmental constraints, psychodynamic processes between leader and led have a great influence. That is not to minimize the context in which leaders operate. But a company can have all the "environmental" advantages in the world—strong financial resources, enviable market position, and state-of-the-art technology—and still fail in the absence of leadership. Without it, environmental advantages melt away and the organization, like a driverless car, runs downhill.

What the clinical orientation to the study of leadership demonstrates more clearly than other conceptual frameworks is that leaders need to recognize that people differ in their motivational patterns (Kets de Vries, 2006a, 2007a). Good leaders see their followers not as one-dimensional creatures but as complex and paradoxical entities, people who radiate a combination of soaring idealism and gloomy pessimism, stubborn short-sightedness and courageous vision, narrow-minded suspicion and open-handed trust, irrational envy and greed and unbelievable unselfishness.

Taking the emotional pulse of followers, both individually and as a group, is essential, but that alone does not comprise effective leadership. The essence of leadership is the ability to use identified motivational patterns to influence others—in other words, to get people voluntarily to do things that they would not otherwise do. Hopefully those things are of a positive nature, but there is nothing inherently moral about motivating people: leadership can be used for bad ends as well as good. History is full of men and women whose leadership was highly "effective" despite pursuing despicable goals—people such as Joseph Stalin, Adolf Hitler, Pol Pot, Saddam Hussein, and Robert Mugabe (Kets de Vries, 2004a; Khurana, 2002). Even well-intentioned leaders are not without a shadow side, unfortunately; if they have a distorted view of reality, they may use their followers to attain goals that benefit neither the organization nor its employees.

The Vicissitudes of Narcissism

When we talk about leaders, we cannot avoid tackling the subject of narcissism, for it lies at the heart of leadership (Kernberg, 1975; Kohut, 1971, 1985; Kets de Vries, 1989, 2001). A solid dose of narcissism is a prerequisite for anyone who hopes to rise to the top of an organization. Narcissism offers leaders a foundation for conviction about the righteousness of their cause. The leader's conviction that his or her group, organization, or country has a special mission inspires loyalty and group identification; the strength (and even inflexibility) of the leader's worldview gives followers something to identify with and hold on to. Narcissism is a toxic drug, however. Although it is a key ingredient for success, it does not take much before a leader suffers from an overdose. The combination of narcissistic disposition and the pressures of a leadership position can have disastrous consequences. The challenge is how to keep sane people sane in insane places.

A closer look at narcissism confirms the link between childhood and adult behavior. When we trace narcissism back to its roots, we return to a person's infancy. We have to remember that the process of growing up is necessarily accompanied by a degree of frustration. During intrauterine existence, human beings are, in effect, on automatic pilot: any needs that exist are taken care of immediately. This situation changes the moment a baby makes its entry into the world. In dealing with the frustrations of trying to make his or her needs and wants known, and in coping with feelings of helplessness, the infant tries to regain the original impression of the perfection and bliss of intrauterine life by creating both a grandiose, exhibitionistic image of the self and an all-powerful, idealized image of the parents (Kohut, 1971). Over time, and with "good enough" care, these two configurations are "tamed" by the forces of reality—especially by parents, siblings, caretakers, and teachers, who modify the infant's exhibitionism and channel the existing grandiose fantasies into socially acceptable behavior. How the major caretakers react to the child's struggle with the paradoxical quandary of infancy—how to resolve the tension between helplessness and the grandiose sense of self found in all children—is paramount to the child's psychological health. The resolution of that tension is what determines a person's feelings of potency or impotence, omnipotence or helplessness. Inadequate resolution of these quandaries due to dysfunctional parenting—understimulation, overstimulation, or highly inconsistent treatment—may leave a legacy of insecurity (Kohut and Wolf, 1978), often producing feelings of shame, guilt, humiliation, rage, envy, spitefulness, a desire for vengeance, and a hunger for personal power and status, which can be acted out in highly destructive ways in adulthood.

We have classified narcissism as either *constructive* or *reactive*, with excess narcissism generally falling in the latter category and healthy narcissism generally falling in the former (Kets de Vries, 1985). Constructive narcissists are those people fortunate enough to have had caretakers who knew how to provide age-appropriate frustration—that is, enough to challenge but not to overwhelm—and who provided a supportive environment, leading to feelings of trust and to a sense of control over one's actions. People exposed to such parenting tend, as adults, to be relatively well balanced; to have a positive sense of self-esteem, a capacity for introspection, and an empathetic outlook; and to radiate a sense of positive vitality.

Although constructive narcissists are no strangers to the pursuit of greatness, they are not searching for personal power alone. Rather, they have a vision of a better organization or society and want to realize that vision with the help of others. They take advice and consult with others, although they are prepared to make the ultimate decisions. As transformational leaders they inspire others not only to be better at what they do, but also to entirely *change* what they do.

Reactive narcissistic leaders, on the other hand, were not as fortunate as children. As a result, they are left in adulthood with a legacy of feelings of deprivation, insecurity, and inadequacy. Some reactive narcissistic leaders may engage in reparative efforts, but that is not the usual scenario. As a way of mastering their feelings of inadequacy and insecurity, they may develop a sense of entitlement, believing that they deserve special treatment and that rules and regulations apply only to others. They may develop an exaggerated sense of self-importance and self-grandiosity and a concomitant need for admiration. Furthermore, not having had many empathic experiences as children, they typically lack empathy and are often unable to experience how others feel.

Many reactive narcissistic leaders become fixated on issues of power, status, prestige, and superiority. To them, life turns into a zero-sum game: there are winners and losers. They are preoccupied with looking out for number one. They are often driven toward achievement and attainment by the need to get even for perceived slights experienced in childhood. (The so-called Monte Cristo complex, named after the protagonist in Alexandre Dumas's *The Count of Monte Cristo*, refers to feelings of envy, spite, revenge, and/or vindictive triumph over others—in short, the need to get even for real or imagined hurts.) Reactive narcissistic leaders are not prepared to share power. On the contrary, as leaders they surround themselves with yes-men. Unwilling to tolerate disagreement and dealing poorly with criticism, such leaders rarely consult with colleagues, preferring to make all decisions on their own. When they do consult with others, such consultation is little more than ritualistic. They use others as a kind of Greek chorus, expecting followers to agree to whatever they suggest.

Many reactive narcissistic leaders learn little from defeat. When setbacks occur, such leaders don't take personal responsibility; instead, they scapegoat others in the organization, passing on the blame. Even when things are going well, they can be cruel and verbally abusive to their subordinates, and they are prone to outbursts of rage when things don't go their way. Likewise, perceiving a personal attack even where none is intended, they may erupt when followers rebel against their distorted view of the world. Such "tantrums," reenactments of childhood behavior, originate in earlier feelings of helplessness and humiliation. Given the power that such leaders now hold, the impact of their rage can be devastating, intimidating followers, who then themselves regress to more childlike behavior.

Transference: The Matrix for Interpersonal and Group Processes

An essential element in the leader-follower interface is transference, or the act of using relationship patterns from the past to deal with situations in the present. Part of the human condition, transference can be viewed as a confusion in time and place (Freud, 1905, 1933; Etchegoyen, 1991; Kets de Vries, 2006a, 2007b). In essence, transference means that no relationship is a new relationship; each relationship is colored by previous relationships. Though the word *transference* conjures up images of the analyst's couch, it is a phenomenon that all of us are familiar with: all of us act out transferential (or historical) reactions on a daily basis, regardless of what we do. The psychological imprints of crucial early caregivers—particularly our parents—cause this confusion in time and place, making us act toward others in the present as if they were significant people from the past, and these imprints stay with us and guide our interactions throughout our life. Though we are generally unaware of experiencing confusion in time and place, the mismatch between the reality of our work situation and our subconscious scenario—colleagues are not parents or siblings, after all—may lead to bewilderment, anxiety, depression, anger, and even aggression.

There are two subtypes of transferential pattern that are especially common in leadership situations (and that are often exaggerated in reactive narcissists): *mirroring* and *idealizing*. It is said that the first mirror a baby looks into is the mother's face. Predictably, one's identity and one's mind are heavily shaped by contact with one's mother, particularly during the early, narcissistic period of development. Starting with that first mirror, the process of mirroring—that is, taking our cues about being and behaving from those around us—becomes an ongoing aspect of our daily life and the relationships we have with others.

For organizations, this mirroring dynamic between leader and follower can become collusive. Followers are eager to use their leaders as mirrors. They use leaders to reflect what they like to see, and leaders rarely mind, finding the affirmation of followers hard to resist. The result is often a mutual admiration society. Membership in that society may encourage leaders to take actions designed to shore up their image rather than serve the needs of the organization.

Idealizing is another universal transferential process: as a way of coping with feelings of helplessness, we idealize people important to us, beginning with our first caretakers, assigning powerful imagery to them. Through this idealizing process, we hope, as mentioned earlier, to combat helplessness and acquire some of the power of the person admired. Idealizing transference thus serves as a protective shield for followers.

Idealizing and mirroring have their positive side: they can generate an adhesive bond that helps to keep the organization together during crisis. Because they temporarily suspend the values of reality testing and self-criticism, they are key tools in the creation of a common vision and the generation of "committed action" on the part of followers. When these transferential patterns persist, however, followers gradually stop responding to the leader according to the reality of the situation, allowing their past (unrealistic) hopes and fantasies to govern their interactions with the leader.

Reactive narcissistic leaders are especially responsive to such admiration. Idealization fatally seduces them into believing that they are in fact the illusory creatures their followers have made them out to be. It is a two-way street, of course: followers project their fantasies onto their leaders, and leaders mirror themselves in the glow of their followers. The result is that disposition and position work together to wreak havoc on reality testing: they are happy to find themselves in a hall of mirrors that lets them hear and see only what they want to hear and see. In that illusory hall, boundaries that define normal work processes disappear—at least for the entitled leader, who feels diminishing restraint regarding actions that are inappropriate, irresponsible, or just plainly unethical. Any follower who calls the leader on such behavior or points out cracks in the mirrors risks inciting a temper tantrum, as noted earlier.

Leader Derailment

Given the pressures leaders are subjected to, it is easy for them to act in inappropriate ways. And given their position of power, their actions can have dire consequences on their organizations. It is always tempting to assign responsibility for the failure factor in leadership to external forces, citing the words of Euripides: "Whom the gods want to destroy they first make mad." But we can find responsibility much closer to home, in the leaders' own shadow sides. We can list some of the more common reasons leaders fall victim to the failure factor.

Isolation from Reality

A major contributing factor to faulty decision making has to do with a leader's isolation from reality—too much information filtering takes place. Followers may, with good or bad intentions, contribute significantly to those misperceptions and misguided actions. Here, as we described above, the role of transference is important.

What happens is that leaders become surrounded by "liars"—people who tell them what they want to hear. Leaders need to recognize that *candor flees authority* and that many of the people who report to them are lying to some degree—whether consciously (for reasons of political expediency) or unconsciously (as a transferential reaction). In hierarchical situations, people have a tendency to tell their superiors what they want to hear. People who don't acknowledge this are fooling themselves. Given the prevalence of mirror and idealizing transference, careless senior executives will eventually find themselves surrounded by sycophants. Guarding against this means creating an organizational culture where frank feedback is encouraged. Leaders need continually to ask themselves whether their own mirror hunger is encouraging dishonesty in the ranks. Many leaders don't realize the extent to which people project their fantasies on them; how much subordinates are inclined to tell them what they want to hear as a way of dealing with their own feelings of insecurity and helplessness; how willing subordinates are to attribute special qualities to someone simply because of the office he or she holds. The process by which executives are corrupted by power is so insidious that without that whispered reminder, they don't sense their humanity slipping away. Even those who recognize these tendencies don't necessarily do anything to counter them. And that failure can lead a company astray. In fact, it's a lucky company that survives it.

Conflict Avoidance

Though we tend to think of leaders as dominant and unafraid, many have a tendency toward conflict avoidance. Often executives have a desperate need to be liked and approved. The need to be loved echoes in every line scripted for their inner theater. Early childhood experiences may have contributed to a fear of rejection. Afraid to do anything that might threaten acceptance, they're unable (or unwilling) to make difficult decisions or to exercise authority. They become mere empty suits, unwilling to accept the fact—and it *is* a fact—that boundary setting sometimes takes precedence over conciliation. Conflict avoidance is neither a successful nor, in the end, a popular management style: the leader who always appeases is like someone who feeds crocodiles hoping that they'll eat him last. There's nothing bad about being nice, but there comes a point when every leader has to say, "My way or the highway." We don't have an exact formula for success, but we know a sure formula for failure, and that's trying to please everybody.

Abrasive Behavior

Another pattern that leads to leadership ineffectiveness is the tyrannization of subordinates. This pattern describes those abrasive (and sometimes sadistically oriented) executives who obviously graduated with honors from the Joseph Stalin School of Management. Former Prime Minister Margaret Thatcher possessed some of these abrasive characteristics. She would make statements such as "I don't mind how much my ministers talk as long as they do what I say," or "I'm extraordinarily patient provided I get my own way in the end." The Iron Lady could be a bit of a bulldozer.

We can make assumptions about the inner theater of these individuals. For example, there's often a history of misplaced parental rejection or hostility—that is, the child has been the inappropriate recipient of parental anger. As the most vulnerable member within the family system, the child is the most convenient outlet for displaced aggression, easy to scapegoat and label as "bad." This sort of treatment leads to feelings of resentment. Some children, faced with the powerlessness of such a situation, simply give up. Others confront it, deny their powerlessness, and attempt to gain the upper hand through provocative, belligerent behavior (Kets de Vries, 2006a).

Furthermore, the tyrannization of subordinates sometimes triggers a response that Anna Freud (1966) called "identification-with-the-aggressor syndrome." Through unconscious impersonation of the "aggressor" (that is, the abusive boss), subordinates assume the leader's attributes and thus transform themselves from threatened to threatening, from helpless victims to powerful actors. This is a defensive maneuver, a way of controlling the severe anxiety caused by the aggressor. The people in the one-down position hope to acquire some of the power that the aggressor possesses. Unfortunately, all they accomplish is to become aggressors themselves, thus increasing the total amount of organizational aggression. The corporate culture created by the key players at Enron is a good example.

Paranoia: The Disease of Kings

Intel's Andy Grove told us long ago that "only the paranoid survive." But this was not a plea for greater mental illness at work. Paranoia exists on a spectrum that moves from normal and sensible vigilance, through paranoid behavior, and on to an ultimately delusional state. Grove argued for vigilance, not manic suspicion.

Still, the paranoid urge may be hard to control once it takes hold of people. They may then succumb to the pervasive and unwarranted suspicion of others, guided by a fantasy that they are out to get them. They believe that trusting others is foolish, because confidential information will be used against them. Other people's actions are misread and misinterpreted.

At the heart of the paranoid disposition there is frequently a negative childhood experience. As children, paranoid individuals may have been exposed to an extremely intrusive and controlling parenting style that fostered feelings of inadequacy or helplessness. Shame and humiliation may have been used as controlling devices by their parents. Early experiences of being spied on, demeaned, depreciated, and/or taken advantage of lay the foundation for a lack of basic trust, creating a need for vigilance at all times to safeguard against trickery, deception, and attack.

Paranoid leaders deploy three defense mechanisms: they split people into camps, they blame others for feelings they themselves possess, and they try to deny the reality of the current situation. They may also fabricate fantasy versions of the truth. Unavoidably, leaders will create some real, nonimaginary enemies. For leaders, healthy suspiciousness can be an adaptive mechanism, a rational response to a world populated by both real and imagined enemies. "Healthy" Groveian paranoia, however, keeps itself in check. If suspicion isn't moderated by a sense of reality, it slips over into paranoia.

Effective leaders ground their behavior in sound political practices that limit and test danger, and they rely on trusted associates to help them stay safe and sane. Unfortunately, leaders with a paranoid disposition are often too isolated to engage in constructive reality testing, seeing hidden meanings and secret coalitions everywhere.

Micromanagement

Another cause for leadership derailment is excessive control. The control freak puts the *micro* in micromanagement. Rules and regulations, order and planning—these are the guiding disciplines of micromanagers. They fear the world will fall apart if they don't adhere to the highest standards at all times, if they don't check every detail, or if the rules are disobeyed. They're obsessed with "shoulds" and "musts" and the need to drive themselves harder. Not trusting anyone else to do a job as well as they can do themselves, micromanagers are unwilling to delegate. As a matter of fact, one of the most difficult transitions for many executives to make is to go from a functional orientation to that of general management. It is hard to give up one's professional identity. Lack of trust in the capabilities of others has a stifling effect on all organizational processes.

For these people, the internalized image of harsh, judgmental parents is ever-present, haunting them and feeding a punitive inner conscience. Thus it appears that people with a controlling disposition are caught in a permanent struggle between obedience and defiance, a troubling unresolved conflict instilled by parental overcontrol; in childhood, they had to live up to parental expectations or risk condemnation.

There is a well-known *New Yorker* cartoon that shows an executive coming home to his wife and saying, "I did it. I just fired all three hundred and twenty-four of them. I'm going to run the plant by myself!" Funny as this cartoon may be, micromanagement clearly isn't the way to get the best out of people. In fact, all it's good for is ruining morale and destroying organizations.

Feeling Like an Impostor

Many of these executives experience feeling like an impostor. People suffering from this problem always doubt that they measure up to others' expectations. They live with the secret conviction that they are less intelligent and competent than they appear to others. High achievers in particular possess a deep-seated fear of being "found out." Despite their obvious successes, they nurture secret, intense feelings of fraudulence. Somehow they are sure that one day, someone will point in their direction and expose them for the real frauds they are. No matter how utterly ridiculous and untrue this is, and all the evidence to the contrary, these individuals have a distorted perception that they are incompetent, clueless, or stupid (Kets de Vries, 2005a).

Characterized by a low sense of self-esteem, they tend to externalize success, attributing it to extreme effort or external factors such as luck, contacts, timing, perseverance, charm, or otherwise having "fooled" others into thinking they are smarter and more capable than they "know" themselves to be. They stubbornly refuse to recognize that they really may be talented and gifted. Failures are interpreted as internal faults or lack of certain abilities. They continue to downplay their strengths and exaggerate or are intolerant of any deficiencies or weaknesses. They live under a Damocles' sword of their own suspension, fearful of their inability to repeat past success. They are their own harshest critics.

The perfectionism of these self-nominated impostors has its positive sides, but can easily become dysfunctional. People who feel imposturous are unable to experience true satisfaction and happiness because they never believe that they are doing things well enough. Their fear of making mistakes contributes to a high state of anxiety.

Since these people believe their successes have been ill gotten, success brings a feeling of guilt and fear. Not surprisingly, these individuals are masters at snatching defeat out of the jaws of victory. Having a tenuous self-view and low expectancy of success may result in their unconsciously engaging in deliberate (albeit self-defeating) ploys to provide an alibi for poor performance. Following extreme over-preparation, these people will worry and suffer acute self-doubt and anxiety—experiences that can result in procrastination and immobility and contribute to failure. Complicatedly, setting high, unattainable goals may provide an alibi for their failure.

Hypomanic Behavior

While hypomania can contribute to creative imagination and expression, research also shows that it can be a highly destructive force. Manic executives, possessed with apparently boundless energy, push themselves and others to the limit. But they're so hyperactive that they don't always notice what it is they're doing (even when what they're doing is completely wrong). Hypomanic executives usually have an inflated sense of self-esteem, as well as an unbending conviction of the correctness and importance of their ideas. Although this sense of conviction can be used for the good, it can also have disastrous consequences. "I'm always right" thinking and behavior tend to disregard valuable alternatives and contribute to poor judgment; this in turn can lead to chaotic patterns of personal and professional relationships. The grandiosity of hypomanics often leads them into impulsive involvement in questionable endeavors, which can jeopardize the stability and success of an organization.

Hypomanic episodes usually alternate with depressive episodes during which people lose interest and enjoyment in normally pleasurable acts and events. Hypomania, being part of the bipolar disposition encompasses a wide range of mood disorders and temperaments, varying in severity from cyclothymia—which is characterized by noticeable (but not debilitating) changes in mood, behavior, and thinking—to full-blown, life-threatening manic-depression. What makes the behavior of people with any of the bipolar variants unique is the cyclical nature of their moods. These people constantly swing back and forth between two opposite poles of emotion, which can cause impairment in professional functioning and in relationships. (Klein, 1948; Jamison, 1993).

Generational Envy

Executives inept at leadership development may suffer from generational envy. One indication of this is resentment of young "upstarts." They're like the mythical figure of Cronus, who ate his own children. They send promising subordinates to the organizational equivalent of Siberia or fire them for supposed incompetence—a "murder" if ever there was one—and then rationalize their fate so effectively that they think they're doing both organization and subordinates a favor.

Many senior executives have a hard time dealing with their successor, even if they themselves have named the crown prince. Archaic Oedipal feelings about parent-child competitiveness seem to reemerge. A major reason is that CEOs are, almost by definition, masters at power calcula-tion; power is an important property to them, and they know how to acquire and manipulate it. Appointing a successor changes the power equation. Power starts to flow away to the newly named candidate, and CEOs experience subtle changes in power relationship patterns almost immediately. Loyalties quickly shift; relationships realign; new power structures begin to emerge. It has often been said, tongue in cheek, that the major task of a CEO is to find his likely successor and kill the bastard. Unfortunately, clinging to power through the derailment of that succes-sor usually has disastrous effects on the organization.

The acid test of excellent leadership is what happens when the leader is no longer there. How seamless is the succession? Does the process occur without too much drama? Is the company still perform-ing successfully after the old CEO is gone? Has the leadership in the company done sufficient planning for leadership succession? If not, give some thought to Charles de Gaulle's comment that the graveyards of the world are full of indispensable men. If after reflection you really believe that you're indispensable, put your finger into a glass of water, withdraw it, and note the hole that you've left.

The Role of the Followers

We should never underestimate the impact of the followers' own need for power, and the detrimental impact their actions can have on the organization. The world is full of Machiavellian followers who deprive their leaders of critical feedback for the purpose of self-enhancement. The desire to satisfy their own addiction to power may cause them to create situations that contribute to leadership derailment. In such instances, political considerations take over from reality. Just as the shadow side of the leader's personality can have devastating effects, so can the shadow side of the followers. It is possible that the more individuals are in pursuit of power, the greater the temptation to contaminate the current process of influence by distorting the leader's perception of reality. No actual or intended leader is immune from taking actions, well intentioned or otherwise, that can lead to the worst of consequences; and no follower is immune from being an active participant in the process.

Given these collusive practices, leaders and followers need to work at understanding themselves, both the positive and the negative parts of their personalities, and being open to all forms of information and feedback. Additionally, and importantly, leaders need to be sensitive to what followers are really telling them. Finally, leaders need to help followers become leaders in their own right. They need to give their followers opportunities to learn; they need to give them constructive feedback. Leaders need to be aware of the emotional needs of subordinates and accommodate them. Leaders need to harness the creativity of individuals within their organizations. The acid test of exemplary leaders, however, is their ability to preserve their own hold on reality, to see things as they are, avoiding the intense pressure from those around them to participate in these distorted mirroring games.

Changing Leaders

It is here where leadership developmental programs can play a critical part. But to have a real impact, these developmental programs should go beyond simple problem solving and help executives better understand their inner world, and the effect their leadership style has on others (Kets de Vries, 2005b; Kets de Vries and Korotov, 2007). In addition, these programs also need to go beyond mere self-understanding and have an action component. The acid test will be to have the executives go beyond having a "dream," and implement whatever good intentions they have to deal better with their personal and organizational dilemmas. To make a leadership program truly transformational, it will be necessary to help executives identify the forces that drive their behavior and contribute to conflicts.

We have learned—having run programs for CEOs for many years—that leaders frequently join executive education programs for more reasons than the obvious ones of gaining additional knowledge and insights into the effective operation of organizations. Frequently, they see it as an opportunity to engage in a form of self-renewal. From our experience, many of the participants in our programs are struggling with complicated personal and organizational issues, including conflicted work relationships, the disappointment of career setbacks, doubts about their leadership capabilities, feeling like a fake or failure, boredom, and even burnout. Additionally, many (as we have suggested earlier) suffer from narcissistic problems, having surrounded themselves with yes-men, creating a kind of "narcissistic soup" that endangers the future of their organizations. Others may have grown too comfortable in their current position and lost the capacity for out-of-the-box thinking, making them incapable of dealing with discontinuous change in a creative way (Kets de Vries, 1989, 2001, 2005a, 2005b, 2006a, 2007b, 2008; Khurana, 2004; Hamel, 2002).

In some instances, the executive (and/or others in the organization) becomes aware of this dysfunctional behavior pattern, which leads to participation in an executive program. In others, although an individual's dysfunctional behavior may not yet be visible, he or she feels a sense of unease and decides that some form of preemptive action is needed to forestall future trouble.

Various crisis points can bring the realization that some form of change is needed, typically the following: loss (separation, divorce, missed promotion opportunity, or job loss); developmental imbalance (certain important life expectations remain unfulfilled); interpersonal conflict; symptomatology reflecting inner turmoil (eating or behavioral disorders, sexual dysfunction, and insomnia); work/life imbalance; and fundamental questions about the meaning of existence and actions (Frankl, 1962; Kets de Vries, 2008). A leadership development program is often seen as a possible solution.

Once executives enter a program, the specific developmental needs of the participants need to be taken into consideration in the program design and delivery to enable change to occur. In guiding executives through a transformational process, we have found a three-triangle framework extremely helpful in conceptualizing some of the dynamics. These triangles can be described as the mental life triangle, the conflict triangle, and the relationship triangle.

The first triangle identifies the need to take both cognitive and emotional processes into consideration if we want to create changes in behavior. The second describes how psychic conflict arises from unacceptable feelings or thoughts that prompt anxiety and defensive reactions. The third, relationship, triangle explains how an individual's childhood experiences create patterns of response that are repeated throughout life.

The Mental Life Triangle

The mental life triangle dictates the script of a person's inner theater and links cognition, emotion, and behavior. It is a distillation of peoples' responses to their motivational need systems, and it is often the basis on which choice is made (Lichtenberg and Schonbar, 1992). Because change is about making new, different choices, executives have to be swayed both cognitively *and* emotionally for any change effort to be successful. People need to understand cognitively the advantages that a change effort will bring. Cognition alone, however, is not enough; people also need to be touched emotionally. Affect and cognition go hand in hand in contributing to specific behavior patterns (McCullough Vaillant, 1997).

Psychotherapists, psychoanalysts, psychiatrists, and leadership coaches help people to make long-lasting personal change. Senior executives, however, are unlikely to seek improvement in their psychological condition via lengthy therapeutic procedures. They look for different, more time-efficient methods to reinvent themselves and tend to look for help only when they are already in trouble or experiencing a considerable amount of discomfort. Years of working with senior managers has made us realize, however, that signing up for a group seminar designed for senior executives will be much less threatening than making an appointment with a therapist. The challenge for faculty becomes to create a meaningful and enduring learning experience, given these executives' short attention span and self-centeredness.

In helping executives on this journey toward personal transformation and change, executive education providers need to find nontraditional ways to overcome participants' resistance. This often necessitates making people aware of problems of a preconscious or unconscious nature. Furthermore, faculty also need to ensure that changes in behavior patterns will be lasting, more than temporary "flights into health"—transient highs of the sort produced by the pulp psychology of too many self-help guides and life coaches of dubious credibility. We need to help these executives realize that it takes a lot of courage to release the familiar and seemingly secure and to embrace the new.

The Conflict Triangle

A part and parcel of the human condition is the "triangle of conflict," the three sides of which are hidden feelings, defensive behaviors, and conflict (Malan, 1963, 1976; Malan and Osimo, 1992). Every individual experiences conflict due to unacceptable feelings or ideas that create anxiety and lead to defensive reactions. Ironically, defensive behavior stirs only a vague awareness of what an individual is protecting him- or herself against, because the exact nature of the unacceptable feelings rarely reaches consciousness. In fact, the suppression of unacceptable feelings can be viewed as the *task* of defensive behavior: it works to avoid the individual becoming aware of them, or experiencing them. Indications of defensive behavior include changing the subject when certain issues are raised, denying that there is a problem (or simply ignoring an admitted problem), and rationalizing questionable acts. When we see these indications, it is our task to help participants explore what such behavior is erecting defenses against. What are the benefits of continuing what seems at first sight a self-destructive path?

The challenge for executives is to overcome defensive barriers and identify the central issue(s) they are trying to deal with. Fortunately, in a transformational leadership program they are not alone in this particular task. Through a process of *confrontation and clarification* by faculty and fellow participants, greater specificity will be created (Menninger 1958; Kets de Vries and Miller, 1984; Etchegoyen, 1991; Kets de Vries, 2006a; Kets de Vries et al., 2007a). Participants work on their issues by presenting them to the other members of the seminar in a plenary or small group setting. *Confrontation* takes the form of probing but not threatening questions about issues and patterns of behavior. These questions, and the kinds of responses they elicit, help to make the participants' defenses more explicit, allowing a better understanding of the underlying feelings and conflicts. It helps create a balance sheet listing the advantages and disadvantages of remaining in their present state. Here the notion of articulating a client's immunity system against change, thus clarifying competing commitments, has been shown to be a highly effective eye opener (Kegan and Lahey, 2001). Furthermore, in helping the person on the road toward change, we have found it useful to clarify the concept of "secondary gain" to our clients—that is, the interpersonal or social advantages gained indirectly from a problem (Fishbain et al., 1995). Only when executives become more cognizant of why they behave the way they do can they engage in lasting change.

The concept of a leadership program as a transformation laboratory presupposes that many risky things can be done within the psychological safety boundaries of this transitional space (Winnicott, 1951; Korotov, 2005). Many executives find themselves for the first time in an environment where they can be genuinely challenged without real risks. What makes the process effective is that each executive finds him- or herself in a challenging situation, but also one where people care and share experiences. The faculty and the other participants serve as guiding figures and sparring partners.

In *clarification*, the problems brought to the fore through confrontation and feedback are analyzed more closely and brought into sharper focus. Clarification helps to sort out cause-and-effect relationships and fosters an appreciation of the connections between past and current patterns of behavior, setting the stage for various forms of interpretation and the creation of greater insight about a specific problem.

Generally, the personal resolutions that grow out of the confrontation and clarification stages lay the groundwork for a considered and detailed reappraisal of dysfunctional patterns, of career and life goals, and for experimentation with new alternatives to deal with organizational and personal issues. Going through this process also furthers the development of new ideas and action plans. By creating greater awareness of a person's inner theater, confrontation and clarification work to decrease ambiguity about what an individual would really like to accomplish, leading to greater peace of mind. The empathy expressed by the other participants, the appreciation that other people truly care, encourages the person to take greater control of his or her life. The support given by the group contributes to the creation of a tipping point to take specific actions executives may have thought about but were never able to implement.

In the creation of a tipping point, some of the concepts of motivational interviewing also have been found extremely helpful. Motivational interviewing is a directive, person-centered, clinical method to help resolve ambivalence and resistance to change, originally developed in addiction counseling (Miller and Rollnick, 2002). Using this very subtle, nonconfrontational intervention technique, clients become ready to reevaluate their perceptions and more prepared to discuss the pros and cons of change. The intervention technique contributing to change talk includes such elements as empathic listening, having the clients (not the facilitator) discuss the ambivalence (and have them argue for change), engage in resistance "judo," and emphasizing self-efficacy.

The Relationship Triangle

The relationship triangle concerns the transference processes mentioned earlier. It points out that all of us, in all situations, have to deal with two kinds of relationship (Freud, 1905; Malan, 1963; Greenson, 1967; Malan and Osimo, 1992; Molnos, 1995). First, there is the "real" relationship between the person and the "other"—a relationship between two colleagues at work, for example, or between an employer and an employee.

This real relationship becomes the context for another, more elusive relationship grounded in the past (Freud, 1905; Racker, 1968; Luborsky and Crits-Cristoph, 1990).Obviously, the relationships that have the most lasting potency, coloring almost every subsequent encounter, are those that we have with our earliest caregivers. Our adult behavior has its roots in those privileged, early relationships.

As we relive our earlier, primary relationships again and again, behavior patterns emerge that direct the way we act toward people in the present: although we are now in a very different situation as adults, our responses are still fundamentally those conditioned in our early child-hood. In other words, without even being aware of it, we are often con-fused about person, time, and place. Like it or not, our past relationships have solidified into organizing themes in our personality structure. In our everyday life, we experience attitudes, thoughts, and emotional responses that, although appropriate to the interpersonal processes gov-erning our earlier years, may have become maladaptive. Anyone hoping to make sense of interpersonal encounters at anything but an intuitive level needs to understand (and be alert to) these transferential processes.

Leadership programs sometimes use the relationships triangle—with its three sides of self, present-other, and past-other—to illustrate the effects of transference. By deconstructing conflict situations, participants come to understand that the earliest feelings they experienced toward others are repeated in relation to people in the present—including, for the duration of the program, the program itself, the other participants, and the faculty. This triangle provides a conceptual structure for assessing patterns of response by pointing out the similarity of past relationships to what happens in the present. It helps explain certain interpersonal prob-lems that the executive may be experiencing at home and at work. Trans-ferential interpretation is a crucial tool in the change toolbox. When a person understands old patterns of interaction and then learns to recog-nize the dysfunctionality of these patterns in current relationships, the process of transformation and change is more likely to be successful.

Facilitating the Process of Change

A leadership program within the context of a business school will encourage executives to look into the original sources of their behavior and start the process of self-exploration. After all, everybody accepts, at least on a rational level, that leading others involves understanding oneself and the way we present ourselves in interactions with others.

Nevertheless, for a true understanding and transformation of self to take place, a number of challenges need to be addressed in the design and delivery of transformational leadership programs.

The Selection of Participants

The first challenge concerns the criteria for selecting program participants prepared to engage in a change effort. In order to create a safe environment where people can play with cognitions, emotions, and behavior, participants need to be willing to engage in self-exploration and self-experimentation. Given the stress that these programs put on their participants, only reasonably well-adapted people will have the psychological strength required to participate and, importantly, to be of help to themselves and others. Fortunately, most successful executives possess a considerable degree of emotional stability. In spite of that, however, we need to be vigilant in assessing the executive's capacity to gain from such transformational programs. And whatever we do, honoring the Hippocratic oath, "Do no harm," is essential.

Among the criteria for acceptance are the level of motivation to learn and change; the capacity to be open and responsive; interpersonal connectedness; emotion management skills; a degree of psychological mindedness; the capacity for introspection; responsiveness to others' observations; the ability to tolerate depression; and flexibility. We believe that all these criteria need to be assessed before the start of the program through a combination of personal interviews with the program faculty and assessment through essay writing (which will reveal the level of a participant's skill at putting thoughts into words). The process of application and interviewing gives the candidate a sneak preview of the program he or she is applying for, and the opportunity to evaluate the initial fit between the program and his or her developmental needs. An in-depth acceptance process also allows faculty to assess whether the candidate will be able to cope with the psychological demands of the program and whether he or she will fit with the group. This pre-program work is the first step in the change process, as it not only brings many psychological issues to the fore, but is de facto the start of the program as it will be the beginning of the process of self-discovery.

Finding the Focal Issue

The second challenge concerns the identification of the focal issue that each participant needs to work on and how to fit this into the overall structure and content of the program. In order to change, executives need to be clear about what it is that they *want* to change. They have to identify their central problem(s) and be able to formulate explicit, tractable improvement goals. When people tell their life story (and listen to the stories of the other participants), they are often able to identify specific themes that began in their past and continue into the present. We have noted that, more often than not, the stories people tell about themselves center on seemingly insoluble dilemmas grounded in misguided perceptions of the world.

The act of articulating one's personal narrative takes on a major transformational role (Loewenberg, 1982; Spence, 1982; McAdams, 1993; Rennie, 1994; McLeod, 1997). It becomes a way of exploring the self, leading to questions such as the following: Who am I? Where am I going? How will I get there? Working through internal crises and developmental challenges helps participants to arrive at meaningful personal life integration. In addition, listening to others' stories is a highly effective way of understanding one's self. What we have learned from the feedback given by the participants is that every story resonates with the listeners.

In order to maximize the benefits of storytelling, opportunities must be created for people to tell their stories and for the audience (the other participants) to identify the issues together and talk them through. Every story will reveal specific present-day dilemmas that have grown out of underlying problems—dilemmas that can be remedied by addressing those deeper issues. These dilemmas will be the basis for "change contracts" between the presenter and the rest of the participants.

In our programs, we create opportunities for each participant to take a "hot seat" and present his or her stories to the rest of the group, or to participate in small group coaching sessions in which participants take turns presenting their stories, supported by the creation of a "self-portrait," a debrief of the results of a 360-degree leadership feedback package, a review of personal feedback from work and nonwork environments, and observations and reflections of other participants (Kets de Vries, 2004b, 2004c, 2005b, 2006b, 2007a; Kets de Vries et al., 2007c).

Trust is, of course, essential. As the program unfolds, participants develop the trust necessary to be able to open up and learn from each other. We have observed that programs consisting of several modules that give people an opportunity to interact with each other over a longer period of time (both in class and through structured out-of-class activities, like working together on assignments or via conference calls) have a significantly higher chance of making a lasting impact on executives than the temporary highs created by one event.

Creating Transitional Space

The third challenge concerns the creation of a safe transitional space. Exploring oneself, one's emotions, and one's behavioral patterns is a stressful undertaking. Change is difficult, and changing oneself is often the most difficult task executives have to handle in their life or career. Even the best-intentioned people rarely manage it single-handedly. Asking for help is difficult, too, especially for successful executives who are closely watched by their internal and external organizational stakeholders. So a major challenge of leadership education providers is how to get others involved in helping the executive initiate and carry through the process of change.

For that purpose our efforts are directed toward creating a transitional space—a safe and empathic identity laboratory—that allows executives the opportunity to "play," to climb out of the rut they find themselves in, helping them to pick up the threads of stagnated development (Winnicott, 1951, 1975; Korotov, 2005). Leaders may be stuck in a psychic prison, trapped by their job or personal circumstances in a life devoid of learning, playfulness, creativity, and pleasure. We go to great lengths to create opportunities for them to reinvent themselves. We help them realize that they *do* have options, that they *can* make choices, and that these options and choices are often within close reach.

As well as short-term dynamic psychotherapy and motivational interviewing, we use a number of eclectic intervention methods to encourage the sense of trust and support that the holding environment of an identity laboratory requires, including positive reframing, encouragement, and the anticipation or rehearsal of difficult situations. *Reframing* is a cognitive technique used to assist people in diffusing or sidestepping a painful situation, thus enhancing self-esteem. An essential part of reframing is assessing a person's strengths—looking not only at what has gone wrong but also at what has gone right in his or her life (Seltzery, 1986; Seligman and Csikszentmihalyi, 2000; Cooperrider and Whitney, 2005). Psychological strengths can then be drawn on to deal with conflicted areas. *Encouragement*, which is closely related to reframing, encompasses reassurance, praise (which, to be helpful, must affirm something that the recipient considers praiseworthy), and empathic comments (Rogers, 1951). *Anticipation* allows a person to move through new situations hypothetically and to weigh different ways of responding. Allowing someone to become better acquainted with a situation reduces anticipatory anxiety. *Rehearsal* allows a person to practice more appropriate ways of engaging in future events, expanding his or her adaptive repertoire (Kilburg, 2000). The purpose of all these interventions is to help the person acquire a greater sense of self-efficacy (Bandura, 1997).

Constructive suggestions about what and how to change are also needed. Within the holding environment of the leadership program, those suggestions should come from both faculty and fellow participants, who can point out better ways of doing things, building on what they have learned listening to each others' stories. Unsurprisingly, many participants have great problem-solving skills.

A safe holding environment gives the individual experimenting with change an opportunity to make a *public commitment* about what changes he or she would like to make. Public commitment accelerates the personal transformation process, because it doubles momentum: it not only influences the person making the commitment (cementing willingness to confront a difficult situation) but also enlists the cooperation of others, a strong reinforcement for change. By taking a public stance, the speaker issues a self-ultimatum: go through with the change or lose face (bearing in mind that there will be a follow-up). Facetiously, we sometimes say that our major allies in the change process are the forces of shame, guilt, and hope.

Again, a multimodular program allows participants to try new behavior patterns, experimenting outside the class, and then report back to the group on the results and learning points of the experiment they staged. Further clarification of goals then takes place, new alternatives are assessed, and new commitments can be made.

Making Change Last

The fourth challenge is concerned with problems of internalization and lasting change. Once workshop participants have identified the focal problems and practiced alternative approaches to dealing with them, they face the critical task of maintaining acquired gains. They need to arrive at a state of self-efficacy. They need the skills to edit the script for their inner theater, even if they fall short of rewriting it. But this kind of inner transformation can only take place once a new way of looking at things has been *internalized* (Kets de Vries, 2005b).

Internalization is a gradual process by which *external* interactions between self and others are taken in and replaced by *internal* representations of these interactions. In these leadership programs, telling (and retelling) one's own story, listening to others' stories, and recognizing similarities between them all consolidate this process of internalization. Work between modules, conference calls with other participants, and peer-coaching sessions held as part of the learning process also contribute to internalization. Once participants leave the group, they have to try to hold on to the insights they have acquired through the internalization process, even though the group is no longer there to provide external reinforcement.

Advantages of Group Intervention

If leadership interventions like this are done within a specific company context (a "natural" top executive working group), they will bring the additional advantage of helping to create a high-performance team. Everyone in the team will have a stake in the other executives' leadership development plans, increasing the chances that something will be made to happen. It also contributes to a boundaryless organization as the members of the top executive team become less focused on defending their turf and develop a more holistic attitude to the organization, a great advantage, given today's highly complex organizational structures. Finally, it will give true meaning to the term "knowledge management," which is more than just setting up a shared database. Knowledge management needs another essential—people have to trust each other. Without trust, there will be no exchange of information. If there is trust, people will engage in constructive problem solving and be more committed and accountable, and organizations will have better results (Kets de Vries, 2005b). (For a summary of the group intervention process, see figure 7-1.)

The Leader-Faculty Dance

We draw on many different intellectual sources to help our clients in the change process, including concepts from psychoanalytic and developmental psychology, group dynamics, management theory, and behavioral/cognitive insights. One theoretical approach that offers

FIGURE 7-1

Group leadership coaching

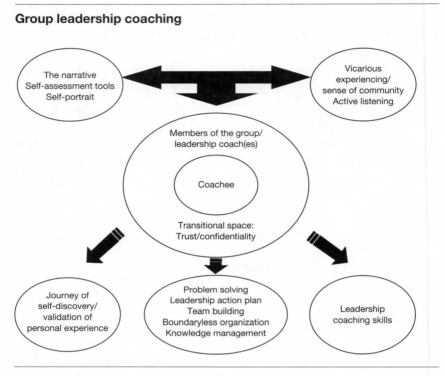

considerable promise in accelerating the process of change has come
from experiments in short-term dynamic and group psychotherapy
(Balint, 1957; Balint et al., 1972; Bion, 1959; Mann, 1973; Sifneos,
1979; Rosenbaum, 1983; Horowitz et al., 1984; Strupp and Binder,
1984; Yalom, 1985; Gustavson, 1986; Molnos, 1995; Groves, 1996;
Rutan and Stone, 2001; Rawson, 2002). These interventions, together
with the motivational interviewing technique (Miller and Rolnick,
2002), overcoming immunity systems (Kegan and Lahey, 2001, 2009),
appreciative inquiry (Cooperrider, Whitney, and Stavros, 2003), and
paradoxical interventions (Weeks and L'Abate, 1982) have been of
great help in creating a tipping point for change. Faculty members
and facilitators trained in these techniques find that, when combined
with a solid dose of empathy and psychological support, they often
result in remarkable progress for their program participants. (For a
summary of the theoretical concepts used in group leadership
coaching, see figure 7-2.)

FIGURE 7-2

IGLC intervention technique: Conceptual models

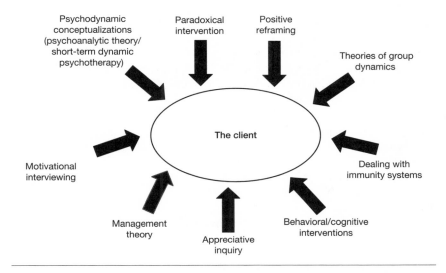

Faculty and facilitators involved in impact-oriented programs should undertake a process of personal self-exploration, experimentation, and change themselves before they try to help others. Creating this kind of transformational laboratory requires a deep understanding of the mental life, conflict, and relationship triangles described earlier. An enormous amount of emotional energy is dispensed when engaging with participants, in order to challenge them while simultaneously showing empathy and care. Last but not least, the time commitment required for these programs is much higher than for more traditional programs.

Although the costs and risks of embarking on transformational leadership programs are high, so are the rewards. These programs allow participants and faculty to become aware that it is the journey of life that counts, not the destination. Embarking on such a journey—letting go of the familiar and secure to embrace the new—takes a lot of courage. But when things no longer make sense, security matters less. In fact, there is more security in adventure and excitement, because there is life in movement and change. As George Bernard Shaw put it, "We don't stop playing because we grow old; we grow old because we stop playing."

References

Balint, M. *The Doctor, the Patient and the Illness.* New York: International Universities Press, 1957.

Balint, M., P.H. Ornstein, and E. Balint. *Focal Psychotherapy.* London: Tavistock, 1972.

Bandura, A. *Self-efficacy: The Exercise of Control.* New York: Freeman, 1997.

Barron, J.W. and M.N. Eagle, eds. *The Interface of Psychoanalysis and Psychology.* Washington, DC: American Psychological Association, 1992.

Bass, B.M. *Leadership and Performance Beyond Expectations.* New York: Free Press, 1985.

Bennis, W., and B. Nanus. *Leadership: The Strategies for Taking Charge.* New York: Harper & Row, 1986.

Bion, W.R. *Experiences in Groups.* London: Tavistock, 1959.

Bowlby, J. *Attachment and Loss.* New York: Basic Books, 1969.

———. *Leadership.* New York: Harper & Row, 1978.

Cooperrider, D.L., and D. Whitney. *Appreciative Inquiry: a Positive Revolution in Change.* San Francisco: Berrett-Koehler, 2005.

Czander, W.M., *The Psychodynamics of Work and Organizations.* New York: Guilford Press, 1933.

DeBoard, R. *The Psychoanalysis of Organisations.* London: Routledge, 1978.

Emde, R.N., "Changing Models of Infancy and the Nature of Early Development: Remodelling the Foundation." *Journal of the American Psychoanalytical Association* 29 (1981): 179–219.

Erikson, E.H., *Childhood and Society.* New York: W.W. Norton, 1963.

Etchegoyen, R. H. *The Fundamentals of Psychoanalytic Technique.* London: Karnac Books, 1991.

Frankl, V. *Man's Search for Meaning: An Introduction to Logotherapy.* Boston: Beacon Press, 1962.

Fishbain, D.A., H.L. Rosomoff, R.B. Cutler, and R.S. Rosomoff. "Secondary Gain Concept: A Review of the Scientific Evidence," *Clinical Journal of Pain* 11, no. 1 (1995): 6–21.

Freud, A. *The Ego and the Mechanisms of Defense.* Madison, CT: International Universities Press, 1966.

Freud, S. (1905). "Fragment of an Analysis of a Case of Hysteria." In *The Standard Edition of the Complete Psychological Works of Sigmund Freud,* edited by J. Strachey. Volume 7. London: The Hogarth Press and The Institute of Psychoanalysis, 1905.

———. "New Introductory Lectures." In *The Standard Edition of the Complete Psychological Works of Sigmund Freud,* edited by J. Strachey. Volume 22. London: The Hogarth Press and the Institute of Psychoanalysis, 1933.

Gabriel, Y. *Organizations in Depth.* London: *Sage,* 1999.

George, A.L., "The 'Operational Code': A Neglected Approach to the Study of Political Leadership and Decision-Making." *International Studies Quarterly* 13 (1995): 190–222.

Greenson, R.R., *The Technique and Practice of Psychoanalysis*. New York: International University Press, 1967.

Groves, J.E., ed. *Essential Papers on Short-Term Dynamic Therapy*. New York: New York University Press, 1996.

Gustavson, J.P., *The Complex Secret of Brief Psychotherapy*. New York: Norton, 1986.

Hamel, G. *Leading the Revolution*. Boston: Harvard Business School Press, 2002.

Heatherton, T., and J.L. Weinberger, eds. *Can Personality Change?* Washington, DC: American Psychological Association, 1994.

Horowitz, M.J., C. Marmor, J.L Krupnick, N. Wilner, N. Kaltreider, and R. Wallerstein. *Personality Styles and Brief Psychotherapy*. New York: Basic Books, 1984.

Jamison, J.R., *Touched with Fire: Manic-Depressive Illness and the Artistic Temperament*. New York: The Free Press, 1993.

Jung, C. *Psychological Reflections: A New Anthology of his Writings*, edited by J. Jacobi. Princeton: Princeton University Press/Bollinger series, 1973.

Kagan, J., and H.A. Moss. *Birth to Maturity: A Study in Psychological Development*. New Haven: Yale University Press, 1983.

Kegan, R., and L. Lahey. *How the Way we Talk can Change the Way we Work*. San Francisco: Jossey-Bass, 2001.

———. *Immunity to Change: How to Overcome It and Unlock the Potential in Yourself and Your Organization*. Boston: Harvard Business School Press.

Kets de Vries, M.F.R., ed. *The Irrational Executive: Psychoanalytic Explorations in Management*. New York: International Universities Press, 1984.

———. "Narcissism and Leadership: An Object Relations Perspective," *Human Relations* 38 (1995): 583–601.

———. *Prisoners of Leadership*. New York: Wiley, 1989.

———. (1994). "The Leadership Mystique," *Academy of Management Executive* 8 (3): 73–92.

———. (2001). *The Leadership Mystique*. London: Financial Times/ Prentice Hall.

———. (2004a). *Lessons on Leadership by Terror: Finding Shaka Zulu in the Attic*. Cheltenham: Edward Elgar, 2004.

———. (2004b). *The Global Executive Leadership Inventory: Facilitator's Guide*. San Francisco: Pfeiffer, 2004.

———. (2004c). *The Global Executive Leadership Inventory: Participant's Guide*. San Francisco: Pfeiffer, 2004.

———. (2005a). "Feeling Like a Fake: How the Fear of Success can Cripple your Career and Damage your Company," *Harvard Business Review* 83, no 8 (2005): 108–116.

———. (2005b). "Leadership Group Coaching in Action: The Zen of Creating High Performance Teams," *Academy of Management Executive* 19, no. 1 (2005): 61–76.

———. (2006a). *The Leader on the Couch*. New York: Wiley, (2006).

———. (2006b). *The Personality Audit*. Fontainebleau: INSEAD (2006).

———. (2007a). "Decoding the Team Conundrum: The Eight Roles Executives Play," *Organizational Dynamics* 36, no. 1 (2007): 28–44.

————. (2007b). "Are You Feeling Mad, Sad, Bad, or Glad?" INSEAD Research Paper Series, 2007/09/EFE, 2007.

————. *Sex, Money, Happiness, and Death: Musings from the Underground.* Forthcoming, 2008.

Kets de Vries, M.F.R., R. Carlock, and E. Florent-Treacy. *The Family Business on the Couch.* London: Wiley, 2007.

Kets de Vries, M.F.R., and K. Korotov. "Creating Transformational Executive Programs," *Academy of Management Learning & Education* 6, no. 3 (2007): 375–387.

Kets de Vries, M.F.R., K. Korotov, and, E. Florent-Treacy. *Coach and Couch.* London: Palgrave, 2007.

Kets de Vries, M.F.R., and D. Miller. *The Neurotic Organization.* San Francisco: Jossey-Bass, 1984.

Kets de Vries, M.F.R., P. Vrignaud, A. Agrawal, and E. Florent-Treacy. "Development and Application of the Leadership Archetype Questionnaire," INSEAD Research Paper Series, 2007/40/EFE, 2007.

Kernberg, O. *Borderline Conditions and Pathological Narcissism.* New York: Aronson, 1975.

Khurana, R. *Searching for a Corporate Savior: The Irrational Quest for Charismatic CEOs.* Princeton, NJ: Princeton University Press, 2004.

Kilburg, R.R. *Executive Coaching.* Washington, DC: American Psychological Association, 2000.

Klein, M. *Contributions to Psychoanalysis, 1921–1945.* London: Hogarth Press, 1948.

Kohut, H. *The Analysis of the Self.* New York: International Universities Press, 1971.

————. *Self Psychology and the Humanities.* New York: W.W. Norton, 1985.

Kohut, H., and E.S. Wolf. "The Disorders of the Self and their Treatment: an Outline." *International Journal of Psychoanalysis* 59 (1978): 413–426.

Korotov, K. *Identity Laboratories.* INSEAD PhD Dissertation. Fontainebleau: INSEAD, 2005.

Levinson, H. *Organizational Diagnosis.* Cambridge, MA: Harvard University Press, 1972.

————. *Organizational Assessment.* Washington, DC: American Psychological Association, 2002.

Lichtenberg, J.D. *Psychoanalysis and Infant Research.* New York: Lawrence Erlbaum, 1991.

Lichtenberg, J.D., and R. A. Schonbar. "Motivation in Psychology and Psychoanalysis." In *Interface of Psychoanalysis and Psychology,* edited by J.W. Barron, M.N. Eagle, and D.L. Wolitzky. Washington, DC: American Psychological Association, 1992, 11–36.

Loewenberg, P. *Decoding the Past: The Psychohistorical Approach.* New York: Alfred A. Knopf, 1982.

Luborsky, L., and P. Crits-Cristoph. *Understanding Transference: The Core Conflictual Relationship Theme Method.* Washington, DC: American Psychological Association, 1998.

Luborsky, L., P. Crits-Cristoph, et al. *Who Will Benefit from Psychotherapy?* New York: Basic Books, 1988.

Mahler, M.S., F. Pine, and A. Bergman. *The Psychological Birth of the Human Infant.* New York: Basic Books, 1975.

Malan, D.H. *A Study of Brief Psychotherapy.* New York: Plenum, 1963.

———. *The Frontier of Brief Psychotherapy.* New York, Plenum, 1976.

Malan, D., and F. Osimo. *Psychodynamics, Training, and Outcome in Brief Psychotherapy.* Oxford: Butterworth Heinemann, 1992.

Mann, J. *Time Limited Psychotherapy.* Cambridge, MA: Harvard University Press, 1973.

McAdams, D.P. *Stories We Live By: Personal Myths and the Making of the Self.* New York: William Morrow and Company, 1993.

McCrae, R.R., and P.T. Costa. *Personality in Adulthood.* New York: Guilford Press, 1990.

McCullough Vaillant, L. *Changing Character.* New York: Basic Books, 1997.

McDougall, J. *Theaters of the Mind.* New York: Basic Books, 1985.

———. *Theaters of the Body.* New York: W.W. Norton, 1989.

McLeod, J. *Narrative and Psychotherapy.* London: Sage, 1997.

Menninger, C. *Theory of Psychoanalytic Technique.* New York: Harper, 1958.

Miller, W.R., and S. Rollnick. *Motivational Interviewing.* New York: The Guilford Press, 2002.

Molnos, A. *A Question of Time: Essentials of Brief Psychotherapy.* London: Karnac Books, 1995.

Pfeffer, J. *The Human Equation: Building Profits by Putting People First.* Boston: Harvard Business School Press, 1998.

Popper, K. *The Logic of Scientific Discovery.* London: Routledge Classics, 2002.

Racker, H. *Transference and Countertransference.* New York: International Universities Press, 1968.

Rennie, D.L. "Storytelling in Psychotherapy: The Client's Subjective Experience." *Psychotherapy* 31 (1994): 234–243.

Rawson, P. *Short-Term Psychodynamic Psychotherapy: An Analysis of the Key Principles.* London: Karnac, 2002.

Rogers, C. R. *Client-centered Therapy.* Boston: Houghton Mifflin, 1951.

Rosenbaum, M. *Handbook of Short-Term Therapy Groups.* New York, McGraw-Hill, 1983.

Scott Rutan, J., and W.N. Stone. *Psychodynamic Group Psychotherapy.* New York: The Guilford Press, 2001.

Seligman, M.E.P., and M. Csikszentmihalyi. "Positive Psychology: An Introduction." *American Psychologist* 55, no., 1 (2000): 5–14.

Seltzery, L.F. *Paradoxical Strategies in Psychotherapy: A Comprehensive Overview and Guidebook.* New York: Wiley, 1986.

Sifneos, P.E. *Short-Term Dynamic Psychotherapy.* Cambridge, MA: Harvard University Press, 1979.

Spence, D.P. *Narrative Truth and Historical Truth.* New York: Norton, 1982.

Spitz, R.A. *The First Year of Life.* New York: International Universities Press, 1965.

Stogdill, R.M. *Handbook of Leadership.* New York: The Free Press, 1974.

Strupp, H.H., and J.L. Binder. *Psychotherapy in a New Key: A Guide to Time-Limited Dynamic Psychotherapy.* New York: Basic Books, 1984.

Weeks, G.R., and L. L'Abate. *Paradoxical Psychotherapy: Theory and Practice with Individuals, Couples, and Families.* New York: Brunner/Mazel.

Westen, D. "The Scientific Legacy of Sigmund Freud: Toward a Psychodynamically Informed Psychological Science." *Psychological Bulletin* 124, no. 3 (1998): 333–371.

White, R. "Motivation Reconsidered: The Concept of Competence." *Psychological Review* 66 (1959): 297–333.

Winnicott, D.W. *Through Paediatrics to Psycho-Analysis.* New York: Basic Books, 1975.

———. "Transitional Objects and Transitional Phenomena." *Collected Papers: Through Paediatrics to Psycho-analysis.* London: Tavistock Publications, 1951.

Yalom, I.D. *The Theory and Practice of Group Psychotherapy.* New York: Basic Books, 1985.

Zaleznik, A. *Human Dilemmas of Leadership.* New York: HarperCollins, 1966.

Zaleznik, A., and M.F.R. Kets de Vries. *Power and the Corporate Mind.* Chicago: Bonus Books, 1985.

8

CLASSICAL SOCIOLOGICAL APPROACHES TO THE STUDY OF LEADERSHIP

Mauro F. Guillén

Introduction

Leadership in organizations, parties, and nation-states has been the subject of much sociological work since the very inception of the discipline in the nineteenth century. Up until the 1970s, sociologists in general, and political sociologists in particular, were the most assiduous students of leadership among social scientists. However, the scholarly literature on leadership has witnessed explosive growth in recent decades. Figure 8-1 plots the number of scholarly articles published each year since 1960 in three fields, namely, business, psychology, and sociology.[1] Until 1969 sociologists published more articles on leadership, especially political leadership, than psychologists or management scholars. By the late 1990s the psychological and management literatures on leadership had increased dramatically.

Author note: I am grateful to the participants in the Leadership Conference at Harvard Business School's Centennial Celebration for insightful comments and suggestions, and especially to Paul DiMaggio, Rakesh Khurana, and Nitin Nohria.

FIGURE 8-1

The scholarly literature on leadership in the fields of business, psychology, and sociology

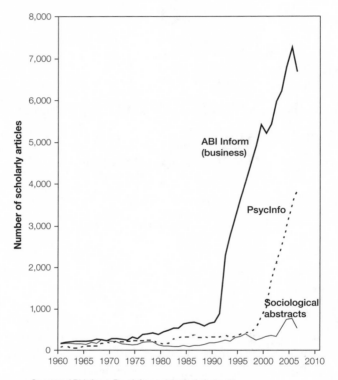

Sources: ABI Inform; Psycinfo; sociological abstracts.

It is interesting to note that one of the most widely cited sociological studies, Lieberson and O'Connor's (1972) paper showing that changes in leadership at the largest U.S. companies accounted for a small proportion of the variance in corporate performance, has attracted much more attention among management scholars than among sociologists. In fact, sociologists have tended to be skeptical about the idea that leadership matters, preferring instead to emphasize structural conditions and constraints on leadership (e.g., Grusky, 1963; Perrow, 1984, 1986).

Historically, most sociologists have undertaken research on leadership not by studying the personal characteristics of the leaders, but rather in terms of the relationship between the leaders and the led, the different paths to leadership positions, and the circulation of elites. Sociologists disagree on the nature of the relationship between the leader and the led, whether leadership is about meaning, domination, or subjugation, and about the performance implications of different leadership styles.

It is revealing to note that although no such thing as a separate sub-field of the sociology of leadership exists, the insights of the sociologists who have worked on this topic have attained wide popularity and even entered the vernacular (e.g., charismatic leadership, the iron law of oligarchy, the power elite, the inner circle, social capital, the strength of weak ties, and so on).

Table 8-1 summarizes the four main schools of thought in sociology when it comes to the study of leadership, namely, Weberian, institutional, neo-Marxist, and relational. They differ from one another in terms of their theoretical assumptions, main postulates, methodology, and main type of evidence used. As a result, they offer different approaches to leadership, although there are some important overlaps as well. This essay describes the theoretical assumptions and arguments of each school. Thus, its emphasis is on the historical origins of current work in the field, rather than on recent empirical research.

The Weberian Approach: The Three Ideal-Types of Authority

Indisputably, Max Weber's main contribution not only to the study of leadership but to sociology in general is his analysis of the three types of authority, namely, the ways in which leaders can secure legitimacy for their rule—that is, justify their authority. His approach was later developed and applied to the world of organizations by Reinhard Bendix (1956). Table 8-2 summarizes the three classic bases of authority: *personal authority* (including charismatic), which is the way in which founders or empire builders justify their claim to be the leaders; *traditional authority*, or the way in which heirs assert their claims; and *legal-rational authority*, or the way in which professional managers establish their legitimacy (Bendix, 2001:xxv–xxviii; Weber, 1978:215–248).

The three types of authority differ substantively from each other. In order to establish their authority, founders of companies, or the "empire builders" who grow them, rely on the ideas of personal gift, talent, exemplary character, demonstrated success, or even divine inspiration.

TABLE 8-1

Main sociological approaches to the study of leadership in organizations

	Weberian	Institutional	Neo-Marxist	Relational
Theoretical assumptions	The leader's authority needs to be legitimate in the eyes of the led.	The leader and led are enmeshed in a relationship of mutual dependence.	The leader and led belong to different, antagonistic social classes.	Leaders and would-be leaders differ in terms of their relational resources.
Main postulate(s)	Social and organizational structures shape leadership ideologies (or styles) and their meaning.	Leadership serves the basic function of integrating a differentiated social system, and is shaped by taken-for-granted symbolic, normative, and cognitive institutions.	Leadership is an epiphenomenon of the underlying class struggle, a mere reflection of social subjugation, which rests on an economic foundation.	Network properties and network position shape advancement to leadership, leadership styles, and leadership performance.
Methodology	Comparative-historical; qualitative; some large-sample multivariate analysis.	Comparative-historical; qualitative; some large-sample multivariate analysis.	Comparative-historical; qualitative.	Social network analysis.
Main type of evidence	Case studies at the organizational and national levels.	Case studies at the organizational and national levels.	Case studies at the organizational and national levels.	Systematic individual social network data within and across organizations.
Main proponents	Weber, 1922; Pareto, 1935; Michels, 1911; Bendix, 1956.	Barnard, 1938; Parsons, 1951; Selznick, 1957; Kerr et al., 1960.	Mosca, 1939; Mills, 1956.	Simmel, 1917; Coleman, 1988; Burt, 1992.
Recent studies	Beckman & Burton, 2007; Fligstein, 1990; Guillén, 1994; Hamilton & Biggart, 1988; Useem, 1984; Walder, 1986.	Khurana, 2002; Ocasio & Thornton, 1999; Cohen & March, 1974.	Mizruchi, 1992.	Baker, 1994; Ibarra, 1992; Podolny and Baron, 1997.

TABLE 8-2

The three types of authority in the firm according to the Weberian tradition

Type of authority	Agent	Staff	Legitimacy	Limitations
Personal, including charismatic	Successful entrepreneur (founder or empire builder)	Confidants, personal retainers, disciples, inner circle	Personal gift, talent, exemplary character, success; business legend; divine inspiration	Employees and customers demand proof of gift and continued success
Traditional	Heir of founder or empire builder	Collaborators of founding entrepreneur or empire builder	Custom or family tradition	Need to show capacity to honor the tradition
Legal-rational	Professional manager	Officials or bureaucrats; other professional managers	Technical competence, formal knowledge, success in other managerial positions, ability to maximize owners' wealth	Failure in the market; anti-bureaucratic or anti-technocratic reactions

Sources: Weber (1978:215–248) and Bendix (2001:xxv–xxviii).

They surround themselves with confidants, personal retainers, and disciples, with an inner circle of unconditional supporters and collaborators who further solidify the founder's grip on the company. The most important limit to their authority is that employees and customers demand proof of gift and continued success.

By contrast, heirs of founders or empire builders face a different task altogether. Their main challenge is to honor the family tradition. As the fictional Thomas Buddenbrook, the heir to a family dynasty of North German businessmen, put it to his sister Antonie, "What we should do, damn it, is to sit ourselves down and accomplish something, just as our forebears did" (Mann, 1901:259). Heirs face a particularly difficult task for a number of reasons. First, they must appear to be modest and hard-working. Thomas Buddenbrook made this point to his wayward brother Christian: "You will impress [the employees] more by behaving as an equal and energetically doing your duty, than by making use of your prerogatives and taking liberties" (Mann, 1901:260).

Second, heirs need to ensure that the collaborators of the founder or empire builder do not undermine their plans and commands. Third, heirs must create the perception that they embody the family tradition:

> Thomas Buddenbrook's prestige was of a different sort. He was not just one man—people honored in him the unique and unforgettable contributions of his father, his grandfather, and great-grandfather; quite apart from his own success in commercial and public affairs, he was the representative of a century of civic excellence. The most important factor, to be sure, was the easy, refined, and irresistibly charming way he had of embodying that history and turning it to his own account. (Mann, 1901:402)

Lastly, heirs must learn to navigate the all-too-frequent feuds within the family. As Johann Buddenbrook put it,

> Father—we sat here so cheerful this evening, it was such a lovely celebration, we were so happy and proud of our accomplishments, of having achieved something, of having brought our firm and our family to new heights, to a full measure of recognition and respect. But this acrimony with my brother, your eldest son, Father—let us not have a hidden crack that runs through the edifice we have built with God's gracious help. A family has to be united, to hold together, Father; otherwise, evil will come knocking at the door. (Mann, 1901:44)

The third classic way of justifying one's authority in the firm is totally different from personal and traditional rule. Professional managers build the legitimacy of their authority on the basis of their technical competence, academic qualifications, formal knowledge, or success in other managerial positions (Kerr et al., 1960:123–124). Failure in the market, or anti-bureaucratic or anti-technocratic reactions from employees or customers, can undermine their authority.

The Weberian themes of authority, power, and elites were further developed by Vilfredo Pareto and Robert Michels. They studied the issues of elite (or leadership) recruitment, homogeneity, interaction, value consensus, solidarity, and integration (for a review, see Putnam, 1976:107–132), themes that were also pursued by the neo-Marxist students of leadership. Pareto's (1935) most important contribution was his theory of the "circulation of elites." He argued that elites are subject to a law of social decadence or entropy, whereby they find it difficult to reproduce themselves over time. He based his arguments not only on sociology but also on psychology, thus building a potential bridge to cognitive approaches to the study of leadership. According to Pareto, change within the elite occurs either because newcomers with new talents displace the established "degenerate elements" within the elite or an entirely new elite replaces the existing elite, as in a revolutionary takeover of power (Putnam, 1976:167). Michels formulated the famous "iron law of oligarchy," a dynamic model of how increasing bureaucratization, organizational complexity, and interorganizational interactions eventually generate vertical differentiation and a distancing between the leaders and the led (Putnam, 1976:136–136).

In order to fully grasp the significance of the Weberian approach to the study of leadership in organizations, it is instructive to summarize the most important study in this tradition, namely, Reinhard Bendix's *Work and Authority in Industry*, originally published in 1956. The book's enduring impact has first and foremost to do with the larger question that it raises, namely, how the ruling classes of different societies deal with the breakdown of traditional patterns of subordination among the people in the wake of industrialization (see p. xxix of Bendix's introduction to the 1974 edition). This is the classic sociological problem that Weber addressed with his three ideal-types of authority. Bendix provides answers as to the various ways in which societies may shift from a traditional to a legal mode of domination by looking at the relationship between the "few" and the "many" in industrial enterprises, a setting that he treats as a microcosm of society at large.

As a true Weberian scholar, Bendix was unhappy about the insufficient attention devoted to the autonomous role of ideas in providing an answer to the transition from traditional to legal modes of authority. As he lucidly observes in the book's very first paragraph, "the few . . . have seldom been satisfied to command without a higher justification even when they abjured all interest in ideas, and the many have seldom been docile enough not to provoke such justifications." This statement sets the tone for the entire book. Bendix certainly presents managerial ideologies as "an effort to interpret the exercise of authority in a favorable light" (p. 13), their purpose being "to promote the interests of 'industry' or 'business' collectively" (p. 343) or "to justify the privilege of voluntary action and association for [the managers], while imposing upon all subordinates the duty of obedience and of service to the best of their ability" (p. xxiii). But he also sees ideologies as inherently ambiguous, as affecting and reflecting action, as a "constant process of formulation and reformulation by which spokesmen identified with a social group seek to articulate what they sense to be its shared understandings" (pp. xxiv, 341–342, 443 n. 16).

Bendix compares industrial leadership in two matched pairs of societies—England and the United States versus Russia and East Germany—to illustrate two different paths from traditional to legal domination, the liberal and the autocratic. His analysis proceeds in two steps. He first establishes the contrast between England and Russia at the inception of industry, and then moves on to compare the United States and East Germany after industry has developed into a large-scale activity and become bureaucratized. Simultaneously, he makes diachronic comparisons to illustrate how bureaucratization affects ideological change. He repeatedly engages in systematic comparisons employing either the method of difference or the method of agreement, depending on the pair of countries being considered. Bendix's comparative scheme is so powerful and neat that it remains unparalleled as a way to lay out the continuities and discontinuities, and the convergences and divergences, in a process of large-scale social change over the long run.

Bendix starts by examining the case of England, where an autonomous class of industrial entrepreneurs sought to reassert itself against the contempt and even opposition of the landed aristocracy. The traditional theory of dependence of the lower class on the upper class had to be abandoned in favor of an ideology of self-dependence and free trade in order for the industrial bourgeoisie to become a ruling class and be able to give labor a role to play. In Russia, by contrast, Bendix paints a landscape of tsarist autocracy with both the upper and lower classes dependent upon its protection and arbitrariness. The state, and not an autonomous class of entrepreneurs, promoted industry, and legitimized draconian methods of leadership and labor management. In the end, the October Revolution was the culminating event in a long process of breakdown of centralized authority during which it became readily apparent that coercion had reached its limits.

After a masterful analysis of the bureaucratization of industry and management, Bendix resumes his historical narrative with the evolution of managerial ideologies in the United States and East Germany.

He describes the transformation of the American ethic of success from its origins in the Puritan ideal to its first scientific conceptualizations under the guise of social Darwinism. He then explains how the increasing complexity of enterprises and the rise of labor unrest rendered such approaches ineffective. While American leadership ideology ultimately pursued a cooperation between workers and managers based on the respect for their "wants" and "qualities," ideologies in the Soviet Union and its satellite states emphasized unity of purpose and practice as interpreted by the totalitarian party. Managers and workers became subject to the controls of an interlocking hierarchy of economic planners and political functionaries, a solution to the demise of the tsarist order that represented a continuity rather than a break.

In recent years the Weberian tradition has been furthered in a variety of ways by a diverse group of scholars. I extended Bendix's classic comparison by examining the more nuanced contrast between liberal and corporatist societies (Guillén, 1994), Fligstein (1990) studied the rise and fall of managerial conceptions of control, Walder (1986) and Hamilton and Biggart (1988) extended the analysis of authority patterns to East Asia, and, among many others, Beckman and Burton (2007) developed a typology of leadership in rising entrepreneurial firms. These studies have continued to emphasize issues of power and legitimacy, but incorporate cultural and cognitive elements. In doing so, they have actually brought the Weberian tradition somewhat closer to the second approach.

A last aspect of the Weberian approach that needs to be mentioned is the one pursued by Michael Useem in his classic book *The Inner Circle* (1984), an astute comparison of corporate governance in the United States and the United Kingdom. Useem follows the strategy of analyzing most similar cases, showing that social extraction and class reproduction through club memberships and interlocking directorates generates a considerable degree of unity of action. His "inner circle" theory emphasizes that corporations and their leaders often make decisions that are beneficial to all large companies as opposed to just their own. Useem's study falls mostly within the Weberian tradition, although some of its themes, especially those having to do with the reproduction of the business elite, have more in common with the approach of C. Wright Mills (1956) than with that of Weber or Pareto.

The Institutional Approach: Leadership and Social Integration

While Weberian sociologists focus their attention on the social bases providing leadership with legitimacy, and hence combine elements of power and ideology, the institutional school is mainly concerned with the mutual dependence between the leader and the led. In the tradition of Émile Durkheim, institutionalists see leadership as an essential feature of a modern, differentiated society, one that fosters social integration, in a largely Parsonsian fashion (Parsons, 1951). Leaders exist because there is a need for order and integration; absent leadership, there is chaos or anomie. They further argue that leadership is shaped by taken-for-granted symbolic, normative, and cognitive institutions.

The most important early proponent of the institutional approach to the study of leadership was Chester Barnard, an executive at New Jersey Bell who wrote an influential book, *The Functions of the Executive* (1938). Barnard proposed the leader as someone who spends the day communicating with the led, motivating them, and ensuring their cooperation. Thus, the leader provides the organization with a common purpose. Interestingly, he was influenced not only by the functionalist sociologist Talcott Parsons but also by the members of the Pareto circle at Harvard, thus overlapping at least partially with the Weberian tradition (Guillén, 1994:60–61). Another key institutional theorist of leadership was Philip Selznick, the author of *Leadership in Administration* (1957), who also defined the subject matter in terms of the functions it is supposed to serve, namely, defining the mission and role of the organization, ensuring its integrity of purpose and action, and resolving conflict by balancing internal and external demands or requirements. Both Barnard and Selznick furthered the idea that the led look toward the leader to find meaning and purpose (Podolny, Khurana, and Hill-Popper, 2005), an idea that may appear to be attractive at first, but one reminiscent also of the process by which fascism and communism captured the imagination of so many from the 1910s to the 1940s, paving the way for the emergence of the most sickening "mass societies" the world has ever witnessed.

As an offshoot of the institutional approach, we find a stream of research on leadership emphasizing decision making and cognition (Cohen and March, 1974; Ocasio and Thornton, 1999). In this view, effective leaders are not seen as visionaries but rather as combining "foolishness and consistency" in order to cope with the pervasive ambiguity and uncertainty of organizations. This view also finds its expression in Khurana's (2002) study of the quest for charismatic CEOs, which leads to suboptimal matching between the leaders and the companies they lead.

The Neo-Marxist Take on Leadership

The essentially idealist view of leadership underpinning both the Weberian and the institutional approaches—albeit yielding sharply different theories because of the primacy of power in the former and the tendency to neglect of social domination in the latter—has its counterpart in the neo-Marxist view of leadership, first outlined in a systematic way by Gaetano Mosca (1939) and later developed by C. Wright Mills in *The Power Elite* (1956). In many ways, the neo-Marxists agree with the Weberians on the importance of studying leadership in terms of authority and power. They are, however, much more explicit about the link between leadership and social classes in the context of capitalist production. As a result, ideas, ideologies, symbols, myths, cognition, and the like are assumed to reflect more fundamental class dynamics and are unceremoniously dismissed as epiphenomenal. Unlike Pareto, the neo-Marxists see elite transformation as the result of political change and not of psychology.

C. Wright Mills (1956) wrote provocatively about the link between elite recruitment and social class, and documented the three-way interactions among business, government, and military elites in the United States. Mills argued that the unity of action of the American power elite—the "higher circles"—was a direct consequence of its social homogeneity and lifestyles. In addition, he was the first social scientist to call attention to the interlocking role that elite members play by virtue of their positions at different types of organizations, either contemporaneously or over time, including companies, the government, the military, universities, and nonprofit organizations. Useem (1984) is perhaps the best subsequent study, one that combined theoretical elements of the Weberian and neo-Marxist approaches, as noted above. The pattern of interlocking elite membership has been documented for virtually every country in the world, including not only capitalist but also communist societies (e.g., Walder, 1986).

More recent work within the neo-Marxist tradition argues and demonstrates that business leaders act in unison only to the extent that they are structurally positioned in ways that generate similarity in behavior, including geographic proximity, common industry membership, cross-shareholdings, and interlocking directorates (Mizruchi, 1992). This approach builds a bridge between the neo-Marxist approach and the subfield of social networks.

Social Networks and Leadership

While Marxist theory is all about the relations of different classes to the means of production, sociologists have also looked at the relational aspects of leadership from a radically different perspective: social networks. The problem is posed not in terms of the relationship between the leader and the led, but more pointedly as the intervention of a third party—the potential leader—in a given system of relationships. The earliest exponent of this view was the German sociologist Georg Simmel (1917), who laid the foundations of modern network analysis with his comparison of power and influence in dyadic and triadic relationships. Specifically, he theorized about the intervention of a third party in a preexisting relationship between two parties. In his analysis, a third party enjoys influence, or can exercise leadership, in four different ways. First, "either two parties are hostile toward one another and therefore compete for the favor of a third element." Second, "they compete for the favor of the third element and therefore are hostile toward one another." Third, the nonpartisan arbiter balances or seeks accord between the two parties in the preexisting relationship. And fourth, the divider-and-ruler "intentionally produces the conflict [between the two parties in the preexisting relationship] in order to gain a dominant position" (Simmel, 1950:146, 155, 162). It is important to note that in the context of triadic relationships, the third party does not necessarily have to exert a huge amount of influence or leadership; rather, "the only important thing is that [the third party's] superadded power give one [of the two preexisting parties] superiority" (Simmel, 1950:157). This last point surely qualifies as one of the most fundamental insights in the sociology of networks.

This line of thought was expanded and formalized by Ronald Burt in a number of publications, culminating in his book *Structural Holes* (1992), in which he theorized about the advantages of individuals (or companies, for that matter) occupying sparse positions in the network of social relationships. "Brokerage advantage" refers to the benefits from regulating flows of information, which presumably enables those possessing it to take the initiative, get ahead, and exercise leadership. In the process of establishing relationships with others, an individual acquires a brokerage advantage to the extent that he or she connects individuals or clusters of individuals not otherwise connected to each other. The broker benefits from his or her ability to bring together separate groups from opposite sides of the so-called structural holes in the network. Thus, an individual with many structural holes around him or her can engage in purposeful action aimed at profitably exploiting his or her position as a broker in the network by regulating information flows and shaping how activities spanning the hole are to take place. The broker enjoys three interrelated advantages, namely, "access to a wider diversity of information, early access to that information, and control over information diffusion," when compared with other individuals (Burt, 1992, 2005:16). Individuals embedded in networks replete with structural holes tend to have a greater number of "weak ties," thus benefiting from access to diverse sources of information (Granovetter, 1973). Such individuals generate more innovative ideas, and enjoy more entrepreneurial opportunities by bringing together disparate parties. Social-network research has resulted in a variety of specific recommendations as to how leaders can improve their career prospects and enhance the success of their organizations (e.g., Baker, 1994). Empirical research has found that individuals with access to diverse information perform better than others (Burt, 1992; Podolny and Baron, 1997). Empirical studies have also shown, however, that individuals of different gender and race obtain unequal returns to their network resources as they attempt to advance their careers (e.g., Ibarra, 1992).

So, What Is Leadership, Sociologically Speaking?

Although based on widely different theoretical assumptions, the Weberian, institutional, neo-Marxist, and network perspectives on leadership offer a series of overlapping insights. First, in sociology leadership is framed as a relationship, not as a characteristic of one individual. This is certainly the case in the Weberian and neo-Marxist traditions because of their shared emphasis on social domination, that is, the agency of one actor over another. The institutional approach, embedded as it is in functionalism, also considers leadership as a relationship between individuals seeking order, in spite of its emphasis on psychology and cognition. It goes without saying that the network tradition takes the relationship between nodes as the unit of analysis.

A second point of coincidence has to do with the multidimensional approach to explaining patterns of leadership, although in the case of the neo-Marxist approach this represents a departure from the original Marxist reductionism. Recent and current research within the Weberian, institutional, and network approaches has clearly honored the commitment to multidimensionality, though striking a delicate balance between breadth of explanation and parsimony. Moreover, the four traditions have converged methodologically, with scholars increasingly recognizing the value of both intensive case-study and large-sample empirical research.

Perhaps a more controversial overlap among the four traditions is the reification of leadership as a phenomenon that manifests itself in a hierarchical way, one in which there are leaders and led. The Weberians and the neo-Marxists certainly see the world as a gigantic structure of domination with the dynamic of power and legitimacy playing itself out at all levels of society, from leadership in small groups all the way to the political leaders of the nation-state. The institutional approach also needs to introduce a hierarchical dimension to leadership in order to make social integration possible. It is important to note that, while the institutional tradition alerted us to the importance of informal social organization, leaders are still necessary to channel the energies of the led in a certain direction. The network approach is perhaps the one that is less necessarily committed to the hierarchical imperative, although much empirical research in the field deals with the role of networks in the context of career advancement in bureaucratized settings.

In my view, the future of the sociology of leadership is discernible, and it will be shaped in large measure by the last of the four traditions discussed in this essay. Over the last two decades, network sociology has revolutionized much of the overall field of sociology, from family, health, migration, and workplace studies to cultural, stratification, organizational, political, and world-system research. Besides its theoretical contributions and methodological tools, network sociology has the potential of helping theories of leadership surmount the view that everything under the sun is, or should be, hierarchical in nature. The flexible, multifaceted, mercurial, even ephemeral aspects of social relationships that the networks tradition seems to accommodate so well will no doubt yield further theoretical insights and help the Weberians, institutionalists, and neo-Marxists arrive at new insights of their own.

Note

1. It is important to note that in 1992 the coverage of the business database was expanded—hence the spike in the number of articles.

References

Baker, Wayne. *Networking Smart: How to Build Relationships for Personal and Organizational Success.* New York: McGraw-Hill, 1994.

Barnard, Chester I. *The Functions of the Executive.* Cambridge, MA: Harvard University Press, 1938.

Beckman, C., and Dianne M. Burton. "Leaving a Legacy: Role Imprints and Successor Turnover in Young Firms." *American Sociological Review* 72 (2007): 239–266.

Bendix, Reinhard. *Work and Authority in Industry.* New Brunswick, NJ: Transaction, [1956] 2001.

Burt, Ronald S. *Brokerage and Closure: An Introduction to Social Capital.* New York: Oxford University Press, 2005.

———. *Structural Holes: The Social Structure of Competition.* Cambridge, MA: Harvard University Press, 1992.

Cohen, Michael D., and James G. March. *Leadership and Ambiguity: The American College President.* New York: McGraw-Hill, 1974.

Coleman, James S. "Social Capital in the Creation of Human Capital." *American Journal of Sociology* 94 (1988): S95–S120.

Fligstein, Neil. *The Transformation of Corporate Control.* Cambridge, MA: Harvard University Press, 1990.

Granovetter, Mark. *Getting a Job: A Study of Contacts and Careers.* Chicago: University of Chicago Press, [1973] 1995.

Grusky, Oscar. "Managerial Succession and Organizational Effectiveness." *American Journal of Sociology* 69, no. 1 (1963): 21–31.

Guillén, Mauro F. *Models of Management: Work, Authority, and Organization in a Comparative Perspective.* Chicago: University of Chicago Press, 1994.

Hamilton, Gary G., and Nicole W. Biggart. "Market, Culture, and Authority: A Comparative Analysis of Management and Organization in the Far East." *American Journal of Sociology* 94, no. s1 (January 1988): S52–S94.

Ibarra, Herminia. "Homophily and Differential Returns: Sex Differences in Network Structure and Access in an Advertising Firm." *Administrative Science Quarterly* 37, no. 3 (1992): 422–447.

Kerr, Clark, John T. Dunlop, Frederick Harbison, and Charles A. Myers. *Industrialism and Industrial Man.* New York: Oxford University Press, [1960] 1964.

Khurana, Rakesh. *The Search for the Corporate Saviour.* Princeton, NJ: Princeton University Press, 2002.

Lieberson, Stanley, and James F. O'Connor. "Leadership and Organizational Performance: A Study of Large Organizations." *American Sociological Review* 37, no. 2 (1972): 117–130.

Mann, Thomas. *Buddenbrooks: The Decline of a Family.* New York: Vintage International, [1901] 1994.

Michels, Robert. *Political Parties: A Sociological Study of the Oligarchical Tendencies of Modern Democracy.* New York: The Free Press, [1911] 1962.

Mills, C. Wright. *The Power Elite.* New York: Oxford University Press, 1956.

Mizruchi, Mark S. *The Structure of Corporate Political Action: Interfirm Relations and Their Consequences.* Cambridge, MA: Harvard University Press, 1992.

Mosca, Gaetano. *Prison Notebooks.* New York: Columbia University Press, [1939] 1996.

Ocasio, William, and Patricia H. Thornton. "Institutional Logics and the Historical Contingency of Power in Organizations: Executive Succession in the Higher Education Publishing Industry, 1958–1990." *American Journal of Sociology* 105 (1999): 801–843.

Pareto, Vilfredo. *Mind and Society.* New York: AMS Press, [1935] 1983.

Parsons, Talcott. *The Social System.* New York: The Free Press, [1951] 1964.

Perrow, Charles. *Complex Organizations.* New York: Random House, 1986.

———. *Normal Accidents.* New York: Basic Books, 1984.

Podolny, Joel M., and James N. Baron. "Resources and Relationships: Social Networks and Mobility in the Workplace." *American Sociological Review* 62 (1997): 673–693.

Podolny, Joel M., Rakesh Khurana, and Marya Hill-Popper. "Revisiting the Meaning of Leadership." *Research in Organizational Behavior* 26 (2005): 1–36.

Putnam, Robert D. *The Comparative Study of Political Elites.* Englewood Cliffs, NJ: Prentice-Hall, 1976.

Selznick, Philip. *Leadership in Administration: A Sociological Interpretation.* Evanston, IL: Row, Peterson, 1957.

Simmel, Georg. *The Sociology of Georg Simmel.* New York: The Free Press, [1917] 1950.

Useem, Michael. *The Inner Circle: Large Corporations and the Rise of Business Political Activity in the U.S. and U.K.* New York: Oxford University Press, 1984.

Walder, Andrew G. *Communist Neo-Traditionalism: Work and Authority in Chinese Industry.* Berkeley, CA: University of California Press, 1986.

Weber, Max. *Economy and Society: An Outline of Interpretive Sociology.* 2 vols., edited by Guenther Roth and Claus Wittich. Berkeley, CA: University of California Press, [1922] 1978.

9

ECONOMISTS' PERSPECTIVES ON LEADERSHIP

Patrick Bolton, Markus K. Brunnermeier, and Laura Veldkamp

Introduction

It is fair to say that leadership in organizations is not a topic that has received a lot of attention by economists. It is only very recently that a small but rapidly growing economics literature on leadership has emerged. The goal of this survey article is to review this literature and to consider how the leadership problem is embedded in the broader context of the managerial theory of the firm.

It is not just the notion of leadership that is foreign to most economists. Even the *raison d'être* of firms in a market economy, the boundaries of firms, and their internal organization are still imperfectly understood. For a long time economists have simply represented firms as a black box, or a production function turning inputs such as labor and raw materials into outputs for consumption. As Coase (1937), Simon (1957), Williamson (1971), and Grossman and Hart (1986) have pointed out, the difficulty with this representation of firms is that it

Author note: We are grateful to Rakesh Khurana for inviting us to provide economists' perspective on leadership.

leaves unanswered the role of firms in a market economy and what the boundaries of the firm should be.

The modern economic theory of the firm pioneered by these authors and others has started addressing these issues by opening this black box and representing the firm as a machine operated by a manager. What is now known as the principal-agent approach has dominated recent economic analysis of firms. In its simplest representation, the principal is the owner of the firm and the agent is the firm's manager. In a few more sophisticated representations, the owner of the firm is the head of a hierarchy of managers and workers. The central issue addressed in this literature is an incentive issue: how to align managers' objectives with those of shareholders (or other stakeholders). Under this approach the basic organization design problem boils down to a contracting problem between the principal and agent, where the principal (or owner) determines the plan of action for the firm as well as a compensation package for the agent (or manager), and the manager executes the plan. In other words, *the principal-agent approach to the firm makes no room for leadership*. What is worse, it makes no room for any significant role for management, because the strategy and operation of the firm are determined in the initial contract between the principal and agent, so that the only role of the manager is to execute the predetermined strategy. In the basic theory there is no room for initiative by the manager, let alone for any leadership role by management.

Although the principal-agent paradigm is a major advance over the neoclassical black-box representation of firms, it is nevertheless deficient and unrealistic. Indeed, more often than not shareholders are in reality looking for guidance by the manager and not the other way around. Similarly, when a firm appoints a new CEO, it may define in broad terms the CEO's compensation package, but otherwise gives *carte blanche* to the CEO in defining and implementing the firm's strategy (subject, of course, to the approval of the board of directors).

Thus, a more accurate representation of how managers run firms than the principal-agent model is to allow for some form of managerial initiative and a leadership role for the CEO. Introducing managerial leadership into the modern economic theory of the firm, however, involves a major departure from the principal-agent model of the firm.

A first step in that direction is to introduce *incomplete contracts*, as Grossman and Hart (1986) have done, so that the entire future of the corporation is no longer determined in a single contract between the owners and the manager. With incomplete contracts, not all decisions are made at the time the contract is signed. As a consequence, the manager has more of a role than just executing what has been agreed. That is, in situations in which the manager has *control rights*, he or she gets to determine how to run the firm when new decision problems arise.

In reality, CEOs don't always have such formal control rights, and yet they are expected to play a leadership role in the firm. To be able to account for an initiative role of CEOs even when they do not have formal control of the firm, the property-rights theory of the firm of Grossman and Hart has to be augmented to introduce the notion of *delegation* of authority, as Aghion and Tirole (1997) have shown.

We begin our discussion of economists' perspectives on leadership in organizations by briefly reviewing the role of incomplete contracts, formal control rights, and delegation of real authority to CEOs with superior expertise or information, because these elements provide the underpinnings that connect the economic models of leadership to the theory of the firm.

Second, we turn to a review of the first generation of economic analyses on leadership and discuss the question of what leadership means to an economist. As we shall see, economists' notions of leadership are much more basic and elementary than the leadership notions discussed in the voluminous management, sociology, organizational psychology, and organizational behavior literatures. However, this does not mean that this burgeoning economics literature should be dismissed as too simplistic or naïve to be of any practical interest. The value of economists' modeling efforts lies in the focus on the *functional aspects* of leadership, the *mechanisms* of leadership, and on what leadership can accomplish for an organization.

Third, after reviewing the main approaches to leadership explored by economists, we outline a general conceptual framework that, in our view, captures some key elements of leadership that economists have focused on. We discuss the key attributes of a leader that are captured by this framework and attempt to identify which important facets it leaves out. We also touch on possible ways of extending the basic framework to incorporate the main missing dimensions of leadership.

To give a first flavor of the aspects of leadership which the economic framework is set up to capture and which it is not, consider the perspectives on leadership recently offered by one of the leading U.S.

corporate executives, Richard Parsons (CEO of Time Warner), in a lecture at Columbia Business School.[1] Parsons identifies five main elements of effective leadership in corporations: (1) setting a *vision*, (2) *communication*, (3) *empowering others*, (4) *execution*, and (5) *integrity*. This may not be an all-encompassing view of leadership, but it includes several elements that are likely to be on many other CEOs' or commentators' lists. In particular the *vision thing* has to be a basic attribute of a leader. This is indeed one important aspect that economists have focused on.

Communication also has to be an integral part of leadership, because a leader's vision can help coordinate an organization's activities around a common goal only if it is clearly and convincingly communicated to all the agents in the organization. Interestingly, Parsons stresses not only the importance of the leader conveying a clear and effective message to all the members of the organization, but also the *two-way street* part of communication and the importance of getting good feedback, ideas, and information from others. Again, economists have suggested and discussed similar aspects.

By empowering others, Parsons means that an effective leader cannot take on the whole burden of running a large organization by himself and has to be able to delegate specific managerial roles to other collaborators in the organization. This is clearly an important aspect of leadership, but also one that often poses a difficult dilemma for the CEO, as the effectiveness of leadership would be undermined if the organization speaks with several voices or if delegation of important leadership roles to young turks invites the most successful and gifted among them to challenge the leader. As important as this aspect of leadership is, it has not received any attention by economists (with a few recent exceptions in the political economy literature).

The fourth element on Parsons's list, *execution*, refers to the responsibility of a leader for seeing things through and for getting her vision implemented. Parsons also alludes to the fact that a leader should be accountable for failing to successfully implement her mission statement. Accountability is an essential aspect of leadership that economists have also highlighted. However, the execution and monitoring role of a leader has generally not been emphasized in the economics literature and clearly merits further attention.

Finally, the fifth element, *integrity*, is a very important and often-stressed quality of a good leader in the management literature. An effective leader should do what he thinks is right and not be overly influenced by market sentiment, or by the changing moods of the common wisdom of the time. As we shall see, the economics literature has also focused on some facets of this element, in particular the idea that a good leader follows his own convictions and is not unduly influenced by others' opinions. However, part of the notion of integrity is also that a leader should be true to himself, and should not cave in to the influence of powerful members of the organization or to controlling shareholders, particularly if he thinks that they are wrong and are trying to steer the organization in the wrong direction. If a leader is unable to resist such pressures or is seen to kowtow to the dominant line, he will lose his power to convince others to follow him. This aspect of integrity is essentially absent from the economics literature, but it is also not clear whether economists have much to say about it.

Control, Delegation, and Leadership

The starting point for Grossman and Hart's (1986) property-rights theory of the firm is the assumption of contractual incompleteness. When contracts are incomplete, new decisions have to be taken or new agreements have to be reached in contingencies not covered by the contract. In their theory, the party who has control, the owner, takes these not-prespecified decisions. As noted in the introduction, although their framework can account for the notion of control rights and the importance of ownership, it cannot explain any role for management unless the manager has formal control. To be able to introduce a role for management even when managers do not have formal ownership of the firm, one has to allow for the possibility of delegation of authority by the owners to the manager.

This is not as straightforward as it appears, for the delegation of authority has to be credible. The owner must find a way to commit not to overrule the manager, or not to fire the CEO if she does not like what he proposes to do. Although economic models of leadership do not make this explicit, any notion of leadership obviously rests first on the ability of the firm's owners to credibly commit to delegate authority to the CEO. To give an example, it will be crucial to the ability of the *Wall Street Journal*'s new managing editor whether the newspaper's new owner, Rupert Murdoch, will be able to credibly delegate editorial authority to the editor. How can this delegation be made credible without transferring formal control?

This is the question that Aghion and Tirole (1997) set out to address. Their proposed answer is that delegation can be credible if the CEO acquires information or expertise superior to the owners'. In particular, when shareholders are widely dispersed and removed from the day-to-day operations of the firm, then the CEO naturally gains real authority over the firm and can begin to assume a leadership role. Aghion and Tirole mainly consider a model with two players, in which each player can first invest in information and in which at a subsequent stage the two agents have to make a decision on which direction to take their organization. In their setup, agents may or may not get a valuable piece of information, and the probability of getting that information is higher the more they invest in information acquisition. If one of the agents has formal control and gets the relevant piece of information, then that agent makes the ultimate decision about which direction to take the company. If the agent with formal authority does not get the piece of information, but the other agent does, then the uninformed agent defers to the informed agent even when he or she has all the control rights.

This is the sense in which expertise or superior information can give real authority to a manager who has no formal control rights. The extent to which the manager will have real control in their model depends on two key parameters: the relative costs of information acquisition for each player and the *congruence* of their objectives (that is, the extent to which they have aligned interests). If a CEO has different goals than the investors, the latter may want to retain formal control, so as to ensure that they get their way at least some of the time. In other words, one reason why shareholders do not want to relinquish formal control is that they then get to monitor the CEO and thus can avoid the worst excesses of CEO power. But holding on to power in this way comes at a cost. It undermines the CEO's incentives to acquire information. Or, to put it in the context of our broader discussion on leadership, formal control in the hands of shareholders may undermine the CEO's ability to be an effective leader because the other members of the organization may worry that the mission statement of the CEO may not be carried out and could be blocked in the future by the board of directors.

As Aghion and Tirole show, the desirability of holding on to formal control and the power to overrule the CEO is less valuable the more congruent the CEO's preferences are with the owners'. Similarly, the more the CEO's goals are aligned with the owners', the less the owners will want to invest in information themselves and the more likely the CEO will be to gain real authority by investing in information himself. The owners may even prefer to give up formal control to the CEO, for example, by letting the CEO handpick his own board of directors, as a way of committing not to interfere and thus maximizing the CEO's incentives to invest in information. This admittedly extreme outcome provides an important insight, which is not generally stressed in either the literature on leadership or corporate governance: namely, that an important prerequisite for successful leadership by a CEO may be a weak board, and generally a weak governance structure. For example, when the financial press criticized the board of General Electric (GE) for granting excessive pay, pension contributions, and perks to its departing CEO, Jack Welch, there were virtually no commentators pointing out that these excesses may have been the price to pay for the exceptional leadership benefits that Jack Welch was able to bring to GE.

An interesting study by Song and Thakor (2008) looks at CEO-board congruence and considers the difference in performance of firms with more or less congruent CEOs and boards. He finds that firm performance is positively correlated with CEO-board alignment and also with CEO longevity. This is consistent with the view that when the board is more friendly to the CEO, the latter's leadership is more credible and therefore more effective.

Of course, for every Jack Welch one can find a Konrad Black, the former CEO of the newspaper empire Hollinger International, who was sentenced for corporate fraud in February 2008. In Konrad Black's case, a more independent and watchful board might in all likelihood have been able to prevent the worst excesses he committed without inhibiting his leadership (see the Breeden Report [2004] for a description of the dysfunctional board meetings at Hollinger under Konrad Black's leadership). Corporations thus face an important dilemma: on the one hand they need to ensure that the corporation is well governed by monitoring the CEO, but on the other hand they also need to make room for managerial leadership and give CEOs the scope to commit to an overall strategy for the firm as a whole. If, as a result of too much board meddling, the CEO's actions and communication are stifled, the sense of commitment to a clear strategy may be compromised and the firm may perform poorly as a result, thus defeating the whole purpose of CEO oversight.

This dilemma is particularly acute at the level of the board of directors. The trend in corporate governance at the level of the board of directors has been toward ever greater independence and accountability of the CEO to the board. While the benefits of this trend in terms of better monitoring are clear, insufficient consideration has been given to the implications of this trend for the ability of CEOs to fulfill their leadership role. If anything, the economic analysis of CEO leadership in the next sections points away from independence and toward greater CEO accountability and more sensitive long-term performance-based compensation.

First-Generation Models of Leadership

Leadership, Communication, and Continual Improvement

Perhaps the earliest economic analysis of leadership in organizations is by Rotemberg and Saloner (1993). A main goal of their article is to propose a first rigorous formulation of what leadership is, how it works, and what it can achieve for an organization. Inevitably, given this objective, their focus is narrower than the broad picture and the five main elements of leadership suggested by Parsons. Rotemberg and Saloner's proposed view of the leadership problem in an organization is that the leader's objective is to try to motivate the other agents in the firm (the followers) to perform. Thus, just as in the principal-agent problem we have mentioned above—where the principal's problem is to incentivize the agent to perform—the leader's problem is to get the followers to exert effort to find and propose improvements to the firm's overall performance.

Their setup focuses mainly on the *communication* element of leadership and specifically on a *bottom-up* vision of leadership, in which the leader induces followers to exert effort in finding improvements by listening to their proposals and by being open to their suggestions. The very prospect that their suggestions for improvement might be carefully evaluated and taken into account by the leader is a sufficient incentive in their model to get followers to exert costly effort. Thus, the fundamental leadership problem they consider is the question of how a leader can credibly become a good listener or communicator. How do followers trust that the leader listens to them when they have already exerted costly effort to find and propose improvements?

Rotemberg and Saloner suggest an idea that is related to the problem of delegation of authority in Aghion and Tirole. They argue that if the leader's objective is mainly to maximize short-term profits, she will not always engage in costly communication with the followers, or she will not implement their proposed improvements as often. Just as the agent with formal authority in Aghion and Tirole's model can deter the other agent from investing in information, the profit-maximizing leader may deter followers from exerting costly effort to find and propose improvements. In contrast, if the leader has the welfare of the whole organization at heart—like Japanese CEOs, who typically follow a lifetime career at their firm—then he can get followers to exert more effort. As one might expect, for some parameter values in their model, this *Toyota-way* leadership model can dominate the more bottom-line-oriented American approach to leadership even in terms of profitability.

The *kaizen* (or continual improvement) model successfully applied by Toyota has been a major managerial innovation in the past quarter century. It has led to fundamental changes in automobile manufacturing around the world and has been an inspiration for many corporations in other sectors. The Rotemberg and Saloner (1993) article proposes an interesting first model of a key aspect of what *kaizen* means and points to an important prerequisite for its implementation: a long-term orientation of management and good communication between employees and management. While it emphasizes one of the five elements of leadership, the Rotemberg and Saloner model leaves out all other key aspects of leadership, however—in particular, the role of the leader in determining a direction or strategy for the firm and thus helping to coordinate the organization's activities around a common goal.

In a later article, Rotemberg and Saloner (2000) extend this model by introducing a role for the leader to define a general direction for the organization. The leader, in their model, does this by outlining in advance which future courses of action the company is unlikely to pursue. For Toyota this might mean announcing that the company will not get involved in any software operating system development for its automobiles and that the company plans to outsource all such information technology activities. The benefit of limiting the firm's activities in this way is that employees will not waste their efforts pursuing too many leads. It can also help coordinate multiple improvements proposed by different workers on the same production process. As Rotemberg and Saloner emphasize, a visionary leader who is able to detect early which directions are worth pursuing could bring enormous benefits to the organization by clearly communicating the general direction the company will take. An obvious example of what the authors have in mind is Toyota's early commitment to the development of a low-cost electric motor for automobiles, and to the hybrid technology. It took vision to see that the technology was within reach and that climate change and the rise of gasoline prices would bring about sufficient demand for hybrid automobiles to make this venture profitable.

Of course, the Toyota way and the technological lead the company has established in hybrid technology are spectacular examples of successful leadership. At the time when a leader commits the company to a particular strategy, it is not obvious whether the strategy will succeed. There are many examples of failed strategies. There is always an element of luck in a successful strategy. The Toyota gamble on the hybrid technology could have failed had oil prices stayed low for a longer period, or had technological progress accelerated the arrival of cheaper and more efficient electric motor technologies. Had this been the case, Toyota might have had to backtrack on its commitment. And had such hesitations been expected by Toyota engineers, researchers, midlevel managers, and workers, the coordination of all these agents' activities around the hybrid project might have been more difficult. Thus an important element of leadership is the credibility of the proposed strategy and the commitment of management to *stay the course*. It is not just that leaders have to define a direction for their company, but also that they have to make it credible for followers that they are willing to go along. This involves both good *communication* and *conviction*, so that followers can rest assured that the strategy will not be modified at the first signs that the strategy might be misguided. These elements are missing from the Rotemberg and Saloner analysis, but we will return to them in the next section.

Leading by Example

The next important economic analysis of leadership is that of Hermalin (1998), who considers *leading by example*. Hermalin's model also involves moral hazard by followers, but the leader's approach to motivating her team members is to lead by example. A key interest of Hermalin's analysis is to show how leadership by example works in situations where agents are self-interested. The main building block Hermalin relies on is the leader's private information about the return to effort for the team as a whole. By exerting high effort herself, the team leader signals to her members that there is a high payoff to exerting effort for the individuals in the team. Interestingly, in his model the leader's signaling activity, which derives from her informational advantage, can result in more efficient outcomes than if all team members were equally informed. The reason is that the signaling encourages followers to also provide effort and thus overcomes their tendency to shirk.

Leading by example is a fundamental element of leadership, which is stressed in many different contexts. Thus, a political leader is more likely to get support and loyalty from followers if he is not seen to enrich himself in office. Similarly, a CEO who is helping himself to too many perks is not in a good position to get his subordinates to implement a painful cost-cutting program. Indeed, some CEOs have voluntarily given up their stock options and cut their salary when their firm hit a rough patch, as a way of convincing their subordinates to accept a pay cut in order to save the firm. Putting in long hours at the office, especially when the firm is facing an unexpected major problem or decision, is also a way for the leader to show that he cares about the firm and others involved in the firm.

Leading by example is not necessarily tied in a direct way to the notion that the leader has private information on the value of effort for the organization. It may simply be a signal that the leader cares about workers as well. One important observation of Hermalin's in this respect is that the leader is only willing to lead by example if his or her compensation is designed to do so. In small organizations, Hermalin shows that the leader's share of profits should be proportionately less than the leader's effort, while in larger organizations it should be proportionately larger. This finding may be relevant to the U.S. corporate environment of the past two decades: when CEO pay reaches the extremely high levels seen in many U.S. corporations today, this compensation could make it more difficult for the CEO to lead by example. The pay is simply so high that employees are likely to conclude that the CEO is just working hard for the money.

The analyses of Rotemberg and Saloner (1993, 2000) and Hermalin (1998) focus mostly on the public good provision aspect of leadership and not so much on the leader's role in coordinating the various activities of the firm. It is worth noting that this focus on public good provision points to leadership models that are quite close to Japanese corporate leadership ideas. Its emphasis is on a long-termist perspective for management, putting the organization's welfare ahead of shareholder value, the importance of communication and eliciting continuous improvements, and finally leadership by example and through pay moderation.

Leadership, Coordination, Conviction, and Execution

More recently, several contributions, including our own (Bolton et al., 2008), have put the spotlight more on the coordination role of the leader. Along these lines, Majumdar and Mukand (2007) have extended Hermalin's analysis by adding another element of successful leadership: the ability of a leader to rally support to be able to make the changes she desires. They consider a model in which the leader's ability to bring about change depends first on how successfully she can communicate to followers that change is feasible and desirable, and second on the leader's level of support from activists who join her cause. That is, in their model, followers make a first move by deciding whether or not they want to lend their support to the leader. Then, the leader commits to a direction, and finally the undecided potential followers choose whether they want to follow the leader. An important observation that emerges from their analysis is that the mere expectation that a leader will be successful can bring about success. That is, their model generates multiple equilibria. If all the followers believe the leader will fail, then indeed she will fail, because she cannot get enough activists to join her in the first place. On the other hand, even if the leader is not particularly able or is not proposing a promising strategy for the organization, she can succeed if the followers expect her to succeed and join her en masse as activists. Majumdar and Mukand argue that in this context the best type of leader for the organization is one who is motivated to act in part but not wholly in self-interest. Her private interest (or ambition) will get her to take initiatives more readily, but it will also make it harder for her to rally activists who do not share the same interests.

Ferreira and Rezende (2007) consider a leadership problem in a two-period model in which information arrives sequentially in both periods. The leader's objective is first of all coordination—getting followers to take actions that are complementary to his—and second adaptation—implementing an overall strategy for the organization that is best suited to the firm's environment in the second period. The leadership facet they focus on is communication. But, in contrast to Rotemberg and Saloner, they emphasize top-down communication. They point to a basic trade-off for the leader in communicating his mission statement for the firm: if he sets too precise milestones and defines the firm's strategy in too specific terms, he takes the risk that he will have to execute the strategy in the future, even when it no longer appears desirable to him in the face of new information. By stating somewhat vague goals for the firm, he keeps more options open and can adapt the execution of the strategy to a changing environment. However, the vaguer the mission statement, the less the leader is able to convince the followers to take complementary action.

In other words, the leader can only gain credibility by being sufficiently specific. Communicating convincingly and credibly incurs costs, which explains why many CEOs are reluctant to do this. The more stable the environment the firm is in, the easier it is for the CEO to be specific and the more effectively he or she can lead by communicating the firm's strategy precisely. But a more uncertain environment, according to their analysis, calls for a more cautious and hesitant approach. Thus, what might appear to be a failure of leadership—a reluctance to commit firmly to a given strategy—may actually be the best way of steering the firm through uncertain times. Their analysis provides one important illustration of the fact that there is no uniquely appropriate leadership style or method. The approach to leadership fundamentally depends on the circumstances the firm finds itself in. We return to this somewhat self-evident but nevertheless important observation in the section below.

Another direction economists have pursued recently is to identify individual characteristics, preferences, or personality traits that make some people particularly effective leaders. A widely accepted view, echoed to some extent in Parsons's analysis of effective leadership and in the economists' writing we have reviewed above, is that a good leader is foremost a *team player*. Interestingly, however, Kaplan et al. (2007) find evidence that somewhat contradicts this view in a first study of CEO characteristics based on a detailed data set of candidates for CEO positions in private equity funded firms. Although the headhunting firm from which Kaplan, Klebanov, and Sorensen received the data had designed its questionnaires partly to be able to identify the team players as promising candidates for CEO positions, the authors found that the CEOs who tended to have better performance were the more self-assured CEOs with exceptional "hard/execution-related skills." These findings are consistent with recent theoretical analyses that have highlighted the potential benefits of CEO overconfidence.

In an early paper exploring the implications of CEO overconfidence, Van den Steen (2005) proposes a model in which managerial overconfidence helps attract and retain employees with similar beliefs. This is a model of the well-known notion of leadership neatly put in the old proverb "He who loves me, follows me." Applied to leadership in organizations, this facet of leadership is most relevant at the founding stage of the firm, when investors and employees have to decide whether they want to commit themselves to this venture.

In a different context, Gervais and Goldstein (2007) explore the benefits of overconfidence in a model similar to Hermalin's, which involves a moral hazard in teams problem. An overconfident leader tends to work even harder than Hermalin's rational leader, and this may help overcome free-riding by other team members. Finally, the study by Blanes i Vidal and Möllar (2007) also emphasizes the potential benefits of leader overconfidence. They study a similar problem of leadership by communication as in Ferreira and Rezende (2007), with the difference that the cost to the leader of communicating too much information is that followers may respond to this information by choosing actions that force the leader to move away from his preferred strategy. They then show that in this context leader overconfidence (or self-confidence, in their terminology) may help the leader to stick to his guns and bring followers around to his preferred strategy.

As this quick tour of the economic literature reveals, several important facets of leadership have been analyzed by economists, the most important ones being *communication* and to some extent *vision*. Conspicuously absent from this literature, however, is any discussion of the idea that a successful leader must know how to *empower others*. Also, the elements of *execution* and *integrity*, while tangentially related to the discussions on CEO compensation on the one hand and to overconfidence on the other, have not been explored in much depth. Moreover, all these early contributions only focus on one or two elements at a time. Finally, none of these contributions explores in any depth what we believe is a fundamental issue for leadership: the credibility of the leader's vision, in settings where the leader is expected to change course in the face of changes in the firm's environment. The next section outlines a general conceptual framework based on our paper (Bolton et al., 2008) that has at its core this credibility problem, but that also includes four of our five elements. The one element still missing is *empowering others*.

Conceptual Framework

The model we outline in this section sheds light on what we believe to be a fundamental problem of leadership, namely, how the leader can credibly convey that he will stay the course so long as a change in strategy is not clearly warranted by new events. The effectiveness of leadership depends on the leader's ability to convey that he will do as best he can to stick to the proposed path for the organization. It is only when followers have the confidence that the firm is committed to a strategy that they are willing to rally around the leader's mission statement for the organization.

The framework we consider has one leader and many followers, which we take to be a continuum indexed by i for analytical simplicity. In contrast to the previous analyses discussed above, this framework applies most clearly to large organizations, in which the typical agent's behavior has a negligible impact on the organization as a whole. The main advantage of focusing on large organizations is that we can abstract from the complexities of gaming inside organizations. The organization's environment is summarized in the parameter θ, which affects payoffs. The leader and followers start with different information or beliefs about the true value of θ. This reflects the idea that most agents in a large organization only have local information about their own department or their market segment, and while the leader has access to global information, he is not fully informed about all the individual activities the firm is engaged in.

The leader's primary role in a large organization is to delineate the overall strategy for the firm. This is captured formally by letting the leader move first and announcing what he believes the environment is, θ_L, to which the firm should try to adapt. Thus, in this framework a strategy is summarized by the goal set for the organization to adapt as closely as possible to the perceived environment θ_L. This is admittedly a somewhat abstract representation of a leader's mission statement for the organization or of the leader's vision. Suffice it to say that the merit of this abstract formulation is generality. Many different strategies in different contexts can be represented in this way.

Of course the leader's vision θ_L is not a fully accurate representation of the environment, and the organization is uncertain as to the true state of the environment. This idea is captured by letting θ_L be a random variable, which is only equal to the true environment on average. For analytical simplicity we take this random variable to be normally distributed: $\theta_L \sim N(\theta, 1)$.

The followers' own information about the environment is given by $\theta_i \sim N(\theta, \sigma_\theta^2)$. They use this information along with the leader's mission statement to determine what action a_i they should take. Finally, after the followers have moved, the leader receives new information about the environment in the form of a signal $S_L \sim N(\theta, \sigma_2^2)$ and then chooses his own action a_L—which can be thought of as the organization's overall course of action—based on his updated beliefs about θ.

Several immediate questions arise. First, why do followers take their own information into account at all? Why not just rely on the global information of the leader? The simple answer is that followers value not just the benefits of coordination but also the benefits of adaptation. But, more interesting, even if followers only cared about coordination, they still need to be able to forecast what the leader's ultimate choice a_L will be, and for that their own information may be helpful. Second, why does the leader pay any attention to the signal S_L? Again, the leader and the organization as a whole care about adaptation to the environment. To the extent that the original mission statement θ_L turns out to be maladapted, the leader will want to change course even if this comes at the expense of some miscoordination. Importantly, however, when the leader makes the final choice a_L he no longer has to worry about how his choice will affect followers' actions a_i, because these actions have already been taken. There is thus a fundamental time-consistency problem for the leader: if he could commit to a choice function $a_L(S_L)$ at the time when he communicates his mission statement he would want to do so, because his ex-ante choice will influence how followers act and will therefore be different from his ex-post choice.

Formally, the objective function for all the agents in the organization can be taken to be as follows:

$$\Pi_i = -(a_i - a_L)^2 - \int_j (a_j - \bar{a})^2 \, dj - (a_L - \theta)^2 \quad \text{for } i \in [0, 1] \cup \{L\}. \quad (9\text{-}1)$$

This objective reflects three concerns for all agents: (1) *coordination with the leader*, or taking an action that is close to the organization's strategy; (2) *coordination among followers*; and (3) *adaptation* to the environment θ.[2]

With this objective function, followers need to forecast the ultimate strategy of the organization, a_L, to be able to determine their own best response, a_i. If they think that the leader's ultimate choice a_L is very sensitive to S_L, they will put very little weight on the leader's mission statement θ_L and more weight on their own information. As a result, the organization will not be well coordinated and there will be a large loss from miscoordination; that is, the term

$$\int_j (a_j - \bar{a})^2 dj$$

will be large. This observation captures in a simple way the concern CEOs and shareholders have with potential failures of leadership. If the firm is not seen to be committed to a clear strategy, there is a risk that there will be lots of coordination failures. Moreover, this risk is highest when senior management is seen to be hesitant and to be waiting for new information before deciding on the overall course for the company. A clear implication is that CEOs should not try to fine-tune the firm's strategy too much; in other words, that *the best is the enemy of the good*.

But how can CEOs credibly convey that they will stay the course? We explore two mechanisms. The first is a form of overconfidence of the leader, which we refer to as *resoluteness* or *conviction*. This is modeled by assuming that the leader overestimates the precision of her prior information. That is, the leader believes that θ_L has variance $\sigma_p^2 \leq 1$. By attaching too high an informational value to θ_L, the leader will put less weight on new information S_L so that her mission statement has more credibility. This is why *conviction brings credibility*.

This is an intuitive and widespread idea. Good leaders are often described to be strong and to have strong convictions along with great vision. In our framework this means that they trust their opinion or information more than those of others and therefore they will not easily be swayed to change course. This mechanism is related to the role of overconfidence discussed in the contributions in the previous section. But resoluteness plays a different role here and is also more specific than overconfidence.

It plays a different role because it serves as a commitment device to achieve greater coordination. And it is more specific because it is precisely overconfidence with respect to prior information that matters. In other words, what matters is the leader's initial conviction, or belief, that she is right. This is what Parsons refers to as the element of *integrity*. Note, however, that if the leader were overconfident with respect to the value of new information, she would be even more fickle than a rational leader and would then undermine the credibility of her mission statement.

To summarize, this framework captures two closely linked leadership problems: the first is that the leader may simply have the wrong vision and chooses a path for the company that may lead to failure; the second is that although the leader ultimately steers the organization in the right direction his mission statement is too vague, poorly communicated, or not fully credible, so that the organization's overall plan of action is implemented incoherently, with substantial coordination failures. The best way to deal with these problems is to appoint a leader who is forceful, even stubborn, has strong convictions, but who is not obstinate to the point where he is willing to take the company in a disastrous direction in the face of overwhelming evidence that his chosen strategy will lead to disaster.

Interestingly, when the leader's or the followers' information is noisier, then, if anything, the firm should appoint a more resolute leader. The reason is that when the leader knows less to begin with, he is more likely to change the firm's strategy in response to new information and therefore is less able to coordinate the followers. A more resolute leader is then desirable even if this means a greater risk of ultimately heading in the wrong direction.

This basic framework can be augmented or modified in several different directions without affecting the fundamental leadership trade-off or the desirability of resolute leadership. Possible modifications of the objective function (9-1) are the following:

1. Replace the term $-(a_i - a_L)^2$ in the leader's objective with

    $$-\int_i (a_i - a_L)^2 \, di$$

    to reflect the idea that the leader does not care only about adaptation of the firm's strategy to the environment but also about coordination with all the followers' actions. With this objective function, leader resoluteness is still desirable, but less so.

2. Add the term $-(\theta - a_i)^2$ to the followers' objective function to reflect the idea that followers also care about adaptation to the environment. This worsens coordination among followers. When followers want to align their action with the leader's,

they do so knowing that the leader's action is partly based on θ_L. Because θ_L is known to all followers, it enables coordination. When followers want to also align their action with the true state, however, they weight θ_L less and coordination deteriorates.

3. Allow for a more general weighting of the different terms in the objective function as follows:

$$-\omega_i(a_i - a_L)^2 - \omega_j\int_j(a_j - \bar{a})^2 dj - (a_L - \theta)^2.$$

As long as the weights on alignment and coordination in the firm's objective function are positive, leader resoluteness is always desirable. But as coordination becomes more important relative to the benefit of alignment, the marginal value of more resoluteness rises. For firms where alignment is crucial (ω_i and ω_j are small), the optimal level of resoluteness will still be positive, but small.

4. Change followers' payoff to

$$-(a_i - a_L) - (\bar{a} - a_i)^2 - (a_L - \theta)^2$$

to reflect the fact that there are only private costs to miscoordination and no public externality costs. In this case, resoluteness is always costly. If followers choose the degree of coordination that is best for the firm on their own, then there is no coordination problem for the leader to resolve. The only issue the leader is then concerned with is to choose the best-adapted mission. Rational leaders perform this task best. This would be a model with an uninteresting role for a leader, in our view, that does not incorporate relevant leadership challenges.

5. Introduce private and public costs to miscoordination in the form

$$-(a_i - a_L)^2 - \int_j(a_i - a_j)^2 dj - (a_L - \theta)^2.$$

With this payoff function, the optimal amount of resoluteness is also lower, because private costs to miscoordination now cause agents to coordinate better. But, again, some resoluteness is still valuable.

6. Add reputation as a commitment device. One way to incorporate reputation costs is to add a fourth term to the leader's payoff function as follows:

$$\Pi_L = -(a_i - a_L)^2 - \int_j (a_j - \bar{a})^2 dj - (a_L - \theta)^2 - c(a_L - \theta_L)^2. \quad (9\text{-}2)$$

The fourth term introduces a penalty for the leader that increases the more the leader ends up deviating from his stated mission θ_L. This term is one way of capturing Parsons's *execution* or accountability element. A leader can be more effective at coordinating followers' actions if he is willing to put his reputation on the line that he won't deviate from the announced mission statement. In our framework this is equivalent to choosing a higher c. Remarkably, as is shown in our companion article, resoluteness remains a valuable attribute of a leader even when the leader can commit to a strategy by staking his reputation. The reason is that a resolute leader is prepared to choose even higher values of c—in other words, is even more willing to put his reputation on the line—because he is more confident that he is right.

To summarize, the framework we have outlined so far can account for four of the five key elements of leadership (at least partially) that we have singled out in the introduction: first, the element of *vision* is captured in the relative precision of the leader's initial information; second, top-down *communication* is reflected in the leader's mission statement; third, *execution* is captured in the leader's willingness to stake her reputation on the successful implementation of the mission; and, fourth, the element of *integrity* is captured in the leader's resoluteness or confidence in her initial information. It is worth noting that overconfidence is often viewed in the economics literature as a *bias* that may lead individuals to make foolish mistakes. In contrast, here, the particular form of overconfidence that results in resoluteness can be a desirable attribute, as has often been noted in the management literature on leadership.

This framework can also be augmented to account for the *bottom-up communication* element of leadership. To introduce a role for communication by followers, it suffices to let the leader's second signal S_L be an aggregate index of followers' actions, which themselves reflect followers' own information:

$$S_L = \int_j a_j dj + \varepsilon,$$

where ε is a noise term—$\varepsilon \sim N(0, \sigma_\varepsilon^2)$—that captures the quality of communication between followers and the leader.

By introducing a two-way communication channel into our framework in this way we obtain several major substantive changes to our analysis. First, a new trade-off arises between greater coordination among followers—achieved by getting followers to found their actions less on their own private information—and less information communication by followers to the leader. In other words, coordinated actions now have both a positive payoff externality and a negative information externality. Second, followers decide to base their actions more or less on their information depending on whether they think that the leader is a *good listener* or not. If they think that the leader will put a lot of weight on S_L (by being a good listener), they expect that θ_L will be less predictive of the leader's final choice of strategy a_L and therefore they will be led to put more weight on their information θ_i. This, in turn, means that S_L is more informative, which confirms their initial belief that the leader will put more weight on S_L. In other words, this two-way communication translates into a fixed-point problem and gives rise to three possible equilibria.

The first equilibrium, which we label *dictatorial equilibrium*, is such that the leader pays no attention to S_L at all. As a result followers only put weight on θ_L and entirely ignore their own information when choosing their actions. This means that the leader is right to ignore S_L, because it conveys no information. As intuition suggests, this equilibrium always exists.

In the other two equilibria, which we label *lead-by-being-led equilibria*, the leader does put a lot of weight on S_L, with the consequence that followers' actions make S_L very informative, albeit at the cost of substantial miscoordination. One of these equilibria is unstable, and we don't focus on it for this reason. In the lead-by-being-led equilibrium, the organization is, of course, better adapted to the environment, because it relies on more information to determine its strategy. This equilibrium does not exist for all parameter configurations. Basically, what is required is that the true precision of the leader's prior information is low, while the precision of agents' private information is high. Also the leader should not be too resolute so that he does indeed put enough weight on S_L, and the environment should not be too uncertain so that miscoordination costs remain within reasonable bounds.

Interestingly, in the dictatorial equilibrium there is so much coordination by the followers that the leader does not need to be resolute at all. However, resoluteness can be a way of selecting the dictatorial over the lead-by-being-led equilibrium. And, paradoxically, in the lead-by-being led equilibrium some leader resoluteness is desirable in some situations to achieve greater coordination. This is the case when the signal the leader sees from the followers' output is already very precise.

In sum, the framework with two-way communication allows for situations in which it is preferable for a leader to be a *good listener* and to be capable of formulating well-adapted missions, as Parsons has been emphasizing. Resoluteness is most valuable when there is lots of uncertainty on the true environment but the leader's prior information is relatively accurate (in other words, when the leader has great *vision*). In these situations, the leader's stubbornness may suppress followers' information and may lead to the wrong strategy choice for the firm, but this risk is reduced by the leader's visionary qualities.

Missing Pieces

As we have already noted, one missing element from our list is *empowering others*. To introduce this element into our framework requires a broader perspective on organizations than our representation of a collection of followers who act in a noncooperative way based on their own information. As Parsons suggests, one important reason why empowering others is so important is that there is a limit to how much a leader can do.

To model leaders' *limited attention*, one would have to put constraints on the leader's ability to process information and to communicate with the whole organization. Our representation of top-down communication in our framework is rudimentary, to say the least. In reality, communication of an overall mission, strategy, or vision for the organization takes a lot of face-to-face meetings during which the strategy can be debated, explained in greater detail, and better motivated. Communication in our framework only takes the form of a message that is broadcast to the whole organization. Many firms have such broad mission statements posted on their Web sites, and they inevitably read like shallow and bland public relations exercises.

Top-down communication is more complex and takes time. To be effective, a leader has to be able to empower others around her in this communication effort. By enlisting the support of a strong team around her, she will be able not only to communicate the mission better but also to signal the credibility of the mission by displaying the level of support in her management team, as Majumdar and Mukand (2007) have argued. Similarly, when it comes to the execution of the strategy, the leader will need to empower others around her to implement all the multiple components of the strategy.

Another reason to empower one's followers is to develop their skills and knowledge base. Followers who rigidly follow a leader's exacting instructions do not develop their own judgment and end up contributing less to their firm than they might if they were allowed to experiment and learn. One way to capture this idea would be to write down a dynamic version of the model outlined above in which followers could learn about the precision of their information over time from seeing their payoff realizations. If they simply followed the leader's instructions, their payoffs would only be related to the leader's information and would teach them nothing about their own information. But if they used their private signals to develop their own course of action, seeing the results of that action would teach them about how to use their information more efficiently in the future. In such an environment, a leader would have to balance the short-term gains from resolute leadership generating well-coordinated outcomes against the long-term costs of strong coordination that results in foregone learning opportunities for followers.

Although there are important benefits in empowering others, this is often one dimension along which many leaders fail. There are several reasons why leaders tend to be reluctant to delegate. A first basic reason is that they are so confident in their own vision and abilities that they do not trust their subordinates to be up to the task. Thus, another drawback of resoluteness (besides leading to greater misadaptation to the environment) may be insufficient empowerment of subordinates.

A second reason is that leaders want to retain their power and fear competition from promising younger, smarter candidates for the job. Thus, in an effort to *entrench* themselves, they will tend to resist empowering others. This idea has been analyzed by economists in the context of a principal-agent model, most notably by Friebel and Raith (2004). It has also been explored in a political economy context by Egorov and Sonin (2006), who argue that an autocratic leader's fear of treason by his viziers is the main reason behind the time-honored practice of appointing weak but loyal subordinates over more competent ones. Another interesting recent analysis on this aspect of political leadership by Myerson (2008) points to the difficulty for the leader of credibly empowering others. The leader can take power or rewards away from his subordinates at any time, and he will do so when he no longer needs them. If his subordinates anticipate this outcome, they will have reduced incentives to work in support of the leader's mission. Myerson's analysis suggests that if the leader wants to credibly delegate power, he needs to subject his authority to a third party, which in the political context of his analysis might be a court with authority to remove the leader. In the corporate context this role could be assigned to an independent board of directors. Note, however, that an independent empowered board could undermine the leader's own credibility, which was already discussed in the introduction.

Another important and related element of leadership that is missing from our framework is the process by which leaders are identified or selected. The board of directors is charged with appointing corporate leaders, but how does the board identify a good leader? Managers compete for leadership positions, and their track record helps establish their leadership credentials. An obvious question that arises in this context is whether this leadership contest results in the appointment of resolute leaders. In an interesting analysis of this question, Goel and Thakor (2008) argue that overconfident managers are more likely to be appointed CEOs. The reason is that overconfidence leads these managers to take greater risks. Even if this risk taking leads overconfident managers to fail more often, the pool of successful managers—from which CEOs are picked—will be overrepresented by overconfident managers. To the extent that overconfidence takes the form of resoluteness, this selection bias toward overconfident managers may be beneficial for the organization, as we have argued above.

Conclusion

As our brief review highlights, the nascent economics literature on leadership has analyzed several important elements of leadership in organizations. Although the starting point of most economic analyses is the principal-agent paradigm of the firm, the ultimate direction of these leadership analyses is an entirely different vision of the managerial firm, in which the main problem is not so much to elicit effort provision by management (or to limit their consumption of perks) but to make sure that management exercises leadership credibly and executes its vision of the firm's mission.

Notes

1. See Aynesley Toole, "Parsons Speaks on Elements of Leadership," December 5, 2007, *The Bottom Line* (Columbia Business School).

2. This basic conceptual framework is similar to the model of organizations by Dessein and Santos (2006), which also considers the organizational trade-off between achieving greater coordination and greater adaptation. However, in their model, agents communicate directly with each other and there is no leader.

References

Aghion, P., and J. Tirole. "Formal and Real Authority in Organizations." *Journal of Political Economy* 105, no. 1 (1997): 1–29.

Blanes i Vidal, J., and M. Möller. "When Should Leaders Share Information with Their Subordinates?" *Journal of Economics and Management Strategy* 16, no. 2 (2007): 251–283.

Bolton, P., M.K. Brunnermeier, and L. Veldkamp. "Leadership, Coordination and Mission-Driven Management." Working paper, 2008.

Breeden, Richard C., et al. "Report of Investigation by the Special Committee of the Board of Directors of Hollinger International Inc." Securities and Exchange Commission, 2004. http://www.sec.gov/Archives/edgar/data/868512/000095012304010413/y01437exv99w2.htm.

Coase, R. "The Nature of the Firm." *Economica* 4, no. 16 (1937): 386–405.

Dessein, W., and T. Santos. "Adaptive Organizations." *Journal of Political Economy* 114, no. 5 (2006): 956–995.

Egorov, G., and K. Sonin. "Dictators and Their Viziers: Endogenizing the Loyalty-Competence Trade-off." Working paper, Harvard University, Cambridge, MA, 2006.

Ferreira, D., and M. Rezende. "Corporate Strategy and Information Disclosure." *RAND Journal of Economics* 38, no. 1 (2007): 164–184.

Friebel, G., and M. Raith. "Abuse of Authority and Hierarchical Communication." *RAND Journal of Economics* 35, no. 2 (2004): 224–244.

Gervais, S., and I. Goldstein. "The Positive Effects of Biased Self-Perceptions in Firms." *Review of Finance* 16 (2007): 453–496.

Goel, A., and A. Thakor. "Overconfidence, CEO Selection and Corporate Governance." *Journal of Finance* 63, no. 6 (2008): 2737–2784.

Grossman, S.J., and O. Hart. "The Cost and Benefits of Ownership: A Theory of Vertical and Lateral Integration." *Journal of Political Economy* 94 (1986): 691–719.

Hermalin, B. "Toward an Economic Theory of Leadership." *American Economic Review* 88 (1998): 1188–1206.

Kaplan, S., M. Klebanov, and M. Sorensen. "Which CEO Characteristics and Abilities Matter?" Working paper, University of Chicago, 2007.

Majumdar, S., and S. Mukand. "The Leader as Catalyst: On Leadership and the Mechanics of Institutional Change." Working paper, 2007.

Myerson, R. "The Autocrat's Credibility Problem and the Foundations of the Constitutional State." Working paper, University of Chicago, 2008.

Rotemberg, J., and G. Saloner. "Leadership Styles and Incentives." *Management Science* 39 (1993): 1299–1318.

——— "Visionaries, Managers and Strategic Direction." *RAND Journal of Economics* 31 (2000): 693–716.

Simon, H.A. *Models of Man: Social and Rational*. New York: John Wiley & Sons, 1957.

Song, Fenghua and Anjan Thakor. "Intrinsically Motivated CEOs, Overbearing Boards, and Diversity in Corporate Governance." Working paper, Pennsylvania State University, 2008.

Van den Steen, E. "Organizational Beliefs and Managerial Vision." *Journal of Law, Economics, and Organization* 21, no. 1 (2005): 256–283.

Williamson, O.E. "The Vertical Integration of Production: Market Failure Considerations." *American Economic Review* 61 (1971): 112–123.

IO

AN ECONOMIC PERSPECTIVE ON LEADERSHIP

Mark A. Zupan

Introduction

Much like Supreme Court Justice Potter Stewart and his struggle with defining pornography ("I know it when I see it"), scholars have been hard pressed to develop a model of leadership. This is not for lack of trying. Each year, scores of books are written on the topic (more than on any other), cataloging traits and operating styles that effective leaders possess and/or providing emblematic case studies and anecdotes. According to Bob Eckert, chairman and CEO of Mattel, Inc., a search on Amazon.com reveals nearly 200,000 matches for books dealing with leadership (Eckert, 2008). Countless speakers like Bob are invited to business schools as well as for university commencement addresses to opine on the subject. And leadership programs continue to sprout within academic, corporate, and government settings.

Notwithstanding the significant effort to arrive at a framework for understanding leadership, precious little progress appears to have been made. Indeed, Warren Bennis's (1959) assertion of nearly a half century

Author note: Helpful comments have been provided by Bob Eckert, Mike Jensen, David Logan, Janice Willett, Steve Zaffron, and Jerry Zimmerman.

265

ago seems to ring even truer today: "Of all the hazy and confounding areas in social psychology, leadership theory undoubtedly contends for top nomination. And, ironically, probably more has been written and less is known about leadership than any other topic in the behavioral sciences."

We intuitively know that leadership matters and can point to settings on the political stage (Lincoln during the Civil War, Gandhi championing the Satyagraha movement, Susan B. Anthony's advocacy of women's rights, Nelson Mandela's nonviolent promotion of racial equality in South Africa) and the military and sports arenas where that seems to be the case. Witness the Fuqua/Coach K Center of Leadership and Ethics built by Duke University's Fuqua School of Business around the highly popular basketball coach Mike Krzyzewski; the accolades bestowed upon and sales of motivational books written by Pat Summitt, coach of Tennessee's Lady Vols basketball team; and the speaking fees currently charged by former military leaders of Operation Desert Storm such as Colin Powell and "Stormin' Norman" Schwarzkopf.

Yet as much as we have learned about leadership, it is fair to say that our conception of it remains much more as an "art" than a "science"—akin to the perceptions of management prior to the establishment of business schools at universities and efforts thereafter to bring intellectual rigor from core academic disciplines such as economics and psychology to bear on the profession. In a modest way, this paper seeks to advance our understanding of leadership and to show that it has the potential to be a science as well as an art. It does so by borrowing an integral concept from economics, the prisoner's dilemma, and showing how effective leadership requires solving this dilemma, a challenge as problematic as the proverbial Gordian knot that confronted Alexander on his way to Great-ness.

In a very fundamental way, leadership involves creating opportunity from a seemingly intractable setting that, if otherwise left to its own resolution, confines us to an inferior equilibrium. To rise above this suboptimal outcome requires reconceptualizing a one-shot play of the prisoner's dilemma into an indefinitely repeated framework. This paper shows how effective leaders make this traverse via vision; enrolling others to participate in the ongoing play of the reformulated prisoner's dilemma; commitment; integrity; communication; and authenticity.

The Prisoner's Dilemma as Leader's Opportunity

The prisoner's dilemma is a well-understood concept in economics. It helps explain why cartels break down, public goods are undersupplied, medical costs burgeon under a system of third-party payment, litigiousness in a society rises when its judicial system taps "deep pockets," and representative democracies tend to run fiscal deficits (Browning and Zupan, 2008). At its core, the prisoner's dilemma illustrates that there are settings in which the pursuit of self-interest leads to suboptimal outcomes, in marked contrast to one of the core insights from Adam Smith's *The Wealth of Nations* (1937) regarding the socially beneficial workings of the Invisible Hand.

Based on the strategy employed by law enforcement agents who are seeking evidence of a greater crime from a set of prisoners who collectively have been picked up for a lesser offense, the prisoner's dilemma is illustrated in figure 10-1 for the simplest 2×2 case. In figure 10-1, two prisoners, Bonnie and Clyde, are interrogated separately by prosecutors and offered the following symmetric payoffs: only one year in prison if they turn state's evidence and confess to the crime while their partner does not (their implicated partner is sent to jail for fifteen years for the more major offense); two years in the slammer if they as well as their partner do not break under the separate interrogations (their partner is also incarcerated for two years in such a scenario for the lesser offense that has been committed); ten years in prison if both parties rat on each other, thereby giving law enforcement agents sufficient evidence to convict both for the major offense and mete out the identical, more

FIGURE 10-1

The prisoner's dilemma

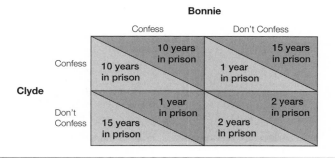

substantial sentence; and fifteen years behind bars if they do not confess but their partner does (implicating them while getting off with the lighter one-year sentence in return for providing the damning evidence).

Note that in this simple example, each party has a dominant strategy to confess. The pursuit of self-interest leads to a pareto inferior income, from Bonnie and Clyde's perspective, relative to the dominated strategy of not confessing (ten years in prison versus the two-year sentence that would accompany being convicted for the lesser crime).

Figure 10-2 recasts the prisoner's dilemma in the case of positive profit outcomes for two symmetric duopolists, Utopia and Artesia, operating in the bottled water market. The two firms can maximize their collective profits by complying with an agreement to cartelize the market, each thereby earning profits of 20. Both firms, however, have an incentive to cheat on the cartel agreement that would maximize their well-being, lowering their individual profit to 10 in the process.

Because the figure 10-2 prisoner's dilemma game has a dominant-strategy equilibrium where all firms cheat, it appears that successful collusion never occurs unless binding contracts are permitted and enforced by an external authority. As is well known, however, such a conclusion is overreaching because firms often interact more than once and the appropriate framework is thus a repeated game as opposed to a one-shot.

With repetition, there is a future. A future gives participating firms a dimension with which to enforce a cartel agreement by punishing one another for cheating, and this critical dimension has been shown to elicit more cooperative outcomes. Indeed, Axelrod (1984) shows that in an indefinitely repeated prisoner's dilemma setting, the equilibrium

FIGURE 10-2

Cheating in a cartel

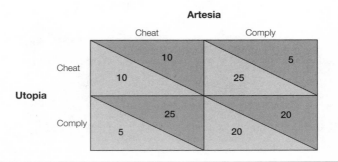

that tends to emerge is the exact opposite of the one predicted by a one-shot framework. Namely, taking steps toward the collaboratively beneficial outcome until one's partner transgresses from such a strategy and then retaliating in kind (the tit-for-tat or Old Testament eye-for-eye approach) consistently outperforms any other strategy put forth in Axelrod's round-robin simulations.

The ability to recast a prisoner's dilemma from a one-shot to an indefinitely lived prisoner's dilemma setting provides a key insight into leadership. In particular, leadership involves the creation of a future and promotion of cooperative behavior by parties enrolled in an endeavor such that more is attained jointly over time than could be realized by individual, self-maximizing behavior in any given period of play. To borrow a well-worn phrase: leaders ensure that the whole is greater than the sum of the parts. The ensuing sections spell out key aspects of leadership within the prisoner's dilemma framework that produce such a successful outcome: vision, enrollment, commitment, integrity, communication, and authenticity.

The First Aspect of Leadership: Vision

Economists are prone to make assumptions as part of practicing our craft. A central assumption of relevance to our discussion here is the existence itself of a prisoner's dilemma that can be played repeatedly and indefinitely. While we may take it for granted ex post, leadership hinges critically on "the vision thing" and seeing it ex ante, where others may not have conceptualized it before but can acknowledge it ex post.

Former University of Notre Dame president Theodore Hesburgh stated, "The very essence of leadership is that you have to have a vision." According to Bennis and Nanus (1997:81–82), a vision is "a target that beckons" and is central to organizational formation/growth and success:

> Over and over again, the leaders we spoke to told us they did the same things when they took charge of their organizations—they paid attention to what was going on, they determined what part of the events at hand would be important for the future of the organization, they set a new direction, and they concentrated the attention of everyone in the organization on it. We soon found that this was a universal principle of leadership, as true for orchestra conductors, army generals, football coaches, and school superintendents as for corporate leaders.

Whether it be Martin Luther King Jr.'s dream of racial equality, John F. Kennedy's announcing, in 1961, the goal of putting a man on the moon by 1970, Bill Gates's entrepreneurial aim to put a computer on every desk in every home, or Mother Teresa's determination to care for Calcutta's destitute, the conceptualization and articulation of targets that beckon is a critical task for any leader hoping to inspire others to sustained collective action.

The Sources of Vision

How does a leader discover, structure, and articulate prisoner's dilemmas that will yield benefits for all concerned if the game is played repeatedly? A common belief is that leaders hatch such ideas de novo in isolated bursts of clarity—much like Athena reputedly sprang from Zeus's head. The leaders then come down from the lofty mountaintops they have scaled in the pursuit of a vision to present their insights to awaiting followers who are ready to be led from the wilderness by the clairvoyant leader.

While there are certainly examples that one can point to in support of the great person view of leadership, there are many others that accord with a more Hayekian (1945) version of how knowledge is developed in society. Indeed, Bennis and Nanus (1997:88) note:

> Historians tend to write about great leaders as if they possessed transcendent genius, as if they were capable of creating their visions and sense of destiny out of some mysterious resource. Perhaps some do, but upon closer examination it usually turns out that the vision did not originate with the leader personally but rather from others.

Personal Administrative Experiences

My personal experience with leadership in business higher education over the past two decades accords with the observation by Bennis and Nanus (1997) on this score. Indeed, of the administrative assignments that I have held at three different academic institutions, the accomplishments that I am proudest of stemmed from insights made by others in the organization that were quite obvious for their rationality and impact once they became articulated but were much less apparent prior to that point in time (much like the reaction one may feel when the rationale is provided for why so-and-so has won a Nobel Prize).

At USC's Marshall School of Business, for example, we convinced a promising MBA applicant to accept our admissions offer over some rival programs. The applicant accepted our offer largely because he saw that USC had the world's top cinema school and that mutually beneficial bridges could be built between the cinema and business schools, located as they are in the entertainment capital of the world. The student's insight, in retrospect, should have been seen by others in the organization decades prior to his arrival. It took his matriculation and bridge building in the early 1990s, however, to create an entertainment management program that now thrives at Marshall (routinely, 20 percent of any incoming MBA class wants to major in the program that the student in the early 1990s helped bring to life at USC).

In 1997, as an incoming dean of the University of Arizona's Eller College of Management, I had expressed the intent of focusing on the MBA program at that institution. Such an objective seemed eminently logical given how much the media rankings spotlight has focused on business schools' full-time MBA programs in recent decades. However, through conversations with stakeholders at Eller, I began to realize how much greater impact a little more emphasis on the undergraduate business program would have on the well-being of that institution. In particular, the most successful Eller College alumni (an overwhelming percentage of whom graduated with a BBA rather than an MBA) would routinely rather meekly note at the end of an initial meeting that while media rankings mattered, their belief was that just a little more attention on the BBA program was merited. Each year, the University of Arizona graduates ten times as many BBA as full-time MBA graduates.

On account of the insights provided by prominent alumni, we were able to make some important enhancements to the Eller College BBA program, including a required interview of all applicants, more rigorous admissions standards in general, a cohort-based approach to delivering the curriculum, and greater emphasis on communication skills building and professional development. Changes such as these led to the school's first-ever top twenty ranking at the undergraduate level in *U.S. News and World Report* and student buy-in and Board of Regents approval for establishing differential tuition at the undergraduate level (something that had been unheard of for a public higher education institution located in a state whose constitution expressly stated that college tuition should be as nearly free as possible).

The incremental revenues from establishing a differential tuition program at the undergraduate level proved to be an important benefit for the college and all of its programs since the funds could be deployed to attract and retain faculty teaching graduate as well as undergraduate students. In addition, prominent alumni, some of whom had been the impetus for the BBA emphasis, began assisting the Eller College philanthropically at dramatically higher levels. Ultimately, the college was able to set its sights on securing at least $100 million in gifts as part of a fundraising campaign versus the initially contemplated $21 million target.

Finally, starting in 2004, as the new Simon School dean at the University of Rochester, I was intent on working with key constituents to enhance what was already an excellent graduate school of business. Those plans did not include paying greater attention to attracting *Early Leaders*—younger applicants with relatively less work experience—to the full-time MBA program (zero to three years' experience versus the traditional average of four to six years of experience that prevails at other leading business schools).

My Simon plans changed after a conversation with a senior faculty member who pointed to the merits of focusing relatively more on traits such as smarts, drive, character, and presence as opposed to sheer years of prior work experience in our admissions decisions. The faculty member noted how business schools admitted candidates straight out of college up through the late 1980s, at which point media rankings appeared and created an incentive to pursue older students by emphasizing average starting salaries as a ratings criterion (the best predictor of post-MBA starting salary is pre-MBA salary).

Diversity suffered on account of the shift toward older full-time students (Brickley and Zupan, 2007). Top-tier business schools are now less female than they were in the early 1980s (28.2 percent in 2007 in the top thirty schools, versus 28.6 percent in 1984). This is in marked contrast to leading medical and law schools, whose graduate programs are roughly 50 percent or more female, still largely select candidates straight out of college, and—probably no coincidence—are not evaluated by media rankings on the basis of their graduates' starting salaries.

Since launching the Early Leaders initiative, the Simon School has experienced significantly greater full-time MBA enrollment growth than other leading business schools (Brickley and Zupan, 2007). Quality, if anything, has been enhanced on many dimensions, as Simon has shown greater increases in incoming GMAT scores and GPAs than most other top-fifty schools ranked by *U.S. News and World Report.*

Diversity has improved—half of Simon School's Early Leaders are female. Recruiters, some of whom were skeptical initially of the initiative, are hiring Early Leaders more quickly than their more experienced counterparts, and the salary penalty they are assigning to youth ($12,000–$15,000 lower average starting salaries) is surprisingly small. The post-MBA starting salary differential is sufficiently small to ensure that, on average, Early Leaders can double, by the age of thirty, the net return of investing in a full-time MBA relative to the option of pursuing the degree as a more experienced student. This sizable difference in return on investment reflects the fact that Early Leaders earn the post-MBA salary jump earlier in their careers and then see it compounded by future year's salary increases. Early Leaders also sacrifice less in terms of forgone salary by opting to pursue the MBA earlier in their careers.

Early Leaders may well end up being the initiative in which I take the greatest ultimate pride in my own administrative career. Importantly, for the purposes of this paper, the ex ante counterintuitive idea that I am now such a champion of ex post was something that welled up from the organization that I was part of through the insight of one of our senior faculty members. Now at the heart of the Simon School's strategic plan, Early Leaders was initially something that I was antithetically opposed to and had, in fact, worked against at previous administrative posts, having sought to ensure a minimum number of years of prior work experience for consideration of MBA admission.

Creating a Vision's Organizational Architecture

Conceptualizing the repeated, indefinitely lived prisoner's dilemma game at the heart of leadership, of course, involves developing the appropriate organizational architecture. This architecture can take explicit and implicit forms. It defines the empowerment of the various participants in the organization and thereby the strategies available to these participants. In addition, the architecture spells out the payoffs associated with the pursuit of various strategies by an organization's participants and includes mechanisms to evaluate individual and group performance.

In a Jensen-Meckling (1976) world where there is imperfect policing of agents by their principals, Brickley, Smith, and Zimmerman (2009) note that there are three key legs to any organizational architecture stool:

the allocation of decision rights, systems to evaluate the performance of individuals as well as groups of individuals within the organization, and the methods of rewarding individuals. These three legs can be seen to boil down to facets that determine the strategies and payoffs in a prisoner's dilemma conception of leadership. Such facets of organizational architecture "facilitate or subvert 'the best-laid plans,'" according to Bennis and Nanus (1997:103).

The Second Aspect of Leadership: Enrollment

The conceptualization of a vision is a necessary but not a sufficient condition for successful leadership. Merely outlining the nature of a prisoner's dilemma game whose repeated and indefinite cooperative play will result in a collective improvement in welfare does not guarantee that the game will actually be played. As economists well know, any game theoretic situation requires three key elements: players, strategies, and payoffs. Yet, just like the existence of a game and its associated strategies and payoffs, economists also tend to merely assume the existence of players.

Leaders worth their salt realize that the voluntary enrollment of others is no small task and is instead a critical aspect of leadership. Scherr and Jensen (2008) note that enrollment is integral for successfully bringing a newly envisioned future into being and cannot just be assumed into existence. Bennis and Nanus (1997:xiii) observe:

> True leaders have an uncanny way of enrolling people in their vision through their optimism—sometimes unwarranted optimism. For them the glass is not half-full, it's brimming. They believe—all of the exemplary leaders that we have studied—that they can change the world or, at the very least, put a dent in the universe. They're all purveyors of hope. Confucius said that leaders are "dealers in hope."

The other aspects of leadership outlined in this paper—vision, organizational architecture, effectiveness of communication, the authenticity and integrity of a leader, demonstrated commitment—all can play key roles in facilitating enrollment. Beyond these aspects, empowerment is a powerful means to encourage others to voluntarily and cooperatively play a repeated prisoner's dilemma game (Bolton, Brunnermeier, and Veldkamp, 2009; Zaffron and Logan, 2008). If others believe that a venture's vision is theirs to help shape, they are much more likely not only to contribute to the development of a compelling vision but also to want to participate in its execution on account of the stake they hold in the venture.

Hayek's (1945) insight, on the eve of the Cold War, as to why communism would ultimately grind itself to a halt stemmed from the fact that command-and-control systems do not provide sufficient incentive to those closest to the bits of information scattered throughout society to act on and profit from valuable knowledge of place, time, and circumstance. This insight leads to an inverse corollary to one of Adam Smith's well-known dictums in the *Wealth of Nations* (1937): "What is prudence in the conduct of every great society can scarce be folly in that of particular ventures within that broader society." Whereas the Pilgrims almost starved themselves to death when the land surrounding Plymouth Colony was owned in common and decisions were made centrally, the willingness to participate in cultivating fields rose dramatically and the colony became self-sufficient when individual settlers were granted rights to farm particular plots of land (Koch, 2007).

The ancient Chinese philosopher Lao-tzu perhaps summed it up best when he observed how critical empowerment was to enrolling others in and then ensuring the long-run success of any great undertaking (Bennis and Nanus, 1997): "Fail to honor people, they fail to honor you . . . The wicked leader is he who the people despise. The good leader is he who the people revere. The great leader is he who the people say, 'We did it ourselves.'"

Getting the Right People on the Bus and in the Right Seats

Integral to the enrollment process is selection. According to Jim Collins (2001:1), the executives who were able to lead their publicly traded companies from good to extended periods of great performance "first got the right people on the bus (and the wrong people off the bus) and then figured out where to drive it."

Focusing on who to get on the bus and in which seats, the publicly traded good-to-great companies analyzed by Collins and his research team realized important advantages, such as being better able to deal with changing circumstances and lowering monitoring costs. Collins notes that "the right people don't need to be tightly managed or fired up; they will be self-motivated by the inner drive to produce the best results and be part of creating something great" (p. 42). Schmidt (2008) makes the related point that in dynamic market settings, agency costs are lower and firms will be more adept at identifying and realizing profitable new opportunities where the right people have been selected for the right corporate seats. Bossidy (2001) provides a further compelling example from his days as CEO of AlliedSignal (1991 through 1999) as to the importance that selection plays in improving organizational performance.

By contrast, companies with the wrong people on the bus or in the wrong seats generally are incapable of achieving greatness even when they have the right direction or seemingly appropriate organizational architecture—see, for example, Schmidt (2008) on the latter facet of this point. Moreover, comparison firms studied by Collins that frequently followed the "genius with a thousand helpers" model—in which a genius leader sets a vision and then enlists a bevy of competent "helpers" to assist with making the vision a reality—tended to perform less well. Indeed, such comparison firms often failed altogether when the resident genius departed.

Collins notes the case of Nucor, a steel manufacturing firm that was one of eleven publicly traded firms out of hundreds examined, which showed a sustained (fifteen-year) period of outperforming the broader market by a factor of at least three to one after a similar period of cumulative stock returns at or below that of the broader market, and outperformed peer firms in the same industry over a sustained period and thus could not merely be explained away as being "lucky." Nucor rejected the old adage that a firm's people are its most important asset. Instead, Collins observes that the Nucor experience underscores that "[i]n a good-to-great transformation, people are not your most important asset. The *right* people are" (p. 51).

The Collins evidence provides strong support for the Hayekian perspective on how visions are developed. Indeed, the evidence even calls into question the primacy of vision before successful enrollment of the right people. According to Collins, "The key point is that 'who' questions come before 'what' decisions—before vision, before strategy, before organization architecture, before tactics" (p. 63).

The Third Aspect of Leadership: Commitment

The first two aspects of leadership noted above focus on structuring the indefinitely lived prisoner's dilemma game at the heart of leadership. Namely, a leader must outline a vision of the game to be played (including the strategies and payoffs) and enroll fellow players. Beyond structuring an indefinitely lived prisoner's dilemma game, however, leaders also shape the process of playing the structured game. They do so through their commitment, integrity, communication, and authenticity. This section and the ensuing ones deal respectively with these four process-related aspects of leadership.

Let us turn first to commitment. As Hermalin (1998) appropriately points out, leadership is distinct from formal authority. It reflects informal authority and requires voluntary followership. Within a prisoner's dilemma setting, there are two ways that a leader can motivate others to put in effort toward promoting the collective good: sacrifice and example. The leader may offer, for example, gifts such as free food or vacation travel to prospective followers to encourage them to render effort on behalf of the collective enterprise—not so much for the private reward associated with the pursuit of the gifts but for the public-goods or signaling value the offer itself provides to prospective followers about a worthwhile activity being promoted. Alternatively, as humanitarian Albert Schweitzer noted, "example is leadership" and leaders can convince followers to engage in a collective activity by being the first to devote effort to the cause.

Commonly, leaders are credited with being the first ones in the office in the morning and the last ones to leave at night and with never asking followers to undertake a task that they themselves are unwilling to perform. Historical instances of leading by example abound and include Rosa Parks refusing to give up her seat on the bus to a white male passenger when ordered to do so by the driver; Teddy Roosevelt leading his Rough Riders up San Juan Hill during the Spanish American War; Colleen Barrett, President Emeritus and former Chief People Officer of Southwest Airlines, developing and living the culture of "LUV" that made her company consistently the most (and only) profitable firm in its business over the last three-plus decades; and Abraham Lincoln being the first Northern elected political leader to visit Richmond within days after its fall to the Union Army in April 1865. "Let 'em up easy" replied Lincoln while touring the Confederate capital at grave personal danger and being asked by a Union general how the defeated Southerners should be treated. Lincoln's remarks echoed his second inaugural address of March 1865 calling for the victorious North to proceed "[w]ith malice toward none, with charity for all . . . let us strive on to finish the work we are in; to bind up the nation's wounds; . . . to do all which may achieve a just, and a lasting peace, among ourselves, and with all nations."

Whether through sacrifice or example, leadership requires commitment to the vision that has been articulated for voluntary followership to occur. Without such a convincing signal being sent, Hermalin shows that rational fellow players will not be induced to follow a leader who otherwise has an incentive to mislead. Furthermore, of the two forms of potential signaling, leading by example is superior to sacrifice because it is a productive action that directly increases welfare, whereas sacrifice merely involves a transfer with no direct impact on welfare.

In the context of the repeated-game prisoner's dilemma model of leadership spelled out earlier, commitment involves leaders making a cooperative first move that then creates a foundation for eliciting mimicking behavior by fellow players in future plays of the game. In a sense, leaders create an extra round to the game during which they convey a signal, through action, as to the strategy they intend to select—cooperation—toward fellow players in future rounds. In an indefinitely repeated game setting, this extra round inserted by leaders in effect primes the pump for cooperative behavior to occur throughout the interaction since it encourages the more rapid spread of the tit-for-tat strategy shown by Axelrod (1984) to otherwise emerge in equilibrium.

The Fourth Aspect of Leadership: Integrity

As Erhard, Jensen, and Zaffron (2008) show, "without integrity nothing works." Once a vision has been articulated, fellow players enrolled, and a commitment made by the leader that elicits cascading consonant commitments from followers, honoring one's declared words through ongoing actions is critical to the success of collective enterprises. In the context of the outlined prisoner's dilemma game, the surest way for a leader to facilitate cooperative behavior on the part of voluntary followers is to take repeated steps in sequential plays of the game that are consonant with the vision for the enterprise. Conversely, as proved by Axelrod (1984), the suboptimality of a relationship's outcome is directly related to the extent to which players are prone to cheat on the vision for the relationship and take steps in any period that are in their more narrow self-interest.

In a very real sense, integrity is a flow variable. "Trust," in turn, reflects the stock that is built up over time through investments in integrity by a player in repeated plays of a prisoner's dilemma interaction.

The greater a player's reputation for integrity, the more likely others will be to entertain entering a relationship with him or her as well as to behave in a cooperative manner once they are engaged in a relationship. Such are the benefits of building up a stock of trust capital through investments in integrity.

Of course, as noted by Erhard, Jensen, and Zaffron (2008), integrity is not the same as morality, ethics, and legality. These related, but alternative, concepts reflect evolved norms of behavior in a particular group, society, and state, respectively. By contrast, integrity involves a condition of wholeness, entirety, completeness, and being unbroken that is a driving factor in a vision's workability. A leader promotes workability through integrity by following through on the commitments to an articulated vision through subsequent actions. Where integrity is lacking, the result will be a breakdown in the relevant prisoner's dilemma game to the detriment of all involved parties. When the leader (or a follower, for that matter) acts without integrity, collective effectiveness will be diminished and supplanted by expediency, broken promises, lack of accountability, and suboptimality. Zaffron and Logan (2009) note that much as one wouldn't want to drive over a bridge that lacks integrity—that isn't whole and complete—so one wouldn't want to participate in a collective vision missing such a vital ingredient.

Integrity, as defined by Erhard, Jensen, and Zaffron (2008), is thus a positive as opposed to a normative aspect of leadership. It is not a normative assessment of the ethics, morality or legality of a vision. Rather, integrity involves a positive assertion of what steps need to be taken to ensure that a vision will become a reality.

The Effect of a Future on the Present Practice of Integrity

While integrity promotes workability and thereby enhances the likelihood that an articulated vision will be realized, there is also an important inverse corollary to this proposition. Namely, leadership as an act that converts a one-shot into an indefinitely repeated prisoner's dilemma game also serves to promote the practice of integrity. Where the future matters, that is, behavior by individual, self-interested parties confronting a prisoner's dilemma will be more consonant with collective well-being.

Consider the research of Scully (1997), who examined the state-sponsored killing of civilians by their own leaders. In the last century, 170 million people were killed by their own political leaders—7.3 percent of the total population and over four times as many as lost their lives to international and civil wars. Scully finds that in a cross-country analysis of killing of civilians by their own leaders, the likelihood of such murder occurring goes down when the future prospective economic contribution of the average civilian to the country is higher. Where citizens' future real GDP contributions promise to be greater, in other words, political leaders show greater respect for the lives of their nation's citizens.

A more recent example involves an examination of the extent to which the resumes submitted by financial service job candidates in the United Kingdom are characterized by integrity.[1] The survey of nearly 4,000 job applications commissioned by Powerchex, the leading London-based pre-employment screening firm, found that graduates of the United Kingdom's least well ranked universities (100+) were three times as likely to have some form of major embellishment hidden in their application, everything else being equal, than graduates of top-20 U.K. universities. This phenomenon is at least consistent with the fact that the future, in terms of professional earnings and accomplishments, is more valuable to degree holders from higher-ranked schools. Because the future matters more, graduates from top-ranked programs have a natural incentive to behave with greater integrity in documenting their accomplishments to date and thereby not put those more valuable future career opportunities and earnings in jeopardy.

Finally, although business students and, more broadly, capitalism often get portrayed in the popular media as lacking integrity, the preceding corollary also stands this conclusion on its head. To the extent that markets and business promote repeat dealing and a future, they serve to facilitate rather than undermine integrity. On top of the virtues of capitalism that have previously been noted (see, for example, McCloskey, 2006), the promotion of integrity merits consideration for inclusion on the list.

An Observation Regarding Religion, Integrity, and the Concept of an Afterlife

While Erhardt, Jensen, and Zaffron (2008) note that integrity is not the same as ethics and morality, there does tend to be some overlap in most major religions. Witness the Old Testament commandment about not bearing false witness, or the admonition from the Koran (17:36) noting that lying is a serious vice and one should not "say that of which you have no knowledge." According to the religion of Islam:[2]

The Prophet . . . stressed the importance of always being truthful and the seriousness of habitual lying, "Truthfulness leads to piety and piety leads to the Paradise. A man should be truthful until he is written down as truthful with God. Lying leads to deviance and deviance leads to the Fire" . . . The malice of lying is tied to hypocrisy as described by the Prophet Muhammad . . . The Prophet's teaching is that we try our best to free ourselves of hypocrisy by keeping our trusts, telling the truth, keeping our promises, and not speaking falsely.

Like markets, most of the world's major religions also promote the concept of an indefinitely lived future. With religion, the relevant future consists of a form of afterlife. The model of leadership outlined in this paper indicates why the creation of such an indefinitely lived afterlife has value in terms of promoting a religion's system of ethics/ morals, including integrity, in the here and now. Namely, the more future payoffs matter (especially if they are perpetual), the greater the likelihood that behavior in one's temporal existence will evidence greater integrity and accord with a religion's other tenets.

Beyond promoting greater meaning and particular systems of morality/ethics, religions thus can be seen as vehicles for fostering integrity in the pursuit of those objectives through their conception of an afterlife. The prospect of endless suffering akin to those vividly described by Dante in his *Inferno* can beneficially affect the personal conduct of those who are still part of the living. Hades, Hell, Gehenna, Jahanan, Avici, Diyu, and Naraka are the types of payoffs and equilibria to be avoided, through adherence to integrity, if human souls truly are subject to the infinitely lived prisoner's dilemma game as conceived by most of our world's major religions.

The Fifth Aspect of Leadership: Communication

The successful exercise of leadership requires effective communication. A vision becomes more beckoning when communicated in a compelling fashion. The ability to articulate the organizational architecture (Bennis and Nanus, 1997) of the prisoner's dilemma game as well as to inspire others to enroll in the game and play for the collective good both hinge critically on a leader's prowess at communication. The capacity to deal with breakdowns (Scherr and Jensen, 2008) that occur in the playing of the prisoner's dilemma game—whether those breakdowns occur due to noise or noncooperative behavior by individual players—expands dramatically through communication. Finally, communication shapes a leader's authenticity and reputation for integrity.

Scherr and Jensen (2008) note the importance that declaration plays in creating a state change by providing a means of communicating a committed vision of leadership. Declaration differs from assertion in terms of the commitment involved. An assertion, which resides in the domain of management, propounds a point of view or idea that the author commits to providing convincing evidence of at a subsequent point in time. The assertion's author presumably is willing to be held accountable that the supporting evidence to be provided will be sufficient to convince the listener of the validity of the assertion. By contrast, declaration lies in the domain of leadership and involves a more powerful and immediate expression of commitment to a future or vision and thereby helps to create that future or vision. The Declaration of Independence aptly illustrates declarative communication as a means to signal commitment to a vision. The signers of the Declaration pledged to each other "their lives, fortunes, and sacred honor" for the purpose of creating a new form of government in the United States dedicated to "life, liberty, and the pursuit of happiness."

As observed earlier, commitment effectively creates an additional period in the playing of an indefinitely lived prisoner's dilemma game. If appropriately channeled, such commitment leads to the realization of collectively desirable outcomes. Importantly, commitment can encompass various potential forms of communication (oral, written, nonverbal as well as verbal, and so on). Such communication involves a leader effectively offering a bond to prospective followers whose value ex post ultimately hinges on the extent to which the leader honors his or her word but ex ante serves as a useful signal to prospective followers to enroll in and contribute to a collective enterprise. As the age-old saying goes, "One's word is one's bond."

Scherr and Jensen (2008) describe how the identity of a declarer and how listeners hear the declarer's words can play essential roles in distinguishing declarations from assertions. They relate the example of a judge in a criminal trial saying a defendant is guilty. When the judge renders such a verdict, the defendant is legally guilty and a state change results from the judge's declaration. By contrast, if the prosecutor in the same trial says that the defendant is guilty, this represents only an assertion, not a declaration.

Beyond the articulation of a vision and signaling commitment to that vision, communication also provides an important degree of freedom to a leader dealing with breakdowns during the play of an indefinitely lived prisoner's dilemma game. As defined by Scherr and Jensen (2008), breakdowns occur when the players involved in bringing a vision to life confront the fact that they will fail to realize the vision if they remain on their current trajectory. Such breakdowns may result from changes in the environment within which the prisoner's dilemma game is being played, changes that adversely affect the expected payoffs involved for the relevant parties. Breakdowns may also stem from one or more parties taking actions more in keeping with their narrow self-interest and contrary to the collective vision.

Economics, focusing as it does on the role of incentives, suggests that players involved in an indefinitely lived prisoner's dilemma game can take certain retaliatory steps when confronted by breakdowns that are perceived to be the result of missteps by other players (whether those missteps are real or the result of unanticipated changes in nature). Indeed, as mentioned earlier, the tit-for-tat or eye-for-eye strategy has been shown to consistently outperform all other intertemporal strategies when it comes to maximizing long-run payoffs and the need to face a bevy of alternative strategies, some of which cheat, at least for certain periods of time, on the collective good (Axelrod, 1984).

Sequential-period retaliation, however, represents just one method to elicit breakthroughs when groups confront breakdowns. Communication offers an important orthogonal means to realize similar breakthroughs. It does so by providing a mechanism to build recognition within the group that a breakdown has occurred; an opportunity for the leader as well as the other members in the group to recommit to the vision (albeit, perhaps, in some modified form); and, most fundamentally, the knowledge that breakdowns are the driving force behind innovation and the breakthroughs that ultimately allow for visions to be realized (Scherr and Jensen, 2008). Rather than being the impetus for nonproductive behavior (finding who to blame or to retaliate against), breakdowns, if channeled through communication in the right way, offer the wellspring to reevaluate and recommit to playing the prisoner's dilemma game at the heart of leadership in a manner that achieves the greatest possible collective outcomes.

Mirrors Versus Windows

Collins (2001) presents a marvelous metaphor for how leaders of good-to-great companies rely on mirrors versus windows in their communication when confronting organizational breakdowns as well as successes. Such transformational leaders "look out the window to apportion credit to factors outside themselves when things go well (and if they cannot find a specific person or event to give credit to, they credit good luck). At the same time, they look in the mirror to apportion responsibility, never blaming bad luck when things go poorly" (p. 35).

By contrast, the leaders of the comparison firms studied by Collins who failed to make the transition from good to great tended to use mirrors and windows in opposite ways. The managers of these firms would look out the window to identify who to blame (e.g., coworkers, bad luck) when organizational breakdowns occurred and gazed first in the mirror when seeking to apportion credit for organizational successes.

Collins's research indicates that the breakdowns as well as successes realized in the process of bringing a vision to life afford opportunities to mete out nonmonetary payoffs, through communication, to the fellow participants enrolled in an enterprise. Leaders are adept at using communication effectively to signal their own ongoing commitment to the enterprise while eliciting continued productive involvement from their fellow participants. Those leaders who are more generous in sharing the credit for successes and stingy when it comes to blaming others for failure are likely to draw, over time, a wider and more willing set of followers. Conversely, leaders who are stingy in sharing the verbal credit for successes and generous at castigating others for failure tend to attract a smaller and less motivated set of followers.

Two-Way Versus One-Way

Effective communication requires that it be two-way and not just one-way. Much like giving others an equity stake facilitates the development of a vision and empowerment, so being open to receiving communication or listening makes a leader more productive than if all the communication travels unidirectionally from leader to followers (Zaffron and Logan, 2009). Rotemberg and Saloner (1993) specifically model a bottom-up approach to leadership and focus on the communication element by which leaders induce followers to exert effort toward collective endeavors by listening to followers' ideas and suggestions for improvement. Just the prospect that their ideas and suggestions for improvement will be listened to by a leader interested in maximizing the long-run value of the venture provides sufficient incentive for followers to exert costly effort on behalf of the venture.

Interaction with Other Aspects of Leadership

Through its impact on authenticity and integrity, communication further influences leadership and its successful exercise. Take the matter of integrity. As defined by Erhard, Jensen, and Zaffron (2008), integrity does not just involve "keeping one's word." Rather, it consists of "honoring one's word." The distinction between these two concepts involves the manner in which individuals address situations where they realize that they will not be able to keep previously made commitments. Honoring one's word in cases like this involves making the situation known as soon as possible to all affected parties. It also requires cleaning up the resulting messes created when commitments cannot be met and making new promises that restore workability to the breakdowns resulting from previous commitments not being kept. Leaders proactively promote integrity, furthermore, by fostering conversations making the topic vital and meaningful for those involved in a collective enterprise (Zaffron and Logan, 2009).

The Sixth Aspect of Leadership: Authenticity

A number of prominent scholars, leaders, and writers have pointed to the importance of authenticity, character, or "being" as an essential aspect of leadership. For example, Bill George (2003:11), former CEO of Medtronic over a thirteen-year period when its market capitalization grew from $1.1 to $60 billion and now a professor of management practice at Harvard Business School, observes:

> After years of studying leaders and their traits, I believe that leadership begins and ends with authenticity . . . This is not what most of the literature on leadership says, nor is it what the experts in corporate America teach. Instead, they develop lists of leadership characteristics one is supposed to emulate. They describe the styles of leaders and suggest that you adopt them. This is the opposite of authenticity . . . They focus on the style of leaders, not their character.

On the opening page of their often-cited book, *Leaders: Strategies for Taking Charge*, Bennis and Nanus (1997:ix) emphasize: "Leadership is about character. Character is a continuously evolving thing. The process of becoming a leader is much the same as becoming an integrated human being." Frances Hesselbein, admired former CEO of the Girl Scouts of America and the Peter Drucker Foundation, notes: "Leadership is a matter of how to be, not how to do. We spend most of our lives mastering how to do things, but in the end it is the quality and character of individuals that defines the performance of great leaders."

Shakespeare perhaps put it best in his play *Hamlet*, when Polonius, the advisor to the king, gave his son, Laertes, some sage advice prior to traveling:

> This above all: to thine own self be true,
> And it must follow, as the night the day,
> Thou canst not then be false to any man.

The reason authenticity, or being true to oneself, carries such a premium in the exercise of leadership is that the most significant "agency costs" (Jensen and Meckling, 1976) within organizations well may stem, as Michael Jensen has observed, from "shirking" against one's own self. Much as a fish starts to rot from the head, so too will organizations flounder where leaders aren't true to themselves and thus impose agency costs on both themselves as well as the other parties involved in an enterprise.

To the extent that leaders are inauthentic and not true to themselves and prospective followers either sense the leaders' inauthenticity or are inauthentic themselves, the losses to the collective enterprise multiply. Whereas leaders may articulate a vision that beckons and enrolls others to participate in an indefinitely lived prisoner's dilemma game, the playing of that game will come to naught if leaders are not true to themselves, let alone if other prospective players sense the leaders' inauthenticity or are inauthentic themselves.

Authenticity carries particular value in a repeated-play prisoner's dilemma game should the leader have the opportunity to create, previously unannounced, a last period to the game. At such critical junctures, inauthenticity by the leader undermines the collective enterprise. For example, if there is expected to be a last period to the game but players (and perhaps even the leader) do not yet know when that period will be and a leader is inauthentic or perceived to be inauthentic, the game will tend to unravel (Selten, 1978), and suboptimal outcomes will be realized by the relevant parties.

Authenticity differs from commitment in that the latter represents actions taken to facilitate the accomplishment of a particular objective, whereas the former reflects being consonant with one's true values/self. Commitment is strategic and serves an important role in the exercise of leadership. Actions taken in service of commitment, however, may not perfectly correlate with the service of one's authentic self. Where there is a discrepancy, commitment in and of itself may be insufficient to ensure effective leadership and the optimal collective outcome.

Like integrity, authenticity is a positive rather than a normative concept. Individuals, that is, can be authentic pursuing evil or noble objectives (however "evil" and "noble" are defined). Like integrity, furthermore, authenticity implies workability. Without authenticity, that is, effective leadership tends to be an oxymoron.

An individual's authenticity is likely to be highly correlated with his or her "emotional intelligence" (Goleman, 1995). Moreover, authenticity can become revealed to the individual as well as to relevant parties through adversity as well as the absence of adversity. For example, the ancient Greek playwright Sophocles observed in his play *Antigone:* "But hard it is to learn the mind of any mortal, or the heart, till he be tried in chief authority. Power shows the man." Analogously, Abraham Lincoln noted that one could truly measure an individual's values only by what he or she did when unconstrained (to an economist, the "bliss point" selected by such an individual faced with no relevant constraints).

Summary and Conclusion

On the question of whether nature or nurture most determines leadership, Bennis and Nanus (1997:207) come down squarely in favor of nurture:

> *Myth 2: Leaders are born, not made.* Biographies of great leaders sometimes read as if they had entered the world with an extraordinary genetic endowment, that somehow their future leadership role was preordained. Don't believe it. The truth is that major capacities and competencies of leadership can be learned, and we are all educable, at least if the basic desire to learn is there and we do not suffer from serious learning disorders. Furthermore, whatever natural

endowments we bring to the role of leadership, they *can* be enhanced; nurture is far more important than nature in determining who becomes a successful leader.

To the extent that nurture indeed does play the more pivotal role, this paper has spelled out the critical aspects that influence the effective exercise of leadership. At its core leadership involves recasting a one-shot prisoner's dilemma into a collectively beneficial indefinitely repeated version of the same game. Leaders accomplish this fundamental transformation by creating a compelling vision, enrolling fellow players to participate in the development and execution of the vision, demonstrating commitment to the vision, exercising integrity, using communication prowess, and being authentic. Of these six identified aspects, the first two involve the setup or structuring of the indefinitely repeated prisoner's dilemma game at the heart of leadership. The remaining four aspects focus on the process by which the structured leadership game is actually played.

Of course, beyond the framework outlined above, much more remains to be explored to add appropriate sinew and skin to the bare-bones skeleton. For example, as posed by Hermalin (1998), what motivates certain individuals to be leaders? Superior information/vision, communication skills, integrity, and authenticity are possible determinants. Individuals can also differ in the utility they derive from having a following and in their perceptions of leadership as a means to gain valued fame, historical approval, or religious rewards.

What factors/traits influence authenticity and integrity? Why are certain individuals more prone to be future-oriented and to not behave in their more narrow self-interest in any individual round of a repeated prisoner's dilemma game? What role do "crucibles" (Bennis, 2003) play in facilitating the key aspects of leadership? To what extent do breakdowns (Scherr and Jensen, 2008) in the playing of an indefinitely repeated prisoner's dilemma game serve as crucibles?

When is remaining committed to a declared vision the wisest course of action? When is it more appropriate to revise a vision given that there are implications for enrollment, organizational architecture, integrity, communication, and so forth? In order to fulfill a particular vision, to what extent does communication matter relative to the appropriate design of a firm's organizational architecture? This question is analogous to the one faced by any parent in raising a child.

The foregoing are just a few of the important issues that await further investigation. For now, suffice it to say that this paper has laid out one economist's vision for conceptualizing leadership. The ultimate success of the vision will, of course, hinge on the extent to which it is effective in gainfully enrolling other scholars in the further study of leadership.

Notes

1. "A Degree of Creativity on CVs." FT.com. July 21, 2008.
2. "The Malice of Lying." IslamReligion.com. December 21, 2008. http://www. islamreligion.com/articles/26.

References

Axelrod, Robert. *The Evolution of Cooperation.* New York: Basic Books, 1984.
Bennis, Warren G. "Leadership Theory and Administrative Behavior: The Problem of Authority." *Administrative Science Quarterly* 4 (1959): 259–301.
———. *On Becoming a Leader.* New York: Basic Books, 2003.
Bennis, Warren G., and Burt Nanus. *Leaders: Strategies for Taking Charge.* New York: HarperBusiness, 1997.
Bolton, Patrick, Markus Brunnermeier, and Laura Veldkamp. "Economists' Perspectives on Leadership." In *Handbook of Leadership Theory and Practice,* edited by Nitin Nohria and Rakesh Khurana. Boston: Harvard Business Press, 2009.
Bossidy, Larry. "The Job No CEO Should Delegate." *Harvard Business Review,* March 2001, 46–49.
Brickley, James A., Clifford W. Smith Jr., and Jerold L. Zimmerman. *Managerial Economics and Organizational Architecture.* 5th ed. New York: McGraw-Hill/Irwin, 2009.
Brickley, James, and Mark A. Zupan. "Early Gains for Early Leaders." Viewpoint, BusinessWeek.com, December 27, 2007. http://www.businessweek.com/ bschools/content/dec2007/bs20071227_410093.htm?chan=search.
Browning, Edgar K., and Mark A. Zupan. *Microeconomics: Theory and Applications.* 10th ed. New York: John Wiley and Sons, 2008.
Collins, Jim. *Good to Great.* New York: HarperBusiness, 2001.
Eckert, Robert A. "Leadership." Unpublished manuscript, 2008.
Erhard, Werner, Michael C. Jensen, and Steve Zaffron. "Integrity: A Positive Model That Incorporates the Normative Phenomena of Morality, Ethics, and Legality." Working paper 06-11, Harvard Negotiations, Organizations, and Markets (NOM); and working paper 03-06, Barbados Group, April 2008. http://ssrn. com/Abstract=920625.
George, William W. *Authentic Leadership: Rediscovering the Secrets to Creating Lasting Value.* San Francisco: Jossey-Bass, 2003.
Goleman, Daniel. *Emotional Intelligence.* New York: Bantam Books, 1995.
Hayek, Friedrich A. "The Use of Knowledge in Society." *American Economic Review* 25, no. 4 (September 1945): 519–532.
Hermalin, Benjamin E. "Toward an Economic Theory of Leadership: Leading by Example." *American Economic Review* 88, no. 5 (December 1998): 1188–1206.

Jensen, Michael C., and William H. Meckling. "Theory of the Firm: Managerial Behavior, Agency Costs, and Ownership Structure." *Journal of Financial Economics* 3, no. 4 (1976): 305–360.

Koch, Charles G. *The Science of Success: How Market-Based Management Built the World's Largest Private Company.* New York: John Wiley and Sons, 2007.

McCloskey, Deirdre N. *The Bourgeois Virtues: Ethics for an Age of Commerce.* Chicago and London: University of Chicago Press, 2006.

Rotemberg, Julio J., and Garth Saloner. "Leadership Styles and Incentives." *Management Science* 39, no. 11 (1993): 1299–1318.

Scherr, Allan, and Michael C. Jensen. "A New Model of Leadership." Research paper 06-10, Harvard Negotiations, Organizations, and Markets (NOM); and working paper 06-02 Barbados Group, 2008. http://papers.ssrn.com/abstract=920623.

Schmidt, Ronald M. "Unpublished Lecture Notes on Leadership." William E. Simon Graduate School of Business Administration, University of Rochester, 2008.

Scully, Gerald. "Murder by the State." NCPA Policy Report no. 211, September 1997.

Selten, Richard. "The Chain Store Paradox." *Theory and Decision* 9 (1978): 127–159.

Smith, Adam. *The Wealth of Nations.* New York: The Modern Library, 1937.

Zaffron, Steve, and Dave Logan. *The Three Laws of Performance.* San Francisco: Jossey-Bass, 2009.

II

LEADERSHIP AND HISTORY

Walter A. Friedman

Introduction

Historians have written a lot about leaders, especially successful ones. Over one thousand biographies of Abraham Lincoln are listed in the catalog of the Harvard University libraries. Comparatively little has been written about the people who lost to him in the presidential election of 1860: John C. Breckinridge (four books), John Bell (three books), and Stephen Douglas (about fifty). There are also many histories of business leaders. The most popular figure, Andrew Carnegie, is the subject of over sixty biographies listed in the Harvard catalog, including several in languages other than English. Carnegie has emerged as the "Lincoln" of the business world, the embodiment, as one historian noted, of the "philosophy of America as a land where one could go from 'rags to riches.'"[1]

In this essay, I look at historians who have studied the functional role of leadership and have aligned it with the Schumpeterian definition of entrepreneurship: a creative-destructive process carried out both by individual agents and by those working in firms. This definition perceives leaders as managers of people, coordinators of resources, and, most important, initiators of change. In particular, I consider the work done at Harvard's Research Center in Entrepreneurial History. During its decade of existence (1948–1958), the Center was a fertile place for historical and economic thinking and home to some of the most prominent scholars of the day in sociology, economics, and history.[2] I pay special attention to the work of two members: one who is little known today, Fritz Redlich, and one of great stature, Alfred D. Chandler Jr.

The term "business leadership" appeared in U.S. newspapers only occasionally during Carnegie's heyday. By the early twentieth century, leadership became a subject of rapidly increasing interest. A popular inspirational and how-to literature on leadership appeared, including books such as Henry L. Gantt's *Industrial Leadership* (1916), which drew on the "scientific management" methods pioneered by Frederick W. Taylor.[3] In 1916 Junior Achievement was founded to mold the business leaders of the future.[4] In the 1920s the Carnegie Institute of Technology developed "mental activity tests" to determine the leadership potential of job applicants.[5] Henry C. Metcalf's edited collection *Business Leadership* (1931) recognized leadership as a phenomenon that escaped easy definition. The book included discussions of the psychological, historical, industrial, and political aspects of the subject.[6]

Redlich and the Research Center

Fritz Redlich (1892–1978) devoted much of his scholarly life to studying business leadership. He grew up in Berlin, the son of a prosperous businessman in the textile industry.[7] He was a student of Gustav von Schmoller and a disciple of the famous Historical School of economics. He earned a doctorate under the great scholar Ignaz Jastrow, writing about the German coal-tar dye industry. Redlich emigrated from Hitler's Germany in 1936 and arrived in the United States at age forty-five, with almost no money, prospects, or connections. He visited the renowned (and German-speaking) economists Frank Taussig and Joseph Schumpeter at Harvard and explained to them his interest in studying German and American entrepreneurs. While neither Taussig nor Schumpeter could offer him a position at the school, both encouraged Redlich to persist and both exerted great influence on his thinking. Taussig had written on the subject of business executives and remained interested in it throughout his career.[8] Schumpeter's work, especially his *Theory of Economic Development* (1911), provided Redlich with a conceptual framework for analyzing entrepreneurs and leaders.[9]

Redlich took teaching assignments at small colleges, such as Mercer in Georgia. He then returned to Cambridge, and from 1948 to

1950 he worked as director of research and statistics for the State Housing Board of Massachusetts. He received modest financial support for his scholarly work from Harvard and the New School for Social Research in New York.[10] Redlich spent some of his most creative time at Harvard Business School, where he worked in several capacities, including advising on the acquisition of books for Baker Library. Arthur Cole, the librarian of Baker Library and an economist, invited Redlich to become a senior associate at the Research Center in Entrepreneurial History, which Cole directed. Here Redlich found a home. Chandler and Kenneth Carpenter, both of whom were Redlich's colleagues, later wrote that "[a]t the Center Fritz Redlich was clearly the major intellectual force. His was its most creative mind."[11]

Redlich was a very productive scholar, publishing fifteen books in German and in English. He focused much of his energy on studying business leaders and leadership. He stayed with the theme of leadership for a long time, writing on it for over twenty years. Among his books and articles on the subject were his *History of American Business Leaders* (1940), which included a detailed study of the businessmen in the iron-and-steel industry, and his two-volume work *The Molding of American Banking, Men and Ideas* (1947 and 1951). Redlich also published several relevant articles in scholarly journals, including "The Leaders of the German Steam-Engine Industry During the First Hundred Years" (1944), "The Business Leader in Theory and Reality" (1949), "The Business Leader as a 'Daimonic' Figure" (1953), and "Business Leadership: Diverse Origins and Variant Forms" (1958).[12]

Despite his seminal influence at the Center, Fritz Redlich never received his due in the wider world of scholarship. His books, in their original format, often look more like typewritten, unpublished dissertations than polished products for a broad readership. *The History of American Business Leaders* is only available in 140 libraries worldwide, and *The Molding of American Banking* can be found only in 476. (For comparison, 1,771 libraries own Alfred Chandler's *The Visible Hand* in its original English, not including translations into many other languages.) Harvard owns two copies of Redlich's *Business Leaders*, one of which was a gift from the author to Taussig. It has been checked out only a dozen times since its publication in 1940. Both of Redlich's major works are oversized, about twice as large as a typical book, with each page having two columns of single-spaced small print. The *Molding of American Banking* alone contains 851 pages.

Part of the reason for the extreme length of his books is that Redlich disliked the trend toward economic theorizing and quantification, which by the 1960s was beginning to dominate the field of economic history.[13] He was interested in "the personal element in economic development." In his books on business leaders, he mentioned by name over six hundred iron-and-steel entrepreneurs—making the text somewhat exhausting for readers. He was emphatically not, however, a mere collector of biography, for he disliked the Great Man theory of history. Redlich insisted that history should be more than descriptive, maintaining that it must be analytical in its approach.[14] He tried to weave the details of people's lives and careers, taken together, into his observations of patterns in industrial development. As one of his colleagues wrote, "His historical universe was not composed of statistical atoms but of human individuals, who could be grouped according to types and by means of analogies but not dissolved into masses of impersonal data."[15]

What were some of his observations on the evolution of leadership? Redlich was greatly influenced by the thinking of Joseph Schumpeter, who taught him about the creative-destructive qualities of capitalism and the critical role of the entrepreneur. Like other members of the Center, Redlich opposed equilibrium models and viewed capitalism as a system of continual change and disruption.[16]

Redlich used the term "leader" or "creative entrepreneur" throughout his books. To many people at the Research Center, including Schumpeter and Arthur Cole, the two terms described similar business functions. In a lengthy article, Redlich described business leaders as *daimonic* characters, meaning that they initiated the creative and destructive elements of capitalism. He wrote that the term "denote[s] the fact that in the economic field hardly any real creation is possible without concomitant destruction." Redlich saw business leaders as being different from commonplace businesspeople: he considered them to be the initiators of change. They were not overseers who implemented enshrined strategy; they did not preserve traditional patterns. Drawing from Schumpeter, Redlich cited the introduction of the power loom, which destroyed the hand weaver's craft. "It did so *ipso facto;* and every new labor-saving device tended in the same direction, . . . the destruction of all hand crafts."[17] Redlich thought it essential for the historian to grasp the idea that the role of business leaders is as much to destroy old traditions and familiar patterns of behavior as it is to initiate new ones, even though "the superficial observer will be inclined to stress the one and to forget the other."[18] Redlich argued that, through this behavior, business leaders brought change in the five ways that Schumpeter had indicated in his path-breaking book *The Theory of Economic Development*: introducing new methods of production, creating new goods, opening new markets, conquering new sources of raw materials, and carrying out new ways of organization.[19]

Redlich argued that business leadership could best be understood in comparative perspective. His book *American Business Leaders* compared traditions of business leadership in various countries. He found, for instance, that in the early development of industry, the English were less likely to enter into combinations, whereas German entrepreneurs were eager to restrict competition and were able to make "loose combinations" work. Thus Germany became "the country of cartels." He also compared attitudes among national business leaders toward the role of research in business. He contrasted the early acceptance of industrial research among German executives in the years prior to World War I with the rapid development of such research by American businessmen after that date, and he noted the slower progress in England and France.[20]

But Redlich pointed out that these national traditions of leadership were hardly stable. The United States and other countries had leadership models that were refreshed by immigration. Some great English leaders had German backgrounds, such as the founders of Barings Bank, Francis and John Barings; George Joachim Goschen, a director of the Bank of England and later Chancellor of the Exchequer; merchant-banker Frederick Huth; and merchant Daniel Meinertzhagen. By contrast, some of the most successful bankers in Germany and Holland were from Great Britain: John Parish and his son David set up their business in Hamburg in the late eighteenth century, and Hope and Company was founded by the Scotsman Henry Hope in seventeenth-century Amsterdam. America both imported and exported business leadership, sending abroad to England Joshua Bates, senior partner at Barings, and bankers George Peabody and Junius Spencer Morgan, the father of J. P. Morgan.[21]

Redlich also perceived business leadership as a generational phenomenon. This was a major point for him. He believed that business-people born within the same span of time formed something of a cohort that often shared similar perceptions and helped to identify the outstanding business problems of the day—they faced "a community of problems and tasks." Generational problems might entail mastering issues of mass production and mass distribution, building up a new industry, converting from a wartime to a peacetime economy, or creating a venture-capital network. Redlich emphasized that leaders should be viewed as those who wrestled with, and defined, the key problems of their generation and thus helped to establish the challenges for the succeeding generation.[22]

Redlich presented a way for historians to make sense of the phenomenon of business leadership as a process, akin to entrepreneurship, of creation and destruction that ended in positive economic growth. The success of business leadership, he argued, is partly measured by the degree of change it brought about. He viewed leadership as a historical phenomenon, in which individuals built upon the major accomplishments of the previous era. As business leaders pushed to create change by enlisting technology, wealth, new organizational forms, or other innovations, they, in a real sense, shaped the economic future.

Redlich's most important idea was that history (the study of change over time) was an indispensable tool for making sense of leadership (which he defined as the creation of positive change over time).[23] Here it is important to remember that Redlich was not writing about *all* business functions—accounting, marketing, finance, and so on—but about the unique characteristics of the leadership process.

While Redlich's works helped to define how historians could identify and make sense of the contours of leadership, they remained scholarly and remote. They did not enlighten a broad audience about the workings of leadership or the real mechanics of industrial change. But the work of Redlich's colleague and protégé at the Center for Research in Entrepreneurial History, Alfred D. Chandler Jr., did accomplish exactly these goals.

Revisiting *Strategy and Structure*

Alfred Chandler's work is not usually associated with leadership. He tended to focus on organizations and industries and, like many of the participants at the Research Center in its later years, not on individuals. In fact, Chandler's work turned many subsequent scholars away from the study of individual businesspeople, influencing them to focus instead on firms and organizations. When Chandler used the term "leader," he was often referring to a company's role in its industry, rather than to a particular person. But there is a great deal in Chandler's work that bears directly on the subject of leadership.[24]

In particular, Chandler's seminal *Strategy and Structure* (1962) highlighted the ways in which individuals (middle managers and executives) shape the organization and the strategic policies of their firms. In doing so, they can bring about real and long-lasting change.[25] *Strategy and Structure* analyzed DuPont, General Motors, Sears, and Standard Oil, showing in minute detail how each of these four companies came to adopt the multidivisional structure. Most of the businesspeople who brought about change within these firms were not well-known personalities. Instead, they were managers and executives who recognized the structural inadequacies of their firm and pointed the way to the future.

Chandler mentioned on several occasions that he gained a lot from working with Fritz Redlich. Redlich was relentless in pressing Chandler to generalize and to tease big lessons out of his excruciatingly detailed research for *Strategy and Structure*. This is evident, for example, toward the end of *Strategy and Structure*, when Chandler went well beyond the four big case studies into a company-by-company enumeration of scores of other firms that did or did not adopt the multidivisional structure—and proceeded to explain why the U-form sufficed perfectly well for firms with small lists of product lines.[26]

Chandler's introduction to *Strategy and Structure* contains a vivid description of the type of history he was writing and its striking relevance to the study of leadership:

> Each case study presents the events from the point of view of the busy men responsible for the destiny of their enterprise. Only by showing these executives as they handled what appeared to them to be unique problems and issues can the process of innovation and change be meaningfully presented. Only in this way can the trials of harassed executives faced with novel and extremely complex problems be clearly pictured, and the impact of specific personalities and of historical or accidental situations on over-all change be adequately presented. Moreover, if the chronological development of the story is kept intact and if it can be presented as it appeared to the actors in the story, the data should have more value to businessmen and scholars interested in the growth and government of the great industrial corporation than if they were selected and arranged to develop or illustrate one particular historian's thesis.[27]

This is a very powerful statement of what business historians do, or should do. The phrases "process of innovation and change," "novel and extremely complex problems," and "specific personalities and of historical or accidental situation" are especially important. Chandler makes it clear that he wants to avoid being present-minded in his assessment of the behavior of individual executives, and his goal is to capture the ambiguity and complexity of the problems they faced.

Chandler's approach was not merely descriptive, nor was it hostile to economic theory.[28] He was arguing for a history in which data are not gathered to illustrate theoretical generalizations, but in which generalizations are derived from data. The "complex decisions, actions, and events are not taken out of context and presented merely to be illustrative, as they would have to be in a general history of American business or of the American economy."[29] Instead, they were being analyzed to develop theoretical propositions.

Chandler's description of his aims for *Strategy and Structure* fits well with the case method used at Harvard Business School. By and large, the case method is a way of teaching about business historically. Most of the cases in the school's curriculum, regardless of subject, are short histories of administrative situations. In some ways, the biggest differences between what historians do and what their colleagues do are (1) that historians go further back in time, and (2) that historians must develop extremely detailed data—mountains of evidence—to document the realities of past economic behavior.

In the first instance, by looking further back, historians reveal the origins of economic institutions and expose the underlying reasons for their appearance and evolution. The multidivisional form had been around for quite some time when Chandler described it and made it the subject for analysis. But he presented, for the first time, a compelling explanation for its development and popularization. His work challenged readers to think about the core problems in the evolution of managerial decision making and the importance of those decisions. For the second criterion, by immersing themselves in the details of day-to-day events of a firm and the decisions of executives, historians ideally serve the function of testing how current economic and social theory relates to past historical realities and thus facilitate new theoretical propositions. Chandler's detailed investigations were, for instance, the basis for his powerful argument that a company's strategy must shape its structure, not the other way around, as often happened.

In *Strategy and Structure*, Chandler captures the details through which important change occurred in business organizations. His account combines the larger perspective of firms undergoing major transitions with the details of individuals who brought it about. This perspective, revealing the entire workings of business from the view of middle managers and executives, is invaluable for any business leader.

Chandler hoped that his method of writing history would find an audience not only among historians and economists, but would also be of interest to businesspeople and to academics who study business. And in fact his work has had great influence in the field of organizational sociology and strategy. Richard Rumelt, Dan Schendel, and David Teece wrote that the founding of the field of strategic management can be "traced to the 1962 publication of Chandler's *Strategy and Structure*."[30]

Most academics who teach business leadership, however, make little use of the type of business history Chandler proposed in *Strategy and Structure*. The nation's military academies have been more receptive to history in their officer training programs than have business schools in their leadership coursework. Among the first textbooks adopted by the new Naval School in 1845 was Alexander Fraser Tytler's *Elements of History: Ancient and Modern*. Today the United States Naval Academy offers "American Naval Heritage—A History of this Country's Navy." West Point, founded in 1802, offered history in its curriculum as early as 1813, and has for most of the years since. In the late 1950s and early 1960s, the school recommended that each graduating officer have "knowledge of military art and science derived from the study of military history."[31] West Point now includes a course on historical perspectives for its future army officers, in the hope that it will make them "sensitive to patterns of continuity and change in the evolution of societies and their military forces." The course description continues: "As students of history learn how to analyze historical events, they gain a deeper understanding of the complexity and ambiguity of current and future events; they also develop analytical reasoning abilities."

In his Pulitzer Prize–winning book *Washington's Crossing*, David Hackett Fischer mentions that American military leaders responded particularly favorably to the work of historian and journalist Douglass Southall Freeman, who, although he wrote a different type of history from Chandler's, also highlighted the messiness of decision making in unique and changing situations. Freeman received a PhD from John

Hopkins and won Pulitzers for his multivolume biographies of Robert E. Lee and George Washington. Fischer wrote of Freeman's contributions to military history:

> [He] began with a mastery of sources, and centered his research and writing on discovering what his protagonist knew when he was making his leadership decisions, rather than on what we know after the fact. This unusual way of studying and writing history has been called (very inaccurately) the "fog of war technique." There was nothing foggy about it. The object was to be very clear about what Washington knew, and when he knew it, and how he reacted to that knowledge. Freeman's account of the battles at Trenton and Princeton were written in that way. The purpose was to learn about leadership from Washington's actions and choices.[32]

Freeman's work, which was published during the years from the Great Depression through the Cold War, proved to be of interest to military and political leaders. Freeman corresponded with Dwight Eisenhower, Chester Nimitz, and George Marshall.[33]

Part of the goal of history for students of leadership is to provide perspective: perspective about the complexities of decision making during periods of uncertainty made by past military leaders or by the "harassed executives" Chandler mentioned; perspective about the traditions of leadership, both ethical and rapacious, exercised in the past; and also perspective about the ways in which present circumstance is like or unlike the past.

Concluding Thoughts

Interest in leadership is growing. The subject will continue to demand a multidisciplinary approach. In reviewing the work of historians on this subject, I have chosen to emphasize two authors and, specifically, two of their books, Fritz Redlich's *History of American Business Leaders* and Alfred Chandler's *Strategy and Structure*, both written a long time ago. I chose them not because there has been little recent work by business historians on leadership. In fact, there has been a great amount of research, including serious analytical studies of business leaders such as German steel magnate August Thyssen; the pioneer of the integrated circuit, Robert Noyce; and Intel president Andy Grove. There have also been comparative studies of ethnic business groups and theoretical studies of entrepreneurship.[34]

I chose one author (Redlich) because his work has been relatively neglected, and the other (Chandler) because his work is usually not thought of as commenting on leadership. This essay suggests that the concept of "leadership" be reconsidered in the light of these works and of the ideas that emerged from the Center for Research in Entrepreneurial History. The point is to encourage historical investigation of the evolution of leadership, on the one hand, and detailed primary-source studies of the dynamics of leadership, on the other.

Following this line of thinking, leadership should be viewed as a Schumpeterian disruptive art, engaged as much in destroying old methods and products as in initiating new ones. It should be studied through the comparative analysis of business practice in various cultures and nations. And it should be studied historically as well as through the many other methods now being used with such fruitful results.[35]

Notes

1. Kenneth T. Jackson and David S. Dunbar, eds., *Empire City: New York Through the Centuries* (New York: Columbia University Press, 2002), 452. There have also been many studies of groups of business leaders. William Miller, Mabel Newcomer, and other scholars have employed statistics to survey the backgrounds and careers of leading businesspeople. There have been enough of these studies to show that Carnegie was not typical, either of his time or of any time since. According to economic historian Peter Temin, approximately two-thirds of business leaders throughout the period from 1870 to 1990 were the sons of business executives or professionals. American business leaders, he wrote in 1997, "are still drawn disproportionately from a small portion of the population, from families which resemble the families of previous members of the elite." (Peter Temin, "The American Business Elite in Historical Perspective," NBER working paper, Historical Paper 104, October 1997, 28–29.) For statistical group studies, see also F.W. Taussig and C.S. Joslyn, *American Business Leaders: A Study in Social Origins and Social Stratification* (New York: Macmillan, 1932); C. Wright Mills, "The American Business Elite: A Collective Portrait," *Journal of Economic History* suppl. V (1945): 20–44; William Miller, "The Recruitment of the Business Elite," *Quarterly Journal of Economics* 44, no. 2 (1950); Suzanne I. Keller, "The Social Origins and Career Lines of Three Generations of American Business Leaders" (PhD diss., Columbia University, 1953); and Mabel Newcomer, *The Big Business Executive: The Factors That Made Him, 1900–1950* (New York: Columbia University Press, 1955). See also Matthew Josephson, *The Robber Barons: The Great American Capitalists, 1861–1901* (New York: Harcourt, Brace, 1934) and Irvin G. Wyllie, *The Self-Made Man in America: The Myth of Rags to Riches* (New Brunswick, NJ: Rutgers University Press, 1954).

2. Ruth Crandall, *The Research Center in Entrepreneurial History at Harvard University, 1948–1958; A Historical Sketch* (Cambridge, MA: Harvard University, 1960); Thomas K. McCraw, *Prophet of Innovation: Joseph Schumpeter and Creative Destruction* (Cambridge, MA: Belknap Press of Harvard University Press, 2007), 472–474; Robert D. Cuff, "Notes for a Panel on Entrepreneurship in Business History," *Business History Review* 76 (Spring 2002): 123–132.

3. Some of these titles include the following: Edward Mott Wooley, *The Junior Partner: The Inner Secrets of Seven Men Who Won Success* (New York: E.P. Dutton, 1912); *Personality in Business: Developing Business Power Through Personality—How Personal Force Dominates in Business* (Chicago: A.W. Shaw, 1916); Frank C. Haddock, *Business Power: A Practical Manual in Financial Ability and Commercial Leadership* (Meriden, CT: Pelton Publishing, 1920); and B.C. Forbes, with Charles M. Schwab, *Ten Commandments of Success, an Interview* (Chicago: La Salle Extension University, 1920).

4. Joe Francomano, Wayne Lavitt, and Darryl Lavitt. *Junior Achievement: A History* (Colorado Springs: Junior Achievement Inc., 1988).

5. Richard Gillespie, "Manufacturing Knowledge: A History of the Hawthorne Experiments" (PhD diss., University of Pennsylvania, 1985).

6. Henry C. Metcalf, ed., *Business Leadership* (New York: Isaac Pitman & Sons, 1931); see also Percy S. Brown's review of this book in *Annals of the American Academy of Political and Social Science* 155, part 1 (May 1931): 243.

7. Hans Jaeger, "Fritz Leonhard Redlich 1892–1978," *Business History Review* 53, no. 2 (Summer 1979): 154–160. Kenneth Carpenter and Alfred D. Chandler Jr., "Fritz Redlich: Scholar and Friend," *Journal of Economic History* 39, no. 4 (December 1979): 1003–1007.

8. Including, with Taussig and Joslyn, *American Business Leaders*; and, with W.S. Barker, *American Corporations and Their Executives* (n.p., 1922).

9. On *The Theory of Economic Development*, see McCraw, *Prophet of Innovation*.

10. Carpenter and Chandler, "Fritz Redlich," 1003.

11. Ibid., 1004.

12. The best was a collection, published in 1970, called *Steeped in Two Cultures*, published by the commercial press Harper's and heavily edited.

13 "Yet, Fritz Redlich himself was dissatisfied with his accomplishments. One reason is that the younger generation turned to quantification, exactly the opposite of his emphasis on the personal element, and he felt that his work for the most part was not built upon. He also felt that inherently the theme of the entrepreneur in history was too narrow and not up to his capacities" (Carpenter and Chandler, "Fritz Redlich," 1005).

14. Ibid.

15. Jaeger, "Fritz Leonhard Redlich 1892–1978," 159.

16. On Schumpeter, see McCraw, *Prophet of Innovation*.

17. "The Business Leader as a 'Daimonic' Figure," *American Journal of Economics and Sociology* 12, no. 2, and 12, no. 3, parts I and II (January 1953): 164; and (April 1953): 289.

18. "The Business Leader as a 'Daimonic' Figure," (January 1953): 163–178; (April 1953): 289.

19. Joseph A. Schumpeter, *The Theory of Economic Development* (Cambridge, MA: Harvard University Press, 1934), 66; Redlich quotes this passage on page 18 of *History of American Business Leaders*.

20. "Business Leadership: Diverse Origins and Variant Forms," *Economic Development and Cultural Change* 6, no. 3 (April 1958): 183.

21. Ibid., 179.

22. Ralph M. Hower, "History of American Business Leaders: A Series of Studies," *Journal of Political Economy* 50, no. 2 (April 1942): 313–315.

23. As Thomas K. McCraw points out in *Prophet of Innovation*, Schumpeter had recognized entrepreneurship as a field best understood through the historical method.

24. Chandler and Redlich coauthored a piece: Alfred D. Chandler Jr. and Fritz Redlich, "Recent Developments in American Business Administration and Their Conceptualization," *Business History Review* 35, no. 1 (Spring 1961): 1–27.

25. Robert Cuff observed: "[T]hroughout all of Chandler's work, the business person most worthy of the designation 'entrepreneur' is someone who puts organization building ahead of financial or short-term deal making" (129–130). In *Strategy and Structure*, Chandler wrote, "I especially want to thank Dr. Redlich for dragooning me into his campaign against empiricism in the writing of business history and his invaluable assistance in developing useful concepts."

26. On this point, I am indebted to Thomas McCraw's recollection of the relationship of these two men.

27. Alfred D. Chandler, *Strategy and Structure: Chapters in the History of the American Industrial Enterprise* (Cambridge, MA: MIT Press, 1962; repr. 1995), 7. All citations are to the 1995 edition.

28. In fact, the economist John H. Habakkuk, in his review of the book, wrote that "Chandler's work is significant, not only for its substantive conclusions, original though these are, but as an example of the way in which fruitful relations can be established between economic and business history." See *Journal of Economic History* 23, no. 3 (September 1963): 348–349.

29. Chandler, *Strategy and Structure*, 7.

30. Richard P. Rumelt, Dan E. Schendel, and David J. Teece, eds., *Fundamental Issues in Strategy: A Research Agenda* (Cambridge, MA: Harvard Business School Press, 1994), 17. See also Richard Whittington, "Alfred D. Chandler, Founder of Strategy: A Lost Tradition and Renewed Inspiration," *Business History Review* 82, no. 2 (Summer 2008): 267–278.

31. From Robert A. Doughty and Theodore J. Crackel, "The History of History at West Point." In *West Point: Two Centuries and Beyond*, ed. Lance Betros (Abilene, TX: McWhiney Foundation Press, 2004), 411.

32. David Hackett Fischer, *Washington's Crossing* (New York: Oxford University Press, 2004), 447.

33. Fischer, *Washington's Crossing*, 447. David Donald, *Lincoln* (New York: Simon & Schuster, 1995) also took the same approach, which some critics did not like, but which had the benefit of showcasing Lincoln's evolution as a leader.

34. For a good overview of relevant recent work, see Geoffrey Jones and Daniel Wadhwani, "Entrepreneurship." In *Handbook of Business History*, eds. Geoffrey Jones and Jonathan Zeitlin (New York: Oxford University Press, 2007). See also Jeffrey R. Fear, *Organizing Control: August Thyssen and the Construction of German Corporate Management* (Cambridge, MA: Harvard University Press, 2005); Leslie Berlin, *The Man Behind the Microchip: Robert Noyce and the Invention of Silicon Valley* (New York: Oxford University Press, 2005); Richard S. Tedlow, *Andy Grove: The Life and Times of an American* (New York: Portfolio/Penguin, 2006); Andrew Godley, *Jewish*

Immigrant Entrepreneurship in New York and London (Basingstoke: Palgrave, 2001); and Yousef Cassis and Ioanna Minoglou, eds., *Entrepreneurship in Theory and History* (New York: Palgrave, 2005).

35. For instance, one of the largest efforts to make sense of leadership, the Global Leadership and Organizational Behavior Effectiveness (GLOBE) Research Project, has recently brought together empirical research from hundreds of scholars and has summarized their findings on the level of assertiveness and the extent of a future orientation in different national economies, all of which can be investigated historically. See the foreword in Robert J. House, Paul J. Hanges, Mansour Javidan, Peter W. Dorfman, and Vipin Gupta, eds., *Culture, Leadership, and Organizations* (London: Sage Publications, 2004).

12

POWER AND LEADERSHIP

Joseph S. Nye, Jr.

L EADERSHIP AND power are changing, but political scientists are not always clear about the relationship between the two.[1] A few decades ago, political scientists such as Robert C. Tucker contrasted a power approach with a leadership approach.[2] In his classic *Leadership*, James MacGregor Burns famously introduced a normative dimension that distinguished leaders from power wielders. More recently, Barbara Kellerman has argued for a positivist definition and written about bad leadership.[3] Moreover, many political scientists in recent years have left the field of leadership studies to psychologists and organizational behavior theorists whose research usually occurs within the narrow boundaries of the laboratory or the organization rather than a wider context of power behaviors.

If one thinks of power as including both the hard power of coercion and the soft power of attraction, leadership and power are inextricably intertwined. Leadership involves power, though not all power relationships are instances of leadership. Bombing an enemy into submission is quite different from persuading others to follow. At the same time, as I argue below, it is difficult to think of a leader without soft power. However, some contemporary theories that define leadership as synonymous with the soft power of attraction and persuasion miss the hard dimension of power. In practice, effective leadership requires a mixture of soft and hard power skills that I call smart power. The proportions differ with contexts. A business executive has more

305

access to the hard power of hiring and firing; a university president or a democratic politician has to rely more on the soft power of attraction and persuasion. I introduced the concept of soft power into the discourse of international politics two decades ago, but it is equally important to the topic of leadership. I define leaders as those who help a group create and achieve shared goals. Some try to impose their own goals while others derive them more from the group, but leaders mobilize people to reach those objectives. Leadership is a social relationship with three key components—leaders, followers, and the contexts in which they interact. One cannot lead without power.

Defining Power

Power is ubiquitous in human relations. We use the word every day, and seldom enter a room or join a group without sensing its power relations. Nonetheless, as James March and others have pointed out, power is hard to measure.[4] But that is also true of love, and we do not doubt its reality simply because you cannot say you love someone 1.7 times more than someone else. Like love (and leadership), power is a relationship whose strength and domain will vary with different contexts. Those with more power in a relationship are better placed to make and resist change. In *Power: A Radical View*, Steven Lukes even defines power in terms of the ability to make and resist change, and empirical studies have shown that the more powerful are less likely to take on the perspectives of others.[5]

The dictionary tells us that power is the ability to affect the behavior of others to get the outcomes one wants. One can do that in three main ways. You can coerce them with threats; you can induce them with payments; or you can attract or co-opt them.

Some people think of power narrowly in terms of command and coercion. They imagine it consists solely of commanding others to do what they would otherwise not do.[6] You say "jump" and they jump. This appears to be a simple test of power, but it is not so straightforward. Suppose, like my granddaughters, they already wanted to jump? When we view power in terms of the changed behavior of others, we have first to know their preferences. What would have happened without the command? A cruel dictator can lock up or execute a dissident, but that may not prove his power if the dissenter was really seeking martyrdom. And the power may evaporate when the context (including your objectives) changes. A tough boss who controls your behavior at work cannot tell you how to raise your daughter (although others outside your family, such as a doctor, can do so.) The domain of your boss's power in this case is limited to work. Power always depends on the context of the relationship.[7]

Sometimes people define power as the possession of resources that can influence outcomes. A person or group is powerful if it is large, stable, wealthy, and so forth. This approach makes power appear concrete and measurable, but it is mistaken because it confuses the results of a power relationship with the means to that end. Some analysts call this the "vehicle fallacy" or the "concrete fallacy." It treats power as something concrete that you can drop on your foot or on a city. But such concrete vehicles as bombs and bullets may (or may not) produce the outcomes you want. People defining power as synonymous with the resources that produce it sometimes encounter the paradox that those best endowed with power resources do not always get the behavioral outcomes they want. After all, the United States lost the Vietnam War to a weaker and more determined opponent, and the richest politicians do not always win the elections. A player holding the highest cards can still lose the game.

Soft Power

Police power, financial power, and the ability to hire and fire are examples of tangible "hard" power that can be used to get others to change their position. Hard power rests on inducements ("carrots") and threats ("sticks"). But sometimes one can get the outcomes one wants by setting the agenda and attracting others without threat or payment. This is soft power—getting the outcomes one wants by attracting others rather than manipulating their material incentives. It co-opts people rather than coerces them.[8]

Soft power rests on the ability to shape the preferences of others to want what you want. At the personal level, we all know the power of attraction and seduction. Power in a relationship or a marriage does not necessarily reside with the larger partner. Smart executives know that leadership is not just a matter of issuing commands, but also involves leading by example and attracting others to do what you want. It is difficult to run a large organization by commands alone unless you can get others to buy in to your values.

Community-based police work relies on making the police friendly and attractive enough that a community wants to help them achieve their shared objectives. Military theories of counterinsurgency stress the importance of winning the hearts and minds of the population, not merely killing the enemy. Similarly, as Gramsci pointed out nearly a century ago, political leaders have long understood the power that comes from setting the agenda and determining the framework of a debate. While leaders in authoritarian countries can use coercion and issue commands, politicians in democracies must rely more on a combination of inducement and attraction. Soft power is a staple of daily democratic politics. Even in the military, attraction and commitment play an important role. As former Army Chief of Staff Eric Shinseki put it, "You can certainly command without that sense of commitment, but you cannot lead without it. And without leadership, command is a hollow experience, a vacuum often filled with mistrust and arrogance."[9]

Of course, in many real-world situations, peoples' motives are mixed. Moreover, the distinction between hard and soft power is one of degree, both in the nature of the behavior and in the tangibility of the resources. Both are aspects of the ability to achieve one's purposes by affecting the behavior of others. Command power—the ability to change what others do—can rest on coercion or inducement. Co-optive power—the ability to shape what others want—can rest on the attractiveness of one's values or the ability to set the agenda of political choices. In real-world situations, hard and soft power are often combined, sometimes with a soft layer of attraction overlaid upon underlying relationships that rest on coercion or payment.[10] A lobbyist may first try to persuade a legislator, but the lobbyist may also make a legal and well-timed campaign contribution. A government may try to persuade young people to forgo drugs with an advertisement campaign featuring attractive celebrities, but if this soft power fails, the hard power of law enforcement remains.

The ability to establish preferences tends to follow from often intangible assets such as an attractive personality, culture, values, and moral authority. If I can get you to want to do what I want, then I do not have to force you to do what you do *not* want. If a leader represents values that others want to follow, it will cost less to lead. Soft power allows the leader to save on carrots and sticks. For example, loyal Catholics may follow the pope's teaching on capital punishment not because of a threat of excommunication, but out of respect for his moral authority. Some radical Muslims are attracted to support Osama bin Laden's actions not because of payments or threats, but because they believe in the legitimacy of his objectives. Even after bin Laden's organization was disrupted by the American military presence in Afghanistan, many terrorist groups around the world organized themselves in his image.

Soft power is not merely the same as influence, though it is one source of influence. After all, influence can also rest on the hard power of threats or payments. The word *influence* is used in various ways. I treat it as synonymous with behavioral power, which is consistent with the dictionary definition. Nor is soft power just persuasion or the ability to move people by argument, though that is an important part of it. It is also the ability to entice and attract. Attraction often leads to acquiescence. In behavioral terms, soft power is attractive power. In terms of resources, soft power resources are the assets—tangible and intangible—that produce such attraction.

People's decisions in the marketplace of ideas are often shaped by an intangible attraction that persuades them to go along with others' purposes without any explicit exchange of tangible threats or rewards taking place. Soft power uses a different currency (not force, not money) to engender cooperation. It can rest on a sense of attraction, love, or duty in a relationship, and appeal to values about the justness of contributing to those shared values and purposes.[11]

Soft power can provide what fundraisers call "the power of the ask." Someone calls and asks you to make a donation. Sometimes you say yes because it is a good cause or in an exchange of favors, but sometimes simply because of the moral authority of the person asking. In a nonprofit organization, the leader may ask you to undertake a task, and you say yes not because they can threaten or pay you, but simply because of who they are. An index of their power is the frequency, size, and range of requests they can successfully make of you. In institutions with flat hierarchies, such as universities and nonprofit organizations, soft power is often the major asset available to a leader.[12] Once that soft power has eroded, little else is left. People just say no. Even in the American presidency, as Richard Neustadt argued, power is mostly the ability to persuade others that they want to do in their own interests what you want them to do.[13] As Dwight Eisenhower put the case for soft power, leadership is an ability "to get people to work together, not only because you tell them to do so and enforce your orders but because they instinctively want to do it for you . . . You don't lead by hitting people over the head; that's assault, not leadership."[14]

The Power of Followers

Why do people follow at all? In ordinary circumstances they have functional needs for meaning, group identity and cohesion, order, and the ability to get work accomplished. Leaders fill these needs by a combination of fear, payment, and attraction—hard and soft power. In some circumstances, people have extraordinary personality needs and develop a culture of permissiveness that transfers enormous hard and soft power to a leader. In 1978 in Guyana, Jim Jones persuaded more than 900 followers to commit mass suicide rather than face the dissolution of his cult, the People's Temple.[15] In 1945, as Soviet troops closed in on Hitler's bunker in Berlin, Joseph Goebbels and his wife killed their children rather than have them face a world without their Führer.

In times of social crisis, such as war or economic depression, temporarily overwhelmed followers may hand over power to leaders that they later find difficult to retrieve. Hitler came to power by elections in Germany in 1933, and then used coercion to consolidate his power. But he also used the soft power of attraction, constructing narratives that turned Jews into scapegoats, glorified the past, and promised a thousand-year Reich as a vision of the future. Followers also helped to create Hitler. As Albert Speer put it, "Of course Goebbels and Hitler know how to penetrate through to the instincts of their audience; but in a deeper sense they derived their whole existence from the audience. Certainly the masses roared to the beat set by Hitler and Goebbels' baton; yet they were not the true conductors. The mob determined the theme."[16]

One can think of Hitler's followers in terms of concentric circles, with true believers like Goebbels, Goering, and Speer as an inner core; they are followed by a next circle of "good soldiers" like the Hamburg Reserve Police Battalion 101, who willingly executed Jews and Poles out of "crushing conformity;"[17] an outer circle of complicit bystanders who knowingly acquiesced; and a further circle of passive bystanders who made no effort to know what was behind the myths and propaganda. Beyond them were those who refused to follow and resisted, many of whom were destroyed or coerced into silence.[18]

Similar circles existed in other totalitarian systems such as Stalin's Soviet Union and Mao's China. Even before the advent of modern totalitarianism, for thousands of years most people have lived under authoritarian political regimes. This has not meant they were totally powerless. Peasants, workers, and religious and ethnic groups have occasionally revolted, sometimes with success. Kings have been killed. Resistance and rebellion are costly, and most subordinates lack the necessary means to succeed. Even when they appear to be docile, however, such subordinates may rebel continuously through withholding effort or quiet sabotage of leaders' orders.[19] Even ostensibly powerless followers may retain a degree of power over the ability of leaders to accomplish their ends.

Some discussions of leadership treat followers as obedient sheep. Followers can be defined by their *position* as subordinates or by their *behavior* of going along with leaders' wishes. But subordinates do not always go along fully with leaders' wishes. Leadership, like power, is a relationship, and followers also have power both to resist and to lead. Followers empower leaders as well as vice versa. This has led some leadership analysts like Ronald Heifetz to avoid using the word *followers* and refer to the others in a power relationship as "citizens" or "constituents."[20]

Heifetz is correct that too simple a view of followers can produce misunderstanding. In modern life, most people wind up being both leaders and followers, and the categories can become quite fluid. Our behavior as followers changes as our objectives change. If I trust your judgment in music more than my own, I may follow your lead on which concert we attend (even though you may be formally my subordinate in position). But if I am an expert on fishing, you may follow my lead on where we fish regardless of our formal positions or the fact that I followed your lead on concerts yesterday.

Regardless of what positions they hold in a group, followers' behavior can be ranked by its intensity and sorted into categories such as alienated, exemplary, conformist, passive, pragmatic, and so forth.[21] And followers' behavior may fit one category on some issues, and another category on another issue. For example, a Republican who is an exemplary supporter of the president on social and fiscal issues may be alienated over the Iraq War. Types of follower behavior vary with the cultural homogeneity, agreement on basic values, and fragmentation over issues that exist in groups and societies. A leader may have a great deal of soft power with followers in one domain, and very little in another.

Even in large organizations, where subordinates have few positional power resources, they may be able to exercise leadership. If a boss has great confidence in an assistant's judgment, she may often follow the assistant's lead. In practice, few of us occupy top positions in groups or organizations. Most people "lead from the middle," attracting and persuading both upward and downward. A successful middle-level leader persuades and attracts his boss as well as his subordinates. Richard Haass uses the metaphor of a compass: "North represents those for whom you work. To the South are those who work for you. East stands for colleagues, those in your organization with whom you work. West represents those outside your organization who have the potential to affect matters that affect you."[22] Effective leadership from the middle often requires leading in all directions of that compass.

Lee Iacocca was a successful executive at Ford Motor Company in the 1980s with great skills at managing the press and was widely regarded as a leader, but not in all directions. "Although Iacocca's self-promotion had a favorable impact on his perception as a leader, it had negative effects as well. Iacocca's increasing recognition as 'the' leader of Ford Motor Company soured his long-standing relationship with Henry Ford [chairman of the board], a situation that was the major factor in his dismissal." His successor, Philip Caldwell, "stressed the importance of everyone's [management's union workers', and key suppliers'] contribution," but he received less public recognition as the leader who turned the company's performance around.[23] Leaders in the middle who forget to attract and persuade in all directions often cease to be leaders.

Whatever they are called, there are no leaders without followers, and followers often initiate group activities. In the possibly apocryphal words of the French revolutionary Comte de Mirabeau, "There goes the mob, and I must follow them, for I am their leader."[24] More seriously, good leaders commonly intuit where their "followers" are trending and adjust accordingly. Followers often have the power to help lead a group. After his New Deal slowed down in the mid 1930s, Franklin Roosevelt reinitiated his legislative programs in response to pressures from new political and social movements in the country.[25] We very often discover that in many groups and organizations, leaders and followers are interchangeable in different situations, and both goals and initiatives can originate among followers.

Even when they do not take initiatives, followers have the power to set constraints on leaders. In hunter-gatherer societies, followers use ridicule, secession, ostracism, and even assassination to limit leaders who try to claim more powers than their followers are willing to grant.[26] Modern liberal democracies constrain leaders with constitutions, laws, and norms. Or to take a current example from the Internet, in open source software communities, members develop a culture that limits the effective authority of leaders, and those exceeding such limits lose their followers.[27] They just log off.

The power of leaders depends upon the followers' objectives that are embedded in their culture. For example, George Washington was an exemplary leader who is often credited with establishing the American republic by refusing a monarchical role. Followers lavished adulation upon him and he was revered as a demigod. His image was everywhere. In exalting Washington, the new Americans exalted their cause, and Washington became the symbol of the nation. He had great soft power, but that power was limited not only by the institutions of Congress and courts, but also by a political culture that was hostile to the exercise of authority. "Washington's great prestige did not provide the foundation for him to become a more dominant political figure because of the ambivalent attitudes Americans had (and have) toward political leaders. The very fact that he was so highly esteemed also made Washington the object of enormous suspicion."[28] Having fought themselves free of one King George, Washington's followers were determined not to allow another.

If leaders of a dominant culture are able to prevent people from having or covertly expressing grievances by completely shaping their worldviews and preferences, then followers have little power.[29] However, such extreme degrees of control are rare. Totalitarian governments have often tried to make subordinates accept their role in the existing order of things through a combination of hard coercive power and an ideological version of soft power, but with only partial success. Even in Stalin's Russia, Hitler's Germany, and Mao's China, it proved difficult to completely overcome all followers' covert forms of resistance, and in most instances, the power relationship between leaders and followers is far from so one-sided.

The Mixture of Hard and Soft Power

A century ago, in asking why people follow or obey, Max Weber identified three ideal types of authority or legitimated power.[30] Two depend on position and one on person. Under traditional authority, a person follows another because the latter is chief or king or emperor by right of some traditional process such as heredity. Under rational/legal authority, a person follows because the other is president, or director, or chair and has been properly elected or appointed based on rationally agreed criteria. Under charismatic authority, a person follows another because the latter embodies a gift of grace or exceptional magnetism. In the first two instances, followers obey because of the power of the position, in the last case because of the power of the person.

The distinction between informal personal power and power that grows out of a formal position is not exactly the same as the distinction between hard and soft power.[31] Some leaders without formal authority, such as gang leaders, may effectively use coercion as well as charisma. And some military officers have the soft power of charisma as well as the hard powers conveyed by their position. Moreover, certain formal positions such as pope or president extract obedience from followers who are attracted by the legitimacy of the institution even if the incumbent has very little personal appeal. But generally, those without formal authority tend to rely more on soft power, whereas those in formal positions are better placed to mix hard and soft power resources. Social movements tend to be volatile and complex formations devoted to causes such as civil rights, women's liberation, or environmental issues, and they rarely have clear and stable structures. Hierarchies are flat or nonexistent. With few material incentives under their control, leaders of social movements have few hard power resources and tend to rely on soft power and inspirational style.[32] Even with authority and structure, however, hard and soft power resources can change over time—witness the experience of lame duck presidents. The position remains the same, but the personal power changes.

There are various types of personal attraction. People are drawn to others both by their inherent qualities and by the effect of their communications. The emotional or magnetic quality of inherent attraction is often called charisma and we can treat it as one source of soft power. Communications can be symbolic (leadership by example) or by persuasion, for example, arguments and visions that cause others to believe, respect, trust, and follow. When such persuasion has a large component of emotion as well as reason, we call it rhetoric. Some communications are designed to limit reasoning and frame issues as impractical or illegitimate in such a way that they never get on the agenda for real discussion.[33] During periods of insecurity, leaders may appeal to patriotic rhetoric to exclude criticism from the public discussion. At this point, persuasion blurs into propaganda and indoctrination.

As for hard power, threats and inducements are closely related. Inducements, rewards, and bonuses are more pleasant to receive than threats, but the hint of their removal can constitute an effective threat.[34] If I can pay you a bonus, I can also threaten to take away your bonus. Some economists argue that there is no power relationship in freely struck market bargains. If you do not like the terms on offer, you can just walk away. But that assumes equal resources and equal needs. If I depend on you more than you depend on me, you have power. Asymmetry in interdependent relationships provides power to the less dependent party.[35] These types of power are summarized in table 12-1.

Hard and soft power are related because they are both approaches to achieving one's purpose by affecting the behavior of others. Sometimes people are attracted to others with command power by myths of invincibility. In some extreme cases known as "the Stockholm syndrome," fearful hostages become attracted to their captors. Adam Smith noted in his *Theory of Moral Sentiments* more than two centuries ago, "We see frequently the vices and follies of the powerful much less despised than the poverty and weakness of the innocent."[36] Or as Osama bin Laden put it more recently in one of his videos, "When people see

TABLE 12-1

Soft and hard power

Type of power	Behavior	Sources	Examples
Soft	Attract and co-opt	Inherent qualities Communications	Charisma Persuasion, rhetoric, example
Hard	Threaten and induce	Threats and intimidation Payments and rewards	Hire, fire, and demote Promotions and compensation

a strong horse and a weak horse, by nature, they will like the strong horse."[37]

Among the great industrial titans, Andrew Carnegie and Thomas J. Watson of IBM led primarily by intimidation; George Eastman of Kodak and Robert Noyce of Intel led primarily through inspiration.[38] Sometimes intimidators have a vision, belief in their cause, and a reputation for success that attracts others despite their bullying behavior— witness the examples of Steve Jobs, Martha Stewart, and Hyman Rickover, the father of the nuclear navy.[39] Rickover was a small man, far from the top of his class at Annapolis, who did not look the part of a warrior or swashbuckling sea captain. His success as a Navy leader came from his bureaucratic skills in cultivating congressional support and resources, and from a rigid discipline that tolerated no failures among his officers. The result was the creation of an efficient and accident-free nuclear submarine force that developed a mystique of success that attracted bright young officers. Able people wanted to join him because Rickover was renowned for implementing an important strategic vision, not because he was a nice boss.[40]

While some studies suggest that bullying is detrimental to organizational performance,[41] Stanford psychologist Roderick Kramer argues that bullies who have a vision and disdain social constraints are "great intimidators" who often succeed. The British Conservative leader John Major was a much nicer person than Margaret Thatcher, but Chris Patten (who served as a minister under both) reports that her bullying made her a more effective prime minister.[42] Machiavelli famously said it is more important for a prince to be feared than to be loved. And while some studies report that Machiavellianism (defined as manipulative, exploitive, and deceitful behavior) is negatively correlated with leadership performance, other studies have found a positive relationship.[43] So where does leadership theory now stand on the roles of hard and soft power?

Hard and soft power sometimes reinforce and sometimes interfere with each other. Although Jim Jones used soft power to persuade his followers to commit mass suicide, he had an inner core of about eight henchmen who used a degree of coercion on followers who threatened to defect. But growing awareness of this use of hard power threatened to "pop the bubble" of the cult's illusions and accelerated its sad end. In responding to Al Qaeda's terrorist attacks on the United States, Vice President Dick Cheney argued that a strong military response would deter further attacks. Certainly the hard power of military and police force was necessary to counter Al Qaeda, but the indiscriminate use of hard power illustrated by the invasion of Iraq, the Abu Ghraib prison pictures, and Guantánamo detentions without trial served to increase the number of terrorist recruits (according to official British and American intelligence estimates).[44] The absence of an effective soft power component undercut the strategy to respond to terrorism.

Almost every leader needs a certain degree of soft power. As mentioned earlier, Burns argued that those who relied on coercion were not leaders but mere power wielders. "A leader and a tyrant are polar opposites."[45] Thus, in his view, Hitler was not a leader. Burns is correct that not all power behavior is leadership, but even tyrants and despots such as Hitler need to have a degree of soft power, at least within an inner circle. As David Hume pointed out more than two centuries ago, no individual alone is strong enough to coerce everyone else.[46] A dictator must attract or induce an inner circle of henchmen to impose his coercive techniques on others. Such masters of coercion as Hitler, Stalin, and Mao attracted and relied on acolytes.

Except for some religious leaders such as the Dalai Lama, who combines personal and positional power, soft power is rarely sufficient. And a leader who only courts popularity may be reluctant to exercise hard power when he or she should. Alternatively, leaders who throw their weight around without regard to the effects on their soft power may find others placing obstacles in the way of their hard power. Psychologists have found that too much assertiveness by a leader worsens relationships, just as too little limits achievement. "Like salt in a sauce, too much overwhelms the dish; too little is similarly distracting; but just the right amount allows the other flavors to dominate our experience."[47] In the words of CEO Jeff Immelt, "When you run General Electric, there are 7 to 12 times a year when you have to say, 'you're doing it my way.' If you do it 18 times, the good people will leave. If you do it 3 times, the company falls apart."[48]

Machiavelli may be correct that it is better for a prince to be feared than to be loved, but we sometimes forget that the opposite of love is not fear, but hatred. And Machiavelli made it clear that hatred is something a prince should carefully avoid.[49] When the exercise of hard power undercuts soft power, it makes leadership more difficult—as President Bush found out after the invasion of Iraq. The ability to combine hard and soft power into an effective strategy is "smart power."

Soft power is not good per se, and it is not always better than hard power. Nobody likes to feel manipulated, even by soft power. Soft power can be used for competitive purposes, and we often talk about "wars of words"—one person's attraction pitted against another's. A president may campaign against legislators in their home districts or run television ads pushing his agenda and attacking theirs. He is using his attraction to combat theirs and thus putting pressure on them. In that sense, soft power can feel "coercive," but it is a very different sense of coercion than what the victim experiences with physical (though not economic) hard power. In a competition with soft power, it matters very much what you and others think. If I shoot you to achieve my objective, it does not matter much what you think.

Like any form of power, soft power can be wielded for good or bad purposes, and these often vary according to the eye of the beholder. Bin Laden possesses a great deal of soft power in the eyes of his followers, but that does not make his actions good from an outside point of view. It is not necessarily better to twist minds than to twist arms. If I want to steal your money, I can threaten you with a gun, I can lure you into a fraudulent get-rich-quick scheme, or I can persuade you with a false claim that I am a guru who will save the world. I can then abscond with your money. The first two approaches rest on the hard power of coercion and inducement, while the third depends solely upon attraction or soft power. Nonetheless, the intentions and result remain theft in all three instances. On the other hand, soft power uses means that allow (on the surface, at least) more choice and leeway to the victim than hard power does. The views and choices of followers matter more in the case of soft power. We will return to these questions in the final chapter about good and bad leadership.

Power and Networks

Long-term trends in the economy and society such as globalization and the information revolution are increasing the importance of networks and changing the context of leadership. Globalization simply means networks of interdependence at intercontinental distances, and it is as old as human history. Early migrations of humans out of Africa populated the empty continents; the silk route connected Asia with medieval Europe; the world economy was more integrated in 1914 than it was again until 1970. What is new today is that global networks are "quicker and thicker." As the columnist Thomas Friedman and others have observed, in today's "flat world" geographical distance no longer protects against competition and threats as well as it once did.[50] That poses new problems for business and national leaders.

In a world of cell phones, computers, and Web sites such as MySpace, Facebook, and LinkedIn, it is commonplace to say that we increasingly live in a networked world. Networks build social capital that leaders can draw upon to get things done. Networks are relationships, and different types of networks provide different forms of power. An airline hub and spokes, a spider web, a bus route, an electricity grid, and the Internet are all networks, though they vary in terms of centralization and the complexity of connections. Centrality in networks can convey power, particularly where there are "structural holes."[51] Think of the hub and spokes of a wheel. If there is no rim connecting the spokes to each other, structural holes exist and the hub gains power from being the central node of communication. As Sir Francis Bacon observed four centuries ago, knowledge is power, and in today's information age, the control of information flows in networks is an important source of power for leaders. So also is the ability to process vast diverse flows so that the information becomes knowledge and not mere noise.

Some networks have strong ties in terms of frequency and reciprocity of contacts, whereas others have weak ties.[52] Think of the difference between friendships and acquaintances. Valuable information is more likely to be shared by friends than among acquaintances. But weak ties that reach out further may provide more novel information. Networks based on strong ties have the power of loyalty, but may become cliques that merely recirculate the conventional wisdom in a group. They may succumb to "groupthink." Weak ties are more effective than strong ties for acquiring novel, innovative, and nonredundant information. Strong ties may provide the power of loyalty but be resistant to change, whereas weak ties may provide "the necessary information and ability to link diverse groups together in a cooperative, successful manner."[53] Democratic leadership rests upon such strategies. Such weak networks are part of the glue that holds diverse societies together. A great democratic politician has to be a person with a great capacity for shallow friendships. Leaders will increasingly need to understand the relationship of networks to power, and how to adapt strategies and create teams that benefit from both strong and weak ties.

One of the open questions about networks will be the effect of the Internet on future leadership styles. In the absence of face-to-face cues, verbal persuasion should become more important, but the study of leadership online is still in its infancy. Will younger generations who spend large parts of their lives in networks that are marked by physical separation and virtual connection have different attitudes? Some early studies suggest that adolescents may be constructing their own styles of leadership and community involvement, with greater emphasis on cooperation, sociability, and soft power. One study of adolescents finds that success in becoming a leader in the online world is less dependent on age and gender than in the offline world and more determined by linguistic skills and the quantity of talk.[54]

Equally interesting for the question of leadership is what globalization is doing to the group question of "who is us?" Beyond a small scale, all human groups and identities are "imagined communities."[55] No one can know everyone else, and leaders' roles in shaping myths of group identity become increasingly complicated when firms often have more than half their employees in countries outside their "native" one; cheap transportation keeps diaspora communities closely connected across national boundaries; and the Internet allows professional, ethnic, religious, terrorist and other groups to create transnational communities. Humans have always been capable of multiple identities, but traditionally they took the form of concentric circles that tended to weaken with distance. In 1914, transnational networks of bankers, labor unions, and socialist movements criss-crossed Europe, but they succumbed to the nation state. The transnational networks collapsed under the demands of national loyalty that overwhelmed them after World War I commenced in August 1914.

In today's global world, a better metaphor might be networks of Venn diagrams. (Think of the overlapping circles that are produced when you put a cold beer bottle down on a dry table top several times.) In such overlapping circles, some identities become intermixed and hard to separate. This raises interesting puzzles for leaders of such networks. Leaders are identity entrepreneurs who increase their power by activating and mobilizing some of their followers' multiple identities at the cost of others. In today's world, national identity usually prevails, but how insular should leaders be in responding to other group's needs? What about conflicting loyalties when groups overlap? This all seems quite abstract until one looks at how leaders have struggled to respond to cases of genocide like Rwanda or Darfur. Intergroup leadership becomes more complex and more important.[56] We will return to the ethical questions raised by these issues in the final chapter.

The other major change in the macro-context of leadership is the information revolution, which simply put means the dramatic drop in the costs of computing and communication. For instance, the cost of computing dropped a thousandfold between 1970 and 2000. If the price of automobiles had dropped that rapidly, you could buy a car today for $5. With such a dramatic drop in costs, the barriers to entry into markets and politics are lowered and more players enter the game. In 1970, instantaneous global communication was possible, but expensive, and thus restricted to large hierarchical organizations with big budgets, such as governments and multinational corporations. Today, anyone with a few dollars can enter an Internet café and have the same communication power that was once reserved to the rich. This has empowered many more actors to be involved in political life. Nonprofit groups devoted to the environment or human rights, such as Greenpeace or Amnesty International, are better placed to challenge governments or launch boycotts against vulnerable corporate brands. Transnational terrorists have also found the Internet to be a particularly powerful tool in recruiting, training, and sending instructions across borders.

If information can create power, it is important to realize that more people have more information today than at any prior time in human history. Technology "democratizes" social and political processes and, for better and worse, institutions play less of a mediating role. A politician makes a mistake, such as George Allen's use of the word "macaca" to refer to a dark-skinned supporter of his opponent in Virginia's 2006 senatorial campaign, and millions of people see it on YouTube within hours and days. In fact, the basic concept of "Web 2.0" on the Internet rests on the concept of user-based content bubbling up from the bottom rather than descending from the top of a traditional hierarchy of information. Institutions such as Wikipedia and Linux are examples of social production that involve very different roles for leaders than do their traditional counterparts, Encyclopedia Britannica and Microsoft.

The information revolution is affecting the structure of organizations. Hierarchies are becoming flatter and embedded in fluid networks of contacts. White-collar knowledge workers respond to different incentives and political appeals than do blue-collar industrial workers.[57] Polls show people today are less deferential to authority in organizations and politics.

In 1930, Ronald Coase tried to explain the rise of the modern corporation. Why not just rely on markets? His answer was transactions costs: anonymous partners were hard to identify, contracts were difficult to manage, and it was more reliable to produce supplies yourself than to count on external networks of suppliers. Today cheap and reliable information makes networks of outsourcing more attractive. The classic economic theory of the firm as a hierarchical organization that internalizes functions in order to reduce transactions costs—think GM—is being supplemented by the notion of firms as networks of outsourcing—think Toyota or Nike. According to the *Financial Times*, "more companies now consist essentially of intangible assets such as patents plus the values embedded in their brands. In a flatter world, the advantages of innovation do not last as long and there are fewer things sheltering companies from competition . . . The proportion of intangible assets to shareholder value at Fortune 500 companies has steadily risen from about 50 percent in 1980 to 70 percent today."[58]

In some cases, one can orchestrate a complex network simply with carefully specified contracts, but the friction of normal life usually creates ambiguities that cannot be fully met in advance. In describing the success of the Toyota and the Linux networks, Philip Evans and Bob Wolf of Boston Consulting Group conclude that "monetary carrots and accountability sticks motivate people to perform narrow, specified tasks. Admiration and applause are far more effective stimulants of above and beyond behavior."[59] Traditional business leadership styles become less effective. Some new styles even seem bizarre. Visitors to the headquarters of a Web 2.0 company in Silicon Valley could be forgiven if they think they have entered a nursery school playroom rather than a corporate office.

According to Samuel J. Palmisano, CEO of IBM, under these new conditions "hierarchical, command-and-control approaches simply do not work anymore. They impede information flows inside companies, hampering the fluid and collaborative nature of work today."[60] A study of a major "bricks and clicks" company (one that combines offline and online operations) found that distributive leadership was essential. "In dynamic, complex, and ambiguous contexts like the dot-com environment, the traditional view of a leaders being decisively in control is difficult to reconcile . . . Effective leadership depends on the use of multiple 'leaders' for capable decision-making and action-taking."[61] John Quelch writes that "business success increasingly depends on the subtleties of soft power."[62] Management gurus refer to "level 5" and "authentic" leadership that is more collaborative and integrative.[63] As one management expert summarized twenty-five years of recent studies, "We have observed an increase in the use of more participative processes."[64]

Politics and government are changing as well. Polls show people today have become less deferential to authority in public institutions and in politics. Levels of trust in large institutions have declined in nearly all advanced countries.[65] The way that governments work is also changing. They are constructing and using market mechanisms for public purposes. Like firms, they are doing more outsourcing and contracting rather than production. More effort goes into negotiating and managing networks of public and private actors. Government work involves less direct production and more indirect regulation. Governments enter more public-private partnerships. To use a crew metaphor, governments do less rowing and more steering than in the past.[66] For example, in a new model of leadership, the Environmental Protection Agency now devotes significant resources to developing regulations in collaboration with its various stakeholders.[67] Success in managing such public and private networks depends on "talent, trust and soft power."[68] In short, new conditions require a new style of public leadership.

Some say these new conditions mean that leaders are finally entering a woman's world, but such stereotypes do not capture the full complexity of the change that is occurring. Postheroic leadership "depends less on the heroic actions of a few individuals at the top and more on collaborative leadership practices distributed throughout an organization."[69] Women are said to have a greater ability to work networks, to collaborate, and to nurture. Their nonhierarchical style and relational skills fill a leadership gap in the new world of knowledge-based organizations and groups that men are less well prepared to fill. In the words of one influential article, "Women leaders don't covet formal authority. They have learned to lead without it."[70]

In the past, in terms of gender stereotypes, when women fought their way to the top of organizations, they often had to adopt a "masculine style," violating the broader social norm of female "niceness," and they were often punished for it. In their view, with the information revolution and democratization demanding more participatory and integrative leadership, the "feminine style" is becoming a path to more effective leadership.

Various social scientific analyses of leadership and gender confirm the increased success of what was once considered a "feminine style of leadership."[71] Nonetheless, women lag in leadership positions, holding only 5 percent of top corporate positions, and a minority of positions in elected legislatures (ranging from 45 percent in Sweden to 16 percent in the United States). One study of the 1,941 rulers of independent countries over the twentieth century found only 27 women, and half of these came to power as widows or daughters of a male ruler. Less than 1 percent of twentieth-century rulers were women who gained power on their own.[72] If leadership opportunities are finally opening for women, it has been a long time coming.

Gender bias, lack of experience, primary caregiver responsibilities, and bargaining style all help to explain this gender gap. The traditional career paths for women do not enable women to gain the requisite experiences for top leadership positions in most organizational contexts. Moreover, women are likely to have a harder time than men negotiating for those resources and opportunities for leadership. Research shows that even in democratic cultures, women are less effective than men at promoting their own self-interest and face a higher social risk than men when attempting to negotiate for career-related resources such as compensation.[73] Women are generally not well integrated into male networks and included in organizations' dominant coalitions.[74] In addition, broader gender stereotypes about the expression of emotions still hamper women who try to overcome such barriers.[75]

Regardless of the disconnect between the ascendance of a new softer style and continuing gender bias, there is a danger in identifying the new type of leadership in gender-stereotypical terms.[76] By using stereotypes, even positive ones, "the great man (or trait) theory of leadership is being applied to women's leadership, but at the group rather than the individual level . . . and that can be perilous for women, men and effective leadership in general."[77] As we saw in the last chapter, leadership should be seen less in heroic terms of command than in sharing and encouraging participation throughout an organization, group, or network. This is becoming increasingly true in the age of globalization and the information revolution. Some situations call for a leader with transformational objectives and an inspirational style. But questions of appropriate style—when to use hard and soft power—in a networked world are equally relevant for men and women, and should not be clouded by traditional gender stereotypes.

Political Skills

Political skills are crucial for effective leadership, but they are more complex than first appears. Politics can take a variety of forms. Intimidation, manipulation, and negotiation are related to hard power, but politics also includes inspiration, brokerage of new beneficial arrangements, and developing networks of trust typical of soft power. Politics can involve success in achieving goals not just for oneself and a narrow group of followers, but also building political capital for bargaining with wider circles of followers. When Roderick Kramer calls "political intelligence" the ability to size up the weaknesses, insecurities, likes, and dislikes of others so that you can turn them into your instruments, he is referring narrowly to the Machiavellian political skills that are crucial for hard power threats and inducements.

Kramer's "great intimidators" employ a variety of tactics to bully and intimidate others in order to get what they want. Abusive language or an aloof attitude can throw others off balance. A calculated loss of temper can be useful at times. Robert McNamara shared intimacies with superiors but never subordinates. Both he and Margaret Thatcher intimidated others by appearing to know it all—even when they did not. Kramer describes former CEO Carly Fiorina of HP and Disney's Michael Eisner as skillful "silent intimidators."[78] Lyndon Johnson, on the other hand, would physically get up front and personal, draping an arm around shorter men, and seizing others by their lapels and argue while pressing his face close to theirs.[79] He would also offer visitors a seat in a low, soft chair while he loomed over them in a tall rocking chair with a high seat. Robert Mugabe uses the silent treatment, "refusing, for example, to say a word in one-on-one meetings, to the deep consternation of the other party."[80]

Kramer contrasts such hard "political intelligence" with the "social intelligence" emphasized by current leadership theorists that stresses empathy and interpersonal skills that attract followers and extract maximum performance from subordinates through soft power. Socially aware executives are also experts at reading the currents of office politics and using political skills in the broader sense of the term, but the starkest point of contrast between these two kinds of leaders is how willing they are to use hard power skills.

Psychologist David McClelland has shown that people with a high need for power have proven more effective leaders, but only if they also develop an internal capacity to restrain their use of power.[81] Kramer points out that his great intimidators are "bullies with a vision," aiming at an objective rather than just manipulating others for its own sake. Pure bullying tends to be counterproductive. Bullying—defined as repeated actions designed to humiliate and dominate others—is a common human behavior. Research on childhood bullying places the percentage of children with bullying characteristics in their personalities at 7 to 15 percent of the school-aged population.[82] In the American workplace, 37 percent say they have been bullied, and of those, nearly half say they left their jobs as a result.[83] As a form of power behavior, bullying can be self-gratifying and tactical or carefully strategic. It can be successful or unsuccessful. The legendary basketball coach Bobby Knight was both a bully and effective.[84] Studies of the workplace, however, have shown that pervasive bullying often lowers performance, and notable bullies like Al Dunlap of Scott Paper created a culture that destroyed the company.[85] In politics, efforts to rate leaders on a scale of Machiavellianism have had mixed results. One study finds Machiavellianism negatively related to leaders' performance, while a study of charismatic American presidents finds a positive relation between Machiavellianism and performance.[86]

Daniel Goleman and his colleagues report that in "some specific business cases, an SOB boss resonates just fine. But in general, leaders who are jerks must reform or else their moods and actions will eventually catch up with them."[87] The politics of fear can be effective, but they are not the only political skills nor the best skills in all circumstances. On the contrary, some leaders build and empower teams. The soft power politics of attraction may be even more effective when they call forth additional effort and loyalty, and thus add leverage to the leader's power. Abraham Lincoln included his rivals for the presidency in his cabinet and then used primarily soft political skills to coax significant contributions from them.[88] Too much hard Machiavellian power can interfere with and deprive leaders of their soft power. Moreover, a style that works in one context may not work in another. In many other nonprofit institutions, presidents have much more limited hard power resources than do their equivalents in government or business. In such a context, once their hard power tactics undercut their soft power, they have few power resources left.

Conclusion

The moral of the story, of course, is not that hard or soft power is better, or that an inspirational or a transactional style is the answer, but that it is important to understand how to combine these power resources and leadership styles in different contexts. A strategy is a plan that relates ends and means, goals and tactics, and such plans must vary with different contexts.[89] Strategic resourcefulness can sometimes compensate for lack of resources, and explain why David can defeat Goliath, or some organizations and social movements succeed where better-endowed ones fail. That suggests that we need more research on contextual intelligence, or the ability to understand context so that hard and soft power can be successfully combined into a smart power strategy.[90] Separating power and leadership is impossible in research, as in life. More must be done to understand the different conditions under which leaders combine hard and soft power resources into strategies of smart power.

Notes

1. This piece is adapted from my book *The Powers to Lead* (New York: Oxford University Press, 2008).

2. Robert C. Tucker, *Politics as Leadership*, rev. ed. (Columbia, MO: University of Missouri Press, 1995), chapter 1.

3. James MacGregor Burns, *Leadership* (New York: Harper & Row, 1978); Barbara Kellerman, *Bad Leadership* (Boston: Harvard Business School Press, 2004).

4. For a classic exploration of this problem, see James G. March, "The Power of Power," in *Varieties of Political Theory*, ed. David Easton (Englewood Cliffs, NJ: Prentice-Hall, 1966), 39–70. See also Steven Lukes, *Power: A Radical View*, 2nd ed. (London: Palgrave, 2005). Classic articles on power by Robert Dahl, John C. Harsanyi, Hebert Simon, and others are collected in Roderick Bell, David V. Edwards, and R. Harrison Wagner, eds., *Political Power: A Reader in Theory and Research* (New York: The Free Press, 1969).

5. Adam Galinsky, Joe C. Magee, M. Ena Inesi, and Deborah Gruenfeld, "Power and Perspectives Not Taken," *Psychological Science* 17, no. 12 (2006): 1068–1074.

6. Robert A. Dahl, *Who Governs? Democracy and Power in an American City* (New Haven, CT: Yale University Press, 1961).

7. David Baldwin, "Power Analysis and World Politics: New Trends Versus Old Tendencies," *World Politics* 31, no. 2 (1979): 161–194. See also David Baldwin, "The Costs of Power," *Journal of Conflict Resolution* 15, no. 2 (June 1971): 145–155.

8. I first introduced this concept in Joseph S. Nye Jr., *Bound to Lead: The Changing Nature of American Power* (New York: Basic Books, 1990), chapter 2. It builds on what Peter Bachrach and Morton Baratz called the "second face of power." See Peter Bachrach and Morton S. Baratz, "Decisions and Nondecisions: An Analytical Framework," *American Political Science Review* 57, no. 3 (1963): 632–642.

9. Thom Shanker, "Retiring Army Chief of Staff Warns Against Arrogance," *The New York Times*, June 12, 2003, A32.

10. A well-known taxonomy of power resources differentiates five types of power: coercive, reward, legitimate, referent, and expert. The first two fall into my hard power category; the latter into soft power. See John R.P. French and Bertram H. Raven, "The Bases of Social Power," in *Studies in Social Power*, ed. Dorwin Cartwright (Ann Arbor, MI: Institute of Social Research, 1959), 150–167. Gary A. Yukl and Cecilia M. Falbe, "The Importance of Different Power Sources in Downward and Lateral Relations," *Journal of Applied Psychology* 76 (1991): 416–423 add persuasiveness and control of information, which I include as soft power resources.

11. Jane J. Mansbridge, *Beyond Self-Interest* (Chicago: University of Chicago Press, 1990).

12. I am indebted to Mark Moore for this point and other discussions.

13. Richard Neustadt, *Presidential Power and the Modern Presidents: The Politics of Leadership from Roosevelt to Reagan* (New York: The Free Press, 1990), 11.

14. Quoted in Alan Axelrod, *Eisenhower on Leadership: Ike's Enduring Lessons in Total Victory Management* (San Francisco: Jossey-Bass, 2006), 120, 283.

15. Charles Lindholm, *Charisma* (Cambridge, MA: Blackwell Publishing, 1990), chapter 10.

16. Christopher Hodgkinson, *The Philosophy of Leadership* (New York: Palgrave Macmillan, 1983), 163.

17. Keith Grint, *The Arts of Leadership* (New York: Oxford University Press, 2000), 332.

18. Barbara Kellerman distinguishes followers (by their level of engagement) as "isolates, bystanders, participants, activists, and diehards." See Barbara Kellerman, *Followership: How Followers Create Change and Change Leaders* (Boston: Harvard Business School Press, 2008).

19. James C. Scott, *Domination and the Arts of Resistance: Hidden Transcripts* (New Haven, CT: Yale University Press, 1990).

20. Ronald A. Heifetz, *Leadership Without Easy Answers* (Cambridge, MA: Belknap Press of Harvard University Press, 1994).

21. Kellerman, *Followership*. See also Robert E. Kelley, *The Power of Followership: How to Create Leaders People Want to Follow, and Followers Who Lead Themselves* (New York: Doubleday/Currency, 1992).

22. Richard N. Haass, *The Bureaucratic Entrepreneur: How to Be Effective in Any Unruly Organization* (Washington, DC: Brookings Institution Press, 1999), 2.

23. Robert G. Lord and Karen J. Maher, *Leadership and Information Processing: Linking Perceptions and Performance* (Boston: Unwin Hyman, 1991), 59.

24. Comte de Mirabeau, quoted in Hodgkinson, *The Philosophy of Leadership*, 163.

25. James McGregor Burns and Susan Dunn, *The Three Roosevelts: Patrician Leaders Who Transformed America* (New York: Grove Press, 2002).

26. Christopher Boehm, *Hierarchy in the Forest: The Evolution of Egalitarian Behavior* (Cambridge, MA: Harvard University Press, 1999).

27. Siobhan O'Mahony, "Governance in Production Communities," unpublished manuscript, 2007.

28. George Edwards, *On Deaf Ears: The Limits of the Bully Pulpit* (New Haven, CT: Yale University Press, 2003), 119.

29. Lukes, *Power*, 11.

30. Max Weber, "Types of Authority," in *Political Leadership: A Source Book*, ed. Barbara Kellerman (Pittsburgh, PA: University of Pittsburgh Press, 1986), 232–244.

31. Gary A. Yukl and David D. Van Fleet, "Theory and Research on Leadership in Organizations," in *Handbook of Industrial and Organizational Psychology*, Vol. 3, 2nd ed., eds. Marvin D. Dunnette and Leaetta M. Hough (Palo Alto, CA: Consulting Psychologists Press, 1992), 147–197.

32. Colin Barker, Alan Johnson, and Michael Lavalette, eds., *Leadership and Social Movements* (Manchester, England: Manchester University Press, 2001).

33. Lukes, *Power*. See also Janice Bially Mattern, "Why Soft Power Isn't So Soft: Representational Force and the Sociolinguistic Construction of Attraction in World Politics," *Millennium* 33, no. 3 (2005): 583–612.

34. Ruth W. Grant, "Ethics and Incentives: A Political Approach," *American Political Science Review* 100, no. 1 (2006): 29–39. Grant distinguishes three forms of power: force, exchange, and speech. My third category of attraction is broader by including charisma and example as well as persuasive speech.

35. Robert O. Keohane and Joseph S. Nye, *Power and Interdependence* (Boston, MA: Little Brown, 1977).

36. Adam Smith, *The Theory of Moral Sentiments* (New York: A.M. Kelley, 1966), 84.

37. Quoted in "A Nation Challenged; Scenes of Rejoicing and Words of Strategy from bin Laden and His Allies," *The New York Times*, December 14, 2001, B4.

38. Richard S. Tedlow, "What Titans Can Teach Us," *Harvard Business Review* 79, no. 11 (2001): 70–79.

39. Roderick M. Kramer, "The Great Intimidators," *Harvard Business Review* 84, no. 2 (2006): 88–96.

40. Jameson W. Doig and Erwin C. Hargrove, eds., *Leadership and Innovation: Entrepreneurs in Government* (Baltimore, MD: Johns Hopkins University Press, 1990).

41. Michael G. Harvey, Joyce T. Heames, R. Glenn Richey, and Nancy Leonard, "Bullying: From the Playground to the Boardroom," *Journal of Leadership and Organizational Studies* 12, no. 4 (2006): 1–11.

42. Chris Patten, *Cousins and Strangers: America, Britain, and Europe in a New Century*, 1st American ed. (New York: Times Books, 2006), 119.

43. Katrina Bedell, Samuel Hunter, Amanda Angie, and Andrew Vert, "A Historiometric Examination of Machiavellianism and a New Taxonomy of Leadership," *Journal of Leadership and Organizational Studies* 12, no. 4 (2006): 50–72. But see Ronald J. Deluga, "American Presidential Machiavellianism: Implications for Charismatic Leadership and Rated Performance," *Leadership Quarterly* 12 (2001): 339–363 and Dean K. Simonton, "Presidential Personality: Biographical Use of the Gough Adjective Check List," *Journal of Personality and Social Psychology* 51, no. 1 (1986): 149–160 for opposing findings.

44. Mark Mazzetti, "Spy Agencies Say Iraq War Worsens Terrorism Threat," *The New York Times*, September 24, 2006, 1.

45. Burns, *Leadership*, 3.

46. David Hume, "Of the First Principles of Government," in *Essays Moral, Political and Literary*, ed. Eugene F. Miller (Indianapolis, IN: Liberty Classics, 1985), 32–36.

47. Daniel R. Ames and Francis J. Flynn, "What Breaks a Leader: The Curvilinear Relation Between Assertiveness and Leadership," *Journal of Personality and Social Psychology* 92, no. 2 (2007): 307–324.

48. Joe Nocera, "Running GE, Comfortable in His Skin," *The New York Times*, June 9, 2007, C9.

49. Niccolo Machiavelli, *The Prince* (New York: New American Library, 1952), chapter 17.

50. Thomas L. Friedman, *The World Is Flat: A Brief History of the Twenty-First Century* (New York: Farrar, Straus and Giroux, 2006); Frances Cairncross, *The Death of Distance: How the Communications Revolution Will Change Our Lives* (Boston: Harvard Business School Press, 2001).

51. Ronald S. Burt, *Structural Holes: The Social Structure of Competition* (Cambridge, MA: Harvard University Press, 1992).

52. Mark Granovetter, "The Myth of Social Network Analysis as a Special Method in the Social Sciences," *Connections* 13, no. 2 (1990): 13–16.

53. Daniel J. Brass and David Krackhardt, "The Social Capital of Twenty-First Century Leaders," in *Out-of-the-Box Leadership Challenges for the 21st Century Army and Other Top-Performing Organizations*, eds. James G. Hunt, George E. Dodge, and Leonard Wong (Stamford, CT: JAI Press, 1999), 179–194.

54. Justine Cassell, David Huffaker, Dona Tversky, and Kim Ferriman, "The Language of Online Leadership: Gender and Youth Engagement on the Internet," *Developmental Psychology* 42, no. 3 (2006): 436–449.

55. Benedict Anderson, *Imagined Communities: Reflections on the Origin and Spread of Nationalism*, rev. ed. (New York: Verso, 1991).

56. Frances Hesselbein and Marshall Goldsmith, eds., *The Leader of the Future 2: Visions, Strategies, and Practices for the New Era* (San Francisco: Jossey-Bass, 2006); Todd L. Pittinsky, R. Matthew Montoya, and Linda R. Tropp, "Leader Influences on Positive and Negative Intergroup Emotions" (paper presented at the 10th Annual Meeting of Research on Managing Groups and Teams, Cornell and Stanford Universities, May 2006).

57. Todd L. Pittinsky and Margaret J. Shih, "Leading the Knowledge Nomad," in *Workforce Wake-up Call: Your Workforce Is Changing, Are You?* eds. Robert Gandossy, Nidhi Verma, and Elissa Tucker (Hoboken, NJ: John Wiley & Sons, 2006), 95–100; Elaine C. Kamarck, *End of Government . . . as We Know It: Making Public Policy Work* (Boulder, CO: Lynne Rienner Publishers, 2007).

58. John Gapper, "Companies Feel Benefit of Intangibles," *Financial Times Special Report on Global Brands*, April 23, 2007, 1.

59. Philip Evans and Bob Wolf, "Collaboration Rules," *Harvard Business Review* 83, no. 7 (2005): 96–104.

60. Samuel J. Palmisano, "The Globally Integrated Enterprise," *Foreign Affairs* 85, no. 3 (2006): 127–136.

61. Michael E. Brown and Dennis Gioia, "Making Things Click: Distributive Leadership in an Online Division of an Offline Organization," *Leadership Quarterly* 13, no. 4 (2002): 397–419.

62. John Quelch, "How Soft Power Is Winning Hearts, Minds, and Influence," *Financial Times*, October 10, 2005, 17.

63. Jim Collins, *Good to Great: Why Some Companies Make the Leap . . . and Others Don't* (New York: HarperBusiness, 2001); Bill George, with Peter Sims, *True North: Discover Your Authentic Leadership* (San Francisco: Wiley, 2007).

64. Victor H. Vroom, "Leadership and Decision Making Processes," *Organizational Dynamics* 28, no. 4 (2000): 82–94.

65. Joseph S. Nye Jr., Philip D. Zelikow, and David C. King, eds., *Why People Don't Trust Government* (Cambridge, MA: Harvard University Press, 1997).

66. David Osborne and Ted Gaebler, *Reinventing Government: How the Entrepreneurial Spirit Is Transforming the Public Sector* (Reading, MA: Addison-Wesley, 1992), 28.

67. I am indebted to Matt Kohut for this example.

68. Evans and Wolf, "Collaboration Rules," 102.

69. Joyce K. Fletcher, "The Paradox of Postheroic Leadership: An Essay on Gender, Power, and Transformational Change," *Leadership Quarterly* 15, no. 5 (2004): 647–661.

70. Judy B. Rosener, "Ways Women Lead," *Harvard Business Review* 68, no. 6 (November–December 1990): 119–125.

71. Alice H. Eagly and Blair T. Johnson, "Gender and Leadership Style: A Meta-analysis," *Psychological Bulletin* 108 (1990): 233–256. See also Gary N. Powell, *Women and Men in Management*, 3rd ed. (Thousand Oaks, CA: Sage Publications, 2003); Deborah L. Rhode, ed., *The Difference "Difference" Makes: Women and Leadership* (Stanford, CA: Stanford University Press, 2003).

72. Arnold Ludwig, *King of the Mountain: The Nature of Political Leadership* (Lexington, KY: University Press of Kentucky, 2002), 22–23.

73. Hannah Riley Bowles and Kathleen L. McGinn, "Claiming Authority: Negotiating Challenges for Women Leaders," in *The Psychology of Leadership: New Perspectives and Research*, eds. David M. Messick and Roderick M. Kramer (Mahwah, NJ: Lawrence Erlbaum, 2005), 191–208. I am indebted to Hannah Bowles for help on this section.

74. Daniel J. Brass, "Men's and Women's Networks: A Study of Interaction Patterns and Influence in an Organization," *Academy of Management Journal* 28, no. 2 (1985): 327–343; Herminia Ibarra, "Personal Networks of Women and Minorities in Management: A Conceptual Framework," *The Academy of Management Review* 18, no. 1 (1993): 56–87.

75. Marjukka Ollilainen, "Gendering Emotions, Gendering Teams: Construction of Emotions in Self-Managing Teamwork," in *Emotions in the Workplace: Research, Theory and Practice*, eds. Neal M. Ashkanasy, Charmine Hartel, and Wilfred Zerbe (Westport, CT: Quorum Books, 2000), 82–96.

76. Nannerl O. Keohane, "Crossing the Bridge: Reflections on Women and Leadership," in *Women and Leadership*, eds. Barbara Kellerman and Deborah L. Rhode (San Francisco: Jossey-Bass, 2007), 87–88.

77. Todd L. Pittinsky, Laura M. Bacon, and Brian Welle, "The Great Women Theory of Leadership? Perils of Positive Stereotypes and Precarious Pedestals," in *Women and Leadership*, eds. Barbara Kellerman and Deborah L. Rhode (San Francisco: Jossey-Bass, 2007), 93–125.

78. Kramer, "The Great Intimidators," 88–96.

79. Robert A. Caro, *Master of the Senate: The Years of Lyndon Johnson* (New York: Knopf, 2002).

80. "Robert Mugabe: The Man Behind the Fist." *The Economist*, March 31, 2007, 28.

81. David C. McClelland and David H. Burnham, "Power Is the Great Motivator," *Harvard Business Review* 54, no. 2 (March–April 1976): 100–110.

82. Harvey et al. "Bullying," 1–11.

83. "As Labor Day Nears, Workplace Bullying Institute Survey Finds Half of Working Americans Affected by Workplace Bullying," Zogby International, August 39, 2007, http://www.zogby.com/news/ReadNews.dbm?ID=1353.

84. Gerald Feris, Robert Zinko, Robyn Brouer, M. Ronald Buckley, and Michael G. Harvey, "Strategic Bullying as a Supplementary, Balanced Perspective on Destructive Leadership," *Leadership Quarterly* 18, no. 3 (2007): 195–206.

85. Barbara Kellerman, *Bad Leadership: What It Is, How It Happens, Why It Matters* (Boston: Harvard Business School Press, 2004), chapter 7.

86. Katrina Bedell, Samuel Hunter, Amanda Angie, and Andrew Vert, "A Historiometric Examination of Machiavellianism and a New Taxonomy of Leadership," *Journal of Leadership and Organizational Studies* 12, no. 4 (2006): 50–72; Deluga, "American Presidential Machiavellianism," 339–363.

87. Daniel Goleman, Richard Boyatzis, and Annie McKee, *Primal Leadership: Learning to Lead with Emotional Intelligence* (Boston: Harvard Business School Press, 2002), 45.

88. Doris Kearns Goodwin, *Team of Rivals: The Political Genius of Abraham Lincoln* (New York: Simon & Schuster, 2005).

89. Marshall Ganz, "Resources and Resourcefulness: Strategic Capacity in the Unionization of California Agriculture, 1959–1966," *American Journal of Sociology* 105, no. 4 (2000): 1003–1062.

90. Here I borrow a term from Anthony Mayo and Nitin Nohria but use it in a political rather than a market context.

The Variability of Leadership

What's Core and Contingent

13

LEADERSHIP AND CULTURAL CONTEXT

A Theoretical and Empirical Examination Based on Project GLOBE

Mansour Javidan, Peter W. Dorfman, Jon Paul Howell, and Paul J. Hanges

Introduction

There is ample evidence that the world of business is increasingly global (Giddens, 1999; Govindarajan and Gupta, 2001; Friedman, 2005; Inkpen and Ramaswamy, 2006). The globalized business world of today provides firms with unprecedented opportunities but also formidable challenges because it represents a higher level of complexity resulting from conditions of multiplicity, interdependence, and ambiguity (Lane, Maznevski, and Mendenhall, 2004).

In a recent article, Samuel J. Palmisano, chairman of the board, president, and CEO of IBM, examined the forces shaping the global world of business and suggested that an increasingly important source of competitive advantage for global corporations is their ability to integrate the various aspects of their global organization:

> Today's global corporations are shifting their focus from products to production—from what things companies choose to make to how they choose to make them, from what services they offer to

335

how they choose to deliver them. Simply put, the emerging globally integrated enterprise is a company that fashions its strategy, its management, and its operations in pursuit of a new goal: the integration of production and value delivery worldwide. State borders define less and less the boundaries of corporate thinking or practice. (Palmisano, 2006:129)

But transforming a global organization to a global network of interconnected and integrated operations is no easy task. From a leadership perspective, it requires the ability to work with and influence individuals inside and outside the corporation, representing a diversity of cultural backgrounds, to help achieve the corporation's goals. Thus, a critical question of importance to management scholars and researchers is the nature and dynamic of leadership in a cross-cultural environment.

In this paper, we build on the foundation of *implicit leadership theory* (ILT) (Lord and Maher, 1990) and *culturally endorsed implicit leadership theory* (House, Hanges, Javidan, Dorfman, and Gupta, 2004; Javidan and Carl, 2004, 2005) to present a theoretical framework linking national culture, organizational culture, and leadership. The paper takes an integrative and multilevel approach to culture, examining the impact of both national culture and organizational culture on implicit leadership profiles. We refer to the simultaneous effect of national and organizational culture as "cultural context." The paper then presents a series of hypotheses on the relationship between specific cultural dimensions and specific leadership attributes. We use the GLOBE database (House et al., 2004) to test these hypotheses and present our conclusions.

GLOBE researchers identified twenty-one primary dimensions of outstanding leadership empirically derived from their survey of over 17,000 managers in sixty-two societies (House et al., 2004). A second-order factor analysis produced a set of six global leadership dimensions, which comprised the *culturally endorsed implicit leadership theory*, or CLT. While the GLOBE findings are the first large-scale rigorous empirical study of the relationship between leadership and culture, the fact that they reduced a very large pool of data into six global leadership dimensions (each consisting of many leadership attributes) resulted in two outcomes: First, rich data ended up being camouflaged. Their quest for parsimony led to a very high level of consolidation and aggregation, thus generating very broad categories. As an example, one of the global leadership dimensions of GLOBE's CLT is Charismatic/Value-Based leadership, which is highly endorsed as a contributor to outstanding leadership in all cultures studied. But one of the primary leadership factors in Charismatic/Value-Based leadership is Self-Sacrificial leadership, which is highly culturally contingent (i.e., endorsed in some cultures but rejected in others). By focusing on the former, GLOBE did not examine the latter, which is among the leadership attributes of study in this paper.

Second, due to the aggregate nature of the *global* leadership dimensions, their *primary* dimensions consisted of leadership attributes that were highly endorsed in all cultures, other attributes that were generally rejected in all cultures, and some attributes that were endorsed in some cultures and rejected in others (i.e., culturally contingent). While the findings regarding the six global leadership dimensions are valuable, they provide a less than precise image of the culturally contingent aspects of leadership.

In this paper, we will attempt to address the above two issues. We will provide a more fine grained analysis of the relationship between cultural context and leadership by focusing on the primary leadership factors, which are by nature more specific and narrower than the six second-order dimensions. Further, we limit our study to those leadership factors that are clearly culturally contingent. In this way, we can provide a more sharply focused and precise understanding of the relationship between culture and leadership. By focusing only on the culturally contingent aspects of leadership, we are better able to discern what dimensions of culture drive which specific dimensions of leadership, and are better able to produce a theoretical basis for our predictions and findings. Simply put, we are interested in the cultural predictors of variability in outstanding leadership across the world.

Leadership and Cultural Context

The literature on the relationship between cultural context and leadership consists of two different levels of analysis: (1) the relationship between organizational culture and leadership, and (2) the relationship between national culture and leadership. The two streams of research are almost mutually exclusive, with little theoretical or empirical linkage. The work of GLOBE is the only rigorous empirical attempt to bridge the two research streams.

Organizational Culture and Leadership

Very few well-conducted empirical or conceptual studies of the relationship between organizational culture and leadership have appeared in the literature. Several writers have suggested that leaders shape organizational cultures (Peters and Waterman, 1982; Deal and Kennedy, 1982; Kouzes and Posner, 2002; Sims and Lorenzi, 1992). Bass (1985) suggested that transactional leaders work within the framework of the organizational culture while transformational leaders transform it. In a study of the U.S. civil service, Hennessy (1998) concluded that leadership played a critical role in reshaping the culture of the organization.

Another stream of thought on the relationship between leadership and organizational culture was proposed by Schein (1992), who argued that organizational life cycle is a key determinant of the connection between leadership and organizational culture. He suggested that in the early part of the life cycle, leaders play a major role in shaping the culture of the organization but that over time, as the organization gains more maturity, its culture influences the actions and behaviors of its leaders. Bass, Avolio, Jung, and Berson (2003) support the dynamic notion of this relationship and view it as an ongoing interplay in which the direction of influence is determined by the maturity of the organization.

While the above literature is intuitively appealing and is almost taken for granted, it lacks empirical scrutiny. There is scant empirical evidence on the relationship between organizational culture and leadership. Ogbonna and Harris (2000) are among the few researchers who have conducted a large-scale study of this issue and they found that leadership styles are associated with organizational culture. In this study of one thousand business units in U.K. firms, they showed that participative leadership style is associated with a competitive organizational culture. More recently, GLOBE researchers provided empirical evidence that both organizational and societal cultural values are predictive of specific global leadership dimensions. For example, they showed that future orientation at both the national and organizational level is negatively associated with autonomous leadership. In the present study we carry the work of GLOBE farther by focusing on the specific primary leadership dimensions that are clearly culturally contingent and relate them to organizational and societal cultural dimensions.

National Culture and Leadership

The second level of analysis relates to the relationship between national culture and leadership. Given the fact that individuals and groups with diverse cultural backgrounds are increasingly working together in the business world, scholars and practitioners have been keen to understand the implications of national culture for a variety of managerial and organizational issues, including leadership. The extant work on the linkage between national culture and leadership tends to focus on one or more of the following questions (Yukl, 2006):

- Differences across national cultures in the conceptualization of leadership behavior

- Differences across national cultures regarding effective leadership behavior

- Differences across national cultures in actual patterns of leadership behavior

- Differences across national cultures in the relationship of leadership behavior to outcomes

There is general agreement among researchers that national culture refers to cognitive systems and behavioral repertoires that are shaped as a result of individuals' common experiences (Hofstede, 1980, 2001; Leung et al., 2002; Smith, Peterson, and Schwartz, 2002; Leung, Bhagat, Buchan, Erez, and Gibson, 2005; Leung and Bond, 2006). Various authors have suggested that such cognitive systems and behavioral repertoires can impact leadership in a variety of ways (Chong and Thomas, 1997; Adler, 1997; House, Wright, and Aditya, 1997; House et al., 2004; Javidan and Carl, 2004, 2005; Dorfman, 2004; Javidan, Dorfman, Sully de Luque, and House, 2006). Leaders are socialized into and internalize the cultural values and practices of the culture they grow up in. They learn, over time, desirable and undesirable modes of behavior. Smith, Peterson, Schwartz, and colleagues (2002) showed that the extent that managers relied on formal rules and supervisors for guidance is related to their cultural background. Geletkanycz (1997) showed that executives' adherence to existing strategy is related to their cultural background in terms of individualism, uncertainty avoidance, and power distance. Rahim and Magner (1996) found that leaders in individualistic cultures tend to put more emphasis on coercive power. Mehra and Krishnan (2005) found that the Indian culture of

Svadharma-orientation (following one's own duty) is related to transformational leadership in that country.

Cultural norms are often enforced in the way people in a society relate to each other (Yukl, 2006). A leader in a high power distance culture is likely to act autocratically not simply because he or she has learned it through experience, but because any other type of behavior may be deemed ineffective by the boss or those outside the organization (Dorfman, 2004; Yukl, 2006; Javidan et al., 2006; Javidan and Lynton, 2005). Dorfman (2004) and Chemers (1997) reviewed the international management literature and assessed the generalizability of leadership theories, behaviors, and processes across national cultures. Both of these authors report mixed results. While some behaviors, such as "supportive leadership" or transformational leadership (Bass, 1985), appear to produce similar effects across cultures, other behaviors, such as "directive leadership," seem to have culturally specific consequences (Dorfman, 2004). Similarly, participative leadership is viewed as a more effective leadership style in societies that have more egalitarian cultures (Carl, Gupta, and Javidan, 2004; Dorfman, Hanges, and Brodbeck, 2004).

Cultural Context and Implicit Leadership Theory

Our approach to the relationship between national and organizational culture and leadership is anchored in the notion of implicit leadership theories of organizational and societal members (Lord and Maher, 1993; House et al., 2004; Javidan and Carl, 2004, 2005). Following the work by Rosch (1975), Lord and colleagues argued that the beliefs and attributes of a leader tend to be clustered together in memory structures called schemas (Lord and Foti, 1986; Lord and Maher, 1990). More formally, a schema is defined as a "cognitive structure that represents knowledge about a concept or type of stimulus, including its attributes and the relations among those attributes" (Fiske and Taylor, 1991:98). Identifying the characteristics within people's leadership schemas is thought to be important because the content of leadership schemas dictates who is perceived as a leader and who is not (Dorfman, 1998; Erez and Earley, 1993; Fiske and Taylor, 1991; House, Wright, and Aditya, 1997; Shaw, 1990). More specifically, during the cognitive categorization process, a person's attributes are compared against the attributes of the "prototypical leader" within a follower's leadership schema. The better the match between the person's attributes and leader prototype, the more likely it is for the person to be considered a leader (Lord and Maher, 1990). Once the label of "leader" is ascribed to a person, that person gains social power (Cronshaw and Lord, 1987) and the label triggers causal attributions and assumptions about the person's ability to motivate and direct others (Konst, Vonk, and Van Der Vlist, 1999).

The early cognitive categorization perspective primarily focused on the content of individuals' schemas. An individual's *implicit leadership theory* is one schema that likely develops over time, although its basic elements may evolve early in life. Individuals' experience with leaders and those in positions of authority make an impression on them and shape their implicit leadership theory. Childhood observations and relations with parents, experiences with teachers, coaches, siblings, and friends, and authority relations with managers as well as political leaders help individuals encode specific attributes as characteristics of leaders or effective leaders. If we see a respected leader being kind to others, we may encode this as humane and deduce that good leaders are humane. This encoding process results in sets of attributes and behaviors that eventually constitute the cognitive categories used to perceive individuals as leaders. More recent work has taken a "connectionist approach," recognizing that the elements in various categories may shift in importance and in how they are grouped together over time and across situations (Hanges, Dorfman, Shteynberg, and Bates, 2006).

While schema content often varies across individuals because of differences in their individual experiences, values, and personality (Lord and Brown, 2004), it is possible that schema content is also shared among individuals. Lord and Emrich described collective cognition as "a socially constructed understanding of the world derived from social exchanges and interactions among multiple individuals in a group or organization" (2000:552). These shared aspects of schemas are especially likely to be found when multiple individuals are sampled from intact groups. Indeed, Shaw (1990) and others (House et al., 1999) have argued that culture is a major determinant of the commonality found in leadership schemas for individuals from the same cultural group. This shared content in the leadership schema of members from an identifiable cultural group was called *culturally endorsed implicit leadership theory (CLT) profiles* in the GLOBE project (Dorfman et al., 2004).

Shaw (1990) suggested three effects that culture can have on leadership schemas. He hypothesized that culture affects (a) the attributes believed to be typical of leaders (i.e., schema content), (b) the cognitive complexity and differentiation among the schema content (i.e., schema structure), and (c) the level of automaticity involved in processing a leadership encounter. Some evidence exists to confirm Shaw's hypotheses about the influence of culture on leadership schemas. A study by O'Connell, Lord, and O'Connell (1990) found that national culture plays a strong role in influencing the content of leader attributes and behaviors perceived as desirable and effective by individuals in that culture. Their study specifically examined the similarities and differences between Japanese and American conceptions of useful leadership attributes. For the Japanese, the personality traits and behaviors of being fair, flexible, a good listener, outgoing, and responsible were highly rated for leadership effectiveness in many domains, such as business, media, and education. For Americans, personality traits and behaviors of intelligence, honesty, understanding, verbal skills, and determination were strongly endorsed as facilitating leader effectiveness in numerous domains. Other studies, such as those by Gerstner and Day (1994) and Offerman, Kennedy, and Wirtz (1994), also provide evidence that ratings of effective leadership attributes and behaviors vary across societies.

The GLOBE project recently found support for Shaw's hypothesized relationship between culture, and leadership schema content (Javidan and House, 2004; Dorfman et al., 2004). Both organizational and societal performance-oriented cultural values were positively associated with participative leadership as a component of respondents' CLT profile (Javidan, 2004). These same researchers also clustered culturally similar societies together (Gupta and Hanges, 2004) and found meaningful differences in the content of the CLT profiles of different clusters (Dorfman et al., 2004).

Thus, although implicit leadership theory was developed with interindividual variation in mind, strong evidence exists that it can be extended to the organizational and national cultural level of analysis. A society's and an organization's culture reflects some collective agreement on meanings and interpretations. Such agreements turn into social influences by producing "a set of compelling behavioural, affective, and attitudinal orientations and values for the members" (House, Wright, and Adytia, 1997:538). Collective interactions and experiences provide important inputs that activate and constrain the selection and retrieval of specific information for cognitive categories such as ILTs. Leadership categories are thus shaped by environmental factors and are revised when contextually inappropriate. For example, Triandis (1994), in a comprehensive review of almost four hundred studies, concluded that the cultural value orientations in a country will determine the optimum leadership profile for that country. He concluded that while there are some universal attributes of management systems, each distinct culture may have a distinct management style that is both moderated and directly influenced by culture.

Numerous examples demonstrate how societal and organizational culture can shape the ILT of their members. In a country with relatively high power distance values (e.g., Russia and Iran), children typically learn that the father is the ultimate authority in the family, and they show strong respect and deference to him. They learn that the father knows what is best and makes decisions for the good of the family. They also learn, through their interactions with their parents, that their role is to comply and follow the decisions and directives made by the father. As a result, in such cultures, the collective ILT reflects elements of power and autocratic leadership. As adults, employees in organizations in such cultures are more accepting of high power distance values and autocratic leadership styles in their organizations.

In contrast, in countries with relatively low power distance values, such as Denmark, family decisions are made with extensive discussion and debate within the family, with the participation of the children. As a result, the predominant ILT in such societies reflects consensus building and participation rather than autocratic decision making. As adults, employees in organizations in such societies are not accepting of high power distance values and autocratic leadership styles in their organizations. Instead, they prefer a more participative and egalitarian approach to leadership.

As another example, in a country with relatively high family-oriented values, such as Mexico, respect for the family and trust among family members tilts the country's ILT toward paternalism and nepotism. The radius of trust tends to be short and the notion of trust takes a personal context. People trust only those with whom they spend much time and get to know deeply. As a result, leaders in organizations tend to support and leverage in-groups and cliques who they can trust to get the work done.

Hypotheses Linking Specific GLOBE Organizational and National Culture Dimensions with Specific Leadership Factors

Having provided a conceptual justification for aggregating ILT to the organizational and national cultural level of analysis, in this section we will propose a set of specific hypotheses to test how cultural context shapes the ILT attributes that are most sensitive to variation across cultures. We will then explain the procedure we used to select among the GLOBE twenty-one primary leadership factors and why each cultural dimension is hypothesized to be associated with specific leadership dimensions.

Culture was conceptualized in terms of nine cultural attributes that, when quantified, are referred to as *cultural dimensions*. GLOBE researchers measured both cultural practices (the way things are) and values (the way things should be) at the organizational and societal levels of analysis. A brief description of each dimension is provided in table 13-1.

TABLE 13-1

GLOBE cultural dimensions

- *Uncertainty avoidance:* The extent to which members of an organization or society strive to avoid uncertainty by reliance on social norms, rituals, and bureaucratic practices to alleviate the unpredictability of future events.

- *Power distance:* The degree to which members of an organization or society expect and agree that power should be unequally shared.

- *Collectivism I—Institutional collectivism:* The degree to which organizational and societal institutional practices encourage and reward collective distribution of resources and collective action.

- *Collectivism II—In-group collectivism:* The degree to which individuals express pride, loyalty, and cohesiveness in their organizations or families.

- *Gender egalitarianism:* The extent to which an organization or a society minimizes gender role differences and gender discrimination.

- *Assertiveness:* The degree to which individuals in organizations or societies are assertive, confrontational, and aggressive in social relationships.

- *Future orientation:* The degree to which individuals in organizations or societies engage in future-oriented behaviors such as planning, investing in the future, and delaying gratification.

- *Performance orientation:* The extent to which an organization or society encourages and rewards group members for performance improvement and excellence. This dimension includes the future-oriented component of the dimension called "Confucian Dynamism" by Hofstede and Bond (1988).

- *Humane orientation:* The degree to which individuals in organizations or societies encourage and reward individuals for being fair, altruistic, friendly, generous, caring, and kind to others. This dimension is similar to the dimension labeled "Kind Heartedness" by Hofstede and Bond (1988).

The leadership attributes were measured through a questionnaire containing 112 leadership items. An initial pool of 382 items was written, along with a brief definition of the item, to reflect a variety of traits, skills, behaviors, and abilities potentially relevant to leadership emergence and effectiveness. Each item was measured on a scale ranging from 1 to 7; a score of 1 means that the attribute greatly inhibits outstanding leadership, and a score of 7 means that the attribute contributes greatly to outstanding leadership. A score of 4 means the attribute neither contributes to nor inhibits outstanding leadership. As pointed out earlier, GLOBE produced a set of twenty-one primary leadership dimensions and then conducted a second-order factor analysis that resulted in six global culturally endorsed implicit leadership theory dimensions, or CLTs. Table 13-2 shows the six such dimensions along with the twenty-one underlying primary dimensions.

As explained earlier, our focus in this paper is on those leadership dimensions that are clearly culturally contingent. We selected those primary leadership dimensions where the scores (aggregated at both the organizational and national level independently) had a range containing the midpoint of 4.0 on a 7-point scale. In other words, these are leadership attributes that are seen as positive in some cultural contexts and negative in others. We did not choose attributes where there was a range of scores but all countries scored either above 4 or below 4 because, in such cases, all cultural contexts viewed the leadership attributes in the same light (positive or negative), although in differing degrees. Instead, we selected the leadership dimensions that were seen as positive in some countries/organizations and negative in other countries/organizations because these were the most subject to variation based on cultural context. The chosen seven culturally contingent leadership dimensions are shown in bold in table 13-2. They are as follows: face saver, bureaucratic (formerly labeled procedural), status conscious, humane, self-sacrifice, autonomous, and internally competitive (formerly labeled conflict inducer). Table 13-3 shows a brief description of each primary dimension and where it fits within the six global leadership dimensions.

GLOBE (House et al., 2004) empirically showed that cultural *values* and not *practices* are predictive of leadership attributes. The authors explained this finding by pointing out that both cultural values and desired leadership attributes reflect an idealized state of what should be, or an ideal end point. Since we are studying these same idealized leader attributes, we also focus on the relationship between cultural values and leadership attributes.

TABLE 13-2

Global culturally endorsed implicit leadership (CLT) dimensions and the twenty-one primary factors

Charismatic/Value-Based	Team-Oriented
1. Charismatic 1: Visionary	7. Team 1: Collaborative team orientation
2. Charismatic 2: Inspirational	8. Team 2: Team Integrator
3. Charismatic 3: Self-sacrifice	9. Diplomatic
	10. Malevolent (reverse scored)
4. Integrity	11. Administratively Competent
5. Decisive	
6. Performance orientation	

Self-Protective	Participative
12. Self-centered	17. Autocratic (reverse scored)
13. Status conscious	18. Nonparticipative (reverse scored)
14. Conflict inducer	
15. Face saver	
16. Procedural (Bureaucratic)	

Humane-Oriented	Autonomous
19. Modesty	**21. Autonomous**
20. Humane orientation	

Note: The leadership dimensions in bold are culturally contingent.

CULTURAL UNDERPINNINGS OF STATUS-CONSCIOUS LEADERSHIP

GLOBE's concept of status-conscious leadership is associated with an elitist view of individuals and relationships (House et al., 1999). Status-conscious leaders are quite aware of their own and others' social position and are strongly motivated by the prospects of an elevated position in their organization. Their behavior toward others is very much moderated by the other person's position in the society or in the organization. They tend to focus on building stronger ties with those who wield a high level of power or status around them.

We postulate that status-conscious leadership is encouraged in societies and organizations that value high levels of uncertainty avoidance

TABLE 13-3

GLOBE culturally contingent leadership factors (including the range of country scores)

1. **Status conscious (2.34–5.81):** This dimension reflects a consciousness of one's own and others' social position; holds an elitist belief that some individuals deserve more privileges than others.

2. **Bureaucratic (formerly labeled procedural) (2.79–4.95):** This dimension emphasizes following established norms, rules, policies, and procedures; habitually follows regular routines.

3. **Autonomous (2.23–4.67):** This dimension describes tendencies to act independently without relying on others. May also include self-governing behavior and a preference to work and act separately from others.

4. **Face saving (2.01–4.75):** This leadership dimension reflects the tendency to ensure followers are not embarrassed or shamed; maintains good relationships by refraining from making negative comments and instead uses metaphors and examples.

5. **Humane (3.31–5.59):** This dimension emphasizes empathy for others by giving time, money, resources, and assistance when needed; shows concern for followers' personal and group welfare.

6. **Self-sacrificial/Risk taking (3.92–6.07):** This dimension indicates an ability to convince followers to invest their efforts in activities that do not have a high probability of success, to forgo their self-interest, and make personal sacrifices for the goal or vision.

7. **Internally competitive (formerly labeled conflict inducer) (2.92–5.04):** This dimension reflects the tendency to encourage competition within a group and may include concealing information in a secretive manner.

because such societies tend to prefer formalized, documented, and orderly relations and encourage clarity in relationships. Titles provide clarity and consistency in such relationships and therefore are held in high esteem. Organizational hierarchy clarifies the formal and encouraged type of relationships. Those in positions of authority and stature enjoy a higher level of deference and privilege in such societies (Brodbeck, Frese, and Javidan, 2002; Sully de Luque and Javidan, 2004).

Status-conscious leadership is also postulated to be viewed positively in societies and organizations that value high levels of power distance because such cultural contexts are typically highly stratified and view power as a source of stability and social order. Those in positions of power tend to enjoy high levels of privilege and have easy access to resources (Hofstede, 1980, 2001; Carl, Gupta, and Javidan, 2004).

Societies and organizations that value gender egalitarianism are postulated to discourage status-conscious leadership because they tend to encourage not just gender egalitarianism, but egalitarianism in general.

Diverse types of individuals will enjoy access to positions of authority, status, participation in decision making, and higher levels of education (Emrich, Denmark, and Den Hartog, 2004) in egalitarian contexts.

Finally, societies and organizations that value assertiveness are postulated to discourage status-conscious leadership because they "value assertive, dominant, and tough behavior for everyone in society" (Den Hartog, 2004:405). They value success and believe that anyone can win if they try hard enough, and value effort and results over status and position (Den Hartog, 2004). In sum, we propose the following hypotheses with regard to the relationship between culture and status-conscious leadership:

> H1.1: Status-conscious leadership is viewed as contributing to outstanding leadership in cultural contexts that highly value uncertainty avoidance.

> H1.2: Status-conscious leadership is viewed as contributing to outstanding leadership in cultural contexts that highly value power distance.

> H1.3: Status-conscious leadership is viewed as inhibiting outstanding leadership in cultural contexts that highly value gender egalitarianism.

> H1.4: Status-conscious leadership is viewed as inhibiting outstanding leadership in cultural contexts that highly value assertiveness.

CULTURAL UNDERPINNINGS OF BUREAUCRATIC LEADERSHIP

GLOBE's concept of bureaucratic leadership is associated with following the established rules and procedures (House et al., 1999). It reflects a risk-averse attitude and support for status quo. It favors stability and certainty over risk, innovation, and new ideas. We postulate that societies and organizations that value uncertainty avoidance tend to encourage this style of leadership because such cultural contexts tend to prefer formal rules and procedures. They are more inclined toward preserving status quo and avoiding risk. They encourage their members to abide by the rules and avoid uncertainty (Brodbeck, Frese, and Javidan, 2002; Sully de Luque and Javidan, 2004).

Bureaucratic leadership is also encouraged in societies and organizations that value high levels of power distance because in such cultural contexts, those in positions of power are expected to be the decision makers. Their direct reports tend to approach them with problems or issues and expect to receive answers or directions. Direct reports tend to avoid making decisions due to the perception that downside risk could be high for them. Making a decision that is not supported by the supervisor can have negative consequences, so individuals learn to pass all issues or decision topics to the next level of authority for decision making, thus creating a bureaucratic and hierarchical approach to decision making (Hofstede, 1980, 2001; Carl, Gupta, and Javidan, 2004).

Bureaucratic leadership is also encouraged in societies and organizations that have high institutional collectivist values because collective harmony is key in such cultural contexts. Employees are typically expected to follow rules and procedures that have evolved to ensure and sustain group harmony, and duties and obligations are important determinants of desirable social behavior (Gelfand, Bhawuk, Nishi, and Bechtold, 2004).

Finally, we postulate that societies and organizations that value performance orientation tend to discourage bureaucratic leadership because they emphasize results over process, and reward performance. They value assertiveness and competition and do not mind bending or breaking some rules if it enhances performance and results. They encourage innovation and initiative and view bureaucratic approaches as an obstacle to individual initiative (Javidan, 2004). In sum, we propose the following hypotheses on the relationship between culture and bureaucratic leadership:

> H2.1: Bureaucratic leadership will be viewed as contributing to outstanding leadership in cultural contexts that highly value uncertainty avoidance.

> H2.2: Bureaucratic leadership will be viewed as contributing to outstanding leadership in cultural contexts that highly value power distance.

> H2.3: Bureaucratic leadership will be viewed as contributing to outstanding leadership in cultural contexts that highly value institutional collectivism.

> H2.4: Bureaucratic leadership will be viewed as inhibiting outstanding leadership in cultural contexts that highly value performance orientation.

Cultural Underpinnings of Autonomous Leadership

GLOBE's concept of autonomous leadership is associated with the tendency to be and act as an independent agent with little interest in interdependent relations (House et al., 1999). It reflects a tendency to prefer to work alone and be self-reliant rather than working with others. Autonomous leaders tend to be suspicious of others' actions and intents and avoid interpersonal relations because they believe they take too much energy and time. They therefore prefer to build and protect their independence.

We postulate that societies and organizations that value in-group or institutional collectivism tend to discourage this form of leadership because they value group harmony either at the small group or at the larger organizational level. They dislike autonomous leadership because of its negative impact on the fabric of the group or the society. In such cultures, interpersonal relations and collective good are paramount, and autonomous leaders, because of their self-reliance and lack of respect for the wishes of others, can damage group relations and harmony (Gelfand, Bhawuk, Nishi, and Bechtold, 2004).

Autonomous leadership is also postulated to be discouraged in societies and organizations that value performance orientation because such cultural contexts are results driven, and autonomous leaders, because of their demotivating effect, can jeopardize results. Such cultures value individual development and training and dislike autonomous leaders because of their self-centered approach and lack of attention to the other members of the organization, especially their team members (Javidan, 2004). In sum, we propose the following hypotheses with regard to the relationship between culture and autonomous leadership:

> H3.1: Autonomous leadership is viewed as inhibiting outstanding leadership in cultural contexts that value in-group collectivism.
>
> H3.2: Autonomous leadership is viewed as inhibiting outstanding leadership in cultural contexts that value institutional collectivism.
>
> H3.3: Autonomous leadership is viewed as inhibiting outstanding leadership in cultural contexts that value performance orientation.

CULTURAL UNDERPINNINGS OF FACE-SAVING LEADERSHIP

GLOBE's concept of face-saving leadership is associated with the tendency to avoid embarrassing anyone (House et al., 1999). It reflects the importance of maintaining a positive relationship with others and the need to be viewed as a good person. A face-saving leader is always cautious not to shame others and not to hurt other people's feelings. He or she is always careful in how to communicate with others and uses indirect and nuanced language peppered with metaphors and analogies. As a result, face-saver leaders are not always easily understood.

We postulate that societies and organizations that value assertiveness and performance orientation tend to discourage face-saving leadership because such cultures tend to prefer assertiveness, competitiveness, tough character, a can-do attitude, a sense of urgency, direct communication, and achieving results (Den Hartog, 2004; Javidan, 2004). In such cultures, overly nuanced and indirect language is viewed as dysfunctional, frustrating, and unacceptable. We also believe that societies and organizations that value humane orientation will encourage face-saving leadership. Leaders do not embarrass people in caring societies. We therefore propose the following three hypotheses:

> H4.1: Face-saving leadership is viewed as inhibiting outstanding leadership in cultural contexts that highly value assertiveness.

> H4.2: Face-saving leadership is viewed as inhibiting outstanding leadership in cultural contexts that highly value performance orientation.

> H4.3: Face-saving leadership is viewed as contributing to outstanding leadership in cultural contexts that highly value humane orientation.

CULTURAL UNDERPINNINGS OF HUMANE LEADERSHIP

GLOBE's concept of humane leadership is associated with concern for others (House et al., 1999). It reflects the tendency to show empathy and be helpful to others; a sincere interest in the well-being of those around the leader, not just from a professional point of view, but also from a personal point of view. Humane leaders are generous and compassionate.

We postulate that humane leadership is encouraged in cultures that value humane orientation because such cultures place importance on caring for others and showing compassion and altruism. They encourage belongingness, sensitivity, empathy, and strong human relationships and expect their members to be supportive of each other (Kabasakal and Bodur, 2004). We also postulate that societies and organizations that value assertiveness tend to discourage humane leadership because they tend to prefer strong character, winning and dominance, and individual self-reliance. They value success and believe that anyone can win if they try hard enough, and value effort and results over relationships and others' feelings. Independence is viewed as more important and valuable than interdependence (Den Hartog, 2004). In sum, we propose the following hypotheses with regard to the relationship between culture and humane leadership:

> H5.1: Humane leadership is viewed as contributing to outstanding leadership in cultural contexts that highly value humane orientation.

> H5.2: Humane leadership is viewed as inhibiting outstanding leadership in cultural contexts that highly value assertive orientation.

CULTURAL UNDERPINNINGS OF SELF-SACRIFICIAL LEADERSHIP

Self-sacrificial leadership is associated with the ability to convince followers to commit to achieving the group's goals and objectives. It is the ability to motivate followers to forgo self-interest in the interest of collective good. Self-sacrificial leaders are willing to take personal risks and demonstrate their own willingness to sacrifice for collective good (House et al., 1999).

We postulate that self-sacrificial leadership is encouraged in societies and organizations that value performance orientation because such societies are focused on results and have a sense of urgency. They prefer demanding targets and value taking initiative (House et al., 2004). We also postulate that cultural contexts that value group and institutional collectivism tend to encourage self-sacrificial leadership due to their focus on collective good either at the group level or the society level. In such cultures, individual interest is subjugated to the interest of a larger community. The self is viewed as interdependent with groups, and social norms and obligations are strong determinants of individual behavior (Gelfand, Bhawuk, Nishi, and Bechtold, 2004). In sum, we propose the following hypotheses with regard to the relationship between culture and self-sacrificial leadership:

H6.1: Self-sacrificial leadership is viewed as contributing to outstanding leadership in cultural contexts that value performance orientation.

H6.2: Self-sacrificial leadership is viewed as contributing to outstanding leadership in cultural contexts that value in-group collectivism.

H6.3: Self-sacrificial leadership is viewed as contributing to outstanding leadership in cultural contexts that value institutional collectivism.

Cultural Underpinnings of Internally Competitive Leadership

The GLOBE notion of internally competitive leadership is associated with the tendency to generate and encourage internal competition within the group, and being highly prescriptive while at the same time being secretive. Internally competitive leaders tend to micromanage but are reluctant to share information that may be helpful in getting the task done. They tend to view information as a source of power and are tight with it. They also believe that by generating competition within their own group, they can motivate their team members to achieve higher results, even if it leads to internal conflict and lack of cooperation. Furthermore, their team members are socialized into hoarding information and not collaborating with their colleagues (House et al., 1999).

We postulate that internally competitive leadership is encouraged in societies and organizations that value power distance because such cultures are typically highly stratified and view power as a source of stability, privilege, and social order. Those in positions of power tend to enjoy high levels of privilege and have easy access to resources and information. They tend to micromanage and make decisions without much input or discussion from their direct reports (Hofstede, 1980, 2001; Carl, Gupta, and Javidan, 2004).

We also postulate that internally competitive leadership is encouraged in societies and organizations that value assertiveness because such cultures "value assertive, dominant, and tough behavior for everyone in society" (Den Hartog, 2004:405). They value success and believe that anyone can win if they try hard enough, and value effort and results over status and position. They enjoy and value competition and are not much concerned about interpersonal relationships (Den Hartog, 2004).

Internally competitive leadership is also postulated to be discouraged in societies and organizations that value gender egalitarianism and in-group collectivism because the former tend to encourage egalitarianism in general, with more ready access to resources, information, and positions of authority (Emrich, Denmark, and Den Hartog, 2004). The latter tend to emphasize group loyalty, collaboration, interdependence, and harmony (Gelfand, Bhawuk, Nishi, and Bechtold, 2004). In sum, we propose the following hypotheses with regard to the relationship between culture and conflict-inducing leadership:

> H7.1: Internally competitive leadership is viewed as contributing to outstanding leadership in cultural contexts that value power distance.
>
> H7.2: Internally competitive leadership is viewed as contributing to outstanding leadership in cultural contexts that value assertiveness.
>
> H7.3: Internally competitive leadership is viewed as inhibiting outstanding leadership in cultural contexts that value gender egalitarianism.
>
> H7.4: Internally competitive leadership is viewed as inhibiting outstanding leadership in cultural contexts that value in-group collectivism.

Research Methodology

Data and Sample

The GLOBE research sample consisted of 17,370 middle managers in 951 organizations within 62 societal cultures. This sample represents local (i.e., non-multinational) organizations within the telecommunications, food processing, and finance industries. To be included in the sample, responses of managers from at least two of the three target industries in each country studied had to be attainable (i.e., responses from managers in a society with a single industry sample were not acceptable). Regardless of the industry that was sampled, half of the respondents from a given organization completed the organizational culture items and the leadership attribute items (i.e., Questionnaire Form Alpha) and the other half completed the societal culture items as well as the leadership attribute items (i.e., Questionnaire Form Beta).

Measures

LEADERSHIP ATTRIBUTES

As described earlier, leadership attributes were measured through a questionnaire containing 112 leadership items that reflected a variety of traits, skills, behaviors, and abilities potentially relevant to leadership emergence and effectiveness. GLOBE researchers identified twenty-one primary leadership factors in the first round of exploratory factor analysis and computed second-order leadership dimensions by factor analyzing the twenty-one primary dimensions to develop what they refer to as the six global culturally endorsed leadership dimensions, or global CLTs. Table 13-2 shows the twenty-one primary dimensions embedded in the six global CLTs. As explained earlier in the paper, the present study focused on seven of these dimensions, which are shown to be culturally contingent. To date, no published research has focused on the twenty-one primary leadership dimensions as they relate to cultural contexts.

CULTURE DIMENSIONS AS ANTECEDENT VARIABLES

Culture was conceptualized in terms of nine dimensions (House et al., 2004). GLOBE researchers measured both cultural practices (the way things are) and values (the way things should be) at the organizational and societal levels of analysis. A brief description of each dimension is provided in table 13-1 of this paper. GLOBE dimensions of societal culture have been validated through the use of unobtrusive measures and independently collected data from the World Values Survey (Inglehart, Basanez, and Moreno, 1998).

The present paper uses the culture dimension *values* in the analyses rather than culture dimension *practices* for two reasons. First, from a conceptual viewpoint, both the culture dimension values and the desired leadership characteristics are similar in that values reflect an idealized state of what should be, and therefore ought to correspond to individuals' implicit beliefs regarding idealized leadership attributes. Furthermore, GLOBE provided empirical support that the secondary (i.e., global) leadership dimensions were most associated with the cultural or organizational *values* orientation (*Should Be* questionnaire responses) rather than cultural or organizational *practices* (*As Is* questionnaire responses).

Thus, for the purposes of explicating salient leadership prototypes among cultures, we followed the same analytical framework, exploring the linkage between cultural values and implicit leadership constructs. As was done with leadership constructs, $r_{wg(j)}$, ICC(1), and ICC(2) statistics were computed for the culture scales, and the results indicated that it is justified to aggregate these measures to the organizational and societal level of analysis.[1]

General Analysis Strategy

Our analysis proceeded in two stages. For stage 1, we determined which leadership dimensions were rated as *culturally contingent*. To do this, we examined all twenty-one primary leadership dimensions and identified those that were universally positive, those that were universally negative, and those whose variability made them likely candidates to be culturally contingent. For the latter, we found that some leadership dimensions varied across countries but were primarily positive contributors in all cultures. Other dimensions also varied but were primarily impediments.

Of the twenty-one primary dimensions, we found five leadership dimensions to be universally positive, two to be universally negative, and fourteen dimensions to not meet the criteria to be either completely positive or negative.[2] To determine which of these latter dimensions were culturally contingent, we used the following criterion. To be labeled "culturally contingent," those dimensions must have a mean (i.e., average) country score whose range transversed the neutral midpoint scale score of 4. For instance, the humane leadership dimension met this criterion because it had a country score range of 3.31 to 5.59—negative in some cultures but positive in others. The seven dimensions that were identified to be culturally contingent were those identified previously as status conscious, procedural (relabeled as "bureaucratic"), autonomous, face saving, humane orientation, self-sacrificial, and conflict inducer (relabeled as "internally competitive").

For stage 2 of the analyses, we conceptualized which aspects of national culture were most predictive of each culturally contingent leadership dimension identified in stage 1. As presented in the previous section, we hypothesized specific cultural values that should be related to specific culturally contingent leadership dimensions. As the primary statistical technique, a hierarchical linear model (HLM) procedure was used to determine the relative impact of organizational and societal cultural values on these leadership dimensions.

Procedure to Identify Cultural Drivers of Culturally Contingent Leadership Dimensions

In the GLOBE model (House et al., 2004), both organizational and societal culture variables were predicted to influence the leadership variables. Since organizations are embedded within societies, the GLOBE sampling strategy produced what is called a nested structure in the database. Middle managers are nested within organizations because multiple middle managers were sampled from each organization. Further, organizations are nested within societies because multiple organizations were sampled from each society. Because of this nested structure, it is likely that covariation among respondents will surface, given that GLOBE was asking middle managers from the same organization and society questions about their organization's and society's culture.

Hierarchical linear modeling (Hofmann, 1997; Hofmann, Griffin, and Gavin, 2000) is an effective tool for analyzing multilevel conceptual models and nested data such as GLOBE's. Specifically, HLM can be thought of as a multistep process designed to test relationships between independent and dependent variables at multiple levels. For instance, a possible hypothesis that we wanted to test is whether middle managers in collective organizations and societies share the perception that being "status conscious" is an effective attribute for leaders. Using this example, it should be noted that there are three levels of variation implicitly specified in this hypothesis. Differences among multiple middle managers from the same organization contribute to individual-level variation in the dependent variable. Differences among the average response across the various organizations represent organizational level variation, and finally, differences in the average response across the various societies represent societal-level variation. We considered all three of these levels in our analysis of our data.

All HLM analyses can be technically described as random intercept models in which three levels (i.e., individual, organizational, and societal) of analysis are specified. Because HLM analyses identify the total amount of variance in the leadership variable that is accounted for by forces at the individual, organizational, and societal levels, this procedure allows us to determine the amount of variance accounted for at each of these levels of analysis considered independently. However, because we are focused on shared leadership belief systems, the individual level of analysis is not of direct concern for us. The HLM procedure allows us to test specific hypotheses concerning the relationship between organizational culture and CLT leadership dimensions as well as societal culture and CLT leadership dimensions. In addition, the HLM results have the advantage of competitively testing several cultural dimensions simultaneously by showing the specific efficacy of a cultural dimension in relation to the other cultural dimensions.

We should again point out that different sets of middle managers completed the two GLOBE questionnaires. GLOBE used Form Alpha responses to obtain the organizational culture and CLT leadership data and used Form Beta responses to obtain the societal culture and CLT leadership data. These separate samples minimized common source variance in the analyses.

To summarize, we used the organizational culture scales that were validated at the organizational level to assess "organizational level culture–CLT effects," and we used the societal culture scales that were developed and validated at the societal level to assess "societal level culture–CLT leadership dimension effects." Thus, we measured our variables and tested our hypotheses in a way consistent with the various levels within the data set.

Results

Correlation Analyses

A correlation analysis was conducted by correlating each of the seven culturally contingent leadership dimensions with the eight cultural values specified in our hypotheses. This analysis does not allow for testing hypotheses, but is presented for the purpose of providing information that may be of interest in providing a more complete picture of all potential relationships among the variables (see tables 13-4 and 13-5). It is important to note that these correlations are not subject to common source variance because data for the leadership responses were obtained from individuals separate from those who completed the organizational or societal culture measures. For instance, correlations for organizational cultural dimensions were obtained from Form Alpha and were computed with ratings of leadership attributes obtained from individuals completing Form Beta. Conversely, correlations for societal culture dimensions obtained from Form Beta were computed with leadership ratings obtained from Form Alpha. However, in the HLM

TABLE 13-4

Mean, range, and correlations between leadership dimensions and cultural values: societal-level analysis

Culturally contingent leadership dimensions	Mean	Range	Cultural values							
			Uncertainty avoidance	Power distance	Institutional collectivism	Humane orientation	Performance orientation	In-group collectivism	Assertiveness	Gender egalitarianism
Status conscious	4.27	2.34–5.81	0.58**	0.10	0.42**	−0.31*	−0.04	0.03	−0.07	−0.35**
Bureaucratic	3.86	2.79–4.95	0.76**	0.34**	0.35**	−0.39	0.06	0.24	0.27*	−0.64**
Autonomous	3.84	2.23–4.67	−0.09	0.25	−0.46**	0.01	−0.26*	−0.16	0.05	−0.12
Face-saving	2.89	2.01–4.75	0.64**	0.38**	0.07	−0.20	−0.26*	−0.15	0.29*	−0.55**
Humane	4.74	3.31–5.59	0.16	0.25	−0.11	−0.10	−0.05	−0.01	0.32*	−0.24
Self-sacrificial	5.00	3.92–6.07	0.16	−0.24	0.34**	−0.12	0.34**	0.35**	0.12	0.16
Internally competitive	3.95	2.92–5.04	0.56**	0.32*	0.19	−0.21	−0.15	−0.09	0.20	−0.58**

Note: N = 60 societies.
*p ≤ 0.05; **p ≤ 0.01

TABLE 13-5

Mean, range, and correlations between leadership dimensions and cultural values: organizational-level analysis

Culturally contingent leadership dimensions	Mean	Range	Cultural values							
			Uncertainty avoidance	Power distance	Institutional collectivism	Humane orientation	Performance orientation	In-group collectivism	Assertiveness	Gender egalitarianism
Status conscious	4.36	1.00–7.00	0.18*	0.00	0.23**	0.023**	-0.01	0.02	-0.13**	-0.13**
Bureaucratic	4.01	1.80–6.50	0.36**	0.21**	0.02	0.15**	-0.10*	0.03	-0.07	-0.32**
Autonomous	3.87	1.00–6.75	0.03	0.06	-0.12**	-0.07	-0.02	-0.04	-0.04	0.01
Face-saving	2.96	1.00–6.33	0.31**	0.18**	0.10*	0.18**	-0.14**	-0.16**	0.00	-0.26**
Humane	4.91	1.00–7.00	0.09*	0.12**	-0.05	0.12**	-0.02	0.03	-0.11**	-0.19**
Self-sacrificial	4.96	1.67–7.00	-0.10*	0.00	0.07	-0.01	0.03	0.21**	0.03	0.01
Internally competitive	4.01	1.67–7.00	0.28**	0.19**	0.01	0.14*	-0.08*	0.01	-0.08	-0.30**

Note: $N = 636$ organizations. Ranges in percentile scores for 5th and 95th percentiles are as follows: Status conscious, 2.50–6.00; Bureaucratic, 2.80–5.30; Autonomous, 2.38–5.17; Face saving, 1.67–4.58; Humane, 3.40–6.43; Self-sacrificial, 3.83–6.17; Internally competitive, 2.83–5.33.

$*p \leq 0.05; **p \leq 0.01$

analysis, to achieve maximum stability of HLM coefficients (presented subsequently), the leadership dimension scores were obtained from the total sample of respondents completing forms Alpha and Beta.

The two tables show that (a) there are many significant relationships between cultural values and the culturally contingent leadership constructs, and (b) the relative size of the correlations are much higher for the relationships between societal cultural values and leadership dimensions than between the organizational cultural values and leadership dimensions.

Hierarchical Linear Modeling Analyses

In the following discussion, statistically significant relationships between the eight societal and organizational cultural values and the seven culturally contingent leadership dimensions are organized around each of the leadership dimensions (similar to the hypotheses described earlier). Recall that HLM analyses considered both the organizational and societal levels simultaneously. Table 13-6 shows the detailed results of the HLM analyses. Table 13-7 presents a summary of significant relationships between the cultural values and the culturally contingent leadership dimensions. For all the HLM analyses, if the predicted relationships among the variables are significant at both the organizational and societal level, we present the findings as *strong support* for the hypotheses; if the predicted relationships are significant among the variables for either the organizational or societal level, we present the findings as *support* for the hypothesis. For ease of discussion, the results are presented in the same order of initial hypothesis presentation.

H1 HYPOTHESES: STATUS-CONSCIOUS LEADERSHIP

We hypothesized that status-conscious leadership contributes to outstanding leadership in cultural contexts that highly value uncertainty avoidance (H1.1) and power distance (H1.2) and inhibits outstanding leadership in cultural contexts that that highly value gender egalitarianism (H1.3) and assertiveness (H1.4).

Three of the four hypotheses regarding status-conscious leadership were either supported or strongly supported. As predicted, status-conscious leadership was viewed as contributing to outstanding leadership in cultural contexts that highly valued uncertainty avoidance (H1.1—strong support) and power distance (H1.2—support). Also as

TABLE 13-6

Hierarchical linear model of cultural values predicting culturally contingent leadership dimensions[a]

Leadership prototype dimension	Coefficient	Standard error	df	t value
Status conscious				
Intercept	4.33	0.07	41	62.41**
Uncertainty avoidance (society)	0.61	0.14	41	4.48**
Assertiveness (society)	−0.30	0.10	41	−3.15**
Power distance (society)	0.18	0.31	41	0.59
Gender egalitarianism (society)	−0.24	0.23	41	−1.03
Uncertainty avoidance (organization)	0.30	0.06	683	5.21**
Assertiveness (organization)	−0.14	0.09	683	−1.52
Power distance (organization)	0.12	0.07	683	1.64***
Gender egalitarianism (organization)	−0.05	0.05	683	−1.01
Bureaucratic				
Intercept	3.91	0.04	41	106.57**
Uncertainty avoidance (society)	0.50	0.06	41	8.23**
Power distance (society)	0.56	0.12	41	4.60**
Institutional collectivism (society)	0.29	0.10	41	3.00**
Performance orientation (society)	−0.01	0.13	41	−0.09
Uncertainty avoidance (organization)	0.34	0.05	683	7.37**
Power distance (organization)	0.16	0.04	683	3.53**
Institutional collectivism (organization)	0.02	0.06	683	0.37
Performance orientation (organization)	−0.05	0.06	683	−0.79

Leadership prototype dimension	Coefficient	Standard error	df	t value
Autonomous				
Intercept	3.90	0.06	41	63.60**
Institutional collectivism (society)	−0.32	0.16	41	−1.94*
Performance orientation (society)	−0.14	0.21	41	−0.66
In-group collectivism (society)	0.02	0.26	41	0.10
Institutional collectivism (organization)	−0.07	0.08	683	0.79
Performance orientation (organization)	0.20	0.13	683	1.53
In-group collectivism (organization)	−0.15	0.14	683	−1.07
Face-saving				
Intercept	2.94	0.08	41	35.33**
Humane orientation (society)	−0.30	0.37	41	0.81
Performance orientation (society)	−0.34	0.23	41	−1.49
Assertiveness (society)	0.34	0.13	41	2.53**
Humane orientation (organization)	0.05	0.09	683	0.54
Performance orientation (organization)	−0.15	0.08	683	−1.86***
Assertiveness (organization)	0.06	0.08	683	0.78
Humane				
Intercept	4.82	0.06	41	74.85**
Humane orientation (society)	0.08	0.28	41	0.30
Assertiveness (society)	0.26	0.09	41	2.92**
Humane orientation (organization)	0.56	0.05	683	11.98**
Assertiveness (organization)	−0.06	0.05	683	−1.27

(Continued)

TABLE 13-6 *(continued)*

Hierarchical linear model of cultural values predicting culturally contingent leadership dimensions[a]

Leadership prototype dimension	Coefficient	Standard error	df	t value
Self-sacrificial				
Intercept	5.05	0.04	41	117.08**
Institutional collectivism (society)	0.28	0.09	41	3.05**
Performance orientation (society)	−0.07	0.16	41	−0.43
In-group collectivism (society)	0.37	0.12	41	2.95**
Institutional collectivism (organization)	0.04	0.05	683	0.77
Performance orientation (organization)	0.09	0.10	683	0.93
In-group collectivism (organization)	0.28	0.09	683	2.91**
Internally competitive				
Intercept	3.93	0.06	41	65.80**
Power distance (society)	0.14	0.24	41	0.55
In-group collectivism (society)	0.04	0.17	41	0.23
Assertiveness (society)	0.00	0.09	41	0.02
Gender egalitarianism (society)	−0.61	0.14	41	−4.39**
Power distance (organization)	0.17	0.04	683	4.24**
In-group collectivism (organization)	0.15	0.07	683	2.08*
Assertiveness (organization)	−0.05	0.03	683	−1.40
Gender egalitarianism (organization)	−0.08	0.04	683	−1.92***

a. Coefficients are multilevel random slopes for hierarchical linear modeling.
*$p \leq 0.05$; **$p \leq 0.01$; ***$p \leq 0.10$.

TABLE 13-7

Summary of proposed hypotheses and results

	Uncertainty avoidance	Power distance	Institutional collectivism	Humane orientation	Performance orientation	In-group collectivism	Assertiveness	Gender egalitarianism
Status conscious (H1)	++	++					– –	–
Bureaucratic (H2)	++	++	++		–			
Autonomous (H3)			– –		–	– –		
Face-saving (H4)				+	– –		–	
Humane (H5)				++			–	
Self-sacrificial (H6)			++		++	++		
Internally competitive (H7)		++				–	+	–

Note: +, positive relationship hypothesized; ++, positive hypothesis and results that support hypothesis; –, negative relationship hypothesized; – –, negative hypothesis and results that support hypothesis.

predicted, status-conscious leadership inhibited outstanding leadership in cultural contexts that highly valued assertiveness (H1.4—strong support). No support was found for the hypothesized relationship between status-conscious leadership and gender egalitarianism (H1.3).

H2 Hypotheses: Bureaucratic Leadership

We hypothesized that bureaucratic leadership contributes to outstanding leadership in cultural contexts that highly value uncertainty avoidance (H2.1), power distance (H2.2), and institutional collectivism (H2.3) and inhibits outstanding leadership in cultural contexts that highly value performance orientation (H2.4).

Three of the four hypotheses regarding bureaucratic leadership were either supported or strongly supported. As predicted, bureaucratic leadership was viewed as contributing to outstanding leadership in societal cultures that highly valued uncertainty avoidance (H2.1—strong support), power distance (H2.2—strong support) and institutional collectivism (H2.3—support). The hypothesized relationship between bureaucratic leadership and performance orientation was not supported (H2.4).

H3 Hypotheses: Autonomous Leadership

We hypothesized that autonomous leadership inhibits outstanding leadership in cultural contexts that highly value in-group collectivism (H3.1), institutional collectivism (H3.2), and performance orientation (H3.3).

Two of the three hypotheses regarding autonomous leadership were supported. As predicted, autonomous leadership was viewed as inhibiting outstanding leadership in cultural contexts that highly valued institutional collectivism (H3.2—support) and in-group collectivism (H3.1—support). No support was found for the predicted negative relationship between autonomous leadership and performance orientation (H3.3); it was significant, but in the positive direction.

H4 Hypotheses: Face-Saving Leadership

We hypothesized that face-saving leadership contributes to outstanding leadership in cultural contexts that highly value humane orientation (H4.3), and inhibits outstanding leadership in cultural contexts that highly value performance orientation (H4.2) and assertiveness (H4.1).

Only one of three hypotheses regarding face-saving leadership was supported. As predicted, face-saving leadership was viewed as inhibiting outstanding leadership in cultural contexts that highly valued performance orientation (H4.2—support). It was not significantly related to humane orientation (H4.3). The significant relationship between face saving and assertiveness (H4.1) was in the opposite direction than predicted (i.e., positive rather than the predicted negative relationship).

H5 Hypotheses: Humane Leadership

We hypothesized that humane leadership contributes to outstanding leadership in cultural contexts that highly value humane orientation (H5.1) and inhibits outstanding leadership in cultural contexts that highly value assertiveness (H5.2).

One of the two hypotheses regarding humane leadership was supported. As predicted, humane leadership was viewed as contributing to outstanding leadership in cultural contexts that highly valued humane orientation (H5.1—strong support). While humane leadership was significantly related to assertiveness (H5.2), it was in the opposite direction than predicted (i.e., positive in contrast to our negative prediction).

H6 Hypotheses: Self-Sacrificial Leadership

We hypothesized that self-sacrificial leadership contributes to outstanding leadership in cultural contexts that highly value performance orientation (H61.), in-group collectivism (H6.2), and institutional collectivism (H6.3).

All three hypotheses regarding self-sacrificial leadership were either supported or strongly supported. As predicted, self-sacrificial leadership was viewed as contributing to outstanding leadership in cultural contexts that highly valued in-group collectivism (H6.1—strong support), institutional collectivism (H6.3—support), and performance orientation (H6.2—support).

H7 Hypotheses: Internally Competitive Leadership

We hypothesized that internally competitive leadership contributes to outstanding leadership in cultural contexts that highly value power distance (H7.1) and assertiveness (H7.2), and inhibits outstanding leadership in cultural contexts that highly value gender egalitarianism (H7.3) and in-group collectivism (H7.4).

Two of the four hypotheses regarding internally competitive leadership were supported. As predicted, internally competitive leadership was viewed as contributing to outstanding leadership in societal cultures that highly valued power distance (H7.1—support) and inhibited outstanding leadership in cultural contexts that highly valued gender egalitarianism (H7.3—support). It was not significantly related to assertiveness (H7.2), and in contrast to our prediction, it was positively related to in-group collectivism (H7.4).

In summary, we found support for 65 percent of our hypotheses tested (fifteen of twenty-three). We note that the highest support for our predictions was found for the leadership dimensions of status-conscious, bureaucratic, autonomous, and self-sacrificial leadership. The highest support for our predictions with respect to specific cultural dimensions were for uncertainty avoidance, institutional collectivism, in-group collectivism, and power distance cultural values.

Discussion

In this paper, we first provided a conceptual framework linking national culture, organizational culture, and leadership attributes. We then conducted a series of HLM analyses using the GLOBE data from over 17,000 middle mangers to empirically verify their interconnections.

Our findings confirm strong empirical support for the notion, argued by a few authors (Peters and Waterman, 1982; Deal and Kennedy, 1982; Kouzes and Posner, 2002; Sims and Lorenzi, 1992), that organizational culture and leadership attributes are connected. Our results also show that, as suggested by others (Chong and Thomas, 1997; Adler, 1997; House et al., 1997, 2004; Javidan and Carl, 2004, 2005; Dorfman, 2004; Javidan, Dorfman, Sully de Luque, and House, 2006), national culture and leadership attributes are also connected.

The paper builds on the work of GLOBE and, similar to GLOBE, provides a unique analysis of the simultaneous impact of national and organizational culture on culturally endorsed leadership theory (CLT). It also goes beyond GLOBE and contributes in two specific ways: first, it provides a stronger theoretical framework, and second, it presents a new series of more in-depth and fine-grained analyses to help us better understand the relationship between national and organizational culture and leadership attributes.

Our analyses show that national culture and organizational culture do matter to leadership. Power distance and institutional collectivist values at the national or organizational level are predictive of three culturally contingent leadership attributes: status conscious, bureaucratic, and internally competitive for power distance, and bureaucratic, autonomous, and self-sacrificial for institutional collectivism. Other cultural values are predictive of at least one leadership attribute. Furthermore, three leadership attributes—bureaucratic, self-sacrificial, and internally competitive—are predicted by three cultural values each.

An important implication of these findings for researchers is that a multilevel approach to the study of leadership is a profitable line of research. Given the globalized nature of the world of business, and the increasing globalization of corporations, it is not sufficient any more to examine the relationship between organizational culture and leadership and national culture and leadership in isolation. Global managers are increasingly tasked with integrating or balancing corporate culture and national cultures in host countries. To be helpful, researchers need to explore and understand the resultant complexities that global managers have to deal with.

The GLOBE project and this paper provide insights into the new path for research. We have shown, both theoretically and empirically, that how managers evaluate their leaders, what they expect from their leaders, and what they consider facilitators or impediments of outstanding leadership can be predicted by a confluence of national and organizational values.

An obvious next step for GLOBE researchers was to examine the actual behavioral manifestation and outcomes of the identified leadership attributes. In its latest phase, GLOBE has identified what being bureaucratic actually means in different cultures. What are the specific behaviors associated with it in various cultures? Furthermore, the research team has examined the extent to which compliance with such behaviors results in some important outcome, positive or negative. The data collection in twenty countries has been completed, and the results will be published in the next eighteen months.

Our findings also have important implications for global leaders. At its core, the role of global leaders is to influence individuals, groups, and organizations from other parts of the world (Javidan, Hitt, and Steers, 2007; Beechler and Javidan, 2007). Some of these stakeholders may belong to the global leader's organization (e.g., employees), while others may be independent (e.g., clients and customers or regulatory agencies).

It is the diversity of the targets of influence that signifies and distinguishes the task of global leaders. We have shown in this paper that middle managers, a natural target of influence for global leaders, develop their implicit leadership theory based on their cultural upbringing and their organizational values. An intuitive assumption, yet to be empirically verified, is that global leaders who conform to middle managers' culturally endorsed implicit leadership theory are better equipped, and are more likely, to influence them. It is therefore incumbent upon global leaders to understand the cultural lens that is used to assess them in different parts of the world and leverage it in building a strong relationship with their stakeholders (Beechler and Javidan, 2007). GLOBE and this paper have taken important steps in providing such information to global managers. But simply having relevant information is not sufficient. The task of mastering cross-cultural leadership is indeed complex:

> Crossing business borders—borders of business unit, of market, of product, of function, and of customer—although important, is fundamentally different from crossing borders of country and culture. Dealing with multiple business elements, however arranged, adds layer upon layer of complexity and contributes to ambiguity, anxiety, and uncertainty, but the impact on executives is primarily cognitive or intellectual. Although the problems may be more complex, they are, at bottom, business problems, not personal problems. It is the crossing of cultural lines that is an assault on the identity of the person. When the task becomes managing differences of country, culture, language, and values, the assumptions we make about ourselves and other people are brought into question. Effective executive performance when crossing country and cultural borders often demands a kind of transformation of who we are and how we see ourselves. (McCall and Hollenbeck, 2002:22)

To succeed, global leaders need to navigate across a wide range of culturally endorsed implicit leadership theories. An important tool to help such navigation is what several authors refer to as the global mindset (Javidan, Hitt, and Steers, 2007; Beechler and Javidan, 2007; Levy, Beechler, Taylor, and Boyacigiller, 2007). Beechler and Javidan (2007) define global mindset as a set of individual attributes that enable global leaders to influence those that are different from them. Their construct of global mindset consists of three major ingredients: intellectual capital, psychological capital, and social capital. This line of work is a potentially profitable approach to help global leaders assess their potential in dealing with culturally diverse groups and identify new ways of assisting leaders in their global contexts.

Notes

1. The average $r_{wg(J)}$ for both the organizational and societal cultural values scales was 0.80. The average ICC(1) for the GLOBE organizational and societal cultural values scales was 0.27. The average ICC(2) for the organizational cultural values scales was 0.94, and the average ICC(2) for the societal cultural values scales was 0.95. In summary, these analyses support the appropriateness of aggregating these culture scales to the organizational and societal level of analysis.

2. **Universally Endorsed Leadership Dimensions.** The current project used the same criteria for determining which of the twenty-one primary leadership *dimensions* are universal as was done previously with individual *attributes*. That is, we established the following criteria for leadership dimensions to be considered universally endorsed as contributing to outstanding leadership: (a) 95 percent of the societal averages for the dimension had to exceed a mean of 5 on a 7-point scale, and (b) the worldwide grand mean score for that dimension (considering all sixty-two cultures together) had to exceed 6 on a 7-point scale.

Using the criteria above, the following four primary leadership dimensions met both standards for universal endorsement. A fifth dimension was included because it met one of the standards and came close to meeting the other criterion:

1. Integrity (grand mean score = 6.10; 95% > 6.58)
2. Charismatic–Inspirational (grand mean = 6.08; 95% > 6.52)
3. Performance Oriented (grand mean = 6.04; 95% > 6.52)
4. Charismatic–Visionary (grand mean = 6.03; 95% > 6.50)
5. Team Oriented (team integrator) (grand mean = 5.90; 95% > 6.48)

Universally Refuted Leadership Dimensions. GLOBE criteria for specific dimensions to be universally considered as impediments to effective leadership mirrored that of previous GLOBE findings regarding universal negative leadership attributes. The requirements were that (a) the dimension grand mean for all cultures had to be less than 3 on a 7-point scale, and (b) 95% of culture scores on the dimension item had to be less than 3 on a 7-point scale.

Using the criteria above, the following two primary leadership dimensions met our standard for universal refutation:

1. Malevolent (grand mean = 1.79; 95% < 2.45)
2. Self-Protective (grand mean = 2.17; 95% < 2.17)

Culturally Contingent Leader Dimensions. Fourteen primary leadership dimensions did not meet the criteria of either universal endorsement or refutation. One might argue that this entire set of fourteen leadership dimensions that did not meet the criteria for universal endorsement or refutation should be considered "culturally contingent." After all, they are culturally variable in that there exists a fairly large range of scores among countries. However, about half of these fourteen remaining dimensions are either mostly positive (e.g., participative) or mostly negative (e.g., autocratic), but the range of country scores does not cross the "neutral threshold" score of 4. For example, the range of societal scores for the primary leadership dimension labeled Diplomatic ranges from 4.80 to 6.25. While there clearly is a range of scores for this variable, it does not meet the definition of "strongly culturally contingent" since it is always a positive factor in each society (i.e., it is never an impediment to outstanding leadership). Because we anticipated that this could happen, we added the criterion that to be considered culturally contingent, the country mean scores must also transverse the neutral score of 4. Thus, the following seven primary leadership dimensions were found to be culturally contingent:

1. Face saving (mean societal score = 2.89; range 2.01–4.75)
2. Autonomous (mean societal score = 3.84; range 2.23–4.67)
3. Bureaucratic (formerly labeled procedural) (mean societal score = 3.86; range 2.79–4.95)
4. Internally competitive (formerly labeled conflict inducing) (mean societal score = 3.95; range 2.92–5.04)
5. Status conscious (mean societal score = 4.27; range 2.34–5.81)
6. Humane (mean societal score = 4.74; range 3.31–5.59)
7. Charismatic–self-sacrificial (mean societal score = 5.00; range 3.92–6.07)

References

Adler, N. *International Dimensions of Organizational Behavior.* 3rd ed. Cincinnati: South-Western College Publishing, 1997.

Bass, B.M. *Leadership and Performance Beyond Expectations.* New York: The Free Press, 1985.

Bass, B.M., B.J. Avolio, D.I. Jung, and Y. Berson. "Predicting Unit Performance by Assessing Transformational and Transactional Leadership." *Journal of Applied Psychology* 88, no. 2 (2003): 207–218.

Beechler, S., and M. Javidan. "Leading with a Global Mindset." In *Advances in International Management.* Vol. 19, *The Global Mindset*, edited by M. Javidan, M.A. Hitt, and R.M. Steers, 131–170. Oxford, UK: Elsevier, 2007.

Brodbeck, F., M. Frese, and M. Javidan. "Leadership Made in Germany: Low on Compassion, High on Performance." *Academy of Management Executive* 16, no. 1 (2002): 13–15.

Carl, D., V. Gupta, and M. Javidan. "Power Distance." In *Culture, Leadership, and Organizations: The GLOBE Study of 62 Societies*, edited by R. House, P. Hanges, M. Javidan, P. Dorfman, and V. Gupta, 513–563. Thousand Oaks, CA: Sage Publications, 2004.

Chemers, M.M. *Integrative Theory of Leadership.* London: Lawrence Erlbaum, 1997.

Chong, L.M.A., and D.C. Thomas. "Leadership Perceptions in Cross-Cultural Context: Pakeha and Pacific Islanders in New Zealand." *Leadership Quarterly* 8, no. 3 (1997): 275–293.

Cronshaw, S.F., and R.G. Lord. "Effects of Categorization, Attribution, and Encoding Processes on Leadership Perceptions." *Journal of Applied Psychology* 72 (1987): 97–106.

Deal, T.E., and A.A. Kennedy. *Corporate Cultures.* Reading, MA: Addison-Wesley, 1982.

Den Hartog, D.N. "Assertiveness." In *Culture, Leadership, and Organizations: The GLOBE Study of 62 Societies*, edited by R.J. House, P.J. Hanges, M. Javidan, P.W. Dorfman, and V. Gupta, 395–431. Thousand Oaks, CA: Sage Publications, 2004.

Dorfman, P. "Implications of Vertical and Horizontal Individualism and Collectivism for Leadership Effectiveness." In *Advances in International Comparative Management*. Vol. 12, edited by L.C. Change and R.B. Peterson, 53–65. Greenwich, CT: JAI Press, 1998.

———. "International and Cross Cultural Leadership Research." In *Handbook for International Management Research*, edited by B.J. Punnett and O. Shenkar, 265–355. Ann Arbor, MI: University of Michigan Press, 2004.

Dorfman, P., P. Hanges, and F. Brodbeck. "Leadership and Culture Variation: The Identification of Culturally Endorsed Leadership Profiles." In *Culture, Leadership, and Organizations: The GLOBE Study of 62 Societies*, edited by R.J. House, P.J. Hanges, M. Javidan, P.W. Dorfman, and V. Gupta, 669–719. Thousand Oaks, CA: Sage Publications, 2004.

Emrich, C.G., F.L. Denmark, and D.N. Den Hartog. "Cross-Cultural Differences in Gender Egalitarianism: Implications for Societies, Organizations, and Leaders." In *Culture, Leadership, and Organizations: The GLOBE Study of 62 Societies*, edited by R.J. House, P.J. Hanges, M. Javidan, P.W. Dorfman, and V. Gupta, 343–394. Thousand Oaks, CA: Sage Publications, 2004.

Erez, M., and P.C. Earley. *Culture, Self-Identity, and Work*. New York: Oxford University Press, 1993.

Fiske, S.T., and S.E. Taylor. *Social Cognition*. 2nd ed. New York: McGraw-Hill, 1991.

Friedman, T.L. *The World Is Flat: A Brief History of the Twentieth Century*. New York: Farrar, Straus, and Giroux, 2005.

Geletkanycz, M.A. "The Salience of Culture's Consequences: The Effects of Cultural Values on Top Executive Commitment to Status Quo." *Strategic Management Journal* 18 (1997): 615–634.

Gelfand, M.J., D.P.S. Bhawuk, L.H. Nishi, and D.J. Bechtold. "Individualism and Collectivism." In *Culture, Leadership, and Organizations: The GLOBE Study of 62 Societies*, edited by R.J. House, P.J. Hanges, M. Javidan, P.W. Dorfman, and V. Gupta, 437–512. Thousand Oaks, CA: Sage Publications, 2004.

Gerstner, C.R., and D.V. Day. "Cross-Cultural Comparison of Leadership Prototypes." *Leadership Quarterly* 5, no. 2 (1994): 121–134.

Giddens, A. *Runaway World: How Globalization Is Reshaping Our Lives*. London: Profile Books, 1999.

Govindarajan, V., and A.K. Gupta. *The Quest for Global Dominance*. San Francisco: Jossey-Bass, 2001.

Gupta, V. and P.J. Hanges. "Regional and Climate Clusters of Societal Cultures." In R.J. House, P.J. Hanges, M. Javidan, P.W. Dorfman, and V. Gupta, eds. *Culture, Leadership, and Organizations: The GLOBE Study of 62 Societies*, 178–215. Thousand Oaks, CA: Sage Publications, 2004.

Hanges, P.J., P.W. Dorfman, G, Shteynberg, and A. Bates. "Culture and Leadership: A Connectionist Information Processing Model." In W.H. Mobley & E. Weldon (eds). *Advances in Global Leadership*. Vol. 4, 7–37. NY: JAI Press, 2006.

Hennessey, T.J., Jr. "'Reinventing' Government: Does Leadership Make the Difference?" *Public Administration Review* 58 (1998): 522–531.

Hofmann, D.A. "An Overview of the Logic and Rationale of Hierarchical Linear Models." *Journal of Management* 23, no. 6 (1997): 723–744.

Hofmann, D.A., M.A. Griffin, and M.B. Gavin. "The Application of Hierarchical Linear Modeling to Organizational Research." In *Multilevel Theory, Research, and Methods in Organizations,* edited by K.J. Klein and S.W. Koslowski, 467–511. San Francisco: Jossey-Bass, 2000.

Hofstede, G. *Culture's Consequences: International Differences in Work Related Values.* London: Sage Publications, 1980.

———. *Culture's Consequences: Comparing Values, Behaviors, Institutions and Organizations Across Nations.* 2nd ed. Thousand Oaks, CA: Sage Publications, 2001.

Hofstede, G., and M.H. Bond, "The Confucian Connection: From Cultural Roots to Economic Growth,' *Organization Dynamics"* 16 (1988): 5–21.

House, R.J., P.J. Hanges, S.A. Ruiz-Quintanilla, P.W. Dorfman, M. Javidan, M. Dickson, et al. "Cultural Influences on Leadership and Organizations: Project GLOBE." In *Advances in Global Leadership.* Vol. 1, edited by W.F. Mobley, M.J. Gessner, and V. Arnold, 171–233. Greenwich, CT: JAI Press, 1999.

House, R.J., P.J. Hanges, M. Javidan, P.W. Dorfman, and V. Gupta, eds. *Culture, Leadership, and Organizations: The GLOBE Study of 62 Societies.* Thousand Oaks, CA: Sage Publications, 2004.

House, R.J., N. Wright, and R.N. Aditya. "Cross-Cultural Research on Organizational Leadership: A Critical Analysis and a Proposed Theory." In *New Perspectives on International Industrial/Organizational Psychology,* edited by P.C. Earley and M. Erez, 535–623. San Francisco, CA: New Lexington Press, 1997.

Inglehart, R., M. Basanez, and A. Moreno. *Human Values and Beliefs: A Cross-Cultural Sourcebook.* Ann Arbor: University of Michigan, 1998.

Inkpen, A., and K. Ramaswamy. *Global Strategy: Creating and Sustaining Advantage Across Borders.* Oxford, UK: Oxford University Press, 2006.

Javidan, M. "Empirical Findings." In *Culture, Leadership, and Organizations: The GLOBE Study of 62 Societies,* edited by R.J. House, P.J. Hanges, M. Javidan, P.W. Dorfman, and V. Gupta, 235–281. Thousand Oaks, CA: Sage Publications, 2004.

Javidan, M., and D. Carl. "East Meets West: Searching for the Etic in Leadership." *Journal of Management Studies* 41, no. 4 (June 2004): 665–691.

———. "Leadership Across Cultures: A Study of Canadian and Taiwanese Executives." *Management International Review* 45, no. 1 (2005): 23–44.

Javidan, M., P. Dorfman, M. Sully de Luque, and R.J. House. "In the Eye of Beholder: Cross Cultural Lessons in Leadership from Project GLOBE." *Academy of Management Perspectives* 20, no. 1 (February 2006): 67–91.

Javidan, M., M.A. Hitt, and R.M. Steers, eds. *Advances in International Management.* Vol. 19, *The Global Mindset.* Oxford, UK: Elsevier, 2007.

Javidan, M., and R.J. House. "A Nontechnical Summary of GLOBE Findings." In *Culture, Leadership, and Organizations: The GLOBE Study of 62 Societies,* edited by R.J. House, P.J. Hanges, M. Javidan, P.W. Dorfman, and V. Gupta. Thousand Oaks, CA: Sage Publications, 2004.

Javidan, M., and N. Lynton. "The Changing Face of the Chinese Executive." *Harvard Business Review* 83, no. 12 (December 2005): 28–30.

Kabasakal, H., and M. Bodur. "Humane Orientation in Societies, Organizations, and Leader Attributes." In *Culture, Leadership, and Organizations: The GLOBE Study of 62 Societies*, edited by R.J. House, P.J. Hanges, M. Javidan, P.W. Dorfman, and V. Gupta, 564–595. Thousand Oaks, CA: Sage Publications, 2004.

Konst, D., R. Vonk, and R. Van der Vlist. "Inferences About Causes and Consequences of Behaviors of Leaders and Followers." *Journal of Organizational Behavior* 20 (1999): 261–271.

Kouzes, J.M., and Z.P. Posner. *Leadership Challenge*. 3rd ed. San Francisco: Jossey-Bass, 2002.

Lane, H., M. Maznevski, and M. Mendenhall. "Globalization: Hercules Meets Buddha." In *The Blackwell Handbook of Global Management: A Guide to Managing Complexity*, edited by H. Lane, M. Maznevski, M. Mendenhall, and J. McNett, 3–25. Malden, MA: Blackwell Publishing, 2004.

Leung, K., R.S. Bhagat, N.R. Buchan, M. Erez, and C.B. Gibson. "Culture and International Business: Recent Advances and Their Implications for Future Research." *Journal of International Business Studies* 36 (2005): 357–378.

Leung, K., and M.H. Bond. "Psycho-logic vs. Echo-logic: Insights from Social Axiom Dimensions." In *Individuals and Cultures in Multilevel Analysis*, edited by F. van de Vijver and D. van Dermert. Mahwah, NJ: Lawrence Erlbaum, 2006.

Leung, K., M.H. Bond, S. Reimel de Carrasquel, C. Muñoz, M. Hernández, F. Murakami, S. Yamaguchim, G. Bierbrauer, and T.M. Singelis. "Social Axioms: The Search for Universal Dimensions of General Beliefs About How the World Functions." *Journal of Cross Cultural Psychology* 33 (2002): 286–302.

Levy, O., S. Beechler, S. Taylor, and N. Boyacigiller. "What Do We Talk About When We Talk About Global Mindset: Managerial Cognition in Multinational Corporations." *Journal of International Business Studies* 27 (2007): 802–807.

Lord, R.G., and D.J. Brown. *Leadership Processes and Follower Identity*. Mahwah, NJ: Lawrence Erlbaum, 2004.

Lord, R.G., and C.G. Emrich. "Thinking Outside the Box by Looking Inside the Box Extending the Cognitive Revolution in Leadership Research." *Leadership Quarterly* 11, no. 4 (2000): 551–579.

Lord, R.G., and R.J. Foti. "Schema Theories, Information Processing, and Organizational Behavior." In *The Thinking Organization*, edited by H.P. Sims, D.A. Gioa, et al., 20–48. San Francisco: Jossey-Bass, 1986.

Lord, R.G., and K.J. Maher. "Alternative Information-Processing Models and Their Implications for Theory, Research, and Practice." *The Academy of Management Review* 15, no. 1 (1990): 9–28.

———. *Leadership and Information Processing: Linking Perceptions and Performance*. Vol. 1. Cambridge, MA: Unwin Hyman, 1993.

McCall, Morgan and G. Hollenbeck. *Developing Global Executives: The Lessons of International Experience*. Boston, MA: Harvard Business School Press, 2002.

Mehra, P., and V.R. Krishnan. "Impact of Svadharma-Orientation on Transformational Leadership and Followers' Trust in Leader." *Journal of Indian Psychology* 23 (2005): 1–11.

O'Connell, M.S., R.G. Lord, and M.K. O'Connell. "Differences in Japanese and American Leadership Prototypes: Implications for Cross-Cultural Training." Paper presented at the Academy of Management, San Francisco, 1990.

Offerman, L.R., J.K. Kennedy Jr., and P.W. Wirtz. "Implicit Leadership Theories: Content, Structure, and Generalizability." *Leadership Quarterly* 5, no. 1 (1994): 43–58.

Ogbonna, E., and L.C. Harris. "Leadership Style, Organizational Culture and Performance: Empirical Evidence from UK Companies." *International Journal of Human Resource Management* 11, no. 4 (2000): 766–788.

Palmisano, S.J. "The Globally Integrated Enterprise." *Foreign Affairs* (May/June 2006).

Peters, T.J., and R.H. Waterman Jr. *In Search of Excellence: Lessons from America's Best Run Companies.* New York: Harper & Row, 1982.

Rahim, M.A., and N.R. Magner. "Confirmatory Factor Analysis of the Bases of Leader Power: First-Order Factor Model and Its Invariance Across Groups." *Multivariate Behavioral Research* 31, no. 4 (1996): 495–516.

Rosch, E. "Universals and Cultural Specifics in Human Categorization." In *Cross Cultural Perspectives in Learning*, edited by R. Brislin, S. Bochner, and W. Lonner, 177–206. Beverly Hills, CA: Sage Publications, 1975.

Schein, E.H. *Organizational Culture and Leadership.* 2nd ed. San Francisco: Jossey-Bass, 1992.

Shaw, J.B. "A Cognitive Categorization Model for Study of Intercultural Management." *Academy of Management Review* 15, no. 4 (1990): 626–645.

Sims, H.P., Jr., and P. Lorenzi. *The New Leadership Paradigm: Social Learning and Cognition in Organizations.* Newbury Park, CA: Sage Publications, 1992.

Smith, P.B., M.F. Peterson, and S.H. Schwartz. "Cultural Values, Sources of Guidance, and Their Relevance to Managerial Behavior: A 47 Nation Study." *Journal of Cross Cultural Psychology* 33, no. 2 (2002): 188–208.

Sully de Luque, M., and M. Javidan. "Uncertainty Avoidance." In *Culture, Leadership, and Organizations: The GLOBE Study of 62 Societies*, edited by R.J. House, P.J. Hanges, M. Javidan, P.W. Dorfman, and V. Gupta, 602–653. Thousand Oaks, CA: Sage Publications, 2004.

Triandis, H.C. "Cross-Cultural Industrial and Organizational Psychology." In *Handbook of Industrial and Organizational Psychology.* Vol. 4, edited by H.C. Triandis, M. Dunnette, and L.M. Hough, 103–117. Palo Alto, CA: Consulting Psychologist Press, 1994.

Yukl, G. *Leadership in Organizations.* 6th ed. Upper Saddle River, NJ: Pearson Prentice Hall, 2006.

14

Women and Leadership

Defining the Challenges

Robin J. Ely and Deborah L. Rhode

In 1999, when Carly Fiorina assumed leadership of Hewlett-Packard (HP), she announced: "I hope that we are at the point that everyone has figured out that there is not a glass ceiling" (Markoff, 1999). Seven years later, in a memoir chronicling her highly public ouster from HP, Fiorina recounted endless examples of the sexism she had earlier denied, including routine descriptions of her as a "bimbo" or a "bitch" (Fiorina, 2006). That about-face well captures America's contemporary ambivalence about women and leadership. The increasing prominence of leaders like Carly Fiorina, Hillary Clinton, Nancy Pelosi, and Condoleeza Rice underscores the changes in gender roles over the last half century. More than 90 percent of surveyed Americans are willing to vote for a qualified female presidential candidate, up from a third in the 1930s. Yet only half think the country is ready to elect one (Mandel, 2007:291–292). In Gallup polls, 61 percent of men and 45 percent of women believe that the sexes have equal job opportunities (Jones, 2005). But a cottage industry of studies makes clear that women's under-representation in leadership positions is at least partly attributable to traditional gender expectations and practices (Eagly and Carli, 2007a; Rhode and Kellerman, 2007).

Initially, the hope was that filling the pipeline would take care of the problem, but it is now clear that time alone is not the answer. For more than two decades, women have been earning about one-third of the MBAs awarded in the United States, yet they constitute only 2 percent of *Fortune* 500 CEOs and 8 percent of top leadership positions (Wilson, 2006). For almost a quarter century, women have made up more than 40 percent of new entrants to the legal profession, but they are still less than one-fifth of law firm partners, federal judges, and *Fortune* 500 general counsels. The gap widens for women of color, who account for only about 4 percent of congressional legislators, and 1 to 2 percent of corporate officers, top earners, law firm partners, and general counsels (Center for American Women in Politics, 2006). Women constitute a majority of American voters, but hold only 16 percent of congressional seats (Center for American Women in Politics, 2006; Center for Women in Government and Civil Society, 2006). In other nations, the patterns are similar. Although gender quotas for public positions have brought women an increasing share of political leadership, they lag far behind in corporate and elite professional settings (Dahlerup, 2007:227; Eagly and Carli, 2007a). In Europe, women account for about a third of managerial positions but only 3 percent of CEOs (European Commission, 2007).

These statistics point up the barriers women face in gaining leadership roles, but as Carly Fiorina's experience suggests, traditional gender expectations and practices also shape people's experiences even after they reach the top. A fundamental challenge to women's leadership arises from the mismatch between the qualities traditionally associated with leaders and those traditionally associated with women (Catalyst, 2007; Eagly and Carli, 2007a). The assertive, authoritative, and dominant behaviors that people link with leadership tend not to be viewed as typical or attractive in women (Catalyst, 2007; Eagly and Carli, 2007b). Reactions to Hillary Clinton's candidacy for the 2008 Democratic presidential nomination are illustrative. She has been roundly criticized for lacking "people skills" (Vedantam, 2007) and opposed by online groups bearing such names as "Life's a B*tch, Don't Vote for One . . . Anti Hillary Clinton '08" and "Hillary Clinton Is a Man and I Won't Vote for Him." Yet when she has publicly expressed caring and compassion, people have questioned both her authenticity and her toughness. "Can Hillary Cry Her Way Back to the White House?" asked *New York Times* Op Ed columnist Maureen Dowd (2008:A21). Clinton is in good company. Reflecting on the "myth of the iron lady,"

Washington Post staff writer Shankar Vedantam notes a pattern in the phrases used to describe many countries' first female leaders: "England's Margaret Thatcher," he notes, "was called 'Attila the Hen.' Golda Meir, Israel's first female prime minister, was 'the only man in the Cabinet.' Richard Nixon called Indira Gandhi, India's first female prime minister, 'the old witch.' And Angela Merkel, the current chancellor of Germany, has been dubbed 'the iron frau.'"

Although attitudes toward women as a group are generally positive, even more positive than attitudes toward men (Eagly and Mladinic, 1989), these views do not hold for women who occupy traditionally male roles, especially when they excel in those roles (Eagly, Makhijani, and Klonsky, 1992; Heilman et al., 2004; Rudman and Glick, 2001). In experiment after experiment, when women achieve in distinctly male arenas, they are seen as competent but are less well liked than equally successful men (Heilman et al., 2004:416). By the same token, when women performing traditionally male roles are seen as nice, they are liked but not respected (Rudman and Glick, 2001:744). In short, women, unlike men, face trade-offs between competence (i.e., success) and likability in traditionally male roles.

In leadership contexts, these biases play out on several levels: in the ways that organizations structure leadership paths and positions, in the ways that people perceive women leaders, and in the ways that women leaders perceive themselves and what they must do to succeed (Hogue and Lord, 2007). At each level, a woman's qualifications for leadership are called into question. Organizations consistently, if unwittingly, communicate that women are not well-suited for leadership roles. Just as others may view her leadership through a cultural lens distorted by gender bias, so too may a woman have difficulty developing a viable view of herself as a leader. Recent theory suggests that individuals who are unable to firmly ground their self-identity in the leadership role may be missing a critical requirement for leadership development (Lord and Hall, 2005). In that respect, gender bias presents a significant problem not only for women but also for organizations (Hogue and Lord, 2007:370).

Women leaders clearly navigate a different societal and organizational terrain from their male counterparts, a terrain deeply rooted in cultural ambivalence. In this chapter, we explore this landscape, how women leaders might navigate it more effectively, and how organizations might support them and stand to gain in the process. Specifically, we examine how ambivalence about women emerges in organizational structures and practices, as well as in individual attitudes; how the resulting double bind women face shapes their experiences and identities in leadership roles; and how these dynamics in turn may limit their capacity to exercise leadership effectively. Drawing on recent theory about the role of identity in developing leadership expertise, and applying a goal-based approach to the self, we speculate about how women might succeed and how organizations might assist them. Finally, we propose a research agenda to investigate these issues at both the individual and organizational level.

Barriers to Women's Leadership

Some women achieve leadership positions in spite of barriers to their advancement, but these barriers nonetheless shape their developmental and leadership experiences. In this section, we briefly review the research on structural and attitudinal obstacles to women leaders' advancement and speculate about the effects on career patterns.

Structural Barriers

Differential structures of opportunity and power block women's access and advancement to leadership positions (Kanter, 1977; Reskin, 1988; Ridgeway, 1993; Strober, 1984). For example, men's predominance in positions of organizational power, together with differences in the composition of men's and women's social and professional networks, give men greater access to information and support (Burt, 1992; Ibarra, 1992; Podolny and Baron, 1997). Women in traditionally male-dominated settings often have difficulty breaking into the "old boys" loop of advice and professional development opportunities (Catalyst, 2003; Hefferman, 2004; O'Brien, 2006; Ragins, 1998). Isolation and exclusion are particularly likely for women of color (American Bar Association, 2006; Bell and Nkomo, 2001; Catalyst, 2003, 2004a). Surveys of upper-level American managers find that almost half of women of color and close to one-third of white women cite a lack of influential mentors as a major barrier to advancement (Catalyst, 1999, 2004a). In law, 62 percent of women of color and 60 percent of white women, but only 4 percent of white men, felt excluded from formal and informal networking opportunities (American Bar Association, 2006).

The problem of exclusion is compounded by organizational structures and practices that tend to reflect and support men's experiences (Acker, 1990; Bailyn, 2006; Martin, 1996; Rapoport et al., 2002). For example, women are disadvantaged by the convergence of their biological and professional clocks and by the escalating time demands of leadership positions. The increasing pace and competitiveness of organizational life, coupled with technological advances, have created a culture of constant accessibility and blurred the boundaries of home and work. With BlackBerrys, cell phones, e-mails, and faxes, leaders remain tethered to their offices. Although such technologies have made it easier for a woman to work from home, they have also made it harder not to. Excessive hours are a major reason that many highly qualified women step off the leadership track (Stone and Lovejoy, 2004). Some evidence suggests that women of color are particularly likely to face challenges given their greater responsibilities as single parents or caretakers of elderly and extended family members (Catalyst, 2003; Hewlett, Luce, and West, 2005).

Excessive workloads also leave limited time for the informal socializing and mentoring that promote professional development. The small number of women in top positions cannot begin to provide adequate support for every subordinate who needs it, and some female leaders worry about appearances of favoritism if they focus their effort on other women (Rhode and Kellerman, 2007). Junior women who are scrambling to build careers while raising children have similar difficulty finding time for the social activities that help forge professional relationships. After the workday ends, men are picking up tips over golf and drinks; women are picking up "laundry, dinner, and the house" (Wellington and Catalyst, 2001).

Although men have assumed an increasing share of household responsibilities over the last quarter century, women continue to shoulder the major burden. Government data indicate that about one-fifth of men engage in some kind of housework on an average day, while more than half of women do (U.S. Bureau of Labor Statistics, 2006). Women put in about twice as much time on childcare as men (Bianchi, Robinson, and Milkie, 2006). In one representative survey of high-achieving women, four of ten felt that their husbands created more domestic work than they contributed (Hewlett and Vita Leon, 2001). In another study involving well-educated professional women who had left the paid workforce, two-thirds cited their husbands' role as a reason for the decision, including their lack of support in childcare and other domestic tasks, and their expectation that wives should be the ones to cut back on employment (Stone and Lovejoy, 2004). Unlike most male leaders, most aspiring female leaders lack the support of spouses who are full-time homemakers or who are working only part-time (Williams, 2000). Women with families also face more constraints on travel and relocation than similarly situated men. Until the home becomes an equal opportunity employer, women will pay the price in the world outside it.

Employment policies reflect and further reinforce gender differences in family roles and responsibilities. The vast majority of American workplaces fail to offer the same paid parental leave to fathers as to mothers, and few men take any extended period of time away from their jobs for family reasons (Rhode and Williams, 2007). In law, three-quarters of those with part-time schedules are female (National Association of Law Placement, 2007). Similar leave and part-time patterns prevail in other professions, as well as in other nations, except in the small minority of countries that mandate "use it or lose it" paid leave for fathers. Work/family policies that disadvantage men also disadvantage women. The effect is to entrench unequal family responsibilities, which perpetuates unequal workplace opportunities.

Related problems stem from the lack of flexible schedules, meaningful part-time positions, and affordable quality childcare. Although women in top managerial and professional positions often are in workplaces that offer reduced or flex-time arrangements, few of these women take advantage of them. Most believe, with reason, that any limitation in hours or availability would jeopardize their career prospects, and that they would end up working more than their status and compensation justified (Crittendon, 2001; Rhode and Williams, 2007). So, for example, almost all of America's large law firms (98 percent) permit part-time schedules, but only about 5 percent of lawyers use them (National Association of Law Placement, 2007). Supervisors now would rarely greet a pregnancy with the advice that the CEO of Archer Daniels once received: "Get yourself fixed and put it on your expense account" (Birger, 2006). But such attitudes remain embedded in workplace cultures and reward structures.

Taken together, these inadequate workplace policies and unequal family responsibilities help account for gender differences in paid leadership positions. Almost 20 percent of women with graduate or professional degrees have stepped out of the labor force, compared with only 5 percent of similarly credentialed men (Wallis, 2004). In a study by the Center for Work-Life Policy of some three thousand highly educated Americans, nearly four in ten women reported voluntarily leaving the workforce at some point over their careers. The same proportion reported sometimes choosing a job with lesser compensation and fewer responsibilities than they were qualified to assume in order to accommodate family responsibilities. By contrast, only one in ten men left the workforce primarily for family-related reasons (Hewlett and Luce, 2005). Although other surveys find some variation in the number of women who opt out to accommodate domestic obligations, all of these studies find substantial gender differences. Yet the overwhelming majority of these women want to return to work, and most do so, although generally not without significant career costs and difficulties (Hewlett and Luce, 2005; Rhode and Williams, 2007). Similar obstacles arise in other advanced industrial nations (Foroohar, 2006; International Labor Organization, 2004).

Societal and organizational structures that heighten women's willingness to reduce or suspend their workforce participation carry an unwelcome by-product. The effect is to reinforce assumptions about women's lesser career commitment and to make them seem less worthy of mentoring, training, and challenging assignments (Rhode and Williams, 2007). These assumptions are buttressed by other cognitive biases. People are, for example, more likely to notice and recall information that confirms their prior stereotypes than information that contradicts them; the dissonant data are filtered out (Festinger, 1957). For example, if employers assume that a working mother will sometimes give priority to family over job, they will more easily remember the times when she left early than the times when she stayed late. The result is often to reduce women's opportunities for career development, which increases their willingness to step off the leadership track. Women's attrition, in turn, reinforces stereotypes about women's lesser commitment and creates a self-perpetuating cycle of gender inequalities (Deutsch, 2005; Hewlett and Luce, 2005).

In organizations with few if any women in positions of power, gender is particularly salient and negatively affects women lower in the organizational ranks, despite balanced representation at those levels.

In a study of women associates in law firms, gender roles were more stereotypical and more problematic in firms with low proportions of senior women (Ely, 1995). Compared with women in firms with higher proportions of senior women, these women associates were more likely to consider feminine attributes as a hindrance to success, and were less able to develop professional styles that were both personally satisfying and consistent with the firm's requirements for success. Women's representation in upper-level positions also influenced the quality of their relationships with each other. Women associates in firms with few senior women were less likely to experience their shared gender as a positive basis for identification with women, less likely to perceive senior women as role models with legitimate authority, more likely to experience competition in relationships with female peers, and less likely to find support in these relationships (Ely, 1994). These findings suggest that women's relative presence or absence in powerful organizational positions affects the conditions that their junior female colleagues need to succeed.

Attitudinal Barriers

To be sure, the bias that Virginia Schein once labeled as "think manager—think male" has diminished over time (Koch, Luft, and Kruse, 2005; Schein, 2001:675–676). Women are becoming more like men in their career aspirations and achievements and are more willing to see themselves as having characteristics associated with authority (Dennis and Kunkel, 2004; Eagly, 2005:459–474; Koch et al., 2005). So too, recent theories of leadership have stressed the importance of interpersonal qualities commonly attributed to women, such as cooperation, collaboration, and interpersonal sensitivity. An emerging body of scholarship suggests that the most effective style of leadership in today's world is "transformational" (Avolio et al., 2004; Luthans and Avolio, 2003; May et al., 2003). Leaders who take this approach emphasize gaining the trust and confidence of followers and empowering them to develop their own potential. Meta-analyses of studies involving thousands of leaders suggest that women are somewhat more transformational than men, especially in providing support for subordinates (Eagly, Johannesen-Schmidt, and van Engen, 2003). Women are also less likely than men to engage in the leadership styles judged least effective: "laissez-faire" hands-off approaches and transactional "passive management by exception" approaches that call for intervention only when situations become extreme (Eagly et al., 2003; Judge and Piccolo, 2004).

Yet despite these trends, the legacy of traditional gender stereotypes remains. Women have long suffered from a double standard and double bind in the exercise of authority. They are thought too aggressive or not aggressive enough, and what appears assertive in a man appears abrasive in a woman (Eagly and Carli, 2007b; Eagly and Karau, 2002; Rudman and Glick, 2001; Babcock and Laschever, 2003). In its report *The Double-Bind Dilemma for Women in Leadership: Damned If You Do, Doomed If You Don't,* Catalyst documented the persistence of this double standard among senior American and European business leaders (Catalyst, 2007). As noted above, women who conform to traditional feminine stereotypes are often liked but not respected: they are judged too soft, emotional, and unassertive to make tough calls and project the necessary "presence" in positions of authority (Catalyst, 2007; Eagly and Carli, 2007b). Asian women are particularly likely to be stereotyped as passive, reserved, and lacking in ambition, and Latina women are frequently viewed as overemotional (Catalyst, 2003; Giscombe and Mattis, 2002).

By contrast, women who adopt more masculine traits are often respected but not liked: they are seen as domineering, strident, and cold. "Dragon Lady" and "Bully Broad" are epithets of choice (Babcock and Laschever, 2003; Eagly and Karau, 2002). Self-promoting behavior that appears self-confident or entrepreneurial in men often looks pushy and "unfeminine" in women. African American women are especially vulnerable to such stereotypes, and risk being seen as overly aggressive and confrontational (Catalyst, 2004a). A review of more than a hundred studies found that women are rated lower when they adopt authoritative, masculine styles, particularly when the evaluators are men (Butterfield and Grinnell, 1999; Catalyst, 2006; Cleveland, Stockdale, and Murphy, 2000). In effect, women face a trade-off between competence and likability in circumstances where effective leadership requires both.

Recent research suggests that two coexisting and complementary forms of sexism—one benevolent and the other one hostile—lie at the root of this dilemma. Benevolent sexism is "a subjectively favorable, chivalrous ideology that offers protection and affection to women who

embrace conventional roles" and is used to reward women who conform to traditional gender role expectations. Hostile sexism is "antipathy toward women who are viewed as usurping men's power" and is
used to punish women who challenge the status quo (Glick and Fiske,
2001:109). Taken together, these two forms of prejudice reflect ambivalence about women, promoting polarized responses to them. Women
who appear feminine are at risk for benevolent sexism, which disquali-
fies them for leadership. Women who demonstrate the masculine traits
associated with leadership may evoke hostile sexism, which leads to
ostracism and rejection.

This double bind helps account for why women continue to be
rated lower than men on most of the qualities associated with leadership (Catalyst, 2005; Eagly and Carli, 2007b). People more readily
credit men with leadership ability and more readily accept men as leaders (Eagly and Carli, 2007b; Rudman and Kilianski, 2007). More
Americans prefer a male to a female boss, and women have a stronger
preference than men (Carroll, 2006). An analysis of some sixty-one
studies in which the leadership behavior of men and women was similar, or their paper credentials were equal, revealed that overall men
were rated higher, particularly for male-dominated positions (Eagly,
Makhijani, and Klonsky, 1992). Such findings are consistent with other
studies on gender bias in performance evaluations and in explanations
of success and failure (Foschi, 1996; Valian, 1999). Even in experimental situations where male and female performance is objectively equal,
women are held to higher standards and their competence is rated
lower (Foschi, 1996). In another meta-analysis of fifty-eight studies,
when women did well on traditionally masculine tasks, the common
explanation was hard work; when men did well, the assumed reason
was generally competence (Swim and Sanna, 1996).

Such biases are compounded by in-group favoritism, especially
among groups with high status. Extensive research documents the
preferences and presumptions of competence that individuals accord
to those who are like them in important respects, including gender.
Members of high status in-groups tend to attribute accomplishments
of fellow members to intrinsic characteristics, such as intelligence,
drive, and commitment. By contrast, the achievements of low status
out-group members are often ascribed to luck or special treatment
(Crocker, Major, and Steele, 1998; Foschi, 2000). Accordingly, the men
who dominate leadership positions tend to support and channel career

development opportunities to male subordinates who appear more likely to succeed than their female counterparts. Women's effective performance may not be enough to break the pattern if it is attributed to factors other than ability. In one recent study of 2,800 managers, supervisors who rated female subordinates somewhat higher than men in competence still rated the women lower in long-term leadership potential (Coughlin, 2005).

When women perform consistently and substantially above expectations in male-dominated contexts, however, their effectiveness may carry special positive weight. This effect is particularly true of women of color, who routinely encounter lower expectations of competence (Eagly and Carli, 2007a). When small numbers of women occupy prominent roles, they are subject to special scrutiny and polarized assessments (Kanter, 1977). Superstars attract special notice and receive higher evaluations than their male counterparts, but women who are just below that level tend to get disproportionately lower evaluations (Biernat and Kobrynowicz, 1997; Heilman, 2001; Heilman, Martell, and Simon, 1998). At the same time, the presence of a few highly regarded women at the top creates the illusion that the glass ceiling has been shattered for everyone else. And when superstars fail or opt out, their departures attract particular notice and reinforce stereotypes about women's lesser capabilities and commitment (Kephart and Schumacher, 2005; Stanley, 2004).

These perceptions about performance can, in turn, prevent women from getting assignments that would demonstrate their abilities, thus creating a cycle of self-fulfilling prophecies. In professional contexts, women, particularly women of color, are left off the partnership track, and in corporate sectors, they receive fewer line responsibilities that lead to top executive positions (International Labor Organization, 2004; Wilkins and Gulati, 1996). In a recent study by the American Bar Association (2006), 44 percent of women of color and 39 percent of white women, compared with only 2 percent of white men, reported being passed over for desirable work assignments. The absence of important line experience is the major reason that surveyed CEOs gave for women's under-representation in leadership positions (Wellington, Kropf, and Gerkovich, 2003).

Many women also internalize these stereotypes, which creates a psychological glass ceiling. In general, women see themselves as less deserving than men of rewards for the same performance and as less qualified for key leadership positions (Babcock and Laschever, 2003; Barron, 2003). This lesser sense of entitlement may discourage them from engaging in assertive, self-promoting behaviors and from taking risks that are critical for developing key leadership skills (Hogue and Lord, 2007). As one comprehensive overview of gender in negotiations put it, "Women don't ask" (Babcock and Laschever, 2003). Part of the reason is that women who do ask confront other problems. For example, experimental research on negotiation also suggests that male participants penalize women more than men for their attempts to negotiate greater compensation (Bowles and McGinn, 2008). An unwillingness to seem too "pushy" or "difficult," and an undervaluation of their own worth, often deter women from negotiating effectively for what they want or need. Their reluctance is understandable in settings where men's dislike of assertive women can undermine career advancement. In one Catalyst survey, 96 percent of female executives said that it was critical or fairly important "to develop a style with which male managers are comfortable" (Catalyst, 2004c). In short, the legacy of gender stereotypes subjects aspiring female leaders to higher standards and greater constraints than their male counterparts.

Individual, Organizational, and Societal Consequences

Research findings concerning barriers to women's leadership raise an obvious question. What difference does it make? Are the consequences for individuals, organizations, and society sufficient to justify expending considerable time and resources to address these problems?

To many observers, women's underrepresentation in positions of influence is unproblematic; women's absence reflects women's choices. As one *New York Times Magazine* cover story famously put it: "Why don't women run the world? Maybe it's because they don't want to" (Belkin, 2003). Or at least they don't want to make the personal and family sacrifices that leadership demands. Yet the assumption that individual preferences explain social inequalities ignores all the evidence of bias summarized above, as well as the constraints that drive career patterns. A focus on the choices of women also deflects attention from those of men and the way that their decisions as spouses, employers, and policy makers limit the options available to women. In fact, recent evidence suggests that the sexes have increasingly similar employment aspirations and that women's unequal opportunities to realize their potential ill serves all concerned.

In a comprehensive 2007 assessment, Alice Eagly and Linda Carli reviewed studies on women's career preferences and workplace commitments. In general, they found that gender differences have weakened among men and women in similar occupations, although women still place a higher priority on good hours and working with or helping other people, and young men particularly value leisure time (Eagly and Carli, 2007a). Although women are still much more willing than men to assume full-time homemaker roles, employees who are similarly well established in managerial careers report similar leadership ambitions (Catalyst, 2004b; Eagly and Carli, 2007a). Among those with comparable jobs and family situations, female employees report greater work effort than men (Bielby and Bielby, 1988).

Moreover, many of the women who step off the leadership track are not entirely happy with the decision. For some, the decision reflects less a desire to become a full-time homemaker than frustration with inadequate professional opportunities or work/family accommodations (Rhode and Williams, 2007). For others, the problems surface only later when women discover the long-term career costs of even relatively short absences (Crittendon, 2001; Hewlett and Luce, 2005). In one study by the Columbia Center for Work-Life Policy, a quarter of those who wanted to return to work were unable to find jobs, and a majority failed to obtain full-time professional employment (Hewlett and Luce, 2005).

The result is to shortchange both individuals and employers. The barriers to women's advancement undermine organizational performance and compromise fundamental principles of equal opportunity and social justice. Some research suggests that having more women in leadership positions has tangible payoffs. In weak corporate governance firms, boards with fewer women performed worse (Adams and Ferreira, 2007). A lack of gender diversity can also limit an organization's opportunities for learning and renewal. Women tend to engage in different social relations and economic activities from men and bring different experiences and perspectives to their workplaces. Organizations that fail to tap this knowledge miss out on a valuable resource for rethinking and improving their performance (Ely and Thomas, 2001; Meyerson and Ely, 2003; for an example, see Groysberg, 2008).

A further consideration is demographic. Women are now a majority of college and master's degree graduates and represent an equal share of the talent available for leadership. Reducing the obstacles to women's success also reduces the costs of attrition. It increases employees' morale, commitment, and retention, and decreases the expenses associated with recruiting, training, and mentoring replacements (Rhode and Williams, 2007). Removing barriers also helps to ensure that women are able to develop to their fullest potential. In an increasingly competitive and multicultural environment, organizations cannot afford to squander their human resources.

So too, society as a whole has a stake in ensuring that people are able—and believe they are able—to contribute fully to public and private sector institutions. Our economy depends on effective corporate performance, and our political system depends on public confidence in meritocratic processes. As the United States Supreme Court recognized in a decision sustaining law school affirmative action programs, "In order to cultivate a set of leaders with legitimacy in the eyes of the citizens, it is necessary that the path to leadership be open to talented and qualified individuals of every race and ethnicity" (*Grutter v. Bollinger*, 2003). The same is true of gender. By diversifying leadership opportunities, organizations leverage their talent, create role models, challenge stereotypes, and enlarge aspirations among underrepresented groups. To that end, we need to focus more attention on how to develop women's leadership goals and skills.

Identity, Gender, and the Development of Leadership Skills

How people become leaders and who they are as leaders are fundamentally questions about identity (Lord and Hall, 2005; for a review, see van Knippenberg et al., 2004). To develop the deep cognitive structures associated with leadership expertise, the leadership role must become a central part of one's sense of self (Lord and Hall, 2005:592). In this view, as leaders progress from novice to expert, they shift from an individual-oriented identity focused on self to a collective-oriented identity focused on self-and-others. The novice's central concern is with emulating leadership behaviors in order to project an image of the self as a leader. By contrast, the expert develops an increasing capacity to pursue internally held values and personalized strategies in service of goals that include others. In short, the leader's focus shifts from "doing" to "being," from "how I behave" to "who I am."

Our focus here is on how structural and attitudinal barriers to women's leadership interfere with this crucial developmental process. The result is to make it difficult for talented, enterprising, motivated women to seek and benefit from the sorts of developmental experiences that are more readily available to their similarly credentialed male counterparts. Women, we argue, can become stuck in *doing*.

Drawing from the theories of Robert Lord and colleagues, we provide a brief overview of this perspective on leadership development (see, for example, Hogue and Lord, 2007; Lord and Hall, 2005). We then suggest how gender may play out in this process. Finally, we propose a research agenda to develop and test these ideas, one focused on both individuals and organizations.

Identity and the Development of Leadership Skills: From Doing to Being

With leaders' shift from an individual to collective orientation comes a qualitative change both in their information processing skills and in the types of knowledge these skills enable leaders to use. Individually oriented leaders are concerned with differentiating themselves from others and with learning leadership behaviors that will lead others to accept them as leaders (Lord and Hall, 2005:596). Learning the surface structures of leadership—how to meet the accepted definitions of what leaders should be and do—is the first central skill leaders acquire. Such definitions are based largely on an idealized representation of what leadership involves, from which the novice formulates general heuristics and applies them to all superficially similar situations (Lord and Hall, 2005:598–599). At this stage, relevant skills include displaying the emotions seen as appropriate for leaders. Social interactions serve to validate (or challenge) the individual's self-view as a leader (Lord and Hall, 2005:596). The developmental work of novices involves proactively seeking and experimenting with provisional identities—images they adapt from role models as trials for possible but not yet fully formed "selves" (Ibarra, 1999).

As leaders gain experience, these identities become more firmly established. Different self-concepts emerge in different situations (Lord and Hall, 2005:592). As contexts change, different identities become salient, eliciting different skills, goals, and self-regulatory structures. Increasingly oriented toward a relational rather than individual identity, leaders at this stage begin to consider others in their self-definition as a leader (Andersen and Chen, 2002; Fletcher, 2006). Greater motivation to attempt new leadership activities further enhances these leaders' skill and identity development.

Finally, expert leaders rely on deep structures of knowledge, drawing on principles and values rather than surface features to respond to situational requirements, and adjusting their identities accordingly. This approach necessitates a deliberate shift in focus away from concerns about self to concerns about others, the organization, and even society as a whole. Increased cognitive capacity enables expert leaders to gauge their progress in various tasks and interpersonal activities and to adjust their behavior accordingly (Lord and Hall, 2005:593). A personal understanding of identity and core values is an important source of flexibility in applying leadership skills. By no longer patterning their behavior on others, these leaders can rely on more sophisticated and personalized strategies for managing their emotions and responding to those of others, particularly during times of crisis. Expert leaders also build relevant knowledge and leadership capacities in subordinates, making effective delegation possible (Lord and Hall, 2005:603).

In sum, a leader's identity solidifies with experience as leadership roles and skills become more central to his or her sense of self. Those skills become increasingly contextualized and their application more driven by internally held values, further strengthening the link between one's personal identity and the leadership role. Thus, the leader's identity takes on an increasingly important function in guiding knowledge acquisition, goal formation, and interpretations of social situations.

The Challenge for Women

This perspective on leadership sheds new light on gender-related barriers by placing them in a developmental context. If a central developmental task is to integrate the leadership role into the core self, then this task is fraught at the outset with an inherent contradiction for the woman leader—a contradiction between her female identity and the masculine traits associated with leadership. With little support or direction, a woman leader must convey a credible image—one that strikes just the right blend of masculinity and femininity—to an audience that is deeply ambivalent about her authority. From this viewpoint, the likability-competence trade-off would be most critical in the novice phase of development, when learning to behave in accordance with idealized images of leadership is the key task. With this framing, the double bind is a problem to be addressed as a means to an end, rather than as an end in itself. Accordingly, many of the structural and attitudinal barriers women leaders face may compromise their early developmental experiences and impede their transition to later stages.

Research suggests that in the evolution from follower to leader, men and women both experience a gap between their identity and the image they wish to convey, but that the strategies they use to bridge the gap differ (Ibarra, 1999; Ibarra and Petriglieri, 2007). In a study of identity development among young professionals transitioning to a managerial role, men relied on imitation strategies, which involved experimenting with traits and behaviors selected from a broad array of role models. By contrast, women tended to rely on true-to-self strategies, transferring to the new role behaviors that had worked for them in the past (Ibarra, 1999). Further analysis revealed differences in self-presentation styles as well (Ibarra and Petriglieri, 2007). Men were more "acquisitive," aggressively seeking to signal credibility by displaying behaviors that conformed to their firm's norms, even when they felt insecure, while women engaged in "protective" self-presentation, modestly asserting more neutral, uncertain, or qualified images in an effort to avoid disapproval. With clients, women sought to prove their competence by demonstrating technical mastery over the long term; in contrast, men were intent on making a positive first impression. Women cited their reliance on "substance rather than form" as a more "authentic" strategy than their male counterparts', and thus as a source of pride. Nevertheless, because displaying technical competence drew on already well-honed self-presentation skills, women's strategies failed to close the gap between identity and image in their new role. Men not only built a broader repertoire of possible selves, they also experienced more congruence between their provisional identity and the kind of professional they aspired to become. When the best of their male counterparts have built the foundations of a new identity and are ready to move on, equally high-potential women may still be searching for the raw materials.

These differences partly reflect men's and women's different structural positions in their workplaces and cultural attitudes about gender and leadership. To further leadership skills, novices need to identify role models, proactively experiment with provisional identities, and evaluate experiments against internal standards and external feedback (Ibarra, 1999). Yet women generally have fewer supports than men for learning how to convey the image of a leader, receive less latitude for making mistakes in the learning process (Foschi, 1996), and experience less social acceptance for their leadership attempts (Hogue and Lord, 2007). These challenges may be particularly acute for women of color (Giscombe and Mattis, 2002). In the study of identity development described earlier, women reported having few role models whose styles were feasible or congruent with their self-concepts and worried that either "acting like a man" or "acting like a woman" would diminish their credibility (Ibarra and Petriglieri, 2007:19). These findings are consistent with research showing that in firms with few women in powerful positions—the norm in most professions and industries—junior women had difficulty identifying with senior women, seeing them as credible role models (Ely, 1994), and finding ways of being a woman that were both personally satisfying and professionally valued (Ely, 1995). For many women transitioning into a leadership role, the provisional self may be an "impossible self" (Ibarra and Petriglieri, 2007).

An Agenda for Future Research

The self-help shelves of bookstores are overstocked with strategies to promote women's leadership: "how-to" publications that advise aspiring women to be more like men, less like men, or simply more savvy in managing their career development and family obligations (Eagly and Carli, 2007a; Rhode and Kellerman, 2007). These "leadership lite" publications offer such commonsense homilies as don't sleep with your supervisor, advertise mistakes, show bad manners, or neglect relationships; the best also echo experts' suggestions about the need to demonstrate competence, seek high-visibility challenging assignments, and develop a style that blends assertiveness and warmth (Catalyst, 2006; Eagly and Carli, 2007a).

The jazzed-up, dumbed-down sound bites available in publications like *Play Like a Man*, *Ten Secrets of Successful Women*, and *Nice Girls Don't Get the Corner Office* may sell books, but they won't level the playing field because they erroneously assume that the essence of leadership lies simply in *what leaders do*. If leadership is also about *who leaders are*, and the contexts in which they lead, then this advice may be shortsighted.

We wish to reframe the problem at both the individual and organizational levels. At the individual level, one central problem is developmental: the way gender biases affect capacities for developing leadership identity. At the organizational level, the primary problem is structural: the way unconscious biases and workplace practices constrain women's leadership opportunities and performance. Our research agenda examines the difficulties on both dimensions.

Identity Processes in Women's Leadership Development

Although theory is rich on how leaders develop, we have little direct empirical evidence about how these processes may differ for women and men and less still about how they unfold in organizations. Herminia Ibarra and Jennifer Petriglieri's (2007) qualitative accounts of women and men's identity transitions in the shift from individual-contributor to managerial roles are a promising start, but many questions remain unanswered.

One set of questions concerns whether, in light of cultural attitudes toward women in authority and the small number of effective female role models, women's leadership identity might need to develop differently from men's. Drawing on a "goal approach" to the self (for reviews, see Dweck, Higgins, and Grant-Pillow, 2003, and Crocker, Moeller, and Burson, 2010), we explore what the process might look like for women. A growing body of social psychological research suggests that personal goals form the core of self-systems. Peoples' different goals influence their emotional states, attributions, expectancies, and relationships with others.

PERFORMANCE VERSUS LEARNING GOALS

A large body of research on goals for the self concerns people's orientation toward performance versus learning (for reviews, see Dweck and Leggett, 1988, and Dweck et al., 2003). When people hold *performance* goals, they want to *demonstrate* a valued attribute and validate a self-image that includes this attribute. This is both a private strategy designed for self-reinforcement and a public impression-management strategy designed for others. By contrast, when people hold *learning* goals, they want to *develop* a valued attribute. In theory, a novice leader might focus on either demonstrating or developing attributes associated with leadership and could construct a provisional self with either goal orientation. We suspect, however, that because this process involves image construction, it more readily lends itself to performance goals.

More than two decades of research attest to the differences these goals make. Those seeking to validate a self-image prefer tasks that will make them look smart over tasks that will foster learning, and prefer partners who will reinforce them rather than challenge them to grow. Compared with those holding learning goals, people with performance goals are more likely to greet new tasks with apprehension or anxiety than with excitement, more likely to experience difficulty on a task as failure, and less likely to take actions to remedy their deficiencies. When a task is used as a means to validate the self, a setback decreases enjoyment of the task, dampens intrinsic motivation, and implies inability, which lowers subsequent expectations of success. Performance goals also lead to more superficial processing of information (e.g., rote memorization) aimed at demonstrating competence rather than increasing understanding, and that focus diminishes performance. Ironically enough, on difficult tasks, performance goals undermine performance. Learning goals enhance it. Although efforts to project the image of leadership may encourage both men and women to seek performance goals, we suspect that the particular identity challenges confronting women leaders often heighten their concerns about how others view them and increase their tendency to pursue a performance-oriented strategy. Moreover, although performance goals can be self-defeating for anyone, they may be particularly so for women, whose identity task is more difficult than men's. Seeking external validation for an image that reflects the perfect blend of seemingly incompatible attributes—those of a leader and those of a woman—is almost surely a losing proposition. Research might fruitfully explore the impact of performance versus learning goals on novice leaders' identity transitions and whether these goals have a differential effect on women's and men's success.

Prevention Versus Promotion Strategies

A second line of research considers the strategic and motivational character of the pursuit of goals. Those who emphasize *prevention* primarily seek to avoid failure. By contrast, those who emphasize *promotion* are primarily driven to approach success. *Prevention* strategies derive from an internalized sense of what one *ought* to do and focus on responsibilities, safety, and security. *Promotion* strategies derive from an internalized sense of what one would ideally *like* to do and focus on aspirations, advancement, and accomplishments (for reviews, see Dweck et al., 2003; Higgins, 1997). Those with a protection focus generally use fewer means to pursue their goals compared with those with a promotion focus.

The catch-22 women experience in the workplace—too feminine or not feminine enough—may encourage a prevention-oriented approach to leadership identity. So, for example, in Ibarra and Petrigleiri's (2007) study, women tended to prefer a protective style, seeking to avoid disapproval. Men's more acquisitive approach to identity construction may reflect a promotion focus, which is easier for them than for women to adopt because their gender identity is not inconsistent with the masculine traits associated with leadership. These differences may help to explain why the women in the Ibarra–Petrigleiri study produced a narrower repertoire of strategies than men.

Research on women's and men's strategies for developing leadership identities may further illuminate the gender dynamics of leadership. For example, we suspect that women leaders' prevention-focused identity strategies may elicit more negative competence ratings from followers, whereas promotion-focused ones may elicit more negative likability ratings. Whether leaders view situations as threats or as opportunities can trigger different motivational structures in followers (Avolio et al., 2004; Lord and Brown, 2004). Research suggests that labeling situations as threats may elicit in followers a more cautious orientation (Lord and Hall, 2005). If women's leadership already raises anxiety (Kram and McCollom-Hampton, 1998; Lerner, 1981), then cautious, prevention-focused strategies may trigger further concerns about competence. By contrast, viewing situations as opportunities should foster a more creative orientation in followers (Avolio et al., 2004; Lord and Hall, 2005). Yet gender stereotypes may lead followers to experience women's use of promotion-focused strategies as inappropriate or over-claiming. In short, the strategic choices women face during identity transitions to leadership roles may also constitute a double bind.

Research has demonstrated that although people differ substantially in the goals that are most immediately accessible to them, clear situational cues can induce different goals, along with their allied affects and strategies (Dweck et al., 2003:249). In other words, goals are malleable and open to intervention. With such intervention in mind,

Jennifer Crocker and her colleagues have proposed an alternative to performance goals—one that is compatible with learning but more encompassing (see Crocker et al., 2010). This alternative may facilitate women's leadership development by providing a more viable path to the integrated, values-based identity that is characteristic of expert leaders. Although systematic scrutiny of these ideas has only just begun, this framework is consistent with a great deal of psychological theory and research, and has the potential to inform future study of women and leadership.

Egosystem Versus Ecosystem Motivation

An understanding of women's career development may also benefit from exploring distinctions between "egosystem" and "ecosystem" motivations. In essence, performance goals are part of individuals' ego-system, which makes self-worth contingent on having desirable qualities and having those qualities recognized by others. When people operate in an egosystem framework, they seek validation of their desired qualities and thus are oriented toward performance goals. The self is primarily experienced as an object to be judged.

By contrast, ecosystem motivation assesses the self as part of a larger whole, a system in which individual actions have consequences for others and repercussions for the system as a whole. Under this approach, people view the relationship between the self and others as positive rather than zero sum—what is good for oneself can also be good for others. They prioritize the needs of others, not out of virtue or self-sacrifice, but rather out of a commitment to collective well-being, through such goals as fostering teamwork, an organizational mission, or broader social ideals. In this framework, the self is not an object but an agent acting in service of common ends. Although ecosystem motivation may encourage self-evaluation, its objective is not simply to assess one's self-worth or standing, but rather to identify strengths and weaknesses in order to accomplish broader goals. Feelings of self-worth may be a by-product of such goals, but positive self-evaluations or feelings of self-worth are not an end in themselves. Because they are not focused on self-image, ecosystem goals facilitate openness to learning. They motivate people to use their ignorance as a signal that they need to draw on the talents and skills of others; failure becomes a clue that assumptions may be faulty, and a mistake becomes a signal to reassess practices. These goals may not quell fears and anxieties about rejection or incompetence in the short term, as do self-validation goals, but they provide a powerful reason to move forward in spite of those fears and anxieties (Ely, Meyerson, and Davidson, 2006). In addition, while egosystem motivation narrows the focus of attention to cues that are relevant to the needs of the self, ecosystem motivation broadens it, encouraging a long-term perspective on personal goals. This perspective enables people to become more mindful, to notice a broader array of social and environmental cues, and to develop a wider repertoire of strategies. Ecosystem goals can push in different directions than a desire to be "nice" or "likeable." Acting on ecosystem motivation sometimes involves making others uncomfortable or unhappy, as in the case of a manager who must lay people off or give unsettling feedback to those whose performance is deficient. As this example suggests, there can be a trade-off between these two types of goals. Being overly concerned with self-image can lead one to overlook what is best for the organization as a whole, and acting on behalf of the organization can sometimes damage one's image.

What is critical about these motivational systems is that they refer to goals or intended consequences, not to specific behaviors. Almost any action can be taken with an egosystem or an ecosystem motivation. For example, one can be generous to enhance one's reputation as a virtuous person or to benefit others without regard for self-enhancement. Withholding support could similarly serve either objective. For example, a person might say "no" to a request in order to appear tough-minded or in order to prod the other person to become more independent.

This framework suggests that ecosystem goals may be a more constructive path to leadership for women. Focusing their attention on collective goals rather than simply on self-image may help women to escape the double bind. An experimental study of the effects of leaders' mindfulness on evaluations of women leaders is consistent with this suggestion (Kawakami, White, and Langer, 2000). Among women leaders with a masculine style, those who sought to make a genuine connection with their audience were rated higher in warmth, genuineness, and leadership skill than those who focused on a script.

Moreover, although much of the theory on ecosystem motivation remains untested, early findings suggest that holding these goals may foster precisely the kinds of behaviors that are essential for leadership expertise (Avolio et al., 2004; Lord and Hall, 2005). Compared with people who chronically seek to validate their self-images, those who chronically seek to be constructive and supportive of others are clearer about their goals, more open to learning from failure, and evidence better self-regulation (Crocker et al., 2010). Over time, holding collectively oriented goals produces upward spirals of giving and receiving support and increases interpersonal trust (Crocker and Canevello, 2008). By replacing self-image goals with more collective concerns, women may be better able to develop the identity orientation characteristic of expert leaders.

The Organizational Context

Women's capacity for leadership, of course, depends not simply on their individual development of goals and identities, but also on the organizational contexts within which opportunities for leadership arise. Organizations can either reinforce or disrupt sex-based roles and practices, and thus are key sites for intervention and reform (Ely and Meyerson, 2000; Ely and Padavic, 2007). They are correspondingly critical sites for research. (For examples, see Ely and Meyerson's [2007] analysis of how organizational conditions disrupted masculinity on offshore oil platforms and Meyerson, Ely, and Wernick's [2007] speculation on how such conditions may affect women's leadership.)

One set of questions involves how organizational structures affect leadership identity. For example, how might organizations alter norms and practices to better support women's identity and role transitions? Can men also benefit from such organizational changes? What organizational conditions encourage a focus on self-image versus collective goals, and are these conditions related to women's rise into leadership positions? How does the organization's demographic structure (e.g., the proportion and placement of women in senior positions) affect junior women's identity transitions when moving into leadership roles? How does this structure influence how women conceptualize and take up authority? These questions call for research that focuses on the interplay between organizational features and individual-level processes. Organizational scholars are uniquely positioned to conduct such studies by examining how organizational features "magnify and blunt" individual cognitive, emotional, and behavioral processes (Staw and Sutton, 1992:26).

A second cluster of research questions involves how to create cultures that value and promote gender diversity and equity in leadership positions. Scholars and practitioners generally agree that the most important factor in ensuring equal access to leadership opportunities is a commitment to that objective, which is reflected in workplace priorities, policies, and reward structures (Rhode and Kellerman, 2007; Ridgeway and Correll, 2000; Powell, 1998; Wellington et al., 2003). Yet we know little about what causes some organizations to develop and sustain this commitment. Why did the heads of Deloitte Touche embrace the business case for diversity when so many other accounting firms with the same problems failed to respond, even after seeing the extraordinary payoffs that Deloitte achieved from gender-related initiatives?

For organizations that fail to treat diversity as a bottom-line issue, what strategies are most effective in promoting change? Under what circumstances does greater transparency produce constructive responses? What kind of pressure is most effective, and how can it be mobilized? For example, some evidence suggests that most female investors would like to see their pension funds support companies with good track records on women's issues, but we know little about how such preferences might translate into organizational leverage (Calvert Group, 2004; Grosser and Moon, 2005). Other research suggests that certain kinds of pressure, such as class action suits brought by women, provoke more resistance and harassment than litigation brought by other groups, such as racial minorities (James and Wooten, 2006). More systematic evaluation of different forms of political and legal pressure should be a priority.

We also need to know more about the effectiveness of particular governmental interventions and internal initiatives. In countries that require companies to report data on women's representation and advancement (Grosser and Moon, 2005), do the requirements result in significant improvements? In this country, what information is available indicates that many employers now invest substantial time and money in diversity programs that have no significant or measurable impact on outcomes. Although some small-scale studies find that diversity training may improve awareness and attitudes, more systematic, large-scale studies find no effects (Kalev, Dobbin, and Kelly, 2006), or evidence of backlash from white male participants (Bendick, Egan, and Lofthejelm, 1998; Krawiec, 2003; Nelson, Acker, and Melvin, 1996). Many ostensible beneficiaries of these programs express doubt about their effectiveness; only a third of woman of color surveyed by Catalyst felt that diversity efforts created a supportive environment for their group (Giscombe and Mattis, 2002). Virtually no evidence documents improvements in the representation of women in upper-level positions as a result of such training (Kalev et al., 2006; Krawiec, 2003).

Mentoring initiatives also merit attention, especially in light of the role they might play in the development of leadership identity. Although virtually all experts agree about the value of mentors, less than a quarter of surveyed female managers have expressed satisfaction with the availability of mentoring at their workplaces (Catalyst, 2004c). Similar unhappiness is common in other professional contexts, such as large law firms (American Bar Association, 2006). Yet inadequate attention has focused on analyzing the underlying causes and assessing institutional responses, such as formal and electronic mentoring systems and women's networks (Headlam-Wells, 2004). We know that relationships that arise from formal assignments are rarely as successful as those that arise naturally (Catalyst, 2004c; Cleveland et al., 2000). But we know too little about what kinds of incentives and oversight might make required or voluntary mentoring work better. We also lack sufficient data about the significance of women's networks that are emerging in workplaces and professional associations. These networks sponsor a range of activities that build career skills, forge policy coalitions, and link managerial and professional employees with colleagues and potential clients and customers (Kalev et al., 2006; Nance-Nest, 2006; Rhode and Kellerman, 2007). Given the significant time and money now invested in these networks, it would be useful to know more about their effectiveness in generating business and advancement opportunities.

Work/family policies similarly require more systematic assessment. In surveys of high-achieving women, between two-thirds and four-fifths identify work/family issues as a major part of the problem and the solution for women's advancement. Most of these women rate scheduling flexibility as more important than compensation (Hewlett and Luce, 2005; Wellington et al., 2003). Organizations have responded with a wide array of initiatives concerning flex time, part time, telecommuting, and leave policies, as well as childcare assistance and reentry support. Programs that are accessible in principle, however, are often inadequate in practice. Many women who opt for flexible or reduced schedules find that their hours are not respected, their compensation is not proportionate to performance, and their second-class status deprives them of desirable assignments and career development opportunities (Rhode and Williams, 2007). New ways to address these concerns are beginning to emerge. A growing number of employers are offering consulting arrangements and career assistance for women who have temporarily left the labor force, and executive education programs are beginning to target women seeking to transition back (McGinn, 2006). Law firms are experimenting with alternative structures that allow different hours and compensation trade-offs, or that eliminate up or out partnership tracks entirely and match attorneys with cases that fit their expertise and scheduling preferences (Belkin, 2008; Jones, 2007). Nonprofit research and policy organizations are developing more innovative scheduling and compensation structures that enable individuals to have a life as well as leadership opportunities.

All of these initiatives deserve more attention from the academic community. Business, professional, and public policy schools should be at the forefront of teaching and research on gender, diversity, and leadership. Society has an enormous stake in ensuring equal access to leadership opportunities and effective development of leadership potential. To make that possible, we need more knowledge about what works in the world. Research institutions have a unique opportunity and corresponding obligation to help fill the gap.

References

Acker, J. "Hierarchies, Jobs, Bodies: A Theory of Gendered Organizations." *Gender and Society* 4 (1990): 139–158.

Adams, R., and D. Ferreira. "Gender Diversity in the Boardroom." Working paper, London School of Economics, 2007.

American Bar Association, Commission on Women in the Profession. *Visible Invisibility: Women of Color in Law Firms.* Chicago: ABA Foundation, 2006.

Andersen, S.N. and S. Chen. "The Relational Self: An Interpersonal Social-Cognitive Theory." *Psychological Review* 109 (2002): 619–645.

Avolio, B.J., W.L. Gardner, F.O. Walumbwa, F. Luthans, and D.R. May. "Unlocking the Mask: A Look at the Process by Which Authentic Leaders Impact Follower Attitudes and Behaviors." *Leadership Quarterly* 15 (2004): 801–823.

Babcock, L., and S. Laschever. *Women Don't Ask: Negotiation and the Gender Divide.* Princeton University Press, 2003.

Bailyn, L. *Breaking the Mold: Redesigning Work for Productive and Satisfying Lives.* Ithaca, NY: Cornell University Press, 2006.

Barron, L. "Ask and You Shall Receive? Gender Differences in Negotiators' Beliefs About Requests for a Higher Salary." *Human Relations* 56 (2003): 635–662.

Belkin, L. "The Opt Out Revolution." *New York Times Magazine*, October 26, 2003, 42.

————. "Who's Cuddly Now? Law Firms." *The New York Times*, January 24, 2008, 1.

Bell, E., and S. Nkomo. *Our Separate Ways*. Cambridge, MA: Harvard Business School Press, 2001.

Bendick, M., M. Egan, and S. Lofthejelm. *The Documentation and Evaluation of Anti-discrimination Training in the United States*. Washington, D.C.: Bendick and Egan Economic Consultants, 1998.

Bianchi, S., J. Robinson, and M. Milkie. *Changing Rhythms of American Family Life*. New York: Russell Sage Foundation, 2006.

Bielby, D., and W. Bielby. "She Works Hard for the Money: Household Responsibilities and the Allocation of Work Effort." *American Journal of Sociology* 93 (1988): 1031–1059.

Biernat, M., and D. Kobrynowicz. "Gender and Race-Based Standards of Competence: Lower Minimum Standards but Higher Ability Standards for Devalued Groups." *Journal of Personality and Social Psychology* 72 (1997): 544–557.

Birger, J. "The Outsider." *Fortune*, October 16, 2006, 137.

Bowles, H., and K. McGinn. "Untapped Potential in the Study of Negotiation and Gender Inequality in Organizations." *Academy of Management Annals* 2 (2008): 99–132.

Burt, R. *Structural Holes*. Cambridge, MA: Harvard University Press, 1992.

Butterfield, D.A., and J.P. Grinnell. "'Re-viewing' Gender, Leadership, and Managerial Behavior: Do the Decades of Research Tell Us Anything?" In *Handbook of Gender and Work*, edited by G. Powell, 223–238. Thousand Oaks, CA.: Sage Publications, 1999.

Calvert Group. *The Calvert Women's Principles: A Global Code of Conduct for Corporations*. Bethesda, MD: The Calvert Group, 2004.

Carroll, J. "Americans Prefer Male Boss to Female Boss." Gallup Brain, 2006. http://institution.gallup.com/content/Default.aspx?ci=24346.

Catalyst. *Women of Color in Corporate Management: Opportunities and Barriers*. New York: Catalyst, 1999.

————. *Advancing Asian Women in the Workplace: What Managers Need to Know*. New York: Catalyst, 2003.

————. *Advancing African-American Women in the Workplace: What Managers Need to Know*. New York: Catalyst, 2004a.

————. *The Bottom Line: Connecting Corporate Performance and Gender Diversity*. New York: Catalyst, 2004b.

————. *Women and Men in U.S. Corporate Leadership: Same Workforce, Different Realities*. New York: Catalyst, 2004c.

————. *Women Take Care, Men Take Charge: Stereotyping of Business Leaders Exposed*. New York: Catalyst, 2005.

————. *The Double Bind Dilemma for Women in Leadership: Damned If You Do; Doomed If You Don't*. New York: Catalyst, 2007.

Center for American Women in Politics. *Election Results Show Advances for Women*. New Brunswick, NJ: Eagleton Institute of Politics, Rutgers, State University of New Jersey, 2006.

Center for Women in Government and Civil Society. *Women in State Policy Leadership 1998–2005*. Albany, NY: State University of New York Center for Women in Government and Civil Society, 2006.

Cleveland, J., M. Stockdale, and K. Murphy. *Women and Men in Organizations: Sex and Gender Issues at Work*. Mahwah, NJ: Lawrence Erlbaum Associates, 2000.

Coughlin, L. "The Time Is Now: A Leader's Personal Journey." In *Enlightened Power: How Women Are Transforming the Practice of Leadership,* edited by L. Coughlin, 1–16. Hoboken, NJ: John Wiley & Sons, 2005.

Crittendon, A. *The Price of Motherhood: Why the Most Important Job in the World Is Still the Least Valued.* New York: Metropolitan/Owl, 2001.

Crocker, J., and A. Canevello. "Creating and Undermining Social Support in Communal Relationships: The Role of Compassionate and Self-Image Goals." *Journal of Personality and Social Psychology* 95, no. 3 (2008): 555–575.

Crocker, J., B. Major, and C. Steele. "Social Stigma." In *Handbook of Social Psychology,* edited by D.T. Gilbert, S.T. Fiske, and G. Kubdzey, 504–553. Boston: McGraw-Hill, 1998.

Crocker, J., S. Moeller, and A. Burson. "The Costly Pursuit of Self-Esteem: Implications for Self-Regulation." In *Handbook of Personality and Self-Regulation,* edited by R. Hoyle, forthcoming.

Dahlerup, D. "Will Gender Balance in Politics Come By Itself?" In *Women and Leadership: The State of Play and Strategies for Change,* edited by B. Kellerman and D. Rhode, 251–270. San Francisco: Jossey Bass, 2007.

Dennis, M.R., and A.D. Kunkel. "Perceptions of Men, Women, and CEOs: The Effects of Gender Identity." *Social Behavior and Personality* 32 (2004): 155–172.

Deutsch, C. "Behind the Exodus of Executive Women: Boredom." *The New York Times,* May 1, 2005.

Dowd, M. "Can Hillary Cry Her Way to the White House?" *The New York Times,* January 9, 2008, A21.

Dweck, C., E. Higgins, and H. Grant-Pillow. "Self-Systems Give Unique Meaning to Self Variables." In *Handbook of Self and Identity,* edited by M.R. Leary, 239–252. New York: Guilford, 2003.

Dweck, C., and E. Leggett. "A Social-Cognitive Approach to Motivation and Personality." *Psychological Review* 95 (1988): 256–273.

Eagly, A. "Achieving Relational Authenticity in Leadership: Does Gender Matter?" *Leadership Quarterly* 16 (2005): 459–474.

Eagly A., and L. Carli. "Overcoming Resistance to Women Leaders." In *Women and Leadership: The State of Play and Strategies for Change,* edited by B. Kellerman and D. Rhode, 127–148. San Francisco: Jossey-Bass, 2007a.

———. *Through the Labyrinth: The Truth About How Women Become Leaders.* Boston: Harvard Business School Press, 2007b.

Eagly, A., M. Johannesen-Schmidt, and M.L. van Engen. "Transformational, Transactional, and Laissez-faire Leadership Styles: A Meta-analysis Comparing Women and Men." *Psychological Bulletin* 95 (2003): 569–591.

Eagly, A., and S. Karau. "Role Congruity Theory of Prejudice Toward Female Leaders." *Psychological Review* 109 (2002): 573–598.

Eagly, A., M.G. Makhijani, and B.G. Klonsky. "Gender and the Evaluation of Leaders: A Meta-analysis." *Psychological Bulletin* 111 (1992): 3–22.

Eagly, A., and A. Mladinic. "Gender Stereotypes and Attitudes Toward Women and Men." *Personality and Social Psychology Bulletin* 15 (1989): 543–548.

Ely, R. "The Effects of Organizational Demographics and Social Identity on Relationships Among Professional Women." *Administrative Science Quarterly* 39 (1994): 203–238.

———. "The Power in Demography: Women's Social Constructions of Gender Identity at Work." *Academy of Management Journal* 38 (1995): 589–634.

Ely, R., and D. Meyerson. "Theories of Gender: A New Approach to Organizational Analysis and Change." In *Research in Organizational Behavior.* Vol. 22, edited by B. Staw and R. Sutton, 105–153. Elsevier, 2000.

———. "Unmasking Manly Men: The Organizational Reconstruction of Men's Identity." Working paper 07-054. Harvard Business School, Boston, 2007.

Ely, R., D. Meyerson, and M. Davidson. "Rethinking Political Correctness." *Harvard Business Review* 84, no. 9 (September 2006).

Ely, R., and I. Padavic. "A Feminist Analysis of Organizational Research on Sex Differences." *Academy of Management Review* 32 (2007): 1121–1143.

Ely, R., and D. Thomas. "Cultural Diversity at Work: The Moderating Effects of Work Group Perspectives on Diversity." *Administrative Science Quarterly* 46 (2001): 229–273.

European Commission, Database. "Social and Economic Domain Decision-Making in the Top Publicly Quoted Companies." 2007. http://ec.europa.eu/employment_social/women_men_stats/out/measures_out438-en.htm.

Festinger, L. *Theory of Cognitive Dissonance.* Stanford, CA: Stanford University Press, 1957.

Fiorina, C. *Tough Choices: A Memoir.* New York: Penguin Group, 2006.

Fletcher, J.K. "Leadership, Power and Positive Relationships at Work." In *Exploring Positive Relationships at Work: Building a Theoretical and Research Foundation,* edited by J. Dutton and B.R. Ragins, 347–370. NJ: Lawrence Erlbaum Press, 2006.

Foroohar, R. "Unlikely Boomtowns." Newsweek.com. July 3, 2006.

Foschi, M. "Double Standards in the Evaluation of Men and Women." *Social Psychology Quarterly* 59 (1996): 237–254.

———. "Double Standards for Competence: Theory and Research." *Annual Review of Sociology* 26 (2000): 21–42.

Giscombe, K., and M.G. Mattis. "Leveling the Playing Field for Women of Color in Corporate Management: Is the Business Case Enough?" *Journal of Business Ethics* 37 (2002): 103–119.

Glick, P., and S. Fiske. "An Ambivalent Alliance: Hostile and Benevolent Sexism as Complementary Justifications for Gender Inequality." *American Psychologist* 56 (2001): 109–118.

Grosser, K., and J. Moon. "Gender Mainstreaming and Corporate Social Responsibility: Reporting Workplace Issues." *Journal of Business Ethics* 62 (2005): 327–340.

Groysberg, B. "How Star Women Build Portable Skills." *Harvard Business Review* 86, no. 2 (February 2008): 74–81.

Grutter v. Bollinger. 539 U.S. 306 (2003).

Headlam-Wells, J. "E-mentoring for Aspiring Women Managers." *Women in Management Review* 19 (2004): 212–218.

Heffernan, M. *The Naked Truth: The Working Woman's Manifesto on Business and What Really Matters.* San Francisco: Jossey-Bass, 2004.

Heilman, M. "Description and Prescription: How Gender Stereotypes Prevent Women's Ascent up the Organizational Ladder." *Journal of Social Issues* 57 (2001): 657–674.

Heilman, M., R. Martell, and M. Simon. "The Vagaries of Sex Bias: Conditions Regulating the Undervaluation, Equivaluation, and Overvaluation of Female Job Applicants." *Organizational Behavior and Human Decision Processes* 41 (1998): 98–110.

Heilman, M., A. Wallen, D. Fuchs, and M. Tamkins. "Penalties for Success: Reactions to Women Who Succeed at Male Gender-Typed Tasks." *Journal of Applied Psychology* 89 (2004): 416–427.

Hewlett, S., and C. Luce. "Off-Ramps and On-Ramps: Keeping Talented Women on the Road to Success." *Harvard Business Review* 83, no. 3 (March 2005): 43–54.

Hewlett, S., C. Luce, and C. West. "Leadership in Your Midst: Tapping the Hidden Strength of Minority Executives." *Harvard Business Review* 83, no. 11 (November 2005): 74–79.

Hewlett, S., and N. Vita Leon. *High Achieving Women.* New York: Center for Work Life Policy, 2001.

Higgins, E.T. "Beyond Pleasure and Pain." *American Psychologist* 52 (1997): 1280–1300.

Hogue, M., and R. Lord. "A Multilevel, Complexity Theory Approach to Understanding Gender Bias in Leadership." *Leadership Quarterly* 18 (2007): 370–390.

Ibarra, H. "Homophily and Differential Returns: Sex Differences in Network Structure and Access in an Advertising Firm." *Administrative Science Quarterly* 37 (1992): 422–447.

———. "Provisional Selves: Experimenting with Image and Identity in Professional Adaptation." *Administrative Science Quarterly* 44 (1999): 764–791.

Ibarra, H., and J. Petriglieri. "Impossible Selves: Image Strategies and Identity Threat in Professional Women's Career Transitions." Working paper, INSEAD, 2007.

International Labor Organization, 2004. "Breaking Through the Glass Ceiling: Women in Management." Geneva Switzerland: International Labor Organization.

James, E., and L. Wooten. "Diversity Crisis: How Firms Manage Discrimination Lawsuits." *Academy of Management Journal* 49 (2006): 1103–1118.

Jones, J. "Gender Differences in Views of Job Opportunity: Fifty-Three Percent of Americans Believe Opportunities Are Equal." Gallup Brain, August 2, 2005. http://brain.gallup.com.

Jones, L. "The Rise of the New Model Firm." *National Law Journal,* May 21, 2007. http:www//.axiom.legal.com.

Judge, T., and R. Piccolo. "Transactional and Transformational Leadership: A Meta-analytic Test of Their Relative Validity." *Journal of Applied Psychology* 89 (2004): 901–910.

Kalev, A., F. Dobbin, and E. Kelly. "Best Practices or Best Guesses: Diversity Management and Remediation of Inequality." *American Sociological Review* 71 (2006): 589–617.

Kanter, R. *Men and Women of the Corporation.* New York: Basics Books, 1977.

Kawakami, C., J. White, and E. Langer. "Mindful and Masculine: Freeing Women Leaders from the Constraints of Gender Roles." *Journal of Social Issues* 56 (2000): 49–63.

Kephart, P., and L. Schumacher. "Has the 'Glass Ceiling' Cracked? An Exploration of Women Entrepreneurship." *Journal of Leadership and Organizational Studies* 12 (2005): 2–15.

Koch, S., R. Luft, and L. Kruse. "Women and Leadership—20 Years Later. A Semantic Connotation Study." *Social Sciences Information* 44 (2005): 3–23.

Kram, K., and M. McCollom-Hampton. "When Women Lead: The Visibility-Vulnerability Spiral." In *The Psychodynamics of Leadership*, edited by E. Klein, F. Gabelnick, and P. Herr, 193–218. Madison, CT: Psychosocial Press, 1998.

Krawiec, K. "Cosmetic Compliance and the Failure of Negotiated Governance." *Washington University Law Quarterly* 81 (2003): 487–544.

Lerner, H. "Early Origins of Envy and Devaluation of Women: Implications for Sex Role Stereotypes." In *Women and Mental Health*, edited by E. Howell and M. Bayes, 26–40. New York: Basic Books, 1981.

Lord, R., and D. Brown. *Leadership Processes and Follower Self-Identity*. Mahwah, NJ: Lawrence Erlbaum, 2004.

Lord, R., and R. Hall. "Identity, Deep Structure and the Development of Leadership Skill." *Leadership Quarterly* 16 (2005): 591–615.

Luthans, F., and B. Avolio. "Authentic Leadership: A Positive Development Approach." In *Positive Organizational Scholarship*, edited by K.S. Cameron, J.E. Dutton, and R.E. Quinn, 241–258. San Francisco, CA: Berrett-Koehler Publishers, 2003.

Mandel, R. "She's the Candidate! A Woman for President." In *Women and Leadership: The State of Play and Strategies for Change*, edited by B. Kellerman and D. Rhode, 283–303. San Francisco: Jossey Bass, 2007.

Markoff, J. "Hewlett-Packard Picks Rising Star at Lucent as Its Chief Executive." *The New York Times*, July 20, 1999, C1.

May, D.R., A. Chan, T. Hodges, and B.J. Avolio. "Developing the Moral Component of Authentic Leadership." *Organizational Dynamics* 32 (2003): 247–260.

McGinn, D. "Getting Back on Track." Newsweek.com, September 25, 2006.

Meyerson, D., and R. Ely. "Using Difference to Make a Difference." In *Women and Leadership: The State of Play and Strategies for Change*, edited by D. Rhode. Stanford, CA: Stanford University Press, 2003.

Meyerson, D.E., R.J. Ely, and L. Wernick. "Disrupting Gender, Revising Leadership." In *Women and Leadership: The State of Play and Strategies for Change*, edited by D. Rhode and B. Kellerman, 453–473. San Francisco: Jossey-Bass, 2007.

Nance-Nest, S. "Wall Street Women: Forming Their Own Inside Circle." April 10, 2006. http://www.womensenews.org/.

National Association of Law Placement. "Few Lawyers Work Part Time: Most Who Do So Are Women." Press release, December 5, 2007.

Nelson, T., M. Acker, and M. Melvin. "Irrepressible Stereotypes." *Journal of Experimental Social Psychology* 32 (1996): 13–38.

O'Brien, T. "Up the Down Staircase." *The New York Times*, March 19, 2006.

Podolny, J., and J. Baron. "Resources and Relationships: Social Networks and Mobility in the Workplace." *American Sociological Review* 62 (1997): 673–693.

Powell, G. *Handbook of Gender and Work*. Thousand Oaks, CA: Sage Publications, 1998.

Ragins, B. "Gender and Mentoring Relationships: A Review and Research Agenda in the Next Decade." In *Handbook of Gender and Work*, edited G. Powell, 347–369. Thousand Oaks, CA: Sage Publications, 1998.

Rapoport, R., L. Bailyn, J. Fletcher, and B.H. Pruitt. *Beyond Work-Family Balance: Advancing Gender Equity and Workplace Performance*. San Francisco: Jossey-Bass, 2002.

Reskin, B. "Bringing the Men Back In: Sex Differentiation and the Devaluation of Women's Work." *Gender and Society* 2 (1988): 58–81.

Rhode, D., and B. Kellerman. "Women and Leadership: The State of Play." In *Women and Leadership: The State of Play and Strategies for Change*, edited by B. Kellerman and D. Rhode, 1–64. Hoboken, NJ: John Wiley & Sons, 2007.

Rhode, D., and J. Williams. "Legal Perspectives on Employment Discrimination." In *Sex Discrimination in the Workplace*, edited by F. Crosby, M. Stockdale, and A. Ropp. Santa Cruz, CA: University of California, 2007.

Ridgeway, C. "Gender, Status, and the Social Psychology of Expectations." In *Theory on Gender/Feminism on Theory*, edited by P. England, 175–198. New York: Aldine Press, 1993.

Ridgeway, C., and S. Correll. "Limiting Inequality Through Interaction: The End(s) of Gender." (Essay for special issue on Utopian Visions). *Contemporary Sociology* 29 (2000): 118.

Rudman, L., and P. Glick. "Prescriptive Gender Stereotypes and Backlash Toward Agentic Women." *Journal of Social Issues* 57 (2001): 743–762.

Rudman, L., and S. Kilianski. "Implicit and Explicit Attitudes Toward Female Authority." *Personality and Social Psychology Bulletin* 26 (2007): 1315–1328.

Schein, V. "A Global Look at the Psychological Barriers to Women's Progress in Management." *Journal of Social Issues* 57 (2001): 675–688.

Stanley, A. "For Women to Soar Is Rare: To Fail Is Human." *The New York Times*, July 13, 2004.

Staw, B., and R. Sutton. "Macro Organizational Psychology." In *Social Psychology in Organizations: Advances in Theory and Research*, edited by J.K. Murnighan, 350–384. Englewood Cliffs, NJ: Prentice Hall, 1992.

Stone, P., and M. Lovejoy. "Fast-Track Women and the Choice to Stay Home." *Annals of the American Academy of Political and Social Science* 596 (2004): 62–83.

Strober, M. "Toward a General Theory of Occupational Sex Segregation: The Case of Public School Teaching." In *Sex Segregation in the Workplace: Trends, Explanations, Remedies*, edited by B. Reskin, 144–156. Washington, DC: National Academy Press, 1984.

Swim, J.K., and L.J. Sanna. "He's Skilled, She's Lucky: A Meta-analysis of Observers' Attributions for Women's and Men's Successes and Failures." *Personality and Social Psychology Bulletin* 22 (1996): 507–519.

U.S. Bureau of Labor Statistics. "News: American Time-use Survey—2005 Results Announced by BLS." 2006. http://wwwbls.gov/news.release/pdf/atus.pdf.

Valian, V. *Why So Slow? The Advancement of Women*. Cambridge, MA: MIT Press, 1999.

van Knippenberg, D., B. van Knippenberg, D. Cremer, and M. Hogg. "Leadership, Self, and Identity: A Review and Research Agenda." *Leadership Quarterly* 15 (2004): 825–856.

Vedantam, S. "The Myth of the Iron Lady." Washingtonpost.com. November 12, 2007, A-03.

Wallis, C. "The Case for Staying Home." *Time*, March 22, 2004, 51.

Wellington, S., and Catalyst. *Be Your Own Mentor*. New York: Random House, 2001.

Wellington, S., S.B. Kropf, and P. Gerkovich. "What's Holding Women Back?" *Harvard Business Review* 81, no. 6 (June 2003): 18–19.

Wilkins, D.B., and M. Gulati. "Why Are There So Few Black Lawyers in Corporate Law Firms? An Institutional Analysis." *California Law Review* 94 (1996): 493–625.

Williams, J. *Unbending Gender: Why Family and Work Conflict and What to Do About It.* New York: Oxford University Press, 2000.

Wilson, M. *Closing the Leadership Gap: Why Women Can and Must Help Run the World.* New York: Feminist Press, City University of New York, 2004.

15

A CONTINGENCY THEORY OF LEADERSHIP

Jay Lorsch

T HE IDEA of a contingency theory of leadership is not novel. In the 1960s several scholars (Fiedler, Tannenbaum and Schmidt, and Vroom and Yetton) conducted research and proposed such an approach, arguing that the style of leadership that would be most effective depended on the situation.[1] This work was an integral part of the wave of organizational behavior research that led to what we labeled a "Contingency Theory" of organizations at the time.[2] Like much of the early contingency work, these efforts on leadership suffered from some limitations. First, although there was an agreement that the appropriate leadership style did depend on situational contingencies, there was not complete agreement about what such factors were. For example, all three of the authors cited indicated that the appropriate leadership style depended on the nature of the task—specifically, how certain or uncertain it was. However, Vroom and Yetton defined the task as decision making, whereas the others were not so specific about the type of task.

Moreover, each of the authors introduced other contingent factors. For example, Fiedler introduced the relationship between the leader and his subordinates and the power of the leader. Tannenbaum and Schmidt were concerned about the group of followers' size, history, and values, as well as the time pressures facing them. Vroom and Yetton

411

were concerned with the group's decision-making style—autocratic, consultative, or group based. In spite of such variations, all agreed that the appropriate dimension of leadership style to consider was directive to participative, although Fiedler also introduced the matter of the leader being task-oriented or relationship-oriented. Another limitation to this work was that it all seemed to be focused on leadership in primary groups and said nothing about leadership in larger organizations.

A final limitation of these studies was that the authors disagreed about how best to achieve the fit they desired between these situations and the leader's behavior. Tannenbaum and Schmidt took the position that leaders could choose their leadership style, as did Vroom and Yetton. In essence, both believed a leader could change his or her style to fit the situation. On the other hand, Fiedler argued that it was easier to change the situational conditions than it was for the leader to change his or her behavior. In essence, Fiedler argued that his ideas could be used to select leaders whose style fit the situation at hand.

In my judgment from the perspective of forty years later, these studies, in spite of such limits, were pointing scholars interested in leadership in the right direction. Unfortunately, scholarship about leadership followed a different path. An example of what happened can be found in Kotter's work. In his early work he took a contingency approach.[3] In his later work he focused on general principles that he argues are relevant to all leaders, but not managers.[4] This distinction between managers and leaders was first made by Zaleznik, and I shall return to what I believe is this false dichotomy shortly.[5] But the point to be made here is that Kotter was not alone in this search for general principles. Many of the most well-known scholars of leadership and organization preceded or joined him. In addition to Zaleznik, there were Bennis, Likert, and McGregor, to name three others.[6] The argument that dominated all these scholars' work was that to be effective, all leaders needed to do the same things. They weren't always pointing to the same precise behaviors, but all believed that all leaders, to be successful, needed their prescriptions, whatever they were. For example, McGregor proposed his famous Theory Y, which in essence was quite similar to Likert's ideas about participative leadership. Kotter, for his part, was focused on leadership as a matter of introducing change, so he prescribed as effective leadership communicating the need for change and building a coalition of those who would support moving in a new direction.

Although these authors seemed to be discussing leadership in the context of organizations that were larger than primary groups, they were not explicit about the settings to which their ideas applied. In essence, they seemed to assume that one type of leadership fit all situations. Even just a few moments of reflection must lead to a recognition that this cannot be. An army lieutenant leading a platoon of soldiers in Iraq has a different leadership challenge than a district sales manager for a consumer products company in Missouri who is responsible for one hundred sales representatives. The CEO of the same company, which has fifty thousand employees worldwide, has yet a different set of leadership issues. Similarly, the senior partner of a prestigious law firm, owned by his partners, has a different set of circumstances, and so does the newly elected governor of one of the fifty states. Clearly, if we are to develop systematic knowledge about effective leadership, we have to recognize the differences that are suggested by these examples, and many others.

Leadership Defined

Before we can begin to consider a way to conceptualize the conditions facing leaders in such diverse circumstances, we have to resolve a more basic question. What do we mean by "leadership"? As I suggested earlier, there is a problem in the leadership literature in this regard. In fact, I discern two issues.

One is that many writers about leadership have assumed that it is such a well understood concept that no explicit definition is necessary. This was a risky approach to begin with, because as so often happens in the social sciences, different scholars use the same term to describe different phenomena. In the hard sciences, in contrast, there is clear agreement about what an atom, cell, or molecule is. However, those of us who study organizations do not have such clarity. We may assume that we all share the same definitions, but we likely do not. This lack of a clear definition has been complicated by the aforementioned distinction drawn first by Zaleznik and then by Kotter and others. According to this view, leaders are individuals who are introducing change. Managers are sustaining the status quo by motivating organization members to work effectively. The further inference is made that it is impossible, or at least difficult, for the same person to be an effective leader and an effective manager.

I know that one of the editors of this volume (Nohria) has used the same distinction and also that many students in leadership classes and courses and other individuals, including many practicing executives, have found this distinction useful.[7] For one thing, it glorifies the notion of leadership, and those who accept this definition enjoy thinking of themselves as high-status leaders rather than mundane managers. Perhaps I should not argue with all this success. However, I believe these definitions are confusing our study of leadership because they create a false dichotomy. It is false in the sense that most effective leaders turn out to be very good managers as well—at least that is my experience. Further, if the only way to be a leader is to be bringing about change, there are an awful lot of us who think we are leading others when, according to this dichotomy, we are not.

For all these reasons I want to provide my own definition of the term *leader*, as I shall be discussing it here. Although some readers may disagree with it, at least they will understand the phenomenon about which I am writing. *A leader is an individual who influences others to follow him or her.* It is a straightforward and simple definition. To be as clear as I can, let me expand on it in two ways. First, I use the word *influence* rather than *power* because I believe leaders gain followers for a number of reasons. For example, it may be the leader's charisma or his superior knowledge that motivates others to follow him. But it may also be the leader's position in the organizational hierarchy and the accompanying right to pass out rewards and punishment. This is positional power, and many leaders are successful with little or no such power, while others rely on it heavily. From this perspective, power is a situational variable that can affect the influence a leader has. However, all leaders, to be successful, must influence others to follow them.

Second, this definition means that an individual is a leader whether she is a senior executive leading an effort to change the strategic direction of her company or is a supervisor leading a group of workers on an assembly line. In both instances she is getting others to do her bidding. True, she faces different task, organizational, and relationship issues, but the goal is the same—influencing others to follow her.

The Value of a Contingency Theory of Leadership

So far I have argued that further developing the contingency approach will create a better understanding of leadership because the various situations confronted by leaders, such as those I have used as examples, are so different. The logic underlying this argument has its roots in the earlier contingency work that I described at the outset. This work is my intellectual roots, and I believe in it deeply. For some readers this may be sufficient justification. However, in case it is not, I want to offer a more conceptual, and I believe a more powerful, argument for moving our inquiry in this direction.

This argument was suggested to me by an article in *Economist* magazine about the field of biology.[8] The title, "All Systems Go," reveals the thrust of the piece. It reports that biologists are moving from reductionism—understanding the functioning of the smallest component—to the study of the biological system of which the component is an interrelated part. Beginning after the 1960s when the original contingency work was done, our study of leadership, like biology and other disciplines, has been aimed at understanding the phenomenon by focusing on the target unit—in this instance, the leader—but not on how the leader's behavior fits into the complex systems that the broader organizational literature suggests organizations are.[9]

In candor, this too is part of my intellectual heritage, and has its roots in *Management and the Worker*.[10] The current organizational literature is rarely explicit about the fact that any valid explanation of behavior in organizations must begin with recognizing their systemic nature. However we choose to define the variable (or variables) of interest to us, it is interrelated to all the other aspects of the organization. Most organizational scholars would not argue with this premise; they just choose to be silent about it.

To illustrate my point, let me use an example different from leadership, but one that is much in the news now: executive compensation. If our goal is to understand how a particular approach to paying executives affects their behavior, we need to comprehend many other interrelated variables in the system that is their organization. First, how important is pay to them? How clearly do they understand the connection between these monetary rewards and their efforts to perform their job?[11] What other rewards are available to them and how important are they compared with pay? Here I have in mind a range of things: intrinsic job satisfaction, promotions, approval from the boss, the values of the culture, and so on. All these factors will interact with the compensation scheme to produce an impact on the executives' behavior.

When it comes to understanding the effect of leaders' behavior, we have the same challenge. We must recognize that it is how a leader's behavior interacts with other elements in the organizational system that determines the outcome. From a normative perspective, my fundamental proposition is that the better aligned these variables, including the leader's behavior, are with each other, the more effective he or she will be.[12] In the balance of this paper I shall suggest those aspects of an organizational system that I hypothesize are likely to have the closest interconnection to the behavior of a leader. My hope is that this exercise will stimulate others to undertake research that will further test my underlying proposition and refine our understanding of how leadership behavior interacts with other elements of the social systems that are organizations.

Selecting Contingent Variables

The early contingent theorists that I mentioned at the outset each had their own sets of contingent variables. Although there were similarities among their ideas, the problem is that they selected relatively similar and simple situations to study. They were similar in that they all chose to look at leadership in primary (small) groups. This was also what made them simple. Such settings were relatively easy to analyze, because the number of contingent variables were few. To use a biological analogy, it was almost as if they had chosen a fruit fly instead of a human to study, which is understandable given the complexity of such contingent relationships. As we have seen, they focused on the nature of the task the group was performing and the predispositions of the group's members. They chose to ignore other factors that also could affect the leader's task—for example, most obviously, the size of the unit being led. If we are serious about developing and testing a contingency theory of leadership, we need to identify contingent variables that differentiate a wider array of leadership situations.

This is what I have set out to do here. In doing so, I have been guided by two basic premises. First, recognizing the complexity of trying to develop such a theory, I have tried to adhere to Occam's razor, and to be conceptually parsimonious. I have used as few variables as I could, and as many as I must. Even so, as the reader will soon see that the model becomes complex. Second, I concluded that the starting point for developing such a theory must be understanding the job of a leader.

Therefore, the first question I needed to explore was how do leaders get others to follow them? Stated another way, why do individuals follow leaders? The second question I needed to explore was in what activities do leaders engage to get others to follow them? To try to find answers to these questions, I began by reviewing a number of well-known, one might even say classic, studies of leadership (e.g., Chester Barnard, James McGregor Burns, John Gardner, and Philip Selznick).[13]

Leaders and Followers

There is a great deal of agreement among these authors that leadership is essentially about the relationship between the leader and his or her followers. In this context, one obvious reason people follow leaders is because leaders have power or influence over them. As Weber pointed out over a hundred years ago, there are three possible sources of such power (or influence).[14] First is positional power, which is the ability to either reward or punish someone because of the office one holds. In the organizational context, "bosses" have such power over their subordinates. They can provide feedback about performance, they can decide to offer or withhold pay increases or promotions, and ultimately they can often terminate those who do not follow their bidding.

A second source of leader power or influence is the often-mentioned charisma. In introducing charisma, I shall also clarify the distinction I draw between power and influence. As my colleague Scott Snook has pointed out, no less an authority on leadership than Machiavelli raised what may be the most fundamental question about leadership: Is it better to be feared or loved? Clearly, positional power has aspects of fear to it, and charisma has aspects of love. If one relies totally on positional power, followers are likely to be fearful that rewards may be withheld or, even worse, that they might be punished for disobeying the leader. In essence, when I use the term *power* I am referring to a property of the leader's position in the organization. The other sources of "power" identified by Weber (charisma and competence) are properties of the individual leader, and these I shall label *influence*.

Another difference between positional power and charismatic influence is that positional power is easy to spot and understand. Charisma, on the other hand, is a less precise commodity. As I have just argued, it is a characteristic of the leader's personality, but it is also in the eye of the follower. For example, John Kennedy had it, as did Ronald Reagan. But did they both have it for the same followers?

A staunch Democrat would clearly agree that Kennedy was charismatic, while a strong Republican would feel the same about Reagan. However, they are less likely to feel attracted to the president who does not share their values and beliefs.

Khurana's account of Jamie Dimon's travails at First Chicago makes this point and places the concept of charisma into an organizational context.[15] According to Khurana, the board of First Chicago selected Dimon to be their CEO because he was charismatic from their perspective. However, it soon became apparent that whatever charisma he had from the board's perspective did not work with the officers of the bank who were supposed to follow him, and he resigned as CEO. So perhaps the most precise we can be about charisma, as a source of influence, is that it is a personal quality of a leader that attracts followers to him or her. As elusive as it is, however, there can be no doubt that it is a source of influence for many leaders.

The third source of leader "power" identified by Weber is the perceived competence of the leader. Again, this is a property of the leader and I shall label it *influence*. To put it plainly, people are likely to follow leaders who seem to know what they are doing. A clear example of this can be seen in professional service firms. The culture of such firms, even more than most organizations, places an immense emphasis on competence within the profession. In these firms the top leaders are usually selected by their peers (partners) and are unlikely to get elected unless they are believed to be competent in the profession. Further, they are unlikely to succeed as leaders unless they demonstrate competence in that role.

So far I have focused primarily on qualities of the leader or his or her position that affect the power and influence he or she has to lead. But I have also touched on qualities in the followers that relate to the leader's effectiveness. Since our focus must be on the relationship between a leader and his or her followers, we need to delve more into the characteristics of followers that cause them to follow a leader—beyond the leader's power and influence, whatever its source. The discussion of charisma and competence earlier suggests another aspect of the leader/follower relationship that the literature points to as important: the extent to which the leader and the followers have shared goals and values. This is most obvious in the political context. Clearly, we vote for and follow leaders with whom we agree. However, it is also important in organizations.

Consider, for example, a leader intent on introducing a change in the structure of an organization that involves new definitions of jobs and reporting relationships. Such change often encounters resistance from the subordinates affected. The resistance may take the form of vocal protests from those affected or a more passive effort to subvert the changes. In either case, the leader's capacity to get followers to do what he or she wants is compromised because the followers do not share the leader's goals.

Such changes also can create anxiety for those affected. New practices and relationships that replace those that are familiar can and do have that effect on many people. In fact, another reason that the leadership literature suggests that followers adhere to leaders' directions is because leaders are like security blankets. They allay the anxiety of their followers.[16]

Thus, my perusal of the classic literature about leadership suggests that any contingency theory of leadership must take into account leader power and influence, as well as the extent to which there is congruence between leader and followers about goals and values. Such a theory must also consider the anxiety present for the followers, and the extent to which the leader can assuage it.

Activities of Leadership

The second question that requires answering concerns what leaders must do to stimulate others to follow them. Again I turned to the classic literature about leaders and leadership for answers. The first conclusion that I reached is that leadership starts with a set of implicit or explicit decisions by the leader. These involve choices about her personal goals for herself and goals for the organization she is leading. What does she intend for it to achieve and what does she want to accomplish through it for herself? Closely connected is how she defines the purpose or mission of the organization. Clearly these are not binary choices, and the answers often involve complicated trade-offs.

A recent example from the nonprofit world illustrates the point. The organization in question was a start-up intended to enable elder citizens in the community to stay in their homes with support from the organization. Although that goal was clear and easy to agree upon, a related question was raised with the organization's paid leader by its board. To what extent should she be encouraging members to volunteer to work in the organization instead of using only paid employees?

Those who argued for more volunteerism made the point that it was critical to the organization's mission. More volunteer involvement would build more membership commitment. However, the leader's concern was that volunteers were unreliable and inexperienced. The more she enlisted, the more complicated her job would be. How this matter was resolved is less important than the fact that it illustrates the type of interrelated choices leaders must make as they define the mission of their organizations.

Obviously, there are multiple factors involved in making such choices. As in the example above, the leader must weigh the various consequences of his decisions. It is worth noting in this connection that one of the most frequent choices leaders must make is between what is in the economic interest of the organization versus what is likely to be most popular with those he seeks to lead. Considering such matters certainly requires an ability to forecast the economic outcomes of the choice being made, but it also means the leader must understand his followers and their likely responses to any decisions or actions he takes.

An essential question for any leader is, how do I understand these people whom I want to follow me? What do they want from me? What motivates them to belong to this organization, and how will this affect their willingness to follow my lead? Where do we have similar values and where do we differ? What do they expect from my leadership, and how can I deliver it? As I pointed out earlier, an important element in an effective leader/follower relationship is shared expectations and values. Clearly, any one who wants to effectively lead must find an alignment between his view of the goals and mission, as he defines them, and what his subordinates want.

The easiest solution for a leader is to choose actions that will be consistent with the goals and values of her followers. However, the world is usually more complicated. For example, a leader may not be clear about what the goals and values of her followers are related to a potential action. When this is the case, the leader has to "listen" to those she would lead. *Listening* is fundamentally a matter of gathering information, not necessarily of direct conversation. A leader of a small unit may be able to meet with and actually listen to people's ideas and views. However, in a larger organization, such understanding may only be possible through a more complicated data-gathering process, such as focus groups or surveys. Of course, leaders can and often do decide to involve their followers in the decision-making process. Again, this is easier to accomplish with a smaller number of followers. When this approach is used, three things are accomplished simultaneously. The leader learns her follower's views, a decision about what a satisfactory alignment entails is jointly made, and the process of communicating what is expected of followers and what they can expect is at least initiated.

When the leader chooses a unilateral approach to deciding a course of action, he is confronted with another challenge—communicating his decision to his followers. Such communication must obviously be clear, to let the followers know what is expected of them, but it must also be persuasive. By this I mean that first it must convince the followers that what they are being asked to do is in their interests. The communication will be most effective, however, if it also conveys an emotional tone that followers find compelling. This, I believe, is where the charismatic leader has an advantage.

As John Gardner has pointed out, another way leaders communicate with followers is symbolically. Leaders communicate what they stand for and what they expect not only by what they say, but also by how they act. For example, I recall earlier in my career doing consulting with executives at United Parcel Service. These leaders were always acting symbolically. To take a simple example, when I was riding in a car with them, they were always on the lookout for UPS trucks. If they saw one, for example, that was dirty, or had broken glass in the window, they jotted down the vehicle number. When I asked what they would do with the information, they replied that they would pass it on to the managers in charge of the relevant facility. The symbolic message to these followers was clear: all vehicles must be in sparkling condition.

Having described the several bases of power and influence that leaders can use to encourage others to follow them, as well as the activities in which leaders need to engage to use these levers of influence and power, I next want to turn to the major contingencies that can affect the degree of difficulty of a leader's job.

Contingent Factors

As I mentioned earlier, leaders act in the context of a social system, and I have focused on factors that vary within such systems. I also have selected factors that are present in purposive organizations, especially businesses. I have done this both because I am most familiar with them, and also to limit the factors that might be considered. After I have described each variable, I shall speculate on how it may relate to a leader's job, ending with a proposition that could be tested in future research.

Followers' Expectations

Since leading is all about the relationship between leaders and followers, I start with what the followers expect from a leader. There are several aspects to such expectations. For example, as one finds in most professional service firms, followers may expect to be involved in decisions affecting their work. At the other extreme is the more typical situation in many businesses (e.g., in manufacturing or service companies), in which followers expect more direction from their leader. Another type of expectation is the extent to which followers want to identify psychologically with the leader. The more they want this emotional connection, the more attracted they may be to a leader who relies strongly on charisma as a source of his or her influence. Similarly, followers may also have expectations about the technical or professional competence of their leader. Returning to the example of professional service firms, employees in such organizations usually expect their leaders to be professionally proficient, and are less likely to follow the leadership of those who are not.

My hypothesis is that the greater the congruence between the leader's goals and his or her source(s) of power and influence and the expectations of followers, the more likely the latter are to follow his or her leadership.

Organizational Complexity

A second set of contingencies that will affect the leader's job is the complexity of the organization. One important aspect of such complexity is the size of the organization. There are several ways to think about organizational size. Perhaps the most obvious is the number of employees who work directly for the leader. It is easier to build and sustain relationships with a small group of followers with whom one can meet face to face. As the number of followers grows, such direct interaction becomes more difficult and, in fact, less and less likely. It is not just the sheer number of followers that makes this so, but also the fact that as organizations become larger there will inevitably be multiple levels of leaders. The leader at the top, for example, a CEO, is leading other leaders, which will complicate the matter of communicating with the wider group of followers. The more levels of leadership that there are in an organization, the more difficulty the top leader is likely to face in getting his or her message out and in understanding the expectations of the wider organization, and therefore the more complicated his or her challenge.

Size also would seem to complicate the use of the various levers of power and influence available to leaders. Charisma and competence both depend on the followers' perceptions of the leader. The larger the organization and the more the intervening levels of leadership, the harder it is in general for the top leader to project these qualities. In fact, he also becomes dependent on the extent to which subordinate leaders demonstrate these qualities. There are obviously exceptions to this generalization, such as when a top leader is able to make a quick connection to a part of his organization through a speech or in some other act that breeches the social and organizational distance and makes the leader seem approachable and likeable. Such events can be spread by word of mouth and be a source of advantage for the leader. However, I would argue that such occurrences are the exception in large organizations. I also would argue that competence is very difficult for an organizationally distant leader to demonstrate. Again, I believe it is likely that the top leader will be dependent on the intervening levels of leadership to be able to demonstrate competence to their followers.

Organizational size also complicates the leader's ability to understand her subordinates and to make decisions that align their interests with hers. Sheer size is part of the problem, but actions and interpretations made by intervening levels of leaders may also complicate the problem of achieving such alignment. Each intervening layer of leadership can act as a dysfunctional filter to the understanding and communication that is so vital in achieving congruent expectations between leader and followers.

In sum, the size of a leader's organization, both in the number of followers and the intervening levels of leaders, is a major contributor to organizational complexity.

International Differences

In considering business organizations, yet another aspect of complexity is the geographic reach of the company. Leading an organization with only one location is obviously an easier task than trying to exercise leadership over many geographic boundaries and time zones. Even if it is a large organization, a leader can interact more easily with followers if they are in one location, rather than in many geographic locations. In a single location the top leader can more easily project his personal qualities and competencies than he can across multiple locations. Similarly, he can understand his followers more easily. Not only is it possible to listen to their concerns directly, but also they are more likely to share common expectations. Followers living in different locations are more likely to have diverse expectations. This is especially true when the different places are across international boundaries, with different economic and legal regimes and different cultures. These factors create different expectations among followers and complicate the leader's task of deciding how best to align his and the organization's interests with those of followers.

Similarly, cross-cultural communication is undoubtedly more complicated. Followers from different cultures may interpret the same message or decision differently. Furthermore, the use of the different levers of power and influence may be interpreted differently in different countries. In fact, the use of positional power may be severely limited, if not impossible, in some locations. For example, in many countries in the European Community, the threat or possibility of terminating an employee is limited by law. Also, the qualities that make leaders seem charismatic in one culture may have a different meaning in another culture.

All of this means that generally the leader of a multinational organization faces significantly greater complexity in using her influence and power, in making decisions which align with followers' interests, and in communicating with these followers. Obviously, the more different locations there are, the more complications the leader faces.

My broad hypothesis is that the greater an organization's complexity, based on its sheer size, the number of levels of leadership, and its international scope, the more difficulties the leader will confront in utilizing the full range of his power and influence and in aligning his and the organization's goals with those of his followers.

This does not imply that leaders cannot deal with these sources of complexity. Obviously, the world is full of examples of business leaders who have been effective in dealing with organizational complexity.

Whether it is Jim Burke and his colleagues at Johnson & Johnson, who knit their decentralized company together by building commitment to their company's credo, or the multiple generations of firm leaders at McKinsey who spread their firm across the globe while maintaining its "one firm" identity, there are ample examples of leaders who have overcome such complexity. The implication of my hypothesis, though, is that this was not easy to do and required great dedication, skill, and tenacity.

The Organization's Task

Yet another factor that will influence the challenge a leader faces is the nature of the task her organization must accomplish. This, of course, was one of the primary factors the original contingency theorists considered. Their original formulation was that tasks could be arrayed along a dimension of "certainty to uncertainty." At one extreme the organization's job was routine and repetitive. At the other extreme it was innovative, novel, and nonrepetitive. Underlying this distinction was the level of uncertainty in the organization's (or group's) work. As Burns and Stalker, along with others, pointed out, the level of uncertainty facing an organization was the most important factor in determining whether a business firm would be most effective with a mechanistic or organic organization.[17] Implicit in this distinction was the sort of management (leadership) style that was appropriate.

If the task was certain (for example, manufacturing an established product), the leader could issue instructions about what to do and how to do it, and all the followers needed to do to perform well was to adhere to these directives. In essence, the leader's job was to motivate followers to do the same routine things day after day. If the task was uncertain, the follower's and the leader's jobs were more complex. The followers had to solve an uncertain problem, whether that might be consultants developing a new strategy, research scientists seeking a new pharmaceutical therapy, or marketing executives developing a new advertising campaign. The leader's challenge was to motivate these followers toward finding such solutions. Leaders in such situations have to encourage their followers to work together to develop creative ideas for solutions to such complicated problems. In sum, when the task was certain, the leaders would find a directive style effective, but when the task was uncertain, leaders would find a more participative style more suitable.

Revisiting these ideas forty years later, as I am, these ideas still seem valid. However, we can now see other reasons for their validity. First, the influence of the leader in a more certain situation can more easily be based on pure positional power. Tell people what you want them to do, and reward them if they do it. You don't need a lot of competence-based influence or charisma to get things to happen, and the task of communication is pretty straightforward. This is not to say that charisma and competence, as well as effective communication, will not have an extra motivational effect. It just is not essential to a workable leader/follower relationship.

The leader confronted with an uncertain task for his organization must motivate followers to use their intellectual and creative powers to resolve the unknowns. Thus, the leader will first of all need sources of influence beyond that of his position. It may be the emotional attraction of charisma, but it will also likely be based on the belief that the leader is competent, that he knows what he is talking about. As I pointed out earlier, one of the functions of being an effective leader is being able to reduce anxiety for followers, and clearly a problem-solving assignment is fraught with such tension for one's followers. It is unlikely that subordinates can engage in such creative activity without encountering frustrations.

Encouraging the involvement of followers in a collaborative process is one way to reduce such anxiety, since it builds group support. Further, the participative process encourages open communication not only among the followers but also between the leader and her followers. Issues can be raised and possible answers explored in a way that encourages the creativity of all involved. Such interaction also keeps the leader aware of the frustrations of her followers. To the extent the leader is involved directly in these discussions, her presence can also be a means to assuage such tensions.

There is another reason that this type of leadership works well in such uncertain task situations. The individuals who do such work are usually highly educated professionals or scientists who have a strong personal preference for being involved in the decisions that affect their efforts. Numerous psychological studies have demonstrated this fact.[18] For such professionals, sharing power with their leader is a key expectation. Without such power sharing there cannot be congruence between the expectations of leaders and followers.

This discussion leads to another hypothesis I would propose. *The style of leading that will be most effective is related to the nature of the organization's task along a continuum of highly certain to highly uncertain. The more certain the task, the more a directive leadership approach is suitable. The more uncertain the organization's work, the more a participative approach to leadership will be effective.*

This hypothesis is obviously directly in line with the assertions of the early proponents of contingency theory. I do not apologize for this fact. If we find a valid relationship, then we should stick with it. Further evidence of the validity of this proposition abounds in the real world. Whether we look at the aforementioned professional service firms or software and Internet companies such as Google or Microsoft, we can see the validity of this hypothesis in practice.

Summing Up

In this essay I have outlined a new contingent approach to understanding leadership in purposive organizations, especially business firms. I have basically argued that effective leadership is dependent on the relationship between the leader and his followers. Followers follow leaders because of a number of qualities of the relationship. First, there must be an alignment between the leader's goals (personal and organizational) and the values and expectations of followers. Second, there must be valid two-way communication between leaders and followers. The leader must know what followers want and what they are experiencing, and the followers must understand what the leader's goals are and how they can contribute to their achievement. Finally, there must be appropriate sources of leader power and influence in the relationship. This includes the bases of power and influence (position, charisma, and competence), the amount of power, and how it is applied on a continuum from directive to participative.

What mix of these factors is needed to ensure an effective relationship is determined by four contingent factors: the leader's power and influence and her personal and organizational goals, the follower's expectations, the complexity of the organization, and the certainty or uncertainty of the task (figure 15-1). For example, I have hypothesized that the greater the organizational complexity (along the dimensions mentioned earlier), the more challenging will be the leader's job. I have

FIGURE 15-1

A new contingency theory of leadership

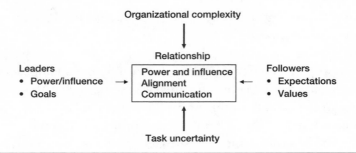

also argued that the certainty of the task will affect the type of relation-ship needed between leaders and followers.

As I also indicated earlier, a critical part of a leader's job is making choices about how to approach the relationship with followers in a way that meets these contingencies, as well as others that I may not have iden-tified. Of course, discussing turning such choices into action might imply that leaders can alter their behavior depending on the situation they face. Clearly many so-called authorities on leadership seem to believe that this is the case, since we have a plethora of business school courses and pro-grams—and in fact entire organizations—devoted to developing leaders.

Although I am likely in the minority, I take a different view of the possibility of altering one's leadership approach. It is my belief that the style a leader uses with his followers is a manifestation of very basic aspects of his personality. I would argue, based on my experience, that leadership skills are learned relatively early in life from role models; parents, grandparents, teachers, scout leaders, and so forth. By the time one becomes a leader in the sorts of organizations I have been consid-ering here, one's personality and the associated leadership preferences are well ingrained. From this perspective, the most leadership educa-tion can accomplish is to enable participants to understand their lead-ership proclivities and their strengths and vulnerabilities. Given this perspective, I would argue that the most important benefit of a modern contingency theory would be to enable individual leaders and those who select them to understand clearly what qualities leaders will need to succeed in different situations. In this regard, I believe I'm returning to Fiedler's assumptions mentioned earlier.

Notes

1. Frederick E. Fiedler, *A Contingency Model for the Prediction of Leadership Effectiveness* (Champaign, IL: University of Illinois Press, 1963); Robert Tannenbaum and Warren H. Schmidt, "How to Choose a Leadership Pattern," *Harvard Business Review* 36, no. 2 (March–April 1958): 95–101; Victor H. Vroom and Philip W. Yetton, *Leadership and Decision-Making* (Pittsburgh: University of Pittsburgh Press, 1973).

2. Paul R. Lawrence and Jay W. Lorsch, *Organization and Environment* (Boston: Harvard Business School Press, 1967).

3. John P. Kotter, *The General Managers* (New York: The Free Press, 1982); John P. Kotter, "Renn Zaphiropoulos," Case 9-480-044 (Boston: Harvard Business School, 1980); and John P. Kotter, "Fred Henderson," Case 9-480-043 (Boston: Harvard Business School, 1979).

4. John P. Kotter, *Leading Change* (Boston: Harvard Business School Press, 1996).

5. Abraham Zaleznik, *Human Dilemmas of Leadership* (New York: Harper & Row, 1966).

6. Warren G. Bennis, *Leaders: The Strategies for Taking Charge* (New York: Harper & Row, 1985); Rensis Likert, *The Human Organization: Its Management and Value* (New York: McGraw-Hill, 1967); Douglas McGregor, *The Human Side of Enterprise* (New York: McGraw-Hill, 1985).

7. Anthony J. Mayo and Nitin Nohria, *In Their Time: The Greatest Business Leaders of the Twentieth Century* (Boston: Harvard Business School Press, 2005).

8. "All Systems Go," *The Economist*, October 27, 2007, 93.

9. Lawrence and Lorsch, *Organization and Environment*.

10. F.J. Roethlisberger, *Management and the Worker* (Cambridge, MA: Harvard University Press, 1939).

11. Edward E. Lawler, *Motivation in Work Organizations* (San Francisco: Jossey-Bass, 1994).

12. Jay W. Lorsch and Thomas J. Tierney, *Aligning the Stars: How to Succeed When Professionals Drive Results* (Boston: Harvard Business School Press, 2002).

13. Chester Irving Barnard, *The Functions of the Executive* (Cambridge, MA: Harvard University Press, 1968); James McGregor Burns, *Leadership* (New York: Harper & Row, 1978); John William Gardner, *On Leadership* (New York: The Free Press, 1990); Philip Selznick, *Leadership in Administration: A Sociological Interpretation* (New York: Harper & Row, 1957).

14. Max Weber, *Economy and Society: An Outline of Interpretative Sociology* (New York: Bedminster Press, 1968).

15. Rakesh Khurana, *Searching for a Corporate Savior: The Irrational Quest for Charismatic CEOs*. Princeton, NJ: Princeton University Press, 2002.

16. Ibid.

17. Tom Burns and G.M. Stalker, *The Management of Innovation* (London: Tavistock Publications, 1966).

18. Jay W. Lorsch and John Morse, "Beyond Theory Y," *Harvard Business Review* 48, no. 3 (May–June 1970): 61–68.

THE PRACTICE OF LEADERSHIP

Agency and Constraint

16

WHAT IS LEADERSHIP?

The CEO's Role in Large, Complex Organizations

Michael E. Porter and Nitin Nohria

WHAT IS the role of the CEO in a large, complex enterprise? What makes a CEO effective? At first blush, these questions seem easy to answer. The CEO represents the epitome of leadership. He or she exercises ultimate power, and is responsible for making the most critical decisions. However, these questions get far more complicated as one contemplates the realities of large organizations. Actually, the CEO cannot make most decisions, or even review them. The CEO is powerful, but multiple constituencies can constrain the CEO's power, starting with the board. The enormous variability in CEO tenure and performance (see chapter 2) reveals that many CEOs misunderstand their role and how to perform it effectively.

We have been examining the CEO role through the vehicle of the New CEO Workshop, an intensive two-day program for newly appointed CEOs we developed at the Harvard Business School

Author note: We are indebted to our colleagues Jay Lorsch and Bill George, who teach the New CEO Workshop at Harvard Business School with us, as well as to the CEOs who have participated in these workshops and so willingly shared their insights. We are grateful to Srikant Datar, Rakesh Khurana, Tony Mayo, Scott Snook, and participants in the colloquium Leadership: Advancing an Intellectual Discipline, held at Harvard Business School on June 10 and 11, 2008, for their comments and feedback. We thank Stephanie Galloway for her superb research assistance.

beginning in the mid 1990s. This program is based on the premise that the CEO's job is different, even from running a large business unit, and even from serving as COO. The workshop creates a peer-based setting in which the role and challenges of becoming a CEO can be examined and a body of knowledge developed about how new CEOs can be effective.

Remarkably, despite the fascination with CEOs, the only in-depth scholarly study of the CEO's job was conducted more than thirty years ago (Mintzberg, 1973). The only other in-depth studies of the CEO's job of which we are aware were conducted by the Conference Board (Stieglitz, 1969, 1985) and in a McKinsey & Company study (McLean et al., 1991). To be sure, much has been written about the general topic of leadership, and CEOs may be used as examples in these studies (e.g., Kotter, 1982, 1990; Bennis, 1985, 2003). There have also been numerous studies of particular aspects of CEO leadership, including CEO compensation (Bebchuck and Fried, 2004), the CEO labor market (Khurana, 2002; Murphy and Zabojnik, 2007), CEO succession (Sonnenfeld, 1988; Bower, 2007), skills and competencies required to be a CEO (Kaplan et al., 2008), the CEO personality (Chatterjee and Hambrick, 2007; Zaleznik, 2008), and the historical evolution of the CEO's background and role (Mayo and Nohria, 2005; Mayo, Nohria, and Singleton, 2006; Tedlow, 2003). Finally, CEOs themselves have written numerous autobiographical accounts of their tenure in office (a popular example is Jack Welch [2001], but there are many others). However, it has been several decades since there has been a study of the nature and challenges of the CEO's role, and the determinants of CEO effectiveness.

In this paper, we report on some preliminary findings from our study of over one hundred CEOs of large, complex organizations who have participated in the New CEO Workshop (see appendix 16-1 for a description of our research program and some summary statistics on these CEOs and their companies). By focusing on CEOs of large, complex organizations, we examine leadership in its most challenging setting. We believe many of our findings will apply to the top leaders of large nonprofits, government entities, and smaller organizations, as well as, to some extent, lower levels of leadership.

The CEO and the Essence of Leadership

The historical evolution of the modern corporation provides the context for understanding the contemporary CEO's job. As Chandler (1977) has documented, the emergence of transportation, communications, and mass-production technologies around the turn of the twentieth century enabled the rise of the large modern corporation—organizations of increasing scale and scope that could no longer be governed by an owner or entrepreneur who was intimately involved in all matters pertaining to running an enterprise. The scale and scope of the modern corporation required mobilizing capital that could not be readily supplied by any individual owner and soon led to the separation of ownership (which was now in the hands of a large number of shareholders) and control (which was now in the hands of a managerial hierarchy that governed the firm). As the modern corporation expanded in scale and scope, so did the elaborate managerial system needed to govern it. At the apex of this extensive managerial hierarchy was the CEO, who was responsible for coordinating the myriad business units, functions, and decisions involved in managing such an increasingly complex enterprise.

The increasing complexity of directing the complex modern enterprise spawned a vast literature on the functions of the manager, including strategy, organization structure, incentives, culture, resource allocation, and management selection. Performing the totality of these functions and making associated decisions is the collective responsibility of all managers in the organization. Although the CEO is ultimately responsible for this collective managerial performance, the CEO cannot humanly be personally involved in every function and every decision. In any large complex organization, there are simply too many functions and decisions. Moreover, the CEO does not always have the best information or the technical ability to make every decision. People who are closer to the situation and have the appropriate expertise or specialization may be better suited to making many decisions. Moreover, organizations often innovate, evolve, and adapt based on the initiative of individuals far removed from the CEO. Even for the decisions the CEO personally makes, he or she will inevitably need to rely on others for input and implementation. Therefore, what needs to be better understood is the allocation of responsibility for these functions and decisions among managers in an organization, and, in particular, the specific role of the CEO. Although much has been written on the overall functions of management, the existing literature has been less precise about the actual role of the CEO in carrying out these functions.

Cataloging all the functions and decisions involved in modern management practice is beyond the scope of this paper. However, these activities can be divided into a number of broad categories that will prove relevant when considering the CEO's role:

1. *Direction:* Setting the *strategy* for the organization, both at the business unit and corporate levels. Closely related to strategy is determining the *specific financial and operating goals* that the organization will seek to achieve. Establishing appropriate *organizational values* and *ethical standards* consistent with the strategy can also be treated as part of setting overall direction.

2. *Organization:* Determining the organization's *structure*, which defines the roles of individuals in the organization, assigns them into units, establishes reporting relationships, and delineates how units will coordinate with each other. An organization's structure should reflect its strategy.

3. *Selection:* Recruiting and developing senior managers and other individuals to perform the various roles in the organization and support the desired direction.

4. *Motivation:* Establishing financial and other *incentives* to encourage ongoing individual and group effort, commitment, and alignment to the organization's objectives.

5. *Systems and processes for implementation:* Establishing *systems* such as planning, budgeting, management development, and performance reviews, and *processes* such as product development and customer service, to ensure the timely and effective implementation of the organization's goals and strategy.

Performing all these functions necessarily involves the collective effort of many people in an organization. The question is: What is the CEO's role?

In each of these broad areas, the CEO's challenge is not only ensuring that the organization collectively makes the right choices and decisions, but also ensuring alignment across them and adaptation over time. *Alignment* means that choices in each area must be consistent with and reinforce others. *Adaptation* implies that these choices need to be reviewed and modified as internal and external conditions change.

The Realities of Being CEO

To understand the role of the CEO in managing the enterprise, it is necessary to first understand some realities of being CEO. The transition to the CEO's job may appear to be just one more step in the evolution of an executive's career. Before becoming CEO, most executives have already been responsible for running a major business or function. Some may even have been a COO or president with operating responsibility for the whole organization. Yet, the newly appointed CEOs in our workshops are often surprised by the realities of the job and how different, not to mention more demanding, the CEO's job is from anything they have done previously.[1]

Broader Scope

New CEOs quickly discover that actually running the business—which was the primary focus of their prior jobs—is a more limited part of the CEO's job than they expected. They are surprised by the range and intensity of new external responsibilities: attending to shareholders, analysts, board members, industry groups, regulators, politicians, and other constituencies that expect to have direct contact with the CEO. This expansion of constituencies often leads to an exponential increase in the types of interactions with which a new CEO has little prior experience (such as appearing before a Senate hearing or managing a board).

As important and demanding as these new external responsibilities are, however, new CEOs recognize that they must still stay in touch with internal constituencies. CEOs cannot afford to neglect how the business is running, because they are still ultimately accountable. But running the business directly is impossible, even if they tried to do so. There is simply too much to know, too much to do, and even too much to monitor. CEOs find that they must depend heavily on others to help run the business, no matter how hard they work to stay involved. Balancing all these inside and outside responsibilities is one of the most salient challenges of the CEO's role.

Reporting to a Board of Directors

Although the CEO must attend to the expectations of numerous constituencies, not all of which are aligned, the board of directors is actually in charge. The board is the only constituency that has the right to fire the CEO, and is the ultimate arbiter of whether the CEO is appropriately meeting and balancing the array of expectations. The CEO must therefore pay special attention to managing and meeting the expectations of the board (Lorsch and Carter, 2003). As boards (especially of public companies) are being pressured to be more vigilant and be more accountable for the conduct of the organization, managing the relationship with the board has become even more important and challenging.

CEOs come to realize that what makes boards especially complex is that they involve not just one or two bosses (as CEOs have previously managed), but a group of bosses who spend limited time together but must approve and support their choices (Lorsch and Carter, 2003).

Most of the CEOs we have studied report spending at least 10 percent of their time managing the board and at least another 20 percent managing external constituencies (e.g., members of the media, analysts, investors, customers). Collectively, these activities take up what many CEOs experience as a surprisingly large fraction of their time and energy (see figure 16-1 for a breakdown of how one CEO we studied in depth distributed time across various constituencies).

Limits of Power

CEOs have the formal power that comes from being at the top of the pyramid, and the formal authority and responsibility to make decisions, allocate resources, and hire and fire. But CEOs soon discover the

FIGURE 16-1

Distribution of the CEO's time inside and outside the company

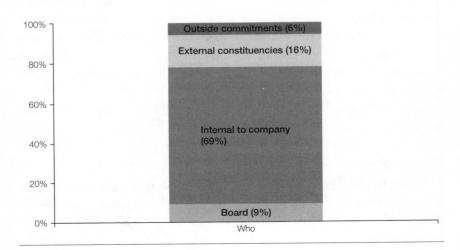

constraints on their expanded power (Pfeffer, 1992). Using power to overrule or make unilateral decisions can have unintended negative consequences, such as undermining the confidence of their team or paralyzing decision making in the organization because others start second-guessing and seeking to ensure that decisions will gain the CEO's approval.

CEOs come to appreciate the limits of their power even over the employees who report directly to them. They learn to be careful to avoid using their formal authority and veto power to make too many decisions, or make them too quickly.

Knowing how best to use their power within these subtle constraints is one of the most challenging realities of the CEO's job.

Obtaining the Right Information

CEOs have formal access to any information they desire, and can ask for a report or a review from anyone on any subject. Getting information is easy, but getting reliable information on what is truly going on in the organization is surprisingly difficult. Individuals who previously shared information with the CEO freely, even close friends and coworkers, suddenly clam up. CEOs get cut off from the informal channels in the organization. Information that is presented to the CEO is typically formal, extensively processed, and synthesized. Also, information is rarely presented to the CEO without some agenda in mind.

It is difficult for a leader to function effectively without good information. CEOs must address the reality that they may not have the information they truly need, and take steps to address this. CEOs must affirmatively seek out a true picture of what is going on inside as well as outside their organization—to learn how people are actually responding to their leadership, sense problems before they become major issues, discover how satisfied customers really are, identify managers with high potential who are languishing under poor bosses, or find the skunk works projects that have the potential to become the next big thing.

What further complicates getting information for CEOs is that they have to be careful about whom they ask for information and how, because they risk undermining their key reports, who might feel that the CEO is going around them. They also have to be careful about how they inquire, because asking questions can be interpreted as signaling the CEO's opinion or priorities.

Visibility

A CEO's every word and action are followed and scrutinized closely—both inside and outside the organization. Word of what the CEO says or does spreads quickly through the organization. Anything the CEO says or does is widely and extensively interpreted, and thus runs the risk of being amplified. The danger, of course, is that the CEO's words and actions can as easily be misinterpreted and distorted, as they can deliver the message the CEO intended.

The new CEOs in our workshops are often surprised by how an innocent remark or action had consequences they could have never imagined. A question is taken as a sign of disapproval; words of praise become a license to invoke the CEO's support. CEOs are equally surprised to learn from others what they are supposed to have said but cannot recall ever saying. Or, the number of times people have tried to invoke their name (e.g., "Frank says . . .") to advance their own agendas. Heightened attention can become a real constraint, as the CEO may inadvertently send unwanted signals. Or, a message designed for one constituency can be problematic to another.

While it adds complexity, the scrutiny paid to the CEO's words and actions also represents a crucial asset in playing the CEO's role. With limited time, CEO actions that will be so closely observed can be used as powerful symbols and signals—to send and spread a message widely. Managing their heightened visibility is another key reality of the CEO's job.

Personify the Company

CEOs identify with and are identified with their organizations—they often personify their organizations—which makes it hard for CEOs to keep their personal identity separate from their professional identity. Because the company's performance is often equated with the CEO's performance, it is hard for the CEO to avoid taking whatever happens in the company personally. This can draw the CEO into being more directly involved in more activities than they should, or getting too caught up in managing public perceptions of their performance—such as the company's stock price or in the media.

CEOs are also the external and internal "face" of the company. Being subsumed by the job is thus a real risk that many CEOs underestimate. Their personal lives (such as their families, their health, and their avocations) may well suffer. Putting everything into a job that demands every ounce of their energy, without losing themselves in the process, is the ultimate personal challenge of the CEO's role.

Time Horizon

CEOs are uniquely entrusted with the long-term health of their organizations. The most important distinction between the CEO's job and all others, according to Jaques (1989), is the time horizon. All the CEOs in our workshop acknowledged and embraced this responsibility. They recognize that their job is to think about the long-term, and to take actions and make investments that will make their organization stronger, enabling them to leave the organization in better shape and with better prospects than when they took charge.

Yet, CEOs must simultaneously attend to short-term matters and deal with short-term pressures, especially if they run publicly traded companies. Consistently delivering on short- and medium-term expectations is important to most CEOs because it builds the internal and external credibility and confidence necessary to achieve their longer-term objectives. Balancing short-term and long-term time horizons pervades the CEO's job.

Expectations of Change

CEOs, and leaders more generally, are expected to drive change (Kotter, 1990). If the organization has performed poorly under the CEO's predecessor, there can be a strong mandate for change. If the organization has performed well, the CEO is expected to make his or her own mark, but sustain the organization's success. CEOs themselves are keen to make some changes—to improve the organization's performance and to leave their own legacy.

Even though they are expected to be agents of change, CEOs simultaneously confront constraints on the changes they can make. There are often widely held assumptions about what kind of changes a CEO will make given his or her background and previous roles (for example, a CEO who was previously a scientist may be expected to invest more in R&D). The history of a company also constrains the changes a CEO may wish to make (Bartlett and Ghoshal, 1998). CEOs inherit people, resources, capabilities, strategies, cultures, processes, market positions, shareholding patterns, and analyst and investor perceptions—all of which limit their ability to act as if they had a blank sheet of paper. Shaping the organization's future while understanding its past and their own history is another key challenge of the CEO's job.

Unpredictability

CEOs are expected to be proactive—to set an agenda, develop plans, and drive action. They are expected to anticipate the future and plan for potential contingencies. However, as much as the CEOs we studied wanted to be proactive, they acknowledged that the job inevitably required them to be reactive as well. It proves to be impossible for CEOs to anticipate or plan for everything, or eliminate ambiguities and uncertainties. There are almost always unexpected external and internal events—whether they are natural disasters, economic downturns, predatory actions by competitors, or the failure of an internal project—which CEOs must react to. These events typically require urgent attention and can be enormously time consuming. The CEO's job thus requires a complex combination of proactive and reactive activities.

Severe Limits of Time

As a consequence of all the above realities, CEOs find that although, ostensibly they are masters of their time, the reality is that the demands on their time are endless. Everyone wants direct contact with the CEO—be it employees, customers, regulators, financial analysts, board members, journalists, or local community leaders. There are also rituals and events at which the CEO's presence is expected, be it the opening of a new plant, speaking to a group of senior managers at a leadership development program, chairing an important investor conference, or attending an industry association annual meeting. Many of these demands, seem "required"—a constant barrage of requests for time over which the CEO feels limited discretion. There are, moreover, some things that only the CEO can do—meetings with the board, testifying before key lawmakers, addressing the annual shareholders meeting, or meeting with a major customer's CEO, to name just a few.

Even though each request may not be important from the CEO's perspective, it is often essential from the perspective of the person who is asking for the CEO's time. Therefore, saying no erodes relationships, affects motivation, and sends signals. For all of these reasons, CEOs often find themselves overcommitted, or spending time on things they regret.

Managing time—doing the things that are highest on the CEO's priority list, while still being responsive to the incessant flow of other demands—proves to be one of the most challenging realties of the CEO's job for workshop participants. It is not just a matter of how much time CEOs should allocate to different matters or to different constituencies, but of how CEOs can best use the time they spend on these various activities.

The Importance of Indirect Influence

What are the implications of the realities of the CEO's job for accomplishing the functions of leadership in managing a large, complex organization? The foremost implication is that the CEO cannot perform even a small fraction of these functions personally. Inevitably, the CEO must principally harness the work of others.

As a result, *indirect levers* of influence are of far greater importance to the CEO's role than the direct exercise of power (giving orders, instructions, or commands or making decisions personally). We define indirect influence as shaping the context so that members of the organization can independently make good decisions, take appropriate actions, and behave in a desired manner. The key to the CEO's job is not what he or she does personally, but what he or she gets done through others in the organization.

The image of the CEO as ultimate decision maker—someone who commands and controls, and who gets involved in every significant decision taken by the organization—is a dangerous way to view the job. In an organization of even modest complexity, there are simply too many decisions to be made (Simon, 1976). Moreover, both the information and the expertise necessary to make good decisions are distributed widely in the organization. If the CEO tries to make too many decisions, the organization can grind to a halt. The CEO lacks the time to make most of the decisions even if he or she wants to. Worse yet, if the CEO starts deciding, others stop deciding; they simply wait for the CEO, rather than risk making decisions that will be disapproved or overruled. CEOs who make excessive use of their direct influence risk sapping the motivation of others in the organization and making poor use of the organizational resources available to them.

This doesn't mean that the CEO is uninvolved in these decisions. As we will discuss, CEO's can be involved in a variety of ways in shaping the decisions that get made in their organizations. The main point here is that CEOs must be wary of viewing their role as personally and directly making most of the important decisions in their organizations. Rather, they must influence others to make good decisions on behalf of the organization.

Indirect levers are not just vital to the CEO's role. Indeed, they become increasingly important to any leader as he or she rises up the organizational hierarchy. However, the CEO's job is uniquely invested with the greatest need, and the greatest potential, for indirect influence. This is because the CEO has the most influence on the important contextual variables that shape an organization's behavior—such as strategy, goals, values, structures, processes, systems, and the management team. These indirect levers operate across different levels of the organization and have powerful multiplier effects, both inside and outside the organization. They allow the organization to get it right without the CEO's involvement in everything.

The Nature of Indirect Levers

Perhaps the CEO's most powerful indirect lever is the organization's strategy (Porter, 1980, 1985, 1996). Strategic choices help clarify how the organization will create value, how it will distinguish itself from its competitors, and how it will gain a sustainable competitive advantage. The essence of strategy is making difficult choices—whether the organization will focus on being a low-cost player or a differentiated player; what kinds of customers and dimensions of the customer experience the organization will focus on; how it will configure its value chain and system of activities to deliver and capture value; with whom it will compete and with whom it will partner.

Why is strategy so important for the CEO? A good strategy helps to bring clarity about what the organization will do and, just as important, what it will *not* do. A CEO who ensures that the entire organization (from the senior team to the front lines) is clear about its strategic choices will help everyone make good choices for the organization without direct supervision. Their actions can reinforce the company's advantages, and their priorities become the organization's priorities.

Goal setting goes hand in hand with strategy as an indirect lever. The CEOs in our workshops spend a great deal of time and energy choosing the appropriate set of goals, metrics, and specific targets against these metrics for their organizations. Goals make strategy concrete, define the relationship between short-term and long-term objectives, and provide a common yardstick by which members of an organization can assess their collective performance—a clear target that everyone can shoot for (Collins and Porras, 1994). Goals also create pressures for improvement and innovation.

Explicitly defined values are another tool for compounding the CEO's influence. Values provide a sense of mission and purpose (Selznick, 1957; Collins and Porras, 1994; Podolny et al., 2005), making the enterprise something truly worthwhile and significant. If goals and strategy establish what members of the organization need to do, values allow the CEO to establish the legitimate and proper means to pursue these ends. Clarifying norms of values versus unacceptable behaviors, which influences the tone and culture of the organization, is another powerful indirect influence (Schein, 1985).

Organization structure is yet another indirect lever as it enables activities and decision rights to be grouped and distributed in different ways. A global product division structure, for example, tilts decision power toward the global product heads versus a regional structure. Centralized structures favor different choices and trade-offs than decentralized ones. The trade-offs inherent in any organization structure allow the CEO to influence the choices and behavior (Eccles and Nohria, 1992; Simons, 2005).

Financial and operating reviews, human resource reviews, and other key systems and processes are indirect levers that enable CEOs to ensure disciplined execution compatible with the organization's goals and strategy (Bossidy and Charan, 2002). These systems and processes also provide vehicles to gain information on how things are going, reinforce direction, promote actions that are compatible with the quality of execution the CEO expects, and identify and correct actions that may be incompatible with the CEO's expectations.

To do these things the CEO has to rely heavily on his or her top management team. The CEO's direct reports enable the CEO to delegate more, carry out a more ambitious agenda, and get good advice (see chapter 17). Developing a good understanding of the strengths and weaknesses of the members of this senior team—knowing how they complement each other, and investing the time to form high trust relationships with them so that the CEO can readily delegate activities to them—was routinely described by CEOs in our workshop as one of the most powerful ways in which they gain leverage and expand their influence. Providing feedback on an ongoing basis to members of this team is vital to ensure that this group stays aligned with the CEO's evolving agenda and priorities. When we ask CEOs later in their tenure what regrets they have or what they might have done differently, the largest number report not acting sooner to replace underperforming members of their top management team. Selecting the right members for their management teams and giving them the appropriate influence to drive the organization collectively is one of the key ways in which CEOs can exercise indirect influence (Collins, 2001).

Many CEOs also pay careful attention to the composition and development of a broader group of top talent in the organization. The selection, training, and motivation of these individuals provide other indirect levers on behavior throughout the wider organization.

Indirect levers are compounded in impact if they are aligned and reinforce each other rather than pull in different directions (Lawrence and Lorsch, 1967; Tushman and Nadler, 1997); for example, when the goals, structure, systems, and processes reinforce the strategy or the people chosen for the senior management team personify the tone and values the CEO wants to set.

CEOs have a unique integrative responsibility to connect the dots for others, to articulate how various aspects of the organization relate to each other. At the nexus of internal and external constituencies, CEOs have the best perspective not only on how well the organization is aligned internally, but also how well it is aligned with its external environment (Lawrence and Lorsch, 1967). As a result, one of the most important responsibilities of the CEO is to sense and identify potential problems and opportunities (March and Weil, 2005). CEOs must be conscious of changes taking place within the organization and its environment and lead the organization to adapt to these changes (Kotter, 1996).

The CEO's Personal Role

Even in these indirect areas of influence, the CEO cannot do everything personally. Strategy, for example, has to be set at all levels of the organization, from corporate strategy to business unit strategy. Clearly, the CEO can't directly participate in making all the strategic choices.

How then should the CEO be personally involved in the various indirect levers they have at their disposal? Using these levers presents the CEO with a subtle set of choices regarding their personal role. Our research suggests that on each of these indirect areas of influence, the CEO's role can vary along three dimensions, namely how the CEO influences the *design* of the decision making process, the extent of the CEO's personal *participation* in the process, and the CEO's role in actually making the *decisions*. Along each of these dimensions, the CEO can play a greater or more limited personal role.

Let's consider the CEO's role in *designing* the decision making process, by which we mean setting parameters such as who is to be involved, what are the questions to answer, what kinds of information to gather and consider, how many meetings they should have, what gets decided in group meetings versus in prior one-on-one sessions, and so on. In some areas, the CEO may play a major role in specifying the design of the decision making process in considerable detail. For example, in order to make corporate strategic choices regarding his company's portfolio of businesses (which to keep, divest, and acquire), one of the CEOs in our workshop designed the process thoroughly, choosing his direct reports and a select group of high-potential managers from lower levels of the organization to be involved in the process, defining the metrics against which each business was to be evaluated, choosing a set of major competitors against which performance was to be benchmarked, setting a time frame of three months to complete the analysis, and establishing weekly three-hour meetings when the whole team was expected to get together to review progress, discuss issues, and agree on next steps. In other cases, the CEO may choose to delegate process design. For example, another CEO delegated to his COO the task of preparing alternative organizational structure recommendations that would achieve certain cost-reduction goals in shared services like HR, IT, and Finance, and left the entire design of the process to the COO.

CEOs must be attentive to their design role, as even simple design choices, such as the number of times the senior management team meets and the agenda of these meetings, can have profound consequences for how a CEO exercises indirect and direct influence.

In addition to the design of the decision-making process, CEOs have to choose the extent to which they want to personally *participate* at various stages of any process or function and at which organizational levels. The CEO we discussed above, who was so active in designing the strategic portfolio review process, chose to personally participate in only the first two and the final two meetings of the process (out of the twelve full team meetings he had designed into the process). He chose the first two meetings as he wanted to set the right tone and direction for the work, but then wanted the team to do its own work without trying to second-guess his opinions. He finally reengaged when the team was ready to present its analysis and recommendations and it was time to make a final set of decisions.

The CEO's personal participation can vary. It may be active at every stage, or the CEO may periodically check in (formally or informally), or the CEO may choose to participate at the very end of the process.

In each of these areas, CEOs also have to make choices about the level of the organization that they are going to personally participate in. CEOs have to decide how much they personally want to be engaged in shaping various indirect levers at different levels of the organization. For example, how do they want to participate in shaping the business-unit strategy, or the marketing function's strategy, or the product development strategy? Although it is fairly straightforward that a CEO should personally participate less in any area the lower the level in the organization, these choices nevertheless need to be made thoughtfully. For example, CEOs may choose to participate in something that is far removed from the top, such as the strategy for a small business unit, or the design of a middle manager executive development program, because they want to signal its importance and shape the outcome. Just as in the design of the processes that collectively shape the work of the organization, CEOs have to be thoughtful about the extent and nature of their personal participation at various stages and levels of these processes, depending on the influence they want to exercise in different areas.

CEOs can also play a more or less active role in actually making the decisions in different areas. On one end, in areas like major mergers and acquisitions or the selection of a key member of the top management team, the CEO may can be the principal decision maker, consulting only a small group of people. On the other end—for example, in deciding the portfolio of new product development projects the company should pursue—the CEO may delegate the decision fully to a member on the senior management team. In other cases—for example, in deciding on a business unit's strategy—the CEO can let others recommend or own the decision, but yet be involved in ratifying or approving these decisions.

The experience of our workshop CEOs suggests that the CEO's personal role varies greatly depending on the indirect lever in question. In some cases, such as the selection of the top management team, the CEO is almost always the driver and decision maker, heavily involved in both the *process* and the *content* of the choice. Although the CEO may consult others in the organization, such as board members or other members of the senior management team, it is a choice he or she ultimately owns and makes.

In other cases, such as setting goals, articulating an overall corporate strategy, or establishing the organization's values, CEOs also tend to be the drivers and decision makers, but are more likely to use a more participative process involving the views and opinions of others in the organization to come up with the answers. Yet the CEOs in our workshop invariably report playing an influential role in shaping the content of these discussions and influencing the final results. They find that they can have the greatest influence, without disempowering others, if they are actively involved early in the process, so that they can frame the issues, ensure that the right questions are asked, the appropriate data are collected, and interject their own views.

On those levers that truly establish the direction of the organization, CEOs are keen to get as much participation and buy-in as feasible, but are equally clear that they need to play a significant personal role throughout the process and in making the final decisions.

On matters such as the organization's structure or systems such as the performance management process, CEOs in our workshop often describe their role more as architecting the process and ratifying or approving the final decisions. They provide a broad framework for how the structure or process should look, but leave it to others to fully flesh it out. Their personal participation in the detailed elaboration of these structures and processes is limited, though they ensure that they are periodically appraised and involved in a full discussion so that the final decisions are compatible and consistent with their overall framework and design principles.

In yet other cases, when the lever is an established organizational process, such as business unit strategic planning, budgeting, or talent management process, CEOs describe their role as primarily setting and enforcing standards. In these situations, CEOs exercise influence by challenging the process, raising the bar, asking tough questions, and demanding better answers. In these cases, CEOs restrain themselves from getting personally involved in making decisions, leaving the final decisions to others to whom decision rights have been delegated.

Finally, there are many processes, such as monthly or quarterly operating reviews (and various other periodic reviews of the various systems or processes within the organization), for which CEOs describe their role as that of a monitor—checking in to make sure things are on track and ensuring that the organization, at all levels is executing as planned. Sometimes, CEOs also describe their role in these settings as that of a coach—educating people, giving them constructive feedback, and helping them to improve their performance.

Although CEOs cannot possibly be involved in shaping all the indirect levers of influence at all levels of the organization and must therefore carefully choose where and how they want to personally be engaged, they also recognize that it is still their ultimate responsibility to ensure that these indirect levers are *aligned* with each other and across all levels of the organization. For example, CEOs know that they cannot possibly be involved in setting goals for each individual and each unit in the organization, but they are still responsible for ensuring that these myriad goals are consistent with the overall corporate goals that they have personally been most actively involved in setting. They also have to ensure that these goals are aligned with other levers such as strategy, structure, systems, etc.

The emphasis we have placed on indirect influence does not imply that CEOs never exercise direct influence. It only suggests they should do so very selectively and deliberately. They must drive decision making when there is an unexpected crisis (such as the Tylenol tragedy) and everyone inside and outside the organization is looking to the CEO to provide direction. CEOs must not hesitate to take direct action when they are presented with an opportunity with big consequences, such as deciding on a major acquisition or divestiture; they must be willing to intervene when things have gone off course to prevent a major mistake (and then later figure out where the indirect levers of influence failed); they must be willing to fire someone on their team who has consistently underperformed or violated some core values.

To some extent, the uses of direct involvement and influence may stem from the CEO's own personal passions and interests (such as getting involved in the design of a product or of a marketing campaign). Also, many CEOs often feel the need to continue to have some direct engagement with the activities of the organization ("keeping their hands dirty," as one CEO put it, or "making sure I am not seen as pure overhead with no ability to add direct value," as another put it).

Whenever a CEO takes direct action, it has a second-order indirect influence as well. A CEO's direct exercise of power sends a powerful message precisely because it is used relatively sparingly. CEOs should, therefore, view their direct involvement also as an opportunity to send a message or align the organization.

In general, though, the realities of the CEO's job require favoring indirect means of influence over the direct exercise of power whenever and wherever possible. The most powerful CEO is the one who uses indirect influence to expand the power of others in the organization.

Managing Presence

Given the enormous range of functions they have to fulfill through the exercise of indirect and direct influence, CEOs have to decide how to best allocate their personal time and presence. At first blush, this seems straightforward. After all, the CEO is in charge and can do whatever he or she wants. In practice, however, everyone wants the CEO's time and attention, whether it is people inside the organization or outside. Most recognize that the CEO can't possibly meet all these demands for his or her presence. Thus, where and how the CEO chooses to be present or get personally involved is a very important signal that accents his or her priorities and interests.

CEOs need to be conscious, mindful, and strategic about how they use their presence. Presence is not just about how the CEO allocates time across various activities and constituencies. It is the nature and quality of involvement the CEO brings to each occasion. CEOs must use their presence to decide, and even more importantly, to amplify the indirect levers they want to shape—by communicating, clarifying, educating, and reinforcing how people inside and outside relate to the organization. Much discussion in our workshops gravitated to how the CEO should allocate their presence, the challenges involved in doing so, and how to overcome these challenges. To inform these discussions, we conducted an in-depth study of how one CEO spent all his time for one full quarter (a three-month period). Although a single in-depth case has limited generalizability, it is instructive when combined with the broader (though less detailed) evidence we gathered from the broader sample of CEOs in our workshops.

Clear Personal Agenda

Given the vast array of issues that demand their attention and the impossibility of personally doing it all, CEOs need a way of differentiating and prioritizing among what is truly important and deserves their personal time and attention, what is important but can be delegated to others, and what is unimportant and should not clutter either their agenda or other senior managers' in the organization. Having a clear personal agenda—a relatively short list of major priorities that are ordered in terms of their time horizon (things that must be accomplished in the short, medium, and long term)—provides CEOs with a clear sense of how to allocate their presence. In the absence of an agenda, CEOs can easily get so consumed by the myriad demands (both from inside and outside the organization), that they dissipate their attention and fail to accomplish anything substantial.

However, having a personal agenda is not just focusing on the few things that only the CEO can do, or concentrating on the "big" issues (such as only matters that have multimillion-dollar consequences). It is dangerous to see the role this way. As we have noted, CEOs should occasionally get personally involved in small things, though mostly to make a bigger point that helps advance their overall agenda.

Having an explicit agenda not only helps the CEO prioritize his or her presence, but also helps others in the organization focus their efforts and energies. If stimulating innovation is topmost on the CEO's agenda, others in the organization know how to direct their own efforts. If, on the other hand, getting costs under control is at the top of the CEO's agenda, others in the organization will focus their attention differently. The benefit of an agenda that is time-sequenced is that it also enables the CEO to be clear about the time horizon of different priorities. When the CEO does not have a clear agenda or the agenda is constantly changing, the rest of the organization tends to become less disciplined about how to use the CEO's time. They may bring more things to the CEO's attention than necessary or may neglect to bring to the CEO's attention what they truly should—because the CEO's unclear agenda does not give them any strong signals of what the CEO expects to be involved in and what the CEO expects to delegate or postpone.

A CEO's agenda needs to be dynamic and adapt over time, but it must be sufficiently stable so that the organization doesn't feel like it's constantly responding to the CEO's changing whims.

Kotter (1982), in a study of divisional general managers, found that those who were effective could be readily discerned from their ineffective counterparts by the clarity of their agenda and the extent to which they spent the majority of their time focused on it. Having a clear agenda is undoubtedly even more important for CEOs. For the CEO whose time we tracked, we found that 52 percent of his time was directly related to his core agenda through meetings, conversations, and other activities (figure 16-2). Discipline in focusing time on his agenda is one of the reasons we believe that this CEO has been unusually effective. Discussions with other CEOs in our workshop revealed that their own personal sense of effectiveness is highly correlated with the clarity with which they can articulate an agenda and the self-discipline they report in allocating their presence in a manner consistent with this agenda.

While CEOs must focus their time and energy on the short-list of priorities on their agenda, they cannot entirely neglect other more routine and lower priority activities that may still be essential for the functioning of the organization as a whole. Such neglect can lead to diminished morale and reduced effectiveness in parts of the organization that feel marginalized by the CEO's exclusive focus on his or her agenda. Striking this balance between allocating the greater part of their presence to their agenda, while still devoting enough presence to make the rest of the organization feel valued is a distinguishing characteristic of effective CEOs.

FIGURE 16-2

Time allocated to core agenda relative to other activities

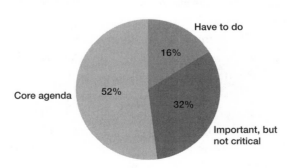

Relentless Communication

To accomplish their agenda, CEO's have to communicate it relentlessly. The CEO's agenda and related message (whether it be about the goals, the strategy, the execution priorities, or the organization's values) need to be communicated and understood as broadly as possible inside and, as appropriate, outside the organization. An effective CEO uses his or her presence ubiquitously to actively communicate and shape how all constituencies think about the organization. Communication helps the CEO frame issues for others, define what's important and relevant, and more generally direct the attention of the organization (Eccles and Nohria, 1992). Communication also has the power to shape the language or discursive practices in the company. Key phrases or ideas a CEO introduces, such as "six-sigma quality" or "balanced scorecard," can have a profound impact on the way members of the organization think, speak, and act.

Even in a moderately sized organization, it is virtually impossible for the CEO to directly communicate with everybody. Moreover, as we have highlighted in our discussion of the realities of the CEO's job, what complicates matters is that the CEO's message may not be transmitted with high fidelity—it may be distorted, amplified, revised, or otherwise modified as it is transmitted. The same message may also be heard differently depending on the perspective and biases of the listener.

The consequence is that most CEOs we have studied report that it is almost impossible to overcommunicate. Indeed, they report that CEOs must find every opportunity to get the message out. They must communicate incessantly—whether in one-on-one meetings, in small groups, in open forums, in town halls, in front of large audiences, and so on. Any occasion—agenda driven, ritual driven, or event driven—wherein the CEO can reiterate and reinforce the direction of the organization and its priorities has to be seized. Besides face-to-face or oral communication, CEOs must also make effective use of other communication media such as organizational newsletters, annual reports, intranets, voice or video messages, e-mails, and blogs to get the message out.

The CEO must be equally clear about communicating with outside audiences (whether it be investors, customers, regulators, or whatever). Unless the CEO is actively shaping the expectations of these constituencies and how they think about the organization, he or she should not be surprised if they then "misunderstand" the organization or its performance.

To communicate effectively across such a broad spectrum of constituencies, it helps if the message is simple, evocative, and memorable. It also helps if the message, as Aristotle advised, simultaneously appeals to the audience's logic, emotions, and values (Eccles and Nohria, 1992). CEOs don't need to be great orators, but they do need to be good communicators. They are the organization's most critical spokesperson. And while others can help, the attention and credibility that the CEO uniquely commands means that this is a job that can never be fully delegated.

Studies of how CEOs spend their time show that the vast majority of their time is spent in some form of communication (Mintzberg, 1973). Our in-depth study of one CEO underscores the importance of communication, especially face-to-face communication, which accounted for 81 percent of this CEO's time at work (figure 16-3).

Continuous Information Gathering

The other side of communication is listening and gathering information. Given the paucity of reliable information available to them and the necessity of having good information to make sound judgments, CEOs make the gathering of information, like communication, a constant personal task. They are constantly asking questions that help them get a better sense of how their business is doing. CEOs in our workshops report being especially interested in informal information

FIGURE 16-3

How the CEO communicates

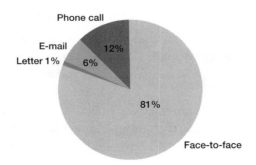

that is not readily available through formal channels. Information gathered through field visits, open forums with employees, customer visits, industry groups, outside consultants, board members—for that matter, any credible source—is prized and valued. In an era in which the media, the Internet, and the blogosphere have become important venues where information about a company circulates, CEOs are discovering the importance of also staying tuned to these channels and directly engaging in them (by writing their own blogs, for example).

Much like the CEOs Mintzberg (1973) observed, the CEOs we studied also resembled the American presidents that Neustadt (1960:153–154) wrote about: "It is the odds and ends of 'tangible detail' that pieced together in his mind illuminate the issues put before him. To help himself, he must reach out as widely as he can for every scrap of fact, opinion, and gossip bearing on his interests and relationships as President. He must become his own director of central intelligence."

The manner in which they get involved in more formal systems and processes, such as management information systems and regular budget review meetings, is also highlighted by CEOs as being vital to their ability to stay informed. CEOs in our workshops emphasize that creating a tone of open dialogue in these settings, pushing for transparency, making conversations a real give-and-take, ensuring that everyone feels included and empowered to voice their opinion (even if it is not going to be popular), being unafraid to ask the "stupid question" themselves, and pushing to understand things more clearly when they appear convoluted or complex are some of the ways in which they ensure that they get better-quality information.

Harnessing Multiplier Effects

Even with a sharply defined agenda, the demands on a CEO's time are still far greater than the time available. The need to constantly communicate and gather information is just an example of how CEOs remain stretched when it comes to their personal presence. Hence, CEOs have to find other ways of leveraging and multiplying their presence. One way in which CEOs (including the one we studied) multiply their presence is to have interactions that involve multiple individuals and groups simultaneously (for example, meetings that include people across the different levels of the organization or that include people from inside the organization and outside the organization such as clients or investment bankers). See figure 16-4 for a diagram showing how the CEO we studied leveraged his time with internal and external constituents.

Another important way in which CEOs can multiply their presence is by involving the people who report to them, especially their top management team. This is another reason why the selection of an effective top management team was viewed as being so important by the CEOs in our study. For the CEO we studied, about 10 percent of his time was spent in one-on-one interactions with his direct reports, but these direct reports were also involved in 36 percent of his other interactions. This involvement helped inform and align direct reports with his agenda (see figure 16-5 for an analysis of how the CEO has leveraged his direct reports with other constituents).

CEOs can also free up their own time and leverage their presence by delegating activities to others on their senior management team. Effective CEOs proactively look for ways to get their top management team to take on activities that may initially appear to warrant CEO involvement, such as getting their CFO to be the primary interface with the financial community, or other senior managers to represent the company in the community or the media. Getting various constituencies comfortable working with trusted team members to whom the CEO delegates certain activities, even when they might have hoped for the CEO's presence, is key to multiplying the CEO's own presence.

FIGURE 16-4

Leveraging time with internal and external constituents

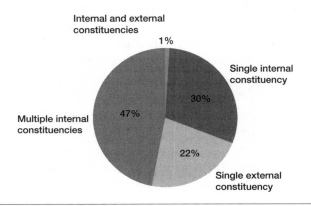

Internal and external constituencies
1%

Single internal constituency

30%

Multiple internal constituencies

47%

22%

Single external constituency

FIGURE 16-5

Leveraging time with direct reports

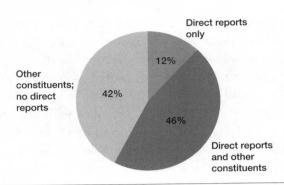

CEOs must inevitably allocate time to routine events and rituals that they are expected to participate in—from visiting customers, to meeting with employees in an open forum, to speaking to investment analysts, to cutting ribbons at various ceremonies, and so on. It may be tempting to dismiss these rituals as unimportant, but effective CEOs recognize that these are also opportunities to communicate their core messages and to signal the importance they attach to all the work of the organization. If a CEO stops making time for such rituals, he or she runs the risk of seeming aloof, remote, and disengaged.

To enable their presence at such rituals, CEOs combine activities so that they can do multiple routine things at once. The CEO whose time we tracked, for example, would combine an industry event that was annually held in New York with visits with investors, meetings with local customers, and a tour of a local facility.

A general lesson that can be drawn from these observations is that CEOs should see every occasion in which they are present as a multiplier opportunity. If they manage their presence mindfully rather than mechanically, they can use their presence to combine various activities, touch different constituencies, communicate their agenda, send signals and messages, or gather valuable information.

Given how often CEOs combine activities or constituencies, it becomes an important signal when they make the time to do just one thing, or spend time with someone one-on-one. Only 21 percent of the CEO's time we tracked was in one-on-one settings (see figure 16-6 below). CEOs, therefore, need to think carefully about how to allocate their dedicated presence.

In general, we found that a CEO is likely to be more effective in leveraging his or her presence if he or she has a clear personal agenda, is relentless about communicating his or her message and gathering information on every occasion, actively works with and delegates to direct reports, uses time to achieve multiple objectives, touch multiple constituencies, and combine activities, and has some disciplined boundaries that protect blocks of personal time.

Leveraging Symbolism

Although the power of the CEO's position is often overestimated, in one respect it is sometimes underestimated—and that is its symbolic significance (Pondy, 1983; Pfeffer, 1981). CEOs we have studied are often surprised by how much their every behavior is scrutinized and the symbolic messages people derive from these behaviors. CEOs are constantly sending signals, as we noted in the first section. What the CEO shows an interest in is quickly interpreted as being important, while what the CEO consciously or unconsciously neglects can be as readily interpreted as being unimportant. For example, if a CEO's questions during a budget review largely center on market share and skip quickly over the part devoted to cost-savings measures, the CEO's interest will signal that he or she is more interested in revenue growth than cost. Moreover, as we have discussed above, how CEOs allocate their presence sends important signals as well.

A CEO's actions and choices are also constantly being assessed relative to expectations. When a CEO fires a manager who makes

FIGURE 16-6

Who the CEO communicates with

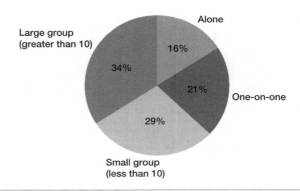

the numbers but violates values, it sends a strong signal about the importance the CEO attaches to values. Equally, if that same person is rewarded, the CEO sends the signal that hitting the numbers is the only thing that matters.

Being aware of this extraordinary symbolic power can prevent the CEO from unwittingly sending unwanted signals. For example, one of our CEOs who had risen through the manufacturing ranks decided that he needed to spend more time visiting other functional areas. In his first year as CEO, he ended up visiting none of the manufacturing sites. To his great surprise and consternation, he discovered a year later that the manufacturing organization felt that it was no longer a high priority for the organization and was demoralized.

CEOs can leverage the symbolic power of presence to send powerful messages about desirable behavior. For example, the first woman to become CEO of one of the world's largest mining companies decided in her first three months to personally visit and descend to the bottom of one of the organization's underground mines with the worst safety record. The fact that she took the time to do this despite other pressing demands on her time sent a very strong signal throughout the organization that she was serious about safety. She showed she was willing to get her hands dirty through direct involvement in the operations of the organization, rather than issue orders from corporate headquarters.

The importance of symbolism amplifies a point we have made earlier. By occasionally choosing to focus their presence on small matters and details (things that the organization ordinarily would not expect them to pay attention to) CEOs can send a powerful signal of the tone they want to set, and the standards they want the organization to embrace. By drawing attention to these seemingly minor or unimportant issues, CEOs model the type of vigilance and attention to detail they expect from all members of the organization. It also helps them communicate that *all* the work of the organization is important.

More generally, CEOs play a powerful modeling role—their every action and behavior is a signal that influences the behavior of others in their organization. People watch the CEO closely and will model their own behavior in a manner that fits what the CEO appears to place importance upon. To be an effective leader, a CEO must therefore be mindful of the great symbolic significance of his or her personal actions and use the unique symbolic power associated with the position strategically.

Establishing Legitimacy

A CEO's most limited resource is his or her presence. CEOs must therefore allocate their presence mindfully to advance their agendas. CEOs must communicate ubiquitously, stay informed, stay in touch with their organization, and find ways of multiplying their presence and symbolizing what's important. To be truly effective in these activities and roles, however, a CEO's most precious resource, which amplifies or diminishes his or her presence, is not the formal authority but the legitimacy he or she enjoys in the eyes of various constituencies. Put differently, legitimacy moderates the relationship between a CEO's actions and outcomes. CEOs with high legitimacy have a greater ability to get desired outcomes from their actions, than CEOs who lack legitimacy.

The high rate of involuntary CEO turnover reminds us that the formal authority granted to the CEO can be readily withdrawn. CEOs have resigned or been fired because they lost the confidence of their board, their employees, their shareholders, their regulators, their customers, or even the public at large (as for example when their personal behavior violates accepted moral standards).

Ultimately, it is legitimacy that gives a CEO the license to lead. A CEO's ability to be an effective leader rests on the extent to which others are voluntarily willing to follow or defer to his or her authority (Barnard, 1938). Moreover, a measure of true leaders is not just the deference given to their formal authority (obedience to their orders) but the extent to which they are able to inspire and mobilize others to voluntarily do their utmost—to rise above duty to give their all. This higher measure of effort and initiative—which the best leaders are able to elicit—depends less on the power they exercise or the incentives they provide, and more on the legitimacy they enjoy. CEOs who enjoy legitimacy motivate loyalty, inspire confidence, and build trust in the organization and in their leadership.

Legitimacy creates trust. Trust, in turn, is a powerful resource in any organization. Trust hinges on the extent to which people believe in the competence, honesty, and benevolence of others (Gambetta, 1988). By enhancing his or her legitimacy, the CEO is able to build trust in himself or herself, as well as the trust individuals are willing to place in the organization as a collective. Enhanced trust increases the sense of psychological safety people feel in exerting effort or giving their all to the organization because they feel confident that others will do the same (there will be few free riders) and that they will be appropriately recognized for their contributions (they will be treated fairly and justly).

Trust, in the experience of our CEOs, is far more effective at getting the most out of people than formal incentives. To the extent people trust the CEO, they will give him or her the benefit of the doubt (to use Barnard's language, the CEO will have a significantly larger zone of authority). They will be more open to making longer-term investments in the organization with uncertain personal payoffs, because they feel confident that they will not be taken advantage of. In short, CEOs who enjoy greater legitimacy and build trust are better able to perform the enormously complex job they are entrusted with—because people give them the moral license to lead.

What, then, allows CEOs to gain and sustain legitimacy? What destroys it?

Formal Authority

CEOs derive some measure of legitimacy from the formal authority of their position. This authority is codified in decision rights and reporting relationships. The presumption in most organizations is that the CEO is in charge, and must be followed. However, the legitimacy that comes from formal authority is limited and only goes so far.

Competence

Legitimacy also comes from the perception of competence. If the CEO is respected for his or her experience, technical knowledge, analytical ability, or other leadership capabilities, the members of the organization will be inclined to follow. A CEO's competence also depends on the extent to which he or she is seen as being connected to reality— aware of the nitty-gritty realities of the organization and its environment rather than appearing divorced and out of touch. Competence reinforces formal authority.

Results

A third source of legitimacy is results. As long as their organization's performance continues to meets expectations (what constitutes good results depends on the situation), the various constituencies will be prone to go along with the CEO. Some believe that the most tangible way for a CEO to enhance or diminish their legitimacy is the results the organization delivers (Hogan and Kaiser, 2005). As one CEO put it, "Although you come in with some money in your bank account because of your prior track record, you have to keep filling it up, keep being seen as someone who is making a difference."

However, the relationship between results and legitimacy is not symmetric. It is hard to be considered an effective leader if the organization's results are chronically poor (whether the results are measured in financial terms or in terms of meeting other expectations). Even a well-liked chief executive who fails to deliver results (think Jimmy Carter in Iran) loses legitimacy. On the other hand, good results typically increase the legitimacy of the leader, but not necessarily. If the results are perceived as temporary or having been obtained using questionable means, the leader's legitimacy may still be contested.

Legitimacy that rests on formal authority, competence, or results alone can be fragile, if for no other reason than that most companies will inevitably go through some tough decisions or periods of shaky performance. In addition, CEOs win true legitimacy from a number of more subtle sources. If a CEO fails to reinforce legitimacy from these deeper sources, the capacity to lead that derives from formal authority, competence, and even good results can be limited and fleeting.

Fairness

CEOs can have a disproportionate impact on the allocation of resources and rewards in the organization. Because the CEO has so much power over the fate of others, CEOs must be perceived to be even-handed to enjoy legitimacy. The CEO, as the person who sets the tone for the rest of the organization, is expected to be caring, fair, and just. Being experienced as fair enhances legitimacy, whereas being experienced as unfair can destroy legitimacy (Hochschild, 1981). If the CEO is seen to be partial to some and hostile to others, to be unfair in the standards used to judge the merits of proposals or people, to show favoritism in meting out praise or criticism and rewards or punishment, the CEO loses legitimacy. When this happens, people withdraw from giving the organization their maximum effort and engage in more self-protective and political behavior.

Integrity

Integrity is a measure of the consistency and coherence between what the CEO espouses and how the CEO behaves (Jensen et al., 2007). The closer the match, the greater will be the legitimacy of the CEO. The wider the gap, the more fragile will be the legitimacy of the CEO. Since the CEO's job is inherently one of communication, the CEO inevitably has a lot to say. Equally, because the CEO's job is the most visible and his or her every behavior is closely watched, it is easy to tell whether the CEO actually walks the talk.

A CEO's integrity gets the greatest boost when he or she shows commitment to his or her espoused values even when doing so is costly. The CEO who shows no hesitation in recalling an unsafe product (whatever the cost), or who continues to fund an important R&D project (even when the company is losing money), or who takes responsibility for a failed investment (even if the decision wasn't entirely his or hers) will enhance his or her integrity and hence legitimacy. Conversely, CEOs who adopt a more expedient approach, who are seen to have forsaken their values when the going got tough, are more likely to diminish their integrity and legitimacy and correspondingly diminish the commitment people put in them and in the organization.

Our CEOs commonly highlighted the courage to do the right thing or make the tough call as a way to gain legitimacy and, with it, greater organizational commitment.

Putting the Company First

Becoming a CEO may be a prize for years of hard work and contribution to the organization, but it is also a privilege and honor. CEOs gain legitimacy to the extent their behavior demonstrates that they put the company's interests above their own. As one of our CEOs put it, "People need to know it's not about you, that you are committed to serving a broader, higher purpose." Most people in an organization don't begrudge the fact that the CEO is paid manyfold more than them or enjoys privileges that they can only dream of. People accept that those who reach the top are rare achievers and must be compensated accordingly. What galls people is when the CEO appears to put self-interest above the company's interests.

When the CEO starts appearing on the cover of every magazine, touting or tacitly accepting that he or she is responsible for the organization's success, the rest of the organization can feel that their contributions are slighted, and the CEO loses legitimacy. CEOs who instead use every opportunity to acknowledge their privilege to lead the company, who are generous in giving others credit for success and quick to assume responsibility for failures, who share sacrifice as much as they share gain, are much more likely to earn legitimacy.

Staying Grounded

To maintain their legitimacy, leaders need to remain grounded and continue to be experienced as authentic (George, 2007). They must be seen as continuing to remain human, humble, and approachable. When CEOs become incapable of looking themselves in the mirror and recognizing what others see, they lose their legitimacy.

Most CEOs do not anticipate that the CEO job will change them as human beings. Yet the evidence is clear that the job can change people (George, 2007). Kramer (2003) has described the risks of the job as structurally induced narcissism. The perks of the CEO job are so numerous and the attention and admiration so constant that it is hard for CEOs not to begin to believe in their own self-importance and their superiority to others in their organization. The New York apartment that seemed like a luxury becomes an absolute necessity. Compensation that may seem obscene to others becomes justified as well deserved. It is but a short step to thinking that CEOs are so much smarter than others that others' opinions are not important, which can lead to a sense of arrogance and infallibility.

Their job demands so much of their time that CEOs often sacrifice time reserved for themselves and their family. Losing themselves in their work can unmoor CEOs from their anchor outside work. Though the costs may not be visible in the short run, the loss of personal time for things like exercise or relaxation or family time can be quite costly in the long run. Some of the ways the CEOs we have studied have gained more control over their time include setting clear boundaries that protect their personal time. For example, the CEO whose time we tracked made it a point to let the organization know that it was important to him to have dinner with his family most nights he was in town. As a result, people had learned that meetings with him would not go past 6:30 in the evening. By setting this boundary clearly, the CEO was able to spend thirty-one out of the thirty-four available evenings (when he was not traveling) at home having dinner with his family (see figure 16-7 for a distribution of his time at work and when he was not at work). Other CEOs have reported setting similar kinds of boundaries to protect the time they need to exercise, meditate, or read; to attend events at their kids' school; or to vacation with their families. Besides their

FIGURE 16-7

Allocation of time to work and nonwork activities

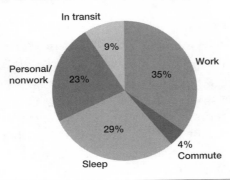

benefits for themselves and their families, these forms of personal discipline also help CEOs remain grounded.

Conclusion

The job of the CEO in a large, complex organization is the epitome of leadership. Yet the reality of the CEO's job is rife with paradoxical opportunities and constraints, and is at odds with the appearance of absolute power and authority associated with the role. The CEO's job has often been conceived in terms of major decisions or functions—such as strategy—that must be accomplished for an organization to perform effectively. However, the CEO does not need to have sole responsibility for fulfilling these functions, nor is this desirable. Rather, the CEO must work with others to perform all the functions within the constraints and realities of the job.

Accomplishing these functions, given the realities of the CEO's job, involves using more indirect than direct levers of influence. The importance of indirect influence requires the CEO to pay special attention to allocating his or her presence (time, attention, and energy), the CEO's most limited, yet crucial, resource. The CEO can only fulfill his or her role, and do so effectively, by enjoying legitimacy in the eyes of those who must be led.

To fulfill these complex roles, becoming an effective CEO requires making a crucial psychological transition, which can be difficult for even the most skilled and experienced operating manager. CEOs need to let go of their previous operating or staff role and the feelings of competence and enjoyment associated with the years of success in them. At the same time as CEO's have to confront the difficulty of letting go, they must embrace aspects of their new role that often feel uncomfortable.

CEOs must learn to cope with the seemingly endless demands placed upon them and the constant spotlight on their every action. They need to adjust to the sudden change in their relationships—even with people they have known for years—and the associated feeling of loneliness. They have to overcome the fear of seeming ignorant, stupid, or at the edge of their competence when dealing with matters they must inevitably get involved in but don't feel deeply informed about.

This discomfort of being exposed, vulnerable, and even overwhelmed is often a precondition of being more in control of the myriad challenges of the role and eventually experiencing a sense of mastery and enjoyment. When CEOs finally start feeling accomplished in their role, they have to find ways of staying grounded and coming to terms with their own egos—the siren calls of fame and fortune that appear everywhere, the enormous latitude to deploy corporate resources for things ranging from corporate jets and corporate suites at sporting events to trophy deals, and the lure of using the company's stock price as a barometer of personal performance.

These psychological challenges of transitioning into the CEO role, and then staying grounded in the job, are rarely anticipated and discussed. This challenge helps explain some of the variability of CEO performance.

The CEO's job is one of the most important leadership positions in society. Understanding the job better is vital to the better functioning of the economy. This article attempts to reinvigorate research on this important topic, which has languished for decades.

Appendix 16-1

Our CEO Research Program

The New CEO Workshop

Initiated in the mid 1990s and expanded after 2002, the New CEO Workshop is an invitation-only Harvard Business School program for newly appointed CEOs of large, complex companies (annual revenues are typically greater than $2 billion).

Since the program's inception, about 110 new CEOs have participated from leading companies representing a wide range of industries. Table 16-1 shows a distribution of companies by the NAIC classification of industries. Table 16-2 provides some other summary statistics on the composition of the companies and CEOs in our sample.

In addition to the initial New CEO workshop, we have reconvened two workshop cohorts (nineteen total CEOs) eighteen to twenty-four months into their tenure to discuss the next set of pressing issues faced once the CEO has made it through the initial phase of his or her tenure. We have also held an Alumni Workshop for past participants (six CEOs) who were six to eight years into their tenure, which has provided a longer-term perspective on the evolving CEO role.

Use of CEO Time

In 2007, we completed a pilot study with one workshop alumnus to examine his use of time in executing the job. For one quarter (three full months) of a year, we cataloged this CEO's every action. Through the diligence of the CEO and his assistant we captured each interaction, from meetings to commutes to how much time he spent with his family. We captured who was involved in each block of time, the subject, and other information. This has allowed us to gain more insight into how CEOs allocate their limited time, presence, and attention. In 2009, we have launched this study with two more alumni and expect to include three more by year's end.

TABLE 16-1

Distribution of companies by NAIC classification of industries

NAIC classification	Percentage
Manufacturing	49
Wholesale trade	7
Retail trade	7
Information technology	7
Transportation and warehousing	5
Waste management and remediation services	5
Finance and insurance	4
Utilities	4
Health care and social assistance	4
Accommodation and food services	4
Professional, scientific, and technical services	3
Agriculture, forestry, fishing, and hunting	2
Mining, quarrying, and oil and gas extraction	2
Real estate and rental and leasing	2
Construction	1
Management of companies and enterprises	1
Other services (except public administration)	1

TABLE 16-2

Characteristics of CEOs in our study (104 CEOs from public companies, 6 CEOs from private companies)

COMPANY

Median company size in revenues	$3.7B
$500M to $1B	25%
$2B–$10B	50%
$10B–$75B	25%

CEO

Average age at appointment	49.7 (Range: 36–63)
Years with company before becoming CEO	Average 14.1 (Range: 0–38)

Tenure as CEO when he or she attended workshop

Less than one year	$N = 110$
Between one and three years	$N = 19$
Three years and beyond	$N = 6$

Appointed CEO as an

Insider	75%
Insider (< 3 years)	7%
Outsider	18%

Chairman appointment

Also chairman when appointed to CEO	12%
Appointed chairman during tenure	29%
Still not appointed chairman	59%

CEO's educational attainment

College	36%
MBA	38%
Other graduate	11%
Doctoral	15%

Note

1. We have described common surprises confronting new CEOs in an earlier article (Porter, Lorsch, and Nohria, 2004). We summarize and extend these ideas in this section.

References

Barnard, C.I. *The Functions of the Executive.* Cambridge, MA: Harvard University Press, 1938.

Bartlett, C.A., and S. Ghoshal. *Managing Across Borders: The Transnational Solution.* Boston: Harvard Business School Press, 1998.

Bebchuk, L.A., and J.M. Fried. *Pay Without Performance: The Unfulfilled Promise of Executive Compensation.* Cambridge, MA: Harvard University Press, 2004.

Bennis, W.G. *Leaders: The Strategies for Taking Charge.* New York: Harper & Row, 1985.

————. *On Becoming a Leader.* Revised ed. Cambridge, MA: Perseus Publishing, 2003.

Bossidy, L., and R. Charan. *Execution: The Discipline of Getting Things Done.* New York: Crown Business, 2002.

Bower, J.L. *The CEO Within: Why Inside Outsiders Are the Key to Succession Planning.* Boston: Harvard Business School Press, 2007.

Chandler, A.D., Jr. *The Visible Hand: The Managerial Revolution in American Business.* Cambridge, MA: Harvard Belknap, 1977.

Chatterjee, A., and D.C. Hambrick. "It's All About Me: Narcissistic Chief Executive Officers and Their Effects on Company Strategy and Performance." *Administrative Science Quarterly* 52, no. 3 (2007).

Collins, J. *Good to Great: Why Some Companies Make the Leap ... and Others Don't.* New York: HarperBusiness, 2001.

Collins, J.C., and J.I. Porras. *Built to Last: Succesful Habits of Visionary Companies.* New York: HarperCollins, 1994.

Eccles, R.C., and N. Nohria. *Beyond the Hype: Rediscovering the Essence of Management.* Boston: Harvard Business School Press, 1992.

Gambetta, D. *Trust: Making and Breaking Cooperative Relations.* New York: Basil Blackwell, 1988.

George, W.W. *True North: Discover Your Authentic Leadership.* San Francisco: Jossey-Bass, 2007.

Hochschild, J.L. *What's Fair? American Beliefs About Distributive Justice.* Cambridge, MA: Harvard University Press, 1981.

Hogan, R., and R. Kaiser. "What We Know About Leadership." *Review of General Psychology* 9 (2005): 169–180.

Jaques, E. *Requisite Organization: The CEO's Guide to Creative Structure and Leadership.* Arlington, VA: Cason Hall, 1989.

Jensen, M.C., W. Erhard, and S. Zaffron. "Integrity: Where Leadership Begins—A New Model of Integrity." Working paper 07-03, Barbados Group, 2007. http://ssrn.com/abstract=983401.

Kaplan, S.N., M. Klebanov, and M. Sorensen. "Which CEO Characteristics and Abilities Matter?" Working paper 14195, National Bureau of Economic Research (NBER), July 2008.

Khurana, R. *Searching for a Corporate Savior: The Irrational Quest for Charismatic CEOs*. Princeton, NJ: Princeton University Press, 2002.

Kotter, J.P. *The General Managers*. New York: The Free Press, 1982.

———. *A Force for Change: How Leadership Differs from Management*. New York: The Free Press, 1990.

———. *Leading Change*. Boston: Harvard Business School Press, 1996.

Kramer, R.M. "The Harder They Fall." *Harvard Business Review* 81, no. 10 (October 2003): 58–66.

Lawrence, P.R., and J.W. Lorsch. *Organization and Environment: Managing Differentiation and Integration*. Boston: Division of Research, Graduate School of Business Administration, Harvard University, 1967.

Lorsch, J.W., and C.B. Carter. *Back to the Drawing Board: Designing Corporate Boards for a Complex World*. Boston: Harvard Business School Press, 2003.

March, J.G., and T. Weil. *On Leadership*. Malden, MA: Blackwell, 2005.

Mayo, A., and N. Nohria. *In Their Time: The Greatest Business Leaders of the 20th Century*. Boston: Harvard Business School Press, 2005.

Mayo, A., N. Nohria, and L.G. Singleton. *Paths to Power: How Insiders and Outsiders Shaped American Business Leadership*. Boston: Harvard Business Press, 2006.

McLean, R.J., Stuckey, J.A., and D. Barton. "Leveraging CEO Time." *McKinsey Quarterly*, no. 4 (1991): 106–115.

Mintzberg, H. *The Nature of Managerial Work*. New York: Harper & Row, 1973.

Murphy, K.J., and J. Zabojnik. "Managerial Capital and the Market for CEOs." Working paper, 2007. http://ssrn.com/abstract=984376.

Neustadt, R.E. *Presidential Power and the Modern Presidents: The Politics of Leadership from Roosevelt to Reagan*. New York: The Free Press, 1960.

Pfeffer, J. *Managing with Power: Politics and Influence in Organizations*. Boston: Harvard Business School Press, 1992.

———. *Power in Organizations*. Marshfield, MA: Pitman, 1981.

Podolny, J., R. Khurana, and M.L. Hill-Popper. "Revisiting the Meaning of Leadership." *Research in Organizational Behavior* 26 (2005): 1–37.

Pondy, L.R. *Organizational Symbolism*. Greenwich, CT: JAI Press, 1983.

Porter, M.E. *Competitive Advantage: Creating and Sustaining Superior Performance*. New York: The Free Press, 1985.

———. *Competitive Strategy: Techniques for Analyzing Industries and Competitors*. New York: The Free Press, 1980.

———. "What Is Strategy?" *Harvard Business Review* 74, no. 6 (November–December 1996): 61–78.

Porter, M.E., J.W. Lorsch, and N. Nohria. "Seven Suprises for New CEOs." *Harvard Business Review* 82, no. 10 (October 2004): 62–72.

Schein, E.H. *Organizational Culture and Leadership: A Dynamic View*. San Francisco: Jossey-Bass, 1985.

Selznick, P. *Leadership in Administration: A Sociological Interpretation*. New York: Harper & Row, 1957.

Simon, H.A. *Administrative Behavior*. New York: Macmillan, 1976.

Simons, R. *Levers of Organization Design: How Managers Use Accountability Systems for Greater Performance and Commitment*. Boston: Harvard Business School Press, 2005.

Sonnenfeld, J.A. *The Hero's Farewell: What Happens When CEOs Retire*. New York: Oxford University Press, 1988.

Stieglitz, H. "The Chief Executive—And His Job." Studies in Personnel Policy no. 214. New York: National Industrial Conference Board, 1969.

———. "Chief Executives View Their Jobs: Today and Tomorrow." New York: Conference Board, 1985.

Tedlow, R.S. *Giants of Enterprise: Seven Business Innovators and the Empires They Built.* New York: Harper Business, 2003

Tushman, M.L., and D.A. Nadler. *Competing by Design: The Power of Organizational Architecture.* New York: Oxford University Press, 1997.

Welch, J. *Jack: Straight from the Gut.* New York: Warner Books, 2001.

Zaleznik, A. *Hedgehogs and Foxes: Character, Leadership, and Command in Organizations.* New York: Palgrave Macmillan, 2008.

17

WHAT MAKES TEAMS OF LEADERS LEADABLE?

Ruth Wageman and J. Richard Hackman

SOME SEVENTY years ago, telecommunications executive Chester Barnard (1938) wrote *The Functions of the Executive*, a classic book explaining what senior leaders must do to help their organizations succeed. The core idea is in the second word of the title: that leadership is a matter of seeing to it that certain necessary *functions*— establishing direction, creating structures and systems, engaging external resources—are fulfilled so that members can accomplish shared purposes. Barnard demonstrates that getting people to collaborate to pursue collective objectives depends on getting those general functions accomplished.

Some two decades later, Joseph McGrath (1962) picked up Barnard's theme and applied it specifically to groups. The leader's main job, he said, "is to do, or get done, whatever is not being adequately handled for group needs" (p. 5). If a leader manages, by whatever means, to ensure that all functions critical to performance are taken care of, then the leader has done well. Thus, a functional approach to leadership leaves room for a wide range of ways to get key functions accomplished, and avoids the impossibility of trying to specify all the particular behaviors or styles that a leader should exhibit in given circumstances (Hackman and Wageman, 2005).

For both Barnard and McGrath, the conceptual focus is identification of the core functions that must be accomplished to promote
social system effectiveness—not who gets them accomplished or even
how that is done. In this view, anyone who helps get critical functions
accomplished in any way they can is exercising leadership. Yet most of
the writing in the functional approach, like scholarly work on leadership more generally, has focused mainly on *individuals* who occupy
leadership roles (see, for example, Hackman, 2002, chap. 7, and
Hackman and Walton, 1986, for a functional analysis of the team
leader role). Little attention has been given to leadership *teams*—that
is, groups of leaders who are collectively responsible for exercising
leadership of a social system, and each of whose members is himself or
herself a significant organizational leader.

The oversight is worrisome, because executive functions increasingly are fulfilled in organizations not by a heroic individual working
alone but rather by leadership teams of various kinds (Ancona and
Nadler, 1989; Hambrick, 1998; Wageman, Nunes, Burruss, and
Hackman, 2008). At the top of organizations, for example, the increasing complexity and interdependence of organizations' environments
may well have made the top leadership role too large for any one person
to accomplish, no matter how talented (Bennis, 1997). Moreover, it is
insufficient for individual senior leaders to merely operate in parallel
these days; instead, their activities must be well aligned, well coordinated, and executed with reference to each other (Henderson and
Fredrickson, 2001; Thompson, 1967). Top management teams appear
to be not merely common in contemporary organizational life but are,
for many enterprises, a necessity.

Yet, as our own research has shown, teams of leaders routinely
underperform their potential (Wageman, Nunes, Burruss, and Hackman,
2008, chap. 1). Are teams of leaders inherently poor at collaboration
and in fulfilling key leadership functions? Some treatments of the subject suggest so. Popular press writings such as those of Lencioni (2002)
and management writer Katzenbach (1997a, 1997b) underscore the
poor processes that characterize most leadership teams and even suggest that the term "team" is something of a misnomer for many of these
entities. Scholarly findings reinforce these pessimistic views of the
forces acting on teams of leaders and their consequent tendency to
fragment (e.g., Berg, 2005; Hambrick, 1995; Li and Hambrick, 2005).

In this paper, we explore the reasons why leadership teams have such difficulty in fulfilling even those functions that are most critical to the effectiveness of their organizations. We show that teams of leaders are characterized by an overriding irony: They have everything they could need to facilitate their performance—the legitimacy to craft team purposes as they please, ample information and resources at their command, talented members who have track records of leadership success, and more. Yet these teams, as we will show, generally perform *less* well than many far-more-constrained teams in their own organizations. Drawing both on the scholarly literature and our own research findings, we analyze four specific ironic features that lie at the root of leadership teams' difficulties. We then identify a number of strategies that can help leadership teams circumvent—or even transcend—these pervasive ironies. We conclude by drawing out the implications of our analysis for how leadership teams themselves can most effectively be led—implications that suggest a final irony that must be dealt with by those who are charged with leading teams of leaders.

We begin by defining what leadership teams are, and then briefly describing the two empirical studies that we draw upon most extensively in our analyses.

Leadership Teams

A leadership team is a group of individuals, each of whom has personal responsibility for leading some part of an organization, who are interdependent for the purpose of providing overall leadership to a larger enterprise. The most commonly written-about kind of leadership team is the one at the top—the top management team. Typically composed of the CEO and his or her direct reports, each member of a top management team has a separate, individual leadership responsibility. In a global for-profit company, for example, that responsibility might be for a geographic region, or for a set of major customers, or for a particular function. But members of such teams also have *collective* responsibility for aligning the various parts of the organization into a coherent whole and fostering its overall effectiveness.

There is a long research tradition examining the influence of top management teams on organizational performance (e.g., Barnard, 1938; Gupta and Govindarajan, 1984; Hambrick and Mason, 1984;

Smith, Smith, Olian, and Sims, 1994; Szilagyi and Schweiger, 1984). Established by Hambrick and Mason (1984), this research stream has focused mainly on the effects of the demographic characteristics of senior team members on organization-level outcomes, on the assumption that a firm's strategic choices are influenced by the backgrounds and preferences of its top managers. Although not focused on teams per se—upper echelons of organizations often are not bounded entities, but rather loose collections of titled individuals at the top—this line of research nonetheless has provided compelling insights about the impact of the senior leaders' characteristics, individually and collectively, on their firms' strategic choices and subsequent organizational performance.

Other research on top management teams has focused more directly on the typical patterns of behavior, both functional and dysfunctional, that occur in such teams (e.g., Ancona and Nadler, 1989; Berg, 2005; Edmondson, Roberto, and Watkins, 2001). Although we draw heavily on findings from previous research on top management teams in this paper, we also extend our analyses to address the challenges faced by leadership teams more generally, not just those at the very top of organizations. In fact, teams of leaders are found throughout most large organizations. For example, one of us recently studied leadership teams in a grassroots environmental organization (described in more detail below). Each member of those leadership teams had personal responsibility for engaging volunteer members in conservation activities and for executing specific roles (e.g., chair of the energy committee, treasurer). But members also *shared* responsibility, as a team, for setting overall direction and for allocating resources across organizational groups and functions. We intend our analyses to be applicable to teams such as that one—indeed, to *any* team whose members all are leaders and who must work together to accomplish the collective leadership of an enterprise.

Two Studies of Leadership Teams
The two recent empirical studies that provide much of the data on which we draw in exploring the dynamics and performance of leadership teams are briefly described below.

Top Management Teams
Our first data source is a study of influences on the effectiveness of 120 top management teams of businesses around the world, all of which

headed entire organizations or major business units (Wageman, Nunes, Burruss, and Hackman, 2008). The focal teams led entities ranging from small, focused organizations to large, multinational conglomerates. Our sample represented a variety of industries, from financial services to retail, natural resources, and consumer goods, as well as some not-for-profit and public sector leadership teams. Teams chose to become part of the research sample for a variety of reasons. Some were led by CEOs who explicitly sought help with ineffective leadership teams; others had undertaken strategic and structural changes to their organizations and sought advice about the implications of those changes for how their leadership teams operated. Some were poor performers, whereas others were fundamentally sound. We assessed the overall effectiveness of every team in providing effective leadership to its enterprise, drawing on the analysis of sixteen expert observers who used an array of archival, survey, and observational data to rate each team on Hackman's (2002) three criteria of effectiveness: (1) how well the team serves its main constituencies, (2) the degree to which the team shows signs of becoming more capable over time, and (3) the degree to which the net impact of the team is more positive than negative on the well-being and development of individual members.

We also assessed the purpose, structure, and leadership of each team to identify those features that most powerfully differentiated superb from struggling leadership teams. Members of all teams completed the Team Diagnostic Survey (TDS) (Wageman, Hackman, and Lehman, 2004). The TDS captures, through a series of descriptive items, a team's main design features, the quality of its work processes, the behavior of team leaders, and the quality of members' relationships.

ACTIVIST LEADERSHIP TEAMS

We also drew on a longitudinal study of leadership teams in a U.S. civic association whose purpose is to mobilize volunteers to protect the natural environment (Ganz and Wageman, 2008). Civic associations have volunteer members, they are governed by elected leaders, and they pursue a public voice as a core organizational outcome. The volunteer leaders in civic associations fulfill essential functions by mobilizing others both to devise and to implement organizational strategies. Leadership tasks include motivating people to work together, dealing strategically with a range of external threats and opportunities, and adapting to the novel and challenging circumstances that accompany the work of advocacy. The leadership of civic teams is challenging, in part because organizational objectives typically are less clear than those of for-profit firms and in part because leaders must do their work without having as much formal authority to require compliance as is available to leaders in other kinds of organizations (Campbell, 2005; Day, 2001; Morris and Staggenborg, 2004).

The unit of analysis for this research was local group or state chapter leadership teams, which in each case was an elected executive committee (ExCom). Chapters and groups engage in local fundraising to support their activities and projects, and chapter leaders decide how to allocate collective resources to their local groups. Our findings about leadership team dynamics were obtained in a longitudinal action research project on leadership development that involved four chapter ExComs and twenty-four local group ExComs. The overall objective of this Leadership Development Project (LDP) was to enhance the structures, skills, and practices of state and local leaders while simultaneously generating research data about what it takes to foster individual and collective leadership competencies.

Our approach to leadership development included structuring interdependent leadership teams, building the relationships necessary to sustain those teams, grounding the teams in shared values, and working with the teams to develop creative organizational strategies that would orient and engage volunteers in advocacy work. In the course of the project, both individual-level and group-level data were collected, including survey assessments of individual motivation for participation in the LDP and in the activist organization, self-evaluations of leadership skills, assessments of the leadership skills of their peers in the team, and analysis of goals set and accomplished by individuals and teams in the course of the project. Members of each participating ExCom also completed the TDS at the beginning of the project, allowing direct comparisons between these activist teams and other types of leadership teams we have studied on their design, leadership, and social dynamics.

Four Ironic Features of Leadership Teams

Our analyses of teams composed of leaders, both in these two research streams and as described in the existing scholarly literature, identified four ironic features that undermine their effectiveness. We describe these ironies below, with special emphasis on their implications for what is needed to transcend them in collectively fulfilling key organizational leadership functions.

Irony I: Leader teams are composed of powerful people—yet they tend to be underdesigned, underled, and underresourced

The basic designs of the leadership teams we studied—both in the international sample of top management teams and in the activist organization—were remarkably poor. Table 17-1 shows the mean scores of the activist teams and the top management teams on overall quality of direction, structure, contextual supports, and coaching as measured by the TDS. Leadership teams, as compared with other kinds of task-performing teams we have studied, are especially likely to have unclear purposes, to work on poorly designed tasks, to suffer from a lack of information and material resources, and to receive insufficient hands-on coaching that could help with their work processes. These findings are not what one would expect, since such teams have unusually high levels of authority to shape their own working contexts.

In Hackman's (2002) terms, these leadership teams are typically *self-governing* teams: they have the authority not just to manage and execute their own work, but also to design their tasks, to alter team composition, to define their purposes, and to commandeer the resources needed to accomplish those purposes. Leadership teams can directly influence their own team designs, whereas teams that perform frontline organizational work often have to exercise deft and persistent upward or outward influence to improve how they are set up and supported.

Top management teams, for example, can simply lay claim to the space, time, information, and material resources that they need to accomplish their work. Yet Ancona and Nadler (1989), consistent with our own observations, note that top management teams generally are "underdesigned" relative to other teams in their organizations. The activist teams similarly can define for themselves precisely which threat to the health of the natural environment will become their core strategic focus. These leadership teams can create a shared purpose that is clear and personally compelling to every individual on the team. Yet, perversely, they show *less* compelling purposes overall than do other kinds of teams that we have studied.

What are the consequences of such poor designs on the functioning of leadership teams? In identifying the most critical functions served by

TABLE 17-1

Quality of design of leadership teams

Type of power	Activist executive committees	Senior teams	Nonleadership teams[a]
Real team	3.75	4.11	4.10
Bounded	3.91	4.51	4.50
Interdependent	3.64	4.02	4.09
Stable	3.71	3.80	3.91
Compelling direction	3.48	3.99	3.84
Clarity	3.28	3.64	3.99
Challenge	3.23	3.83	3.99
Consequentiality	3.95	4.50	4.45
Enabling structure	3.63	3.67	3.78
Team composition	3.47	3.83	3.70
Task design	3.89	3.82	4.00
Group norms	3.49	3.36	3.65
Supportive context	3.11	3.41	3.32
Rewards/ recognition	3.38	3.73	3.53
Information	3.13	3.43	3.25
Education	3.03	3.48	3.43
Resources	2.88	3.02	3.08
Coaching availability	2.98	3.06	3.18

Note: All scales have a minimum of 1 (poor quality) and a maximum of 5 (high quality).
a. Taken from a sample of task-performing teams that also completed the Team Diagnostic Survey in ongoing online data collection.

members of teams, we draw on the model of team performance pro-posed by Hackman and Morris (1975; see also Hackman and Wageman, 2004). Specifically, we posit that team effectiveness is a joint function of three performance processes: (1) the level of *effort* group members col-lectively expend carrying out task work, (2) the appropriateness to the task of the *performance strategies* the group uses in its work, and (3) the amount of *knowledge and skill* members bring to bear on the task. Any team that expends sufficient effort in its work, deploys a task-appropriate performance strategy, and brings ample talent to bear on the work is quite likely to achieve a high standing on the three criteria of work team effectiveness specified earlier. By the same token, teams that operate in ways that leave one or more of these functions unfulfilled—that is, if members expend insufficient effort, use inappropriate strategies, and/or apply inadequate talent in their work—are likely to fall short on one or more of the effectiveness criteria.

Associated with each of the three performance processes is both a characteristic "process loss" (Steiner, 1972) and an opportunity for positive synergy, which we refer to as a "process gain." That is, members may interact in ways that depress the team's effort, the appropriateness of its strategy, and/or the utilization of member talent; alternatively, their interaction may enhance collective effort, generate uniquely appropriate strategies, and/or actively develop members' knowledge and skills.

Our own research and that of other scholars suggests that many leadership teams typically suffer process losses on all three key functions—and show few or no signs of process gains. As is seen in table 17-2, the survey scores of the activist leadership teams and the top management teams show that both have problems in managing their performance processes. Although leadership team members often show intense effort in their *individual* leadership roles, for example, they often are detached, distracted, or not in attendance at leadership *team*

TABLE 17-2

Quality of performance processes

	Activist executive committees	Senior teams	Nonleadership teams
Process criteria	3.65	3.58	4.03
Effort	3.67	3.87	4.05
Strategy	3.52	3.44	4.10
Knowledge and skill	3.82	3.43	3.93

Note: All scales have a minimum of 1 (poor quality) and a maximum of 5 (high quality).

meetings. The work strategies of leadership teams are plagued with mindless routines; as will be seen, these teams habitually disaggregate team tasks into individual activities that members conduct mostly on their own. Finally, leadership teams show few signs of mutual teaching and learning. Instead, they typically rely on individuals providing their expertise in one arena only, and they place heavy emphasis on status in the team as a determinant of whose voice wins the day.

As a consequence, the collective decisions and actions of leadership teams can be ill-chosen, misaligned in execution, or entirely unimplemented. An example from one top management team illustrates how a good team decision can go bad. The CEO of a consumer goods firm asked his team to jointly manage the leadership succession pipeline for the whole firm, rather than division by division. At a meeting, members agreed that corporate human resources would have a hand in the assessment of anyone being considered for one of the leadership jobs identified in the succession plan. One high-status regional business head, however, deliberately complied with the letter of the team's agreement but violated its spirit. When he had a position to fill in his business, he deliberately called corporate human resources only a couple of days before a candidate was scheduled for a final interview. Because his business was headquartered a plane ride away, it was difficult (and on at least two occasions, impossible) for the human resources manager to arrive in time to play a role in the hiring.

Without good design, leadership teams flounder. Why do leadership teams so often fail to use their significant control over resources, and their authority to define team purposes and structure their work, to foster their own effectiveness? One explanation stems from the fact that leadership teams invariably have stewardship responsibilities (Berg, 2005; Jensen and Murphy, 1990). It may be that leadership teams underresource themselves in part because they view their responsibility as guarding resources and providing them to others when a real need can be demonstrated. As highly visible models for other organization members, there is significant pressure on leadership teams not to appear unduly generous to themselves.

Moreover, defining a compelling *team* purpose for leadership teams is an extraordinary conceptual challenge (Wageman, Nunes, Burruss, and Hackman, 2008, chap. 3). Articulating just what a team composed of leaders shares responsibility for, and doing so in a way that is clear, tangible, and motivating, poses special problems for such teams. Although individual responsibilities generally are quite clear, how a collection of leaders together can provide something more than the sum of individuals' responsibilities is difficult for many leaders to articulate. Our data show that many chief executives either leave team purposes unspecified or loosely define them, as, for example, "providing the leadership to accomplish our strategy." This lack of clarity about what the team does together—what leadership functions they fulfill collaboratively rather than individually—impairs the ability of leadership teams to orient themselves and to engage with each other on key organizational issues.

Leadership teams are no less in need of clarity than any other kind of team. Indeed, they may be *more* in need of explicit attention to creating helpful structures than other teams. As Edmondson, Roberto, and Watkins (2001) point out, leadership teams tend to face highly unstructured task streams: continuously changing flows of overlapping problem-solving and decision-making situations. Moreover, teams of leaders have a greater need to deal with unpredictable events in the external environment than do other teams (Berg, 2005; Ancona and Nadler, 1989). The very amorphousness of the work makes the team purposes difficult to specify—but clear purpose, ironically, is one of the most critical ingredients for effective leadership team functioning.

Irony II: Membership is important and coveted—but members often don't know who is on the team, and they do not really want to come to team meetings

Leaders value their membership in leadership teams. Evidence that individual leaders covet membership pervades both our own observations of senior teams and the research literature on their dynamics. In the activist organization, for example, leaders put themselves up for election and volunteered the additional personal time that the demands of the leadership team placed upon them. Business leaders are just as eager to be designated as top team members.

Individuals seek membership on leadership teams for a range of reasons, but most common is the power and status that membership brings (Finkelstein, 1992; Ocasio, 1994). The status of membership often is underlined by the very names of such teams (e.g., the "Executive Committee," the "President's Cabinet"). Moreover, being on a leadership team brings direct access to the leadership team's leader, who invariably has substantially greater power than any other member. Finally, membership is desired because, as a body, such teams have control over resources that can be highly consequential for each member's individual leadership responsibilities.

Ironically, the boundaries of these select teams are unusually porous and blurred. Indeed, members often don't even know that they *don't* know who is on the team. According to their scores on the Team Diagnostic Survey, members have great confidence in their knowledge of leadership team membership. The survey measure of team boundedness included items such as "Team membership is quite clear—everybody knows exactly who is and is not on this team." Members of both the senior leaders and the activists scored in the upper regions of the 5-point boundedness scale ($M = 4.51$ and $M = 3.91$, respectively). But we also asked individual members to report the *number of members* in the team, and these data tell a different story. Of the 120 top management teams we studied, only 11 (9 percent) were in agreement about the number of team members. Of the 25 activist teams, only 10 were in agreement. Moreover, reports of team size were independent of organization size and often high in the double digits, in many cases much larger than the size reported by the chief executive who had formed the team.

Why are leadership teams underbounded and overlarge? One answer to this question has to do with how such teams are composed. Members often are included in leadership teams not because of their capacity to contribute to a *team* task but because they hold particular leadership roles in the organization—roles that bear little relationship to what it takes to perform a team task well. Typically, top management team members are all the direct reports of a CEO and/or are the leaders of major organizational units. In the case of the activists, the individuals are elected by the general membership to fill out a roster of particular roles (e.g., chapter chair, political committee chair, and the like). By contrast, selection to other kinds of task-performing teams more typically begins with an assessment of the team task and the number, skills, and capabilities needed of members to accomplish the work.

We found that leaders of leadership teams were extremely reluctant to alter or to clarify just who is—and who is not—on the team, and when they err, it is on the side of inclusiveness. While that fact may not be surprising for the activist teams—they are, after all, members of a democratic institution with powerful core values about citizen participation and equality—we saw similar tendencies in top management teams as well. Many chief executive officers in our study, for example, assumed that they must have someone from every part of the organization present at the table in order to have adequate information and representation of the whole enterprise.

Moreover, both the activist teams and the top management teams often had "guests" at team meetings, people invited to comment on a specific issue or decision facing the organization. The activists might, for example, invite a member of the broader conservation organization to share her knowledge of mining. Or a top management team might have multiple advisors from the financial function present to provide analysis of a potential acquisition. Sometimes these visitors return for repeat performances—and return again, and again, along with still more guests, gradually both expanding and blurring team boundaries. In one national security organization, for example, crucial policy and operational decisions were made by a very small and high-powered executive team whose name was the time it met every day: "The five o'clock meeting." Over time, attendance at that meeting became so large that the senior executive began to use other, more informal groups for consultation about the most critical decisions.

The high desirability of membership also contributes to the blurring of leadership team boundaries. Leaders of such teams recognize that dis-inviting a member can result in a loss of face for that person, and may engender motivation losses, underground hostilities, or even departure from the organization altogether. The leaders of activist teams, whose purposes often included engaging new volunteers in conservation activities, felt especially irresponsible if they took actions that risked losing from the organization any active participant in the collective work.

The consequences of underbounded and overlarge membership for the work of leadership teams are powerfully negative (Alderfer, 1980; Mortensen, 2008). The more people at the table representing different interests or functions, the harder it can be to define a shared purpose for the team. Leaders of large teams—those with more than a dozen members, for example—struggle hopelessly with questions such as: For what are these individuals interdependent? What work can all of them do together that represents a meaningful leadership function for the organization?

There are four possible answers, not mutually exclusive, to these questions. Figure 17-1 shows four kinds of leadership teams, in increasing order of interdependence from bottom to top. Least interdependent are *information-sharing*, or alignment, teams. These teams exchange information about various organizational matters and bring together in one place external intelligence that may be useful to other parts of the organization or to the enterprise as a whole. They also hear about direction and initiatives from the team leader, which helps make the individual leaders on the team better informed, better aligned, and more able to do their individual jobs well.

The purpose of a *consultative* team is to make the team leader better informed and better able to make his or her own decisions. In contrast to informational teams, consultative teams actively debate key issues, giving members the chance to learn from one another—but the final call is made by the team leader.

Coordinating teams are those whose members come together to coordinate their leadership activities as they execute strategically important initiatives. For example, a top management team at an airline might meet to work through the launch of service to a new country. A successful launch would require coordination across facilities, logistics, marketing, sales, partners, and government affairs—entities that usually operate relatively independently. Members of coordinating teams are highly interdependent, have shared responsibilities, and must work together frequently and flexibly to accomplish their shared purposes. Coordinating teams also serve information-sharing and consultative functions.

Finally, as their name implies, *decision-making* teams make the small number of critical decisions that are most consequential for the enter-

FIGURE 17-1

Four kinds of leadership teams

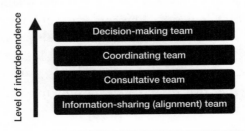

prise as a whole. Although we have seen many leadership teams that are merely information-sharing teams, we have not observed teams that are *only* decision-making bodies. Decision-making teams tend to act at different times as any one of the four types of teams. A decision-making team also tends to serve as the coordinator of core initiatives, as an advisory group for the leader's decisions, and as a vital source of information exchange and learning for the top leaders of the organization (Wageman, Nunes, Burruss, and Hackman, 2008, chap. 2).

In an underbounded and overlarge group, the question "For what is this group of people interdependent?" becomes nearly impossible to define except in highly abstract terms such as "organizational effectiveness." As a consequence, the work of the team typically devolves into mere information sharing among individual members. Each leader presents updates and data about the progress in his or her own individual leadership activities—how things are going in the South Asia region, how the campaign against development near our local wetland is proceeding. Little of what any one member presents is vital or even relevant to any other leader's responsibilities. And nothing is accomplished, debated, or decided *together*.

Thus the least interdependent—and least vital—form of leadership team becomes the most common of all. It may be that this state of affairs contributes substantially to the pessimism of some writers about whether leadership teams ever can function as real interdependent teams at all (Hambrick, 2000; Katzenbach, 1997a).

Irony III: Members are overloaded—but they tend to waste enormous amounts of time in team meetings

Members of leadership teams typically have significant responsibilities as individuals for fulfilling leadership functions in their own parts of the organization. In both settings we studied, many of these leaders were even at serious risk of burnout. The potential to *share* leadership functions with peers and colleagues—thereby reducing the cognitive, emotional, and effort-related strains on individual leaders—is among the compelling reasons to create leadership teams in the first place. Indeed, Andrews et al. (2007) found that civic associations whose leaders worked as interdependent teams were better at strategizing and better able to engage others and to sustain their own energy in accomplishing shared purposes.

The reality, however, is that rather than sharing the burdens of leadership, leadership teams often spend much of their meeting time in wheel-spinning activities. We already have described the tendency to devolve into mere information sharing. But even when leadership teams attempt to engage in shared decision making, they typically waste inordinate amounts of time—thereby making membership on the team an additional burden rather than a source of help and support in fulfilling members' leadership roles.

Leadership teams waste time in three ways. First, they focus on surprisingly trivial matters. They do make decisions together—but often about issues that are not consequential for the team's core leadership work. Survey scores for both the activist teams and the top management teams illustrate. The averages for the meaningfulness of the leadership teams' tasks were $M = 3.89$ and $M = 3.82$, respectively, well below ideal. It is not uncommon for leadership team discussions to focus for surprisingly long periods on issues such as where to have the holiday party or what kind of food to order—hardly vital leadership functions for the constituencies the team serves.

Second, when they do address important matters, leadership teams tend to become caught up in seemingly irresolvable conflicts. Indeed, the potential for unpleasant conflict may be one reason members wind up spending their time on more trivial matters that are unlikely to become fraught with negative emotion. Conflicts in senior teams often stem from members' views that their main responsibilities are to maximize the effectiveness of the unit they lead (Ancona and Nadler, 1989; Berg, 2005). There is a real risk that making decisions together that maximize *overall* organizational effectiveness will result in outcomes that are inconvenient, costly, or demoralizing to the units headed by certain team members. This understandable concern is reinforced by tangible and intangible rewards of the leadership roles that typically are more closely tied to accomplishments attributable to them as individual leaders than to the performance of the leadership team as a *team* (Siegel and Hambrick, 2005).

Moreover, leaders' legitimate roles as representatives of their particular divisions or functions can elicit negative attributions about other team members' motives (Berg, 2005). Members interpret the meaning of each others' statements in a decision-making process as primarily representing the interests of the group they represent. Thus, leadership team dynamics tend to embody and express the intergroup relationships—positive and negative—that pervade the larger organization, especially when those relationships are structurally competitive (e.g., for investments, for talented people, for recognition, and for career opportunities). Finally, the most compelling personal motives of leadership team members generally are more about being individual leaders than about being team members. Together, personal motives, role definitions, and rewards for leadership create a natural tendency for the dynamics of decision-making teams to shift from trying to make the best collective decision possible for the organization to trying to win decision contests with other team members (Lewicki, Saunders, Minton, and Barry, 2000).

As one coping strategy, leadership teams often cut short potentially vital discussions by agreeing to disagree and then moving on. Consistent with their personal preferences, they redefine shared tasks in ways that rely more on individual accomplishment than on collective action. The assumption is that disaggregated tasks and competent individual actions ultimately will add up to a good outcome for the whole enterprise. In the case of the activists, we saw repeatedly that the consequence was dissipated power and thinly spread resources (many things done poorly versus a few things done superbly). For the top management teams, the consequence was a focus on maximizing the performance of leaders' constituent units, even if that meant that enterprise outcomes would be compromised.

Irony IV: Authority dynamics pervade leadership teams and complicate team processes—but members won't talk about them

Leadership teams have all the authority they possibly could need. As noted previously, they are self-governing teams whose members have full authority to chart their own course and to shape their own structure and context. Also as noted, however, such teams ironically underuse that authority, sufficing with suboptimal arrangements that, in many cases, members would not tolerate in their own frontline production or service teams. Part of the reason why many leadership teams do not fully exercise their collective authority is that authority dynamics *within* the team compromise members' ability to take concerted collective action.

Especially challenging to leadership teams are authority dynamics that involve the relationship between the team leader and team members. Members of senior teams, even though each is an organizational leader in his or her own right, tend not to exercise leadership within the team, instead viewing the leadership group as "the boss's team" and therefore the boss's responsibility. Indeed, Ancona and Nadler (1989) report a greater power distance between the leader and members of leadership teams than exists in regular work teams in organizations and a concomitant tendency toward passivity and obedience. Our own research affirms that finding. In one top management team we studied, a newly appointed CEO experienced that power distance for the first time in a dramatic way. Consistent with her practice before she was elevated to the top job, she stood in a hallway "brainstorming" with several of her former peers about needed organizational changes. To her chagrin, she discovered some days later that her colleagues—now her direct reports—had taken her remarks as orders and had already begun to implement them.

It is not lost on team members that personally important outcomes, such as remuneration and career opportunities, are likely to be affected by how a chief executive assesses their behavior in the team and their contributions to its work. That reality can result in subtle jockeying for position and other diversionary activities among members who are supposed to be working *together* to provide leadership of the larger enterprise.

The *leader* of a leadership team, by contrast, generally recognizes that he or she is the one who must establish the team's main purposes and guide members in working together to achieve them. The CEOs we studied did not hesitate to step up to that responsibility; the leaders of the more egalitarian activist teams, however, were more reluctant to specify team purposes and, instead, tended to form committees to generate them or consult extensively about them.

But in both settings, many leaders found it difficult to give the team enough latitude to determine *how* those purposes were to be pursued. Instead, these leaders specified the details of execution, thereby reinforcing members' views that their responsibilities in the team were mainly to do what they were told to do. One member of an activist leadership team in the Southwest, for example, was continually silent during a team planning session about how to energize local members to help stop abusive wildlife control practices in the desert. When asked about his silence, his response reflected the authority dynamics of that team: "This is her [the team leader's] thing. I'll just do what she tells me to."

Some leadership team leaders we studied both articulated a challenging purpose *and* clearly signaled to members that it was their collective responsibility to figure out how to get it achieved. The mistake for these leaders was that they often concluded that their own work was done, that the team would take it from there. When members subsequently failed to work together competently and energetically to achieve team purposes, these leaders eventually lost patience and, in effect, retook control of the process. That is what happened in one activist organization ExCom in the Northwest that was dedicated to preserving local waterways. The chair turned over the design, planning, and execution of a major fundraising event to her team. When she discovered a week later that team members had not yet secured a venue, she created her own plan and began issuing directives to the other team members on all aspects of the event—thereby unintentionally reinforcing members' views that they need not feel personally or collectively responsible for the team's leadership work.

Dynamics of the kind just described are not a caricature, nor are they uncommon. They are documented by the scholars we have cited as well as in our own research. What they show is the power of the *authority dynamics* that pervade leadership teams to shape member attitudes, to complicate team processes, and, not infrequently, to compromise leadership team performance.

Authority dynamics are so powerful that they, more than the demands of the team's actual leadership work, can come to dominate behavior in leadership teams. Members can become quite skilled at keeping behavior in the group smooth and seemingly under control, even when that requires the suppression of strong emotional reactions to what is going on. It is as if a matter does not exist, or at least does not need to be dealt with openly, if it can be kept off the team table. The result is a veneer of courteous and orderly behavior that covers over thoughts and feelings that members are unwilling to personally "own," let alone explore or learn from (Argyris, 1993). When we pressed the activist leader who had remained silent through his team's planning session about why he had not expressed his belief that the leadership team was being harmed by the ExCom chair's dominance, he laughed and said "Why start a fight?"

Sometimes members know what is going on and, like the silent activist, can describe it quite accurately if queried in a private, off-line setting. But other times, authority dynamics operate below the conscious level, as was shown by Wilfred Bion (1961) in his classic analyses of unconscious influences on group life. Bion distinguishes between the *work group*, which is what the group is doing on its manifest task, and the *basic assumption group*, the nonconscious processes that operate in parallel with the work group but are unrecognized by members. Bion identifies three types of basic assumption groups: dependency groups, fight-flight groups, and pairing groups. In each case, the group is operating *as if* its real purpose were to take care of the members (dependency), and/or to engage in battle (fight-flight), and/or to give birth to a new and better world (pairing).

When dependency dynamics are operating, the group implicitly assumes that the leader will take care of everything—and then tries to depose the leader when it becomes clear, as it always will, that he or she is unable to meet their expectations. The obedience/passivity pattern we described above is consistent with Bion's dependency dynamics. When fight-flight dynamics are operating, by contrast, the group implicitly assumes that it is under attack and that it must either fight back or flee. According to Bion, fight-flight can generate excessive conformity and tests of the loyalty of members, who feel they must stick together or be defeated. Finally, when pairing dynamics are operating, the group implicitly assumes that whatever difficulty the group is having can be resolved by sending off two of its members to find a solution—a solution which, if offered at all by the deputized pair, invariably is found wanting.

We are not psychoanalytically inclined, nor do we find in the research literature empirical studies to confirm the specific predictions made by Bion or by others in his intellectual tradition. But our own research has convinced us that authority dynamics in leadership teams do spawn powerful forces of which members are unaware and therefore unable to correct. As much as members may want to fix what ails their team, they cannot correct something they cannot see.

Even group dynamics problems that *are* visible to members can defy resolution, for two reasons. First, as noted above, the norms of leadership teams generally discourage open discussion of precisely those matters that are most problematic to the team and its members (Argyris, 1969; Berg, 2005). Members are disinclined to express their own emotions or to encourage others to do so, especially when the substantive issue at hand also has significant emotional content. And they are even more reluctant to experiment with alternative, unfamiliar, and risky ways of gaining purchase on the team's most difficult problems.

Second, members of leadership teams generally do not have in their repertoires the full complement of skills that would be required to deal competently with issues of power and authority even if they were personally disposed to do so, and even if group norms actively supported their doing so. Members usually are selected for membership on leadership teams because of their technical or functional prowess, coupled with a track record of superb accomplishment as an *individual* leader. They may never have had the opportunity to hone through experience their skills in dealing with thorny, authority-driven group process problems.

So what is the leader of a team of leaders to do? What can be done to minimize the degree to which the dynamics described above will undermine the effectiveness even of teams whose members are strongly committed to providing competent organizational leadership? A tempting answer to that question is that the leader should use his or her authority to put on the team's table even those items—indeed, *especially* those items—that members would rather not deal with, and then help the team work through the ones that are most critical to leadership team performance. But the leaders of leadership teams often achieved their positions in the same way as did team members—namely, through extraordinary individual leadership accomplishment. One cannot count on the leader being ready to provide the kind or level of leadership that is required to deal with thorny authority dynamics that members collude to keep off the table.

An alternative strategy is to create a team design and organizational supports that (1) lessen the pervasiveness and perniciousness of the dynamics we have explored here, and (2) increase the likelihood that those difficulties that *do* arise are amenable to resolution by people who are not necessarily skilled or experienced in dealing with team processes. This, then, is one of the key functions that can be fulfilled by the leader of a team of leaders—creating and maintaining those conditions that make it feasible for leadership team members to notice, deal with, and learn from the authority dynamics that so often compromise the effectiveness of such teams.

Leading Teams of Leaders

Leadership teams have a constellation of characteristics that makes them especially difficult to lead. For all members of such teams, the team role is the second—and lower-priority—job. Typically ill-composed, these teams suffer from amorphous purposes that result in a default task strategy of mere information sharing. Interpersonal dynamics within the team often reflect the tendency of members to seek greater status and recognition, as well as to personally lead rather than to share leadership. These motives, moreover, are reinforced by reward systems that measure and celebrate individual leadership accomplishments. Every element of this constellation is malleable, from purpose to performance measures. But each requires explicit action to shape them.

We address below the five key functions that must be fulfilled to help leadership teams operate well—that is, to serve the organization better, to become a better-operating team in which real learning takes place, and to contribute to the growth and well-being of individual leaders.

1. Creating a bounded entity that is defined by a clear, shared purpose

This first leadership function is basic to any kind of task-performing team. But it has special relevance—and special challenges—for the leaders of leadership teams. First and foremost, it implies that not all individual leaders placed in important leadership roles need be part of the leadership team. A real leadership team with a clear purpose arises when someone defines a circumscribed set of leadership functions to be fulfilled collaboratively, and chooses specific team members whose capabilities will contribute to those purposes.

Fulfilling this function requires first conceptualizing what a leadership team can do *as a team* to provide essential leadership to the larger entity. That kind of cognitive work requires creative conceptualization, something that comes best from an individual rather than from a team. In both research settings we studied, we observed that teams whose leaders—CEOs in one setting, ExCom chairs in the other—attended explicitly to defining their teams' overall purposes made better collective decisions and exhibited higher-quality work processes than did teams whose leaders took a more laissez-faire stance toward team purposes. Fulfilling this first function also requires leadership team leaders to make thoughtful choices about team composition and about ways to keep membership boundaries clear. Defining who is—and who is not—a member of a leadership team is a matter that can pose significant emotional and interpersonal challenges even for experienced leaders.

2. Crafting an agenda so that the work of the team is always focused on meaningful, interdependent activities

Leading a team of leaders requires that someone pay careful attention to the tasks members do in their work together, to prevent an unintended downward slide to mere information sharing or diversions into long discussions about trivial matters. Edmondson, Roberto, and Watkins (2001) point out that there is no single or fixed task list for leadership teams, given the shifting nature of work they perform. What is required, these authors emphasize, is continuous attention by the leader to task demands and team process needs as they evolve over time.

Our observations in both settings confirm that having the CEO or the ExCom chair create a short list of key decisions or activities to address with the team when it convened was significantly related to the level of effort exhibited by team members and to the appropriateness of team performance strategies. Absent explicit attention by the leader, the team as a whole typically generated a long list of small items, each of which was relevant mainly for only one or two leaders at the table—which yielded predictable negative consequences for member attention and effort. Keeping the work both meaningful and interdependent requires selecting team tasks carefully each time the team convenes. It is a function fulfilled repeatedly rather than once in the team's lifetime.

3. Shaping members' construals of their roles

The work of leadership for members of a leadership team involves making collective decisions on behalf of the enterprise as a whole, while simultaneously acting on behalf of their individual constituents. Members of leadership teams do tend to understand their individual leadership roles—but that understanding does not include overall leadership of an enterprise. Construing the leadership job as taking care of one's individual part of the enterprise almost always causes an overfocus on maximizing local performance at the expense of the whole entity.

As Berg (2005) notes, one job of a CEO is to keep senior leaders focused on *both* overall organizational effectiveness and on their individual responsibilities. Our observations are consistent with Berg's analysis. We have observed some top management teams in which the CEO described first to new team members their expectations about the person's role as a member of the leadership team. Only after that aspect of the role was well understood did the CEO discuss expectations about the person's role as the leader of an individual unit or function. Similarly, as the ExComs in the activist organization honed the design of their teams, they emphasized to new members that they had been elected not to a specific post but to a leadership *team*.

In both cases, individual responsibilities were construed as an important part, but only a part, of the overall leadership job. The whole job was about providing leadership for the whole enterprise—both as an individual leader and as a member of the leadership team. Members who perceive their roles in this fashion are considerably more likely in decision-making processes to develop shared criteria for decisions that maximize collective outcomes, and they are more willing to make choices that trade off local for enterprise-wide benefits (Ganz and Wageman, 2008).

4. Articulating explicit norms that promote attention to team strategies and that minimize political dynamics

Well-designed teams develop norms of attentiveness to changes in environmental demands, and thereby craft and execute task performance strategies that are fully appropriate to their task and situation, rather than fall mindlessly into the execution of habitual routines (Gersick and Hackman, 1990; Wageman, 1995, 2001). Such norms are most likely to emerge when the tasks are meaningful and when team purposes are clear (Wageman, 2001). But leadership teams need additional attention to norms about behavior to help them deal constructively with the political dynamics that, as we have seen, emerge because of members' dual roles.

Berg (2005) makes the paradoxical suggestion that leaders "let people have their groups." He advocates norms of making group memberships and representational concerns *discussable* in the team. In his view, a norm that advocates speaking and acting as if one is only considering the big picture has perverse effects because other team members are likely to assume that a position taken is to promote the interests of the leader's own constituency. By making one's concerns on behalf of one's own group explicit, those concerns become part of what the team can discuss.

Consistent with Berg's position, we saw in our research on top management teams that the outstanding teams were significantly more likely to place individual concerns on the table and to have members who displayed high levels of empathy to each others' concerns. The lesson holds for the activist teams we studied as well. Activist teams that developed explicit norms about shared decision criteria that took into account individual concerns were significantly better able to mobilize the whole group and less likely to dissipate their power in multiple, competing activities (Ganz and Wageman, 2008).

High-quality norms are essential for leadership teams, but we found that they do not develop in the absence of active influence from the team leader. Indeed, in our research on top management teams, we found that healthy norms "take" only in teams in which the leader gave explicit attention to modeling the norms and reinforcing them in the team. Although the most effective teams in our sample did help define their norms and eventually took on the role of maintaining them, it took early action by the team leader to get constructive norms established and accepted.

5. Coaching the team

Leadership teams do not get much coaching from their own leaders. As is seen in figure 17-2, of four possible functions that could command team leaders' attention (external activities, structuring the team, coaching individuals, and coaching the team), team coaching came last. But, as is seen in figure 17-3, teams that scored highest overall on our three criteria of team effectiveness had leaders whose focus was evenly balanced between external matters and attention to the team itself.

Hands-on coaching accounted for significant variance in the effectiveness of top management teams, and a high proportion of our sample indicated that they would benefit from a good deal more of it (Wageman, Nunes, Burruss, and Hackman, 2008). Direct intervention into team processes is especially important for teams of leaders because of the high likelihood of process losses that stem from the inherent challenges posed by such teams' structure and context. For one thing, active management of the team process by the team leader can help the team be explicit about and deal constructively with differences in their individual interests (Edmondson, Roberto, and Watkins, 2001). Moreover, competent coaching can help leadership teams develop shared definitions of the very *facts* that they rely on in their discussions (Berg, 2005). Neither of these behaviors is likely to emerge in the absence of deliberate attention and competent facilitation.

FIGURE 17-2

How leaders apportion their attention[*]

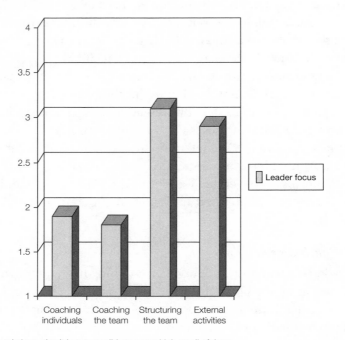

* These scores are *relative* ranks; it is not possible to score high on all of them.

Both the top management teams and the activist teams we studied faced real dilemmas about *who* should provide team coaching. For top management teams, the magnitude of the power distance between CEOs and the rest of the team made coaching attempts by team members extraordinarily risky, and it was viewed as appropriate only when carried out in response to an explicit invitation from the leader. For the activist teams, widely shared norms of equality militated against members claiming the authority to intervene in team processes. In neither case was member coaching impossible, and we did observe it on occasion—but in the main, it was very, very, uncomfortable for all concerned. The transition to shared responsibility for intervening in team processes, we found, occurs most smoothly when team leaders first model good coaching and then explicitly invite other members to join in when they feel they are ready to do so.

FIGURE 17-3

Dual focus of the leaders of outstanding leadership teams*

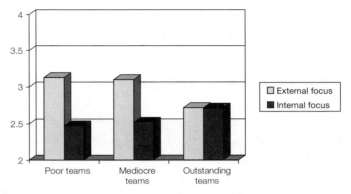

* These scores are *relative* ranks; it is not possible to score high on all of them.

Irony V: Shared leadership may be especially unlikely in teams composed of leaders

Our analysis of the five leadership functions needed to create effective leadership teams suggests our fifth ironic feature of leadership teams. Since all five functions are conditions that are best initiated by a powerful individual—specifically, the leader of the leadership team—shared leadership is especially *un*likely to emerge spontaneously in teams that are composed of people who themselves have extensive experience and expertise as leaders. The combination of authority dynamics, the need for attention to the key elements of high-quality team design, and the inherent challenge in defining a purpose for a leadership team may place such teams especially in need of a single authority, at least early in its life, to fulfill critical leadership functions and to establish the conditions that foster team effectiveness.

Conclusion: The Competencies of the Executive

We close by identifying two essential competencies—one cognitive, one behavioral—that are implied by a functional perspective on leadership teams. These are by no means the only capabilities that can help. Indeed, in our book on top management teams we devote an entire chapter to the competencies that contribute to the competent leadership of senior management teams (Wageman, Nunes, Burruss, and Hackman, 2008, chap. 8). The two competencies we choose to address here are prompted by the analyses we have offered in this paper, which we believe may be especially valuable for the leaders of leadership teams.

Understanding Teams as Social Systems

We have seen that the natural setup of leadership teams, as well as their emergent processes, undermine the accomplishment of key leadership functions. And we have argued that leadership team effectiveness requires identifying the *systemic* conditions that create obstacles to team effectiveness, and then creating design features that can elicit and reinforce effective collaboration in such circumstances. Consistent with these observations, we saw that the best leaders of both top management teams and activist leadership teams were those who were adept both in comprehending the systemic nature of their teams and organizations and in taking actions that respected and took full advantage of systemic forces.

Competent leader interventions require a diagnostic frame of mind, in which one asks "What are the critical functions that are *not* being fulfilled in this system as it presently exists?" That kind of diagnostic question can identify the actions that have the best possible chance of strengthening a leadership team in its particular context. For example, a capable leader of leadership teams must be able to recognize the degree to which unclear purposes or trivial tasks are the root causes of members' seeming disengagement in a leadership team meeting. That recognition allows the leader to take well-aimed action, clarifying purposes or redesigning the team's shared work, as the situation warrants. A diagnostic frame of mind, coupled with an understanding of the main conditions that do elicit and reinforce effective collaboration, defines what we mean by understanding teams as social systems.

The Art of Structuring

The specific conditions that leaders must create to enhance the effectiveness of a particular leadership team vary from context to context. Moreover, the set of actions it will take to get those conditions in place is unpredictable and idiosyncratic. For example, the particular purpose articulated for a team depends on the critical contingencies the enterprise faces at the time the team is convened. How one best articulates that purpose and what themes one chooses to emphasize to energize the team depend on knowledge of the team's history, relationships, and values. The member capabilities that are needed to fulfill those purposes, the specific norms that will adequately support the requisite team processes, the details of how the members should construe their roles in the enterprise—each of these conditions demands attention to the unique circumstances in which the leadership team operates.

Moreover, leadership teams of the kinds we studied face chronic patterns of team dissolution and relaunch. In the case of the activists, team membership is changed with some predictability by the cycle of elections. For top management teams, membership alters as leaders move in and out of the organization. Each time that happens, the leadership team needs to be restructured all over again. There is no recipe or formula for leading a leadership team. As a consequence, effective leaders of leadership teams must have a wide repertoire of ways of enacting these conditions, and of recreating them over time.

The uniqueness of the circumstances leadership teams face over time and the rapid shifts in their composition and leadership suggest that in any given organization, developing leaders' repertoire of structuring skills—and embedding that expertise in the organization, not just in specific individuals—is essential for the long-term effectiveness of leadership teams in any enterprise. Leaders of leadership teams need to develop the art of structuring—and to understand that structuring *is* an art. To get good conditions in place for leadership teams requires leaders to learn to fulfill those functions in whatever way they can, using whatever styles and special capabilities they call their own.

References

Alderfer, C.P. "Consulting to Underbounded Systems." In *Advances in Experiential Social Processes.* Vol. 2, edited by C.P. Alderfer and C.L. Cooper, 267–295. New York: Wiley, 1980.

Ancona, D., and D. Nadler. "Top Hats and Executive Tales: Designing the Senior Team." *Sloan Management Review* (Fall 1989): 19–29.

Andrews, K.T., M. Ganz, M. Baggetta, H. Han, and C. Lim. *Leadership, Membership, and Voice: Civic Associations That Work.* Unpublished manuscript, 2007.

Argyris, C. "The Incompleteness of Social Psychological Theory: Examples from Small Group, Cognitive Consistency, and Attribution Research." *American Psychologist* 24 (1969): 893–908.

———. "Education for Leading-Learning." *Organizational Dynamics* 21, no. 3 (1993): 5–17.

Barnard, C.I. *The Functions of the Executive*. Cambridge, MA: Harvard University Press, 1938.

Bennis, W. (Winter, 1997). "The Secret of Great Groups." *Leader to Leader*, 3.

Berg, D.N. "Senior Executive Teams: Not What You Think." *Consulting Psychology Journal* 57 (2005): 107–117.

Bion, W.R. *Experiences in Groups*. London: Tavistock, 1961.

Campbell, J.L. "Where Do We Stand? Common Mechanisms in Organization and Social Movement Research." In *Social Movements and Organization Theory*, edited by G.F. Davis, D. McAdam, W.R. Scott, and M.N. Zald, 41–68. Cambridge, England: Cambridge University Press, 2005.

Day, D.V. "Leadership Development: A Review in Context." *Leadership Quarterly* 11 (2001): 581–613.

Edmondson, A., M. Roberto, and M. Watkins. "Negotiating Asymmetry: A Model of Top Management Team Effectiveness." Working paper, Harvard Business School, Boston, 2001.

Finkelstein, S. "Power in Top Management Teams: Dimensions, Measurement, and Validation." *Academy of Management Journal* 35 (1992): 505–538.

Ganz, M., and R. Wageman. "Leadership Development in a Civic Organization: Multi-level Influences on Effectiveness." Working paper, Harvard Kennedy School of Government, Cambridge, MA, 2008.

Gersick, C.J.G., and J.R. Hackman. "Habitual Routines in Task-Performing Teams." *Organizational Behavior and Human Decision Processes* 47 (1990): 65–97.

Gupta, A., and V. Govindarajan. "Knowledge Flows Within Multinational Corporations." *Strategic Management Journal* 21 (1984): 473–496.

Hackman, J.R. *Leading Teams: Setting the Stage for Great Performances*. Boston: Harvard Business School Press, 2002.

Hackman, J.R., and C.G. Morris. "Group Tasks, Group Interaction Process, and Group Performance Effectiveness: A Review and Proposed Integration." In *Advances in Experimental Social Psychology*. Vol. 8, edited by L. Berkowitz, 45–99. New York: Academic Press, 1975.

Hackman, J.R., and R. Wageman. "When and How Team Leaders Matter. *Research in Organizational Behavior* 26 (2005): 37–74.

Hackman, J.R., and R.E. Walton. "Leading Groups in Organizations." In *Designing Effective Work Groups*, edited by P.S. Goodman, 72–119. San Francisco: Jossey-Bass, 1986.

Hambrick, D.C. "Fragmentation and Other Problems CEOs Have with Their Top Management Teams." *California Management Review* 37 (1995): 110–131.

———. "Corporate Coherence and the Top Management Team. In *Navigating Change: How CEOs, Top Teams, and Boards Steer Transformation*, edited by D.C. Hambrick, D.A. Nadler, and M.L. Tushman. Boston: Harvard Business School Press, 1998.

Hambrick, D.C., and P.A. Mason. "Upper Echelons: The Organization as a Reflection of Its Top Managers." *Academy of Management Review* 9 (1984): 193–206.

Henderson, A., and J. Fredrickson. "Top Management Team Coordination Needs and the CEO Pay Gap: A Competitive Test of Economic and Behavioral Views." *Academy of Management Journal*, 44 (2001): 96–117.

Jensen, M.C., and K.J. Murphy. "Performance Pay and Top-Management Incentives." *Journal of Political Economy* 98 (1990): 225–264.

Katz, D., and Kahn and R.L. *The Social Psychology of Organizations* (2nd ed.). New York: Wiley, 1978.

Katzenbach, J.R. "The Myth of the Top Management Team." *Harvard Business Review* 75, no. 6 (November–December 1997a): 83–91.

———. *Teams at the Top: Unleashing the Potential of Both Teams and Individual Leaders.* Boston: Harvard Business School Press, 1997b.

Lencioni, P. *The Five Dysfunctions of a Team.* San Francisco: Jossey-Bass, 2002.

Lewicki, R.J., D.M. Saunders, J.W. Minton, and B. Barry. *Negotiation.* New York: McGraw-Hill, 2003.

Li, J.T., and D.C. Hambrick. "Factional Groups: A New Vantage on Demographic Faultlines, Conflict and Disintegration in Work Teams." *Academy of Management Journal* 48 (2005): 794–813.

McGrath, J.E. *Leadership Behavior: Some Requirements for Leadership Training.* Washington, DC: U.S. Civil Service Commission, 1962.

Morris, A.D., and S. Staggenborg. "Leadership in Social Movements." In *The Blackwell Companion to Social Movements*, edited by D.A. Snow, S.A. Soule, and H. Kriesi. Malden, MA: Blackwell, 2004.

Mortensen, M. *Fuzzy Teams: Why Do Teams Disagree on Their Membership, and What Does It Mean?* Unpublished manuscript, 2008.

Ocasio, W. "Political Dynamics and the Circulation of Power: CEO Succession in US Industrial Corporations, 1960–1990." *Administrative Science Quarterly* 39 (1994): 586–611.

Siegel, P.A., and D.C. Hambrick. "Pay Disparities Within Top Management Groups: Evidence of Harmful Effects on Performance of High-Technology Firms." *Organization Science* 16 (2005): 259–274.

Smith, K.G., K.A. Smith, J.D. Olian, and H.P. Sims Jr. "Top Management Team Demography and Process: The Role of Social Integration and Communication." *Administrative Science Quarterly* 39 (1994): 412–438.

Steiner, I.D. *Group Process and Productivity.* New York: Academic Press, 1972.

Szilagyi, A.D., Jr., and D.M. Schweiger. "Matching Managers to Strategies: A Review and Suggested Framework." *Academy of Management Review* 9 (1984): 626–637.

Thompson, J.D. *Organizations in Action.* New York: McGraw-Hill, 1967.

Wageman, R. "Interdependence and Team Effectiveness." *Administrative Science Quarterly* 40 (1995): 145–180.

———. "How Leaders Foster Self-Managing Team Effectiveness: Design Choices Versus Hands-on Coaching." *Organization Science* 12 (2001): 559–577.

Wageman, R., J.R. Hackman, and E.V. Lehman. "The Team Diagnostic Survey: Development of an Instrument." *Journal of Applied Behavioral Science* 41 (2005): 373–398.

Wageman, R., D.A. Nunes, J.A. Burruss, and J.R. Hackman. *Senior Leadership Teams: What It Takes to Make Them Great.* Boston: Harvard Business School Press, 2008.

18

DECISION MAKING AS LEADERSHIP FOUNDATION

Michael Useem

LEADERSHIP REQUIRES a strategic vision and a sense of mission. It requires an ability to excite and to execute. It requires unflinching determination, impeccable character, and a commitment to common cause over private gain. But it also requires an exceptional capacity to make good and timely decisions.[1]

Consider, for example, the final days of investment bank Bear Stearns. During two weeks in March, 2008, its chief executive, his counterpart at J.P. Morgan Chase, and the U.S. Treasury Secretary took critical decisions that had enormous impact on the bank's 13,500 employees, hundreds of clients, and even world financial markets.

Bear Stearns's chief executive, Alan Schwartz, believed on Friday, March 14, that he had just succeeded in buying time: he would have four weeks to find an acquirer for his distressed firm, whose clients had been fleeing in droves and whose share price was plummeting. Earlier that day, the U.S. government had guaranteed a twenty-eight-day loan to Bear Stearns through J.P. Morgan Chase, a bailout of a nonbank by the Federal Reserve that was without modern precedent. The loan would provide Schwartz with the breathing room he would need to find a suitable buyer in an orderly sale.

Having helped arrange the Fed's emergency loan, Treasury Secretary Henry Paulson Jr. realized later the same day, however, that it was proving insufficient to save Bearn Stearns from imminent collapse. Instead of four weeks, Bear Stearns might have forty-eight hours. Paulson called Schwartz on Friday evening to tell him he would have to sell his firm to save the firm—and he would have to do so before the Asian financial markets opened for business on Sunday evening, New York time. Regulators feared Bear Stearns would otherwise fail in the days ahead, pulling other investments banks down and destabilizing equity markets worldwide. The Dow Jones Industrial Average could plunge by 20 percent or more.

J.P. Morgan was already considering a purchase of Bear Stearns, but CEO James Dimon was balking at the unknown risks in a rushed deal. In the wake of Paulson's call, Schwartz understood he had little choice but to make a deal with Dimon. He also knew he was not in a position to expect much from a deal.

Treasury Secretary Paulson called J.P. Morgan CEO Dimon in mid-afternoon on Sunday to check on the prospective buy-out, just hours before the deadline. Dimon reported that his bank was moving toward an offer for Bear Stearns of $4 to $5 a share, a startlingly modest figure given that Bear Stearns's stock price had topped $130 in recent months and was still in the $60s just days before. Paulson told Dimon that even his astonishingly low number was still too high—Paulson worried about the appearance of bailing out Wall Street while distressed homeowners were being foreclosed—and in response Dimon cut his final offer to $2 per share.

Mindful of the Treasury Secretary's warning, Bear Stearns CEO Alan Schwartz told his directors in emergency session later that afternoon that "two dollars is better than nothing." Although board chair and former CEO James Cayne declared he would never approve the deal, when Schwartz challenged his board—"Do I have anyone who's opposed?"—none objected.

The deal would later be repriced at $10 a share, and in an eleven-minute meeting on May 29, Bear Stearns stockholders approved the sale of their company for $1.4 billion, down from a market value of $25 billion in early 2007. In the months that followed, the storm clouds over Wall Street would intensify, and other companies, including AIG, Fannie Mae, Freddy Mac, Lehman Brothers, Merrill Lynch, and Washington Mutual, would become subject to the same momentous decisions that had characterized the final days of Bear Stearns.[2]

The decisions by Henry Paulson to force the sale of Bear Stearns, by James Dimon to buy the company, by Alan Schwartz to accept the offer, and by the Bear Stearns board to approve the deal were gut-wrenching but also life saving. And the choices were certainly not foregone. Others in the same circumstances could have calculated the risks differently, chosen other paths, or taken days to act instead of hours.

The frenzied salvage of Bear Stearns depended much upon the decision quality and timeliness of those in positions of power. How and when those decisions were made determined the fate of Bear Stearns and affected investment banks and equity markets worldwide. Decisions by a few had widespread impact on many.

The same can be said of Lenovo executives and directors when the Chinese personal-computer maker decided to buy IBM's PC division in 2004. It could also be said of Enron executives and directors when they decided to create the special-purpose entities that would cause the firm's downfall in 2001; of Margaret Whitman when she decided to accept an offer to build eBay in 1998; of John F. Kennedy when he decided to confront the Soviet Union over its missiles in Cuba in 1962; of Franklin Delano Roosevelt when he decided to assist Great Britain against Germany in 1940; and of Confederate General Robert E. Lee when he decided to launch an attack led by George Pickett on the Union army at Gettysburg in 1863.[3]

In each case, the principal's choice was neither obvious not foreordained. In every case, the decision was fateful. Appreciating the leadership of Bear Stearns, J.P. Morgan, Lenovo, Enron, Paulson, Whitman, Kennedy, Roosevelt, and Lee thus suggests a closer look at how and why they made their most critical decisions. To understand those decisions is to help us understand their impact on the world they led.

To further that understanding, this chapter first argues that good and timely decisions should be considered a critical feature of organizational leadership. It contends, secondly, that leadership decision making is not a natural capacity, and since those in leadership positions tend to make predictable decision errors, they are also preventable. Third, the chapter suggests that by looking at how company leaders—in this case, company directors—actually make decisions, we can help resolve long-standing conceptual questions about how organizations operate.

Why Good and Timely Leadership Decisions Matter

Making good and timely leadership decisions on behalf of an organization has long been recognized by some scholars and practitioners as a defining aspect of leadership. Academic researcher Gary Yukl, for instance, identified quality decision making as one of the key components of effective leadership, and company executive Jack Welch singled out his ability to make fast decisions without regrets as a defining quality of his own leadership at General Electric.[4]

Other researchers and observers have explicitly linked leadership decisions to organizational outcomes. "Top management teams make strategic decisions," offered one investigator by way of straightforward summary, and their "quality" had direct bearing on "organizational performance." In line with this thinking, many companies now specify effective decision making as one of a dozen select capacities that they expect of high-potential managers moving into their leadership ranks. Both scholars and practitioners view decision making as a vital and impactful function of those who carry leadership responsibilities.[5]

In *The Functions of the Executive*, Chester Barnard characterized the essence of executive decisions as a "choice of means to accomplish ends which are not personal." In keeping with this, we define leadership decisions as those moments when an individual with organizational responsibility faces a discrete, tangible, and realistic opportunity to commit enterprise resources to one course or another on behalf of the firm's objectives. Making no choice in the face of such an opportunity—consciously recognized or not—is also deemed a decision. We extend the terrain of leadership decisions above the executive suite to include decisions by company directors, and below to include midlevel managers.[6]

Detailed study of those in the act of taking leadership decisions, however, has often proven challenging because such actions are usually taken behind closed doors. From his years as an AT&T executive, Chester Bernard observed that "most executive decisions produce no direct evidence of themselves." The absence of direct evidence is one reason that research on corporate governance has focused more often on board membership and published policies than actual decisions taken inside the boardroom. Since "most of the work done by a board takes place in the privacy of the boardroom," concluded two governance researchers, "rarely, if ever," does information "escape to the outside world," and most such decisions are thus largely invisible to the outside world.[7]

The outward invisibility of leadership decisions points to the value of going inside to directly observe their making, or at least drawing information from those who have made them. We concur with one academic team's conclusion that to "appreciate the rich relationship between commitment and action, or to detect the roles of insight, inspiration, and emotion [in decisions] will require researchers to zoom in closer to the people and processes under study." Fresh and fuller insight into how leadership is exercised should thus come from zooming in closer to leaders at those moments when they are making decisions, akin to the close-in observation of senior managers at work conducted by Michael Porter and Nitin Nohria (see chapter 16).[8]

In seeking to make leadership decisions more visible, we work on the implicit premise that leadership decisions can be isolated and evaluated against the firm's goals. The task will be challenging not only because of the shroud of secrecy but also because managers often report that there was no single decision moment behind their company's commitment to launch a product or enter a market. Investigators frequently find that decisions evolved out of numerous discussions, multiple players, and unanticipated events, with few sharp-edged decision moments. And for some organizations, their goals are so ambiguous that the quality of decisions is simply beyond evaluation.[9]

While such challenges no doubt confront our study of many leadership decisions, they should be less of a barrier for decisions taken by those in the most senior positions. It is among executives and directors that the decision context, enterprise goals, and conflicting demands are more sharply delineated, analyzed, and incorporated into decisions. It is here that authority most clearly resides for selecting one organizational path over another. Even at this level, a moment's options are always conditioned by history and market, but executives and directors nonetheless often retain great discretion for choosing among the options. Although the crisis of confidence in Bear Stearns was not of Henry Paulson or James Dimon's making, their discretionary decisions during the crisis proved decisive in resolving it.

Making Optimal Leadership Decisions

All organizations have an interest in ensuring that their leaders make optimal decisions, but effective decision making is not an entirely natural capacity. Our decision-making tools are relatively sound, but we also have a few built-in bugs—design flaws of the mind—that can have adverse consequences. By nature, we are overoptimistic and prone to assign zero probability to events that are merely unlikely. We make choices that justify past decisions and then look for data to support them. Before the *Challenger* disaster in 1986 and the devastation caused by Hurricane Katrina in 2005, for instance, the prevailing government assumption was that the space shuttle's O-rings and New Orleans' levees could never rupture.

Not only do we make these errors, we make them predictably. Leaders tend to fall recurrently into what J. Edward Russo and Paul Schoemaker have termed "decision traps," and a host of reasons for such suboptimal decisions has been identified by a range of investigators.[10]

But predictable errors are preventable errors, and most researchers remain optimistic about the capacity of organizations to help leaders overcome them. Drawing upon a host of studies, for instance, Max Bazerman concluded that "we all have plenty of room to improve our judgment," and self-conscious learning of how to make better decisions is a proven avenue for enhancement. Because the decision making of those in leadership positions has been relatively understudied, however, the roadmap for improving leadership decisions has also remained relatively underdeveloped.[11]

Research studies indirectly touching on this terrain suggest that such a roadmap should make a difference. Two investigators, for example, found that successful work teams were overseen more often than others by managers who were particularly good at acquiring critical information and building good relations between the team and outside constituencies. Put differently, when leaders decided to inform and empower their work teams, the teams performed more effectively, and such capacities are subject to improvement through training and development.[12]

Drawing on academic research and company experience, I identify three areas where leadership decision errors are predictably made but where intervention can also help make them preventable. These are illustrative rather than exhaustive, a sampling of what might appear in a primer on the pitfalls of leadership decision making and their remedies.

Low Preparation, High Stress, and Frail Team

Underpreparation is a major source of suboptimal leadership decisions. Consider one important barrier to good choices: overconfidence, that is, when a leader believes that an outcome is more certain than the facts would warrant. Research confirms that executives are overly audacious when they have to make decisions on products and markets with which they are least familiar. In one study, for instance, the researchers examined confidence among product managers of small computer software and hardware companies when they introduced radically new products to the market. The more pioneering the product—and, thus, the less familiar the market—the more the product managers were likely to view the prospects for success through rose-tinted glasses.[13]

The adverse effects of underpreparation on leadership decisions become more pronounced under high levels of stress, though low levels of stress can have favorable effects. This is the well-known curvilinear relationship between stress and performance: Below the panic point, the adrenaline feed concentrates the mind, mobilizes energies, and eliminates distractions. Above the panic point, however, decision reasoning degrades as stress intensifies. Well-formed leadership teams, however, are better able to insulate themselves against that stress, thereby raising the panic point and reducing suboptimal decisions. That is why the armed forces and firefighters have long seen camaraderie as an essential foundation for their primary combat units. It is also one reason companies often invest in building and developing their leadership teams. When formed into cohesive units, combat, firefighting, and executive teams are better able to reach good and timely leadership decisions in challenging environments.[14]

The Inner and Outer Circles

A small inner circle of trusted advisors can prove important for good and timely leadership decisions. So too can a large outer circle of diverse advisors.

In a study of computer hardware and software companies in Silicon Valley, for example, a researcher reported that one of the distinguishing factors between companies that moved swiftly and those that plodded along was whether their managers sought advice from a small number of experienced and unbiased inside advisers before reaching decisions. The advisers served as a sounding board, guidance givers, and confidence boosters, and when consulting with them, company managers became more comfortable in reaching major decisions in uncertain markets.[15]

The value of such an inner circle was evident at Cisco Systems as it rode the technology wave during the late 1990s and early 2000s. Much of the company's growth came through acquisitions of companies that had developed new technologies. Cisco CEO John Chambers' acquisition success rates were high, and when asked how he had managed to make good and timely acquisition decisions, Chambers referred to the advice provided by Cisco's former CEO and current non-executive chairman, John Morgridge, and Cisco's chief financial officer, Larry Carter. Both individuals, he said, required no briefing on company strategy and they rendered unbiased advice. They knew the company well—and neither was interested in Chambers's job.[16]

At the same time, the absence of a wider and more diverse outer circle can also undermine good and timely decisions. By way of illustration, two investigators studied how managers at a large commercial bank closed deals with corporate customers. When a deal was characterized by a high degree of uncertainty, bankers more often turned for advice to colleagues with whom they had already established strong relationships. The greater the deal uncertainty, the greater the bankers' dependence on their most trusted advisers. But the researchers also found that the larger the reliance of the bankers on their inner circles to the exclusion of a wider and more diverse array of bankers, the less likely were the deal makers to learn what they needed to successfully close the deal. Relying on the inner circle without also turning to the outer circle proved a source of suboptimal leadership decisions.[17]

The 70 Percent Solution

When leaders endlessly compile data in pursuit of perfect knowledge—and thus perfect certainty—they are edging toward "decidophobia," a clinical fear of reaching decisions. And that threatens to thwart the second half of the twin objectives of quality and timeliness in leadership decision making.

The U.S. Marine Corps battles this syndrome with the 70 percent solution. If an officer has 70 percent of the information, has performed 70 percent of the analysis, and feels 70 percent confident, he or she is instructed to decide. The logic is simple: a less than ideal action, swiftly executed, stands a chance of success, whereas no action stands no chance. The worst decision is no decision at all, because it offers no way for learning whether a prospective decision is right or wrong. "Analyze" is the injunction the Marine Corps' Officer Candidates School offers aspirants at its base in Quantico, Virginia, "but do not overanalyze." Analysis and action are both essential for good and timely decisions, and they are reconciled with the 70 percent solution.[18]

The Value of Examining Leadership Decisions

Direct study of leadership decisions provides for not only better understanding how leadership is exercised but also for better clarification of long-standing concepts of what leaders do. Consider one of the long-standing debates about the role of company boards.

We know a great deal about the visible features of corporate governance that make a difference in company behavior ranging from firm profitability and fraudulent activity to protecting the environment and picking a chief. Although the outward features of the governing board, such as the fraction of non-executive directors, separation of CEO and board chair, number of anti-takeover defenses, and director compensation, are useful predictors of company behavior, the board's inside decisions are the drivers of much of that behavior.[19]

By way of example, consider Enron's board just prior to its bankruptcy in December, 2001. Its board had been a model of outward appearance. It was a relatively well-composed board, with prominent independent directors and only two Enron executives serving on the board. An accounting professor had served as its audit committee chair since 1985. The board itself was led by a chairman who was not also the chief executive officer, one more outward sign of good governance. Whatever the outside appearance, however, when directors reached their decisions inside the boardroom, some of their actual decisions proved suboptimal, including suspension of the company's code of ethics and approval of the special-purpose entities that hid Enron's debt from the market. The board's favorable outward features notwithstanding, the directors' inside decisions directly contributed to the company's downfall.[20]

Drawing on such evidence, two theories purport to infer what directors do when they enter the boardroom, each implying that directors focus on a distinct set of issues and use a separate set of criteria in reaching their decisions.

- *Monitoring management:* One well-established conception of the firm views directors as largely serving as the eyes and ears of the shareholders, ensuring that company executives conduct themselves properly on behalf of the owners. The decisions that directors take are therefore presumed to be directed at monitoring the decisions that executives make. This is the formal view that big business sometimes even takes of its own boardrooms. "The board of directors has the important role of overseeing management performance on behalf of shareholders," declared the Business Roundtable, and "directors are diligent monitors, but not managers, of business operations." By way of illustration, directors often take decisions to ensure that their executives do not enrich themselves at the expense of shareholders and that they do not enter into sweetheart deals with other companies controlled by the executives' families.[21]

- *Partnering with management:* A long-standing alternative conception of corporate governance suggests that directors are decision partners with the top executives, joining with them in making the company's most important choices. Directors are seen as coproducers of the firm's strategic decisions. This is the informal view that business executives often take of themselves. The chief executive of a large financial services firm, for instance, spoke for many in describing the decisions that directors reach in his boardroom. They are, he said, those that are "strategically impactful" and those that will "change the future." If a company's executives are seeking to integrate newly acquired international operations, for example, directors may collaborate with the executives in reaching key decisions on how to optimize the process.[22]

To explore these theories, I asked directors and executives of Boeing and Lenovo to describe major decisions by their board during the past several years. I selected these companies for study because their directors and executives were willing to describe their board's decisions and did not insist on anonymity.

Boeing's Directors Decide to Build the 787

In designing Boeing's new 787 aircraft in the early 2000s, company engineers faced thousands of decisions. Individually, none of the design decisions were make-or-break propositions, but together, they could mean the difference between the airplane's success and failure. Sorting through all of them on the way to a final design would cost billions of dollars, and the Boeing board decided that it had to be involved in what then non-executive chairman Lewis Platt called a "bet-the-company decision" on the plane's design.

The board took three major subdecisions in collaboration with the executives as part of the company's overall decision to build the new airliner. First, the Boeing directors decided on a multibillion-dollar budget and a timeline for the aircraft's development. This decision required that the board accurately appraise the future of airline travel. Airbus had already cast its lot with the super-jumbo A380, believing that it would be particularly appealing to airlines operating hub-and-spoke systems with high-volume hubs. The A380 could carry twice the load with the same number of gates, pilots, and takeoffs. The Boeing directors, however, decided that the hub-and-spoke system was not sustainable as passengers increasingly sought nonstop, point-to-point service to their final destination. When Boeing executives made the case for the 787 to the directors, the board initially challenged the executives' assumptions and forecasts. In response to the challenges, management refined its analysis, and the directors finally decided on a budget to develop the 787.

Second, the Boeing directors decided when it was the right time for the company's sales managers to call upon the airlines to discuss the 787's anticipated performance, price, and delivery date. For this subdecision, the directors challenged the executives to prove that they could mold the composites into the fuselage and other large sections that would constitute the 787. Management returned with compelling engineering data, and the board decided in 2003 to authorize the sales team to present the aircraft's specifications to the airlines.

Third, the Boeing directors decided on a final go-ahead in 2004 for production of the aircraft, a decision requiring the company to invest additional billions of dollars long before receiving any cash from its customers. Even after this final subdecision, however, the directors insisted on reviewing both manufacturing progress and order flow to ensure that the 787 production stayed on course. In bringing the 787 into production, then, the directors had co-taken three critical subdecisions on the aircraft's development in collaboration with executives.

The Boeing board's three subdecisions were hardly pro forma. The directors had sought tangible evidence to support each of management's major assumptions. Sometimes it came down to examining the actual test data on very specific functions, such as whether the 787's passenger doors could withstand an accidental slam against a jetway. Only after seeing countless test results and fact-driven forecasts did the directors decide that Boeing's 787 could join its commercial fleet.[23]

Whatever the evidence for the theory that directors serve to monitor management, this evidence from inside the boardroom points toward the theory that directors often serve as strategic decision partners with management. A similar picture emerged from the aftermath of Lenovo's acquisition of the IBM PC division in 2005.

Lenovo's Directors Decide to Build a Global Company

Prior to the IBM acquisition, Lenovo was a largely Chinese company, with headquarters in Beijing and most of its sales and all of its operations in greater China. After the acquisition, it moved its executive offices to Raleigh (North Carolina), Beijing, and Singapore. It divided its research operations among Raleigh, Yamato (Japan), Beijing, Shanghai, and three other Chinese cities. It transferred marketing operations to Bangalore, India. It spread manufacturing operations across Australia, Brazil, China, Hungary, India, Japan, Malaysia, Mexico, the United States, and the United Kingdom. In 2004, none of its personal computer sales came from outside greater China; three years later, it drew more than three-fifths from foreign shores. Symbolizing the international commitment, executive chairman Yang Yuanqing moved his family to the United States.

Lenovo in parallel diversified its ownership. The government's Chinese Academy of Sciences had been the majority holder through Legend Holdings, but after the IBM acquisition, IBM held a significant stake in the company, as did three American-based private equity companies. Lenovo's market and ownership remake also brought a remake of the governing board. In 2003, nonindependent directors outnumbered the independent directors four to three. The postacquisition board, by contrast, was divided between five executive and nonindependent directors, three private-equity directors, and three independent directors. Prior to the acquisition, all seven of the directors were Chinese or of greater China origin. After the acquisition, four of the eleven directors were Americans. Before the acquisition, board meetings had always been conducted in Chinese; after the acquisition, English became the medium of expression. Going into the acquisition, the executive chairman and chief executive were both Chinese; coming out of the acquisition, the executive chairman was Chinese and the CEO American. Of the top management team in 2004, all were Chinese; of the eighteen members of the top management team in 2007, six were from greater China, one from Europe, and eleven from the United States.

In remaking Lenovo's governing board, our interview evidence pointed toward a transformation of the board from a limited version of monitoring management to a partnership with management. Prior to the IBM acquisition, the board had mainly been concerned with company audit and executive pay. The board played a modest monitoring function on behalf of its owners, but was little involved in the firm's strategic decisions. While Lenovo was still the biggest player in the Chinese market, domestic dominance provided no assurance of growth abroad. "If you have a highly successful business in one country," warned CEO William Amelio, "it does not mean that you will have a highly successful business in a global operation," and that is where the counsel of the non-executive directors proved particularly valuable.

The restructuring of the Lenovo board following the IBM purchase also brought the directors into direct guidance of the integration of Lenovo's and IBM's distinct operating styles. IBM had built up strong, enduring relations with its select corporate customers; in contrast, Lenovo had created a largely "transactional" exchange with its many retail customers. While large enterprise relations had been the staple of IBM's PC sales, management anticipated greater growth among small consumers. But identifying the optimal areas for growth outside of China and effective ways of reaching them were uncertain and risky judgment calls. In making them, management sought director guidance.

Facing many decisions of this kind in the wake of the IBM PC acquisition, Lenovo formed a strategy committee, charged with vetting the company's mid- and long-term decisions on behalf of the board. In CEO William Amelio's words, the role of the directors on the strategy committee was to pick from an array of choices "the right idea that is going to maximize the core competence of the company." A host of other major issues—how long to retain the IBM logo, what acquisitions to make, which "adjacencies" such as servers to consider, and whether to build devices that bridge laptops and telephones—now came to the directors for vetting and decision making. Before the acquisition, the board had virtually no role in business decisions, but afterward, it took a direct role in formulating strategy.

By peering inside the Boeing and Lenovo boardrooms, we witness a world of active decision making in collaboration with management. While monitoring of management has not necessarily diminished, directors have become active partners with executives in reaching major company decisions. Instead of rubber-stamping management's plans, the directors grappled with and modified them. Both directors and executives were at the table when the major decisions were taken.

Several implications directly follow this evidence from inside the boardroom. As new directors are recruited to their boards, a premium will likely be placed on director capacity to work with executives at critical choice points and on their ability to make good and timely strategic decisions. A changing skill set for executives can also be expected, with stronger executive ability to work with directors at major choice points and less inclination to hold directors at arm's length. Institutional investors will be more likely to look for directors and executives who can collaboratively engage in the firm's most important decisions, not just directors who can monitor management.

The Difference That Director Decisions Make

To close with a final illustration of the difference that director decisions can make, we turn to the moment on May 29, 1953, when Sir Edmund Hillary and Tenzing Norgay summited Mount Everest. Behind that accomplishment was an earlier board decision that was to prove critical.

The U.K.'s Himalayan Committee originally chose veteran mountaineer Eric Shipton to lead the assault on the summit. Shipton's lightly equipped and nimble climbs had shown creative flair. But he was known to be inattentive to detail and planning, and the governing body worried that his style might not be up to the competition. A year earlier, a Swiss team had come within a few hundred feet of the summit. And should the British fail this time, there were German and French expeditions ready to launch assaults soon thereafter. Fearful of another failure and believing that logistics would make the difference, the Himalayan Committee fired Shipton just six weeks after choosing him. In the resulting uproar, one climber resigned. Others protested about Shipton's replacement, a career military man, called John Hunt, who was known for his management savvy but barely known to mountaineering.

In replacing its expedition CEO, the board had changed its strategy. As expedition leader, John Hunt indeed focused on logistics. His approach called for an array of climbers and Sherpas who would methodically move up the mountain, placing supplies at ever-higher camps. The goal was to deliver just two climbers to the summit, although ten mountaineers were in the running. The final choice,

Hunt declared, would depend on who was climbing well and who was in high camp when the weather cleared. On May 28, 1953, Hunt selected two men for immortality and, at 11.30 a.m. the next day, Edmund Hillary snapped the iconic photo of Tenzing Norgay atop the summit.[24]

The Himalayan Committee had decided that Everest's conquest would require a well-organized team to succeed, and it decided on a new executive for its new strategy. Whatever its formal membership and policies, the board had taken two history-making decisions behind closed doors that made the difference.

Conclusion

All organizations have an interest in ensuring that their leaders make optimal decisions, but effective decision making is not a natural capacity, and universities and companies can do much to encourage it. Studies of what Daniel Kahneman terms "systematic biases"—the mental flaws that separate the choices that leaders actually make from what rational agent models expect—reveal that such biases can be reduced when leaders are trained in decision making and have learned from experience.[25]

Both universities and companies carry responsibility for preparing their future and current students to shoulder organizational leadership, and the present analysis implies that they should strengthen the capacities of students and managers to make leadership decisions in work environments that are often demanding and frequently changing. The impact of the decision makers responsible for Bear Stearns, Boeing, Lenovo, and the British expedition to Mount Everest confirm the seminal importance of learning to make good and timely leadership decisions in such programs. Given the impact of increasingly global product and equity markets on company operations, the pressures for quality decision making are likely to intensify in the future, making preparation in leadership decisions even more important for management education in the years ahead.[26]

Many business schools and business firms have established programs on leadership during the past decade, and the evidence reviewed here suggests explicit cultivation of a capacity for making good and timely leadership decisions. How to think strategically, mobilize resources, and act selflessly are often at the core of such courses (including one this author offers to executive MBA students); what is also required is a focus on learning how to make decisions in positions of responsibility when facing discrete, tangible, and realistic opportunities to take the enterprise in one direction or another.

Universities and companies would also be advised to reinforce their classroom lessons on leadership decision making with out-of-classroom learning experiences. Even the best-designed classroom-based leadership curriculums do not succeed as well as they might in engendering the capacities of leadership, and they may be particularly inadequate for developing an ability to make good and timely leadership decisions. Out-of-classroom learning experiences would do well to place future or current managers in the shoes of decision makers such as those in and around Bear Stearns.

Out-of-classroom learning experiences need not be limited to company incidents. By examining decision moments in venues ranging from Civil War battlefields and Himalayan mountain ascents to White House crises and Wall Street convulsions, future and current managers should gain improved and enduring insight into the perils and pluses of decision making in their own settings. Programs to achieve this would include explicit exposure to decision making under stress, a fostering of team cohesion, creation of inner and outer circles, and building a culture that emphasizes a 70 percent solution. Akin to action-learning projects that many companies have come to use for much the same purpose, such experiences would be advisedly designed to be tangible and engaging but also analytically informed if they are to be instructively memorable. With greater appreciation for how to make good and timely leadership decisions, more mountain summits and fewer company meltdowns could well be in store.[27]

Notes

1. Jim Collins, *Good to Great: Why Some Companies Make the Leap . . . and Others Don't* (New York: HarperBusiness, 2001); Howard Gardner, with Emma Laskin, *Leading Minds: An Anatomy of Leadership* (New York: Basic Books, 2003); William George, *Authentic Leadership: Rediscovering the Secrets to Creating Lasting Value* (San Francisco: Jossey-Bass, 2004); Warren Bennis, *Becoming a Leader* (New York: Basic Books, 2003); John Gardner, *On Leadership* (New York: The Free Press, 1993).

2. Kate Kelly, "Lost Opportunities Haunt Final Days of Bear Stearns," *The Wall Street Journal*, May 27, 2008, A1; Kate Kelly, "Fear, Rumors Touched Off Fatal Run on Bear Stearns," *The Wall Street Journal*, May 28, 2008, A1; Kate Kelly, "Bear Stearns Neared Collapse Twice in Frenzied Last Days," *The Wall Street Journal*, May 29, 2008, A1.

3. Graham T. Allison and Philip Zelikow, *Essence of Decision: Explaining the Cuban Missile Crisis*, 2nd ed. (New York: Longman, 1999); Stephen W. Sears, *Gettysburg* (Boston: Houghton Mifflin, 2003); Ian Kershaw, *Fateful Choices: Ten Decisions That Changed the World, 1940–1941* (New York: Penguin Press, 2007); Bethany McLean and Peter Elkind, *The Smartest Guys in the Room: The Amazing Rise and Scandalous Fall of Enron* (New York: Portfolio, 2004).

4. Gary Yukl, "Managerial Leadership: A Review of Theory and Research," *Journal of Management Development* 15 (1989): 251–289; Jack Welch and John A. Byrne, *Jack: Straight from the Gut* (New York: Warner Books, 2001).

5. A.C. Amason, "Distinguishing the Effects of Functional and Dysfunctional Conflict on Strategic Decision Making: Resolving a Paradox for Top Management Teams," *Academy of Management Journal* 39 (1996): 123–148; Gordon Donaldson and Jay W. Lorsch, *Decision Making at the Top: The Shaping of Strategic Direction* (New York: Basic Books, 1984); Sydney Finkelstein and Donald C. Hambrick, *Strategic Leadership: Top Executives and Their Effects on Organizations* (Minneapolis/St. Paul, MN: West Publishing, 1996).

6. Chester I. Barnard, *The Functions of the Executive* (Cambridge, MA: Harvard University Press, 1971), 186.

7. Ibid, 193; Colin B. Carter and Jay W. Lorsch, *Back to the Drawing Board: Designing Corporate Boards for a Complex World* (Boston: Harvard Business School Press, 2004).

8. Also see A. Langley, H. Mintzberg, P. Pitcher, E. Posada, and J. Saint-Macary, "Opening up Decision-Making: The View from the Black Stool," *Organization Science* 6 (1995): 260–279.

9. See, for instance, Scott Snook, *Friendly Fire: The Accidental Shootdown of U.S. Black Hawks over Northern Iraq* (Princeton, NJ: Princeton University Press, 2002).

10. J. Edward Russo and Paul J.H. Schoemaker, *Decision Traps: Ten Barriers to Brilliant Decision-Making and How to Overcome Them* (New York: Simon & Schuster, 1990); J. Edward Russo and Paul J.H. Schoemaker, *Winning Decisions: Getting It Right the First Time* (New York: Currency Doubleday, 2002); John Hammond, Ralph L. Keeney, and Howard Raiffa, *Smart Choices: A Practical Guide to Making Better Decisions* (Boston: Harvard Business School Press, 1999); Daniel Kahneman, "Maps of Bounded Rationality: Psychology for Behavioral Economics," *American Economic Review* 93 (2003): 1449–1475; Daniel Kahneman, Paul Slovic, and Amos Tversky, eds., *Judgment Under Uncertainty: Heuristics and Biases* (New York: Cambridge University Press, 1982); J. Frank Yates, *Decision Management: How to Assure Better Decisions in Your Company* (San Francisco: Jossey-Bass, 2003); Reid Hastie and Robyn M. Dawes, *Rational Choice in an Uncertain World: The Psychology of Judgment and Decision Making* (Thousand Oaks, CA: Sage, 2001); J. Keith Murnighan and John C. Mowen, *The Art of High-Stakes Decision-Making: Tough Calls in a Speed-Driven World* (New York: Wiley, 2002); Robert E. Rubin, with Jacob Weisberg, *In an Uncertain World: Tough Choices from Wall Street to Washington* (New York: Random House, 2003); *Fortune*, special issue on decision making, June 27, 2005; *Harvard Business Review*, special issue on decision making, January 2006.

11. Max Bazerman, *Judgment in Managerial Decision Making*, 6th ed. (Hoboken, NJ: J. Wiley, 2006).

12. V.U. Druskat and J.V. Wheeler, "Managing from the Boundary: The Effective Leadership of Self-Managing Work Teams," *Academy of Management Journal* 46 (2003): 435–457.

13. Mark Simon and Susan M. Houghton, "The Relationship Between Overconfidence and the Introduction of Risky Products: Evidence from a Field Study," *Academy of Management Journal* 46 (2003): 139–149.

14. Kenneth R. Hammond, *Judgments Under Stress* (New York: Oxford University Press, 2000); Gary Klein, *Sources of Power: How People Make Decisions* (Cambridge, MA: MIT Press, 1998); Gary Klein, *Intuition at Work: Why Developing Your Gut Instincts Will Make You Better at What You Do* (New York: Currency/Doubleday, 2003); Michael Useem, James Cook, and Larry Sutton, "Developing Leaders for Decision Making Under Duress: Wildland Firefighters in the South Canyon Fire and Its Aftermath," *Academy of Management Learning and Education* 4 (2005): 461–485.

15. Kathleen M. Eisenhardt, "Speed and Strategic Choice: How Managers Accelerate Decision Making," *California Management Review* 32 (1990): 39–54.

16. Michael Useem, *The Go Point: When It's Time to Decide* (New York: Crown Business, 2006).

17. Mark S. Mizruchi and Linda Brewster Stearns, "Getting Deals Done: The Use of Social Networks in Bank Decision-Making," *American Sociological Review* 66 (2001): 647–671.

18. David H. Freedman, *Corps Business: The 30 Management Principles of the U.S. Marines* (New York: HarperBusiness, 2000).

19. P. Gompers, J. Ishii, and A. Metrick, "Corporate Governance and Equity Prices," *Quarterly Journal of Economics* 118 (2003): 107–155; E. Kang and A. Zardkoohi, "Board Leadership Structure and Firm Performance," *Corporate Governance: An International Review* 13 (2005): 785–799; T. Perry and A. Shivdasani, "Do Boards Affect Performance? Evidence from Corporate Restructuring," *Journal of Business* 78 (2005): 1403–1431; S.L. Gillan, "Recent Developments in Corporate Governance: An Overview," *Journal of Corporate Finance* 12 (2006): 381–402; A. Yawson, "Evaluating the Characteristics of Corporate Boards Associated with Layoff Decisions," *Corporate Governance: An International Review* 14 (2006): 75–84.

20. Jeffrey A. Sonnenfeld, "What Makes Great Boards Great," *Harvard Business Review* 80, no. 9 (September 2002): 106–113; U.S. Senate Permanent Subcommittee on Investigations of the Committee on Governmental Affairs, *The Role of the Board of Directors in Enron's Collapse*, 107th Congr., 2nd sess., S. Rep. 107-70, 2002.

21. Eugene F. Fama and Michael C. Jensen, "Separation of Ownership and Control," *Journal of Law and Economics* 26 (1983): 301–325; Business Roundtable, *Principles of Corporate Governance* (Washington, DC: Business Roundtable, 2005), 5.

22. R. Leblanc and J. Gillies, *Inside the Boardroom: How Boards Really Work and the Coming Revolution in Corporate Governance* (Toronto: J. Wiley & Sons Canada, 2005); C. Sundaramurthy and M. Lewis, "Control and Collaboration: Paradoxes of Governance," *Academy of Management Review* 28 (2003): 397–415; T. McNulty and A. Pettigrew, "Strategists on the Board," *Organizational Studies* 20 (1999): 47–74; Michael Useem and Andy Zelleke, "Oversight and Delegation in Corporate Governance: Deciding What the Board Should Decide," *Corporate Governance: An International Review* 14 (2006): 2–12.

23. Michael Useem, "How Well-Run Boards Make Decisions," *Harvard Business Review* 84, no. 11 (November 2006): 130–138; Michael Useem and Neng Liang, "Globalizing the Company Board: Lessons from China's Lenovo," in *Leading Corporate Boardrooms: The New Realities, the New Rules*, ed. Jay Conger (San Francisco: Jossey-Bass, forthcoming).

24. John Hunt, *The Conquest of Everest* (New York: Dutton, 1954); Eric Shipton, *That Untravelled World: An Autobiography* (New York: Charles Scriber's Sons, 1969); Stephen Venables, *Everest: Summit of Achievement* (New York: Simon & Schuster, 2003).

25. Kahneman, "Maps of Bounded Rationality," 1449–1475; R.E. Boyatzis, E.C. Stubbs, and S.N. Taylor, "Learning Cognitive and Emotional Intelligence Competencies Through Graduate Management Education," *Academy of Management Learning and Education* 1 (2002): 150–162.

26. David V. Day, "Leadership Development: A Review in Context," *Leadership Quarterly* 11 (2000): 581–613.

27. D.L. Dotlich and J.L. Noel, *Action Learning: How the World's Top Companies Are Recreating Their Leaders and Themselves* (San Francisco: Jossey-Bass, 1998); G. Hirst, L. Mann, P. Bainc, A. Pirola-Merlod, and A. Richvera, "Learning to Lead: The Development and Testing of a Model of Leadership Learning," *Leadership Quarterly* 15 (2004): 311–327.

19

LEADING CHANGE

Leadership, Organization, and Social Movements

Marshall Ganz

Introduction

Social movements emerge as a result of the efforts of purposeful actors (individuals, organizations) to assert new public values, form new relationships rooted in those values, and mobilize the political, economic, and cultural power to translate these values into action.[1] They differ from fashions, styles, or fads (viral or otherwise) in that they are collective, strategic, and organized.[2] They differ from interest groups in that they focus less on allocating goods than on redefining them—not only on winning the game, but also changing the rules.[3] Initiated in hopeful response to conditions adherents deem intolerable, social movement participants make moral claims based on renewed personal identities, collective identities, and public action. In the United States, they have been the major drivers of social and political reform since the American Revolution.[4]

Leadership is accepting responsibility to create conditions that enable others to achieve shared purpose in the face of uncertainty. Leaders accept responsibility not only for their individual "part" of the work, but also for the collective "whole." Leaders can create conditions interpersonally, structurally, and/or procedurally. The need for leadership (a need often not met) is evident when encounters with the uncertain demand adaptive, heuristic, or innovative response: past practices are breached, new threats loom, a sudden opportunity appears, social conditions change, new technology changes the rules, and so on.[5]

The role of leadership in social movements goes well beyond that of the stereotypical charismatic public persona with whom they are often identified. Social movements are organized by identifying, recruiting, and developing leadership at all levels. This leadership forges a social movement community and mobilizes its resources, a primary source of social movement power.[6] Sometimes those who do this leadership work, especially when they work at it full time, are called *organizers*, or, more colorfully, *lecturers, agents, travelers, circuit riders, representatives,* or *field secretaries.* Sometimes they are simply called leaders. The Grange, for example, a rural organization key to the agrarian movement of the late nineteenth century, enjoyed a membership of 450,000 organized in 450 chapters, a structure that required recruiting men and women for 77,775 voluntary leadership posts, of which 77,248 (99.3 percent) were local, 510 at the state level, and only 17 at the national level. One of every 5 members occupied a formal leadership post at any one time. More recently, a mainstay of the Conservative movement, the 4-million-member NRA, rooted its activities in 14,000 local clubs, governed by some 140,000 local leaders, 1 of every 25 members.[7] And the Sierra Club, a 750,000-member environmental advocacy organization with some 380 local groups organized in 62 chapters, must recruit, train, and support volunteers for some 12,500 leadership posts, of which 10,000 are local: 1 of every 57 members.[8]

Because social movements are dynamic, participatory, and organized primarily to celebrate collective identity and assert public voice, their structures of participation, decision making, and accountability are more like those of other civic associations that celebrate collective identity (churches, for example) or assert public voice (advocacy groups) than of those that produce goods or services.[9] They interact with constituents, not customers or clients.[10] Authority rests on moral suasion more than on economic or political coercion. Outputs depend on the motivated, committed, and voluntary participation of members and supporters.[11] They are often incubators of social movements in the way that black churches, student groups, and NAACP chapters incubated the Civil Rights movement.[12]

Despite the deep roots of leadership studies in sociology,[13] especially within radically different authority regimes, social movement scholars have, with few exceptions, eschewed the project.[14] A structural bias in social movement studies seems to have made it more productive for scholars to identify the constraining conditions that make certain outcomes more probable than to focus on enabling conditions that make many outcomes possible. Agency, however, is more about grasping at possibility than conforming to probability.

One of the few scholars to address the challenges of leadership in voluntary associations, not only social movements, is James Q. Wilson:

> In most voluntary associations, authority is uncertain and leadership is precarious. Because the association is voluntary, its chief officer has neither the effective power nor the acknowledged right to coerce the members—they are, after all, members and not employees. In a business firm, the chief officer may, within limits, hire and fire, promote or demote, his subordinates . . . In most associations, power, or the ability to get a subordinate to do what the superior wants, is limited, and authority, or the right to exercises such power as exists, is circumscribed and contingent.[15]
>
> Though the authority of many association leaders is weak, the demands of the office are great. The chief officer of a voluntary organization must usually combine the executive task of maintaining the organization with the leadership task of defining and advancing its objectives . . . [M]aintenance needs are better served by having vague or broadly stated goals, whereas task achievement is facilitated by having explicit and concrete ones.[16]

In this paper I focus on leadership in social movements: a volatile context in which motivational, relational, strategic, and action skills—and the capacity to develop these skills in others—play key roles. I draw on examples from the first social movement about which I learned, the Exodus; the Civil Rights movement; the farmworkers' movement; the women's movement; and American politics.

Social Movement Leadership: Who Does It, Where Does It Come From, and Why?

At least since Moses, social movement leadership—exercised by individuals or by teams—has come from conflicted backgrounds. Moses, a Jew, the oppressed, was raised in the house of the Pharaoh, the oppressor. He struggles to link a desire for change (freeing his people) with a capacity to make change (as an Egyptian prince). His reaction, killing an Egyptian taskmaster, doesn't work, bringing down upon him censure from other Jews. He flees to the desert (where you go to get your act together in the Bible) and assumes a third, quite liminal, identity as neither Jew nor Egyptian, but as the son-in-law of a Midianite priest, a shepherd.

Remaining curious, one day he steps off a path to attend to a strange light, a burning bush, where, it turns out, God is waiting for him, challenging him to accept a call to return to Egypt, confront Pharaoh, with whom he grew up, and free his people. He accepts this charge only when God promises him the help of a brother, Aaron, and a sister, Miriam. He learns how he can combine his desire for change with a capacity to make change, but only by engaging with God, his family, and his people. Importantly, however, in Exodus 18, after he has brought his people out of Egypt he is visited by his father-in-law, Jethro, who teaches him two things: he reminds him he has a family that requires his attention and he observes that Moses is burning himself out—and burning the people out—by trying to do all the work himself. He proposes a structure in which among every ten men, one is recruited to provide leadership, and among every ten of those, one, and so on. In this way he turns Moses's attention to the critical role of leadership development that his movement will require if it is to grow strong.[17]

Leading in social movements requires learning to manage the core tensions at the heart of what theologian Walter Brueggemann calls the "prophetic imagination": a combination of criticality (experience of the world's pain) with hope (experience of the world's possibility), avoiding being numbed by despair or deluded by optimism.[18] A deep desire for change must be coupled with the capacity to make change. Structures must be created that create the space within which growth, creativity, and action can flourish, without slipping into the chaos of structurelessness, and leaders must be recruited, trained, and developed on a scale required to build the relationships, sustain the motivation, do the strategizing, and carry out the action required to achieve success.

The need for committed, hopeful leadership on a large scale is one reason that social movement leadership is often drawn from among the young (other than Moses). Dr. King was 25 when he was chosen to lead the bus boycott. César Chávez was 25 when recruited as a professional organizer and 35 when he initiated the farmworkers' movement. Some attribute the affinity of young people with social movements as due to "biographical availability" (having the time, but no family).[19] Although this may hold the "costs" of activism down, it says little about the benefits. It has much more to do with Brueggemann. Young people often come of age with a critical eye, an evaluation of their parent's generation, and a hopeful heart, almost a biological necessity. As we can see in the presidential campaign that unfolded before our eyes, the combination can be transformational.

Leadership Practices: Relationship, Story, Strategy, Action

Building Relationships

Because social movements are new, the leaders who initiate them learn to form interpersonal relationships that link individuals, networks, and organizations. In the absence of formal structures, the voluntary commitments people make to one another create the fabric from which formal structures may be woven. In this context, relationships can be viewed as exchanges of interests and resources between parties (figure 19-1).[20] An exchange becomes a relationship, however, only when a mutual commitment of resources is made to a shared future.

FIGURE 19-1

The nature of relationships in social movements

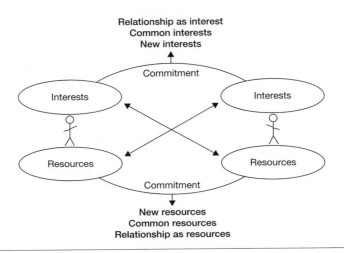

Commitment to a shared future and the consequences of a shared past transform an exchange into a relationship.

Because relationships are beginnings, not endings, they create opportunity for interests to grow, change, and develop. Similarly, participant resources irrelevant to the initial exchange may become relevant—and the basis for new forms of exchange—over time. Participants may also discover common interests of which they were unaware. And most important, participants may develop an interest in the relationship itself, creating what Robert Putnam and others describe as "social capital": a "relational" capacity that can facilitate collaborative action of all kinds.[21]

In social movement organizations, relationships among peers are as significant as those among leaders and between leaders and members. One joins a movement not only by entering into relationship with a leader—or organizer—but also by entering into a set of peer relationships with other members. Interpersonal relationships are thus critical to forging the shared understandings, commitments, and collaborative action that constitute a movement. And as Mark Granovetter taught us, the kinds of relationship—or networks—to which one commits make a big difference. Strong ties facilitate trust, motivation, and commitment, and weak ties broaden access to salient information, skills, and learning.[22] Successful movements learn to combine both.

The challenges of forging movement organizations across lines of race, class, culture, generation, and ethnicity are considerable, and rarely engaged successfully in the abstract or as a matter of principle. For example, the organizers of the Greater Boston Interfaith Organization (GBIO)—a community organization of over one hundred churches, synagogues, mosques, community development corporations, unions, and other groups—devoted their first two years of work almost entirely to holding "one-on-one meetings," a relational practice that has achieved ritual quality in an organization that operates across so many traditional boundaries. On May 27, 2009, GBIO, which shares major responsibility for the Massachusetts health care reform, celebrated its tenth anniversary with an assembly of some 1,700 people, drawn from all these communities, attended by the mayor, speaker of the assembly, and governor.[23]

Because relational resources are so central to social movements and entering into new ones and sustaining old ones so labor intensive, scale can be achieved only if leaders at all levels are recruited to accept the responsibility. The challenge is to cast a net widely enough to recruit others to do this work, create the capacity to train them, and offer the coaching to support their development.

Most active social movements thus train participants in some form of one-on-one meetings as well as "house meetings," a way to grow a movement utilizing preexisting relational networks.[24] In a one-on-one meeting, organizers recruit a host who will commit to invite members of his or her network to his or her home to meet the organizer, share experience, and discuss the movement. Attendees are then recruited to organize a similar meeting of their own, and so forth. The advantage this approach offers from a movement perspective is that it identifies potential community leaders—those successful in hosting a meeting—and avoids reliance on existing organizations and institutions that may be resistant to change. In the movement-like Obama campaign in South Carolina, for example, organizers had conducted some four hundred house meetings by October 2007, attended by some four thousand people, the foundation for a mobilization that deployed fifteen thousand Election Day volunteers, most of them active politically for the first time.[25]

Because relational work is so foundational for a social movement and can only be conducted to scale by many leaders skilled in this practice, a capacity to train leadership—not only at the top—is a core social movement competency.

Telling the Story

A social movement tells a new "story." Learning how to tell that story, the craft of what I call *public narrative*, is a second important leadership practice. And, like relationship building, its contribution to a movement depends on sharing the practice widely.

VALUES, EMOTION, AND ACTION

A puzzle social movement scholars of an earlier era faced was the question of why grievances produced protest in some cases but not in others. Scholars of moral economy showed that actionable "grievances" were experienced as an injustice, not simply an inconvenience, but as a wrong that demanded righting.[26] Psychologists showed that grievance leads to action only if combined with efficacy, or hope.[27] Thus, action on a grievance becomes more likely when it is experienced as an injustice, coupled with the presence of the sense of efficacy, solidarity, and hopefulness required to undertake the sacrifice, make the commitments, and take the risks that acting to create change entails. The discursive challenge, then, is not only to articulate grievances but also to muster the moral energy, especially the hope, to drive the whole project. And although we tend to attribute this work to a single, visible, charismatic leader, it is a leadership practice required at all levels if a movement is to flourish.

Psychologist Jerome Bruner argues that narrative is how we learn to exercise agency—choice in the face of uncertainty. We interpret the world in analytic and narrative modes.[28] Cognitively mapping the world, we can discern patterns, test relationships, and hypothesize empirical claims—the domain of analysis. But we also map the world affectively, coding experience, objects, and symbols as good for us or bad us for us, fearful or safe, hopeful or depressing, and so on. When we consider responding to a challenge with purposeful action, we ask ourselves two questions: why and how. Analytics helps answer the "how question"—how to use resources efficiently, detect opportunities, compare costs, and so on. But to answer the "why question"—why this matters, why we care, why we value one goal over another—we turn to narrative. The why question is not why we think we *ought* to act, but rather, why we *do* act, that which actually moves us to act, our motivation, our values. Or, as St. Augustine wrote, it is the difference between "knowing" the good, an ought, and "loving the good," a source of motivation.

Moral philosopher Martha Nussbaum argues that because we make choices based on values we experience via emotion, making moral choices without emotional information is futile.[29] She supports her argument with research on people afflicted with lesions on the amygdala, a part of the brain central to our emotions. When faced with decisions, they can come up with one option after another, but cannot decide because decisions rest on judgments of value. If we cannot experience emotion, we cannot experience values that orient us to the choices we must make.

Facilitating Purposeful Action

Some emotions inhibit agency expressed as purposeful action, whereas others facilitate it (figure 19-2). Exploring the relationship between emotion and purposeful action, political scientist George Marcus points to two of our neurophysiologic systems—surveillance and disposition.[30]

FIGURE 19-2

Emotions that inhibit and facilitate purposeful action

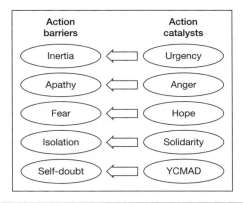

Our surveillance system compares what we *expect* to see with what we *do* see, tracking anomalies that, when observed, translate into anxiety. Without this emotional cue, Marcus argues, we operate out of habit. When we do feel anxiety, we say to ourselves, "Hey! Pay attention! There's a bear in the door!" Our *dispositional system*, on the other hand, operates along a continuum from depression to enthusiasm, or, as we might also describe it, from despair to hope. If we link an experience of anxiety with despair, our fear kicks in, or our rage, or we freeze—none of which facilitates adaptive agency. On the other hand, if we are hopeful, our curiosity will be provoked to explore the novelty in ways that can facilitate learning, creative problem solving, and intentional action. Thus, our capacity to consider action, consider it well, and act on our consideration depends on what we feel.

Social movement leaders mobilize the emotions that make agency possible. When we experience the "world as it is" in deep dissonance with values that define the "world as it should be," we experience emotional dissonance, a tension only resolvable through action. Organizers call this *agitation*. For example, because I depend on my job, I fear upsetting the boss (teacher, parent, employer); however, this may conflict with my self-respect if the boss violates my dignity. One person may become angry and challenge her boss, another may "swallow her pride," and another may resist the organizer who points out the conflict. Any of these options is costly, but one may serve a person's interests better than another.

As figure 19-2 illustrates, inertia—the security of habitual routine —can blind us to the need for action, but urgency and anger get our attention. Fear can paralyze us, driving us to rationalize inaction; amplified by self-doubt and isolation, fear can cause us to become victims of despair. On the other hand, hope inspires us and, in concert with self-efficacy (the feeling that you can make a difference) and solidarity (love, empathy), can move us to act.

Urgency that captures our attention creates the space for new action and is more about priority than time. An urgent need to complete a problem set due tomorrow supplants the important need to decide what to do with the rest of life. The urgent need to attend to a critically ill family member supplants the important need to attend a long postponed business meeting (or ought to?). The urgent need to commit a full day to turning out voters for a critical election supplants the important need to review the family budget. Because commitment and focused energy are required to launch anything new, creating a sense of urgency is often the only way to get the process started.

What about inertia's first cousin, apathy? As discussed earlier, we can counter apathy with anger—not rage, but outrage or indignation. Constructive anger grows out of experiencing the difference between *what ought to be* and *what is*—the way we feel when our moral order has been violated.[31] Sociologist Bill Gamson describes this as using an "injustice frame" to counter a "legitimacy frame."[32] As scholars of "moral economy" have taught us, people rarely mobilize to protest inequality as such, but they do mobilize to protest "unjust" inequality.[33] In other words, values, moral traditions, and a sense of personal dignity can function as critical sources of the motivation to act.

Where can we find courage to act despite our fear? Trying to reduce our fear by eliminating external provocation is often a fool's errand because it locates its source of courage outside, rather than within our own hearts. Trying to make ourselves "fearless" is counterproductive when acting more out of "nerve than brain." Leaders can inoculate against this tendency by warning others that the opposition will threaten them with this and woo them with that. The fact that these behaviors are expected reveals the opposition as more predictable and thus less to be feared. But in reality, it is the choice to act in spite of fear that constitutes courage. And of the sources of courage, perhaps the most important is hope.

Where do we go to get hope? One source of hope is the experience of "credible solutions," not only reports of success elsewhere, but also direct experience of small successes and small victories. Another source of hope for many lies in faith traditions, spiritual beliefs, cultural practices, and moral understandings. Many of the great social movements—Gandhi, Civil Rights, and Solidarity—drew strength from religious traditions, and much of today's organizing occurs in faith communities. Relationships offer another source of hope. We know people who can inspire hope just by being around. "Charisma" can be understood as a person's capacity to inspire hope in others, of believing in himself or herself. Psychologists who study the role of "positive emotion" give particular attention to the "psychology of hope."[34] More philosophically, Moses Maimonides, the Jewish scholar of the twelfth century, argued that hope is belief in the "plausibility of the possible" as opposed to the "necessity of the probable."

Leaders counter self-doubt by enhancing others' sense of self-efficacy, the sense that *you can make a difference*, or YCMAD. One can inspire this sentiment by framing action in terms of what we *can* do, not what we *can't* do. A leader who designs a plan requiring each new volunteer to recruit one hundred people but provides no leads, training, or coaching will only exacerbate feelings of self-doubt. Recognition based on real accomplishment, not empty flattery, can help. In other words, there can be no *real* recognition without accountability. Accountability does not show lack of trust, but is evidence that what one is doing really matters.

Finally, social movement leaders counter feelings of isolation with the experience of belovedness or solidarity. This is the role of mass meetings, celebration, singing, common dress, and shared language.

The Power of Story
The discursive form through which we all translate our values into action is story. A story is crafted of just three elements: *plot, character*, and *moral* (figure 19-3). The effect depends on the *setting*: who tells the story, who listens, where they are, why they are there, and when.

Plot. A plot engages us, captures our interest, and makes us pay attention. "I got up this morning, had breakfast, and came to school." Is that a plot? Why? Why not? How about: "I was having breakfast this morning when I heard a loud screeching coming from the roof. At that very moment I looked outside to where my car was parked, but it

FIGURE 19-3

Narrative structure

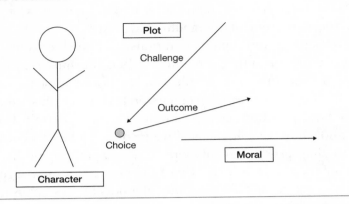

was gone! All I could find was a grease spot!" Now what's going on? What's the difference?

A story begins. The protagonist moves toward a desired goal. But the unexpected intervenes, a challenge looms. The plan is up in the air. The protagonist must figure out what to do. This is when we get interested. We want to find out what happens.

Why do we care?

Dealing with the unexpected defines the texture of our lives. There are no more tickets at the movie theater. You lose your job. Our marriage is on the verge of break-up. We are always learning how to deal with uncertainty, the greatest source of which is other people. The subject of most stories is therefore about how to interact with other people.

As human beings we are capable of agency: making choices in the present based on remembering the past and imagining the future. When we act from habit, we don't choose; we just follow the routine. Only when the routines break down, when the guidelines are unclear, when no one can tell us what to do, do we make real choices and become the creators of our own lives, communities, and futures. It is in these moments, as frightening as they are exhilarating, that we become the agents of our own fate.

A plot consists of just three elements: a *challenge*, a *choice*, and an *outcome*. Attending to plot is how we learn to deal with the unpredictable. Researchers report that most of the time that parents spend with young children is in storytelling—stories of the family, the child's stories, stories of the neighbors. Bruner describes this as *agency training*: the way we learn how to process choices in the face of uncertainty.[35] Because our need to learn how to handle the unexpected is infinite, we invest billions of dollars and countless hours in films, literature, and sports events—not to mention religious practices, cultural activities, and national celebrations.

Character. Although a story requires a plot, it only works if we experience its emotional content by identifying empathetically with the protagonist. That is how we learn what the story has to teach to our hearts, not only our heads. As Aristotle wrote, the protagonist's tragic experience touches us and, perhaps, opens our eyes.[36] Arguments persuade with evidence, logic, and data. Stories persuade through empathetic identification. Have you been to a movie where you couldn't identify with a single character? It's boring. We may identify with protagonists that are only vaguely "like us"—like the road runner (if not the coyote) in the cartoons. Other times we identify with protagonists very much like us in stories about friends, relatives, and neighbors. Sometimes the protagonists of a story are *us*, as when we find ourselves in the midst of an unfolding story in which we are the authors of the outcome.

Moral. Stories teach. We've all heard the ending "And that is the moral of the story." Have you ever been at a party where someone starts telling a story and goes on and on? Someone may say (or want to say), "Get to the point!" We deploy stories to *make a point* and to evoke a response.

The moral of a successful story is emotionally experienced understanding, not only conceptual understanding—a lesson of the heart, not only the head. When stated only conceptually, many a moral becomes a banality. Saying "haste makes waste" does not communicate the emotional experience of losing it all because we moved too quickly—but it can remind us of that feeling, learned through a story. Nor can we expect morals to provide technical information. We do not retell the story of David and Goliath to learn how to use a slingshot. The story teaches us that a "little guy" with courage, resourcefulness, and imagination can beat a "big guy," especially one with Goliath's arrogance.

We feel David's anger, courage, and satisfaction and feel hopeful for our own lives because he is victorious. Stories thus teach how to manage our emotions, not repress them, so we can act with agency to face our own challenges.

Stories are not simply examples and illustrations. When well told, we experience *the point*, and we feel hope. It is that experience, not the words, that moves us to action. Because sometimes that is the point—we have to act.

Setting. Stories are told. They are not a disembodied string of words, images, and phrases. They are not messages, sound bites, or brands, although these rhetorical fragments may reference a story. Storytelling is fundamentally relational. As we listen, we evaluate the story, and we find it more or less easy to enter, depending on the storyteller. Is it his or her story? We hear it one way. Is it the story of a friend, a colleague, or a family member? We hear it another way. Is it a story without time, place, or specificity? We step back. Is it a story we share, perhaps a Bible story? Perhaps we draw closer to one another. And even as he tells his story, the storyteller attends to our reactions, modifying the story if need be to make the desired point. Storytelling is how we interact with each other about values; how we share experiences with each other, counsel each other, comfort each other, and inspire each other to action.

Public Narrative: Self, Us, and Now

Social movement leaders tell new public stories: a story of self, a story of us, and a story of now (figure 19-4). A story of self communicates

FIGURE 19-4

Telling a public story

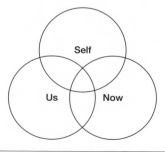

the values that call one to action. A story of us communicates the values shared by those in action. A story of now communicates an urgent challenge to those values that demands action now. Participating in a social movement not only often involves a rearticulation of one's story of self, us, and now, but also marks an entry into a world of uncertainty so daunting that access to sources of hope is essential. In this section I'll draw examples from the first seven minutes of Senator Barack Obama's speech to the Democratic National Convention in July 2004 (see chapter appendix).

Story of Self. Telling one's story of self is a way to communicate our identity, the choices that have made us who we are, and the values that shaped those choices—not as abstract principle, but as lived experience. We construct stories of self around *choice points*—moments when we faced a challenge, chose, experienced an outcome, and learned something. We can access the values that move us—and communicate them—by reflecting on these choice points and describing what happened to another person. And because storytelling is a social transaction, one that engages our listener's memories as well as our own, we often adapt our story of self in response to feedback so the communication works. We construct our identity, in other words, as our story. What is utterly unique about each of us is not a combination of the categories (race, gender, class, profession, marital status) that include us, but rather, our journey, our way through life, our personal text from which each of us can teach.[37]

A story is like a poem. A poem moves not by how long it is, nor how eloquent or complicated. A story or poem moves by evoking an experience or moment through which we grasp the feeling or insight the poet communicates. Because we are gifted with episodic memory, based on our ability to visualize past experience, we can imagine ourselves in the scene described.[38] The more specific the details we choose to recount, the more we can move our listeners, and the more powerfully we can articulate our values, what moral philosopher Charles Taylor calls our "moral sources."[39]

Some believe their personal stories don't matter, that others won't care, or that we shouldn't talk about ourselves so much. But if we do public work, we have a responsibility to give a public account of ourselves—where we came from, why we do what we do, and where we think we're going. Aristotle argued that rhetoric has three components —*logos*, *pathos*, and *ethos*—this is the ethos.[40] The logos is the logic of the argument. The pathos is the feeling the argument evokes. The ethos is the credibility of the person who makes the argument.

One who serves in public leadership really has little choice as to telling his or her story of self. If we don't author our story, others will—and may tell our story in ways that we may not like. Not because they are malevolent, but because others try to make sense of who we are by drawing on their experience of people whom they consider to be like us.

Social movements often serve as crucibles within which participants learn to tell new stories of self interacting with other participants. Stories of self can be challenging because social movement participation is often prompted by the "prophetic" combination of criticality and hope. In personal terms, this means that most participants have stories of both pain and of hope. If we haven't talked about our stories of pain very much, it can take a while to learn how to manage it. But if others are to understand who we are, and we omit the pain, our account will lack authenticity, raising questions about the rest of the story.

In the early days of the women's movement, people participated in "consciousness raising" group conversations that mediated changes in their stories of self, who they were, as women. Stories of pain could be shared, but so could stories of hope.[41] In the Civil Rights movement, blacks living in the Deep South who feared claiming the right to vote had to encourage one another to find the courage to make the claim—which, once made, began to alter how they thought of themselves and how they could interact with their children, as well as with white people, and each other.[42]

In Senator Obama's "story of self," he recounts three key choice points: his grandfather's decision to send his son to America to study, his parents' "improbable" decision to marry, and his parents' decision to name him Barack ("blessing"), an expression of hope for a tolerant and generous America. Each choice communicates courage, hope, and caring. He tells us nothing of his resume, preferring to introduce himself by telling us where he came from, and who made him the person that he is, so that we might have an idea of where he is going. In his presidential campaign, a key element of the training provided for organizers, leadership teams, and volunteers was in learning to tell their stories of self. Although many arrived expecting they would have to learn Obama's biography, become public policy experts, or both, they discovered that their own experience could provide them with all the stories they needed to communicate their own motivations, and to motivate others to join them.[43] One of these personal stories, told at a South

Carolina house meeting by twenty-three-year-old organizer Ashley Baia, provided the conclusion to Obama's historic speech on race, "A More Perfect Union," delivered in Philadelphia on March 18, 2008.

Story of Us. Our stories of self overlap with our stories of us. We each participate in many us's: family, community, faith, organization, profession, nation, or movement. A story of us expresses the values, the experiences, shared by the us we are evoking at the time. But a story of "us" not only articulates values of our community; it can also distinguish our community from another, reducing uncertainty about what to expect from those with whom we interact. Social scientists often describe a "story of us" as collective identity.[44]

Our cultures are repositories of stories. Stories about challenges we have faced, how we stood up to them, and how we survived are woven into the fabric of our political culture, faith traditions, and so on We tell these stories again and again in the form of folk sayings, songs, religious practice, and celebrations (e.g., Easter, Passover, Fourth of July). And like individual stories, stories of us can inspire, teach, offer hope, advise caution, and so on. We also weave new stories from old ones. The Exodus story, for example, served the Puritans when they colonized North America, but it also served Southern blacks claiming civil rights in the freedom movement.

For a collection of people to become an "us" requires a story-teller, an interpreter of their shared experience. In a workplace, people who work beside one another but interact little, don't linger after work, don't arrive early, and don't eat together never develop a story of us. In a social movement, the interpretation of the movement's new experience is a critical leadership function. And, like the story of self, it is built from the choice points—the founding, the choices made, the challenges faced, the outcomes, the lessons learned.

In Senator Obama's speech, he moves into his "story of us" when he declares, "My story is part of the American story" and proceeds to list American values that he shares with his listeners—the people in the room, the people watching on television, the people who will read about the speech the next day. And he begins by going back to the beginning, to choices made by the founders to begin this nation, a beginning that he locates in the Declaration of Independence, a repository of the value of equality, in particular. He then cites a series of moments that evoke values shared by his audience. And in his presidential victory speech, delivered in Chicago on the evening of November 4, 2008, he declared:

> If there is anyone out there who still doubts that America is a place where all things are possible; who still wonders if the dream of our founders is alive in our time; who still questions the power of our democracy, tonight is your answer . . . It's the answer spoken by young and old, rich and poor, Democrat and Republican, black, white, Latino, Asian, Native American, gay, straight, disabled and not disabled—Americans who sent a message to the world that we have never been a collection of Red States and Blue States: we are, and always will be, the United States of America.

Story of Now. A story of now articulates the urgent challenge to the values that we share that demands action now. What choice must we make? What is at risk? And where is the hope?

In a story of now, we are the protagonists and it is our choices that shape the story's outcome. We must draw on our "moral sources" to respond. A powerful articulation of a story of now was Dr. King's talk, often recalled as the "I have a dream" speech, delivered on August 23, 1963. People often forget that he preceded the dream with a challenge, white America's long overdue debt to African Americans. King argued that it was a debt that could no longer be postponed—it was a moment possessed of the "fierce urgency of now."[45] If we did not act, the nightmare would grow worse, never to become the dream.

In the story of now, story and strategy overlap because a key element in hope *is* strategy—a credible vision of how to get from here to there. The "choice" offered cannot be something like "we must all choose to be better people" or "we must all choose to do any one of this list of fifty-three things" (which makes each of the items trivial). A meaningful choice is more like "we must all choose—do we commit to boycotting the buses until they desegregate or not?" Hope is specific, not abstract. What's the vision? When God inspires the Israelites in Exodus, he doesn't offer a vague hope of "better days" but describes a land "flowing with milk and honey" (Exodus 3:9) and what must be done to get there. A vision of hope can unfold a chapter at a time. It can begin by getting the number of people to show up at a meeting that you committed to bring. You can win a small victory that shows change is possible. A small victory can become a source of hope if it is *interpreted* as part of a greater vision. In churches, when people have a "new story" to tell about themselves, it is as "testimony"—a person shares an account of moving from despair to hope, the significance of the experience enhanced by the telling of it.

Hope is not to be found in lying about the facts, but in the *meaning* of the facts. In Shakespeare's version of his speech on the eve of the Battle of Agincourt, King Henry V stirs hope in his men's hearts by offering them a different view of themselves. No longer are they a few bedraggled soldiers led by a young and inexperienced king in an obscure corner of France who are about to be wiped out by an overwhelming force. Now they are a "happy few," united with their king in solidarity, holding an opportunity to grasp immortality in their hands, to become legends in their own time, a legacy for their children and grandchildren.[46] This is their time! The story of now is that moment in which story (why) and strategy (how) overlap and in which, as poet Seamus Heaney writes, "Justice can rise up, and hope and history rhyme."[47]

Senator Obama moves to his "story of now" with the phrase, "There is more work left to do." After we experience the values that we identify with America at its best, he confronts us with the fact that they are not realized in practice. He then tells stories of specific people in specific places with specific problems. And as we identify with each of them, our empathy reminds us of pain we have felt in our own lives. But, he reminds us, all this could change. And we know it could change. It could change because we have a way to make the change, if we choose to take it. And that way is to support the election of Senator John Kerry. Although that last part didn't work out, the point is that he concluded his story of now with a very specific choice he called upon us to make. And in his presidential campaign, Obama appropriated Dr. King's "fierce urgency of now" to mobilize voters on behalf of his cause.

Through public narrative, social movement leaders—and participants—can move to action by mobilizing sources of motivation, constructing new shared individual and collective identities, and finding the courage to act.

Devising Strategy

A third function of social movement leadership is creative strategizing. Just as storytelling is key to meeting the motivational challenge, so strategy is key to dealing with the resource challenge: the fact that challengers of the status quo rarely have access to the conventional resources that its defenders do. Challengers must therefore find ways to compensate for resources with resourcefulness. And, because of the participatory, decentralized, and voluntary structure of most social movement organizations, the gifts of one entrepreneurial "genius" will not do—the practice must be learned throughout the movement for its potential to be realized.

As I have argued elsewhere, for the social movement strategist, the story of David and Goliath is most instructive.[48]

> And there went out a champion out of the camp of the Philistines, named Goliath . . . whose height was six cubits and a span. And he had an helmet of brass upon his head, and he was armed with a coat of mail . . . and he had greaves of brass upon his legs . . . and the staff of his spear was like a weaver's beam; and his spear's head weighed six hundred shekels of iron . . . And he stood and cried to the armies of Israel . . . Choose you a man for you . . . If he be able to fight with me, and to kill me, then will we be your servants; but if I prevail against him, and kill him, then shall ye be our servants . . . Give me a man that we may fight together. When Saul and all Israel heard those words of the Philistine, they were dismayed and greatly afraid . . .
>
> And David said unto Saul, Let no man's heart fail because of him; thy servant will go and fight with this Philistine. And Saul said to David, Thou art not able to go against this Philistine to fight with him: for thou art but a youth, and he a man of war from his youth . . . David said . . . The Lord that delivered me out of the lion, and out of the paw of the bear, he will deliver me out of the hand of this Philistine. And Saul said unto David, Go, and the Lord be with thee. And Saul armed David with his armour, and he put an helmet of brass upon his head; also he armed him with a coat of mail. And David girded his sword upon his armour, and he assayed to go; for he had not proved it. And David said unto Saul, I cannot go with these; for I have not proved them. And David put them off him. And he took his staff in his hand, and chose him five smooth stones out of the brook, and put them in a shepherd's bag which he had . . . ; and his sling was in his hand: and he drew near unto the Philistine . . . And when the Philistine looked about, and saw David, he disdained him: for he was but a youth, and ruddy, and of a fair countenance . . . Then said David to the Philistine, Thou comest to me with a sword,

and with a spear, and with a shield; but I come to thee in the name of the Lord of hosts . . . And David put his hand in his bag, and took thence a stone, and slang it, and smote the Philistine in his forehead; and he fell upon his face to the earth.[49]

When Goliath, veteran warrior, victor of many battles, arrayed in full battle gear, challenges the Israelites, their military leaders cower in fear. It is David, the young shepherd boy, to whom God gives the courage to face the giant. David's success begins with his courage, his commitment, and his motivation. But it takes more than courage to bring David success. David thinks about the battle differently. Reminded by five stones he finds in a brook, he reflects on previous encounters in which he protected his flock from bears and lions. Based on these recollections, he reframes this new battle in a way that gives him an advantage. Pointedly rejecting the offer of shield, sword, or armor as weapons because he cannot use them effectively against a master of these weapons, David conceives a plan of battle based on his five smooth stones, his skill with a sling, and the giant's underestimation of him.

The strategic challenge that social movement leaders face is how to successfully challenge those with more power. In an interdependent world of competition and cooperation, using one's resources to achieve one's goals often requires deploying those resources to influence the interests of others who hold a resource one needs—power. Although no one is entirely without resources, people lack power when unable to mobilize or deploy their resources in ways that influence the interests of critical others. A person's labor resource, for example, can become a source of power vis-à-vis an employer if mobilized collectively. Strategy is how actors translate their resources into power to get "more bang for the buck."

Opportunities occur at moments when actors' resources acquire more value because the environmental context changes. Actors do not suddenly acquire more resources or devise a new strategy, but find that resources they already have give them more leverage in achieving their goals. A full granary, for example, acquires greater value in a famine, creating opportunity for its owner. Similarly, a close election creates opportunity for political leaders who can influence swing voters. A labor shortage creates opportunity for workers to get more for their labor. This is one reason timing is such an important element of strategy.

Strategy is how we turn what we have into what we need to get what we want—a hypothesis that if we do x, y, and z, then a will result. Rooted in a theory of change, it orients current action toward future goals, adapting to an ever-changing environment, especially the actions and reactions of other actors. In fixed contexts in which rules, resources, and interests are given, strategy can be assessed in the analytic terms of game theory. But in settings in which rules, resources, and interests are emergent—such as social movements—strategy has more in common with creative thinking. Strategic action is thus an ongoing creative process of understanding and adapting new conditions to one's goals.

Development of effective strategy is thus more likely to occur under conditions in which strategists are highly motivated, enjoy access to diverse sources of salient knowledge, and employ deliberative practices committed to learning—what I call *strategic capacity* (figure 19-5).

- *David committed to fight Goliath before he knew how he would do it. He knew* why *he* had *to do it before he knew* how *he* could *do it.* Motivation influences creative output because it affects the focus one brings to one's work, the ability to concentrate for extended periods of time, persistence, willingness to take risks, and ability to sustain high energy. Motivated individuals are more likely to do the work to acquire needed knowledge and

FIGURE 19-5

Strategic capacity

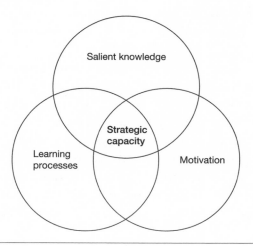

skills. Individuals think more critically and reflectively, overriding programmed modes of thought, if they are intensely interested in a problem, dissatisfied with the status quo, or have experienced a schema failure as a result of sharp breaches in expectations and outcomes. To the extent that success enhances motivation, it not only generates more resources but also may encourage greater creativity.

- *David did not know how to use King Saul's weapons, but he did know how to use stones as weapons.* A second element of creativity is possession of skills, mastery of which is requisite for developing novel applications. Creative jazz piano players have learned how to play the piano very well. In terms of strategy, mastery of specific skills—or tactics—is relevant, but so is access to local knowledge of constituencies with which one is interacting. We expect effective military strategists to command skills required for battlefield success and to understand the troops, the enemy, the battlefield, and so forth. The better our information about how to work within a domain—local knowledge—the more likely we are to know how to deal with problems arising within that domain. Since environments change in response to initiatives, however, regular feedback is especially important in evaluating responses to these initiatives.

- *David could use his skill with stones because he had imaginatively recontextualized the battlefield, transforming it into a place where, as a shepherd, he knew how to protect his flock from wolves and bears.* An outsider to the battle, he saw resources others did not see and opportunities they did not grasp. Goliath, on the other hand, the insider, failed to see a shepherd boy as a threat. When we face novel problems, we can use heuristic processes to devise novel solutions, recontextualizing data or synthesizing data in new ways. But to think creatively, we must recognize our problems as new ones—at least to us—that require new solutions. Innovative thinking is facilitated by encounters with diverse points of view, whether based on the life experience of individuals or diversity of experience within a group. Access to a diversity of salient knowledge not only offers multiple routines from which to choose, but also contributes to the "mindfulness" that multiple solutions are possible.

Structurally, strategic capacity is most effectively developed among a leadership team, rather than in the head of a single individual. It will be most productive if it includes insiders and outsiders to relevant constituencies, leaders with strong and weak ties to those constituencies, and persons experienced with diverse repertoires of collective action. Social movement leaders can make the most of these factors if they conduct regular, open, authoritative deliberations; establish accountability to key constituencies; and can draw critical resources from these actions.

I offer one example of how strategic capacity works from the early days of the California farmworkers' movement led by Cesar Chavez. In February 1966 in Delano, California, grape workers had been on strike for union recognition for five months. In November the season had ended with no breakthroughs, and a boycott called in December against Schenley Industries, a major liquor company with four thousand acres of grapes, had produced no results. So Chavez convened a meeting of leadership at a supporter's home near Santa Barbara to devote three days to figuring out how to move on Schenley, prepare for the spring, and sustain the commitment of strikers, organizers, and supporters. I quote from my notes of that meeting:

> As proposals flew around the room, someone suggested we follow the example of the New Mexico miners who had traveled to New York to set up a mining camp in front of the company headquarters on Wall Street. Farm workers could travel to Schenley headquarters in New York, set up a labor camp out front, and maintain a vigil until Schenley signed. Someone else then suggested they go by bus so rallies could be held all across the country, local boycott committees organized, and publicity generated, building momentum for the arrival in New York. Then why not march instead of going by bus, someone else asked, as Dr. King had the previous year. But it's too far from Delano to New York, someone countered. On the other hand, the Schenley headquarters in San Francisco might not be too far—about 280 miles which an army veteran present calculated could be done at the rate of 15 miles a day or in about 20 days.
>
> But what if Schenley doesn't respond, Chavez asked. Why not march to Sacramento instead and put the heat on Governor Brown to intervene and get negotiations started. He's up for reelection,

wants the votes of our supporters, so perhaps we can have more impact if we use him as "leverage." Yes, some one else said, and on the way to Sacramento, the march could pass through most of the farm worker towns. Taking a page from Mao's "long march" we could organize local committees and get pledges not to break the strike signed. Yes, and we could also get them to feed us and house us. And just as Zapata wrote his "Plan de Ayala," Luis Valdez suggested, we can write a "Plan de Delano," read it in each town, ask local farm workers to sign it and to carry it to the next town. Then, Chavez asked, why should it be a "march" at all? It will be Lent soon, a time for reflection, for penance, for asking forgiveness. Perhaps ours should be a pilgrimage, a "peregrinación," which could arrive at Sacramento on Easter Sunday.[50]

On March 17, farmworkers began their *peregrinación*, carrying banners of Our Lady of Guadalupe, patron saint of Mexico, portraits of *campesino* leader Emiliano Zapata, placards proclaiming *peregrinación*, *penitencia*, *revolución*—pilgrimage, penance, revolution—and signs calling on supporters to boycott Schenley. One striker, Roberto Roman, carried a six-foot-tall wooden cross, constructed of two-by-fours and draped in black cloth. Timed to coincide with a visit by Senator Robert Kennedy for U.S. Senate Subcommittee on Migratory Labor hearings in Delano, the march attracted public attention from the start. Televised images of a line of helmeted police temporarily blocking the marchers' departure evoked images of police lines in Selma, Alabama, the year before. A crowd of more than one thousand welcomed them to Fresno at the end of the first week. Reporters profiled strikers, examining why they would walk three hundred miles, and analyzed what the strike was all about. The march articulated not only the farmworkers' call for justice, but also the Mexican American community's claims for a voice in public life. At an individual level, as Cesar Chavez described it, the march was also a way of "training ourselves to endure the long, long struggle, which by this time had become evident . . . would be required. We wanted to be fit not only physically but also spiritually."

On the afternoon of April 3, as the farmworkers arrived in Stockton, a week's march south of Sacramento, Schenley's lawyer reached Chavez by phone. Schenley had little interest in remaining the object of a boycott, especially as the march's arrival in Sacramento promised to become a national anti-Schenley rally. As a result, just three days before the march would arrive, Schenley signed the first real union contract in California farm labor history. So Saturday afternoon, a crowd that had grown to two thousand gathered on the grounds of Our Lady of Grace School in West Sacramento, on a hill looking across the Sacramento River to the capital city that they would enter the next morning. During the Easter vigil service that evening, more than one speaker compared them to the ancient Israelites camped across the River Jordan from the Promised Land. That night Roberto Roman carefully redraped his cross in white and decorated it with spring flowers. The next morning, barefoot, he bore it triumphantly across the river bridge, down the Capitol mall, and up the Capitol steps, where he was met by a crowd of ten thousand farmworkers and supporters who launched the farmworker movement.

A key challenge social movement leaders face, one overcome in the above example, is that of focusing the use of movement resources, a function of participant commitment, on a single strategic outcome for a sustained period of time. Individual participants often identify with a particular issue or position. And when identity is at stake, strategic choices can become very difficult. Given a fragile governance structure, leaders often try to avoid conflict by saying "yes" to everyone. This "thousand flowers" approach, however, diffuses effort, squanders resources, confuses supporters, and trivializes the value of individual contribution. One strength of the Montgomery Bus Boycott, for example, was the clarity of its strategic objective: desegregating buses in Montgomery, Alabama, a goal to which almost every member in the community could contribute resources by withholding bus fare. Had the organizers fragmented their resources by attacking voting rights, housing, and lunch counters as a way to accommodate the preferences of various groups of participants, the campaign could easily have failed.

A strength of the Civil Rights movement leadership was creation of a mechanism, the Leadership Conference on Civil Rights, which, roughly from 1956 to 1967, provided a venue in which strategic focus was considered. This focus was not achieved without debate, conflict, and argument, some of it very intense. Its duration was limited, and at times multiple campaigns would be in play. But one clear reason for this relative success was the creation of organizational structures within which this work could be done at local, regional, and national levels. One of the most salient challenges faced by the climate change movement today is precisely one of bringing strategic focus to its efforts.

Catalyzing Action

Action refers to the work of mobilizing and deploying resources to achieve outcomes. It is the bottom line of the relational, motivational, and strategic work. Social movements are, in the end, about changing the world, not yearning for it, thinking about it, or exhorting it. The resources a social movement can mobilize are those held by their participants—time, skills, and effort—and are matters of voluntary commitment.

How leaders mobilize resources affects how they can be deployed; how they are deployed affects how they can be mobilized. Resources mobilized from participants can be deployed with accountability solely to participants in ways that empowers them to achieve results.[51] Outside resources entail accountability to donors, who often place limits on how they can be used, creating a counterproductive dependency rather than empowerment. When foundations began to prioritize the environment, for example, inner city organizations dependent on foundation funding found that constituency interests could now be served by focusing on environmental programs.[52] Similarly, if one's resource advantage is numbers of people, using tactics that require money makes little sense. On the other hand, action based on resources that participants can commit may limit tactics to those in which they are willing to participate.

A key strategic question social movement leaders face is where to emphasize "collaboration" or "claims making." Collaboration builds power "with" others, interdependently, making the most of participant resources—for example, credit unions, death benefits, and cooperative day care. Claims making challenges actors who use their power over the participants in ways that compromise participant interests. This might include getting the city to allocate funds to new community needs, an employer to raise wages, or Congress to pass a law. Collaborative work often is required to create enough "power with" to challenge "power over."

Some action generates new resources, whereas other action drains resources. Union success, for example, yields more members, more dues, and more leadership. When faith-based community organizations do parish renewal work among member churches, their human and financial capacities grow. Grant-based action programs, in contrast, often fail to generate new resources through their work, holding themselves in a state of perpetual dependency. There is no consistently "right" answer to the appropriate interaction of resources and action. But understanding the relationship is essential so leaders can make conscious choices about how to improve the odds that their movement will succeed in its goals.

Perhaps the greatest social movement "action" challenge is consistently translating intent into outcome: making things happen, on time; counting them; and evaluating them for continual improvement. Developing such a "culture of commitment" is critical if a movement is to use its most precious resource, volunteer time, well. Meeting the challenge is not a matter of exhortation, but of establishing norms, processes, and structures to make commitment real, coach excellent performance, and realize motivational benefits of intrinsic reward generated by well-designed work.

The key to social movement action is the craft of getting *commitments*. And it is a leadership skill that people find most difficult to master. A commitment is a specific pledge of time, money, or action. "Can we count on you to be at the meeting at 7:00 p.m.? Can we count on you for your phone bank shift at 4:00 p.m.? On the one hand, a person asking another to commit may "underask" to avoid getting a "no" and having to deal with the feeling of rejection that can go with it. On the other hand, they may underask to avoid getting a "yes" and the reciprocal commitment that goes with it. A game of "face work," as sociologist Erving Goffman describes it, often develops around commitment.[53] Just as I pretend not to see the soup you spilled on your shirt, so you pretend not to see that I see, and I, in turn, pretend not to see that you see that I see—all in the interest of avoiding embarrassment. Those asking others for commitment often ignore a response that falls far short ("I'll try") to avoid the tension of clarification. The fact that we avoid making commitments we do not intend to keep points to their power of calling forth behavior that is consistent with the commitment.[54] Securing commitment is thus the primary means by which social movements can get resources that they need to do their work. Whatever the reasons, it takes courage, training, and dedication to develop a movement culture of asking for and getting real commitments.

A second key to effective action is turning strategy into *specific measurable outcomes with real deadlines*. Without clear outcomes, neither leaders nor participants have any way to evaluate success or failure, to learn, or to experience the feedback essential to motivation. An advantage of electoral campaigns is that a specific number of votes are required to win an election. Even in that setting, however, intermediate outcomes are often avoided. One of the main reasons movements avoid commitment to specific outcomes is a fear that failure will diminish the motivation needed to sustain the movement. The cost of avoiding this risk, however, is not only strategic, but motivational as well—only at the front end. One of the most important leadership challenges in a social movement is learning to handle loss. In part, it is a matter of narrative interpretation whether a setback is experienced as "contaminating" the enterprise or as a necessary cost of "redemption."[55] But it is also a function of building in outcome evaluation as a routine practice, allowing participants to experience it as a source of learning, rather than of negative judgment. One possible tactic is organizing physical space to focus on outcomes—for example, turning the number of votes secured through phone calls and house meetings into a large chart that hangs in the line of sight of anyone who enters headquarters. "When you walk through an organizing office, it ought to remind people of what needs to be done, what's important, what things should happen next. The place should have an orienting effect."[56]

A third key factor is designing volunteer tasks in such a way as to avoid the "grunt work" experience in favor of the far more motivational experience of intrinsic reward. This need not be a pipe dream, because the principles of motivational work design are well established in the work of Richard Hackman and others.[57] In a project with the Sierra Club more fully described later in this chapter, my colleague Ruth Wageman and I trained volunteer leaders in how to redesign tasks, such as phone banking, so as to make them more rewarding. This required attention to the skill variety, task identity (a whole task), task significance (meaningful impact), autonomy (choice as to how to achieve the outcome for which one is responsible), and feedback (seeing the results of one's work).[58] This approach to the design of volunteer work remains almost entirely untapped.

Securing excellent outcomes requires consistent *coaching*, a practice I address more fully later in the chapter as leadership development. In social movements, because "new" people are usually trying to make "new" things happen under novel conditions, ongoing learning and teaching is required. On the one hand, performance feedback, especially short-term failure, is critical for adapting tactics and strategy.[59]

On the other hand, to develop the leadership skills of those with less experience, leaders must learn to coach, avoiding both micromanagement on the one hand and hands-off management on the other. This requires making time to meet before an action, during an action if need be, and afterward to evaluate the action. Managing an effective team means scheduling time for the team to meet, to learn, to coach each other, and to receive expert coaching. Regular "learning" meetings can become the eye in the hurricane, the order at the core of what can feel like a chaotic enterprise. For this to work, however, it must be sacred. When I was coordinating the organizing of Nancy Pelosi's first campaign for Congress in 1987, I looked for an opportunity to establish this practice. We had just begun our daily coordinators meeting when someone came running into the room shouting, "Nancy's on the phone! Nancy's on the phone! She's got to talk to you right away!" All eyes turned to me. Was our time really sacred or not? "Please tell Nancy that we're in our coordinators meeting," I said. "I'll call her as soon as we're done." A big sigh of relief. From that point on, we never had any problem sticking to our daily meeting.

Finally, the world of social movements is a world of *contingency:* almost everything that can go wrong likely will. Someone forgets to unlock the hall, the sound system is missing a cable, someone forgot to order the chairs, the map got printed backward, half the flyers didn't get printed on time, someone's car has a flat tire, the date was mistranslated in the Spanish version, and so on. In a setting in which new recruits are trying to achieve daunting tasks, under pressure of time and with fewer resources than they need—typical of most social movements—disaster lurks just around the corner. Because most contingency is outside our control, however, effective leaders focus on that over which they can have some control. For example, making a reminder call two hours before a meeting may persuade someone who was on the fence to come, or it may reveal that no one is coming, allowing one to save his or her valuable time. The best way to handle contingency, however, is to remain in learning mode: resilient, creative, and ready to adapt practices in real time.

Structuring Social Movements

Paleontologist Stephen Jay Gould wrote that time is sometimes a "cycle" and sometimes an "arrow."[60] Thinking of time as a cycle helps us to maintain our routines, our normal procedures, our annual budget, and so forth. Thinking of time as an arrow, on the other hand, focuses us on making change: we begin at a specific moment, we end at a specific moment, and in between is change.

Social movements generally operate within the time-as-an-arrow framework, more generally described as a *campaign*, a way to organize that most valuable, yet widely distributed, resource: time. As Connie Gersick's work shows, organizations have a temporal life as well as a spatial one.[61] Work governed by the internal rhythm of an organization may be more or less well "entrained" with the rhythm of events in its environment. Student groups, for example, need to start a new project in the first weeks of the semester or they won't get started at all. After mid-semester, the rhythm changes as people focus on completing what they have begun. Managing timing is especially important for organizations that must be attuned to the sudden appearance of opportunities; on the one hand, making the most of the opportunity, but, on the other hand, not operating in such a reactive mode that forward momentum is lost.

Campaigns unfold over time with a rhythm that slowly builds a foundation, gathers gradual momentum with preliminary peaks, culminates in a climax when the campaign is won or lost, and then achieves resolution (figure 19-6). When done well, campaigns strengthen the organizations that give rise to them.

A campaign is a strategic and motivational way to organize change activity. It is strategic because it is a way to target effort. It is

FIGURE 19-6

Campaigns

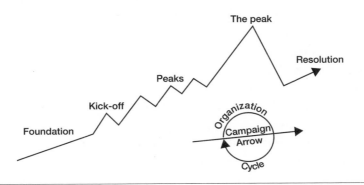

motivational because it enacts an unfolding story of the hope that we can achieve our objective. As it progresses, we find we can make a difference. Our work acquires the urgency of genuine deadlines. The solidarity of collaborating with others in a common cause energizes us.

Campaigns facilitate *targeting* specific objectives, one at a time. Creating something new requires intense energy and concentration—unlike the inertia that keeps things going once they have begun. We can invest energy for a limited number of days, weeks, or months at levels we cannot—and should not—sustain for long periods of time. As a campaign ends, we consolidate our wins or our losses, we return to normal life, we regroup, and perhaps we undertake another campaign in the future. The "adventurous" quality of a campaign facilitates the development of relationships more quickly—and with greater intensity—than would ordinarily be the case. We more easily come to share a common story that we all take part in authoring.

Campaign *timing* is structured as an unfolding narrative. It begins with a foundation period (prologue), starts crisply with a kick-off (curtain goes up), builds slowly to successive peaks (act one, act two), culminates in a final peak determining the outcome (denouement), and is resolved as we celebrate the outcome (epilogue). Our efforts generate momentum not mysteriously, but as a snowball. As we accomplish each objective, we generate new resources that can be applied to achieve the subsequent greater objective. Our motivation grows as each small success persuades us that the subsequent success is achievable—and our commitment grows. The unfolding story of our campaign makes the unfolding story of our organization more credible and, thus, more achievable. Timing has to be carefully managed because a campaign can peak too quickly, exhausting everyone, and then fall into decline. Another danger is that a campaign may heat up faster in some areas than in others, as some people burn out and others never get going.

Campaigns provide an opportunity for learning by allowing for small losses in the early days of a campaign. As Sam Sitkin argues, creating space for small losses early in an undertaking affords participants the opportunity to try new things, which is essential to learning how to do them.[62] It also affords the organization as a whole a chance to learn how to get it right. In most campaigns, we know the first rap we write will be changed once the rubber hits the road and we begin to use it. Of course, it is important to use the early phase of a campaign "mindfully" in this way so it isn't just a preview of what we will do wrong on a large scale.

As is the case with strategy, campaigns are nested. Each campaign objective can be viewed as a "mini-campaign" with its own prologue, kick-off, peaks, climax, and epilogue. The campaign also "chunks out" into distinct territories, districts, or other responsibilities for which specific individuals are responsible. A good campaign can be thought of as a symphony of multiple movements, each with an exposition, development, and recapitulation, but which together proceed toward a grand finale. A symphony is also constructed from the interplay of many different voices interacting in multiple ways but whose overall coordination is crucial for the success of the undertaking. If this seems an overly structured metaphor, you may prefer a jazz ensemble.

Leadership Development

Social movement leadership requires not only adapting to the rhythm of change, but also structuring the space in which effective leadership can grow. Social movement leaders face particular challenges given the decentralized, self-governing, and voluntary mode in which movements operate. Command and control structures alienate participation, inhibit adaptation to local and often rapidly changing conditions, and curb organizational learning.[63] On the other hand, as sociologist Jo Freeman famously noted, antipathy to structure creates a "tyranny of structurelessness" in which authority is exercised in opaque ways, off the books, so to speak, with little or no public accountability.[64] And while decentralization has benefits, it too can inhibit learning, constrict resources, and inhibit strategic coordination.

The challenge has become particularly difficult in recent years because institutional mechanisms that equipped large numbers of people with basic civic skills are in eclipse. De Tocquville's "great free schools of democracy," the extensive three-tiered civic associations that, along with churches, structured our participation in public life for most of our first 180 years of our history, have fallen into sharp decline since the 1960s.[65] These organizations created extensive leadership development opportunities, especially at the local level. Leadership roles, expectations, and obligations had an almost ritualized clarity; collective deliberation and decision making were established practices; and opportunities for learning, development, and growth were afforded by frequent conventions and multitiered leadership ladders. They came apart, however, confronting the combined challenges of race, gender, and generational change (most of them had been gender and race segregated); the development of new communications and, especially, fundraising technologies that marginalized the role of local groups; and the professionalization of advocacy.[66] The vacuum created by this atrophy of collective action leadership skills has so far not been filled by the Internet, a tool far better suited to creating new marketplaces than to forging organizational commitments. The Obama campaign, however, was an important exception in that it combined large-scale training in organizing skills with the development of innovative new media techniques to support the organizers and their local leadership teams in putting those skills to work.[67]

Three structural challenges that social movements face today are in the organization of leadership; processes for effective deliberation and decision making; and mechanisms of genuine accountability. In recent research on the Sierra Club, Ruth Wageman and I employed three approaches to address these challenges: team design, deliberative practice, and mechanisms of accountability.[68]

We restructured leadership practice away from the dominant model of a heroic individual, standing firm in the face of cosmic challenge, to a team approach. Individuals acquired skills in a context in which they would use them,[69] the skills they learned were inherently collaborative,[70] and accountability and motivation embedded in team membership enhanced the odds that new practices would persist, thus creating new capacity. Adapting the work of Hackman and Wageman on "real teams" to this setting, we found that restructuring volunteer leaders as bounded, stable, and interdependent teams with a common purpose, specified roles, and clear norms encouraged goal attainment and learning.[71] The experience of the Obama campaign, where we also introduced this team-based approach, was that volunteers affiliated with teams volunteered ten hours more per week, on average, than those who were unaffiliated.[72]

To address the challenge of decision making that veered from autocracy to consensus and from an overreliance on process to chaos, we introduced deliberative practices that enabled teams to engage conflict without suppressing it, and to differ without personalizing differences. These are much easier to cultivate when the group has done the work of articulating its shared values, identifying its common purpose. In this context a process of defining the problem, establishing outcome criteria, generating alternatives, evaluating alternatives, making a decision, and learning from the decision proved quite positive.

In terms of accountability, we noted that participants were reticent to claim authority, especially when it came to holding each other accountable to commitments, a common refrain being "you can't fire volunteers." In the absence of accountability practices available to traditional social movements, we focused on naming the problem, identifying norms that could help solve the problem, and institutionalizing those norms—something real only in the context of an entire team. Recognizing the centrality of commitment to volunteer effort, we focused on equipping teams to confront (offer feedback to) those who did not honor their commitments, celebrate those who did, and provide coaching to each other across the board. We found that teams with clear norms contributed more effort to their tasks, developed better work strategies, and used talent more efficiently. They also did far better in accomplishing goals.

Conclusion

Social movements make a vital contribution to our capacity for economic, social, political, and cultural adaptation and renewal. Their very nature, however, as broadly based harbingers of change creates unusual leadership challenges: they are voluntary, decentralized, and self-governing; they are volatile, dynamic, and interactive; participants are motivated by moral claims, but results depend on strategic creativity; and their capacity to make things happen depends on their ability to mobilize broad levels of commitment. As a result, perhaps their most critical capacity is consistent formal and informal leadership development.

Appendix 19-1

Senator Barack Obama, "The Audacity of Hope"

Democratic National Convention, Boston, MA, July 27, 2004

Thank you so much. Thank you. Thank you. Thank you so much. Thank you so much. Thank you. Thank you. Thank you, Dick Durbin. You make us all proud.

On behalf of the great state of Illinois, crossroads of a nation, Land of Lincoln, let me express my deepest gratitude for the privilege of addressing this convention.

Tonight is a particular honor for me because, let's face it, my presence on this stage is pretty unlikely. My father was a foreign student, born and raised in a small village in Kenya. He grew up herding goats, went to school in a tin-roof shack. His father—my grandfather—was a cook, a domestic servant to the British.

But my grandfather had larger dreams for his son. Through hard work and perseverance my father got a scholarship to study in a magical place, America, that shone as a beacon of freedom and opportunity to so many who had come before.

While studying here, my father met my mother. She was born in a town on the other side of the world, in Kansas. Her father worked on oil rigs and farms through most of the Depression. The day after Pearl Harbor my grandfather signed up for duty; joined Patton's army, marched across Europe. Back home, my grandmother raised a baby and went to work on a bomber assembly line. After the war, they studied on the G.I. Bill, bought a house through F.H.A., and later moved west all the way to Hawaii in search of opportunity.

And they, too, had big dreams for their daughter. A common dream, born of two continents.

My parents shared not only an improbable love, they shared an abiding faith in the possibilities of this nation. They would give me an African name, Barack, or "blessed," believing that in a tolerant America your name is no barrier to success. They imagined—They imagined me going to the best schools in the land, even though they weren't rich, because in a generous America you don't have to be rich to achieve your potential.

They're both passed away now. And yet, I know that on this night they look down on me with great pride.

They stand here—And I stand here today, grateful for the diversity of my heritage, aware that my parents' dreams live on in my two precious daughters. I stand here knowing that my story is part of the larger American story, that I owe a debt to all of those who came before me, and that, in no other country on earth, is my story even possible.

Tonight, we gather to affirm the greatness of our Nation—not because of the height of our skyscrapers, or the power of our military, or the size of our economy. Our pride is based on a very simple premise, summed up in a declaration made over two hundred years ago: "We hold these truths to be self-evident, that all men are created equal, that they are endowed by their Creator with certain inalienable rights, that among these are Life, Liberty and the pursuit of Happiness."

That is the true genius of America, a faith—a faith in simple dreams, an insistence on small miracles; that we can tuck in our children at night and know that they are fed and clothed and safe from harm; that we can say what we think, write what we think, without hearing a sudden knock on the door; that we can have an idea and start our own business without paying a bribe; that we can participate in the political process without fear of retribution, and that our votes will be counted—at least most of the time.

This year, in this election we are called to reaffirm our values and our commitments, to hold them against a hard reality and see how we're measuring up to the legacy of our forbearers and the promise of future generations.

And fellow Americans, Democrats, Republicans, Independents, I say to you tonight: We have more work to do—more work to do for the workers I met in Galesburg, Illinois, who are losing their union jobs at the Maytag plant that's moving to Mexico, and now are having to compete with their own children for jobs that pay seven bucks an hour; more to do for the father that I met who was losing his job and choking back the tears, wondering how he would pay 4,500 dollars a month for the drugs his son needs without the health benefits that he counted on; more to do for the young woman in East St. Louis, and thousands more like her, who has the grades, has the drive, has the will, but doesn't have the money to go to college.

Now, don't get me wrong. The people I meet—in small towns and big cities, in diners and office parks—they don't expect government to solve all their problems. They know they have to work hard to get ahead, and they want to. Go into the collar counties around Chicago, and people will tell you they don't want their tax money wasted, by a welfare agency or by the Pentagon. Go in—Go into any inner city neighborhood, and folks will tell you that government alone can't teach our kids to learn; they know that parents have to teach, that children can't achieve unless we raise their expectations and turn off the television sets and eradicate the slander that says a black youth with a book is acting white. They know those things.

People don't expect—People don't expect government to solve all their problems. But they sense, deep in their bones, that with just a slight change in priorities, we can make sure that every child in America has a decent shot at life, and that the doors of opportunity remain open to all.

They know we can do better. And they want that choice.

In this election, we offer that choice. Our Party has chosen a man to lead us who embodies the best this country has to offer. And that man is John Kerry.

Notes

1. Thomas Rochon, *Culture Moves: Ideas, Activism, and Changing Values* (Princeton, NJ: Princeton University Press, 1998).

2. Gary T. Max and Doug McAdam, "Collective Behavior in Oppositional Settings: The Emerging Social Movement," in *Collective Behavior and Social Movements* (Englewood Cliffs: Prentice Hall, 1993), chapter 4.

3. Mario Diani, "The Concept of Social Movement," in *Readings in Contemporary Political Sociology*, ed. Kate Nash (New York: Blackwell Publishing, 2000), 158–176.

4. Eric Foner, *The Story of American Freedom* (New York: W.W. Norton, 1998); Theda Skocpol, Marshall Ganz, and Ziad Munson, "A Nation of Organizers: The Institutional Origins of Civic Voluntarism in the United States," *American Political Science Review* 94, no. 3 (September 2000): 527–546; Marshall Ganz, "'Left Behind': Social Movements, Parties, and the Politics of Reform" (paper presented at the annual meeting of the American Sociological Association, Montreal, August 2006).

5. Ronald Heifetz, *Leadership Without Easy Answers* (Cambridge, MA: Harvard University Press, 1998).

6. Marshall Ganz, "What Is Organizing?" *Social Policy* 33 (2002): 16–17; Theda Skocpol, "From Membership to Management," in *Diminished Democray* (Norman, OK: University of Oklahoma Press, 2003), 127–174.

7. Marshall Ganz, Public Leadership Project, Harvard University, Cambridge, MA, 2003.

8. Kenneth T. Andrews, Marshall Ganz, Matt Baggetta, Hahrie Han, and Chaeyoon Lim, "Leadership, Membership, and Voice: Civic Associations That Work," unpublished manuscript, 2007.

9. Joyce Rothschild-Whitt, "The Collectivist Organization: An Alternative to Rational-Bureaucratic Models," *American Sociological Review* 44, no. 4 (August 1979): 509–527; Kathy L. Schiflett and Mary Zey, "Comparison of Characteristics of Private Product Producing Organizations and Public Service Organizations," *Sociological Quarterly* 31, no. 4 (Winter 1990): 569–583.

10. Mike Gecan, "Three Public Cultures," in *Going Public: An Organizer's Guide to Citizen Action* (New York: Anchor, 2004), 151–166.

11. David Knoke and David Prensky, "What Relevance Do Organization Theories Have for Voluntary Associations?" *Social Science Quarterly* 65 (1984): 3–20; David Horton Smith, *Grassroots Associations* (Thousand Oaks, CA: Sage Publications, 2000).

12. Doug McAdam, *Political Process and the Development of Black Insurgency, 1930–1970* (Chicago: University of Chicago Press, 1982); Aldon Morris, *The Origins of the Civil Rights Movement: Black Communities Organizing for Change* (Chicago: The Free Press, 1986).

13. Robert Michels, *Political Parties* (New York: Dover, 1959); Max Weber, *From Max Weber: Essays in Sociology*, trans. and ed. H.H. Gerth and C. Wright Mills (New York: Oxford University Press, 1946).

14. Marshall Ganz, "Resources and Resourcefulness: Strategic Capacity in the Unionization of California Agriculture (1959–1967)," *American Journal of Sociology* 105, no. 4 (January 2000): 1003–1062; Aldon D. Morris and Suzanne Staggenborg, "Leadership in Social Movements," in *The Blackwell Companion to Social Movements*, eds. David A. Snow, Sarah A. Soule, and Hanspeter Kriesi (Malden, MA: Blackwell Publishing, 2004), 171–198; Colin Barker, Alan Johnson, and Michael Lavalette, "Leadership Matters: An Introduction," in *Leadership and Social Movements*, eds. Colin Barker, Alan Johnson, and Michael Lavalette (Manchester, England: Manchester University Press, 2001), 1–23.

15. James Q. Wilson, *Political Organizations* (New York: Basic Books, 1973).

16. Ibid.

17. "Exodus," in *The Five Books of Moses: A Translation and Commentary*, ed. Robert Alter (New York: Norton, 2004).

18. Walter Brueggemann, "The Alternative Community of Moses," in *The Prophetic Imagination* (Minneapolis, MN: Fortress Press, 2001), 1–19.

19. Sharon Erickson Nepstad and Christian Smith, "Rethinking Recruitment to High-Risk/Cost Activism: The Case of Nicaragua Exchange," *Mobilization: An International Quarterly* 4, no. 1 (April 1999): 25–40.

20. Peter Blau, *Exchange and Power in Social Life* (New York: Wiley, 1964).

21. Robert Putnam, "Social Capital and Institutional Success," in *Making Democracy Work: Civic Traditions in Modern Italy* (Princeton, NJ: Princeton University Press, 1994), 163–185.

22. Mark Granovetter, "The Strength of Weak Ties," *American Journal of Sociology* 78, no. 6 (May 1973): 1360–1379; Malcolm Gladwell, "Six Degrees of Lois Weisberg," *The New Yorker*, January 11, 1999, 52–63.

23. Adrian Walker, "Transcending Race, Class," *The Boston Globe*, May 27, 2009.

24. Ian Simmons, "On One-to-Ones," in The Next Steps of Organizing: Putting Theory into Action, Sociology 91r Seminar, 1998.

25. Kelly Candaele and Peter Dreier, "The Year of the Organizer," *American Prospect*, February 1, 2008.

26. James C. Scott, *The Moral Economy of the Peasant: Rebellion and Subsistence in Southeast Asia* (New Haven: Yale University Press, 1977).

27. Jo Freeman, "The Tyranny of Structurelessness," *Berkeley Journal of Sociology* (1970).

28. Jerome Bruner, "Two Modes of Thought," in *Actual Minds, Possible Worlds* (Cambridge, MA: Harvard University Press, 1986), 11–25.

29. Martha Nussbaum, *Upheavals of Thought: The Intelligence of Emotions* (New York: Cambridge University Press, 2001).

30. G.E. Marcus, The *Sentimental Citizen* (University Park, PA: Penn State University Press, 2002).

31. Anger at the contrast of is and ought.

32. W.A. Gamson, *Talking Politics* (New York: Cambridge University Press, 1992).

33. Scott, *The Moral Economy of the Peasant*.

34. Martin E.P. Seligman and Mihaly Csikszentmihaly, "Positive Psychology: An Introduction," *American Psychologist* 55 (2000): 5–14.

35. Bruner, *Actual Minds*, Possible Worlds.

36. Aristotle, *The Poetics*, ed. Richard McKeon (New York: Random House, 1941).

37. Phillip L. Hammack, "Narrative and the Cultural Psychology of Identity," *Personality and Social Psychology Review* 12, no. 3 (2008): 222–247.

38. E. Tulving, "Episodic Memory: From Mind to Brain," *Annual Review of Psychology* 53 (2002): 1–25.

39. Charles Taylor, *Sources of the Self: The Making of Modern Identity* (Cambridge, MA: Harvard University Press, 1989).

40. Aristotle, *The Rhetoric*, ed. Richard McKeon (New York: Random House, 1941).

41. Francesca Polletta, "Ways of Knowing and Stories Worth Telling," in *It Was Like a Fever: Storytelling in Protest and Politics* (Chicago: University of Chicago, 2006), 109–140.

42. Richard A. Cuoto, "Narrative, Free Space, and Political Leadership in Social Movements," *Journal of Politics* 55, no. 1 (February 1993): 57–79.

43. Alec MacGillis, "Obama Camp Relying Heavily on Ground Effort," *The Washington Post*, October 12, 2008, A 04.

44. Alasdair Macintyre, "The Virtues, the Unity of a Human Life, and the Concept of a Tradition," in *Memory, Identity, Community: The Idea of Narrative in the Human Sciences*, eds. Lewis P. Hinchman and Sandra K. Hinchman (Albany, NY: State University of New York, 2001), 241–263; Margaret Somers, "Narrativity, Narrative Identity, and Social Action: Rethinking English Working Class Formation," *Social Science History* 16 (1992): 591–629; Margaret Somers, "The Narrative Constitution of Identity: A Relational and Network Approach," *Theory and Society* 23 (1994): 605–649.

45. Martin Luther King Jr., "I Have a Dream" (Washington DC, August 28, 1963).

46. William Shakespeare, *Henry V*, Act IV, Scene 3.

47. Seamus Heaney, *The Cure at Troy* (New York: Farrar, Straus, and Giroux, 1991).

48. Marshall Ganz, "Why David Sometimes Wins: Strategic Capacity in Social Movements," in *Psychology of Leadership: New Perspectives and Research*, eds. David M. Messick and Roderick M. Kramer (Mahwah, NJ: L. Erlbaum Press, 2004).

49. 1 Samuel 17:4–49 (King James Version).

50. Ganz, "Resources and Resourcefulness," 1003–1062.

51. Pam Oliver and G. Marwell, "Mobilizing Technologies for Collective Action," in *Frontiers in Social Movement Theory*, eds. A. Morris and C.M. Mueller (New Haven, CT: Yale University Press, 1988), 251–271.

52. J. Craig Jenkins and Robert J. Brulle, "Foundation Funding for Environmental Advocacy," Nonprofit Sector Research Fund, Aspen Institute, Washington, DC, 2003.

53. E. Goffman, *The Presentation of Self in Everyday Life* (New York: Doubleday, 1956).

54. R.B. Cialdini, *Influence: Science and Practice*, 4th ed. (Needham Heights, MA: Allyn & Bacon, 2001).

55. Dan P. McAdams and Philip J. Bowman, "Narrating Life's Turning Points: Redemption and Contamination," in *Turns in the Road: Narrative Studies of Lives in Transition* (Washington DC: American Psychological Association, 2001), 3–34.

56. Interview with Paul Milne, July 2005.

57. J. Richard Hackman, "Designing Work for Individuals and for Groups," in *Perspectives on Behavior in Organizations*, eds. J. Richard Hackman, Edward E. Lawler, and Lyman W. Porter (New York: McGraw-Hill Book Company, 1977), 242–257.

58. Marshall Ganz and Ruth Wageman, "Leadership Development in a Civic Organization: Multi-level Influences on Effectiveness," working paper, Harvard Kennedy School of Government, Cambridge, MA, 2008.

59. Sim Sitkin, "Learning Through Failure: The Strategy of Small Losses," *Research in Organizational Behavior* 14 (1992): 231–256.

60. Steven Jay Gould, *Time's Arrow, Time's Cycle: Myth and Metaphor in the Discovery of Geological Time* (Cambridge, MA: Harvard University Press, 1987).

61. Connie Gersick, "Pacing Strategic Change: The Case of a New Venture," *Academy of Management Journal* 37, no. 1 (February 1994): 9–45.

62. Sitkin, "Learning Through Failure."

63. Richard Walton, "From Control to Commitment in the Workplace," *Harvard Business Review* 63, no. 2 (March–April 1985): 77–84.

64. Freeman, "The Tyranny of Structurelessness."

65. Skocpol, Ganz, and Munson, "A Nation of Organizers."

66. Skocpol, "From Membership to Management."

67. Sarah Lai Stirland, "Obama's Secret Weapons: Internet, Databases and Psychology," *Wired*, October 29, 2008.

68. Ganz and Wageman, "Leadership Development in a Civic Organization."

69. Chris Argyris, "Some Limitations of the Case Method: Experiences in a Management Development Program,"*Academy of Management Review* 5 (1980): 291–298.

70. Amy C. Edmondson, R.M. Bohmer, and G.P. Pisano, "Disrupted Routines: Team Learning and New Technology Implementation in Hospitals," *Administrative Science Quarterly* 46 (2001): 685–716; S.W.J. Kozlowski, S.M. Gully, E. Salas, and J.A. Cannon-Bowers, "Team Leadership and Development: Theories, Principles, and Guidelines for Training Team Leaders and Teams," in *Advances in Interdisciplinary Study of Work Teams*, Vol. 3, eds. M.M. Beyerlein, D.A. Johnson, and S.T. Beyerlein. (Greenwich, CT: JAI Press, 1996), 253–291.

71. R. Wageman, "Interdependence and Group Effectiveness,"*Administrative Science Quarterly* 40 (1995): 145–180; J.R. Hackman and R. Wageman, "When and How Team Leaders Matter," *Research in Organizational Behavior* 26 (2005): 39–76.

72. Jeremy Bird, Ohio general election coordinator, interview by author. Chicago, IL, November 8, 2008.

20

LEADERSHIP IN A GLOBALIZING WORLD

Rosabeth Moss Kanter

W HAT DO leaders do? And what will they do in the future? Is this any different in a globalizing world—that is, one in which there are plural public spheres—than in other contexts?

This paper offers a sociological, empirically grounded view of leadership that is both descriptive and normative. It is based on holistic case studies of international companies that examined the perspective of employees and managers on the ground in their local/national setting as they addressed, used, and influenced global frameworks.[1] In short, the research, which is reported fully in my book, *Supercorp: How Vanguard Companies Create Innovation, Profits, Growth, and Social Good,* examined the widest possible geographic context in which leadership is exercised. A focus on the context for leadership illuminates the work of leadership, and that, in turn, illuminates the skills and qualities of persons who are chosen for leadership roles. In short, a sociological approach begins with the context and assumes that the characteristics of leaders must fit the context, mediated by the nature of the tasks leaders must perform in order to master the context.

The paper begins with generalizations (admittedly sweeping ones) about macro-trends—the meaning of globalization. The trend analysis is the basis for a simplified construct for how three aspects of globalization (increased uncertainty, complexity, and diversity) shape the work leaders must perform. Three big tasks follow from the three conditions:

- Institutional work to deal with uncertainty

- Integrative work to deal with complexity

- Identity work to deal with diversity

I then illustrate the nature of these leadership tasks and how they can be carried out effectively with examples from my research. There is a great deal of continuity with enduring tasks performed by leaders but also some challenging differences of kind or extent that make it important to develop new knowledge about leadership for the future. The naturalistic observations and frameworks in this paper raise questions for further research.

The Context: Global Trends That Impact Leadership

Macro-trends set the context for exercising leadership, and thus we must begin with a little history.[2] International trade and the international scope of business are long-standing phenomena, and some of the companies in my research have been "international" in scope for a century. But even those companies are quick to point out the differences introduced by the current wave of globalization. The current wave, which has had several phases, can be traced to technological and geopolitical changes starting in the 1980s. These changes were themselves the outgrowth of technological and economic developments following World War II.

The 1980s included several important events that shaped global communication and competition: the development of personal computers and widespread use of computing technologies, the fax machine and early Internet increasing communication speed, and the rise of Japanese industry and European community deliberations causing industry restructuring. A series of events around 1989 marked geopolitical change: the fall of the Berlin Wall heralding the end of communism in Eastern Europe, the liberalization of Asian financial markets, the democratization of some Latin American regimes, and preparations to release Nelson Mandela from prison in South Africa.

The 1990s were characterized by the supposed (note the modifier) triumph of free market ideology, the formation of regional trade blocs, rapid growth in developing countries, and the opening of China and India to more significant foreign direct investment. The creation of the World Wide Web in 1993 and the subsequent Internet business boom facilitated global communications connectivity.

However, agents of globalization had also overshot the mark, resulting, among other things, in the Asian financial crisis in 1998 and the dotcom crash in 2001. The opening years of the twenty-first century brought global terrorism, political backlash and protectionism, and the return of overtly socialist regimes in Latin America. For a time globalization was discredited and criticized, as the developed world faced slow growth and tightened national security, as well as skirmishes and war in the Middle East and Central Asia. But at the same time, the 2000s also brought Web 2.0—a more interactive form of the Internet—and continued growth opportunities in BRIC nations (Brazil, Russia, India, and China) and other attractive emerging markets. Educated populations competed for high-skilled jobs with developed countries, technology expertise and engineering talent was increasingly found in developing countries, and multinational companies no longer had to rely on expatriates to staff their operations outside of their home countries. The loss of developed country advantages and the rise of emerging country giants (including those in my research) led to declarations that the world is now "flat," that is, a level playing field in terms of technology and industrial might.[3]

Over these three decades, the response of businesses to global opportunities and pressures has fed further globalization. Industry consolidation in financial services, consumer products, and basic industries such as steel and auto manufacturing, to attain economies of scale and wider scope, has had a global as well as national dimension, while competitors from emerging countries have threatened established players. As governments loosened regulations, cross-border alliances and mergers have occurred in formerly controlled industries such as air transportation and telecommunication. Service industries, such as advertising, management consulting, and systems integration, have sought mergers to ensure global scope, as illustrated by the rapid growth of Publicis Groupe, one of the companies in my research, from a European company toward the bottom of the top twenty in the industry worldwide to the fourth largest player and number one in some areas, such as digital services.

When businesses cross country lines, the business/society relationship becomes more visible and salient. It is not surprising, then, that a globalizing world has moved the concept of corporate social responsibility—recently reframed by some companies as corporate citizenship—from periphery to mainstream, on every continent. The movement, embraced by employees as well as pushed by external activists, brings private companies into the public arena. The public role of privately owned companies is reflected in the importance of interaction with government. Walter Wriston, legendary chairman of Citigroup, one of the first extensive global banks, prematurely declared the death of sovereignty.[4] Business can define strategy as though it is a borderless world, as Kenichi Ohmae proposed,[5] but there are still border patrols in every country attempting to secure more of the flow of capital within the country's own boundaries while also opening markets to attract investment and growth. There is a delicate relationship between politicians and multinational—that is, foreign—companies. The business/society relationship requires management beyond the market. Ben Heineman, former general counsel for General Electric, argues that companies need their own "foreign policy."

Taken together, these changes represent forces that cannot be ignored, nor can they be reversed by the actions of individual companies. They spread through the local ecosystem through the interactions among companies across their extended family of suppliers, distributors, customers, and investors—for example, the way that Publicis's desire to retain Nestlé's business requires finding a way to be present in all the places that Nestlé operates. This becomes a self-fueling dynamic. Globalization itself adds pressure on companies to be global—"world class"—in orientation, sourcing, and standards if not market scope, and to thrive domestically by joining global networks.[6]

Global competition forces change even in domestic players. For example, Shinhan, a bank in Korea formed in 1982 to serve the middle market (while large established banks focused on the chaebols, or conglomerates), grew profitably and survived the Asian financial crisis of 1998, while established banks needed government bailouts. Noting international banks entering its markets, Shinhan decided in 2003 to acquire one of the largest of the old banks from the government (I began to study Shinhan in the postmerger phase) and simultaneously prepare for global growth by obtaining a listing on the New York Stock Exchange. By 2006 it was the largest financial group in Korea and one of the twenty-five Asian stocks tracked by the *Wall Street Journal*, outmaneuvering both domestic and international competition in its home market by incorporating global standards.

Deconstructing Macro-Trends: Organizational Challenges and the Work of Leaders

It is popular today to view leadership as a skill and activity set apart from and different from that of management, even though popular parlance also tends to conflate leaders with those occupying positions of managerial authority. For purposes of this paper, I will confine the work of management to oversight of the technical or functional aspects of an organization, and use leadership as a more dynamic effort to shape the direction of an organization beyond its technical core. Management, or the idea of technical functionaries, is a concept rooted in the industrial age. Max Weber was thinking about government agencies, not factories, when he conceptualized bureaucracies as perfect impersonal vehicles for organizing and perpetuating routines. But it was in factories that mass production flourished and analytics dominated, keeping his idea alive. It was considered negative rather than positive by many (but not all) management theorists that the less rational human side of enterprise kept intruding on rationally engineered organizations.

Management emerged as a science in an era defined by machines and inward-focused machinelike business organizations. Much of management theory and practice in the industrial age, and the remnants in factories for services, were technocratic. There was less need to think about leadership. Indeed, Weber seemed to have an underlying disdain for the irrationality behind the appeal of charismatic leaders, and seemed relieved that once they founded organizations, agitators might continue to appeal to emotions but administrators could take over and run the place.

So much of management theory, especially as overtaken by economists, was based on a series of simplifying assumptions associated with industrial era thinking, which tended to ignore the broader ecosystem context. These assumptions were of the following:

- Relatively stable activities with clear boundaries (high routinization)

- Relatively simple structures (clear chains of decisions and reporting)

- Relatively homogenous populations (dominant majorities of similar types)

- Relatively high control over organizational and individual information (privacy and secrecy)

With such assumptions about organizations, no wonder there was not much attention given to work beyond the technocratic, and there was not much attention to leadership. Once an organization was designed, managers had control, and everyone knew what they were supposed to do—or so it was assumed.

But scholars, consultants, and practitioners have increasingly challenged those simplifying assumptions during the same three decades that I have called the current wave of globalization. There have been numerous critiques of the pathologies of bureaucracies and calls for new paradigms that would supplant command-and-control, tall hierarchies for decisions, impersonal management by money, rigid structures, and so forth (even while some processes have become even more scientific, such as the emphasis on Total Quality Management and then Six Sigma). Matrix organizations, interorganizational relationships, and networks were all discovered by theorists as they came to be used in practice. There have been numerous calls for leaders to replace managers.

Thus, there has been a search for a paradigm that stresses leadership as a skill and activity above and beyond management. It's not literal globalization (that is, greater international contact) that has produced this quest for a new paradigm, nor is it global sales. Rather, change stems from the broadening of horizons, enlarging sources of ideas as well as supplies—which is why the term *information* should be added to the term *global* in defining the globally connected information era. But certainly those companies working across national borders and viewing themselves in global terms as examples of global rather than local standards, such as the companies in my research, represent the fullest flowering of globalization's impact on organizations.

Clearly, the old simplifying assumptions are obsolete. We cannot create valid theories based on assumptions of stability, simple structures, population homogeneity, and secrecy. Instead, we must contend with four contrasting phenomena:

- *Uncertainty:* More frequent, rapid, unexpected change

- *Complexity:* More moving parts, more variables in play simultaneously

- *Diversity:* More variety of people and organizations, more dimensions of difference among those in contact

- *Transparency:* More information known about more people and organizations in more places

Organization theory has already moved away from some obsolete assumptions, as can be seen in the important emphasis on social networks and network analysis, both within and across organizations.[7] But practice has been ahead of theory when it comes to seeing what difference all this makes for leaders and how to frame and conceptualize the nature of leadership under globalization.

First, leadership has an interpersonal dimension, although it is not purely interpersonal. An ongoing, defining task of leaders is to inspire their followers—to guide and motivate performance, to instill confidence in advance of victory. Leaders have always performed inspirational work, and they always will. A second aspect involves setting standards for what is good conduct and serving as models for meeting those standards—leaders as the laureates of the true and beautiful, who are leaders in their field while not always necessarily leaders of people. In short, integrity. Integrity work is also classic and enduring, but it does increase in importance in a globalizing world because of the fourth aspect of globalization: increased information flow and pressures for transparency, from regulatory bodies policing companies and companies assessing governments, and NGOs examining both. Misconduct is more readily exposed and risks to reputation more readily communicated by watchdog groups using Internet tools, so the task of ensuring that the organization meets high standards grows in importance and takes on global dimensions. The impending death of privacy and secrecy makes ensuring integrity in oneself and others more central to the definition of leadership. Leadership is not about financial results alone.

Those two classic I's of the tasks of leaders—inspirational work and integrity work—are just the starting point. The global forces I have identified shape the context for three important tasks for leaders as they guide organizations and influence other people:

- To deal with uncertainty, *institutional work*

- To deal with complexity, *integrative work*

- To deal with diversity, *identity work*

Top leaders perform this work personally, on behalf of the organization, and they set the framework for many people throughout the organization to do this work in addition to their technical tasks. Particularly at the top, leaders operate through the messages they espouse (what they say), the models leaders exemplify (what they do), and the mechanisms they establish (what leaders enable others to do).[8] But in a globalizing world, leadership is not confined to the top positions (those which traditionally have been the most highly compensated and carry the most command over resources). Top leaders rely on many people exercising these responsibilities of leadership—the essence of integrative work, which is to facilitate connections rather than exercise command.

This paper offers these three kinds of work of leaders as the future of leadership in organizations, as a kind of universal that itself is global in scope. In any country, in any culture, in any particular organization, there may be a range of individual and interpersonal styles characteristic of that entity—the cross-cultural differences often invoked in international management texts. But focusing on country norms of behavior does not get us very far in understanding leadership effectiveness and organizational performance, and it could be a futile, stereotypical dead end. Across the twenty countries in my project, three are certainly differences in leadership style—for example, loudness of voice or directness of manner—but there is also convergence at a higher level as leaders address the common tasks they must accomplish.

I will now turn to the three big tasks one by one, illustrating with empirical examples how leaders from the companies in my project perform them. I will ask readers to bear in mind four caveats: that these tasks are not easy and must be performed beyond all the technical work; that the companies in my study might not be representative of the vast majority of businesses; that no one of the companies or their leaders meets the ideal that the skeptical public holds out for perfect conduct in every respect; and that the new conditions often have a downside of unintended consequences or pernicious effects.

Leading Under Uncertainty and Rapid Change: Institutional Work

The era of globalization is characterized by frequent, rapid, and sometimes unpredictable change, both done by leaders and done to them by events in the external world. Globalization increases the speed of change, as more competitors from more places produce surprises. System effects send ripples that spread to more places faster—innovations in one place proving disruptive in others, problems in one economy triggering problems in others. Although geographic diversification is a hedge against local risk, geographic consolidation to gain economies of scope can expose companies to risks that cannot be contained. For example, this is a concern for IBM leaders about consolidating certain data storage or processing functions in fewer places, which increases global vulnerability from local events.

Furthermore, companies acquire, divest, or are acquired; the business mix of globalizing companies changes frequently; and jobs levels fluctuate across countries. So what exactly is the same that makes us say this is the same company? Bank of America is the surviving name after numerous mergers, but the underlying surviving bank is Nation's Bank, which gave up its name but not its headquarters, management cadre, or culture. And where are the sources of certainty that permit people to take action in an uncertain world? "Management is temporary, returns are cyclical," IBM CEO Sam Palmisano said, explaining to me why he puts so much emphasis on values and culture.

The answer to the question of who we are in the future is that we are not our current widgets, but we are our values, and that can help us find the right new widgets to serve society. Globalization seemingly detaches organizations from particular societies only to require the internalizing of society and its needs (many societies) in organizations. Institutional certainty can balance business uncertainty.

Thus, leaders can compensate for uncertainty by institutional grounding—identifying something larger than transactions or today's portfolio that provide purpose and meaning. Institutional frameworks permit diverse, self-organizing people to gain coherence. Joel Podolny and Rakesh Khurana have argued that meaning-making is the central function of leaders.[9] I am arguing that the meaning that is most important for institutionalizing an organization is a purpose and values that provide a rationale beyond the transactions or activities of the moment. Institutional work involves active efforts to build and reinforce aspects of what is loosely called organizational culture—but it is also much more than that. Culture, as generally used, is often a by-product of past actions, a passively experienced outgrowth of history. Institutional work is an investment in activities and relationships that do not yet have an instrumental purpose or a direct road to business results but that instead show what the institution stands for and how it will endure.

Institutional work is a survival strategy. Globalization increases the likelihood of shorter organizational life cycles, as a result of mergers and acquisitions, industry consolidation, and intensified competition driving out weaker competitors. It is plausible to hypothesize that the extent and depth of institutional work can divide the survivors from those subsumed by global change, equivalent to the difference between long-lived and short-lived utopian communities in my earlier research about commitment and survival.[10] The leaders whose organizational heritage lives on even if names change are likely to be masters of institutional work.

For example, ABN AMRO, a Dutch international bank, was a takeover target in 2006–2007 because of undervalued assets. Meanwhile, its Brazilian subsidiary, Banco Real, was a high-performer growing in size, reputation, and financial performance. This was widely attributed to institutional work by CEO Fabio Barbosa and other top leaders to infuse the bank with values of environmental and social responsibility. These values give larger purpose to daily work and stimulate innovation to serve customers and society with practices that meet high standards. Starting around 2001, in response to the most recent phase of globalization, Barbosa made corporate social responsibility (CSR) the core of the business strategy—the bank's key point of differentiation. In 2006, when the Dutch parent ABN AMRO was on the auction block, producing enormous uncertainty and anxiety in Brazil, Barbosa turned again to the Banco Real's culture. He reminded managers that the best protection was high performance stemming from intensified efforts to showcase institutional values. He told them at smaller meetings and larger conferences that certainty came from their knowledge that they were "doing the right things the right way every day" (a slogan he often repeated). In April 2007, a consortium bought ABN AMRO, and ownership of Banco Real shifted from the Netherlands to Spain's Santander, which bought the Brazilian assets to add to the branches it already operated in Brazil. But the spirit of Banco Real involved much more than the assets. Fabio Barbosa was named CEO of the combined entity, and the Banco Real culture and values were to be infused throughout Santander Brazil. Banco Real is the institution that lives on; Barbosa is adding 25,000 new people from Santander to the 30,000 he had already led.

Institutional work infuses meaning into the organization, "institutionalizing" it as a fixture in society with continuity between past and future. Institutional work is such a broad idea that it is hard to single it out from integration, identity, and integrity tasks, all of which contribute to the grand institutional mission of being more than a bundle of business assets and transactions. The institutional work of leaders involves establishing and reinforcing values and principles throughout the organization through conversations and actions. In so doing, leaders help the organization internalize society and societal goals.

Establishing and Transmitting Values: Conversations About Higher Purpose

Having a statement of values has become common, but the institutional work of leaders goes beyond the mere posting of a set of words. In recent years, CEOs of companies in my project headquartered in the United States, Mexico, the United Kingdom, and Japan all allocated considerable resources to breathing new life into long-standing values statements, engaging multiple levels of junior leaders in this institutional task of identifying and communicating values. The point was not the exact words themselves but the living process: to begin a dialogue that would keep the sense of social purpose in the forefront of everyone's mind and use that as a guidance mechanism for business decisions. That was how Procter & Gamble leaders saw the company's PVP (statement of purpose, values, and principles); CEO A. G. Lafley and Vice Chairman Bob McDonald spent much of their time teaching about and discussing the PVP in formal programs and in visits to locations around the world.

Omron's new CEO, Sakuta-san, led a restructuring of this Japanese global electronic sensors company from 2002 to 2006. But he says that he considers something beyond rearranging the business portfolio or technical engineering prowess more important to the long-term endurance of Omron: Omron's Principles. The Principles, which had been created many years earlier, were rewritten in 2002 and then transmitted through a massive communication process that could have seemed a distraction from the managerial work of restructuring. It proved instead the glue that helped Omron through business ups and downs. Today, groups of employees begin each workday by reciting the core slogan, salespeople start conversations with customers by talking about the Omron Principles, and representatives invoke the Principles first when meeting with companies they are vetting and courting for acquisition. (The analogy with religious ritual is apparent.) CEO Sakuta-san fully expects that 35,000 people in Omron might have different interpretations—maybe 35,000 different ones—but that the engagement and discussion is the important thing. He said, "Whenever I speak with employees, I tell them your answer should not be a set answer. Please tell what you understood, and how you can express it using the language of the Principles. I also promote discussion among peers, colleagues, and teams to share these understandings with each other." He puts this in terms of a very long time horizon: "No matter how different the workplaces are in terms of race, value sets, geographical locations, etc., as long as we can continue this debate and discussion, we are able to maintain our attractive and strong work environment and Principles with a flexible attitude to respond to any changes to come in 50, 100, 200, 300 years. And I believe we will be able to refine the Principles by doing so."

IBM CEO Sam Palmisano's process for refreshing IBM's values for the twenty-first century was itself a dialogue on a scale beyond anything any company had ever done. By 2000, IBM had outlived others prominent in the industry twenty-five years earlier but was hardly the same company from a business perspective. It had downsized or sold manufacturing (later selling the ThinkPad to Lenovo), grown in software and services, emphasized the Internet over mainframes, had nearly as many employees in India as in the United States, and was targeting growth in all the BRIC nations. So what was IBM? One of the early leadership actions that Sam Palmisano took when he became chairman and CEO in 2002 was to refresh the IBM values through a unique participative process involving Web chats open to over 350,000 IBMers worldwide. He wanted people to have pride in IBM as an institution, not to be following a leader: "The values are the connective tissue that has longevity."

Corporate Diplomacy Writ Large: Elevating Each Society

One paradox of globalization is that it is accompanied by a greater need for deep national and local connections in many more places, in plural public spheres. To thrive in diverse geographies and political jurisdictions, companies must build a base of relationships with government officials, public intermediaries, and customers that can ensure alignment of agendas even as circumstances (and public officials) change. In some places, these external stakeholders are interested in the quality and sustainability of the institution as a local contributor as much as the transactional capabilities of the organization. The global organizations themselves want both an extended family of relationships that can endure and a seat at the policy table for matters affecting their ability to do business in the future. So the institutional work of leaders extends outside the enterprise.

For example, IBM's Palmisano circumnavigates the globe six or seven times a year to meet with national and regional officials, bringing regional leaders with him, discussing how to help the country achieve its goals. This is not sales, not even marketing, but rather a high-level conversation to indicate IBM's interest in being an enduring institution contributing to that country. Such contacts help other IBM leaders get seats at the table discussing the country's future. That certainly provides an opening for discussion of the company's policy agenda (which is more technical than political). But any instrumental goal would not be achievable without first contributing to efforts clearly benefiting the country.

Institution building requires effort by many people. Top leaders involve others in leading diplomacy, such as representing the company to the community at conferences and civic or charitable dinners and serving communities directly through service projects.

I hypothesize, based on the companies in my research, that the more interested top leaders are in institution building for the long term, the more likely they are to involve more people in institutional work and reward it with recognition and resources. A Cemex manager in his first country manager post expressed surprise to the chairman, Lorenzo Zambrano, at how much time he had to spend making relationships with government officials and wondered if he should be doing it. "Welcome to top management," Zambrano told me he replied.

Relatively few people hold formal responsibility for these external interfaces as their primary jobs, and indeed, institutional work is less effective in terms of impact on external stakeholders when it appears to be "just a job." So instead, many others perform institutional work as volunteers, giving meetings and community service projects a ring of authentic motivation. This is not a hard sell for people either native to the area or long-term residents, because there is an emotional pull of place that makes institutional work desirable, so they are willing to volunteer personal time to do it, sometimes initiating efforts and taking others in the company with them. For others whose careers take them across geographies, institutional work is a way to connect their internal roles with the place they now live, making them feel less rootless and more at home.

Leaders from global companies operating in developing countries are often asked to advise on emerging issues where global experience could be useful. That requires special diplomatic skill: being able to appear neutral and interested in the host country, rather than interested in the company or home country. A leader in India was typical in presenting the company's agenda to the Minister of Commerce as a slate of future-oriented issues that would help ensure India's competitiveness.

Corporate diplomacy is particularly important where country interests differ or there is active conflict (or long historical memories)—for example, U.S.-headquartered companies in the Middle East, or Japanese companies in China. Add to that challenge suspicion of foreigners and concerns about their hidden agendas. Leaders must find ways to show that they act or advise in the interests of society, beyond politics, as a company that is not tied to a specific government or interest group but serves humanity. If the values are real, then leaders are willing to invest in ways that reflect them, not as a quid pro quo but as a sign that they will be locally involved. An Indian company entering Europe faced hostility from some government officials. Company leaders, who could draw from a long tradition of social responsibility, chose to make community investments that heralded their high standards, and leaders spoke with officials primarily about their values and how, once in a country, they would remain committed to its prosperity.

When leaders come to see themselves in terms of societal purpose, even across countries, they choose to perform institutional work, including self-initiated unofficial international diplomacy. In May 2007, the chairman of IBM Greater China organized his own diplomatic mission to Washington, DC, meeting with senators, members of Congress, and White House officials on both sides of the China issue to build bridges and find areas of collaboration, such as environmental issues, because of his conviction that his role in a global company gave him a unique perspective on both countries and a desire to see both thrive as allies.

Claims of serving society are made credible and tangible when leaders allocate time, talent, and resources to national or community projects without seeking immediate returns, and when they encourage people from one country to serve another.

Internalizing Society: Leading Service Beyond the Business

Corporate citizenship increasingly means more than corporate philanthropy; it is important institutional work that helps leaders reinforce the purpose that endures in the face of business uncertainty.

IBM's approach to corporate citizenship was closely connected to its business competence—to harness the power of innovation in service to the social and educational goals of the broader society. Leaders even at middle levels saw this as a task worth their time. A Latin American executive responsible for the small and midsized business sector felt that IBMers were increasingly using an external or societal lens to view IBM: "I see a change in the way we think about social responsibility. Twenty years ago, I think the focus was, do the right thing internally. Before, it's like I see a problem in the society, in the community, and I don't care, because this is not inside IBM, so I have nothing to do with it. The change right now is to leverage the size of IBM and do the right thing outside our organization, into the whole supply chain with providers and customers."

A wide range of services can be performed at various levels, from international activities in collaboration with the United Nations (e.g., P&G's Children's Safe Drinking Water partnership with UNICEF), large national projects in collaboration with government ministries, products addressing unmet societal needs, or leading employees and/or other stakeholders in short-term volunteer efforts (e.g., IBM's response to the Asian tsunami, or Cemex's engagement of small distributors in Latin America in community service days).[11]

Like Omron, Cemex's attention to social needs in particular places generated ideas that led to significant innovations: antibacterial concrete, which was particularly important for hospitals and farms; water-resistant concrete helpful in flood-prone areas; or used tires converted to road surface for countries with rapid growth in road construction. An idea from Egypt for saltwater-resistant concrete, helpful for harbor and marine applications, became a product launched in the Philippines. This was an emphasis of CEOs in both companies.

Institutional work has the greatest impact, and more people are likely to engage in it, when leaders link values with company capabilities, solidifying the institution and resting it on firm foundations. The leader of IBM for Europe and the Middle East encouraged IBMers in Egypt to work on a voluntary basis on an initiative called Building Bridges to the Arab World in partnership with the National Council of Women in Egypt, chaired by Egypt's First Lady. Building Bridges to the Arab World combined technology (a Web portal for Arab women), community service, diversity goals and women's empowerment goals, and government relations opportunities both in Egypt and for a U.S. company in an Arab region.

Institution building connects an extended family of partners across an ecosystem. Cemex started Construrama, a distribution program for small hardware stores, in 2001 in response to competition from Home Depot and Lowes, U.S. construction product companies that were then entering Latin America. Cemex drew on its values to seek dealers with integrity who were trusted in their communities; the company rejected high-growth/high-margin candidates whose business tactics didn't meet Cemex's ethical standards. Construrama offers training, support, brand recognition, and easy access to products for small hardware stores, including sometimes the first computers and Internet access for these small enterprises. By the mid 2000s, this network in Mexico and Venezuela was the equivalent of the largest retail chain in Latin America, and it was expanding to other developing countries. Cemex owns the Construrama brand and handles promotion but doesn't charge distributors, operate stores, or have decision-making authority, although service standards must be met. About a third of the Construrama management team at headquarters spends six to eight months working at the stores. Partners participate in councils on a rotating basis. Among the Cemex values that are disseminated to partners is participation in community-building philanthropic endeavors, for example, contributing people and materials to expand an orphanage or improve a school. A Cemex executive referred to the societal sensitivity that produced Construrama as "understanding the last link in the value chain."

Widespread opportunities for individuals to use company resources to serve society further institution-building goals. In 2003, when IBM's business emphasis had shifted to on-demand computing, the company launched On Demand Community, an intranet site for technology tools designed to improve schools and community organizations. Three years later, 75,000 employees (over 20 percent of the population) had performed nearly 3.5 million hours of service. IBMers can clock their volunteer time and at 50 hours get a certificate of recognition from their country head and be eligible to apply for a grant for that organization based on IBM worldwide standards. Many people love the service for its own sake and forget to clock their hours.

Values Evangelists: Communicate Iconic Stories to External Stakeholders

The stories leaders tell reflect strategic choices about which capabilities to highlight or which relationships are valued—and thus, what future choices might be made in an uncertain world. For Omron, the safety and health benefits of their products and their particular concern with people with disabilities reflects Omron values but also the continuing potential for future contributions to society that are important to industrial customers and acquisition targets who want to know that Omron will endure.

Procter & Gamble's Children's Safe Drinking Water (CSDW) initiative, in partnership with the United Nations, shows that the company values societal benefits for children sufficiently to fund a nonprofit to continue the distribution of an unprofitable product. CSDW is the next incarnation of an unsuccessful effort to establish a market for water purification tablets in Africa; instead of abandoning the product, P&G converted it from a for-profit commercial category to a contribution to a nonprofit organization. The story of the rapid evacuation of all P&G people to Egypt during the war in Lebanon is another iconic demonstration of the company's PVP, making real the value of putting people first.

For IBM, disaster relief efforts are one of many similar examples, showing that IBM is there to serve humanitarian needs quickly. IBM's cultural heritage preservation projects in Egypt, Russia, and China; an African American oral history Web site in the United States, and an English-Arabic social networking project all serve many institutional purposes beyond goodwill in the marketplace or with government officials. They highlight the company's desire to build long-lasting relationship with particular groups and honor their cultures. Such projects also help to alleviate some fears about globalization by showing that a global company can support the deepest emotions of national and local pride

Iconic stories give employees a way to talk about social purpose that show that the company can make big commitments without an immediate business goal and deliver on them: "Much better than talking about the weather," an executive in Egypt said, "and it demonstrates that the company cares about more than maximizing sales, especially important for an off-shore company." "If we are participating in the community, people see that we are willing to make commitments for the long haul, that we're a company oriented toward building long-lasting relationships," an executive in India said.

The external value from investing in principles reinforces internal commitment as well as motivation to continue institutional work. A Latin American executive told this story: "Last year, a good friend of mine that works for another large international company called me because a family member had an accident and became disabled. He said, 'Marcelo, I know that IBM has very good programs. Is there anything that you can do to help me to help my family, because I know that IBM is the best company for this.' When you receive this kind of phone call, it's the prize—this is the momentum that outsiders see, a company that is here helping society." Many others had similar stories.

Toward Institutional Charisma

Charisma is a powerful force for emotional attraction, a kind of social magnetism that motivates and inspires and can keep believers adhering to a cause even with uncertainty of outcomes or uneven direction—like the ancient Israelites of Judeo-Christian lore wandering in the desert for forty years searching for the Promised Land. But, as Rakesh Khurana has argued, it is an ephemeral and misleading basis for organizational viability, and it puts too much reliance and emphasis on a single leader and his or her individual qualities.[12]

Thus, the top leader's task is paradoxical. He or she has to express and exemplify the values while routinizing charisma so that it spreads throughout the organization, with many people performing institutional work so that the entire organization holds emotional appeal, and successors can convey the founding ethos and take it in new directions. Reverence for a founder or purpose-establisher must be readily transferable to anyone representing the organization. That leader must continue to fuel the passion at the heart of institutional work while remaining aware of the distinction between organization and person. He or she must convey that the institution is larger than any one person, so that people are not following a leader but rather are following the values and principles of the institution.

When institutional work is done well, the ultimate results might not be apparent for years; survival and longevity can't be known in the short term of financial reporting periods. But the emotional impact can be immediate and powerful, and that can be measured by loyalty and commitment in the face of alternative choices, recruitment of others to join, expressions of belief, and efforts by individuals to volunteer for institutional tasks, above and beyond their jobs. Institutional grounding in purpose and values might attract and hold customers that are not solely transaction-oriented. And if the institution has coherence and an enduring purpose, then the inevitable change of an uncertain world should be less threatening.

Sustaining the institution also requires resource attraction, so financial performance matters. But some leaders are willing to sacrifice short-term financial opportunities if those are incompatible with institutional values—for example, Banco Real walking away from customers that did not meet its tests of environmental and social responsibility. Sometimes this is justified in risk reduction terms, but it is a signal that the interests of the institution in the long term transcend short-term transactions.

Leading Under Complexity: Integrative Work

Globalization brings more moving parts, more variables in play simultaneously, and more dimensions of interest. There is a rapid flow of people, money, and ideas in and around the organization. An intensely competitive global information economy places a high premium on innovation, the faster the better, and innovation itself often reflects a new connection between previously unrelated elements or entities that now require further integration. Information has a short half-life—"use it or lose it." So there is more need to get ideas connected to tangible products and services, and to connect innovations with applications and users. Mergers and acquisitions add further complexity, and their success rests on the effectiveness of integration among the previously unconnected organizations. The important challenges and opportunities lie across boundaries.

Open access and communication irrespective of levels are increasingly apparent everywhere in the world, even in countries with more authoritarian traditions. Information technology facilitates direct access and rewards those who seek and spread information. Some of this is generational; younger employees, even in elder-revering countries, are less hesitant than older employees to e-mail the CEO directly.

Integration in the face of complexity is harder to effect through formal structures, which are too rigid to reflect the many multidirectional pathways for resource or idea flows. Informal, self-organizing, shape-changing, and temporary networks are more flexible and can make connections or connect bundles of resources more quickly. Formal positions come to resemble a home base for people who are highly mobile in terms of daily tasks, projects, work relationships, group membership, and physical location. Matrix organizations, in which individuals report to two bosses representing two dimensions of their tasks (e.g., reporting to a functional head and an industry head or a geographic head), become what I dub a "matrix on steroids." In a multidimensional matrix, people are accountable along many dimensions simultaneously and consecutively, with multiple projects and with multiple interfaces that enable them to assemble resources for those projects.

Globalization thus magnifies the integrative work that leaders must perform. Leaders must ensure that ideas are captured and people connected. Top leaders must facilitate integrative work on the part of others in the organization. They must enable more people to make more connections, establishing roles and processes for connectors or integrators who link other people or link any set of resources to one another— serving as idea scouts and transfer agents. As they do so, they must let go of full control—so that self-organizing can take place, or decisions can be made by integrators connecting across boundaries. Leaders do not stand "above" on a vertical dimension; they lead by facilitating horizontal, diagonal, or multidirectional connections. The decisions that top leaders retain involve choices about which potential pathways to endow with resources to start them moving—that is, which broad initiatives to fund or which pieces of the organization to combine formally in order to facilitate closer connections between related parts.

"Management by Flying Around": Convening, Connecting, and Building Social Capital

MBWA ("management by walking around," a famous Hewlett-Packard practice that built a strong culture in its early days of growth) is too slow for a globalizing world (and many people might be out of the office anyway). More appropriate for leaders is MBFA, or management by flying around.

MBFA is literally true for IBM's CEO; when Palmisano circumnavigates the globe, the company plane picks up key executives for certain legs, providing integration in the air as well as on the ground for the key customer or official meetings. Large numbers of other IBMers log more conventional air miles. Though tools and technology can be globally integrated and support routine work and problem solving (e.g., a test engineering system that can diagnose and solve problems in any plant from any location, remotely), nonroutine issues call for physical presence. A senior leader said, "If there's a problem or a critical situation, we darken the skies"—that is, send people to the problem.

Integrative work at the top involves frequent convening of groups cutting across the organization along many dimensions and expecting them to collaborate as well as serve as connectors between and among their home units. Groups might meet based on responsibility for a step in the value-creating process—for example, global technology, strategy, and operations—or various cuts through the organization, including geography leaders, functional leaders, or product/service leaders. There might be issues groups, permanent or ad hoc. They might meet face to face at longer intervals but hold conference calls at shorter intervals—voice communication is used even in technology companies for substantial conversations, with e-mail relegated to short factual messages.

Leaders' investments in face-to-face meetings build their capacity to integrate. A Latin American executive said, "The leaders, they have to like people. They have to have a strong relationship with people, a face-to-face relationship," he said. He visits people in the nine countries in which they work to build trust—and also because he needs direct observation to make difficult decisions, as in cases of poor job performance. Even though his team of direct reports at Latin American headquarters does not work in the same building, he convenes them often, which is important for conveying the same messages to everyone, providing a common platform for autonomous action. Another executive in the region shares that belief, so she provides incentives for her country-based team to spend an occasional week working in another country.

Letting Go at the Top: Lowering the Center of Gravity and Encouraging Self-Organizing

To realize his goal of transforming IBM into a globally integrated enterprise in which the best of IBM from anywhere could get to customers quickly, CEO Sam Palmisano is seeking to lower the center of gravity. The idea is to locate decision making lower in the organization and into the points of connection with customers. In his theory, those dealing with customers should be the ones to integrate IBM, taking innovation to apply to customer needs with a minimum of organizational or operational barriers by requesting and negotiating for resources directly, without going up one hierarchy and down another. Circles of influence should replace chains of command, and people should be trusted to set priorities responsibly, starting with the customer as the focus for integration, as stated in the IBM values.

To realize this theory in action, Palmisano has made a few radical, symbolic changes. Rather than maintaining the tradition that career progression involves moves upward, ever closer to regional and global headquarters, he stressed other dimensions. In Europe, he moved about five thousand people and two hundred executives above the country level out of European headquarters and back into country organizations. He elevated the role of account manager to high status, signaling its importance, by asking a few key executives to move from what had been top vertical positions to become executives for big accounts. A Latin American executive responsible for the relationship between IBM and customers—pre-sales, post-sales, and continuing customer satisfaction—said "It's a difficult mission, but I like it. I like it because I believe that this is the most important position inside the company. Because we have to integrate the other organization, we have to put the customer interest in front." For example, his group would determine the best platform for a customer (UNIX, Intel) and then persuade the hardware organization to supply it.

For Fabio Barbosa, CEO of Banco Real in Brazil, a measure of his success in leading the bank to embrace social and environmental responsibility as its mission is that he lost control of the effort, as he put it. In the beginning, projects started with top leaders identifying priorities. But a few years after the new direction was established, managers started contacting one another to create and execute on initiatives that he knew nothing about. Now they work across departments to integrate the organization themselves. Similarly, when companies such as P&G expect innovation to come from the field and from outside the organization, leaders are lowering the center of gravity to permit people to go directly to the source of ideas and then find the resource to execute, within P&G principles. Shinhan Financial Group accomplished a high-payoff integration of Shinhan and Chohung Banks, even before an agreement with Chohung's union permitted formal integration, by establishing a large number of task forces linking the lower-level people at the two banks to discuss issues; that produced self-generated modification of practices without top leader direction.

Nick Donofrio, IBM executive vice president, encourages nearly 190,000 technical people to think of themselves as working for him, and he tries to answer hundreds of daily e-mails personally, counting on this as a major bottom-up source of information about issues, opportunities, and developments. Following the successful dialogue in 2002 that led to the IBM values, Palmisano sponsored a second huge conversation, an Innovation Jam in the summer of 2006, in which 140,000 people identified possibilities for innovation.

Self-organizing communities, operating outside of formal structures, are a valuable resource if top leaders can accept that they are not in control but can take advantage of the results of lower-level integrative leadership. The driving force for self-organized groups is curiosity and interest on the part of the people themselves, if left free to conduct the dialogue. In India, a group of engineers self-organized after the tsunami to provide support for disaster relief, asking their nominal bosses to endorse commitments they had already made and place a few phone calls to government officials on their behalf.

For IBM, a recent self-organized virtual worlds community got IBM involved in this new technology, which burst on the scene in 2003 with Second Life. At least a hundred people interested in and experimenting in virtual worlds found each other through company chat and created an ad hoc virtual universe community. They started informally, then found an IBM executive to support them as a more-or-less official activity. Dozens of people chatted via their avatars on Second Life, and later, other platforms. There were weekly calls, and the phone line was open when in the virtual world; dozens of people would participate, though mostly not by phone. A participant said, "This was one of the most exciting years I've spent in IBM, to watch this group come together outside of every structure IBM has. We acted like a bottom-up corporation or a corporation of free-lancers. People were doing it on their free time." Eventually, virtual worlds was designated an emerging business opportunity with official funding for three years. CEO Palmisano provided public endorsement of the concept in Beijing in November 2006 when he announced the results of the Innovation Jam and a partnership with the Chinese Ministry of Culture by showing his avatar entering the Forbidden City. More recently, in another example with significant implications for the business, a self-organizing group in the United Kingdom started IBM's "green computing" initiative.

Relying on the Middle: More Leaders at More Levels

The complexity of globalization tends to induce and favor distributed rather than concentrated leadership. That is, fewer people act as power-holders monopolizing information or decision making, and more people serve as integrators using relationships and persuasion to get things done, a hallmark of a flatter organization.

Formal assignments as integrators or connectors are common in global companies, and integrative work is an expectation for many more people. A large number of people juggle multiple responsibilities and work with a large set of peers drawn quite broadly throughout the organization, sometimes leading initiatives, sometimes leading the flow of ideas that keep other initiatives moving. Some jobs are explicitly devised to connect a mix of projects and initiatives to ensure that they align with major strategic priorities for ever-larger chunks of the business. These are leadership tasks requiring persuasion to keep resources over which the person has no direct control on the same track toward the same destination.

At a large European multinational company, leaders recalled the time when country organizations operated separately and only the few top executives in each geography were in contact with the rest of the company. Now this occurs at many levels, as people engage in regular direct communication with their peers in other geographies, especially as they take responsibility for marketing, distribution, and product innovations. For Cemex such direct contact is part of spreading local innovations quickly to ensure that everyone can tap best practices. People speak of needing to understand much more about how Cemex operates elsewhere, including corporate strategy, so as to figure out how to combine the thinking of various locations.

Mentoring becomes a much more important part of the leadership role under such circumstances because of the need to transmit knowledge faster that increases people's ability to use their judgment and tap a network of relationships—that is, to acquire and use what is now called social capital. Cemex expects managers to train backups so the managers can travel, in essence embedding a leadership sensibility at lower levels. The founder of Infosys in India refers to his current position as "Chairman and Chief Mentoring Officer." At IBM, the best leaders coach large numbers of people. The chairman of IBM Greater China, considered one of the top information technology executives and best CEOs in China, personally mentors about one hundred people: twenty-five formal and active mentees, twenty-five informal mentees, and around fifty "graduates"—former mentees with whom he maintains a close personal relationship. Sam Palmisano stopped only because he became the CEO; he said that his staff told him that if he maintained mentoring relationships it might be misinterpreted as a sign of who was favored. Palmisano spends about 20 to 25 percent of his time on executive development; planning for future jobs and for successions; developing skills, culture, and climate; and thinking about the personal characteristics associated with leadership

Those doing integrative work sometimes wear many hats. For example, a woman in Egypt serves as communications manager for the country, reporting to the country general manager and the communications head in Europe; regional manager for diversity for the Middle East (Arab countries and Pakistan), reporting to Europe; and liaison for community relations, reporting to a manager in the United Kingdom. She works closely with the human resource (HR) department and government relations in Egypt and in Europe on other initiatives, but she calls herself a volunteer on these projects, because they are not part of her formal appraisal. Her effectiveness as a leader and her ability to wield influence derives not from what she does in any one of the areas but because she connects all of them; she is a significant idea conduit. She contrasts the current approach with the past: "Before, you only have your region, and there is a ceiling you cannot see through. If you go to a higher level, then you are escalating. Now I can exchange e-mails with any corporate director. This is the beauty of the matrix organization—you find the know-how anywhere, any time. The moment you ask for support, you will find it."

At IBM, rising stars among leaders manage cross-cutting roles and relationships of many kinds and do integrative work well beyond their formal titles. In Russia, the research lab director feels responsible for helping customer-facing teams and business partners leverage IBM research technologies; she regularly attends sales meetings with customers to add a technology perspective. She was instrumental in encouraging IBM to locate a lab in Moscow in the first place, making the case that a lab in Russia is part of a global ecosystem strategy, providing technology experts on the ground who could collaborate with sales teams, clients, and business partners to answer questions, learn, and bring back ideas for worldwide projects. She reports locally to the country general manager and worldwide to a vice president of development in the systems and technology group in the United States. She has dotted-line relationships to the other product lines on which the lab was working. She is a member of the IBM Academy of Technology, three hundred technology professionals that advise on technology policy and direction, for which she led a team studying globalization issues related to technology. She also interacts with U.S. headquarters as a member of informal teams with people in strategy, sales, services, and research. She works with labs in Mainz, Germany; Poughkeepsie, New York; and Beijing, China, and participates in bimonthly lab directors' meetings to set priorities and assign projects among labs. And, to top it all off, she maintains numerous informal relationships. She fields near-daily instant messages from a colleague in California that he sends before he goes to the gym in the morning to learn from her, ten time zones away, if there are any issues he should address during the day.

Deploying Social Capital: Politics and Persuasion

When integrators lead projects or initiatives that require cross-cutting groups, they are often working with people whose participation has a voluntary component. Broad priorities can be set by high-level leaders, but within those there is often freedom to negotiate the work itself with the team and the managers—although negotiations can sometimes be drawn out and politely contentiousness, slowing down the speed of project delivery, and there is always the issue of whether people can leave a project in the middle to go to a sudden high-priority task. It is challenging to get the right people to the right tasks, especially as technology changes and some regions enjoy rapid growth. A leader said, "Can you find the talent fast enough, and if you do, will they let you move it, and how many fights do you have to have before it finally moves?" Cemex managers were expected to train backups so that they could leave their posts for three months to two years to work on rapid integration and upgrade of operations coming from acquisitions.

Leaders below the top who guide such integrative groups often must attract both financial and human resources for projects, with their team thus enlarging and shrinking like an accordion. The money often comes from multiple budgets and the people from many different groups, recruited as individuals or because an intact team took on one aspect of a project at a particular point in time, so leaders must be beggars and borrowers. Project leaders knock on doors for resources, stop to see many people, and engage in arguments over priorities, because managers of other efforts do not want to lose good people. In general, integrative projects get support because they meet two tests: they are strategic to the business (which attracts capital) and motivational to the individual (which attracts talent). In China, a young woman relatively new to IBM said that although she thought her manager was a very good boss, she did not need to go through him to make decisions or find resources; she went directly to her peers. She assembled a team by using personal persuasion and the appeal of her project to encourage already-overscheduled IBMers to join her. Access across boundaries frees people from constraints, such as waiting to be told what to do, while adding to their responsibilities for taking initiative. A distributed organization has more ears to the ground, but people have to do something with what they hear. Success in many jobs requires spotting opportunities, generating ideas, and getting them moving.

Finding the resources to beg for in the first place is often a function of leaders' social capital—their stockpile of personal relationships with many people. Though technology tools are increasingly common to help people find one another, I found that even tech-savvy leaders still rely on their own personal networks to get to the right resource quickly. The director of IT for a company's Middle Eastern technology center observed that he relied on "the old-fashioned way, the knowing people type thing: I know a person who might know a person." IBM's executive vice president for technology and innovation felt that personal networks of people one had met or worked with were often better sources for key assignments than databases of resumes.

Note that this mode of operating has characterized fast-moving, highly innovative companies in technology fields since the opening of the global information age, as this observation from my 1983[13] book, *The Change Masters*, makes clear:

> Though innovators are diverse people in diverse circumstance, they share an integrative mode of operating which produces innovation: seeing problems not within limited categories but in terms larger than received wisdom; they make new connections, both intellectual and organizational; and they work across boundaries, reaching beyond the limits of their own jobs-as-given. They are not rugged individualists as in the classic stereotype of an entrepreneur but

good builders and users of teams, as even classic business creators have to be. And so they are aided in their quest for innovation by an integrative environment, in which ideas flow freely, resources are attainable rather than locked in budgetary boxes, and support and teamwork across areas are the norm.

> [J]ust about all innovating has a "political" dimension, . . . [b]ut I am using "political" not in the negative sense of backroom deal making but in the positive sense that it requires campaigning, lobbying, bargaining, negotiating, caucusing, collaborating, and winning votes. That is, an idea must be sold, resources must be acquired or rearranged, and some variable numbers of other people must agree to changes in their own areas for innovations generally cut across existing areas and have wider organization ripples, like dropping pebbles into a pond.[14]

Leading Under Diversity: Identity Work

Classic international trade of past decades could be carried out with relatively few points of contact between operations in a variety of countries, and within each, organizations could rely on somewhat homogeneous workforces, with expatriate home-country representatives at the top of the pyramid who might even be housed in segregated enclaves echoing home-country conditions. Although there were often great differences within a country in ethnicity and race, as well as gender divides, these were often managed by other forms of segregation and subordination. Only relatively recently have even pluralistic countries recognized diversity as a matter of legal rights and overt discussion— meaning that people would not have to pretend that differences do not exist and cannot be mentioned.

Globalization has heightened attention to workforce composition and has been accompanied by growth in the number of countries with equal opportunity legislation—and that references diversity merely within a country. Many of the geopolitical conflicts of this era have involved ethnic or religious groups engaged in identity politics writ large, sometime with a national dimension, sometimes with an ethno-religious dimension. Within companies, today's global leaders must acknowledge and contend with much greater heterogeneity under conditions that make it impossible to maintain myths regarding the homogeneity of internal and external players. Globalization increases the variety of people who potentially interact as well as the dimensions of difference among them. Heterogeneity is introduced within organizations through mobility, the dispersion of people from particular locations across other locations, as well as through structures that require communication across locations. Although the number sent on long-term international assignments might be a small percentage of the population, the number of people who regularly communicate with counterparts in culturally different locations is a larger proportion, and, arguably, a growing proportion as global integration increases. In short, leaders must become adept at identity work.

Some kinds of differences are obvious and task-relevant, such as linguistic differences. Some are matters of private life, including religious preferences, that are increasingly salient because of geopolitical conflicts. Some are immutable, such as gender or skin color, with the meaning ascribed to them varying itself according to differences based on location, nationality, or ethnicity. The structural point is merely that there are more dimensions of difference recognized, more types of bundles of those differences, and greater likelihood of encounters with strangers carrying those differences.

The sorting of people into social categories carries assumptions about the attitudes, approaches, capabilities, and biases of people in those categories, and categories can become bases for self-identity and the formation of identity groups based on those categories. Differences can also become the basis for rankings of superiority and inferiority and thus for systems of dominance by people of some types over those of another type—such as a bias for home-country natives or a preference for the approaches or interests of those who have typically held power.

Company identities also create an inclusion challenge when they reflect not only company culture differences in operating styles but also loyalties that influence individual identities. Merger and acquisition activity, whether cross-border or within a country, poses another diversity challenge for leaders: how to manage differentiated identities and integrate people and their work effectively.

Identities, whether of individuals, groups, or an organization as a collective, become clear when encountering others who are different. Identity is differentiation, so it takes the experience of an "Other" for "me" to know what is "not me," and therefore "what I am." At the risk of anthropomorphizing, I can argue that even organizations often do not bother with explicit articulation of what they are and stand for—their values—as long as they can recruit people for similarity and then slowly and carefully socialize people into their tacit culture, thereby assuring sufficient homogeneity for operating purposes. Procter & Gamble, for example, was long known for promotion from within and for a conformist culture; this was captured in the characterization of its employees as "proctoids." It was only when P&G made a very large acquisition (Richardson-Vicks) that the company formalized its institutional identity by crafting the PVP (purpose, values, and principles).

Social and linguistic differences and the identities that flow from them constitute a leadership challenge. They can produce miscommunication, misunderstanding, mistrust, divisiveness, distraction, inequalities, and resentment of inequalities—in short, centrifugal forces within an organization as people view how "people like me" are treated and as they must encounter otherness. Externally, they can complicate the task of diplomacy, or securing what the organization needs from power holders whose identity and interests are different.

Some progressive U.S.-headquartered companies have dealt with diversity by encouraging formal networks for people representing social categories assumed to have a harder time fitting into the mainstream, which is assumed to be white, male, and American—thus there are networks for women, African Americans, Hispanics, Asian Americans, gays and lesbians (and related sexual orientations), and so forth. For one such company, diversity and inclusion are called centerpieces of its human resource strategy. The company counts more than forty networks in the United States alone, and supports their meeting on company time if they help recruit people like them to join the company. There are many positive changes as a result. The company has increased the numbers of people from previously excluded categories and given them a vehicle for meeting others like them, trained managers about what various groups might want or need from the workplace, and spread some U.S.-originated policies (e.g., regarding work/family issues) to other countries. But the company is still deliberating about how to develop global leaders capable of working across countries in a globally integrated fashion, because diversity has come to mean fragmentation. Diversity in practice requires choosing to join a special interest group. Moreover, diversity training has reinforced stereotypes by trying to show how people from previously underrepresented social categories might be different from prevailing norms, even if actual people do not always fit into a single social category. For that company, it is not clear what to do beyond the numbers game or policy changes. What skills do leaders need in a world of diversity?

This is the leadership challenge in a globalizing world of greater contact among people of many varieties. Global leaders must confront identity issues in a way that unites people while acknowledging individuality. Leaders must become much more interpersonally aware than was the norm when whoever they were or whatever group they came from was automatically mainstream and dominant, and others (from subordinate groups to "lesser" nations) adjusted and accommodated to those in leadership positions without anyone explicitly saying anything about it—it just happened. Today, dominance-and-subordination models are fading from the best global companies. Home-country nationals can no longer claim superiority, and they must create relationships of reciprocity in order to work effectively across borders and boundaries. Even without the pressures for fairness reflected in equal opportunity laws in a growing number of countries (for women and minorities within those countries), companies originating from homogeneity-preferring countries must deal with more pluralistic norms in other places where they do business.

Identity work involves shaping awareness and action in terms of both differentiation (acknowledging differences) and inclusion (finding points of commonality). What is called "identity politics," which consists of hostility and conflict, occurs when neither of these conditions are met—when people feel that their differences go unacknowledged and yet they do not feel membership in the wider group.

Tuning into Others: Respect for Differences

Leaders must develop their consciousness about others, noting the things that are important to other people. They need an awareness of differences and a willingness to honor them. American social theorists in the school known as symbolic interactionism argued that all human interaction depends on the ability to put oneself in the shoes of another, but they wrote at a time when people could count on a common vocabulary with roughly the same interpretive categories. Empathy, an important aspect of what is now called "emotional intelligence," is made more difficult and becomes a higher, more conscious skill when dimensions of difference multiply.

Effective leaders in a globalizing world must attempt to read others and put them at ease by managing their perception of the situation. This is not the front-stage/backstage impression management and facework described by Erving Goffman, which had the ring of inauthenticity and manipulation, akin to the photo opportunities of smiling political figures at contentious international summits. Instead, it involves gestures of respect and inclusion.

The CEO of Publicis Groupe, Maurice Lévy, is a master of identity work. He personally led the courtship of advertising agencies considered unattainable to grow Paris-based Publicis into the world's fourth-largest advertising and communications group, catapulting it from far behind to highly profitable and able to continue to acquire effectively. When I say "personally," I mean by himself, unaccompanied at intimate dinners with heads of target companies by aides, staff, lawyers, or investment bankers. In three cases—the acquisitions of Hal Riney in San Francisco, Saatchi & Saatchi in London, and Leo Burnett in Chicago—Lévy devoted considerable time to personal bonding sessions with the relevant CEOs, in which he revealed details of his own family history (his father escaped from the Nazis) to show his values and also observed carefully to see what mattered to each of the CEOs. The courtship metaphor is often used, but Lévy went deeper, and he saw how they—from each of their vantage points—viewed a Frenchman and the feelings they would have about being part of a French company. (Indeed, the Saatchi acquisition got a disproportionate share of media in the United Kingdom for its size or value, under headlines indicating that the French were conquering the British.) When Saatchi's CEO, Kevin Roberts, said that he didn't want to have a boss, Lévy took note—and seeing the value of many Saatchi practices, proceeded to treat the merger as a reverse takeover. But Roberts also became so enamored of Lévy that he would do anything for him should Lévy but hint—which made Lévy the boss without anyone losing face.

An important part of identity work is holding one's own ego in check in order to honor something important to others. At the first post-deal meeting of Publicis and Saatchi executives, when the executive teams were introduced to each other for the first time, the Saatchi chairman, who was British, made his opening speech entirely in French, although he did not consider himself fluent—a gesture of respect that required humility (made even though Publicis executives were all good English-speakers). Leaders of an Indian company that acquired a French company suspended their rule of no alcohol at work to serve French wine during the workday at their facilities, including their headquarters in India.

Cross-cultural savvy is especially important for leaders who travel frequently across countries, work on international teams, or meet with their counterparts from other locations. A Mexican woman based in Brazil who leads a Latin American function commented on contrasts in behavior in staff meetings: "People from certain countries are very direct and very passionate to say something. And from another country, very soft and tentative, but it is not because that person is not involved or interested in his or her point." The differences are clear, whether stemming from country norms or individual characteristics, but what effective leaders do is acknowledge that without making a value judgment, and expect the same of the rest of the group.

Effective leaders also point to the importance of listening and adapting one's own style. Listening involves catching the meaning in a range of accents. When Patricia Menenes got a global assignment to manage from Brazil, she found an English teacher nearby who gave her lessons over the phone so that she could recognize words in different accents on telephone calls. An executive in Egypt is also sensitive to accents, even within his country, deliberately using a thicker accent with English words when talking with government customers, to make them feel at ease.

Many IBMers who have worked across geographies have stories about cultural tendencies, some told with admiration—for example, an American expressing appreciation for Japanese culture because of team members who are punctual, courteous, and willing to talk in the middle of their night. But for the most part, leaders in cross-cultural or multi-cultural situations seem drawn not to generalize about differences but to find commonalities with other IBMers or with customers in other countries. Indeed, in interviews, they minimize the effect of differences. An American IBM veteran leading a technical function in Moscow answered my question "What's different about doing business in Russia?" by jokingly replying, "They speak Russian here." Only then, after establishing that people are people did she mention Russia's unique historical legacy of communism and shaky business practices that were increasingly and rapidly changing to an international model. A Brazilian who led the implementation of a global model in Italy, Ireland, and Vietnam could point to the differences in how governments were organized or differences in accents but was most inspired by the similarities everywhere in people's passion for their children and families. Other IBMers similarly downplay country differences and are quick to point to cultural differences within countries that require equal or more sensitivity—north versus south in Brazil, regions and ethnic suburbs in the United States and India—or even differences across functions—a British engineer described adjusting his style to differences between research teams and customer-facing teams in Russia.

One important lesson from IBM's diversity focus is that leaders need not a set of stereotypes about countries or types of people but the ability to see people as individuals and to put themselves in others' shoes. What leaders provide in their messages about diversity is permission for people to talk to one another more openly, to learn what it is like for other people with different life experiences. "They take it home, to their neighborhood, to families. Some people say it helps make them much better people," a Latin American leader said.

When leaders model and encourage acknowledgment of differences, individuals feel freer to express more aspects of their identity at work, and sometimes that becomes a useful source of innovation. Because of P&G's long-standing commitment to respect in the face of diversity, an executive in Brazil who was a native of Egypt served Middle Eastern food in São Paulo to an American visitor—and, more important for the business, he used an Egyptian artifact with his team to stimulate thinking that led to an important process innovation.

Forging a Common Identity: Toward an Overarching Membership

Helping people to operate as members of a community rather than isolated in fragmented groups has both technical and emotional components. Without the right technical facilitators, communication is awkward and insufficient. Community requires a common language, a common platform for communication, and processes—which is why Cemex created "the Cemex Way" to make explicit and easy to learn all of those routines that would help people in acquired companies feel part of One Cemex and able to work out differences without contention. The technical infrastructure is important, because it increases objectivity and makes certain things givens, not arenas for conflict.

The technical side is not enough, however; that can be just bureaucracy. The main leadership work is on the emotional side, to forge a common identity, a common feeling of membership, above and beyond the ability to conduct transactions. Although the common language of engineering or of managerial processes can provide a basis for connection, it cannot fully produce a sense of community. That feeling of membership comes from being included as a whole person (feeling that "people like me" have a place), having the opportunity to form emotional bonds with others, and experiencing a kind of shared consciousness, which helps people feel that they can understand each other and come to think alike. P&G and IBM managers say almost the same words when asked to explain why overt conflict is so rare and why people insist they do not take it personally if a request is turned down. One said: "It's the notion of an IBMer. We understand each other really very well, and we speak the same language, and we share the same beliefs and values. When issues arise, we are making some business decisions, and it's just done. Everyone understands."

Omron leaders feel that the Omron Principles help them create community not only within Japan, but also with acquired companies. They use the Principles as a basis for dialogue, to find a commonality of values that then makes it easier for people from the acquired company to identify themselves as members of the Omron community. Executives from two very different U.S. companies acquired by Omron mentioned this, and noted that it helped them work through the differences with a Japanese company and educate Omron leaders in Japan about the U.S. market.

For P&G, use of the PVP facilitated the smooth integration of Gillette in 2006, its largest acquisition. A P&G country manager created the basis for a new shared identity from day one of the formal integration, when he moved absolutely everyone to a new office. Jim Kilts, Gillette's chairman and CEO who sold Gillette to P&G, described Gillette as a "team" but P&G as a "family." Not intended entirely as a compliment (families don't cut off low-performing members the way teams do), this comparison indicates something about the quality of community P&G has built that arguably makes it the stronger company in terms of community, or at least the surviving one. (P&G has since adopted some of Gillette's get-the-team-to-perform practices.)

Global leaders must not only emphasize a common identity, but also take active steps to reinforce it against all the centrifugal forces of fragmentation. Shinhan Bank, a smaller, newer bank in Korea, acquired Chohung Bank, a much larger and older bank with strong pride among its employees; leaders proceeded to put "emotional integration" (their term) at the center of their merger integration strategy. The Chohung union protested the acquisition announcement, with 3,500 union members shaving their heads and piling the hair in front of Shinhan headquarters in Seoul—a dramatic example of identity politics becoming high-cost conflict. Negotiating with the union, Shinhan agreed to suspend formal integration for three years—and then proceeded to integrate in all but name well before the stand-still period was up. It did this by emphasizing membership in a common endeavor through three streams of activity. First was "dual bank"—separate but equal, and ready to learn from one another, as people rooted in their Chohung or Shinhan identity met in task forces discussing their practices without any assumption of superiority or inferiority and no pressure to do anything but talk. By feeling pride in their former identity as a source of best practices, people could start to feel connected to the other bank. Second was "one bank," the stream of activities designed to produce feelings of membership in something beyond their jobs, which was also part of the institutional work Shinhan leaders performed to infuse Shinhan Financial Group with meaning. Under the "one bank" umbrella, for example, 1,500 managers climbed a mountain together at one of Korea's most historic shrines. The third stream, called "new bank," involved people on teams explicitly creating the future—a new concept that would be owned and embraced by everyone together.

Sensitivity to dimensions of identity—that is, cultural differences and how to overcome them—is striking in these instances of merger integration because it is so obviously lacking in many mergers that fail. A feeling of common membership comes from activities that by definition lie outside of anyone's task role. That's why joint community service is so powerful as a way to transcend the many things that can divide people. The "community" that leaders build overlaps with the organization but is not identical with the formal structure and boundaries (for one thing, it might include suppliers of critical services, alumni, or retirees).

Challenges

In many ways, all leadership is intergroup leadership, as I argue in another paper,[15] and the enduring skills that help leaders respect differences but forge a common membership are merely applied on a larger scale, to more dimensions and combinations of differences, in a globalizing world. Leading under diversity is difficult, both as leaders manage themselves and as they set the context for others. There are many reasons for this, stemming from biases to historical legacies to the politics of interest groups to a common tendency for the identification of differences to immediately turn into rankings of superiority and inferiority. Furthermore, as people become more conscious of social categories or aspects of their own identity, and as they see leaders willing to permit them to express it, they push for more expressions of difference at work. One global company that bans discussions or expressions of politics or religion at work—which has helped considerably with maintaining professionalism and business success as it does business in conflict-ridden regions—is now facing an employee push to allow decorations on cubicles during religious holidays.

At the organizational level, it is still a struggle for many companies to get away from home-country dominance. P&G people talk about Cincinnati, IBMers about Armonk, and Cemex people about Monterrey as though these places were persons. Cemex is referenced as though divided between "Mexicans" and Others (though "Mexican" was loosely used to encompass native Spanish-speakers from Latin America and Spain). The huge global scope of these companies poses another challenge in itself, and one not handled by the Internet. The sensing part of sensitivity blossoms when there is face-to-face contact and time for discussions that are not solely task-oriented.

The very difficulty surrounding diversity has moved it out of the HR department and into the C-suite more generally. Leaders must consider identity work critical for their personal success and that of their organizations.

Conclusion: Trends, Leadership Qualities, and Further Research

This paper has outlined three kinds of leadership work that are particularly important in a globalizing world. Organizations are being turned upside-down (e.g., lower centers of gravity, self-organizing communities) and inside-out (e.g., internalizing society and social identities while having more people on the boundaries connecting to society).

The argument in this paper describes a much more open-ended aspect to leadership than what emerged from the so-called heroic or Great Man theories of the past. The top leaders in the companies referenced seem most effective in leading change or stimulating innovation, for example, when they establish the process but do not overly constrain the outcome, when they set challenges or define problems rather than offer answers. They are confident in other people on their team or in their organization and believe that, with an empowering framework and strong capabilities, answers will emerge.

The top of any organization has always dealt heavily in symbols as well as strategies.[16] The forces of globalization make leaders' ability to think through the symbolic consequences of their actions or to find symbols that create meaning even more important, because there is so much information and so much flux.

It is easy to generate a list of qualities that leaders should possess in the context that has been emerging over the past three decades, and many writers have done so: systems thinking, initiative-taking, persuasion and diplomacy, a cosmopolitan outlook with a concern for collaborative solutions good for many people. Leaders need intellectual skills in pattern recognition, seeing similarities and differences, systems thinking, and framing and conceptualizing. Leaders need emotional skills in empathy, self-awareness, warmth and respect, and ego management. It helps to be curious. It helps to like people. It helps to communicate with drama and clarity.

Perhaps effective leaders have always possessed these qualities. But now they must exercise them with many more variables in mind, with resources they cannot control, with attention to the hearts and minds of other people who might have different assumptions or interests, and with the utmost of diplomacy. Whatever their job description, they must add the three important tasks encouraged by globalization: institutional work, integrative work, and identity work.

This analysis raises questions for further research, at both sociological (macro) and social psychological (micro) levels. Among them are the following:

- How much of the time of leaders, and at which levels, is spent performing institutional, integrative, and identity work in addition to routine or technical responsibilities, and how does this change with the amount of globalization? Can these aspects of the work of leaders be deconstructed to make them scalable, so they can be studied, analyzed, and used in practice? How does the performance of these aspects of leadership work correlate with overall business performance and longer-term business sustainability?

- What difference does top team diversity make? Does international diversity on the top team increase effectiveness or produce competitive advantages? If so, of what kinds? What are the mediating variables? And how are truly global top leaders developed?

- How does the relative tolerance or restrictiveness of a national/local context affect the ability of global leaders to function effectively? Are global leaders more likely to emerge from some contexts rather than others? What impact can they have in contexts that are dissimilar?

- In terms of leader qualities, does globalization mean that leaders' ability to send messages (i.e., to communicate their themes or visions) must be balanced by leaders' ability to receive and interpret messages from a diverse set of others?

- In globalizing companies, do leaders' national origins and/or education tilt decisions in particular directions? That is, are there patterns in terms of strategic choices, process preferences, and public engagement based on the national origins and formative experiences of leaders? Or are those differences irrelevant?

- Can a social contract be forged with the public across diverse countries with conflicting societal needs and requirements? As the ecosystem for business reaches its theoretical limits, encompassing potentially the entire world, how can leaders maintain the national/local bonds that provide legitimation? Will the bases for legitimacy shift, as global bodies legitimate if not authorize companies, and will something resembling a global society be created—like the cosmopolitan citizens suggested by some writers?

- What are the circumstances under which universal values truly guide behavior? And what are the consequences? Will that create convergence among countries or merely provoke particularistic backlash?

It is clear that the study of leadership in a globalizing world has a world's worth of potential to enrich the interplay between theory and practice. In addition, to the extent that global leaders are developed and mobilized by companies that operate under more universalistic values, those leaders themselves have enormous potential to improve the state of the world. Thus, global leaders are not only worthy of study, they should be actively developed at all those institutions of higher learning at which researchers are encouraged to translate their findings to the classroom.

Notes

1. The research is described fully in my book, *Supercorp: How Vanguard Companies Create Innovation, Profits, Growth, and Social Good*, New York: Crown, 2009. The project involved a multi-year study of more than 15 companies with international scope, based on approximately 350 interviews in 20 countries. The companies were chosen opportunistically because of their expressed interest in further globalizing and their willingness to allow access (in several cases I was invited as a consultant), but all have been externally identified by at least one group as high reputation and high performance. All of them made significant changes to their strategies and structures between 1998 and 2003 in response to global challenges and aspirations. The companies anchored in developed countries increased their investment in emerging market countries, and several of the companies from emerging economies increased investment in the developed world. Even the oldest companies in this group, with international operations for one hundred years or more, changed their international strategies and organizational structures or processes after the year 2000. All of the companies have CEOs who are widely admired, some of whom led turnarounds following predecessors who stumbled.

The companies I studied can be arrayed along a continuum in terms of degree of globality. At the least global end, although the company earned 90 percent of its revenues outside its home country, about 80 percent of its employees were natives of the headquarters country, even those working in international facilities. The company anchoring the most global end of the continuum in my research operated in 170 countries and was reshaping its organizational model to be "globally integrated" rather than "multinational."

2. Anthony J. Mayo and Nitin Nohria, *In Their Time: The Greatest Business Leaders of the Twentieth Century* (Boston: Harvard Business School Press, 2005).

3. Thomas Friedman, *The World Is Flat: A Brief History of the Twentieth Century* (New York: Farrar, Straus, and Giroux, 2005).

4. Walter B. Wriston, *The Twilight of Sovereignty: How the Information Revolution Is Reshaping Our World* (New York: Scribner, 1992).

5. Kenichi Ohmae, *The Borderless World: Power and Strategy in an Interlinked World*, rev. ed. (New York: Collins, 1999). See also the classic book by Christopher Bartlett and Sumantra Ghoshal, *Managing Across Borders: The Transnational Solution*, paperback ed. (Boston: Harvard Business School Press, 2002).

6. Rosabeth Moss Kanter, *World Class: Thriving Locally in the Global Economy* (New York: Simon and Schuster, 1995).

7. Ranjay Gulati, *Managing Network Resources: Alliances, Affiliations, and Other Relational Assets* (New York: Oxford University Press, 2007).

8. Rosabeth Moss Kanter, *Confidence: How Winning Streaks and Losing Streaks Begin and End* (New York: Crown, 2004), chapter 11.

9. Joel Podolny, Rakesh Khurana, and Marya Lisl Hill-Popper, "Revisiting the Meaning of Leadership," *Research in Organizational Behavior* 26 (2004): 1–36.

10. Rosabeth Moss Kanter, *Commitment and Community* (Cambridge MA: Harvard University Press, 1972).

11. Rosabeth Moss Kanter, *Supercorp: How Vanguard Companies Create Innovation, Profits, Growth and Social Good* (New York: Crown, 2009).

12. Rakesh Khurana, *Searching for a Corporate Savior* (Princeton, NJ: Princeton University Press, 2002).

13. Rosabeth Moss Kanter, *The Change Masters* (New York: Simon and Schuster, 1983).

14. Ibid.

15. Rosabeth Moss Kanter, "Creating Common Ground: Propositions About Effective Intergroup Leadership," in *Intergroup Leadership*, ed. T.L. Pittinsky (Boston: Harvard Business School Press, 2008).

16. Rosabeth Moss Kanter, "How the Top Is Different," in *Life in Organizations*, eds. R.M. Kanter and B.A. Stein (New York: Basic Books, 1979).

2 1

Unlocking the Slices of Genius in Your Organization

Leading for Innovation

Linda A. Hill, Maurizio Travaglini, Greg Brandeau, and Emily Stecker

T HERE IS a widespread consensus that innovation is fast becoming the principal source of differentiation and competitive advantage in today's knowledge-intensive economy.[1] In a global survey of 1,000 CEOs and leaders of institutions across the public and private sectors, executives painted a surprisingly consistent portrait of the traits they believe will lead to outstanding performance. Two of the five characteristics identified were "innovative beyond customer imagination" and "disruptive by nature."[2] The message was clear—to be fit for the future, organizations have to innovate fast and boldly: "The Enterprise of the Future radically challenges its business model, disrupting the basis of competition. It shifts the value proposition, overturns traditional delivery approaches and, as soon as opportunities arise, reinvents itself and its entire industry."[3]

But until we reframe our understanding of what innovation and leadership are all about, we fear that innovation will remain an "unnatural

Author note: We would like to thank the leaders who have allowed us to study their companies over the past few years. They are co-designers in this work, as are the individuals on their teams and in their organizations. We would also like to thank Anthony Mayo, Nitin Nohria, Rakesh Khurana, and Ranjay Gulati for their valuable insights on our work.

611

act" in many corporations. Most of our leadership theories were developed at a time when work was different, workers were different, and the economy was not as dynamic or global. Thus, it is not surprising that the mental models we have propagated are not well suited to meet the current and future challenges of corporations. We need to understand a great deal more about the essential conditions for innovation and, with that understanding, redefine what it takes to be an effective leader. A sizeable body of research on engendering innovation exists; too little of this knowledge appears to have infiltrated the notions of leadership espoused in the literature or in practice.

We have been engaged in a collaborative project on leadership for innovation. We came together because of a shared passion: to develop business leaders who can make a positive difference in the world. We consider ourselves optimists, yet grounded in reality. We are an interdisciplinary team and have introduced each other to the classic works in our respective fields. Our perspective has been shaped not only by relevant research in the social sciences, but also by writings on agile software engineering, architecture, and urban planning. Over the past three years, we have had the privilege to research and work with individuals in organizations across the sectors and around the globe.

Through participative observation and hundreds of interviews, we have become intimately acquainted with the leaders and inner workings of some of the world's most highly innovative teams and organizations. Our focus has been on leaders of teams or organizations that have produced breakthrough innovations more than once, as well as on leaders who have managed to transform teams into hotbeds of innovation. Ultimately, we decided to focus on ten research sites that span from Silicon Valley, California, to Dubai to India and Korea, from entertainment and e-commerce to legal services and luxury goods. The ten leaders include women and men of seven nationalities, at varying levels of their organizations. Given our methodology, we cannot prove that leadership matters for innovation, but we believe that our findings are suggestive of its importance and offer promising avenues for future research. In our work, we consider four questions: (1) how leaders of innovative teams and organizations think, (2) what they do, (3) how they do it, and (4) who they are and how they got to be that way.

In the pages below, we will focus on how leaders of innovative teams and organizations think and what they do.[4] We will share some of our thoughts about who they are. We will not say much about how they do their work. That story must be left for another time, when we can write in narrative form, for the beauty is in the detail, and also in the dynamic unfolding of events.[5] We will end by outlining a research agenda for the future. We will provide rather extensive quotations— some from the leaders in our study, but most from other experts on innovation, from the academy and from practice. Their rhetoric matters; it is our window into how they think about and frame the challenges and opportunities of leadership for innovation.

Early in our research journey, we discovered that if we wanted to visit the world of innovation, Pixar Animation Studio was a choice destination.[6] Pixar's track record of success stands out when it comes to producing artistic and technological breakthroughs. One of our number has spent over a decade at the studio; the rest of us have spent considerable time there. Because we know Pixar so well and, more important, because it is an exemplar of so many aspects of the innovative process, we turn our spotlight on Pixar quite often in this chapter, relying on it as an empirical touchstone to illustrate our argument. In the coming pages, the leader at Pixar you will learn about is Ed Catmull, a founder of Pixar and its current CEO.

Our argument is admittedly a rather complex one, so a brief summary is in order. We have only recently completed the analyses of our data; perhaps parsimony will come. But in the spirit of the innovation process, we ask your indulgence. Our conclusions are as follows:[7]

- Innovation is about *co-design: creative abrasion, creative agility,* and *integrative problem-solving*. Co-design is collaborative work that entails the exacting leadership task of unleashing and harnessing the diverse "slices of genius"™ (talents) in an organization for a collective good.

- The art of leadership for innovation is about (1) *creating a world to which people want to belong*—one in which individuals are affirmed in their identity (unleashing their slices of genius and values) and able to be a part of and contribute to something larger than themselves (harnessing the diverse slices of genius to develop innovative solutions for a collective purpose) and (2) *developing the individual and collective capacity for co-design*.

- Leadership for innovation is more about *leading from behind* than leading from the front. It is about shaping individual and collective experiences to foster innovation rather than about setting direction and mobilizing people to follow.

How Leaders of Innovation Think: Facing the Realities of Innovation

To frame our research, it is important to define what we mean by innovation and the innovative process. Innovation is about producing something that is novel (creative) and useful. The innovation can be a new product, service, process, business model, industry, or way of organizing. Some innovations are incremental, while others are breakthrough or disruptive. Myths about innovation abound, and like the mistaken notion that leadership is about charisma, they appear to die hard.

Many still hold a misguided view that exaggerates the importance of genius and of the initial idea; they conceive of innovation as a solitary act, a flash of creative insight in the mind of a genius. In his seminal book on the creative genius of individuals such as Freud, Einstein, and Picasso, Howard Gardner made the following admission, "As a psychologist interested in the individual creator, I was surprised by this discovery of the intensive social and affective forces that surround creative breakthroughs."[8] Although prodigies are born, it is clear they are then *made* through their social interactions. Keith Sawyer's incisive review of the research on innovation in organizations begins with this revealing vignette:

> The Wright brothers lived together, ate together, and discussed their project every day. Their collaboration was visible to everyone around them, and it speaks from every page of their journals. But many creative collaborations are almost invisible—and it's these largely unseen and undocumented collaborations that hold the secrets of group genius.[9]

Sawyer continues:

> The Wright brothers had lots of small ideas, each critical to the success of the first powered flight . . . The mountain bike wasn't commercially viable until many distinct ideas came together . . . Sigmund Freud is credited with creating psychoanalysis, but in fact these ideas emerged from a vast network of colleagues. The French impressionist painting associated with Claude Monet and Auguste

Renoir emerged from a closely connected group of Parisian painters. Albert Einstein's contributions to modern physics were embedded in an international collaboration among many teams. Psychoanalysis, impressionism, and quantum physics emerged over many years of interactions, trial and error and false starts—not in a single burst of insight.[10]

The most significant breakthroughs often represent years of sustained activity with others, even for prodigies. Thomas Edison registered more than one thousand patents in a "six-decade inventive odyssey."[11] Tim Brown, the CEO of IDEO, the renowned innovation and design firm, made the following observation of what he considered to be Thomas Edison's greatest contribution, his artisan-oriented shops—a new way of organizing and getting innovative work done:

> Many people believe that Edison's greatest invention is the modern R&D laboratory and methods of experimental investigation. Edison wasn't a narrowly specialized scientist but a broad generalist with a shrewd business sense. In his Menlo Park, New Jersey, laboratory he surrounded himself with gifted tinkerers, improvisers, and experimenters. Indeed, he broke the mold of the "lone genius inventor" by creating a team-based approach to innovation. Although Edison biographers write of the camaraderie enjoyed by this merry band, the process also featured endless rounds of trial and error— the "99% perspiration" in Edison's famous definition of genius.[12]

The parallels between Thomas Edison's principles of innovation and those outlined by Ed Catmull at Pixar are especially illuminating. It is interesting to note that Steve Jobs, perhaps the Thomas Edison of our times, purchased Pixar from George Lucas and served as its chairman until 2006, when Pixar was acquired by The Walt Disney Company. Catmull commented:

> People tend to think of creativity as a mysterious solo act, and they typically reduce products to a single idea: This is a movie about toys, or dinosaurs, or love, they'll say. However, in filmmaking and other kinds of complex product development, creativity involves a large number of people from different disciplines working effectively together to solve a great many problems. The initial idea for the movie—what people in the movie business call "the high concept"—is merely one step in a long, arduous process that takes four to five years.

A movie contains literally tens of thousands of ideas. They're in the form of every sentence; in the performance of each line; in the design of characters, sets, and backgrounds; in the locations of the cameras, in the colors, the lighting, the pacing. The director and the other creative leaders of a production do not come up with all the ideas on their own; rather, every single member of the 200- to 250-person production group makes suggestions. Creativity must be present at every level of every artistic and technical part of the organization. The leaders sort through a mass of ideas to find the ones that fit into a coherent whole—that support the story— which is a very difficult task. It's like an archeological dig where you don't know what you're looking for or whether you will even find anything. The process is downright scary.[13]

Well over a decade of R&D culminated in the release of *Toy Story* in 1995, the world's first computer-animated feature film. In the following years, Pixar has released eight other films that have achieved critical and financial acclaim. Like many companies doing cutting-edge work, Pixar has to solve problems of a scope, scale, and complexity that go far beyond the capabilities of any individual.[14] Pixar's films require a collaborative group, and Catmull and his colleagues contend that world-class companies need world-class talent.[15] Indeed, there are many stars with incessantly active minds from diverse backgrounds at Pixar. But perhaps equally important is the conviction that everyone has a "slice of genius." This is not to imply that all are equally talented. But Catmull, like the leaders we have studied, can be considered a humanist who believes that there is creative potential in everyone. These slices of genius are the resources organizations can amplify and leverage for innovation.

The research supports what Catmull has learned from experience: most innovation is generated from the bottom up, by self-organizing teams of talented individuals. The earliest work on creativity found that those who produced more creative ideas were slightly above average in intelligence but were not necessarily "geniuses." They were better than average, though, in generating lots of ideas.[16] Innovation generally represents the work of interdisciplinary groups willing and able to engage in the long, hard collaborative process of what we will call co-design. Co-design consists of three activities that take place in parallel: (1) creative abrasion, (2) creative agility, and (3) integrative problem solving. We arrived at this conceptualization of the innovation process as the result of an inductive analysis of our data, informed by a careful reading of the voluminous work in this area.[17]

The Co-design Process

Creative abrasion refers to the process of creating a marketplace of diverse ideas, generating as many ideas, options, or alternatives as possible and then refining, editing, and developing those ideas, options, or alternatives.[18] Sawyer, in his analyses of both historical and contemporary breakthrough innovations, observes that collaboration drives creativity and that insights always emerge from a series of sparks, not in a single flash. In those teams that produce significant innovations, the members play off one another, each person's contributions providing the spark for the next:

> Even a single idea can't be attributed to one person because ideas don't take on their full importance until they're taken up, reinterpreted and applied by others . . . Individual creative actions take on meaning only later, after they are woven into other ideas, created by other actors . . . Participants are willing to allow other people to give their action meaning by building on it later.[19]

There is considerable research that suggests that diversity and conflict are essential ingredients for innovation.[20] In innovative teams, differences in perspective, expertise, and intentions are amplified and used as resources. John Seely Brown, the former head of Xerox PARC, contends that innovation results from the friction of multiple views coming together. He explains: "Breakthroughs often appear in the white space between crafts . . . These crafts start to collide, and in that collision radically new things start to happen."[21] There is growing evidence that places where these collisions occur are magnets for talented individuals. Regional development economist Richard Florida refers to these individuals as "the creative class"—people in science, engineering, architecture, education, and the arts who "share a common creative ethos" and gravitate to communities that "provide the stimulation, diversity and richness of experiences that are wellsprings of creativity."[22] Leaders of innovation seek out communities and organizations where creative abrasion is likely to occur. Florida notes, "Diversity also means 'excitement' and 'energy.' Creative-minded people enjoy a mix of influences . . . a place seething with the interplay of cultures and ideas . . . They also happen to be qualities conducive to innovation, risk-taking and the formation of new businesses."[23]

Creative agility refers to the process of experimentation and iteration that innovation entails.[24] Thomas Edison was "always afraid of anything that worked the first time"; invention often came from serendipity.[25] From his earliest days, he believed in the "cut and try" methodology to bring to bear the broadest conceivable range of options into focus upon the narrowest possible range of a challenge over time.[26] Neil Baldwin, Edison's biographer, compared Edison's approach to innovation to that of a great French chemist:

> "[Antoine Lavoisier] was to carry his mind into his laboratory, and to make of his alembics and cucurbits instruments of thoughts, giving a new conception of reasoning as something which was to be done with one's eyes open, by manipulating real things instead of words and fancies." Thus, did Edison, with endless drawings and working models and incessant collaborative attempts, dwell extremely in the world of experience. And equally thus did he have the alchemical capacity to exploit that hard experience.[27]

The most innovative teams adopt a strategy of "try early and often," or as IDEO puts it, "fail often to succeed sooner."[28] Missteps, "failures," and rework are considered inevitable. Instead of driving out variation and treating it as error, innovative companies introduce variation, do multiple low-cost experiments to test assumptions, and produce real-time feedback. Hence, they engage in rapid prototyping, experimentation, and iterative adaption, with a willingness to proceed in entirely unexpected directions as a consequence of what is learned. Multiple teams are sometimes created to work on the same problem independently; they are brought together to allow for cross-fertilization and the blending of ideas and approaches only later in the process. Innovative teams favor responding to change and maneuverability over following a plan.

The third collaborative process, *integrative problem solving*, refers to the process of taking a systems perspective and using difference and conflict to create a solution in which the whole is truly more than the sum of the parts. An effort is made to see problems and opportunities in their entirety, as a means of taking into account all the salient aspects of a problem or opportunity—even those that appear in opposition. Through this process, multidirectional and nonlinear relationships among the various facets of the problem are explored. Instead of set-tling for choice A or B, teams that engage in integrative problem solving create an innovative third way that combines elements of and improves on both. An integrative solution is an approach that solves a conflict by accommodating the real demands of all the parties involved.[29] The result is often represented more aptly as a mosaic rather than a melting pot of the varied talents and perspectives of those involved.

Mary Parker Follett, a social worker and political scientist by educa-tion, provides one of the most insightful accounts of integrative problem solving. In her book *Creative Experience*, she writes, "It is possible to conceive of conflict as not necessarily a wasteful outbreak of incompati-bilities but a normal process by which socially valuable differences register themselves for the enrichment of all."[30] She continues: "We do not want adjustment. We want the plus-values of the conflict . . . we do not want to do away with differences but to do away with muddle."[31] As Follett describes, there are three methods of resolving conflict: domina-tion, compromise, and integration.

Integration is perhaps the hardest and rarest method found in organizational life, but it is integration that leads to novel ways of framing and hence solving problems. She goes on to acknowledge that differences cannot always be reconciled and that it is often difficult to decide whether a solution is a "true integration or something of a compromise."[32] But as she points out, signs of even partial integration, or signs that people want integration rather than domination or compromise, must be encouraged.[33] Unlike her contemporaries in the human relations movement, Follett saw conflict as an important function in the "inven-tion process," not evidence of dysfunction.[34] Like Follett, Roger Martin, a strategic management professor and author of *The Opposable Mind: How Successful Leaders Win Through Integrative Thinking*, laments the scarcity of integrative thinking in organizational life. He stresses the importance of developing what he calls an "opposable mind":

> Why is this potentially powerful but generally latent tool used so infrequently and to less than full advantage? Because putting it to work makes us anxious. Most of us avoid complexity and ambiguity and seek out the comfort of simplicity and clarity. To cope with the dizzying complexity of the world around us, we simplify where we can. We crave the certainty of choosing between well-defined alternatives and the closure that comes when a decision has been made.

For these reasons, we often don't know what to do with fundamentally opposing and seemingly incommensurable models. Our
first impulse is usually to determine which of the two models is
"right" and by the process of elimination which is "wrong." We may
even take sides and try to prove that our chosen model is better than
the other one. But in rejecting one model out of hand, we miss out
on all the value that we could have realized by considering the
opposing two at the same time and finding in the tension clues to a
superior model. By forcing a choice between the two, we disengage
the opposable mind before it can seek a creative resolution.[35]

Both Follett and Martin identify leadership as one of the major
obstacles to integrative problem solving. When in a group, many leaders are more comfortable in the role of visionary or expert, the one with
the most foresight and insight who is prepared to act decisively. There
is no individual glory or "thrill of victory" or conquest in integrative
problem solving.[36] When it is working, it is often hard to ascertain
where an idea originated, let alone assign credit to specific individuals.

Setting the Foundation for Innovation: Community Building

It is clear that innovation is a social and developmental process for even
the most gifted.[37] Innovation comes from the tension that arises as individuals with widely different talents and points of view engage in co-
design. With these tensions come feelings of vulnerability and anxiety.
Individuals crave social support and the associated feelings of psychological safety to sustain them through what can be a highly charged and
taxing experience.[38] Interestingly, in her work on urban design, Jane
Jacobs found that the most effective way to improve safety in cities was
not to add more police but, rather, to create well-defined neighborhoods with narrow, crowded, multi-use streets where diverse people
could interact and get to know each other in the course of completing
their daily routines.[39] It is not surprising that the research suggests that
keeping organizational life on a "human scale" is an important
determinant of innovation; smaller is better than larger when it comes
to the size of the group or organization, because the former makes
conversation, connection, and flexibility easier. When work groups
get too big—two hundred seems to be the limit—innovative companies

tend to break them into smaller units, even if operational costs increase. Consequently, the structure of the innovative companies we have studied seems to fit what Karl Weick found in his work presented in *The Social Psychology of Organizing*. He described the structures as "loosely coupled" or network-like organizations formed of relatively autonomous building blocks (smaller units) that were brought together, disassembled, or reconfigured as necessary.[40]

The quality of interactions and relationships matters. Individuals are only willing to share their slice of genius when they feel a sense of collective identity with others; that is, when they have a sense of belonging to and a sense of civic engagement with a community whose purpose, values, and norms they embrace.[41] Leaders of innovation appreciate the critical role community building plays in creating the most seminal precondition for co-design: unleashing slices of genius. To illustrate, it is instructive to return to Pixar. Unlike the rest of those in the movie industry, Pixar has rejected free-agency practices. They have never bought scripts or movie ideas from the outside; everything is done internally by what Catmull refers to as their "community of artists." He explains:

> What's equally tough, of course, is getting talented people to work effectively with one another. That takes trust and respect, which we as managers can't mandate; they must be earned over time. What we can do is construct an environment that nurtures trusting and respectful relationships and unleashes everyone's creativity. If we get that right, the result is a vibrant community where talented people are loyal to one another and their collective work, everyone feels that they are part of something extraordinary, and their passion and accomplishments make the community a magnet for talented people.[42]

Jim Highsmith and Alistair Cockburn, two founders of the "agile software development" vanguard, advocate a strikingly similar worldview. Their belief that working code should be "shipped, modified, or scrapped, but it is always real" harkens back to Thomas Edison's "cut and try" method. Perhaps most important, they understand that organizations are human, complex, and adaptive systems:

> Agile methods stress . . . the effectiveness of people working with goodwill . . . Using people effectively achieves maneuverability, speed, and cost savings. People can transfer ideas faster by talking face to face than by writing and reading documents. Few designers

sitting together can produce a better design than each could produce alone. When developers talk with customers and sponsors, they can iron out difficulties, adjust priorities, and examine alternate paths forward in ways not possible when they are not working together.

One aspect of agile development is often missed or glossed over: a world view that organizations are complex adaptive systems. A complex adaptive system is one in which decentralized, independent individuals interact in self-organizing ways, guided by a set of simple, generative rules, to create innovative, emergent results.

Most methodologies provide inclusive rules—all the things you could possibility do under all situations. Agile methods offer generative rules—a minimum set of things you must do under all situations to generate appropriate practices for special situations. Teams that follow inclusive rules depend on someone else to name in advance the practices and conditions for every situation. A team that follows generative rules depends on individuals and their creativity to find ways to solve problems as they arise.[43]

The shared purpose and values vary across the innovative groups and organizations we studied, but the norms of civic engagement are relatively consistent and mirror what we understand about what it takes to build effective work relationships. Work relationships are more effective when the concerned parties have a sense of mutual expectations, mutual influence, and mutual trust.[44] Those of us in the corporate world have much to learn from the community activists who are involved in capacity building in some of the world's most beleaguered neighborhoods. For a community to work, its members must accept both rights and privileges (opportunity to influence their world) as well as duties and obligations (accountability to behave consistently with the values and norms of their world). In *Community*, Peter Block outlines what it takes to weave and strengthen the social fabric of communities so that they can develop innovative solutions to the problems they face:

- *Accountability and commitment.* The essential insight is that people will be accountable and committed to what they have a hand in creating. This insight extends to the belief that whatever the world demands of us, the people most involved have the collective wisdom to meet the requirements of the demand. And if we can get them together in a room, in the right context and with a few simple ground rules, the wisdom to create the future or solve a problem is almost always in the room. All you need to ensure this is to make sure the people in the room are a diverse and textured sample of the larger world you want to affect.

This insight is an argument for the collective intelligence and an argument against expensive studies and specialized expertise. That is why this thinking finds a skeptical ear from the academy, most expert consultants, and the leadership that espouses democracy but really only trusts patriarchy and cosmetic empowerment.

- *Learning from one another.* The key to gathering citizens, leaders, and stakeholders is to create in the room a living example of how I want the future to be. Then there is nothing to wait for, because the future begins to show up as we gather. One of the principles is that all voices need to be heard, but not necessarily all at one time or by everybody. What makes this succeed is that most everything important happens in a small group. Which expresses another principle, that peer-to-peer interaction is where most learning takes place; it is the fertile earth out of which something new is produced. In this small group you place the maximum mix of people's stories, values, and viewpoints, and in this way each group of six to twelve brings the whole system into the space.[45]

The insight that freedom is what creates the willingness to be held accountable for the well-being of the whole is often misunderstood. We have all seen leaders and those in their organizations collude to avoid a sense of interdependency; they resist accepting responsibility for the well-being of others. We propose a reframing of leadership for innovation that implies revolution for both the leader and the led. We can see why leaders might resist this change in the redefinition of effective leadership, for it requires leaders to be generous with their power and willing to let others help shape critical organizational processes and outcomes. They must have a capacity to trust, to be comfortable with the ambiguity and surprise associated with the co-design process. Our framing of leadership stretches individuals in the organization as well. They must embrace the privileges of freedom—such as being a co-creator of their own experience—and also accept the responsibilities that accompany this freedom. Some are ill-prepared to accept the duties and obligations that come with being a member of a community; they may even prefer the leader as benevolent dictator model characterized by Thomas Hobbes in *Leviathan*.[46] Such individuals have no place in innovative organizations and, once discovered, are often rejected by their peers, no matter how gifted. If leaders are going to allow for individual difference and freedom, they have to make sure those individuals are committed to a superordinate goal. One of our colleagues opined, "If you want to build a car with a powerful engine, you have got to make sure it has powerful brakes."[47]

Leadership Is About Creating a World to Which People Want to Belong

If leaders expect to unleash and harness diverse slices of genius for a collective good, they should think of the members of their organization as volunteers who show up by choice, not obligation, to join the community and do the hard work of innovation.[48] Thus, the leader's primary task is to create a world to which people want to belong. This kind of world is one in which their individual identity is affirmed (their values and talents) *and* they can contribute to something larger than themselves. They are willing to contribute to something larger than themselves because they see themselves as part of a community with a common purpose and values; they are able to contribute because their individual capacity and the collective capacity for co-design have been nurtured. Leaders who successfully create and maintain these worlds focus on shaping experience; it is worth noting that there are parallels between our work and that of Podolny, Khurana, and Hill-Popper on leadership as meaning-making.[49]

Sam Palmisano, CEO of IBM, provides an apt example of a leader who understands the importance of returning to an ethos of community and a sense of shared purpose and values if innovation is of paramount concern. IBM, with 320,000 employees in nearly two hundred countries, is not an easy place to instill a sense of belonging and civic engagement. But that is exactly what Palmisano sought to create when he became CEO in 2002. Palmisano knew that vision setting was not the answer.[50] He knew that in order for IBMers to believe in the company values, they had to be involved in the process of developing them. He explained:

> We traditionally were viewed as a large, successful, "well-managed" company. That was a compliment. But in today's fast-changing environment, it's a problem. You can easily end up with a bureaucracy of people overanalyzing problems and slowing down the decision-making process . . . So how do you channel this diverse and constantly changing array of talent and experience into a common purpose?[51]

Palmisano's solution was a ValuesJam on IBM's intranet. The worldwide conversation was an experiment on a scale yet unseen—and one that would have been impossible without IBM's proprietary technology. Over the three days, 50,000 employees posted nearly 100,000 comments about their values, purpose, and IBM. Having helped define the company values themselves, IBMers were inspired to pursue a common, collectively articulated purpose. Palmisano commented:

> I feel that a strong value system is crucial to bringing together and motivating a workforce as large and diverse as ours has become. We have nearly one-third of a million employees serving clients in 170 countries . . . forty percent of those people don't report daily to an IBM site . . . half of today's employees have been with the company for fewer than five years.
>
> So how do you channel this diverse and constantly changing array of talent and experience into a common purpose? How do you get people to *passionately* pursue that purpose? You could employ all kinds of traditional, top-down management processes. But they wouldn't work at IBM . . . More than 200,000 of our employees have college degrees. The CEO can't say to them, "Get in line and follow me." Or "*I've* decided what *your* values are." They're too smart for that.[52]

The information technology (IT) industry, like many others, changes at breakneck speed. Today, leaders are increasingly recognizing that they lack the clairvoyance to know what the future will bring. As one leader of innovation put it, if he expects his group to produce something brand new or original, by definition, he does not know in which direction the group should go. When doing truly innovative work, a leader-generated vision is a rather limited tool. Knowledge workers often want to participate in the creation of the company direction. As one star engineer at one of our research sites declared, "I do not want to be managed or led." Leaders of innovation understand that just as the process of defining a community's purpose matters, so does the purpose's content. Maximizing shareholder returns does not energize many for long. Many of the innovative companies we have studied have intensified their efforts to make sure that the corporate purpose speaks to the loftier aspirations of their people.

What Leaders of Innovation Do: Managing the Paradoxes of Innovation

Leaders of innovative teams and organizations conceive of their primary role as that of a social architect, shaping the individual and collective interactions and experiences of those in their organizations.[53] Creating the world to which people want to belong is to lay the foundation. Building the individual and collective capacity for co-design comes next; unlocking the slices of genius in the organization is tough work. Implicit in the many accounts of co-design is the fact that there are a set of tensions inherent in the innovation process. To at once unleash and harness diverse slices of genius is a process of continually recalibrating a set of five paradoxes: (1) affirming individual identity (individual talents and values) *and* collective identity (community purpose and values); (2) providing support *and also* confrontation; (3) fostering learning and development *and also* performance; (4) promoting improvisation *and* structuring; and (5) encouraging bottom-up initiatives *and* top-down interventions (figure 21-1).

Getting the center of gravity in the right place on each of these paradoxes is a continual struggle. Below we consider each of the paradoxes in turn; it will become apparent quickly how interrelated they are. As one leader put it, he often feels like he is at the edge of chaos, engaged in a perpetual game of tug-of-war.

Affirm Individual Identity and Collective Identity

We have already discussed, at some length, the first and most fundamental paradox: the need to embrace individual differences while pursuing organizational purpose. The innovation process demands a mix

FIGURE 21-1

The paradoxes

Unleash		Harness
Individual identity	————————————	Collective identity
Support	————————————	Confrontation
Learning and development	————————————	Performance
Improvisation	————————————	Structuring
Bottom-up	————————————	Top-down

Copyright © 2007 by Hill, Brandeau, and Stecker.

of diverse individuals with regard to talents and perspectives. For the organization to benefit from this diversity, norms and processes that allow for the expression of varied perspectives, priorities, and styles must be established. Some leaders comment that one of their most important responsibilities is to make sure the "minority voice is heard." Others note that they feel responsible for ensuring that the "fresh perspectives" of the inexperienced do not get drowned out by those of the experts. When these different voices are brought out into the open, conflict among team members is inevitable. Hopefully, there will also be healthy competition, although too much conflict and competition can lead to a "win/lose" mind-set instead of an integrative problem-solving approach. Thus, the challenge is to integrate the individual differences and mobilize them in pursuit of the common purpose.

People will only take the risks necessary to share their talents with others when they feel psychologically safe, and safety comes from knowing they are part of a community of like-minded people with regard to purpose and values. Although the co-design process embodies the signature characteristics of intrinsically motivating work, the collective purpose matters.[54] It is what energizes the group, and more important, keeps the group members committed to the common welfare. Consequently, many leaders have intensified their efforts to make sure that the corporate purpose speaks to the loftiest aspirations of their people, especially the emerging generation of socially minded individuals.[55]

Foster Support and Confrontation Among Members

If member diversity is to be acknowledged and differences encouraged, the group must develop mutual influence and trust so that the members will want to support one another. Without a sense of social support, individuals may find that the negative emotions and stress that accompany the creative process outweigh the benefits. Individuals in supportive groups are open to accepting the leadership and influence of others; in many cases they seek out opportunities to have their ideas refined, revised, tested, and edited by others. They are encouraged to be active listeners and to inquire of each other as much as they advocate, adopting a more Socratic method of mutual coaching and learning.[56] The norm is to focus critique on the quality of the ideas, not the person who generated them. Often, we have heard members of highly innovative teams say, "I'd rather be successful than right."

However, if the members become *too* supportive of one another, they may stop confronting each other. In very cohesive groups, strong norms to preserve harmonious and friendly relationships can evolve, and "groupthink," as opposed to critical thinking, can occur. In this state, individuals stop critiquing each other's decisions and actions, suppressing their own thoughts and feelings, sometimes at considerable personal cost.[57] This squelches the free exchange of ideas and the team's ability to adapt. If and when a dispute finally comes out into the open, members are likely to become polarized around the particular issue; because of their pent-up frustration, they just want to get their way instead of problem-solving about the matter constructively. The team's dysfunctional quest for innovative solutions is likely to end in compromise or concession. But innovation cannot happen when groups use a "weighted average" approach. Group members need to learn how to be comfortable making others uncomfortable when needed.

One final comment is in order about this paradox. Many of the leaders in our study espoused that necessity is often the mother of invention. They felt strongly that resource constraints often spurred innovation. The leader was often the one who confronted the group with critical deadlines or budget realities, in part to spur creative thinking, the evaluation of key assumptions, and the reframing of opportunities. As one of our leaders said, "Our creative process will go on forever unless there is a hard stop. Constraints seem to sharpen thinking because they force the team to find ways to get around them."

Focus on Learning and Development and Performance

The third paradox—to simultaneously focus on learning and development and performance—is an ever-perplexing one, especially given short-term competitive pressures. Innovation requires an investment of time, energy, and other organizational resources.[58] Some of the leaders we have studied call innovation "a numbers game." The challenge is to produce as many ideas and options as possible and to pursue as many avenues of inquiry as possible; inevitably, some waste is produced. Economies of scale and efficiency may suffer in the short run as teams engage in the creative agility and integrative problem-solving processes. Leaders must be willing to let their teams experiment, iterate, debrief, learn, and start the process over again if necessary.

Missteps are to be treated as sources of learning rather than reasons for punishment if risk taking and hence development and innovation are to occur. When the inevitable mistakes or failures happen, innovative groups adopt a joint problem-solving approach. One leader notes that because his organization is so selective, if a person makes "a really big mistake, we assume they are working on a really tough problem." Team members are held accountable to high standards—in fact, a premium is placed on excellence, and the aspiration is breakthrough, not incremental innovation. "Supportive autonomy" with transparency is the name of the game. Critical metrics and information on key drivers of the business are often made available for all to see. One of the leaders we are studying has even put his 360-degree feedback up on the company intranet—and he has encouraged other senior leaders to do the same. Indeed, many innovative teams rely heavily on healthy competition and peer review systems.

In environments like these, people are encouraged to take charge of and continually commit to their own personal development and reinvention. They are particularly encouraged to broaden their "bandwidth," their expertise and point of view; in short, to be more "T" shaped, as Morten Hansen describes in his work on creating horizontal value in organizations.[59] The leaders of many of the companies in our study invest considerable funds in providing educational opportunities throughout their organizations. Not surprisingly, many rely heavily on distance learning to reach people across the globe. The larger organizations have thriving corporate universities at which people are encouraged to broaden their horizons in their choice of studies, in order to "gear up for the future." Other companies, in an effort to enhance creative agility, encourage people to periodically "retool themselves" and rotate onto different projects or departments.

Promote Improvisation and Structuring

The only way individual voices can be expressed and heard is to treat people fairly, which means to treat people differently. Individuals want and need different things if their potential is to be realized. Effective leaders know the power that comes from putting the right people in the right roles. The key is to find ways to match individuals' unique and deeply embedded interests with the business of the organization. Timothy Butler and James Waldroop describe this process as job-sculpting, "the art of matching people to jobs that allow their deeply embedded life interests to be expressed."[60] In almost all of the innovative teams and organizations we have seen, individuals are given choice and discretionary time to pursue their particular passions. In these organizations, there is a recognition that individuals need both engagement and independence to do their best work. Individuals need intellectual and emotional space and solitude; mastering a field or developing an idea often demands discipline and focus.

In highly innovative teams and organizations, positions often cut across traditional boundaries. Work assignments are more project-like. They often reflect shared accountabilities because the scale and scope of the task is bigger than one person. One leader explains that her team is "like a bowl of spaghetti." It is hard to know where one person's role begins and the other ends. The overlapping roles allow them to "tap into one another's varied strengths," but they also slow down the decision-making process at times. Another leader, in an effort to eradicate silos, encouraged her team to do a "crabwalk"; when appropriate, individuals with complementary talents would even job-share. Leaders of innovation aspire for their teams to operate more like an "improvisational jazz ensemble" or "tennis-doubles team," to use Peter Drucker's analogy for self-managed work teams.[61] In these teams, only the group performs; individual members contribute to this performance. They cover their teammates, adjusting as necessary to teammates' talents, weaknesses, and preferred working styles. The research is clear: mutual expectations, influence, and trust are requisites for such teams.

Teams and organizations capable of improvisation have an action orientation to structure. In his extensive work on global, knowledge-intensive corporations, Nitin Nohria refers to this as "structuring," as opposed to structure.[62] They continually adapt the shape and size of the various groups in the organization based on who should be involved in making key decisions and on where vital resources or expertise may reside. Like chameleons, these organizations adapt to the needs of the ever-changing lineup of insiders and outsiders involved in a particular co-design effort.

Leaders of highly innovative teams view structure as a tool for facilitating the co-design process. They also understand it to be an essential lever for encouraging patterns of communication and interaction conducive to innovation. For example, one leader was careful to "cluster together" individuals with diverse skills and to encourage impromptu conversations and networking. Not only do these leaders think about the overall structure of the organization, they also think about what structure to put in place to encourage the right kind of minute-to-minute interactions of a particular co-design effort. It is no accident that Peter Block's *Community* bears *The Structure of Belonging* as its subtitle. Block proposes:

> The way we bring people together matters more than our usual concerns about the content of what we present to people. How we structure the gathering is as worthy of attention as grasping the nature of a problem or focusing on the solutions that we seek . . . Transformation hinges on changing the structure of how we engage with each other.[63]

In the spirit of structuring, leaders of innovation are always prepared to adapt the structure as necessary, so they watch what patterns of interaction emerge, reflect, and then course-correct (or recalibrate, in our language) when necessary. In so doing, they seem to rely on biological models when it comes to making structure decisions. Many put in place "a few simple principles" from which they hope a complex social system conducive to co-design will emerge.[64] The principles are mostly about how people are to interact with each other or about boundary conditions that are never to be crossed. W. L. Gore & Associates, a technology and manufacturing company, is a nice illustration. Gore is recognized as one of America's most innovative companies.[65] Founded by an engineer determined to create an innovator's paradise, Gore is a nearly $3 billion global business with over eight thousand employees— and its foundation is a few simple principles. The four principles by which the company lives are fairness, freedom, commitment, and waterline (shorthand for a ship metaphor, this word represents the notion that associates should make decisions on their own, as long as the downside risk does not threaten the survival of the company).[66] From these principles, a set of robust beliefs and practices have emerged to hold together what has become a diverse global workforce.

At Gore and other organizations, when the rules of engagement or boundary conditions are breached, appropriate sanctions result. Other things being equal, an effort is made to keep structure to a minimum; unnecessary complexity is avoided. In fact, many of the leaders in our study have an aversion to excessive rules—and to rule books; they prefer to "manage by exception." They have learned that relying on informal means or social structure (shared values, norms, social networks, and peer pressure) for guiding and controlling behavior is most effective.

These leaders are quick to utilize the tools—technological and otherwise—at their disposal to add structure where it facilitates co-design. Many have invested in the latest social networking and real-time communication technologies. They have also encouraged the development of compelling, data-rich intranets to facilitate information sharing and worldwide conversation. In many cases, leaders use intranets to articulate shared rhetoric—both to ease communication and to enhance the sense of community. They understand the potential for miscommunication that globalization brings. One of the leaders we are studying hired a social scientist to map out the informal social network in her organization, to make sure that paths of communication were robust. When the pace of growth accelerated and people no longer recognized each other as fellow employees of the company, one leader instituted a series of working retreats in different locations across the world to which individuals from different levels, functions, and geographies were invited. It was expensive, but this leader felt it was an important investment in community building for innovation.

The care with which these leaders tend to structuring their teams and organizations is often matched by attention to the physical structure of the work space. Herman Miller, a leading global provider of office furniture, has an entire division dedicated to the design and development of space and furniture for collaborative innovative work.[67] In *How Buildings Learn: What Happens After They Are Built*, Stewart Brand discusses the kinds of buildings that encourage innovation. A perhaps surprising finding is that the most creative work often happens in "un-precious" spaces that the inhabitants are not afraid to adapt. Brand illustrates this point with an example about MIT's beloved Building 20, a temporary structure that was supposed to be torn down at the end of World War II. It has been described as "The only building on campus you can cut with a saw." Brand explains:

> Like most Low Road buildings, Building 20 was too hot in the summer, too cold in the winter, Spartan in its amenities, often dirty, and implacably ugly. Whatever was the attraction? The organizations of the 1978 exhibit queried alumni of the building and got illuminating answers. "Windows that open and shut at will of the owner! . . . The ability to personalize your space and shape it to various purposes. If you don't like a wall, just stick your elbow through it." . . . "We feel our space is really ours. We designed it; we run it. The building is full of small microenvironments, each of which is different and each a creative space."[68]

As it turns out, since World War II, Building 20 has been the home of legendary innovators, from the Research Laboratory of Electronics, which founded much of modern communication science, to Noam Chomsky and to the first generation of "hackers."[69]

Encourage Bottom-Up Initiative and Selective Top-Down Intervention

The final paradox involves achieving a delicate balance between bottom-up initiatives and top-down intervention. The leaders in our study understand that innovation is often the result of grassroots efforts. Hence, they encourage and reward both autonomy and attempts at co-design. These leaders encourage peer-driven processes of self-organizing and self-governing. Much like we see in Web 2.0 practices, online multiplayer games, and social networking sites, innovative organizations are places where "natural hierarchies" often replace more formal ones as groups advance in the co-design process.[70] Influence and status are determined more by contribution than they are by title. In some of these organizations, teams elect their own leader; in others, leaders self-nominate.

To be clear: hierarchy is alive and well in these organizations, but it is used on an as-needed basis. These leaders accept final accountability for their teams' performance, yet conceive of themselves as the first among equals. Most of the leaders are very hands-on, and many have grown up in their organizations. Having been embedded in the process of co-design, they know what people in their teams and organizations are doing and feeling. They pay attention to the emotional state of their people; they are acutely aware of how threatening and stressful co-design can be. As such, they are vigilant about the individual and collective experiences of their people and are deeply engaged in the continual recalibration of the five paradoxes.

Part of this vigilance is being thoughtful about when to intervene and when to let the group continue to grapple with its challenges. As Skarzynski and Gibson describe in *Innovation to the Core*, honoring both sides of the tensions inherent in the innovation process is an enormously subtle challenge.[71] It takes great skill to avoid becoming hostage to one side or the other. They compare it to raising children: "Parents need to somehow find the right mix of both love and discipline and give their children what they need at the right moment, in the right way."[72] In some ways, the analogy is a dangerous one; the individuals in the organizations in our study are adults and expect to be treated accordingly.

Top-down behavior occurs sparingly by these leaders as they participate in the co-design process. Sometimes they are the author of ideas; in fact, many of the leaders in our study are visionaries in their fields. More often, these leaders serve as editors or integrators of ideas. When conflicts verge on becoming dysfunctional, they step in to encourage the group to reframe the problem. Other times, they step in by procuring needed resources; a favorite resource, it seems, is people who can offer new perspectives. Given their unique organizational vantage points, these leaders serve as bridgers, helping people make the connections, both inside and outside the company, necessary to gain access to the different points of view or expertise required.[73] Because there is a high degree of trust between the leaders and their people, the leaders are given considerable latitude. Their interventions are generally accepted. And because of the relatively high degree of candor in these organizations, when there is discomfort with a leader's actions, he or she usually hears about it. That said, the leaders are all too aware that if they shoot the messenger, their credibility and access to information about the most sensitive aspects of group life—people's feelings and deepest concerns—will be seriously damaged.

Who These Leaders Are: Leading from Behind

The leaders of innovation that we have studied lead from behind, as opposed to leading from the front—a common metaphor in the leadership literature.[74] Nelson Mandela, a social innovator of the highest order, described leading from behind like this, when recalling how a leader of his tribe talked about leadership: "A leader . . . is like a shepherd. He stays behind the flock, letting the most nimble go out ahead, whereupon the others follow, not realizing that all along they are being directed from behind."[75]

This shepherd image embodies the kind of leaders we increasingly need. We need leaders who see their principal role as creating a world or work environment in which others can share their diverse talents and realize their potential for the well-being of the team or organization. It is an acknowledgement that leadership, like the co-design process, is a collective and fluid activity in which different people at different times—depending on their particular slice of genius or "nimbleness"—come forward to move the group in the direction it needs to go. It also hints at the agility of a group that does not have to wait for and then respond to a command from the front. We should also take this opportunity to emphasize that leading from behind is not about abrogating responsibility. After all, the shepherd makes sure that the flock stays together. He uses his staff to nudge and prod if the flock strays too far off course or into danger. As we saw earlier, unleashing and harnessing the slices of genius of diverse and passionate individuals is delicate and difficult work. While diverse along many dimensions, the leaders we have studied share a common set of characteristics worth consideration. Interestingly, these qualities sometimes contradict conventional notions of what effective leaders look like.

Leaders of innovation are idealists, yet pragmatists with well-developed inner compasses to keep them grounded. They are builders, investors, and developers. They are committed to creating a better world for the people in their organizations as well as stakeholders outside their organizations; for some, this includes broader society. Many conceive of their work in the grandest terms—whether it's organizing the world's information through Internet search, enhancing the world's beauty and culture through design, or promoting a global nomad lifestyle through luxury goods. Relative to many leaders we have met, they take the long-term view, but are well aware of the need to do so in a manner that takes seriously competitive realties. As one publicly proclaimed during a time of unprecedented economic turmoil, "We will leave no one behind and we will do what is necessary to maintain the vibrancy of the business."

Most important, the leaders see the extraordinary where others see the ordinary. They look for slices of genius in others, and they act as if everyone matters—because they do. They help people discover and develop their personal slice of genius. One of the leaders in our study is a high-powered litigator from one of the world's largest law firms. A member of her team noted, "It seems like she can see things that other people can't see. She detects people's strengths and channels them toward a client's needs. It is one of the ways she leverages herself—and this leverage has allowed her to build a very large practice. Plus, it helps her retain the best and brightest, even when we could have our own practices elsewhere. It's widely known that if you work with her, you get exposed to the most exciting cases and you will continually develop." Indeed, our leaders have an unusual capacity for trust and risk taking.

Leaders of innovation have the talent of soloists—and the temperament of orchestra players.[76] These leaders are perfectly capable of leading from the front. Many in our study are considered gurus in their respective fields. But they choose to work collaboratively. Take, for example, the international design partnership in our study. In an industry where firms often bear their founders' names and fade with retirements, this firm, which was founded on the "principles of generosity and equality," has endured for decades. In one profile of the firm, the author wrote that the firm has a "socialist ethos." But be assured they are capitalists. To become a partner, an individual has to meet three requirements: have an international reputation, a demonstrated ability to run a business, and "the social skills to make intriguing, pleasant company." Individuals join because they believe that the creative abrasion that comes from being with other talented individuals from different disciplines (five design disciplines are represented in the firm) elevates the quality of their individual and collective work. Twice each year, partners gather to present their work to one another. The formal leadership of Pentagram rotates, and incidentally, one of the most important roles of the rotating chair is to select an interesting cultural locale for the meeting. The process of peer critique has been described as "cacophonous"; many partners note that showing their work to their colleagues is the scariest thing they do. The creative abrasion is both painful and enjoyable; it's something these talented individuals seek. One partner, referred to by some as a "rock star" and by others as a "legend," considers this work environment to be his "postgraduate education."

In addition, leaders of innovation are systems thinkers with an action orientation. They are integrative thinkers able to use both the right and left sides of their brains; they cope well with considerable amounts of cognitive complexity. They have a high tolerance for ambiguity and uncertainty. Inquisitive by nature, they are often voracious readers with vivacious imaginations and broad interests. They enjoy unraveling complex technical and organizational issues down to their core. It is no surprise that they serve as role models for others in their organization about how to approach the co-design process.

When it comes to innovation, an action orientation is a must, and actions are all the more powerful when they are formulated through systems thinking. We have been struck by the sophistication with which the leaders in our study understand organizational dynamics. They conceive of organizations as systems, and they see the world in shades of gray. Unlike those who are paralyzed by the notion that every action ignites a series of reactions, these leaders act with thoughtful decisiveness. They have the psychological and emotional maturity to weather the dark and stormy times of the co-design process. They are often regarded as empathic, even those who are also described as "gruff" or "rather stoic." They "spread calm during chaos" when others are overwhelmed.

Another characteristic of the leaders we have studied is their generosity. Fundamentally, they are comfortable sharing power. Despite all the talk about empowerment, many leaders are too afraid to give up the control it implies. Leaders of innovation are secure enough in themselves to share credit. A member of one of the teams in our study said of his leader, "It's as though she enjoys getting the credit just so she can give it away." A leader's generosity is important for enhancing the commitment of individuals in the collective, and for creating the conditions of psychological safety that are critical for risk taking and hence innovation. Sometimes generosity comes in the form of leaders offering support at just the right moment in just the right way. A team member at one of the technology companies in our study noted the following about his group's leader: "He is the best manager I have ever had. He encourages me to be a disruption, to put myself out there without worry, to question everything, and to just find interesting things to work on. When he identifies that someone is really capable, the reins are off. He has deep trust in his engineers; he knows we'll do the right thing."

Trust, generosity, and empathy are not to be mistaken for faint-heartedness. Leading from behind often takes tremendous courage, even audacity. Listen to one of our leaders describe his company's three-phase strategy: "The final stage will be a radical shift in the business model. With the industry changing so rapidly, I do not have a firm vision of what this will look like, although I plan that 50 percent of our revenue will come from services that do not exist today." The time frame to which this leader is referring is just five years. Clearly, leading from behind is not a style reserved for the uninspiring or indecisive. In fact, like the leader just quoted, many people who lead from behind are perfectly capable of leading from the front—and when it's appropriate, they do. Some of these leaders have to actively fight their natural tendency to intervene because they know how fragile the co-design process can be; they understand how willing people will be to delegate up when they feel stuck or stressed. These leaders elect to shape rather than direct—to be nuanced in their actions, like the shepherd.

Despite formidable accomplishments and healthy doses of confidence, these leaders are humble. They feel privileged to lead—and to have been born in a place and time where their talents are valued.[77] This extends to their teams and organizations as well; perhaps it's the nature of innovation itself. An engineer at one of the companies commented, "We've always invented things as we go along. When we start, we literally do not have the technical ability to get it [the job] done. It's like jumping out of an airplane and building a parachute as you drop—the release date, like the ground, doesn't budge. This has given us a vague inferiority complex, and that's a healthy thing. Success can be damaging."

The leaders in our study are exceptional in many ways, but they are imperfect, like the rest of us humans. They report having their share of bad days, and all can cite instances in which they mismanaged the co-design process. They know their strengths and weaknesses. They know they don't have to have all the answers. They surround themselves with great people who can cover for them when necessary. They are committed to continually developing themselves. They are insatiable learners—constantly seeking new information and learning from mistakes. Importantly, they instill this learning orientation to their teams, which enhances the co-design process.

One of these leaders proclaimed that leadership is "fundamentally about humanity." Where do we find more leaders like this? We need leaders who understand that leadership is not about setting a vision and getting everyone to follow, but creating a world to which others want to belong. Perhaps the more pertinent question is this: How do we *develop* leaders capable of leading from behind? Those who lead from behind do not often exhibit the take-charge, direction-setting behavior so often associated with traditional notions of leadership (although many do have what might be thought of as "quiet charisma"). Much of their time is devoted to doing the invisible work of co-design. When co-design really works, the whole is much more than the sum of the parts, making it hard to ascertain individual contributions. Indeed, some of what they have to learn to live with is the frustration of being overlooked, especially in the short run, before the fruits of their labor become apparent. As one reported, it helps to deal with frustrations if you stay focused on the purpose of the work.

The Future Research Agenda

We actually know a great deal about the innovation process, especially if we read beyond the disciplines most often found in business schools. We have proposed that innovation in organizations be conceived of as a process of co-design: creative abrasion, creative agility, and integrated problem solving. We know much about the kind of contextual factors that foster the three collaborative processes. Much of the research on leadership for innovation is macro in its orientation, focusing on the organizational factors that impact innovation and spelling out the implications for best practice.[78] There is comparatively little research on leadership for innovation that looks at micro-level phenomena or their connection with macro-level phenomena. Hence our research questions: (1) how leaders of innovation think, (2) what they do, (3) how they do it, and (4) who they are and how they got to be that way.

In terms of management theorists, we found Mary Parker Follett's work especially enlightening for our areas of inquiry. As Rosabeth Moss Kanter discussed in a preface to a collection of Follett's works, Follett was way ahead of her time.[79] She was admittedly a utopian and romantic, but she had a profound appreciation for human relations and was one of the earliest systems thinkers. She saw all people as equals and would understand the notion that everyone has a slice of genius. The power of the dialectic of individual and collective identity resonated with Follett; consider her words: "We find the true man only through group organization. The potentialities of an individual remain potentialities until they are released by group life."[80] Moreover, she sung the virtues of difference and conflict in organizational life. In the 1920s she was encouraging leaders to replace bureaucracy with empowered group networks with a common purpose. In a discussion of Follett's contribution, John Child wrote:

> There was, for example, a very significant divergence between Follett's concept of constructive conflict . . . and [Elton] Mayo's deep abhorrence of conflict in any form. Follett believed that people at all levels in an enterprise could come rationally to accept the "law of the situation" and that therefore, through discussion, a mutually acceptable and innovative integrative solution could be found to many conflicts. She anticipated that integration could be achieved through participation in decision-making, on the basis of the functional knowledge that each party to an issue had could offer. Mayo and his colleague, by contrast, assumed that ordinary employees were largely governed by a "logic of sentiment," which was of a different order from managers' rational appraisal of the situation in terms of costs and efficiency. Conflict with management was thus an aberration that threatened the effectiveness of organizations.[81]

Now, with the premium being placed on innovation as a key differentiator and source of competitive advantage, it is time we all reread her work. In the same vein, we recommend the work of urban planners.[82] It is not surprising that the ideas of Horst Rittel, an eminent urban planner and designer, are very much in vogue. Rittel found that traditional planning and problem-solving methods were inadequate for the ill-structured problems he encountered in city planning. Like Follett he often found himself working on what he termed "wicked problems," problems that, among other things, cannot really be understood until they are solved.[83] Rittel invented what he described as a "structure for rational discourse":

> With wicked problems, the determination of solution quality is not objective and cannot be derived from following a formula. Solutions are assessed in a social context in which "many parties are equally equipped, interested, and/or entitled to judge [them] and these judgments are likely to vary widely and depend on the stakeholders' independent values and goals."[84]

We hope we have provided some insight into three of the four questions outlined above. It is with some frustration that we have not had much to say about how effective leaders of innovation do what they do. As many leaders have told us, this is knowledge they crave. They know what to do; they just do not know how to do it. We need more research on implementation, especially empirical work that examines effective leaders of innovation in action and in context. In particular, we would argue for comparative field study work so that a collection of "teaching parables" can be produced. In this regard, we suggest not only more action research but also the use of social science portraiture, a genre of inquiry and representation that joins science and art. Sara Lawrence-Lightfoot has articulated the virtues and complexities of this method:

> Portraiture is a method of qualitative research that blurs the boundaries of aesthetics and empiricism in an effort to capture the complexity, dynamics, and subtlety of human experience and organizational life. Portraitists seek to record and interpret the perspectives and experiences of the people they are studying, documenting their voices and their visions—their authority, knowledge and wisdom. The drawing of the portrait is placed in social and cultural context and shaped through dialogue between the portraitist and the subject, each one negotiating the discourse and shaping the evolving image. The relationship between the two is rich with meaning and resonance and becomes the arena for navigating the empirical, aesthetic, and ethical dimensions of authentic and compelling narrative.[85]

To our minds, portraiture is a perfect vehicle for expert leaders of innovation to share their slices of genius with each other. It represents a tool for co-design between academics and those in practice. The academic's task would be to harness leaders' varied experiences to create an action theory of leadership better suited to our times.

As we embark on this endeavor, we would advocate the adoption of a global view. Too much of leadership research is conducted in the United States or western Europe. This is despite the reality that some of the most disruptive leadership practices and new business models are coming out of the emerging markets, as they abandon labor arbitrage and begin to move up the value chain. Established enterprises in the developed economies are discovering with some chagrin that their most formidable competitors are coming from the BRICs.[86] One of our U.S. leaders has developed an innovative response to his competitors in the emerging economies. In an effort to build community around a worthy cause and to develop leaders capable of co-design, he has sought volunteers (people in the company willing to work on their own time) to come together and start up profitable business lines in the so-called bottom of the pyramid markets. The teams have set specific profitability and poverty eradication targets. C. K. Prahalad has noted that some of the most breakthrough business strategies, models, processes, and ways of organizing have come from teams building profitable businesses directed at those economically less fortunate.[87] This leader is tapping into employees' passion—and creating a fertile context for innovation. And in so doing, he is creating a world to which people want to belong.

An Inquisitive Brain Trust

As an experiment, we have begun to introduce the ten leaders in our study to each other to create a "brain trust" on leadership for innovation. We selected these leaders because they are very good at what they do, but the reality is that they are constantly struggling with the trade-offs and dilemmas inherent to the innovation process. As described earlier, they are all committed to excellence and constant improvement. From their conversations and common concerns, we have identified three arenas as particularly fruitful for further exploration: community-building in large global companies; reframing the innovation-versus-efficiency dichotomy; and developing leaders who are willing and able to lead from behind.

1. What does it take to create and maintain a community with human scale in a large global company so that co-design is possible?

   - How do you build a sense of community in a group of demographically diverse individuals? How do you build a sense of community in a group that is globally dispersed? Is this asking people to go against human nature? How can we develop both the individual and collective capacity to be truly open-minded, encourage creative abrasion, and embrace integrative problem solving? Perhaps the work on conflict resolution in peace studies departments or on community capacity building from urban planning and community development can offer insight into these questions.

- Just how fast can you grow a company and maintain a sense of community? Some of the companies we are studying, particularly those in emerging markets, are growing in excess of 30 percent each year.

- How can leaders design work spaces more conducive to co-design? The main building at Pixar shares many of the traits of Building 20 at MIT, only it is aesthetically quite pleasing—and of the finest quality. Every brick has been hand-laid; the building's steel is bolted together, not welded, to lend it a rehabbed factory feel. It is structured to facilitate inadvertent encounters and to enhance the sense of community.

- How can leaders better exploit information technology for innovation (in building community and facilitating co-design)?[88] What can we learn from the open-source and agile programming movements about distributed leadership and new organizational forms? What lessons can we learn, for instance, from the evolution of Linux, which emerged from a collaborative web of teams sometimes working independently and other times collectively without any guiding plan?[89]

- What is the role of rhetoric in community building and innovation?[90] Language profoundly shapes the way we see the world, and oral history and storytelling have been important tools for cultural transmission and teaching throughout the ages. Do we need a new rhetoric that humanizes the languages of business and leadership? How do we go about building a language with new metaphors to create a new mind-set about leadership and organizational life?

2. In the effort to allow for creative agility and improvisation, many questions arise about the relationship between innovation and efficiency and whether they are inherently in conflict. Superficially, it appears they might be, but perhaps this is a false dichotomy. If so, how can we devise a more integrative way of framing this issue so that it can be addressed more constructively?

- How much complexity and improvisation can people cope with? Will the work on neuroscience and organizational phenomena help us answer this query? Are there other perspectives that should be brought to bear?

- What structuring needs to be in place to make it easier to innovate? We know more about what barriers need to be removed than we know about what tools or resources need to be put in place. Can insights from the open-source movement or multiplayer computer games help us address the latter?[91]

3. We know what those capable of leading for innovation do, how they think, and who they are. How do we go about developing a new generation of leaders who excel at solving the challenges listed above?

  - It is logical that the leaders most suited for today's—and tomorrow's—world are different from those who excelled in times past.[92] Will the new generation of leaders come from leading business schools, the military, and elite consulting firms? Are there new sources of talent we should pursue? Emerging markets? Different educational backgrounds? Different sectors?

  - Few organizations today cite "generous with power" and "see the extraordinary where others see the ordinary" as markers of leadership potential. How should we assess leadership potential?

  - We need more study of the developmental experiences of leaders capable of building communities and developing individual and collective capacity for co-design. What experiences were formative for these leaders? What do they find most difficult to master? How can they best share their wisdom and judgment with others?

  - With the entry of Generation Y into the workforce, will our notion of the ideal leader change? There is a growing speculation that multiplayer computer games represent more than a mere foreshadowing of how leadership might evolve. These games, and the generation that has grown up with them, may end up being catalysts for change in business leadership. Among other things, those raised on these games will expect more distributed and fluid leadership models, rapid change, hyper-transparency, and customizable, intrinsically motivating work.

- Will it be easier for individuals from some cultures to learn to lead from behind than it is for others? Consider two quotes. One is from a Western perspective: "Leadership involves finding a parade and getting in front of it." The other is from an Eastern perspective: "To lead the people, walk behind them."[93]

- How can we educate leaders to be better at managing diversity? After all, this is integral for being able to engage in creative abrasion. Florida may have found that the "creative class" flocks to cities because of the diversity they will find there, but most of those cities are made up of neighborhoods segregated by socioeconomic status, race, and ethnicity. Let's face it: we all find it easier to trust and build relationships with people who are similar to us. Will forging ties with diverse others be easier for the younger generations, given their life experiences (global travel, fluency with Web 2.0 and social-networking technology)?[94]

- How do we educate future leaders to be integrative problem solvers? As a first step, they need to have "opposable minds" that resist the temptation of dichotomous thinking. They need to have a more systems (as opposed to an interpersonal) orientation to organizational life. Without this, it will be hard for them to master the art of recalibrating the five paradoxes.[95]

The real challenge, of course, is to translate integrative and systems thinking into action. We have no doubt that the capacity to do the collaborative work for innovation will be an imperative for the next generation of leaders. Of course, integrative problem solving is only one of the three co-design processes. The other two, creative abrasion and creative agility, are equally as important. Expectations for business leaders are rising; they are expected not only to build competitive businesses, but also to do so in a manner that positively impacts broader society.[96] "Do no harm" is only the beginning; moral leadership and courage on the part of business leadership is being called for by stakeholders from nearly every corner of the globe.[97] Business leaders are being asked to join with those from other sectors to develop innovative solutions to the intractable challenges of our times, from terrorism to global warming to education and poverty.

While daunting, these questions are also a source of inspiration. A comparison with the equivalent questions from one hundred years or even ten years ago speaks to just how far we have come. It is not easy to forecast the future, and like anyone attempting prognostication, we are bound by our inherently limited frames of reference. We are well beyond the phase where signals indicating that a new type of leadership is needed are weak. Frankly, we believe we have reached an inflection point in the field of leadership. The trend is clear: disruptive innovations coming increasingly from nontraditional players are putting pressure on established companies to increase the type and pace of innovation. The leaders whose companies can innovate and continually change the rules of the game—or the game itself—in their competitive space will be able to command premium positioning and pricing. Another trend is clear as well: businesses are increasingly being expected to play a role in the development of innovative solutions to our global sociopolitical challenges. The leaders whose companies can meet this aspiration will play a critical role in creating a better world for those within the confines of their corporate communities as well as the larger global community.

The business leaders of today and the foreseeable future must know how to turn their organizations into innovative communities instead of practicing what Gary Hamel has referred to as "creative apartheid"—a scenario where only a few "gifted individuals" are given responsibility for innovation, with the other members of the organization seen as unimaginative.[98] It is time to recognize that creativity is widely distributed and that innovation comes from nurturing the slice of genius in everyone. The time has come for a revolution in our thinking about what makes an effective leader.

Notes

1. Many works emphasize the criticality of innovation in today's economy. See, for example, Rebecca Henderson, "Managing Innovation in the Information Age," *Harvard Business Review* 72, no. 1 (January–February 1994): 100–107; and John Kao, *Innovation Nation: How America Is Losing Its Innovation Edge, Why It Matters, and What*

We Can Do to Get It Back (New York: The Free Press, 2007). See also Rosabeth Moss Kanter, John Kao, and Fred Wiersema, eds., *Innovation: Breakthrough Thinking at 3M, GE, DuPont, Pfizer, and Rubbermaid* (New York: HarperCollins, 1997). For classic work on the role of economic development in innovation, see Joseph Schumpeter, *The Theory of Economic Development: An Inquiry into Profits, Capital, Credit, Interest and the Business Cycle* (Piscataway, NJ: Transaction Publishers, 1982).

2. IBM, *The Enterprise of the Future: Global CEO Study* (Armonk, NY: International Business Machines Corp., 2008).

3. Ibid., 9.

4. Unless otherwise noted, in this chapter, "leaders" refers to the individuals with formal authority on a team or in an organization.

5. There are many examples of narratives that capture the micro-level dynamics of innovation in organizations. See, for instance, Tracy Kidder, *The Soul of a New Machine* (New York: Avon Books, 1981).

6. For in-depth accounts of Pixar Animation Studios, see Karen Paik, *To Infinity and Beyond! The Story of Pixar Animation Studios* (San Francisco: Chronicle Books, 2007); and David A. Price, *The Pixar Touch: The Making of a Company* (New York: Alfred A. Knopf, 2008).

7. One of this chapter's coauthors, Linda A. Hill, started down this path of inquiry over a decade ago. In 1999, she was asked to write a chapter on the future of leadership. While the ideas have evolved considerably since then, many of the central ideas in this chapter were first published in 1999. See Linda A. Hill, "Leadership as Collective Genius," in *Management 21C: New Visions for the New Millennium*, ed. Subir Chowdry (New York: Financial Times Publishing, 1999), 45–65.

8. Howard Gardner, *Creating Minds* (New York: Basic Books, 1993), 44.

9. Keith Sawyer, *Group Genius: The Creative Power of Collaboration* (New York: Basic Books, 2007), 5.

10. Ibid., 8–9.

11. For an in-depth look at Edison's life, see Neil Baldwin, *Edison: Inventing the Century* (Chicago: University of Chicago Press, 2001).

12. Tim Brown, "Design Thinking," *Harvard Business Review* 86, no. 6 (June 2008): 84–92. For more on IDEO, see Tom Kelley, *The Art of Innovation: Lessons in Creativity from IDEO, America's Leading Design Firm* (New York: Doubleday, 2001).

13. Ed Catmull, "How Pixar Fosters Collective Creativity," *Harvard Business Review* 86, no. 9 (September 2008): 66.

14. Writers like James Surowiecki offer insights into the power of groups. See, for example, James Surowiecki, *The Wisdom of Crowds* (New York: Random House, 2004).

15. For more on how companies attract and develop world-class talent, see Claudio Fernandez Araoz, *Great People Decisions* (Hoboken: Wiley, 2007). For more work on "stars," see Robert Kelley and Janet Caplan, "How Bell Labs Creates Star Performers," *Harvard Business Review* 71, no. 4 (July–August 1993): 128–139.

16. See for example, Jacob Getzels and Mike Csikszentmihalyi, *The Creative Vision* (Hoboken, NJ: Wiley, 1976); or Keith Sawyer, *Explaining Creativity: The Science of Innovation* (New York: Oxford University Press, 2006).

17. Much has been written about the creative process. For a cultural and historical look at the key relationships and social contexts of some of the most creative people of our time, see the work of Howard Gardner and also of Vera John-Steiner. See Gardner, *Creating Minds*; Howard Gardner, *Extraordinary Minds: Portraits of Four Exceptional Individuals and an Examination of Our Own Extraordinariness*

(New York: Basic Books, 1998); and Vera John-Steiner, *Creative Collaboration* (New York: Oxford University Press USA, 2006). Other works on creative people include Mike Csikszentmihalyi, *Creativity: Flow and the Psychology of Discovery and Invention* (New York: Harper Perennial, 1997); and Getzels and Csikszentmihalyi, *The Creative Vision*. In addition, the research of Teresa Amabile has been especially influential on our thinking. In particular, see Teresa Amabile, *The Social Psychology of Creativity* (New York: Springer-Verlag, 1983); Teresa Amabile, *Creativity in Context* (Boulder, CO: Westview Press, 1996); and Teresa Amabile et al., "Affect and Creativity at Work," *Administrative Science Quarterly* 50, no. 3 (2005): 367–403. There are many other works that explore the creative process in organizational life. See, for example, John Kao, *Jamming: The Art and Discipline of Business Creativity* (New York: Collins Business, 1997); R. Keith Sawyer, *Explaining Creativity: The Science of Human Innovation* (New York: Oxford University Press, 2006); and Robert Sutton and Andrew Hargadon, "Brainstorming Groups in Context: Effectiveness in a Product Design Firm," *Administrative Science Quarterly* 41, no. 4 (1996): 685–718.

18. The term "creative abrasion" was coined by Jerry Hirshberg. See Jerry Hirshberg, *The Creative Priority* (New York: HarperCollins, 1998). Dorothy Leonard's work on creative abrasion has been helpful to us. See, for example, Dorothy Leonard and Walter Swap, *When Sparks Fly: Igniting Group Creativity* (Boston: Harvard Business School Press, 1999). Bennis and Biederman's book on organizing genius is also relevant: Warren Bennis and Patricia Ward Biederman, *Organizing Genius* (New York: Basic Books, 1998).

19. Sawyer, *Group Genius*, 15.

20. Our conceptualization of creative abrasion has also been strongly influenced by David Thomas and Robin Ely's work on leveraging diversity. See Robin Ely and David Thomas, "Cultural Diversity at Work: The Effects of Diversity Perspectives on Work Group Social Processes and Outcomes," *Administrative Science Quarterly* 46, no. 2 (2001): 229–273. Another important perspective comes from Scott Page. See Scott Page, *The Difference: How the Power of Diversity Creates Better Groups, Firms, Schools, and Societies* (Princeton, NJ: Princeton University Press, 2007).

21. This John Seely Brown quotation is in Mark Stefik and Barbara Stefik, *Breakthrough: Stories and Strategies of Radical Innovation* (Cambridge, MA: MIT Press, 2004), 169–170.

22. Richard Florida, *The Rise of the Creative Class . . . and How It's Transforming Work, Leisure, Community, and Everyday Life* (New York: Basic Books, 2002), 8, 15.

23. Ibid., 227.

24. Stefan Thomke's work is useful for understanding the process and importance of what we call creative agility. See Stefan Thomke, "Enlightened Experimentation: The New Imperative for Innovation," *Harvard Business Review* 79, no. 2 (February 2001): 67–75. See also Stefan Thomke and Eric von Hippel, "Customers as Innovators: A New Way to Create Value," *Harvard Business Review* 80, no. 4 (April 2002): 74–81. The work on process innovation is also helpful. See Gary Pisano, *The Development Factory: Unlocking the Potential of Process Innovation* (Boston: Harvard Business School Press, 1996).

25. Baldwin, *Edison*, 83.

26. Ibid., 73–74.

27. Ibid., 74.

28. Kelley, *The Art of Innovation*, 232.

29. This quote is from Mary Parker Follett's 1924 book, *Creative Experience*. Many of the passages from *Creative Experience* can be found in a collection of Follett's work that is edited by Pauline Graham. See Pauline Graham, ed., *Mary Parker Follett, Prophet of Management: A Celebration of Writings from the 1920s* (Washington, DC: Beard Books, 2003), 20. For further elaboration on these ideas, see Mary Parker Follett, *Creative Experience* (Bristol: Thoemmes Press, 2001).

30. Graham, *Mary Parker Follett*, 20.

31. Ibid., 20.

32. Ibid., 70.

33. Ibid., 71.

34. Ibid., 86.

35. Roger Martin, *The Opposable Mind: How Successful Leaders Win Through Integrative Thinking* (Boston: Harvard Business School Press, 2007), 4.

36. Follett used the term "thrill of victory" in a January 1925 paper that she presented before a Bureau of Public Administration conference. For quotes from the paper, see Pauline Graham, ed., *Mary Parker Follett, Prophet of Management: A Celebration of Writings from the 1920s* (Washington, DC: Beard Books, 2003), xviii.

37. For more on community building and social capital, see Robert Putnam, "Bowling Alone: America's Declining Social Capital," *Journal of Democracy* 6, no. 1 (1995): 65–78. Henry Mintzberg also writes about community. See his 2007 working paper entitled "Developing Management as Community."

38. For research on the importance of psychological safety, see Amy Edmundson, "Psychological Safety and Learning Behavior in Work Teams," *Administrative Science Quarterly* 44, no. 4 (1999): 350–383. Also useful is Edmudson's article on organizations that foster "execution-as-learning." See Amy Edmundson, "The Competitive Imperative of Learning," *Harvard Business Review* 86, nos. 7–8 (July–August 2008): 60–67.

39. Jane Jacobs, *The Death and Life of Great American Cities* (New York: Random House, 1961).

40. Karl Weick, *The Social Psychology of Organizing* (New York: McGraw-Hill, 1969).

41. Gerben S. van der Vegt and J. Stuart Bunderson, "Learning and Performance in Multidisciplinary Teams: The Importance of Collective Team Identification," *Academy of Management Journal* 48, no. 3 (2005): 532–547.

42. Catmull, "How Pixar Fosters Collective Creativity," 66–67.

43. Alistair Cockburn and Jim Highsmith, "Agile Software Development: The Business of Innovation," *Computer* 34, no. 9 (2001): 121.

44. See John J. Gabarro, *The Dynamics of Taking Charge* (Boston: Harvard Business School Press, 1987).

45. Peter Block, *Community: The Structure of Belonging* (New York: Berrett-Koehler Publishers, 2008), 24.

46. Thomas Hobbes, *Leviathan* (New York: Penguin Classics, 1985), 21.

47. As we write, we are in dire economic times. A colleague made this comment in a seminar on financial innovation run amok convened for Harvard Business School faculty. He raised an interesting question about what happens when there is too heavy a reliance on individual integrity, especially when there are weak social norms. Both businesses and larger society must consider the trade-offs between regulation versus social norms. Systems must be balanced by equally weighted opposing tensions.

48. The social movement and community building literature is helpful in this regard. See, for example, Gerald Davis et al., *Social Movements and Organization Theory* (London: Cambridge University Press, 2005); and Rosabeth Moss Kanter, *Commitment and Community: Communes and Utopias in Sociological Perspective* (Boston: Harvard University Press, 1972). See also John Pepper, *What Really Matters: Service, Leadership, People and Values* (New Haven, CT: Yale University Press, 2007).

49. See Joel Podolny, Rakesh Khurana, and Mary Hill-Popper, "Revisiting the Meaning of Leadership," *Research in Organizational Behavior* 26, no. 1 (2005): 1–36. Another person working in this vein, with a focus on identity, is John Clippinger. See John Clippinger, *A Crowd of One: The Future of Individual Identity* (New York: PublicAffairs, 2007).

50. Kotter and Bennis both make the distinction between leadership and management. Leadership is about coping with change: setting direction, aligning people, and motivating and inspiring. Management is about coping with complexity: planning and budgeting, organizing and staffing, controlling, and problem solving. They both found that many companies lack agility and the capacity to adapt to new competitive environments because they are overmanaged and underled—a very important observation. Note that their work was focused on change, not innovation—these are related but different phenomena. See John Kotter, *Leading Change* (Boston: Harvard Business School Press, 1999); John Kotter, *What Leaders Really Do* (Boston: Harvard Business School Press, 1999); and John Kotter, *The Heart of Change* (Boston: Harvard Business School Press, 2002). Also see Warren Bennis and Burt Nanus, *Leaders: The Strategies for Taking Charge* (New York: HarperBusiness, 1997).

51. Samuel J. Palmisano, "Leading Change When Business Is Good," *Harvard Business Review* (December 2004): 60–70.

52. Ibid., 65.

53. Leaders of innovation focus on shaping individual and collective experiences. In understanding the mechanisms at play in shaping experience, we have found some of the research on the "experience economy" insightful. See, for example, B. Joseph Pine II and James Gilmore, *The Experience Economy: Work Is Theatre and Every Business a Stage* (Boston: Harvard Business School Press, 1999).

54. For more on intrinsic motivation, see J. Richard Hackman and Greg R. Oldham, "Motivation Through the Design of Work: Test of a Theory," *Organizational Behavior and Human Performance* 16, no. 2 (1976): 250–279. For more on intrinsic motivation and on the effective leadership of teams, see, for example, J. Richard Hackman, *Leading Teams: Setting the Stage for Great Performances* (Boston: Harvard Business School Press, 2002).

55. Similar considerations exist with individuals from emerging markets. Two of the authors of this chapter were engaged in a project on talent management in emerging markets. We found that many job candidates in emerging markets prize a company with a game-changing business model, where they can be a part of redefining their nation's place in the world economy. These individuals are attracted to corporations that include in their purpose helping the unfortunate—many have experienced poverty first hand and express the value of global citizenship. See Doug A. Ready, Linda A. Hill, and Jay A. Conger, "Winning the Race for Talent in Emerging Markets," *Harvard Business Review* 86, no. 11 (November 2008): 62–70.

56. In fact, the innovative teams and organizations in our study bear striking resemblance to many of the principles outlined by Peter Senge in his work on learning

organizations. See Peter M. Senge, *The Fifth Discipline: The Art and Practice of the Learning Organization* (New York: Random House, 2006).

57. For more on groupthink, see Irving Janis, *Groupthink: Psychological Studies of Policy Decisions and Fiascoes* (Boston: Houghton Mifflin, 1982).

58. For more on the ingredients of positive workplace energy and how these lead to innovation, see Lynda Gratton, *Hot Spots: Why Some Teams, Workplaces and Organizations Buzz with Energy—and Others Don't* (New York: Berrett-Koehler Publishers, 2007).

59. For more on "T-shaped managers," see Morton Hansen, "Introducing T-Shaped Managers: Knowledge Management's Next Generation," *Harvard Business Review* 79, no. 3 (March 2001): 106–116.

60. Timothy Butler and James Waldroop, "Job Sculpting: The Art of Retaining Your Best People," *Harvard Business Review* 77, no. 5 (September–October 1999): 144–152.

61. Peter Drucker, "There's More Than One Kind of Team," *The Wall Street Journal*, February 11, 1992.

62. See Nitin Nohria's 1995 working paper for more insights on structuring: Nitin Nohria and J.D. Berkley, "From Structure to Structuring: A Pragmatic Perspective on Organizational Design," working paper 96-053, Harvard Business School, Boston, 1996. For other insights into structuring, see Lowell Bryan and Claudia Joyce, *Mobilizing Minds: Creating Wealth Through Talent in the 21st Century Organization* (New York: McGraw-Hill, 2007); Anne S. Miner, Paula Bassoff, and Christine Moorman, "Organizational Improvisation and Learning: A Field Study," *Administrative Science Quarterly* 46, no. 2 (2001): 304–337; and Clay Shirky, *Here Comes Everybody: The Power of Organizing Without Organizations* (New York: Penguin, 2008).

63. Block, *Community*, 25.

64. The work on complexity theory has been influential for us. A good introduction to the idea of deep simplicity can be found in John Gribbin, *Deep Simplicity: Bringing Order to Chaos and Complexity* (New York: Random House, 2004).

65. In fact, Gore has captured the attention of academics and journalists for years. For more on Gore, see Gary Hamel and Bill Breen, *The Future of Management* (Boston: Harvard Business School Press, 2007).

66. Charles C. Manz and Henry P. Sims Jr., *Business Without Bosses: How Self-Managing Teams Are Building High-Performing Companies* (New York: John Wiley and Sons, 1995), 137.

67. The work of Christopher Alexander has been helpful for our understanding of patterns of interaction and behavior. For insights into the role of space on patterns of interaction, see Christopher Alexander, *A Pattern Language: Towns, Buildings, Construction* (New York: Oxford University Press USA, 1977).

68. Stewart Brand, *How Buildings Learn: What Happens After They're Built* (New York: Penguin, 1994), 27–28.

69. Ibid, 28. The author notes that The Tech Model Railroad Club, located on the third floor, was the source in the early 1960s of most of the first generation of "hackers," who set in motion a series of computer technology revolutions. This is a compelling example not only of the impact of context (physical space) on innovation, but also of the power of the relationship between meaningful work (work that affirms the individual's identity and allows them to contribute to something larger than themselves) and innovation.

70. For more, see Eric von Hippel, *Democratizing Innovation* (Cambridge, MA: MIT Press, 2005); and Shirky, *Here Comes Everybody*.

71. Peter Skarzynski and Rowan Gibson, *Innovation to the Core: A Blueprint for Transforming the Way Your Company Innovates* (Boston: Harvard Business School Press, 2008), 264.

72. Ibid., 265.

73. Henry Chesbrough discusses the importance of bringing in valuable ideas from outside of the organization. See Henry Chesbrough, *Open Innovation: The New Imperative for Creating and Profiting from Technology* (Boston: Harvard Business School Press, 2006).

74. We should qualify that this is a common metaphor in Western scholarship and writing about leadership. Beyond the West, we see some different notions of leadership. Some have noted that while Western conceptions of leaders tend to focus on leading from the front ("trailblazing"), Eastern views often focus on leaders leading from behind ("trailing the group"). The latter may be more in line with our own research on the leaders of innovation. See Tanya Menon, Jessica Sim, Jeanne Ho-Ying Fu, Chi-yue Chiu, and Ying-yi Hong, "Blazing the Trail Versus Trailing the Group: Culture and Perceptions of the Leader's Position," working paper, University of Chicago, 2007.

75. Nelson Mandela, *Long Walk to Freedom* (London: Little, Brown & Company, 1995), 22.

76. See, for example, J. Keith Murninghan and Donald E. Conlon, "The Dynamics of Intense Work Groups: A Study of British String Quartets," *Administrative Science Quarterly* 36, no. 2 (1991): 165–186.

77. In fact, the leaders in our study seem to share some of the qualities of what researchers have referred to as "servant leaders" or "steward leaders." See James Autry, *The Servant Leader: How to Build a Creative Team, Develop Great Morale, and Improve Bottom-Line Performance* (New York: Three Rivers Press, 2004); Peter Block, *Stewardship: Choosing Service Over Self-Interest* (New York: Berrett-Koehler Publishers, 1993); and Max Depree, *Leadership Is an Art* (New York: Doubleday Business, 2004).

78. For work that is macro in scope, see, for example, James I. Cash, Michael J. Earl, and Robert Morison, "Teaming Up to Crack Innovation and Enterprise Integration," *Harvard Business Review* 86, no. 11 (November 2008): 90–100; Kim B. Clark and Rebecca Henderson, "Architectural Innovation: The Reconfiguration of Existing Product Technologies and the Failure of Established Firms," *Administrative Science Quarterly* 35, no. 1 (1990): 9–30; Clayton M. Christensen, *The Innovator's Dilemma: When New Technologies Cause Great Firms to Fail* (Boston: Harvard Business School Press, 1997); Clayton M. Christensen and Michael E. Raynor, *The Innovator's Solution: Creating and Sustaining Successful Growth* (Boston: Harvard Business School Press, 2003); Gary Hamel and C.K. Prahalad, *Competing for the Future* (Boston: Harvard Business School Press, 1996); Eric von Hippel, *The Sources of Innovation* (New York: Oxford University Press, 1988); Rosabeth Moss Kanter, *The Change Masters: Innovation and Entrepreneurship in the American Corporation* (New York: Simon and Schuster, 1983); Nicholas Negroponte, "Creating a Culture of Ideas," *Technology Review* (February 2003): 34–35; C.K. Prahalad and M.S. Krishnan, *The New Age of Innovation: Driving Cocreated Value Through Global Networks* (New York: McGraw-Hill, 2008); Michael Schrage, *Serious Play: How the World's Best Companies Simulate to Innovate* (Boston: Harvard Business School Press, 2000); and Michael Tushman and Charles O'Reilly, *Winning Through Innovation: A Practical Guide to Leading Organizational Change and Renewal* (Boston: Harvard Business School Press, 2002).

79. Kanter wrote about utopias herself. See Rosabeth Moss Kanter, "Commitment and Social Organizations: A Study of Commitment Mechanisms in Utopian Communities," *American Sociological Review* 33, no. 4 (1968): 499–517.

80. Pauline Graham, "Mary Parker Follett (1868–1993): A Pioneering Life," in *Mary Parker Follett, Prophet of Management: A Celebration of Writings from the 1920s,* ed. Pauline Graham (Washington, DC: Beard Books, 2003), 18.

81. John Child, "Commentary on Constructive Conflict," in *Mary Parker Follett, Prophet of Management: A Celebration of Writings from the 1920s,* ed. Pauline Graham (Washington, DC: Beard Books, 2003), 89.

82. For a classic collection of readings on urban planning, see Richard LeGates and Frederic Stout, *The City Reader* (London: Routledge, 1996). Richard Florida also examines the role that cities play in innovation. See Richard Florida, *Who's Your City? How the Creative Economy Is Making Where You Live the Most Important Decision of Your Life* (New York: Basic Books, 2008).

83. For this definition and more information on what Rittel defines as "wicked problems," see his work as discussed in Jeff Conklin, *Dialogue Mapping: Building Shared Understanding of Wicked Problems* (Hoboken, NJ: Wiley, 2005). For more on wicked problems, see John Camillus, "Strategy as a Wicked Problem." *Harvard Business Review* 86, no. 5 (May 2008): 98–106.

84. Conklin, *Dialogue Mapping*, 7.

85. Sara Lawrence-Lightfoot and Jessica Hoffman Davis, *The Art and Science of Portraiture* (San Francisco: Jossey-Bass, 2002), xv.

86. BRIC is an acronym that stands for Brazil, Russia, India, and China. According to Goldman Sachs, these developing countries will play an increasingly important role in the global economy in the future. For more details, see Goldman Sachs Global Economics Paper no. 99, October 1, 2003.

87. See C.K. Prahalad, *The Fortune at the Bottom of the Pyramid: Eradicating Poverty Through Profits* (Philadelphia: Wharton School Publishing, 2004). It may also be useful to read Prahalad and Krishnan, *The New Age of Innovation.*

88. For more on succeeding in the digital age, see Rosabeth Moss Kanter, *Evolve! Succeeding in the Digital Culture of Tomorrow* (Boston: Harvard Business School Press, 2001).

89. We recognize that a debate exists about whether Linux represents incremental or breakthrough innovation.

90. Eccles and Nohria offer insights into the importance of rhetoric. See Robert Eccles and Nitin Nohria, *Beyond the Hype* (Boston: Harvard Business School Press, 1992).

91. For research on the impact of the open-source and Web 2.0 movements on innovation, see von Hippel, *Democratizing Innovation.* For an account of how online multiplayer games may influence the leadership styles of the future, see Byron Reeves, Thomas W. Malone, and Tony O'Driscoll, "Leadership's Online Labs," *Harvard Business Review* 86, no. 5 (May 2008): 58–66. It is also worth looking at the work on social networks and innovation. This work reveals that innovation happens when teams are autonomous and independent, yet connected with each other. See, for example, Brian Uzzi and Jarrett Spiro, "Collaboration and Creativity: The Small World Problem," *American Journal of Sociology* 111, no. 2 (2005): 447–504.

92. For a discussion of where we will find the next generation of leaders, see Linda A. Hill, "Where Will We Find Tomorrow's Leaders? A Conversation with Linda A. Hill," *Harvard Business Review* 86, no. 1 (January 2008): 123–129. Also, for a

volume of leadership lessons transferred from one generation to another, see Warren Bennis, Gretchen Spreitzer, and Thomas Cummings, eds., *The Future of Leadership: Today's Top Leadership Thinkers Speak to Tomorrow's Leaders* (New York: Jossey-Bass, 2001).

93. These quotes appear in the 2007 working paper by Menon et al., "Blazing the Trail Versus Trailing the Group."

94. For an insightful perspective on how work and the workforce are changing, see James O'Toole, Edward Lawler, and Susan Meisinger, *The New American Workplace* (New York: Palgrave Macmillan, 2007).

95. This new generation of leaders must also apply a systems approach to the role of business in society. Sharon Parks has interesting observations and recommendations in this regard. She notes: "Again, their [MBA students] sense of power as individuals (or at least their sense of power as individuals in the role of CEO) seems to be constrained by the limits of an interpersonal imagination; they express little sense of power or imagination in relationship to the socioeconomic fabric of their wider public life. As their generation stands on the threshold of significant new challenges from Asian economies, a unifying Europe, and a reordering of the former Soviet political and economic order, these students await initiations into a more adequate and precise articulation of the dynamics and goals of democratic capitalism. They appear to engage business in an interpersonal mode, as yet unaware of the systemic reach of their personal energy, both actual and potential." See Sharon Parks, "Is it Too Late? Young Adults and the Formation of Professional Ethics," In *Can Ethics Be Taught? Perspectives, Challenges and Approaches*, eds. Thomas R. Piper, Mary C. Gentile, and Sharon D. Parks (Boston: Harvard Business School Press, 1993), 40.

96. See Peter Senge et al., *The Necessary Revolution: How Individuals and Organizations Are Working Together to Create a Sustainable World* (London: Nicholas Brealey Publishing, 2008).

97. For more discussion of the role that business schools can play in preparing leaders for these responsibilities, see Linda A. Hill, "Exercising Moral Courage: A Developmental Agenda," in *Moral Leadership: The Theory and Practice of Power, Judgment, and Policy*, ed. Deborah L. Rhode (San Francisco: Jossey Bass, 2006), 267–290. See also Lynn Sharp Paine, *Value Shift: Why Companies Must Merge Social and Financial Imperatives to Achieve Superior Performance* (New York: McGraw-Hill, 2003), 199–226.

98. Gary Hamel made this comment about "creative apartheid" at "Management 2.0™: Inventing the Future of Management," a May 28, 2008, meeting of MLab in Half Moon Bay, CA. The MLab is a "renegade brigade of academics, CEOs, consultants, entrepreneurs, and venture capitalists," brought together by Gary Hamel, to lay out a roadmap for reinventing management for the twenty-first century. For more of Hamel's thoughts on management innovation, see Gary Hamel, "The Why, What, and How of Management Innovation," *Harvard Business Review* 84, no. 2 (February 2006): 72–84.

THE DEVELOPMENT OF LEADERS

Knowing, Doing, and Being

22

IDENTITY-BASED LEADER DEVELOPMENT

Herminia Ibarra, Scott Snook, and Laura Guillén Ramo

A person does not gather learnings as possessions but rather becomes a new person with those learnings as part of his or her new self.

Bennis (1989:38)

MUCH HAS been written about forms of leader development and the learning processes on which they are based (Avolio and Gardner, 2005; Bennis and Thomas, 2002; Day, Zaccaro, and Halpin, 2004; Kets de Vries and Korotov, 2007; McCall, Lombardo, and Morrison, 1988; McCauley, Moxley, and Van Velsor, 1999; Murphy and Riggio, 2003; Parks, 2005; Tichy and Cohen, 1997). It is now taken for granted that managers learn leadership skills by observation and practice, and therefore learn most from direct work experiences. Consequently, one of the most significant advances in executive development has been the increasing reliance on methods that take place *in situ*, notably action learning and coaching (Boud and Garrik, 1999; Day, 2001; Goldsmith and Lyons, 2006; Kets de Vries and Korotov, 2007). Much attention has been devoted to helping people bridge the interval between gaining new insight ("knowing") and translating that insight into new behavior ("doing") (Hirst, Mann, Bain, Pirola-Merlo, and Richver, 2004; Pfeffer and Sutton, 1999).

In recent years a new perspective has been emerging that explicitly links leadership and identity (Hogg, 2001; Lord and Hall, 2005; Pittaway, Rivera, and Murphy, 2005; Snook and Khurana, 2004; van Knippenberg, van Knippenberg, De Cremer, and Hogg, 2005), calling attention to the importance of a leader's self-concept and focusing on the potential gap between "doing" and "being." Lord and Hall (2005), for example, posit a model of development in which increasingly sophisticated systems guide a manager's behavior, knowledge, and perceptions; these systems develop along with emerging personal identities in which leadership roles and skills become more central to a person's sense of self. A compelling argument that the development of leadership skills is inextricably integrated with the development of the person's self-concept as a leader is emerging. But, research and theorizing on leadership development have yet to specify the processes and moderating conditions that account for this identity transformation.

Our objective in this chapter is to consolidate and extend this burgeoning line of thinking under the label *identity-based leader development*. The chapter situates itself within a stream of literature that links role transitions and identity processes (Ashforth, 2001; Ebaugh, 1988; Hill, 1992; Ibarra, 1999, 2003a). It builds on several of the key insights that have emerged from this literature, notably the idea that people make work role transitions by publicly experimenting with provisional selves that serve as trials for possible, but not yet fully elaborated, professional identities (Ibarra, 1999; Lord and Hall, 2005), and the notion that "becoming a leader" is a process involving movement through the separation, transition, and incorporation phases shared by all rites of passage (Dubouloy, 2004; Kets de Vries and Korotov, 2007; Turner, 1969; Van Gennep, 1960). We extend current thinking by explicitly applying these ideas to the process of becoming a leader and suggesting ways in which leadership development can be fostered by designing experiences and training that take identity processes into account.

Our essay is divided into two sections. In the first, we briefly review thinking to date on identity change in role transition, and on leadership and identity. The second section outlines our identity-based perspective as it addresses three critical questions about leader development: (1) What changes? (2) How does it change? and (3) What conditions make a difference? Throughout we identify promising directions suggested by this perspective for future research on leader development, as well as the practice of developing leaders.

Identity Change in Transition to Leadership Roles

Identity refers to the various meanings attached to oneself by self and others (Gecas, 1982; Gergen, 1971). These meanings are based on the social roles and group memberships a person holds (social identities), as well as the personal and character traits they display and that others attribute to them (personal identities) (Ashforth, 2001; Gecas, 1982; Gergen, 1971). A professional identity combines both personal and social identities, as the relatively stable and enduring constellation of attributes, beliefs, values, motives, and experiences in terms of which people define themselves in a professional role (Schein, 1978). Professional identities are claimed and granted in social interaction (Cooley, 1902; Goffman, 1959) and evolve over time with varied experiences and meaningful feedback that allow people to gain insight about their central and enduring preferences, talents, and values (Schein, 1978).

But identities are not only historical constructions, nor are they limited to the social negotiation of current roles; identities are also projections about the future (Markus and Nurius, 1986). An important component of the self-concept is a person's possible selves—the images an individual has about who he or she might become, would like to become, or fears becoming in the future (Markus and Nurius, 1986). Possible selves play a key role in identity change because images of future selves act as attention screens and motivational devices, shaping one's interpretations of, and responses to, unfolding opportunities or constraints, and serving as incentives for future behavior (Markus and Nurius, 1986:955–956). We argue that possible selves are a critical part of leader development because they provide a structure around which relevant knowledge can be organized and provide the motivation to seek out developmentally relevant opportunities (Chan and Drasgow, 2001; Eccles, Nohria, and Berkley, 1992; Lord and Hall, 2005).

Transition to Leadership Roles

Key work-role transitions place new claims on the self (Van Maanen, 1998). As moments that force a person to "take stock, re-evaluate, revise, resee, and rejudge" (Strauss, 1959), they can precipitate identity revision (Ashforth, 2001). Charan, Drotter, and Noel (2001) identified a number of these key passages, those entailing significant quantitative and qualitative leaps in the progression of a person through the formal ranks of an organization—for example, the transition from producer to manager and from functional to general manager. Successfully negotiating these passages, they argue, requires not only skill development but also significant changes in the work values and time allocations that reflect managers' assessments of what kind of work is important. Because managers frequently continue allocating their time to tasks they value and have been rewarded for in the past (Charan et al., 2001), these junctures are rife with derailment potential.

People must learn different things as they move up the "leadership pipeline" (Charan et al., 2001). Whereas novice leaders acquire the fundamentals of management, experienced leaders learn more complex organizational and strategic knowledge that requires extended socialization and influencing skills (Mumford, Marks, Shane Connelly, Zaccaro, and Reiter-Palmon, 2000). Common hurdles associated with moving into more senior leadership roles include adopting a more businesswide perspective (Charan et al., 2001), managing change processes and key stakeholders so as to execute strategy successfully (Charan et al., 2001; Kotter, 1990), learning to communicate with, and work through, informal networks of people outside one's direct control (Ibarra and Hunter, 2007; Kotter, 1990), and adapting one's leadership styles to better delegate and develop others (Avolio and Gardner, 2005; Bass, 1985; Goleman, Boyatzis, and McKee, 2002).

Taking on any of these challenges may be problematic for several reasons intimately tied to questions of identity. First, aspiring leaders may not do these things especially well and thus are faced with the need to spend much of their time on tasks in which they do not feel effective (Bandura, 1977). Second, because they may not yet value this kind of work, aspiring leaders are also likely to feel inauthentic as they first start working differently (Ibarra, 1999). For example, while many managers understand intellectually that they have to learn to work through informal networks, they also balk at engaging in "instrumental" relationships that do not feel "genuine" (Ibarra and Hunter, 2007). Finally, development of this sort often involves painful unlearning and identity loss (Hedberg, 1981; Schein, 1996) because these new behaviors entail spending less time and energy on the activities and relationships that have defined a person's professional identity to that point.

Identity Change in Role Transition

Socialization researchers have long noted that identity changes accompany role transitions. Because new roles require new skills, behaviors, attitudes, and patterns of interactions, they are likely to produce fundamental changes in an individual's self-definitions (e.g., Ashforth, 2001; Becker and Carper, 1956; Hall, 1976; Hill, 1992; Schein, 1978). As contextual demands require people to draw from, elaborate, or create new repertoires of possibilities, various aspects of one's professional identity that have been relatively stable may change markedly. Although all roles carry behavioral scripts about how to act the part (Goffman, 1959; Settles, 2004), adaptation unfolds as a negotiated process in which people exercise much leeway as they strive to improve the fit between themselves and their work environment (Ashford and Taylor, 1990; Ibarra, 1999; Nicholson, 1984; Schein, 1978). With experience, they improve their understanding of the new role and refine their emerging notions of who they want to be in that role (Bandura, 1977; Hill, 1992), adapting aspects of their identity to accommodate role demands and modifying role definitions to preserve and enact valued aspects of their identity.

A view of leadership development as an identity transition has been suggested by numerous researchers (e.g., Anderson, 1987; Ericsson and Charness, 1994; Glaser and Chi, 1988; Patel and Groen, 1991), who not only identify critical junctures such as the transition from "doer" to "manager" (Hill, 1992), from junior to senior professional (Ibarra, 1999), and from more junior to more senior managerial levels (Charan et al., 2001; Lord and Hall, 2005) but also define these transitions as constituting a profound transformation in what people think, feel, and value. For example, Hill (1992:5) observed that new managers need not only to make time for planning and coaching others, but must also come to "view this other-directed work as mission-critical to their success . . . [T]hey value being producers and they must learn to value making others more productive" (Charan et al., 2001:18). Later in a manager's career the key hurdles include letting go of a functional or otherwise parochial perspective in favor of a systems or organizational view, and replacing a shorter-term operational outlook with longer-term visionary thinking (Charan et al., 2001).

Just how people reinvent their self-concepts, however, has not been explored. In recent years, multiple aspects of this identity crafting have been conceptualized as the development of an authentic self-concept (Avolio and Gardner, 2005; Goffee and Jones, 2006), in which key events or "crucibles," and how a person interprets them, play an important role in forging a leader's sense of self (Bennis and Thomas, 2002). Although this body of work makes a compelling case for leadership development as an identity transition, it has yet to articulate the mechanisms and process underlying identity's dynamism in the development process or how knowledge of this process can guide the design of formal development efforts.

Toward an Identity-Based View of Leader Development

Our identity-based model posits that leader development unfolds as an identity transition in which people disengage from central, behaviorally anchored identities while exploring new possible selves and, eventually, integrate a new, alternative identity. Old and new identities coexist in the interim, as people try on provisional selves that are refined through task, social, and emotional feedback or abandoned if found to be either ineffective or blatantly inauthentic (Ibarra, 1999, 2003a).

An example from recent empirical research grounds our view in the experience of change agents. Huising (2006) describes becoming an organizational change agent as a process of personal transformation. As a result of their participation in business process redesign (BPR) projects, managers, accountants, production supervisors, and engineers from five different organizations experienced an "awakening" or transformation of self. The actual transformation (what changed) consisted of a new way of thinking about the organization and its purpose, and a concomitant redefinition of future possibilities. The transformation process began as employees selected to participate in the change programs detached from old activities and relationships as they built new ones centered on BPR. Over time, they came to see the work of the organization as a whole and understood their prior perspective to be partial and particularistic. As new actions and interpretations became increasingly possible and desirable, participants became more peripheral or less embedded within their home organization and consequently sought further occasions to enact their new commitments and understandings. After the projects ended, some did not want to return to their old roles, but rather reconsidered career plans and pursued opportunities for continued participation in change.

We use this example to illustrate our arguments for two reasons. First, it highlights a definition of leadership as behaviors that can be enacted at any level of an organization's hierarchy. Second, if managers learn mostly from direct experience, then we need to understand what happens in instances of organic (nonprogrammatic) leadership development such as this one in order to design formal interventions that replicate, facilitate, or accelerate on-the-job transformation processes.

While building on well-established notions of experiential learning and change processes that entail moving through phases of exploration, provisional commitment, and integration (Brown and Starkey, 2000; Ibarra, 1999), we aim to extend current thinking in three major areas. First, we contrast our approach to prevalent competency models of leadership development and develop further the argument for self-concept change. Second, by conceptualizing leadership development as an identity transition, our model calls attention to the dynamics of a "liminal"—betwixt and between—transition period in which people linger between old and new identities before grounding a deeper change based on their own experience and practice. Third, acknowledging the robust finding that people typically relapse when attempting significant changes, we consider conditions that increase or decrease the likelihood of "deep change" (Quinn, 1996; Ibarra, 2003a). Below we do not attempt to review the extensive literature and divergent perspectives on why, how, and when people change, but rather build on the Huising (2006) example and identity literature to construct our identity-based perspective and to explore potentially fruitful aspects of formal programs that might also spark similar transformations.

What Changes?

Without attempting to summarize a voluminous literature, our perspective on leader development must be grounded in a clear understanding of the essence of leadership itself. Two basic assumptions ground our perspective. First, we define leadership as a type of work or process rather than a formal position or the mere exercise of formal authority. Second, we assume that self-understanding and experience are mutually constitutive. To return to the change agents described by Huising (2006), their transformation extended beyond new competencies to a new way of thinking about the organization and its purpose, and a concomitant redefinition of self-conceptions, work values, and future possibilities. Change agents spoke of becoming "systems thinkers," described a shift in values ("the reason for all work must be the customer"), and began to consider alternative careers in similar roles in which they felt a "sense of making a difference."

Following a tradition of distinguishing leadership from management (Kotter, 1990; Zaleznik, 1977), and technical from adaptive work (Heifetz and Laurie, 2001), we use the term *leadership* to refer to behavior that creates a departure from routine and current practice, creating instead new learning, innovation, and patterns of behavior. From this perspective, therefore, what changes in leadership development is a person's capacity to use interpersonal influence to move and shape complex social systems by aligning and motivating diverse stakeholders (Bass, 1985; Burns, 1979; Kotter, 1990). However, leadership development involves not only skill improvements but also a fundamental evolution of one's system of personal values and motivations (Joiner and Josephs, 2007; Kegan, 1994; Levinson, 1978; Torbert, 2004). Experience does not change only capacity; it also changes the meanings that make new behaviors desirable and creates new standards of judgment or evaluation (Becker, 1953; Schein, 1996). In the case of Huising's change agents, working to change an organization became meaningful to them and motivated them to seek out continued work of this type.

While recent thinking distinguishes between "leader" and "leadership" development, using the term *leader development* to refer to the acquisition of intrapersonal capacity—for example, building self-awareness—while reserving the term *leadership development* for efforts to build interpersonal competencies and networks that enhance cooperation on organizational tasks (Day, 2001), we focus here on efforts that necessarily involve the inextricable relationship between "being" and "doing." As such, personal insight and self-renewal divorced from an increased capacity and motivation to change or influence a social system are outside the scope of our concern in this chapter.

How Does the Self Change?

A large variety of conceptual models identify phases of change and their associated tasks. Van Gennep's (1960) three phases of a rite of passage—separation, transition, and incorporation—provide a foundation for most models of role transition, while organizational identity researchers (e.g., Ashforth, 2001) have built on Lewin's theory of unfreezing, changing, and refreezing and notions of alternating phases of exploration, provisional commitment, and integration (Brown and Starkey, 2000; Ibarra, 1999) to conceptualize identity transformation. The present model of identity transition builds on these various frameworks, combining ideas about how possible selves are elaborated with a view of identity development as an evolutionary process involving separation from established identities, transition, and integration of new self-conceptions.

Separation

A significant body of work in the social sciences converges on the idea that all forms of learning and change start with some form of dissatisfaction, rupture, loss, or data that disconfirm expectations (e.g., Bridges, 1980; Schein, 1996; Senge, 1990). In the Huising (2006) study, for example, the change agents experienced a rupture as they were reassigned away from their existing functional roles to the process redesign projects. For many this entailed a loss of formal authority and organizational position as well as physical dislocation and a psychological "separation" from doing work that was familiar and that they did well. At the same time, they were immersed in the business process community, which provided a theoretical frame and "narrative" for their work as well as a network of like-situated members. As members' activities, relationships, and narratives changed, their disrupted organizational role identity was slowly replaced by that of change agent.

From an identity perspective, physical or social separation is as important as psychological separation, although a formal role change is not necessary. Indeed, people may assume greater leadership responsibilities without a formal title change or promotion. As people's work activities change, novel behaviors often challenge their sense of who they are (i.e., a current identity) or want to become (i.e., possible selves). Role changes are often accompanied by new reference groups that generate novel self-conceptions (Lieberman, 1956), providing both a point of reference and reflected appraisals that shape the focal person's self-understanding (Baumeister, 1998; Cooley, 1902). By doing new things and interacting in different networks, people make new meaning of who they are and who they want to become. At the same time, an eroding commitment to former roles and their norms and referents unfolds with decreased social activity in the old sphere. New activities and relationships allow people to try out possible selves on a limited but tangible scale; at the same time, they diminish the hold of the old self by providing potentially viable alternative ways of being. Leadership programs designed to reproduce these sort of dynamics by creating projects that separate participants from their home organizations as they immerse them in a new peer community might provide an interesting laboratory to further explore the uses and dynamics of separation.

TRANSITION

To be in transit is to be in the process of leaving one thing, without having fully left it, and at the same time of entering something else, without being fully a part of it (Levinson, 1978). The notion of *limen* (which means *threshold* in Latin) was introduced by Van Gennep (1960) to refer to the middle phase of the separation-transition-incorporation process, in which "subjects pass through a period and area of ambiguity, a sort of social limbo." Despite its central importance in most theoretical models, being "in between," or on the threshold—a key feature of the change process—has received little conceptual attention.

Studies of a broad range of role transitions, from leaving a religious order to exiting an occupation, indicate that people in transition invariably feel "in-between" identities, describing their state in terms of being "in a vacuum," "in midair," "neither here nor there," and "at loose ends" (Bridges, 1980; Ebaugh, 1988; Ibarra, 2003a; Osherton, 1980; Settles, 2004). While the most commonly discussed forms of liminality in occupational life concern retirement and job loss, in which a person is literally devoid of a valued identity (Ashforth, 2001; Hermans and Oles, 1999; Newman, 1999; Robbins, 1978), people making major work-role transitions may experience liminality as a period of acute identity ambiguity or conflict (Ibarra, 2003a; Osherton, 1980; Settles, 2004) in which a person either lacks a clear role identity, or alternatively, experiences a "multiple-defined self, whose multiple definitions are incompatible" (Baumeister, 1986:199).

For example, joining a business process redesign team disrupted the conventional organizational roles and authority bases of the change agents described by Huising (2006), forcing them to enter a liminal state in which "team members feel disconnected from the established status hierarchy and placed into a situation where both their rank and esteem in the organization is no longer clear to them." Studies of voluntary career changes, by contrast, suggest that liminal states also arise as people develop competing commitments to, and investments in, two or more seemingly incompatible futures (Ibarra, 2003a; Osherton, 1980). For example, as star producers begin to assume organizational leadership roles, new demands and possible futures compete with well-established role requirements and self-conceptions (Lorsch and

Mathias, 1987). Simple role conflicts become identity transitions when the conflict extends beyond short-term time allocations to deeper questions about alternative career trajectories. What role leadership development efforts can play in helping people manage a liminal period characterized by coexisting, competing identities to which a person is partially but not fully committed has yet to be investigated.

INCORPORATION

As Lord and Hall (2005) note, "to sustain interest for the months and years required to develop and practice complex leadership skills, it is also likely that the leadership role needs to become part of one's self-identity." *Incorporation*, or *internalization*, refers to the gradual process by which external interactions between self and others are taken in and replaced by internal representations of these interactions (Kelman, 1958). While various theorists have emphasized the importance of practice and feedback in internalizing behavioral changes (e.g., Goleman et al., 2002), adult change depends not only on experiential learning but also on mechanisms that allow individuals to evaluate results and consider alternative courses of action.

Ibarra (1999) argued that people use internal and external feedback to evaluate provisional identities. They make internal assessments by comparing their public behavior with their representations of the kind of person they "really" are or would like to be; conclusions about what selves to keep or reject depend on feelings of congruence or authenticity. But the incorporation of a new identity also requires participation in a "sequence of social experiences during which the person acquires a conception of the meaning of the behaviour, and perceptions and judgement of objects and situations, all of which make the activity possible and desirable" (Becker, 1953:235). External assessments based on the observations and reactions of role-set members who offer explicit or implicit feedback are therefore essential; decisions about what possibilities to retain hinge on whether provisional selves secure the personal validation as full-fledged role occupants by relevant parties.

To conclude with the Huising (2006) example, internalizing the change agent identity hinged on becoming active participants in the practices of a large industrywide community of process practitioners. Abstract knowledge about process tools such as root cause analysis and basic flowcharting "did not situate BRP in a larger context or provide team members with a variety of cultural resources through which they can conceptualize and narrate what they learn" (p. 15). Contact with the "gurus" and consultants as well as others like themselves across a large number of organizations provided role models and a reference group, as well as a durable network and cultural milieu built around the idea of process redesign. The lesson from both identity theory and this example is that formal leadership development programs that do not take into account or actively manage the socially grounded nature of incorporation processes are unlikely to produce sustainable identity change.

What Conditions Matter?

Developmental Readiness

Most perspectives on executive development largely ignore the larger life context in which development occurs, or "the process of self-construction over the lifespan" (Laske, 2003:577). Theories of adult development, by contrast, map out significant patterns of personal and professional change over the span of a person's life and underscore the basic but implicit assumptions about what is desirable and possible that shape critical life choices (Joiner and Josephs, 2007; Kegan, 1982, 1994; Levinson, 1978; Torbert, 2004). While a thorough treatment of these approaches is beyond the scope of this chapter, most developmental theories lay out a sequence of predictable stages through which people pass, and share a perspective on work and personal life as intersecting systems. Although executives frequently enroll in executive education for personal reasons (Kets de Vries and Korotov, 2007), the idea of linking personal development and leadership effectiveness (e.g., Joiner and Josephs, 2007) has been underexploited in both the theory and practice of leader development.

A person's stage of development influences "what" he or she is ready for; furthermore, the relative stability of an individual's developmental stage also affects how open a person is to experiencing confirming or disconfirming information as well as his or her capacity to recognize and take advantage of developmental opportunities. From this perspective, leadership development programs that focus on developing skills and abilities while ignoring basic psychosocial development levels and processes are likely to be ineffective in achieving the desired results (Bartone, Snook, Forsythe, Lewis, and Bullis, 2007), because the full engagement of the participants in managing their career proactively is a prerequisite for continued development.

Among potentially promising areas for research is the idea of situating a person with regard to important life issues (Pittaway et al., 2005) or age-related stages (Levinson, 1978). Although professional identities evolve over the course of a person's career, they tend to come up for revision and questioning at critical junctions in the adult life cycle (Erikson, 1959; Jung, 1930; Kegan, 1982; Levinson, 1978). People who enter formal programs in a state of life transition may be more open to self-examination and personal exploration than those settled or already committed to a given lifestyle or career path. While life-stage issues may have always been implicit in leader development programs that bring together participants of similar age, key personal concerns such as midlife renewal are rarely leveraged in the service of leadership development. We have not begun to define what it means to take into account the specific developmental needs of participants in designing and delivering leadership programs.

TRANSITIONAL TIME AND SPACE

Because Van Gennep's notion of liminality pertained exclusively to primitive rites, Turner (1969) extended the concept to a broader range of experiences in which the normal rules of everyday life are suspended for a concentrated period during which "anything goes" and curiosity, exploration, frivolity, and *joie de vivre* govern behavior. Turner noted that these "liminoid" experiences often share dedicated time, space, and guiding figures such that the person in transition can "violate the rules" or experiment with new identities without fear of danger or sanction. This idea of a protected time and space is also present in developmental psychology, notably Winnicott's (1989) view of transitional periods "in between" more clearly defined stages of maturity, in which children imagine various possibilities for themselves in the future and play out these possibilities via games, imagination, and make-believe. Transitional objects, such as toys and blankets, serve as bridges between the external world of reality and constraint and the internal world of fantasy and future possibility. Transitional figures, initially the mother, provide a safety zone in which the child can give rein to his or her imagination. The mother and the play objects demarcate a boundary region in which the child can gradually define and test out a newly emerging self, protected from any danger.

The operating principles shared by the notions of liminal experience and transitional phenomena are psychological safety, suspension of the rules, separation from "real life", and the opportunity to "play" (Ibarra and Petriglieri, forthcoming; Kets de Vries and Korotov, 2007). In organizational life, liminoid settings demarcate a psychological space and time that creates safety, provides relief from the pressure of social validation, and legitimizes exploration. Spatial boundaries, such as those around laboratories, scenarios, simulations, off-sites, and role-plays, encourage departures from existing norms and procedures by allowing people to suspend normal requirements for consistency and rationality and, as they play with possibilities, develop new skills or self-images that can be transferred back to the mainstream (Brown and Starkey, 2000; Schein, 1996; Schrage, 1999; Senge, 1990). Similarly, temporal boundaries, such as those defined by sabbaticals, educational programs, vacations, and extracurricular activities, buffer people from institutional obligations and thus grant license to play with new ways of being (Turner, 1969).

Extending these notions to leadership development, several authors have begun to incorporate the concepts of "transitional space" and "holding environment" in their description of business school courses as places that facilitate professional and even personal transitions (Dubouloy, 2004; Kets de Vries and Korotov, 2007; Petriglieri and Petriglieri, forthcoming; Snook, forthcoming). Conditions and design features that make for more or less productive holding environments, however, have not been explored conceptually or empirically. The current variety of leadership development offerings, ranging from concentrated one- and two-year-long programs to evening, weekend, and multisession courses, provides an excellent laboratory in which to explore diverse forms of separation and encapsulation (Greil and Rudy, 1984). One might hypothesize, for example, that multisession interventions in which people move back and forth from organization reality to a "liminal" classroom will create more lasting changes than single-dose concentrated programs (Kets de Vries and Korotov, 2007); alternatively, one might also argue that the greater the extent of identity transformation desired, the longer the separation needed from the activities, relationships, and operating norms of the former role (Baumeister, 1986).

Acknowledging the importance of transitional time and space also suggests greater research attention to the extracurricular or "ephemeral" roles that may play a critical role in leader development.[1] Although this has been the principle behind the use of role-play and simulation methods, the current trend toward leadership development by involving people in extracurricular activities, typically in the social sector (e.g., community service, nonprofits, nongovernmental organizations, development organizations), merits further investigation as a potentially more realistic and sustained laboratory for experimenting with new leadership behaviors (Hart, Southerland, and Atkins, 2003).

GUIDES AND REFERENCE GROUPS

Social comparison theory suggests that information about the self is only meaningful in relation to others, who both provide a point of reference and whose reflected appraisals shape the focal person's self-understanding (Cooley, 1902; Festinger, 1954; Mead, 1934). Successful self-changes are often instigated, motivated, or supported by others because self-concept change depends on enlisting other people to lend social legitimacy to the desired changes (Baumeister, 1998). Despite a noticeable increase in "relational methods" for leader development, such as coaching, mentoring programs, or using company executives as faculty for in-house programs (Drath and Palus, 2004; Mintzberg, 2004), the relational context for leadership development has been understudied. While the importance of mentors and role models in early leader development has been amply documented (Kram and Kahn, 1994), how helping relationships affect later career processes—when access is potentially more limited—has been virtually ignored. An identity-based perspective suggests greater research attention to exploring the importance of coaches as "guiding figures" and peer reference groups.

Scholars as far back as Vygotsky (1978), Strauss (1959), and Levinson (1978) noted the key role of guiding figures in helping people in transition endure the ambiguity of the transition period by conferring blessings, giving advice, embodying new possibilities, and, most important, believing in his or her "dream," which at first is "poorly articulated and only tenuously connected to reality" (Levinson, 1978). The bond that develops between the person in transition and the guiding figure forms a transitional space within which a possible self starts becoming a reality (Strauss, 1959). Recent developments, including cross-company mentoring programs for senior executives and the increasing use of professional coaches (Kets de Vries and Korotov, 2007), provide a context for comparing and contrasting the transition process with different degrees or forms of guidance.

Even more rarely studied is the role of peers in leader development, although comparison with, and social validation from, a different reference group is a key determinant of behavior change (Schein, 1996). The greater the ambiguity about the future, the greater the influence of the reference group, because people who are uncertain about their beliefs are more likely to seek support for them from others (Festinger, 1954). People who are engaged in self-exploration and experimentation, for example, need to feel that others similar to themselves are experiencing similar issues and can form a network of potential future support (Kets de Vries and Korotov, 2007). Interventions such as group coaching methodologies, which by design create a support group for change (Kets de Vries and Korotov, 2007), are a recent means that explicitly makes use of this peer dynamic to foster leadership development.

If no good models or referents are available, or if one wants to craft a more genuinely unique leadership identity, different development processes may come into play (Schein, 1996). One potentially rich context for studying this issue concerns leadership development processes for women in demographically skewed organizations, where available role models are frequently perceived as either unsuitable or unappealing stylistically (Ely, 1995; Ibarra and Petriglieri, 2007). The currently popular women's leadership executive programs have not yet been examined with regard to their underlying pedagogical assumptions. Among the various mechanisms potentially at work is the creation of an alternative peer or reference group.

PRE- AND POST-FORMAL-PROGRAM EXPERIENCE

While leadership development programs are often billed as "transformative," a wealth of research and thinking suggests that fulfilling this potential requires much greater attention to the underappreciated "bookends" of development (Snook, 2008), and the "takeoff" (before) and "reentry" (after) phases of formal programs (Ibarra, 2003b). Current critics of MBA programs (e.g., Mintzberg, 2004), for example, argue that a lack of prior managerial experience significantly limits the potential learning from an MBA program for young adults. In executive education, it is often noted that while great personal learning may be catalyzed by a program, transferring that learning back home—to the team, unit, or organization—is much harder, if it happens at all (Ibarra, 2003b). With few exceptions (e.g., Boyatzis, Stubbs, and Taylor, 2002; Evers, Bouwers, and Tomic, 2006; Yorks, Beechler, and Ciporen, 2007), little empirical research has investigated how differences in pre- and post-program experience affect outcomes.

The issue of what makes change stick has been treated extensively in a psychological literature that treats relapse or backsliding as a common occurrence (e.g., Prochaska, DiClemente, and Norcross, 1992). Most people taking action to modify dysfunctional behaviors do not successfully maintain their gains on their first attempt. New Year's resolvers, for example, report five or more years of consecutive pledges before maintaining their behavioral goal for at least six months (Norcross and Vangarelli, 1989). As a result, behavior change scholars propose a spiral dynamic model of change in which people often regress to an earlier stage in making progress through a sequence of precontemplation, contemplation, preparation, action, and maintenance stages. People may recycle several times through the preparation and action stages before achieving long-term maintenance. The more action taken and the greater the preparation for maintenance, the better the prognosis; both are enhanced by a "sense that one was becoming the kind of person one wanted to be" (Prochaska et al., 1992:1109). More research is needed, however, to distinguish those who learn from their backsliding from those who do not. As leadership development providers increasingly experiment with follow-up tools and support after a formal intervention, these efforts may also shed further light on how people can manage their inevitable relapses more effectively.

Conclusion

As Hackman and Wageman (2007) note, the right question about leadership development is not *what* should be taught in leadership courses, but *how* leaders can be helped to learn. This chapter suggests that helping people to learn requires a view of leadership development as ultimately about facilitating an identity transition. While the idea of crafting one's leadership identity has become more prevalent in treatments of leadership development (Avolio and Gardner, 2005; Lord and Hall, 2005; van Knippenberg et al., 2005), the underlying processes have not been fully articulated or systematically linked to theory and research on identity and transition in professional life. We argue that the notion of identity transition is a useful lens for conceptualizing and designing developmental experiences because it points to previously ignored issues, including how people shed the outdated identities that hinder change, how the adult life cycle plays into the course of leadership development, and how features of time and space designed by leadership development practitioners can form a bridge between old and new selves.

Leadership development may be one of the most important yet understudied areas in leadership research (Day, 2001). An identity-based view of leader development calls attention to the need for creating opportunities to practice (and make mistakes with) new possible selves, and to the fact that this kind of learning is constrained by a general lack of safe environments in which to practice and make such errors. Future research and theorizing that takes into account these identity processes, we argue, will allow us to better discern the conditions that promote identity-based leader development.

Note

1. Zurcher (1970:174) defines an ephemeral role as "a temporary or ancillary position-related behaviour pattern chosen by the enactor to satisfy social psychological needs incompletely satisfied by the more dominant and lasting role he or she must enact in everyday life positions."

References

Anderson, J.R. (1987). Skill acquisition: Compilation of weak-method problem solutions. *Psychological Review*, 94, 192–210.

Ashford, S.J., and Taylor, M.S. (1990). Adaptation to work transitions: An integrative approach. In G.R. Ferris and K.M. Rowland (Eds.), *Research in Personnel and Human Resource Management* (pp. 1–39). Greenwich, CT: JAI Press.

Ashforth, B.E. (2001). *Role Transitions in Organizational Life: An Identity-Based Perspective*. Mahwah, NJ: Lawrence Erlbaum Associates.

Avolio, B.J., and Gardner, W.L. (2005). Authentic leadership development: Getting to the root of positive forms of leadership. *Leadership Quarterly*, 16, 315–338.

Bandura, A. (1977). *Social Learning Theory*. Englewood Cliffs, NJ: Prentice Hall.

Bartone, P.T, Snook, S.A., Forsythe, G.B., Lewis, P., and Bullis, R.C. (2007). Psychosocial development and leader performance of military officer cadets. *Leadership Quarterly*, 18(5), 490–504.

Bass, B.M. (1985). *Leadership and Performance Beyond Expectations*. New York: Free Press.

Baumeister, R.F. (1986). *Identity: Cultural Change and the Struggle for Self*. New York: Oxford University Press.

———. (1998). The self. In D.T. Gilbert, S.T. Fiske, and G. Lindszey (Eds.), *The Handbook of Social Psychology* (4th ed., pp. 680–740). Boston: McGraw-Hill.

Becker, H. (1953). Becoming a marijuana user. *American Journal of Sociology*, 59, 235–242.

Becker, H.S., and Carper, J.W. (1956). The development of identification with an occupation. *American Journal of Sociology*, 61(4), 289–298.

Bennis, W.G. (1989). *On Becoming a Leader*. Reading, MA: Addison-Wesley.

Bennis, W.G., and Thomas, R.J. (2002). Crucibles of leadership. *Harvard Business Review*, 80(9), 39–45.

Boud, D., and Garrick, J. (1999). Understandings of workplace learning. In D. Boud and J. Garrick (Eds.), *Understanding Learning at Work* (pp. 1–13). London: Routledge.

Boyatzis, R.E., Stubbs, E.C., and Taylor, S.N. (2002). Learning cognitive and emotional intelligence competencies through graduate management education. *Academy of Management Journal on Learning and Education*, 1(2), 150–162.

Bridges, W. (1980). *Transitions: Making Sense of Life's Changes.* Cambridge, MA: Perseus.

Brown, A.D., and Starkey, K. (2000). Organizational identity and learning: A psychodynamic perspective. *Academy of Management Review*, 25(1), 102–121.

Burns, J.M. (1979). *Leadership.* New York: Harper & Row.

Chan, K., and Drasgow, F. (2001). Toward a theory of individual differences and leadership: Understanding the motivation to lead. *Journal of Applied Psychology*, 86(3), 481–498.

Charan, R., Drotter, S., and Noel, J. (2001). *The Leadership Pipeline: How to Build the Leadership-Powered Company.* San Francisco: Jossey-Bass.

Cooley, C.H. (1902). *Human Nature and the Social Order.* New York: Scribners.

Day, D.V. (2001). Leadership development: A review in context. *Leadership Quarterly*, 11(4), 581–613.

Day, D.V., Zaccaro, S.J., and Halpin, S.M. (2004). *Leader Development for Transforming Organizations: Growing Leaders for Tomorrow.* Mahwah, NJ: Lawrence Erlbaum Associates.

Drath, W.H., and Palus C.J. (2004). *Making Common Sense: Leadership as Meaning Making in a Community of Practice.* Greensboro, NC: CCL Press.

Dubouloy, M. (2004). The transitional space and self-recovery: A psychoanalytical approach to high-potential managers' training. *Human Relations*, 57(4), 467–496.

Ebaugh, H.R.F. (1988). *Becoming an Ex: The Process of Role Exit.* Chicago, IL: University of Chicago Press.

Eccles, R.G., Nohria, N., and Berkley, J.D. (1992). *Beyond the Hype: Rediscovering the Essence of Management.* Boston: Harvard Business School Press.

Ely, R.J. (1995). The power in demography: Women's social constructions of gender identity at work. *Academy of Management Journal*, 38(3), 589–634.

Ericsson, K.A., and Charness, N. (1994). Expert performance: Its structure and acquisition. *American Psychologist*, 49, 725–747.

Erikson, E.H. (1959). *Identity and the Life Cycle.* New York: International University Press.

Evers, W., Bouwers, A., and Tomic, W. (2006). A quasi-experimental study on management coaching effectiveness. *Consulting Psychology Journal: Practice and Research*, 58(3), 174–182.

Festinger, L. (1954). A theory of social comparison processes. *Human Relations*, 7, 117–140.

Gecas, V. (1982). The self-concept. *Annual Review of Sociology*, 8, 1–33.

Gergen, K.J. (1971). *The Concept of Self.* New York: Holt, Rinehart and Winston.

Glaser, R., and Chi, M.T.H. (1988). Overview. In M.T.H. Chi, R. Glaser, and M.J. Farr (Eds.), *The Nature of Expertise* (pp. xv–xxviii). Hillsdale, NJ: Lawrence Erlbaum.

Goffee, R., and Jones, G. (2006). *Why Should Anyone Be Led by You?* Boston: Harvard Business School Press.

Goffman, E. (1959). *The Presentation of Self in Everyday Life.* Garden City, NY: Doubleday.

Goldsmith, M., and Lyons, L. (2006). *Coaching for Leadership: The Practice of Leadership Coaching for the World's Greatest Coaches.* San Francisco: Pfeiffer.

Goleman, D., Boyatzis, R.E., and McKee, A. (2002). *Leadership and Emotional Intelligence.* Boston: Harvard Business School Press.

Greil, A.L., and Rudy, D.R. (1984). Social cocoons: Encapsulation and identity transformation organizations. *Social Inquiry,* 54, 260–278.

Hackman, J.R., and Wageman, R. (2007). Asking the right questions about leadership. *American Psychologist,* 62(1), 43–47.

Hall, D.T. (1976). *Careers in Organizations.* Santa Monica, CA: Goodyear.

Hart, D., Southerland, N., and Atkins, R. (2003). Community service and adult development. In J. Demick and C. Andreoletti (Eds.), *Handbook of Adult Development* (pp. 585–597). New York: Plenum.

Hedberg, B. (1981). How organizations learn and unlearn. In P.C. Nystrom and W.H. Starbuck (Eds.), *Handbook of Organizational Design* (pp. 3–27). New York: Oxford University Press.

Heifetz, R.A., and Laurie, D.L. (2001). The work of leadership. *Harvard Business Review,* 79(11), 131–141.

Hermans, H.J.M., and Oles, P.K. (1999). Midlife crisis in men: Affective organization of personal meanings. *Human Relations,* 52, 1403–1426.

Hill, L.A. (1992). *Becoming a Manager: Mastery of a New Identity.* Boston: Harvard Business School Press.

Hirst, G., Mann, L., Bain, P., Pirola-Merlo A., and Richver, A. (2004). Learning to lead: The development and testing of a model of leadership learning. *Leadership Quarterly,* 15, 311–327.

Hogg, M.A. (2001). A social identity theory of leadership. *Personality and Social Psychology Review,* 5, 184–200.

Huising, R. (2006). Becoming (and being) a change agent: Personal transformation and organizational change. Paper presented at the annual meeting of the American Sociological Association, Montreal Convention Center, Montreal, Quebec, Canada, August 10, 2006.

Ibarra, H. (1999). Provisional selves: Experimenting with image and identity in professional adaptation. *Administrative Science Quarterly,* 44(4), 764–791.

———. (2003a). *Working Identity: Unconventional Strategies for Reinventing Your Career.* Boston: Harvard Business School Press.

———. (2003b). Managing take-off and re-entry. *European Business Journal,* 14.

Ibarra, H., and Hunter, M. (2007). How leaders create and use networks. *Harvard Business Review,* 85(1), 40–47.

Ibarra, H., and Petriglieri, J.L. (2007). Impossible selves: Image strategies and identity threat in professional women's career transitions. INSEAD Working Paper 2007/69/OB.

———. (forthcoming). Identity work and play. *Journal of Organizational Change Management.*

Joiner, S.A., and Josephs, S.A. (2007). *Leadership Agility: Five Levels of Mastery for Anticipating and Initiating Change.* San Francisco: Jossey-Bass.

Jung, C.G. (1930). The stages of life. In *The Structure and Dynamics of the Psyche* (R.F.C. Hull, Trans.). Princeton, NJ: Princeton University Press.

Kegan, R. (1982). *The Evolving Self: Problem and Process in Human Development.* Cambridge, MA: Harvard University Press.

———. (1994). In *Over Our Heads: The Mental Demands of Modern Life.* Cambridge, MA: Harvard University Press.

Kelman, H.C. (1958). Compliance, identification, and internalization: Three processes of attitude change. *Journal of Conflict Resolution*, 2, 51–60.

Kets de Vries, M.F.R., and Korotov, K. (2007). Creating transformational executive education programs. *Academy of Management Learning and Education*, 6(3), 375–387.

Kotter, J.P. (1990). *A Force for Change: How Leadership Differs from Management*. New York: Free Press/Collier Macmillan.

Kram, K.E., and Kahn, W.A. (1994). Authority at work: Internal models and their organizational consequences. *Academy of Management Review*, 19(1), 17–50.

Laske, O. (2003). Executive development as adult development. In J. Demick (Ed.), *Handbook of Adult Development* (pp. 565–584). New York: Plenum/Kluwer.

Levinson, D.J. (1978). *The Seasons of a Man's Life*. New York: Ballantine Books.

Lieberman, S. (1956). The effects of changes in role on the attitudes of role occupants. *Human Relations*, 9, 385–402.

Lord, R.G., and Hall, R.J. (2005). Identity, deep structure and the development of leadership skill. *Leadership Quarterly*, 16, 591–615.

Lorsch, J., and Mathias, P. (1987). When professionals have to manage. *Harvard Business Review*, 65(4), 78–83.

Markus, H., and Nurius, P. (1986). Possible selves. *American Psychologist*, 41, 954–969.

McCall, M.W., Lombardo, M.M., and Morrison, A.M. (1988). *The Lessons of Experience: How Successful Executives Develop on the Job*. New York: The Free Press.

McCauley, C.D., Moxley, R.S., and Van Velsor, E. (1999). *The Center for Creative Leadership Handbook of Leadership Development*. San Francisco: Jossey-Bass.

Mead, G.H. (1934). *Mind, Self and Society*. Chicago, IL: University of Chicago Press.

Mintzberg, H. (2004). *Managers Not MBAs: A Hard Look at the Soft Practice of Managing and Management Development*. San Francisco: Berrett-Koehler Publishers.

Mumford, M.D., Marks, M.A., Shane Connelly, M., Zaccaro, S.J., and Reiter-Palmon, R. (2000). Development of leadership skills: Experience and timing. *Leadership Quarterly*, 11(1), 87–114.

Murphy, S.E., and Riggio, R.E. (Eds.). (2003). *The Future of Leadership Development*. Mahwah, NJ: Lawrence Erlbaum Associates.

Newman, K.S. (1999). *Falling from Grace: Downward Mobility in the Age of Affluence*. Berkeley: University of California Press.

Nicholson, N. (1984). A theory of work role transitions. *Administrative Science Quarterly*, 29(2), 172–191.

Norcross, J., and Vangarelli, D. (1989). The resolution solution: Longitudinal examination of New Year's change attempts. *Journal of Substance Abuse*, 1, 127–134.

Osherton, S.D. (1980). *Holding On and Letting Go: Mean and Career Change at Midlife*. New York: Free Press.

Parks, S.F. (2005). *Leadership Can Be Taught: A Bold Approach for a Complex World*. Boston: Harvard Business School Press.

Patel, V.L., and Groen, G.J. (1991). The general and specific nature of medical expertise: A critical look. In K.A. Ericsson, and J. Smith (Eds.), *Toward a General Theory of Expertise: Prospects and Limits* (pp. 93–125). New York: Cambridge University Press.

Petriglieri, G., and Petriglieri, J. (forthcoming). Identity workspaces: The case of business schools. *Academy of Management Learning and Education*.

Pfeffer, J., and Sutton, R.I. (1999). *The Knowing-Doing Gap: How Smart Companies Turn Knowledge into Action*. Boston: Harvard Business School Press.

Pittaway, L., Rivera, O., and Murphy, A. (2005). Social identity and leadership in the Basque region: A study of leadership development programmes. *Journal of Leadership and Organizational Studies*, 11(3), 17–29.

Prochaska, J.O., DiClemente, C.C., and Norcross, J.C. (1992). In search of how people change: Applications to addictive behaviors. *American Psychologist*, 47(9), 1102–1114.

Quinn, R. (1996). *Deep Change: Discovering the Leader Within*. San Francisco: Jossey-Bass.

Robbins, P. I. (1978). *Successful Midlife Career Change: Self-Understanding and Strategies for Action*. New York: Amacom.

Schein, E.H. (1978). *Career Dynamics: Matching Individual and Organizational Needs*. Reading, MA: Addison Wesley.

———. (1996). Kurt Lewin's change theory in the field and in the classroom: Notes toward a model of management learning. *Systems Practice*, 9(1), 27–47.

Schrage, M. (1999). *Serious Play: How the World's Best Companies Simulate to Innovate*. Boston: Harvard Business School Press.

Senge, P.M. (1990). *The Fifth Discipline: The Art and Practice of the Learning Organization*. New York: Random House.

Settles, I.H. (2004). When multiple identities interfere: The role of identity centrality. *Personality and Social Psychology Bulletin*, 30, 487–500.

Snook, S. (2008). *Leader(ship) Development*. Boston: Harvard Business School Publishing.

———. (forthcoming). *Becoming a Harvard MBA: Confirmation as Transformation*. Cambridge, MA: Harvard University Press.

Snook, S., and Khurana, R. (2004). Developing 'Leaders of Character': Lessons from West Point. In R. Gandossy and J. Sonnenfeld (Eds.), *Leadership and Governance from the Inside Out* (pp. 213–232). Hoboken, NJ: John Wiley & Sons.

Strauss, A.L. (1959). *Mirrors and Masks: The Search for Identity*. New Brunswick, NJ: Transaction.

Tichy, N., and Cohen, E. (1997). *The Leadership Engine: How Winning Companies Build Leaders at Every Level*. New York: HarperCollins.

Torbert, W. (2004). *Action Inquiry: The Secret of Timely and Transforming Leadership*. San Francisco: Berrett-Koehler Publishers.

Turner, V. (1969). *From Ritual to Theatre: The Human Seriousness of Play*. Chicago: Aldione.

Van Gennep, A. (1960). *The Rites of Passage* (M.B. Vizedom and G.L. Cafee, Trans.). Chicago: University of Chicago Press. (Original work published 1908)

Van Knippenberg, B., van Knippenberg, D., De Cremer, D., and Hogg, M.A. (2005). Research in leadership, self, and identity: A sample of the present and a glimpse of the future. *Leadership Quarterly*, 16, 495–499.

Van Maanen, J. (1998). Identity work: Notes on the personal identity of police officers. Paper presented at the Annual Meeting of the Academy of Management, San Diego, CA, 9–12 August.

Vygotsky, L.S. (1978). *Mind in Society*. Cambridge, MA: Harvard University Press.

Winnicott, D.W. (1989). *Psychoanalytic Explorations*. London: Karnac Books.

Yorks, L., Beechler, S., and Ciporen, R. (2007). Enhancing the impact of an open-enrolment executive program through assessment. *Academy of Management Learning and Education*, 6(3), 310–320.

Zaleznik, A. (1977). Managers and leaders: Are they different? *Harvard Business Review*, 55(5), 67–78.

Zurcher, L.A., Jr. (1970). The "friendly" poker game: A study of an ephemeral role. *Social Forces*, 49(2), 173-186.

23

The Experience Conundrum

Morgan W. McCall Jr.

Introduction

But the fact is that no book, consultant, class, or series of classes, including an MBA, can teach anyone how to lead even a small team, let alone a big organization. It is a craft you can learn only through experience. This lesson about leadership is evident throughout history, and remains true despite all the training and business knowledge that has been amassed.
—Pfeffer and Sutton, *Hard Facts, Dangerous Half-Truths, and*
Total Nonsense

Ah, experience! The school of hard knocks that teaches lessons learned only in the trenches for which there is no substitute. Yet few concepts (is it a concept?) produce so many contradictions. "Some people have twenty years of experience, while others have one year of experience twenty times." Experience is said to be "the best teacher," yet the number of years of experience does not predict expert performance, executive effectiveness, or, ironically, teaching ratings.

Author note: This chapter is an edited version of a paper in the 2008 proceedings of "Leadership: Advancing an Intellectual Discipline," celebrating the Harvard Business School's 100th anniversary.

It is not difficult convincing executives that experience is essential in developing leadership, even when they believe that leadership ability is largely a gift: a gift must be developed and that development comes largely through experience. But using experience to develop leadership talent is far easier to espouse than to do. On the one hand it appears deceptively easy: "If you see a guy with talent, you give him a difficult assignment. If he does well, you reward him with another tough assignment," says John F. Smith Jr., retired GM chairman (Welch, 2004:72). Or, as noted by car guru Carlos Ghosn, "You prepare them by sending them to the most difficult places . . . You have to take the ones with the most potential and send them where the action is . . . Leaders are formed in the fire of experience" (Ghosn and Ries, 2005:152). In fact, the very origins of the word "experience," from the Latin roots *ex-*, "out of," and *periri*, "to go through," suggest gaining knowledge by going through trials, being tested.

But what appears to be a simple idea grows increasingly complicated in the face of simple questions. What puts the fire in experience or makes an assignment challenging? What specific lessons are learned from playing with fire? Who are "the ones with the most potential," or talent, and how do you spot them? How do you make sure that, once spotted, the most talented get the experiences that they need when they need them; and, once in those experiences, how do you prevent them from coming out mildly singed, half-baked, or burned out? Indeed, are all fires the same or does experience need to be administered in measured doses? Is variety more important than repeated trials? How much does timing matter?

These "simple" questions are vexing enough, but the whole matter of developing leadership through experience is even more problematic when considering the systematic use of experience to "prepare" a large population of people with "potential" for a multiplicity of senior roles. How many and what kinds of difficult assignments are available? Can the fires of experience be programmed? Can progress be measured? Are the results predictable? Do all talented future executives need all the same experiences? Some? Many?

Despite the increasing recognition that development is forged by powerful experiences, whether in crucibles (McCall, Lombardo, and Morrison, 1988; Bennis and Thomas, 2002), through personal and professional transitions (Dotlich, Noel, and Walker, 2004), or negotiating the passages in the leadership pipeline (Charan, Drotter, and Noel, 2001), the practical questions remain and define a research agenda for years to come. While much has been learned in the twenty-plus years since *Lessons of Experience* focused attention on the role of experience in developing executives, and while corporations have made increasingly sophisticated use of that knowledge (e.g., Yost and Plunkett, 2009), each step forward, instead of answering the questions, seems to raise new ones. The purpose of this chapter is to take stock of where we are today in our knowledge of the role of experience in developing leadership talent, and to suggest where we might go next in our quest for wisdom.

State of the Craft

Translating the use of experience to develop leadership talent from an intuitive act into a systematic process has not been an easy road and is far from complete. For this author, ending up on this road, like most things in life, was serendipitous. It began innocently enough, with an interest in what managers actually do as opposed to the popular abstractions of the time concerning leadership styles. Diary and observational studies of managerial work (see McCall, Morrison, and Hannan, 1978, for a review) pioneered by people such as Rosemary Stewart (1967) and Henry Mintzberg (1973) suggested a dynamic, fragmented world that bore little resemblance to the simplified models of the day (e.g., Fiedler, 1967). At the same time, it was a daunting challenge to actually study people "who dash around all the time" in dynamic environments.

Finding a way to hold the environment so that behavior within it could be examined more closely led to a multiyear project to develop a realistic simulation of managerial jobs in which practicing managers could be turned loose to do their thing under the watchful eyes of researchers. Looking Glass created a known, standardized, and valid environment to study how managers made decisions, shared information, built and used relationships, and dealt with the myriad of issues, trivial and titanic, presented by a day in organizational life. It was observing managers and executives at work and seeing the obvious power of simulation to stimulate learning (Lombardo and McCall, 1981; McCall and Lombardo, 1982) that inspired our research on experience and what it could teach.

Starting from what managers do rather than what they are like leads to a focus not on attributes of the individuals we might call effective leaders but on the experiences that teach lessons that might, over time, produce effective leaders. Instead of defining the Holy Grail as the characteristics that effective leaders have in common (McCall and Hollenbeck, 2002), this approach acknowledges that effective leaders have different personalities and different styles, and behave in different ways. Despite these differences, they can be equally effective if they are able to meet the demands of the environments in which they find themselves. With that as a starting point, our focus was on how people learned to handle the demands, and the experiences that taught them.

Experiences That Matter

In our first effort to understand experience and what it teaches, we used personal interviews and open-ended surveys to find out from successful executives (as identified by their corporations) what experiences had changed them in some significant way and what they had learned from those experiences (McCall, Lombardo, and Morrison, 1988). Qualitative analyses of these data produced sixteen types of experiences, ranging from challenging assignments to significant other people to personal challenges, and thirty-two categories of lessons. The "core elements" that made an experience a significant learning event were such things as facing difficult relationships, playing for high stakes, confronting adversity, and dealing with scope and scale. The factors that make an experience a powerful learning event were later elaborated by McCauley et al. (1994) and appear in table 23-1.

The same year saw two seminal studies that supported the notion that challenging experiences lead to significant development of managerial and executive ability. Nicholson and West (1988) surveyed over two thousand managers about transitions and their effects, concluding:

> [T]he job changes managers experience are, more often than not, radical in the altered situations they represent and the new demands they make. It is common for the job changer to have to adapt simultaneously to new organizational settings, the responsibility of altered status, the demand to practice new skills, and involvement in a range of new relationships . . . [A]djustment to novelty acts as a stimulus to personal change. (p. 117)

Adding to the evidence, Howard and Bray (1988), in their classic longitudinal study of managerial progress at the old AT&T, found that "the men[1] who advanced the furthest tended not to be promoted in a

TABLE 23-1

Core elements of powerful developmental experiences

Job transitions

Handling unfamiliar responsibilities

Having to prove yourself

Task-related characteristics

Creating change

      Responsible for developing new directions

      Inherited problems

      Reduction decisions

      Problems with employees

High level of responsibility

      High stakes

      Managing business diversity

      Job overload

      External pressure

Influencing without authority

Obstacles

Adverse business conditions

Lack of top management support

Lack of personal support

      Difficult boss

Source: Adapted from McCauley, Ruderman, Ohlott, and Morrow (1994).

straight line through the same type of function. Movement between departments was common, as was movement to different geographical locations" (p. 174). They went on to note that "it had been important, then, regardless of the men's level in early years, to provide them with stimulation, challenge, and enough freedom to develop their own resourcefulness" (p. 175).

There is little question, then, that long-held managerial beliefs that leadership is learned on the job are supported by the empirical evidence accumulated over the last two decades. Indeed, research has developed the wisdom of the trenches into an understanding of what makes an experience challenging, the kinds of experiences that present those challenges, and even what can be learned from mastering them. These findings have been extended to the global stage (McCall and Hollenbeck, 2002), as shown in table 23-2.

But confirming that "leaders are formed in the fire of experience" has not solved the problems associated with using experiences to "form" leaders. We know that all experiences are not created equal and that the developmental potential of experiences lies not in job titles or levels or descriptions, but in the challenges they present that force new learning. In other words, where there is smoke there is not always fire. We know that variety trumps more of the same, but it isn't as simple as jumping boundaries of business, geography, or function—what matters is what is jumped into and how that differs from what has gone before. Doing a start-up in one part of the business and then another start-up somewhere else may require less learning than a start-up followed by doing a turnaround, whether in the same or a different part of the business.

Further, there is some sketchy evidence that the sequence of experience matters (McCall et al., 1988; Charan et al., 2001; Jaques and Clement, 1991). We know, for example, that the first managerial job can be an extremely important experience, and that the transition from individual contributor to manager offers crucial lessons (Hill, 1992). Having learned these early lessons appears necessary for learning the different and more complex lessons of even more demanding experiences (such as growing a business or handling a difficult turnaround). Some managers, lacking the foundation provided by an early transition, learn what they should have learned earlier when they hit a major line assignment—and fail to learn the lessons offered by the more challenging experience.

The issue of sequence takes on even more importance when the serendipitous nature of experience is taken into account. Even if learning from experience were programmable—give them a first supervisory job, a turnaround, a divorce, and, voilà: *executive*—which it isn't, powerful experiences are not always available to those who need them when they need them, and many priorities other than development dictate who gets what experience. Often the organization's short-term needs come first, and selection is dictated by past performance or track record rather

TABLE 23-2

Potential powerful developmental experiences

Setting the stage

Early work experiences

First supervisory job

Leading by persuasion

Special projects

Staff assignments

Headquarters posting

Leading on line

Start-ups

Turnarounds

Growing the business

Other people

Excellent bosses

Terrible bosses

Hardships

Traumatic events

Career setbacks

Changing jobs

Mistakes

Difficult subordinates

Culture shock

Miscellaneous events

Courses and programs

Family, school, community

Source: Adapted from McCall, Lombardo, and Morrison (1988); and McCall and Hollenbeck (2002).

than by developmental need. Sometimes it works the other way, as when individuals refuse developmental opportunities that don't appear to be promotions or that require them to make big personal sacrifices. The realities of organizational existence make it fortunate that the order in which experience occurs isn't always critical, and shows why career paths and other lock-step approaches to development have never worked well.

In summary, here's what we have reason to believe is true about developmental experiences:

- They cover a variety of domains, from personal to jobs to other people.

- They are developmental because they *force* learning by providing novel challenges.

- All experiences are not created equal—they teach different things.

- Variety over time matters, but it is not programmable.

- Sequence sometimes matters.

- Opportunities are often serendipitous.

This means that using experience effectively will never be, and cannot be, a precise science or practice. Above all it confirms and informs why developing leadership talent is highly individual and becomes more so over the course of a career. It also suggests that an organization is limited in how much it can determine individual development. Because of this, it is even more important that organizations do what they can to create a context supportive of developing leadership talent. The callous practice of simply throwing talented people into fires to see who survives may be better than doing nothing, and given a sufficiently large pool of potential talent may even be sufficient, but it fails to capitalize on what we know about experience. In that sense it is both inefficient (because it does not use the limited resource of experience efficiently) and costly (if the most talented people are the ones thrown into the fires, then the ones who do not survive are wasted talent—talk about burned out!).

Given that learning from experience is, in the end, up to the person having it, and that an organization cannot make anyone develop, finding the leverage points that increase the probability of developing more effective leaders is the central challenge. One might begin by identifying experiences that have developmental potential.

Leveraging Experience

LEVERAGE POINT 1: IDENTIFYING DEVELOPMENTAL EXPERIENCES

The easiest place to start is by having people who know the organization identify developmental projects, start-ups, and turnarounds, exceptional bosses, and so on—those experiences in table 23-2 that are available in an organizational setting. In many cases assignments can be developmentally enriched, without requiring the incumbent to actually change jobs, by including the elements that make experiences powerful (see table 23-1). Although this buffet of potent experiences is demonstrably loaded with potential learning, not all of the lessons available are equally valuable to the organization. Besides, life is too short for anyone to have all of the available experiences. For this reason it is important to prioritize developmental needs in light of the organization's strategy or business model and values (if any).

The logic goes something like this. First, translate the organization's strategy into the leadership demands it implies: if this is what we need to do, then what will our leaders need to deal with effectively? Note that we are not asking what skills or attributes leaders will need, but rather what situations, demands, or challenges they will face as a result of the strategic direction. Then, if we assume that leadership talent can be developed, and that some people are more likely to develop it than others, we can ask what experiences would increase the ability of talented people to handle those kinds of situations (see McCall, 1998). If, for example, the growth of the business will be driven by mergers and acquisitions, what experiences would we give our best people to help develop their competence in dealing with mergers and acquisitions?

This immediately leads to questions about where those kinds of experiences exist in the organization, or, if they don't exist, what alternatives can be found or fabricated to prepare leaders for that future. It also raises at least two other crucial issues: how do we know who has the potential to learn from the experiences and become, over time, the leaders we need; and how do we ensure that those people, once identified, actually get the experiences that they need?

LEVERAGE POINT 2: IDENTIFICATION OF POTENTIAL

The current reverence for competency models[2] has distracted research-ers and practitioners from developing more sophisticated and realistic approaches to understanding leadership, and this distraction has been particularly destructive when it comes to identifying leadership poten-tial (McCall and Hollenbeck, 2007). Assuming that all effective leaders or executives or managers are alike, whether in personality or style, or that they all share the same set of attributes, is an appealing simplicity that flies in the face of everyday experience. Toyota's Fujio Cho is hardly a Jack Welch in personality, style, or behavior, yet both were undeniably effective leaders.

A more useful approach, and one with more promise for improving leadership development, assumes that different people have different attributes that they bring to situations and that there are different ways to handle the same situation effectively. The challenge is to provide opportunities for people to learn how to handle important situations effectively without making assumptions about some finite set of attri-butes that everyone must have. The measure of effectiveness here is increased competence in handling the demands and challenges of a lead-ership role, not acquiring an arbitrary set of competencies that may or may not be necessary or sufficient to get the desired results. This is an interesting parallel to research on the performance of world-class experts in a variety of domains that focuses on the path to mastery (McCall and Hollenbeck, 2008) rather than on a search for universal traits or styles.

Applied to the leadership domain, the mastery perspective suggests looking for people who have the potential to become increasingly com-petent through learning from experience. More simply, we would want to give valuable developmental experiences to the people most likely to learn from them—people with the ability to learn from experience, variously defined as an "openness to learning" (McCall, 1998; Spre-itzer, McCall, and Mahoney, 1997) or "learning agility" (Lombardo and Eichinger, 2001).

The ability to learn from experience, as defined by the various authors, seems to include a variety of attitudes (e.g., acting as if there is something to learn, openness to feedback), skills (e.g., creating condi-tions that produce valid feedback, listening to feedback), and behaviors (e.g., taking opportunities to learn). This is an area crying out for more research on whether learning from experience is the product of a unique set of attributes (unlikely) or of several different but equally effective sets, whether the ability to learn from experience is itself learned from experience, and how learning from experience may change over time or in the context of different kinds of experiences. It seems, from anecdotes and observation, that people drawn to managerial and executive careers are rarely reflective learners, so conventional approaches to how people learn may not apply. Altogether different types of skills may be involved in learning on the fly and in learning while performing (there is even some evidence of an alarming negative relationship between performance demands and development).

Access to developmental experiences often is restricted to those considered to have "high potential." Membership in high-potential pools is, in turn, usually determined by senior manager nomination, reflecting, in theory at least, a track record of high performance plus a dollop of prediction about how many more levels a person might rise. Setting aside that this prediction may be made by someone who is not considered high potential, or who has not held the position at higher levels at which the prediction is aimed, the high-potential individual's ability to learn from experience is only implied by successful performance (the assumption being that only a learner could have progressed this far). However, if the ability to learn from experience is not essential to effective performance in a particular situation (as may be the case in promotions that don't require the development of new skills, such as doing more of the same with perhaps larger scope), or if learning from different kinds of experiences requires different learning abilities, then identifying "potential" based on current or past performance is problematic. Assessment of demonstrated potential requires an understanding of the type of learning ability demonstrated by the candidate, the circumstances under which it was exhibited, and how the learning requirements may differ in future experiences.

Defining potential in terms of an individual attribute such as "ability to learn from experience" does not address the cumulative learning from experiences required for eventual mastery. Indeed, the trek to mastery is characterized by fits and starts and discontinuities, but people with potential still should get "better" over time. Given that, how can progress be assessed if it can't be measured against some finite set of competencies that apply to all?

One measure of progress (or mastery of leadership expertise) would be the degree to which the lessons offered by experience are learned and incorporated into behavior. Over time one would expect that the "potential" of individuals could be assessed, however crudely, by evidence of the ability to learn from the experiences they have had, and by progress in the ability to meet the increasingly difficult demands of leadership jobs. Categorizing the lessons (McCall et al., 1988; McCall, 1998; McCall and Hollenbeck, 2002) suggests that the expert leader domain consists of five broad demands that an executive must learn to handle if he or she is to grow in effectiveness as a leader: setting and communicating direction, aligning critical constituencies, setting and living values, developing an executive temperament, and growing self and others (table 23-3).

Assessing mastery of the demands begs the question of current performance, which may or may not be associated with learning. Indeed, going into new experiences is likely to result in lowered performance in the early stages of learning, and learning sometimes results from mistakes and errors that detract from performance. Further, as noted above, high performance does not mean that new learning has necessarily occurred. But to say that results don't matter is to deny the sine qua non of organizational life, even if "results" is an unreliable measure of potential. It is, however, the entry ticket to the game.

In 2300 BCE, Ptahhotep, adviser to the pharaoh, avowed that there were three qualities necessary to pharaoh effectiveness (could this have been the first competency model?). However, before the qualities mattered, the fundamental requirement was to be descended from the Sun god. This is also the reality of organizational life—first performance, then growth. But whatever process is used to control the gate to the high-potential pool, results must be considered in the context of growth, recognizing that there will be occasions when suboptimal results must be tolerated and even expected, even though, over time, those with potential must also be high performers. The irony is that the best performance is likely to be achieved by the person with the least to learn, specifically, the person who has already mastered that experience. A system based on performance alone will by definition destroy itself over time.

In sum, organizations can leverage development by identifying leadership potential and giving those with the most potential access to the experiences they need. Although more research on potential is badly needed, it is safe to assume that it begins with (1) reasonable results, but includes (2) ability to learn from experience and (3) progress toward mastery of the five demands, in the context of the variety of experiences a person has had.

TABLE 23-3

Five demands of leadership based on the "lessons" taught by experience

Setting direction

Technical/professional skills

Business knowledge

Strategic thinking

Taking responsibility

Structure and control systems

Innovative problem solving

Alignment

Political situations

Getting people to implement

What executives are like

Working with executives

Negotiation strategies

Influence without authority

Understanding other perspectives

Dealing with conflict

Directing and motivating subordinates

Developing people

Confronting performance problems

Managing former peers or bosses

Setting and living values

Needing others

Sensitivity to people

Management values

(Continued)

TABLE 23–3 *(continued)*

Five demands of leadership based on the "lessons" taught by experience

Executive temperament

Being tough when necessary

Self-confidence

Coping with situations beyond one's control

Persevering through adversity

Coping with ambiguity

Use of power

Growth of self and others

Balance of life and work

Knowing what excites one

Personal limits and blind spots

Taking charge of one's career

Recognizing and seizing opportunities

Source: Adapted from Hutchison, Homes, and McCall (1987).

LEVERAGE POINT 3: THE RIGHT EXPERIENCE AT THE RIGHT TIME

Assuming a reasonable pool of high-potential talent and a rich selection of strategically relevant developmental opportunities, it would seem we've found pig heaven. All that's left is matching those with developmental needs with the appropriate experiences. But once again the Sun god interferes: organizations need results, and giving rookies, even talented ones, experiences for which they are not fully qualified does not optimize short-term results. Most often the decision on who gets a specific job lies in the hands of the manager of that job (the "hiring manager"). Suppose a leader is needed for an important start-up and there are two candidates, one of whom has successfully led two previous start-ups and one of whom, though talented, has never started anything. The pragmatist needing results is inclined to go for the sure thing. The hiring manager, likely under pressure for results (and quickly), would need a lot of courage (or job security) to risk the lesser-qualified candidate, even though that person would, by definition, learn more from the opportunity. As if more rationalization were necessary, the hiring manager also is aware that choosing the person who might develop the most risks both the success of the start-up and that person's (not to mention the hiring manager's) career. In addition, if the lesser-qualified candidate comes from outside the manager's part of the organization, the lack of firsthand knowledge creates uncertainty about the outsider's abilities. There also may be some costs associated with taking a talented person away from another part of the organization (even if he or she could be persuaded to leave), especially if that person does not succeed in the new environment.

To the extent, then, that using experience for development depends on who gets what experience, there are significant forces working against developmental moves. It is much easier to send someone to a program than to offer up a talented person for an assignment in a different part of the organization, or, conversely, to risk sacrificing results by taking on a developmental candidate. To leave developmental moves in the hands of the hiring managers, especially in results-driven organizations, is to rely overoptimistically on the nobility of leaders. To ensure that cross-boundary developmental moves are considered, some companies (reputedly GE, for example) actually give the hiring manager a slate of candidates from which to choose.

There are several strategies that can be used singly or together in an effort to increase the probability of matching development need to development opportunity. All of them are predicated, of course, on knowing who the people with potential are, what their developmental needs are, and what experiences could meet those needs. The most powerful strategy, and perhaps the hardest to create and maintain, is creating a culture of development in which leaders see it as a natural part of their job to develop others, understand the basics of using experience for that purpose, and act as models for others in that regard.

Even if development is not embedded in the culture, managers can be held accountable for development, just as they are held accountable for other results. That said, accountability for developing others can be a bit tricky to measure. What constitutes adequate performance? Number of moves made? People given up? Numbers promoted? Surveys of direct reports? And how do you reward it? What percentage of a raise or bonus is connected to development as opposed to bottom-line results? The danger in such schemes is that without a supportive culture, they can be gamed by savvy managers who find ways to make the numbers without truly committing to developing talent.

In many organizations, the primary vehicle, other than the hiring manager, for matching high-potential individuals to jobs is the succession planning process. As typically conducted, such a process involves a senior management team assessing managers at some number of levels below them and identifying who has the "potential" to fill the key jobs in the organization. Frequently these candidates are assessed in terms of how much more seasoning is needed (ready now, ready in two years, etc.), and diversity goals are taken into account as well. Sometimes the developmental needs of individuals are discussed, especially for the "not yet ready" candidates. In organizations with leadership pipeline problems, higher-level succession planning is closely monitored by the board. The primary purpose of the exercise is to make sure there are replacements for key positions and key executives, and to identify weak spots in the executive bench—not to develop talent.

While there is some debate about how often the people in the succession charts actually take the positions for which they were slated, there is no doubt that succession planning is potentially a valuable tool for managing leadership talent. With some relatively minor modifications it could be considerably more valuable in developing that talent. Not to diminish the importance of replacement planning for key positions, imagine an additional session devoted to developmental planning. Utilizing leverage points 1 and 2 above, this session might begin by using the business plan to identify *strategically* relevant assignments, experiences, and bosses. Each of these could be further elaborated by analyzing what could be learned by a talented person who was given the opportunity. Then a subset of managers, identified as high potential in the terms described in leverage point 2, could be discussed[3] and matched to the opportunities. Taken one step further, each person given a developmental experience could be told about the assessment and what she or he would be expected to learn from this assignment. Further, a similar conversation with the person's boss-to-be could be used to create a supportive context and accountability for the learning objective.

The advantages of such a session would extend far beyond the developmental opportunities afforded to the talented individuals matched to needed experiences. The senior management team would gain a better understanding of the leadership talent pool and the developmental needs within it. By explicitly talking about the leadership challenges implied by the business strategy and about the developmental experiences that would prepare people for those challenges, senior management would themselves develop deeper insight into their organization's leadership needs. By providing useful developmental feedback to individuals and their bosses, senior management would convey by example the importance of development and accountability for it, thereby creating a culture for development. And possibly, over time, by sharing talented managers' progress through these developmental experiences, senior managers would begin to incorporate growth into the replacement decisions made in the traditional succession planning exercise, thereby promoting developmentally oriented people into key positions.

In sum, organizations can gain leverage over development by taking actions to better match developmental needs to developmental experiences. This can be achieved by a variety of means, including making sure that hiring managers understand the development process and expectations around it, building a culture for using experience for development, modeling appropriate behavior through the actions of senior managers with their people as well as themselves, increasing accountability by measuring and sanctioning developmental activities, creating processes to enhance movement across experiences (such as candidate slates), and doing succession planning with a developmental twist.

Even with all of these efforts to create a context for development, there are no guarantees. For various reasons, many of them legitimate, some people may refuse to accept a developmental assignment. Others may accept developmental opportunities but, even if motivated to grow, may fail to learn the lessons they offer. The latter case presents an organization with another point of leverage.

Leverage Point 4: Increasing the Odds That Learning Will Occur

Do what you might, an experience challenging enough to be developmental does not necessarily yield up its lessons easily: "There are always an infinite number of generalizations that a learner can draw from a finite set of inputs" (Pinker, 2002:101). Instead of simply taking away the wrong message, we sometimes manage to escape altogether the lessons we are offered. Perhaps this is why the first rule of development through experience is that the experience has to get your attention. But it's no footnote that even after investing enormous effort in getting it right—identifying those with potential, finding or creating relevant experience, investing in matching the two—no development, or worse, undesirable change, may come of it. In a nutshell, everyday life has taught us that people may learn nothing, learn the wrong thing, or forget what was learned, and that they do such things on a regular basis. If we are intent on throwing people into fires—even the right people into the right fires at the right time—then it behooves us to do what we can to ensure that they learn what we threw them in there to learn.

At first that seems a simple task, especially since so many tools are available to help managers learn. The development arsenal is packed with 360-degree feedback instruments, internal and external coaches, educational programs of every shape and size, books loaded with development advice, motivational speakers, elaborate performance management systems with at least annual feedback, human resource (HR) staffs with a mission, action learning models, and more. There is no doubt that each of these can be extremely powerful. But with all of these resources available, it's nothing short of miraculous that so many managers manage to maintain mediocrity.

Despite the resources listed above, wrenching meaning from experience remains a challenge. Some of the reason is that these tools are often disassociated in space and time from the experience in which they are needed. Sometimes they are simply misdirected, for example, by providing feedback on competencies that have little to do with competence. Sometimes they are based on a model of learning and reflection that is not how many managers learn.

The truth is, although drawing meaning out of experience can be simple, creating the circumstances in which it happens predictably, and as intended, is quite complex. It begins with what we have already covered. We have some idea what experiences are important and what they can teach, but the relationship between experience and its lessons is not precise. Even more important, people come into experiences with particular histories that affect their perspectives. They bring differing tapestries of strengths and weaknesses, and differing motivations and expectations. They are at different places in their lives and may be more or less open to what is possible. It is no understatement to say we are dealing, minimally, with an interaction of personal attributes, experience, timing, history, and context.

The author experienced this complexity first hand while on sabbatical as a director in a high-tech company. By following newly appointed executives as they worked their way through the first year of the new job, the project aimed at understanding what helped and what hindered their learning from the experience. Interviews were conducted with the executives, some of their bosses, HR business partners, executives in the mentor program of the company, and executives in charge of executive development. While in retrospect the results may be obvious, they are no less discouraging. For almost every type of resource or intervention that might help learning in one situation, its absence or opposite was crucial in another. Good bosses, bad bosses, and absent bosses could be helpful (although interestingly no one learned much of anything from mediocre bosses). Abundant, adequate, or inadequate resources. Coaching or having to do it on one's own. Authority or the lack of it. Help as needed or no help at all. Adequate staff or no staff. Feedback or no feedback. On and on.

Thank goodness for tenure, because no academically acceptable paper resulted from all this work—the qualitative data raised more questions than answers. Clearly there is a version of Heisenberg's famous uncertainty principle at work here, because the newly arrived individual changes the nature of the experience, and having the experience changes the individual (not to mention the impact of the researcher on both). But no answer is sometimes an answer as well, especially when it suggests that the wrong question was asked. Of course learning from experience is highly—*highly*—individual. Ergo, interventions that facilitate it also need to be considered on an individual basis. So if what we are dealing with is a judgment call based on the circumstances, that raises a different set of questions. Who makes the judgment? What matters in deciding whether to intervene or not? If development is ultimately the responsibility of the people who are developing, then what context can be set to actually accept that responsibility?

Obviously a different research project is needed to answer these questions (if there is some formula that might be found), but there are some hints that might help guide that research or the practitioner seeking some guidance on what to try. From all those interviews it appears that, other than the incumbent, the immediate boss has the most impact, pro or con, on development. Not only does the boss control access to potentially valuable experiences, but also he or she sets the objectives, evaluates performance (and often potential), controls many resources, and essentially determines the nature of the work. It should be no surprise, then, that development-oriented bosses made judgment calls about critical aspects of experience. Few of those bosses behaved like good coaches in the athletic sense of that word, but many were wise (often unconsciously) in creating a context in which a lot of growth could occur. Using their judgment of the individual and of the situation, these bosses:

- Made sure that the work was challenging, stretching the incumbent by putting her in novel situations or by pushing him to the edge of his competence.

- Gave the appearance of autonomy while indirectly keeping an eye on how far the incumbent was pushed—and the better ones were prepared to "make a diving catch" to rescue the incumbent if circumstances got too far out of hand.

- In setting objectives, included specific learning goals as if they were just as important as other kinds of results, sometimes stating them in results language so that the incumbent might not even know he or she was learning goals. This ensured accountability for growth as well as for performance.

- Made sure that there was feedback, preferably from some other source, on learning (or progress toward a learning objective, however stated), and not just on performance.

- Judiciously meted out resources, depending on whether their presence or absence would help (or sometimes force) the incumbent to learn.

- Cleverly designed the work so the incumbent had to do new things rather than spend his time doing what he already knew how to do. If, for example, he was already accomplished at marketing, the boss might make sure that an extremely competent marketing person was on the incumbent's staff.

- Used other staffing decisions (e.g., peers) to make sure that the incumbent had access to advice and perhaps support or monitoring from sources other than the boss.

- Were willing to give up their very talented people when the experiences needed for further growth were unavailable in their part of the organization.

No doubt there are many other things a boss can do to facilitate learning from experience, but even these examples suggest why bosses are so important to development and why so few are very good at it. It requires significant wisdom to help others develop, so much so that it is perhaps the boss who needs coaching more than the person being developed! And because bosses are usually under considerable pressure to get results, they may need help with some of the development responsibilities. This is the best argument we've seen for developing human resource business partners who understand the business, the jobs, and the people, and who, because of that knowledge, can provide an executive with sound guidance in developing talent. It also suggests that it might be worthwhile to explore how people other than the immediate boss might play bigger roles in the development process.

The other critical player in learning from experience, and perhaps the most critical, is the person being developed. Obviously no one can make someone else develop, and equally obviously the incumbent is unlikely or unable to do for himself or herself many of the things the boss must do. The desire to learn, to take on challenges that stretch one, and to seek out feedback, advice, and support all come from within. More research would be helpful on why some people have or develop the motivation for mastery and why some people are willing to make the sacrifices required to learn and practice new skills. Some of it is genetic, no doubt (see Arvey et al. [2006] for research on twins that suggests about 30 percent of leadership emergence is heritable), but much of it comes from the combination of a passion for leadership with an understanding of how leadership ability is acquired. It can make a substantial difference if there is a context that provides inspiration for talented individual contributors to consider taking on leadership roles and that drives existing managers to aspire to become more expert leaders. Ironically, from that perspective, developing leaders boils down to leadership, for it is a leadership act to create such a context.

In sum, one of the most neglected and highest-payoff leverage points is doing whatever is possible to enhance learning of the desired lessons from ongoing experience. The goal, after all, is not to test whether a talented person can figure it out, but to have a talented person grow more capable. The field of human resources has developed many helpful tools and processes that, if used selectively and connected in space and time with experience, can be very helpful. But the more influential factor in learning from experience is the immediate boss, who controls directly so much of the learning context. Perhaps the most effective strategy over the long haul is to promote and reward bosses who "get it": those people who value and understand their role in helping others grow. Things that effective bosses do to foster development from experience, such as finding ways to provide feedback, accountability, support, and the like, can be done by other people as well. The key is that it gets done, whether by a business partner, a coach, or a peer—which suggests enlisting as many different people as possible in the development process.

In the final analysis, it all boils down to the person who is developing. All too often, however, organizations use that fact to abrogate their responsibility for creating the opportunities for growth and for providing the soil that supports it. At a minimum, a person who wants to develop needs the information, tools, and opportunities to do so.

Leverage Point 5: A Career-Long Perspective and a Focus on Transitions

Time and resources are always limited, and development of talent, as important as it is, is not the first priority of most (if any) organizations. In developing talent, as with any other strategic choice, resources must be concentrated in the places with the greatest potential impact. The leverage points described above represent such places, but the recommendations are largely systemic whereas the phenomenon is highly individual.

For individuals, life and development do not unfold in the neat chunks dictated by organizational review cycles. As we have learned from studies of experts, mastery, if ever achieved at all, can be the result of a lifelong, or at least career-long, process. And, as we have learned from numerous psychological (e.g., Levinson, 1978; Bridges, 1980) and organizational (e.g., Charan et al., 2001; Dotlich et al., 2004) studies, life and development require significant transitions. It seems logical, then, that bringing the individual into the development process requires attention to growth as it unfolds over time and to the key transitions that are required in moving from one level of mastery to the next.

Unfortunately, individual progress in most organizations is measured once or twice a year in a performance management process aimed primarily at assessing past performance and using that assessment to make pay and promotion decisions. Development, which is often included as a part of that process, is typically a secondary outcome embedded in the annual cycle, connected to a particular boss, and limited to low-power actions such as attending programs or involvement in certain meetings or projects. In many cases, individuals essentially start over each year or, at best, with each new boss. Development, however, does not fit neatly into such a pattern, so there needs to be some other way to keep track of growth over time: a way to keep track of experiences, what was learned from them, and any evidence of increased mastery of the leadership domain.

Such a longitudinal perspective will also highlight key transition points, those times when an individual is required to make a major change in attitudes and skills. We know, for example, that the move from individual contributor to manager is one such transition (Hill, 1992) requiring major psychological and behavioral adjustments, and that a demanding expatriate assignment is another (McCall and Hollenbeck, 2002; Osland, 1995; Storti, 1990). Ram Charan and his colleagues (2001) postulate six such transitions, whereas Dotlich and his associates (2004) suggest thirteen "passages" that "make or break a leader."

While one might debate just how many transitions there are on the path to effective leadership, there is little question that these are times when much is on the line. When situations change dramatically, as is the case when a person is given an assignment that is quite different from what she or he has done before, either development or derailment may result. Crucial transitions in earlier times were often marked by rites of passage or initiations (Eliade, 1958; Van Gennep, 1960) during which a great deal of attention was devoted to marking and supporting the change. From a leadership development perspective it is no less important to pay special attention to significant transitions in people's professional lives and to help them get through them successfully. These are times when the individual, in the midst of great challenge, can lose sight easily of what must be left behind as well as what new attitudes and skills are needed.

As onerous as it seems, when it comes to development, timing is everything. As soon as the scope of the challenge shifts to career-long, the necessity to begin development early becomes obvious. Too often serious attention to developing leadership does not begin until a person reaches senior levels. While this is understandable because of cost and sheer numbers, it is no less true that by the time a person reaches senior levels many crucial developmental experiences have either already occurred or have been missed. If the leverage points suggested in this chapter are taken seriously, developmental considerations need to be embedded in recruiting, hiring, retention, promotion, and early job experiences. Because, for example, the first supervisory job can be so critical to development, organizations need to look closely at what those experiences are like, what bosses are involved, and what can be done to make both the transition and the learning successful. Because choosing a managerial path and leaving an individual contributor role is such a big decision for the person and the organization, it only makes sense to give individual contributors significant brushes with leading so they might discover their level of interest prior to making the leap. Because a global perspective is increasingly important and failure in expatriate assignments so expensive, it only makes sense to build in early exposure to international issues and people from other countries.

In the end, then, leverage point 5, following careers and being present at key transitions, is all about connecting what we know about effectively using experience for development with the individuals who need it, when they need it. Organizations likely differ in how many and what kinds of transitions constitute the path to leadership mastery, but identifying them is possible. Organizations certainly differ in the size of their workforce, making a focus on individuals challenging as the number of employees (and proportionately the number with leadership potential) grows larger, but it is less of an information technology problem than one of attention and knowing what needs to be recorded.

The Challenge for Practice

The upshot of all this is that we live in a universe whose age we can't quite compute, surrounded by stars whose distances we don't altogether know, filled with matter we can't identify, operating in conformance with physical laws whose properties we don't truly understand.
—Bill Bryson, *A Short History of Nearly Everything*

It is unlikely that either the next generation of management gurus or more research will provide all the answers to the challenges of leadership development. Ron Heifetz (1994) titled his marvelous book

Leadership Without Easy Answers, and this chapter might well have played off that title by calling itself "Leadership *Development* Without Easy Answers." Unfortunately, there is a tendency to avoid facing up to the complexity when confronted with an important issue and no definitive formula for taking it on. There are substantial bodies of knowledge on how to do pieces and parts of development, such as 360-degree feedback and coaching, so one way to avoid complexity is by incorporating state-of-the-art processes without worrying about their relevance, timing, or tying them together in a meaningful way.

There are corporations with stunning performance (though sometimes only temporary) that, by inference, also must be well led; thus, another path is to emulate what they do to develop talent. General Electric, for example, has had disproportionate impact on corporate practice over the last several decades.

Further, there is no shortage of management consultants dedicated to leadership development who make a living giving advice or coming in as hired guns from the outside to design systems; thus, yet another option is to turn development over to someone else, be it a consultant or an internal HR group.

And there is always the option of avoiding the issue altogether by making the assumption that leadership ability is, after all, one of those mysterious qualities that you either have or you don't. Instead of investing time and money in futile efforts to develop it, the argument goes, effort is better directed at selecting those who have "it" and seeing to it that those people are put in charge of key strategic initiatives. Even if there is some element of development necessary to bring raw talent to fruition, those with the "right stuff," it is assumed, will figure it out. The ultimate way out is simply to assume that leadership doesn't matter, that strategy, technology, and monopoly are the overriding sources of competitive advantage no matter who the leaders are.

It is a matter of faith. If one believes that leadership matters and that leadership talent can be developed, then the absence of a formula is no more daunting in this sphere than it is for other strategic initiatives that require decisions under ambiguity. There are some basic principles to guide action, and there are some clear leverage points where action can make a difference. The fundamental starting point, one that seems supported by experience as well as by research, is that leadership, to the extent that it is developed, is developed primarily through experience. Beginning with that basic premise, it is possible to construct a rational approach to using experience more systematically to develop those who are able and motivated to learn from it. Not all people have both of those necessary qualities—ability to learn and motivation to improve—and because of that, many people will never become masters of leading, no matter what experiences they are offered. But one might venture to guess that many people who find themselves in leadership roles by choice or by chance can get better if given the appropriate experiences, support, and feedback.

As stated earlier, when all is said and done, developing leadership requires leadership.

The Challenge for Research

Whereas practitioners must make decisions and act whether or not there is precedent or adequate information, those choosing to do research on leadership development face a different set of challenges. It is much easier to carry out research on specific human resource topics such as competencies or feedback or training outcomes than it is to tackle the systemic issues raised in this chapter. Unfortunately, even large accumulations of research on these specific topics are not necessarily useful when taken out of the larger context of development, and can sometimes lead into blind alleys. The pros and cons of a focus on competencies, for example, have been debated elsewhere (Hollenbeck, McCall, and Silzer, 2006). Rather than take on the relative merits of more research on HR topics, this foray into using experience to develop leadership raises a number of issues that might be informed by further research with a different focus.

Some researchable issues are largely organization specific. It is possible to identify the experiences and associated lessons, as well as key transition points, that matter in a given organization. It might be possible to develop measures of learning, or to assess the efficacy of certain practices in helping people to learn. These and other projects of applied research are potentially quite useful to any organization seeking to improve practice.

But there are more general issues begging for attention, some of which were raised in this chapter. For instance, is it possible to demonstrate that organizations acting on more or certain combinations of these leverage points actually develop more effective leaders? Is it possible to develop measures of individual differences in ability and motivation to learn that could predict more accurately who will grow through experience? Can we increase our understanding of whether and in what ways the sequence of experience affects learning?

There might be some value in looking more closely at what differences bosses make when it comes to development and providing perspectives other than "the boss as coach." Would it be possible to identify individuals who have a documented track record of spawning leadership talent and then, through observation and interview, document the variety of actions that they take?

Some Concluding Thoughts

I have never been one to subscribe to the idea that leadership doesn't matter, despite some evidence that it may not always be as important as we assume it is (Pfeffer, 1978). There are many factors other than leadership that play a significant part in determining organizational outcomes, and there are obviously times when the situation overwhelms anything a leader might do. But there are no doubt many unqualified, mediocre, or downright incompetent people occupying leadership roles, and the cost of their neglect or mismanagement in human and financial terms will never be known with any precision. It's not the leaders who derail that worry me, it's the ones who should have but are still in place, wreaking havoc. Anyone who has ever suffered under an incompetent leader knows the local toll it takes, and it's not hard to imagine how it multiplies at the highest levels of organization and society.

Considering the damage done by lousy leadership, and the possibilities for good in extraordinary leadership, it seems obvious that it is important, indeed crucial, to invest in developing leadership talent. Even if some leaders are "born," there clearly aren't enough such gifted people to go around, and we need all the help we can get. It is time to move past the naïve notion that mastery of leadership can be achieved in the classroom or through piecemeal application of human resource programs and tools. Taking leadership development seriously means using experience wisely to help those with sufficient dedication and desire to learn the craft. It will not come easily.

Notes

1. The impact of experience is certainly not unique to men. See Morrison et al., 1987.

2. A competency model is typically a handful of attributes and behaviors that are claimed to describe all effective executives or leaders, usually as defined by a specific organization. They often include such things as "strategic thinker," "flexible," "interpersonal skills," and so on.

3. Solid performers not seen as having the potential to advance would be included in the traditional succession planning process as appropriate, and may be considered in this hypothetical session as well because they may be blocking important developmental experiences needed by others. In an ideal world with sufficient resources, all leaders would be expected to continually learn and grow, whether or not they were advancing up the hierarchy, and a session like this would not be restricted to only the high-potential individuals.

References

Arvey, R., M. Rotundo, W. Johnson, and M. McGue. "The Determinants of Leadership Role Occupancy: Genetic and Personality Factors. *Leadership Quarterly* 17, no. 1 (2006): 1–20.

Bennis, W., and R. Thomas. *Geeks and Geezers.* Boston: Harvard Business School Press, 2002.

Bridges, W. *Transitions.* Reading, MA: Addison-Wesley, 1980.

Bryson, B. *A Short History of Nearly Everything.* New York: Broadway, 2003.

Charan, R., S. Drotter, and J. Noel. *The Leadership Pipeline.* San Francisco: Jossey-Bass, 2001.

Dotlich, D., J. Noel, and N. Walker. *Leadership Passages: The Personal and Professional Transitions That Make or Break a Leader.* San Francisco: Jossey-Bass, 2004.

Eliade, M. *Rites and Symbols of Initiation.* Putnam, CT: Spring Publications, 1958.

Fiedler, F. *A Theory of Leadership Effectiveness.* New York: McGraw-Hill, 1967.

Ghosn, C., and P. Ries. *Shift: Inside Nissan's Historic Revival.* New York: Currency Doubleday, 2005.

Heifetz, R. *Leadership Without Easy Answers.* Cambridge, MA: Belknap Press, 1994.

Hill, L. *Becoming a Manager: Mastery of a New Identity.* Boston: Harvard Business School Press, 1992.

Hollenbeck, G., M. McCall, and R. Silzer. "Leadership Competency Models." *Leadership Quarterly* 17 (2006): 398–413.

Howard, A., and D. Bray. *Managerial Lives in Transition: Advancing Age and Changing Times.* New York: Guilford, 1988.

Hutchison, E., V. Homes, and M. McCall. "Key Events in Executive's Lives." Technical report 32, Center for Creative Leadership, Greensboro, NC, 1987.

Jaques, E., and S. Clement. *Executive Leadership.* Oxford: Blackwell, 1991.

Levinson, D. *The Seasons of a Man's Life.* New York: Ballantine, 1978.

Lombardo, M., and R. Eichinger. *The Leadership Machine.* Minneapolis, MN: Lominger Limited, Inc., 2001.

Lombardo, M., and M. McCall. "Leaders on Line: Observations from a Simulation of Managerial Work." Technical report 18, Center for Creative Leadership, Greensboro, NC, 1981.

McCall, M. *High Flyers: Developing the Next Generation of Leaders.* Boston: Harvard Business School Press, 1998.

McCall, M., and G. Hollenbeck. *Developing Global Executives: The Lessons of International Experience*. Boston: Harvard Business School Press, 2002.

———. "Getting Leader Development Right: Competence Not Competencies." In *The Practice of Leadership*, edited by J. Conger and R. Riggio, 87–106. San Francisco: Jossey-Bass, 2007.

———. "Developing the Expert Leader." *People and Strategy* (formerly *Human Resource Planning*) 31, no. 1 (2008): 20–28.

McCall, M., and M. Lombardo. "Using Simulation for Research: Through the Looking Glass." *Management Science* 28 (1982): 533–549.

McCall, M., M. Lombardo, and A. Morrison. *The Lessons of Experience: How Successful Executives Develop on the Job*. Lexington, MA: Lexington Books, 1988.

McCall, M., A. Morrison, and R. Hannan. "Studies of Managerial Work: Results and Methods." Technical report 9, Center for Creative Leadership, Greensboro, NC, 1978.

McCauley, C., M. Ruderman, P. Ohlott, and J. Morrow. "Assessing the Developmental Components of Managerial Jobs." *Journal of Applied Psychology* 79, no. 4 (1994): 544–560.

Mintzberg, H. *The Nature of Managerial Work*. New York: Harper & Row, 1973.

Morrison, A., R. White, E. Van Velsor, et al. *Breaking the Glass Ceiling*. Reading, MA: Addison-Wesley, 1987.

Nicholson, N., and M. West. *Managerial Job Change: Men and Women in Transition*. Cambridge: Cambridge University Press, 1988.

Osland, J. *The Adventure of Working Abroad*. San Francisco: Jossey-Bass, 1995.

Pfeffer, J. "The Ambiguity of Leadership." In *Leadership: Where Else Can We Go?* edited by M. McCall and M. Lombardo. Durham, NC: Duke University Press, 1978.

Pfeffer, J., and R. Sutton. *Hard Facts, Dangerous Half-Truths and Total Nonsense*. Boston: Harvard Business School Press, 2006.

Pinker, S. *The Blank Slate*. New York: Penguin, 2002.

Spreitzer, G., M. McCall, and J. Mahoney. "Early Identification of International Executive Potential." *Journal of Applied Psychology* 82, no. 1 (1997): 6–29.

Stewart, R. *Managers and Their Jobs*. London: Macmillan, 1967.

Storti, C. *The Art of Crossing Cultures*. Yarmouth, ME: Intercultural Press, 1990.

Van Gennep, A. *The Rites of Passage*. Chicago: University of Chicago Press, 1960.

Welch, D. "Toughest Job Yet for This Mr. Fixit." *BusinessWeek*, November 15, 2004, 72–74.

Yost, P.R., and M.M. Plunkett. *Real Time Leadership Development*. Malden, MA: Wiley-Blackwell, 2009.

24

LEADERSHIP DEVELOPMENT INTERVENTIONS

Ensuring a Return on the Investment

Jay A. Conger

A COMMON LAMENT among executives is that their organizations suffer from a shortage of leadership talent. As a result, a broad range of initiatives has appeared over the last two decades to address this critical gap. Yet many of these initiatives appear to have failed. The causes are many and complex (Ready and Conger, 2003). For example, many companies fail to support their development initiatives with corresponding rewards and ongoing support. In some organizations, the cause is too little time and too few resources devoted to leadership development in general. In others, a one-time administration of a 360-degree feedback assessment may be the scope of a manager's formal developmental feedback. Opportunities for professional coaching may be limited to the seniormost executives. A new CEO may radically alter leadership development initiatives, undermining prior investments. For these and other reasons, formal approaches to leadership development have never had the impact that their champions, designers, and sponsors aspire to have.

When deployed in a comprehensive manner with a commitment to the long term, leadership development initiatives can and should play a critical role in deepening the bench of leadership talent of an organization

(Conger and Fulmer, 2003). At a very minimum, programs can heighten managers' appreciation for leadership and in turn strengthen their resolve to develop certain leadership capabilities. In the best case, initiatives can facilitate a common and widespread understanding of the organization's vision and culture and clarify the leadership roles and responsibilities required to advance both. Initiatives can also help with critical leadership transitions by integrating training with job promotions and working to address derailing behaviors. Programs can also help to build champions to lead critical strategic transitions. But they must be well designed in content and process, tightly aligned to the organization's strategy, and supported by talent systems. This chapter explores how formal leadership education and development initiatives can best be deployed to achieve these kinds of impact. It examines the range of approaches and the trade-offs unique to each. It also examines the practices that enhance an initiative's effectiveness as well as identifies common implementation pitfalls facing programs. Before we dive into the different approaches, it is helpful to first explore their historical roots. This examination will frame the evolution of and illustrate the sophistication in our current approaches to leadership development.

Leadership Development: How Far We Have Come

Looking back thirty or forty years ago, leadership development for front-line and middle-level leaders consisted largely of workshops offered by specialized training organizations or in-house training departments. Many of these were built around a simple leadership model, such as Situational Leadership, developed by Paul Hershey and Kenneth Blanchard (Hershey and Blanchard, 1984). Guided by a diagnostic questionnaire, participants would learn that successful leadership involved tailoring one's style to the dynamics of a particular situation. For example, in certain situations, leaders needed to focus more on the task at hand. In other situations, they needed to be more people-oriented. Training, in essence, was designed to help managers assess their situations and then apply the appropriate leadership behavior.

For the more senior levels of leadership, leadership development typically consisted of attendance at a university-based program outside the corporation. Individual managers would attend these programs, which could last anywhere from one week to several months. The learning experience was largely teacher or professor centered, using off-the-shelf case studies, readings, and exercises as instructional vehicles. Participants learned about the latest theories and research by studying what other companies had done and listening to lectures on faculty research. The content was determined primarily by the faculty or training organization and was often more of a mini-MBA than a pure focus on leadership.

During this time, leadership education had primarily a dual role. One was to help managers transition into upcoming roles by broadening their understanding of the business disciplines outside of their functional silos as well as their understanding of the role of leadership. The second was as a reward for "up and comers"—individuals we today call "high potentials." In this era, there was limited customization of learning materials to either organizations or managers, and the leadership models they introduced were relatively simplistic. Executive coaching did exist, but it was primarily reserved for executives whose management styles were highly dysfunctional. Job assignments were considered the primary grooming grounds for leadership. Formal developmental feedback was provided in performance reviews by one's superior and possibly in developmental reviews. Peers and subordinates had few vehicles through which to provide direct feedback to an individual leader unless it was solicited by individual managers themselves.

Also popular during this time period was a more radical form of leadership education called sensitivity training, in the form of encounter groups or T-groups. Whereas university training focused on conceptual or cognitive learning, sensitivity training targeted the manager's interpersonal behavior. In small groups at retreat centers, managers engaged in group dialogues under the supervision of facilitators. There was often no set agenda other than personal and group discovery. Participants learned about themselves as they dealt with group members through the dialogues that emerged. They learned directly from experiencing and reflecting on the needs, attitudes, and interpersonal behaviors that participants demonstrated in the group setting. In contrast to university learning, this was a highly learner-centered experience and relied to a large degree on intense reflection of one's interpersonal style. These experiences were forerunners to the more structured and less emotionally demanding self-assessment tools and action learning experiences of the 1990s and beyond. The experiences also had parallels to the development of what we today call "emotional intelligence" (Goleman, 1996).

Starting in the 1980s, however, the field of leadership development experienced a critical transition. Important shifts were induced by intensifying global competition in the business world. This dynamic drove companies to search for educational experiences that could simultaneously build leadership capability as well as source and speed solutions to the organization's strategic challenges. Suddenly, leadership initiatives had to prove they could deliver more tangible and immediate returns. Under these conditions, the idea of sending one or two managers off to a university program to study cases written about other industries appeared to be a poor choice. The open-enrollment character of university-based programs meant that coursework and materials could not be tailored to a single company or industry. Interest, therefore, grew dramatically in highly customized, in-company programs. You might say we left the Bronze Age of leadership development and entered the Iron Age.

Economics played an important role. As the drive for greater operating efficiencies encouraged corporate cost-cutting, budgets for education and development received more scrutiny. There was strong pressure to show more immediate and tangible paybacks for investments in formal development programs. The economics of customized, in-company programs quickly became more attractive. After all, bringing four university professors in to teach fifty managers was a significantly less expensive proposition than sending fifty managers to open-enrollment programs. Indeed, the growth in customized programs was so strong that by the middle 1990s it was estimated that more than 75 percent of all executive education dollars were spent on these programs (Fulmer and Vicere, 1995).

Other benefits followed with customized programs. Topics and materials could be tailored to the company's needs. CEOs began to realize that programs could be deployed to reinforce companies' cultures and to drive their strategic agendas. They could use leadership development initiatives to create a cadre of change agent leaders. This growing focus on using programs to drive change also helped to promote the educational format of action learning. The approach was popularized by General Electric in programs run at the corporate university in Crotonville, New York. These programs placed managers in team-based experiential exercises aimed at solving real-life problems of immediate relevance to the company (Noel and Charan, 1988). For example, a business unit might be considering new markets in Malaysia.

Action learning teams would conduct market research on these emerging markets. Participants would test ideas for business development, address implementation issues, and present recommendations for company initiatives to company executives. Action learning also incorporated another, more general trend in leadership education: team-based learning, whose roots could be traced back to the earlier sensitivity training.

During this time, 360-degree feedback tools rose in popularity. As leadership concepts and education gained greater currency, it became clear that the "followers" (subordinates) of leaders should share their views on their leaders' effectiveness. With the rise of the organizational matrix and greater cross-functional collaboration, it also became clear that peers would have useful views on the effectiveness of a manager's leadership style. The rise of 360-degree feedback assessments encouraged greater use of competency models built solely around leadership behaviors. Organizations soon had lists of the leadership behaviors they expected their managers to live out.

In conclusion, the role and scope of formalized approaches to leadership development have changed dramatically in the last two decades. Initiatives are far more pervasive and less elitist. The best are designed around an understanding that leadership development is a continuous, lifelong process rather than a single event or program. They deploy more interventions—action learning, coaching, education, feedback assessments, and formal coaching (Conger and Fulmer, 2003; Fulmer and Conger, 2004)—and they do so more intensely. Initiatives are better integrated with the actual work of the organization and better integrated with organizational support systems such as performance management, rewards, and succession. They also involve far more stakeholders than the approaches of yesterday. The best initiatives strive to advance the strategic and cultural objectives of the organization while simultaneously developing a deep bench of leadership talent.

The following sections examine how the target population of formal leadership initiatives has also evolved. In earlier days, there was a more singular emphasis on individual development. Today's more sophisticated approaches strive to do far more. They attempt to develop cadres of managers and to enlist company leaders in strategic change. What follows is a typology of today's approaches along with guidance on best practices and common implementation pitfalls.

A Typology of Formal Leadership Development Approaches

Formal leadership development initiatives can be organized into four general categories: (1) individual skill development, (2) socialization of the corporate vision and values, (3) strategic interventions that facilitate a major strategic shift throughout an organization, and (4) targeted action learning designed to address specific organizational challenges and opportunities.

Individual skill development has the oldest roots of the four approaches. Its primary aim has been to help managers learn the essential concepts and skills of leadership. The second approach seeks to socialize the corporate vision, values, and mission of an organization throughout its leadership ranks. In recent years, this has become an immensely popular approach. The third approach—facilitating a major strategic change—is the least common of the four but potentially the one with the most significant payoffs for the organization. These educational experiences focus on building a cadre of change agents who are engaged in implementing organizational initiatives that facilitate and accelerate a major strategic change. The emphasis is on having participants take ownership for leading change initiatives at their level of the organization. The fourth approach—action learning—uses team-based projects that explore opportunities or dilemmas facing the organization as a development vehicle for mid- to senior-level leaders. We examine each of the four approaches in the discussions that follow.

Individual Leadership Development Interventions

Leadership is often conceived of as an individual capability; therefore, not so surprisingly, leadership development has long emphasized learning at the individual level. For example, leadership experts such as James Kouzes and Barry Posner (1987) argue that leadership development is very much about "finding your own voice." The objective of this approach has been to expose developing leaders to the essential and often behavioral dimensions of leadership, have them reflect on their capabilities along these dimensions, and in turn stimulate their desire to seek out developmental experiences. Individually oriented programs tend to be relatively short and employ a variety of development methods. Such formal programs can provide one of the few windows for managers to objectively look at their own leadership style in a low-risk environment. Studies have shown that these programs can encourage self-evaluation and insight (Schmitt, Ford, and Stults, 1986)—factors that in turn can lead to improved individual performance.

To illustrate the design of a program focused on individual development, the example of one program developed for a manufacturing business will be used. Two professors, experts in leadership, were hired to design and deliver the program. The leadership framework for the course was derived from research by the professors. It consisted of four dimensions: leadership vision, communications capabilities, role-modeling behavior, and motivational/empowerment approaches. On the first day of the program, a 360-degree survey feedback assessment based on the four dimensions provided participants with benchmark data on their own capabilities related to each dimension. Case studies, practice sessions, and reflective exercises conveyed and taught the four dimensions in some depth. The emphasis was on individual participants' learning and mastery of the leadership framework.

BEST PRACTICES FOR INDIVIDUAL DEVELOPMENT PROGRAMS

The following best-practice dimensions are essential for success in the deployment of these types of programs.

1. *Build the program around a single well-delineated leadership model.* Research confirms that a well-defined and simple model or framework of leadership improves participants' learning (Fulmer and Conger, 2004; Conger and Benjamin, 1999). In contrast, the use of multiple models increases the probability that participants will forget essential components or find themselves confused about the different frameworks. Multiple models make it more difficult to cover individual dimensions in depth. In other words, the number of different dimensions hinders a genuine and deep understanding of any one. This results in participants having difficulty gaining mastery over individual dimensions. In contrast, a single model provides a clear focus for both participants and designers, makes for tighter alignment of learning materials as well as assessment tools, and removes the probability of conflicting points of view.

The more effective models are typically built around a set of tangible leadership behaviors or competencies. Competencies, in turn, form the skill categories that participants learn in exercises and on which they receive personalized feedback. Later in this chapter, I will discuss the distinct advantages and disadvantages of competency-based programs.

2. *Conduct pre-course preparation.* By sending out exercises and materials in advance that encourage participants to reflect on their leadership, pre-course preparation can heighten an appreciation for the upcoming learning experience. It can also facilitate potential links between the daily challenges of participants and the development program that lies ahead. Although an obvious point, it is of course critical that the course experiences link directly to the pre-course work. Ideally the pre-course work should be a combination of reflective and workplace application exercises as well as preparation for actual course experiences.

3. *Use multiple learning methods.* Adult learning theory shows that individuals differ in their learning styles. Some learn best from experiential exercises, others from reflective methods, and others from traditional classroom methods. Multiple learning methods increase the likelihood that at least one, if not several, methods will be compatible with an individual participant's style (Conger, 1992). Also, learning occurs at several levels. For instance, it is useful to have a conceptual/cognitive understanding of the basic roles and activities of leadership. At the same time, there are behavioral skills that the learner can acquire through actual practice and experimentation. Personalized feedback is useful to target the learner's attention and awareness. Learning that taps into the psychological and emotional needs of individuals is also necessary to stimulate their interest in seeking out developmental experiences after a formal program.

4. *Structure learning around extended learning periods and multiple sessions.* Research on the transfer of learning from training shows that information gleaned over distributed periods of training is generally retained longer than that from a one-time

formal program (Naylor and Briggs, 1963). Furthermore, feedback-oriented programs that span multiple periods appear to move participants from awareness to an increased probability of effecting change in their behavior and perspectives (Young and Dixon, 1996).

The research that sheds the greatest light on why extended and multiple periods of learning are required for developing leadership comes from a growing body of research on how individuals become experts in different fields. Becoming an expert takes time. Ten years of experiences appears to be the norm, and often the period is longer (Ericsson, Krampe, and Tesch-Romer, 1993). During this extended time, developmental experiences must take place that involve deliberate, focused, and repeated practice (Ericsson and Charness, 1994). Practice ensures the acquisition of critical tacit knowledge. It must be learned through multiple and varied exposures to the area in which one is to become an expert. The expertise literature makes an important distinction between exposure to knowledge and deliberate practice or application. Exposure does not suffice. Training built around a few days of practice is insufficient. It takes a longer-term orientation with multiple, focused sessions occurring over a period of years.

5. *Support learning with organizational processes.* One of the common dilemmas facing participants who return from formal programs is a lack of reinforcement for exhibiting the leadership behaviors taught in the program. To succeed, organizations must align their performance management systems to incorporate the demonstration of leadership behavior. There must be extrinsic and intrinsic rewards for exhibiting leadership behavior.

The attitudes and styles of superiors are a critical factor in the transfer of learning. In fact, studies (e.g., Huczynski and Lewis, 1980) that examine the factors that facilitate or inhibit learning show that the participant's application of new learnings on the job is largely dependent on his or her superior's support. Through praise, incentives, coaching, feedback, and challenging assignments, the supervisor can reinforce the leadership behavior of his or her subordinates. To further motivate learning, superiors can discuss program learning and benefits both beforehand and afterward as well as set action goals for the individual concerning learning and implementing specific behaviors or actions. The superior's own role modeling can also influence subordinates' behavior (Sims and Manz, 1982). In the ideal case, superiors would model behavior that is congruent with the development initiative's emphasis. Finally, supervisors can support new behaviors through rewards and by providing opportunities to practice new skills. Work assignments following training experiences can reinforce and deepen learnings. Yet rarely is this connection made.

COMMON PROBLEMS WITH INDIVIDUAL DEVELOPMENT APPROACHES

If an organization wishes to expand its cadre of leaders, the individual development approach can be a relatively slow path to achieving this outcome. Skills-based programs may focus so much on one's personal development that they overlook opportunities to instill company philosophies or to tie leadership to new company strategies and their implementation. These are but a few of the common shortcomings of initiatives focused on individual development. What follows is a description of the most common design pitfalls. Several of these are also problems associated with other types of leadership development initiatives.

1. *Failure to build a critical mass.* One of the principal drawbacks of individual development programs is that they are not always geared to cohorts of individuals from a single workplace— especially programs offered outside the organization, such as at universities. When participants return, they may discover that their learning is little appreciated or understood by others. The dilemma is tied to the fact that work is a collaborative experience. As Brown and Duguid (1991) have shown, an individual's learning is inseparable from the collective learning of their work group.

   What gives new learning and insights the potential for taking hold is that one's work group also endorses, promotes, and reinforces them. Without social support and group pressure, new ideas and behaviors may receive neither sufficient reinforcement nor rewards to survive for long. Moreover, an integral part of a workplace learning community is a shared language and a set of stories about what is valued (Brown and Duguid, 1991). If only a single individual or a handful of individuals attends a program, there may not be a sufficient mass of participants returning to the workplace to fully spread the learning. Having no experience with the development lessons, coworkers will have little comprehension or appreciation for the knowledge and language that participants might share with them. As a result, the normally powerful influence of the workplace community is hindered from both spreading and reinforcing an individual's learning.

2. *Limits of competency-based leadership models.* Although competency models are the foundation for most initiatives, there are at least three characteristics of competency-based programs that pose dilemmas for leadership development. Their dimensions can be complicated, conceptual, and built around past or current realities (Conger and Ready, 2004). Because many of the frameworks themselves are based on research on a wide range of managerial and leadership behaviors, there is a tendency for them to be complicated—in other words, to contain many dimensions. For example, it is not uncommon for some competency frameworks to contain between thirty to fifty or more different behaviors. This creates a program with complicated content. Yet it is far from clear whether managers can focus developmentally on more than a few behaviors at a given time. Certain coaching experts argue that managers can and should focus on only one to two behaviors at most (Goldsmith, 2003). Although programs built around multiple competencies may capture the complex reality of leadership, they dilute not only the attention they get but also an understanding of which competencies are priorities for the individual's current role or situation.

   From a program design perspective, a large number of competencies may similarly lessen an appreciation for the real priorities. In his autobiography, Louis Gerstner Jr. (2002), who was chairman and CEO of IBM from 1993 until 2002, describes his experience with the firm's use of a competency model to drive changes in leadership behavior within the company. Using a set of eleven competencies (customer insight, breakthrough thinking, drive to achieve, team leadership, straight talk, teamwork, decisiveness, building organizational capability, coaching, personal dedication, and passion for the business), training and evaluation was designed to reinforce these behaviors with the aim of producing a new culture at IBM. Although Gerstner did indeed witness changes in behavior and focus as an outcome, he concluded there were simply too many competencies. In the end, they were clustered into three categories: win, execute, and team. Thus, although competencies played a role in developing a new generation of leaders at IBM, the model was simplified. That said, Gerstner did find that they created a common language, a sense of consistency, and a basis for performance management and rewards.

The second limitation is that competency-centric programs are based on an idealized concept of leadership—in other words, the concept of a universal best-in-class leader capable of functioning across all situations. Few managers are outstanding examples of the full range of leadership behaviors that these models promote. As a result, they reinforce the notion of a "perfect" leader, and such individuals rarely exist in reality. Moreover, to ensure the advantage of consistency, organizations have moved toward universal competency models for their leadership development programs. Yet a "universal" model fails to recognize that leadership requirements vary by level and by situation. For example, leadership skills at the executive level are often significantly different from those at the midlevel ranks. Different functions and operating units may also demand different leadership capabilities given their unique requirements.

Most important, the underlying assumption behind the conceptualization of competency models of leadership is that an effective leader is the sum of a set of competencies (Hollenbeck and McCall, 2002). This does not reflect the reality of the manager's world (for a debate of this issue, see Hollenbeck, McCall, and Silzer, 2006). The logic of these models follows that if we develop each competency to the point of mastery one after the other, a manager will emerge as a successful leader.

Morgan McCall and George Hollenbeck, two experts on leadership development, argue that there are a myriad of ways of accomplishing a leader's job, especially at the executive level: "No two CEOs do the same things much less in the same ways, or have the same competencies. To define especially executive leadership around nine or ten universal behavioral dimensions oversimplifies a highly complex role. This conclusion is not only obvious on its face, it is evident when we observe outstanding leaders, whether military officers, heads of states, or CEOs—one cannot but be struck by the differences rather than the similarities in their makeup" (Hollenbeck and McCall, 2002).

At best, there is a loose coupling between the results a leader achieves along with the means to those results and any specific set of behaviors and competencies. McCall and Hollenbeck argue that the focus of developmental needs must move away from behavioral models to "strategic demands." Organizations need their senior leaders to define the strategy of the business and from there identify the leadership challenges implied by these objectives. Experiences could then be identified that provide sufficient preparation for managers to meet such strategic challenges. Succession management processes would begin by focusing on the essential question: what types of jobs, special assignments, bosses, and education are needed to build the leadership capability to successfully achieve our business strategy? These experiences would be identified and safeguarded by the senior team as essential to the succession management process.

The last concern is that competency-centric programs tend to be focused on past or current leadership behaviors—in other words, their frameworks are developed using today's high-performing leaders as benchmarks. Moreover, the models themselves tend to stabilize themselves in organizational systems—after all, they require extensive resource and psychological investments as performance and feedback systems are revised, managers are educated in the new models, and new expectations are set for the behavior that will be rewarded. Unfortunately, the competencies that helped current leaders succeed may not be appropriate for the next generation of leaders. Younger leaders may require different competencies for the challenges ahead, and yet they may be trained and rewarded for today's competencies.

3. *Insufficient time spent on developing individual skill areas.* One of the most common dilemmas facing individual leadership development initiatives is the lack of follow-up. When the program ends, there may be no additional experiences to reinforce learning or ongoing programs of feedback to gauge their development efforts regarding specific leadership competencies. Many of the problems related to follow-up initiatives can be traced back to the issues of ownership, time, and rewards. For example, who claims responsibility for learning after a program is over? Who makes certain that learning gets extended throughout the organization?

   Often the burden of ownership falls on both the program designers and leaders and on the participants. But in many cases these groups do not control the needed resources or have the political clout necessary to make changes in the structures and systems of the organization. In addition, follow-up assignments are commonly done in one's spare time, beyond normal working hours. As a result, they rarely receive the time and dedication needed to succeed. Rewards may be limited or nonexistent for one's follow-up efforts. It is critical that organizations accept greater responsibility for post-program activities. This means providing a method of monitoring participants' progress toward meeting certain prescribed development goals. One solution to the follow-up dilemma is to provide participants with formal coaching and mentoring. Another is to hold the boss accountable for the individual's development progress.

Socializing Leadership Vision and Values Interventions

One of the most important functions of senior leaders is to define and reinforce the strategic parameters and cultural values that will guide the decisions and actions of organizational members. Executives instill these by building a shared understanding of what the organization is about and how it should operate. It is important that the next generation of leaders accurately understand and embody the vision and values that they are expected to perpetuate. Recognizing this, these leadership development initiatives focus on socializing crucial strategic and cultural elements. They do so with two broad objectives in mind: to indoctrinate leaders to the company's core vision and cultural values and to facilitate career transitions by involving leaders in a dialogue about their upcoming roles and responsibilities. These initiatives try to build a shared interpretation of the organization's key strategic objectives and a commitment to the values and assumptions that underlie its culture. Consequently, they focus less on developing individual skills and talents and more on imparting a collective sense of culture and a leadership philosophy that are acted upon as much as they are acknowledged.

The U.S. Army's approach to leadership development exemplifies this particular model. For example, the Army strongly emphasizes its leadership culture in almost every program and operational assignment that officers take part in. More important than its formal doctrine and programs, the informal mentoring and role modeling by Army officers along with on-the-job training experiences instill the leadership in the culture and daily activities of Army life. Through an extensive socialization process, officers learn and internalize the Army's leadership creed through years of direct interaction with more experienced leaders. Through this integrated approach of formal classroom instruction, on-the-job training, informal mentoring, role modeling, and self-development, the Army leadership development system clarifies and reinforces the Army's vision and leadership values along with the duties and expectations associated with carrying them out at each level of management.

BEST PRACTICES FOR SOCIALIZING VISION AND VALUES INITIATIVES

Certain design features enhance the effectiveness of such initiatives designed for socialization of an organization's leaders. Following are descriptions of the best-practice features and their contribution to the socialization process.

1. *Select program participants carefully.* Leadership programs aimed at socialization must pay particular attention to the selection of program participants. These programs ideally seek to provide leadership development primarily to those individuals who have demonstrated significant leadership potential through their past performance and who do or can embody the values and styles consistent with the existing leadership culture. Selectivity

increases the probability that participants will hold values similar to the stated values of the corporation. Such consistency serves to strengthen communication both within the learning environment and later, when the participant returns to the job. Second, selecting only those individuals who consistently demonstrate certain traits and values confirms that such characteristics are critical to the organization and that they will be rewarded. This encourages other managers to develop similar capabilities.

2. *Ensure a well-articulated organizational vision and philosophy.* Although this point seems obvious, I have seen organizations fail on this dimension. Programs cannot effectively socialize a corporate vision and philosophy if the organization itself is conflicted about its own vision and values or if these entities are in flux and in question. It is therefore crucial that the organization possess a vision and value set that are reasonably well articulated and well lived by leaders.

3. *Have practicing leaders provide instruction.* Although a well-known leadership expert can provide insight into the latest theories on leadership, outside experts typically have less to say about the strategies and practices that work well for one's own firm. Moreover, outsiders are likely to have superficial knowledge about the firm's culture and history. Using organizational leaders as instructors facilitates the socialization of junior leaders in a number of ways. First, by providing interaction with leaders who embody the company's values and live its philosophy, the company offers living role models of the ideology it hopes to perpetuate through successive generations. Second, using practicing leaders ensures that learning remains grounded in the reality of the workplace and culture. Leaders directly convey their beliefs, experience, and expectations to program participants, thereby facilitating the transmission of cultural knowledge. Finally, a system of leaders teaching leaders creates a two-way exchange of information and learning. By increasing interaction between new and existing leaders, leadership development programs can improve the probability that new information and insight will be properly integrated within the firm's culture.

4. *Move beyond singular initiatives.* To be truly successful, socialization of leadership capabilities depends on continual, progressive, and sequential development. A single program cannot be sufficient. In addition, organizational leaders must be unified in their understanding of the corporate vision and in the values considered important in achieving the vision. Organizational systems need to be properly aligned to send consistent messages about what is valued and what is not. Consistent work processes, performance metrics, succession systems, promotions, and reward systems must maximize the probability that the values and assumptions instilled during the development program will be reinforced and supported once leaders return to the job.

Common Problems with Socialization Initiatives

Socialization programs hold the promise of embedding a company's vision and values deep into its cadre of leaders, but they are difficult to implement and require a long-term commitment from senior executives. They can also be expensive, as they are often supported by an in-house educational center such as General Electric's Crotonville and FedEx's Leadership Institute. Following are descriptions of common problems facing these types of initiatives.

1. *Participant selection criteria are poorly defined or enforced.* As noted earlier, participants for these types of programs are selected on their ability to demonstrate leadership behaviors and to embody the organization's values. In reality, selection criteria are often poorly defined or poorly enforced. Maintaining a focused selection process means that those responsible for nominating and selecting participants must clearly understand and support the selection criteria and the rationale behind them. They must be able to apply these criteria reliably and concretely when making judgments about potential candidates. Selection often becomes muddied as programs begin to develop a reputation. People watch to see who attends programs and what promotion opportunities present themselves to graduates. Once a program is perceived as a critical marker that participants are on a fast track, managers can begin to plot how to get themselves into such programs. At the other end of the spectrum, programs may be viewed as

a fad or simply a waste of time. In this case, managers work hard to exempt themselves from nominations to a program. Who is chosen to nominate can also pose a challenge. For example, senior executives may be the nominators, but they may have limited information on those they nominate, especially if candidates are several levels below them. Similarly, programs that focus on new directions may involve senior-level nominators who themselves are not necessarily advocates of the new direction.

2. *Hidden challenges in using company executives as teachers.* It would be a mistake to assume that company leaders do indeed make the best instructors or that their use is not without special challenges. Several important dilemmas must be addressed with executive instructors. They need to be role models for leadership. They should have "icon status" within the organization. In contrast, when executives who are poor role models are used for instruction in programs, they often generate cynicism among program participants and in turn undermine the credibility of the program itself. Beyond the dilemma of poor role models, there is the risk that company insiders will reinforce organizational paradigms and worldviews. If the external environment is changing rapidly and moving away from the organization's paradigm, this reinforcement from senior leaders could inhibit the organization's ability to adapt. One approach would be to choose iconoclastic leaders with a track record of being at the forefront of important trends. With rare exceptions, executive instructors and their message should not be the driving factor behind a program design. Rather, the internal and external leadership needs of the organization should be the primary design drivers.

Preparation of the executive instructor, his or her materials, and instruction formats all need careful attention. The program designer must be prepared to coach the executive instructor on certain common problems. For example, part of the designer's task is to convince the executive instructor that effective learning best occurs when the participants are involved in dialogue. Executive instructors must learn to allow participants to reach their own conclusions rather than to simply feed them information and points of view. Program designers need to sit in during program sessions and provide executive instructors with feedback on their teaching style, participant reactions to content, how discussions are progressing, and session timing.

3. *Organizational downturns or serious business challenges undermine programs.* It is not unusual in a business downturn for leadership development budgets to be among the first to be cut. As a result, socialization initiatives can often die out. Importantly, a symbolic message is sent throughout the organization that the values and leadership behaviors were perhaps not as essential as employees were led to believe. Crises can produce events that undermine the very behaviors and values that organizations are socializing.

Strategic Leadership Interventions

Leaders today face a marketplace characterized by change and great complexity. There are strong indications that learning how to lead the direction, intensity, and speed of strategic and organizational change will be the key driver of corporate success in the years ahead. Moreover, this learning will be required not only of the organization's most senior leaders but of leaders at all levels. No longer will executives be able to rely on simply top-down command-and-control tactics. A more collaborative form of leadership is required to successfully implement strategic change initiatives.

As a result, some organizations are deploying leadership development interventions to address strategic shifts and the leadership capabilities required for their successful implementation. This approach is more customized and tightly integrated to the organization's strategic agenda. These programs facilitate efforts to communicate and implement the corporate strategy, to build strategic unity throughout the organization, and to create a cadre of change agents. In other words, they simultaneously build leadership capabilities while facilitating progress toward critical strategic objectives.

An illustrative example would be an initiative deployed by a European technology company for the radical repositioning of its strategy to close performance gaps with its competition. The company wanted to engage approximately a quarter of a million employees spread across fifty-two countries. The leadership initiative was built around three components. First was an effort to translate the new corporate vision into local goals and programs. Some thirty thousand leaders representing the top four levels of the company were brought together in groups of thirty to seventy for a three-day program. These leadership team meetings translated the company's new strategic vision of the change process into actions and goals for the business units and product divisions. The second component involved twenty-two task forces examining important aspects of the company's strategy, marketing, research, products, and management skills. This initiative identified and addressed issues that were the key drivers for the future strategy. Each task force was headed by a champion who had a track record of performance in the area being examined. This component reached some two hundred thousand employees, using up to four hundred town meetings at each plant to discuss the implications of the strategic change for individual work situations. The third component involved two separate days of interactive satellite discussions for the entire European workforce. The first session day was held soon after the start of the overall initiative, and the second session day occurred one and a half years later. These sessions focused on how the company could become more customer focused and quality driven. As this example illustrates, these types of strategic initiatives are very ambitious and often involve the entire organization.

BEST PRACTICES FOR STRATEGIC LEADERSHIP INITIATIVES

To the extent that an organization's senior leaders have a clearly defined change agenda and the accompanying change leadership requirements, these programs can be extremely effective mechanisms for rapidly building a shared sense of the new strategic vision and a cadre of change agents. Certain design elements, however, are critical for success. These include the following.

1. *Ensure that a clear strategic framework drives program content and design.* The foundational feature of these programs is a clearly articulated strategic framework that guides the organization's collective efforts. If the new strategy is vague or clouded by competing initiatives, the development effort will simply surface underlying conflicts, create frustration, and ultimately increase opposition to the change effort. In short, these programs should be undertaken only when there is a consensus regarding the strategic agenda or vision.

2. *Ensure that the strategy is translated into corresponding leadership behaviors and mind-sets and company capabilities and culture.* Once the new strategy is clear, a critical second step must take place: clarifying the behaviors and mind-sets that company leaders must embody to implement the strategy successfully and to create a noticeable competitive advantage in behavior, organizational capability, and culture. For this reason, off-the-shelf leadership competency models will not work. The initiative must identify and ingrain a handful of distinctive leadership behaviors that deliver on the promise of the new strategy. Of the three approaches mentioned to this point, the strategic leadership initiatives require the greatest degree of alignment with supporting organizational systems and processes to ensure that the new leadership behaviors are adopted with consistency throughout the organization.

3. *Design the curriculum to elicit group discussions between units and across levels.* These initiatives are highly dependent on individuals coming together, sharing experiences, and jointly constructing a common interpretation of the information and events around them. Group discussions across functions and levels are critical for developing a common understanding of a firm's larger strategic vision and, in turn, a shared interpretation of how that vision can be implemented at the local level. Because strategic implementation efforts require a complicated transition from abstract ideas to clearly defined directives and goals, facilitated group discussions are essential for determining how an organization's strategy can unfold to become an effective course of action. The best programs therefore include multiple sessions built around discussions that generate support for the new strategy and its leadership requirements but that also effectively translate the overarching strategy into tangible local initiatives.

4. *Deploy trained facilitators to provide critical process assistance.* Given that much of what occurs in these initiatives is through discussions, well-designed programs employ trained facilitators. With discussions centered on issues that are complex and charged, facilitators keep the participants focused and

constructive in their conclusions. They are also instrumental in organizing and codifying group discussions and in keeping groups from getting distracted by tangential issues. The facilitators ideally not only enhance group process but also challenge and push participants to think in different ways. In particular, outside facilitators can challenge status quo thinking and implicit assumptions when participants may be unable or uncomfortable to do so. Moreover, facilitators can model for the participants effective team facilitation skills. Finally, they can serve as nonthreatening providers of information across the organization. They can bridge gaps in information and disseminate information more broadly through their sessions with participants.

5. *Cascade the learning experiences down and across multiple levels and operations.* A multilevel approach is necessary. This ensures that all levels of the organization have a consistent understanding of the organization's strategic direction, the leadership demands in light of that direction, and the implementation steps essential to moving the organization forward. This is called "cascading initiatives." In other words, there are similar initiatives running at each level of the organization's hierarchy, often in tandem. They use the same methodology but are seeking outcomes specifically tailored to each level. In the best cases, these initiatives overlap levels so that senior- and middle-level leaders are interacting with one another in the same program. Cascading initiatives powerfully helps to translate what a particular vision or change initiative means to leaders to each level. Research (Finkelstein and Hambrick, 1996) shows that senior leaders are generally too far removed from day-to-day operations to determine the best ways to implement the vision in every unit, function, and situation. By cascading an initiative down into the organization, frontline leaders can determine the most appropriate local structures, strategies, and tactics for their level and in turn feel a greater sense of ownership. Cascading can also ensure better integration across levels when senior leaders actively participate in conveying their own understandings to those below them. Finally, by discussing the vision, encouraging comments,

answering questions, and incorporating feedback, senior leaders demonstrate their commitment to the change agenda and model for others the types of behavior necessary for interactions with the next level.

6. *Put in place continuous or real-time feedback mechanisms.* It is critical to be able to monitor the reactions of program participants to implementation challenges and to track the progress of initiatives in meeting objectives and timelines. Active feedback approaches can take a variety of forms, including direct interaction, follow-up interviews, and surveys. Methods that allow a greater flow of information and ideas are the best. Regardless of the form, it is critical to gather feedback from a representative sample of participants across the organization. This ensures that the information gathered provides an accurate picture of how the program is being received and adapted. Technology can play an important role in this feedback process via online discussions and intranet forums and surveys.

Common Problems with Strategic Leadership Initiatives

These types of initiatives tend to be extremely complicated and demanding. The greatest risk is that they will be seen as a discrete event or set of events rather than as part of an ongoing change process. They also raise expectations. Employees leave with a sense of momentum, which places a burden on the program sponsors and designers to maintain the energy and focus of the initiative. The following are additional pitfalls common to strategic leadership initiatives.

1. *Poor modeling by corporate leaders.* Given the overriding emphasis on the strategic direction of the organization, these programs tend to raise expectations about the organization's senior leaders. They raise expectations that senior leaders will model the very behaviors and mind-sets that the program aims to instill in others. In addition, immediately following each stage of the initiative, employees will watch to see what initiatives emerge from the executive suite as tests of the senior team's commitment to the overall initiative. Modeling by top leaders becomes critical. In one organization, the CEO emphasized his commitment to two-way communications at the start of a strategic leadership initiative. The program itself

contained exercises illustrating how best to implement two-way communications. The CEO himself, however, failed to change his own behavior. As managers down the line continued to experience top-down, one-way communications, they discounted the initiative and in turn reinforced the old behaviors.

2. *Entrenched managers and the legacy of past relations limit program impact.* In any change effort, there are supporters and resisters. Because strategic intervention designs rely on local managers and their work groups, resisting managers can block the impact of learning initiatives in their units. Such managers can create intractable problems for an intervention initiative. For example, they may have a history of past relationships that prevent the interaction and dialogue needed to effect learning and change. In one company, supervisors in one unit boycotted a kickoff event and follow-up sessions. Their subordinates concluded that their own efforts to participate and to develop a local vision would be futile. It is therefore critical to both identify and engage managers who are likely to resist the initiative.

3. *Competing initiatives distract sponsor support.* The initial momentum created by these strategic initiatives may begin to wane as time passes. Senior leaders may turn their attention elsewhere even if they consider the program important. As the firm's top leaders become less directly involved, the momentum behind the program can begin to decrease. It is critical that senior leaders continually communicate their commitment and demonstrate it in follow-up initiatives. Otherwise, employees will see it as a one-time event or fad.

4. *Lack of consistent reinforcement.* For a number of reasons, many of these strategic development initiatives lack systematic follow-up and reinforcement. Program sponsors may be promoted or transferred or leave the organization. The daily challenges and time demands of a major change effort, added to one's regular work, can make individuals less supportive of subsequent events that require additional time and energy. The natural rhythms of the business cycle, as well as unexpected events such as mergers or market downturns, may divert attention to more immediate pressures. Finally, top management naïveté about the need for follow-up can lead to

a lack of reinforcement. That said, the best programs succeed because they ensure systemic change across a number of important support systems. Incentive systems, job assignments, performance measures, reporting relations, training, and organizational structures all may need to be realigned to support the larger change initiative.

5. *Limitations of facilitators.* Despite their advantages, facilitators are often in a precarious position. If they challenge too strenuously, they may jeopardize their own employment. They are also asked to help address issues yet are given few resources or formal power. Many facilitators are not strategy consultants and are generally limited in their ability to help teams develop more of a strategic mind-set.

Action Learning Development Interventions

Action learning describes developmental approaches in which participants learn by working on critical issues facing their own organization. These development formats involve a continuous process of learning and reflection built around working groups of colleagues. Most therefore emphasize learning by doing, are conducted in teams, address real organizational challenges or opportunities, place participants in a problem-solving mode, and require that team decisions be formally presented. For example, a typical action learning project might have participants conduct a team-based investigation of new markets for the organization's products or services.

The stages of an action learning experience are fairly standardized (Dotlich and Noel, 1998). Typically, after receiving project assignments and background materials, learning teams travel to locations where the issues reside and conduct other forms of field research. The participants have access to key managers involved in the issue. As their findings and recommendations progress, they are reviewed by consultants or advisors who identify gaps in the analysis and assist in mapping out concrete and viable recommendations. The conclusion of this effort results in presentations, often to the senior leaders of the business unit involved and sometimes to the organization's executives. From the standpoint of leadership development, the projects are used to ensure that up-and-coming leaders are exposed to the next generation of emerging issues and challenges facing the organization that require a broad enterprise perspective.

From the standpoint of critical design features, the following are essential: (1) careful selection of projects, (2) project outcomes that are clearly defined at the start, (3) multiple opportunities for reflection, (4) active involvement by senior management, and (5) expert facilitation, coaching, and consultation.

1. *Select projects with great care.* A thorough and rigorous approach to selecting projects is an imperative. Projects must have a direct link to a business imperative. The most valued experiences are those where teams are given responsibility for initiating a strategic shift or a significant organizational change or a new venture that the organization is committed to implementing. It is also important to ensure that projects are structured for success. In the ideal case, projects would also be chosen in which individual leadership development can be addressed while simultaneously tackling the business imperative. Finally, in selecting projects, there must be a clear sponsor of the project who is highly motivated to support the team and who has significant influence within the organization. In other words, the sponsor can ensure that the proposed solutions of the team can actually be implemented. Naturally, there needs to be a high probability that this individual will act upon the recommendations of the team.

2. *Be certain that project deliverables are extremely clear.* On the dimension of clearly defined outcomes, it is best to ensure that the sponsors be very clear at the front end about what their outcome expectations are for a successful project. Problems regarding outcomes often arise when there are joint sponsors. Each party may communicate different expectations. There can also be too many objectives or objectives that are hidden or in dispute among sponsors.

3. *Design multiple opportunities for reflection.* From the vantage point of participant learning, it is important that program designers incorporate multiple opportunities for reflective learning. Coaches, facilitators, company leaders, and teammates are all sources of useful feedback in action learning experiences. Feedback and reflection should be focused on as many different levels of learning as possible—from lessons

about the issue being explored to team processes to individual reactions and styles. Reflections should also be staged at regular intervals rather than just at the end of the program.

4. *Ensure active involvement by senior management.* The importance of active senior management direction, support, and feedback cannot be overemphasized. Participants often expect some form of special recognition for their investment of time and energy in their projects. Visible recognition by executives is one powerful form of recognition. Senior management participation signals the importance of the programs, rewards participants, and conveys to the larger organization that such programs are valued.

5. *Provide facilitation and coaching by topic experts.* Because a significant portion of the learning experience occurs in team-based discussions, facilitators and coaches play a vital role. Participants often find themselves bombarded by information. Facilitators help them process and structure information. They can also help the group more effectively utilize frameworks and concepts that coursework may introduce. They can help the group reflect on their process.

Common Problems with Action Learning Initiatives

The pitfalls that action learning programs face are numerous, from make-work projects that have little or no real meaning to a lack of follow-up on a team's recommendations by sponsors. The business units providing the projects must be committed to taking some form of action, which ranges from providing access to critical information and resources to getting support for project proposals to the actual implementation of recommendations. A lack of any of these can completely undermine the meaningfulness of the initiative.

Dysfunctional team dynamics are another common pitfall. Teams that do not develop strong norms of candor and include a diversity of perspectives typically produce inferior outcomes. Teams in which one individual or function dominates tend to produce far less insightful and innovative recommendations.

Finally, a failure to include follow-up learning is a common fault of many programs. Often when the action learning project ends, it is assumed that the learning ends—quite literally. There is an assumption that the learning has fully taken place. Yet nothing could be farther from the truth. Participants need to learn what actually happens to their recommendations. Which ones are implemented and why? Which ones are not implemented and why? What were common implementation challenges for the various recommendations and how did the recommendations need to be adapted to be useful?

Conclusion

If we think of leadership as a form of expertise, we can begin to appreciate the long gestation period required to successfully develop leaders. Research shows that experts in most fields require ten years of learning and development before they reach a state of true expertise. This means that senior leaders must appreciate the long time horizons required to truly develop their leadership talent. They must also look beyond simple solutions such as a three-day training program or the one-time administration of 360-degree feedback. The four leadership development approaches described above are only some of the complex and rich ways in which leaders are developed. Supplementing them must be the organization's talent management processes, performance management and reward systems, culture and core values, and the behaviors and actions of the senior team (Ready and Conger, 2007). These all profoundly influence the development of leadership talent within organizations. As a result, we cannot think of leadership as the product of an event or a particular program but rather as a deep commitment embodied in ongoing actions, systems, and values of the organization.

Although our knowledge of leadership development has advanced greatly in the last decade and a half, we still have much to learn. Research is needed that explores how robust the program design and derailment factors identified in this chapter are in terms of truly influencing positive outcomes. There are also likely to be numerous other design elements that have been overlooked. Thus, future research is needed to rigorously tease apart the many factors contributing to successful leadership development and to provide a deeper sense of the impact of individual dimensions.

In addition, we need to examine far more carefully the role of follow-up interventions. These would include after-program initiatives such as 360-degree feedback or coaching or boss/subordinate activities. Participants, their bosses, and their organizations are often distracted in their attention to development. This is a great tragedy because we know that development is an ongoing process. It never ends when a program or initiative ends. We must identify new and more enduring means for after-program development. We must move from seeing leadership development as an event to an ongoing process without an actual end.

References

Brown, J.S., and P. Duguid. "Organizational Learning and Communities-of-Practice: Towards a Unified View of Working, Learning, and Innovation." *Organizational Science* 2, no. 1 (1991): 40–57.

Conger, J.A. *Learning to Lead.* San Francisco: Jossey-Bass, 1992.

Conger, J.A., and B. Benjamin. *Building Leaders: How Successful Companies Develop the Next Generation.* San Francisco: Jossey-Bass, 1999.

Conger, J.A., and R.M. Fulmer. "Developing Your Leadership Pipeline." *Harvard Business Review* 81, no. 12 (December 2003): 76–84.

Conger, J.A., and D.A. Ready. "Rethinking Leadership Competencies." *Leader to Leader* (Spring 2004): 41–47.

Dotlich, D.L., and J.L. Noel. *Action Learning.* San Francisco: Jossey-Bass, 1998.

Ericsson, K.A., and N. Charness. "Expert Performance." *American Psychologist* 49, no. 8 (1994): 725–747.

Ericsson, K.A., R.T. Krampe, and C. Tesch-Romer. "The Role of Deliberate Practices in the Acquisition of Expert Performance." *Psychological Review* 100, no. 3 (1993): 363–406.

Finkelstein, S., and D.C. Hambrick. *Strategic Leadership.* St. Paul, MN: West Publishing, 1996.

Fulmer, R.M., and J.A. Conger. *Growing Your Company's Leaders: How Organizations Use Succession Management to Sustain Competitive Advantage.* New York: AMACOM, 2004.

Fulmer, R.M., and A.A. Vicere. *Executive Education and Leadership Development: The State of the Practice.* University Park, PA: Penn State Institute for the Study of Organizational Effectiveness, 1995.

Gerstner, L. *Who Says Elephants Can't Dance?* New York: Collins Publishers, 2002.

Goldsmith, M. "Helping Successful People Get Even Better." *Business Strategy Review* 14, no. 1 (2003): 9–16.

Goleman, D. *Emotional Intelligence: Why It Can Matter More Than IQ.* New York: Bantam Books, 1996.

Hershey, P., and K.H. Blanchard. *The Management of Organizational Behavior.* Englewood Cliffs, NJ: Prentice-Hall, 1984.

Hollenbeck, G., and M.W. McCall. "Competence, Not Competences: Making Global Executive Development Work." Working paper, Center for Effective Organizations, University of Southern California, 2002.

Hollenbeck, G., M.W. McCall, and R.F. Silzer. "Leadership Competency Models." *Leadership Quarterly* 17 (2006): 398–413.

Huczynski, A.A., and J.W. Lewis. "An Empirical Study into the Learning Transfer Process in Management Training." *Journal of Management Studies* (1980): 227–240.

Kouzes, J.M., and B.Z. Posner. *The Leadership Challenge*. San Francisco: Jossey-Bass, 1987.

McCall, M., M. Lombardo, and A. Morrison. *The Lessons of Experience: How Successful Executives Develop on the Job*. Lexington, MA: Lexington Books, 1988.

Naylor, J.C., and G.E. Briggs. "The Effect of Task Complexity and Task Organization on the Relative Efficiency of Part and Whole Training Methods." *Journal of Experimental Psychology* 65 (1963): 217–224.

Noel, J.L., and R. Charan. "Leadership Development at GE's Crotonville." *Human Resource Management* 27, no. 4 (1988): 433–447.

Ready, D., and J.A. Conger. "Why Leadership Development Efforts Fail." *Sloan Management Review*, April 15, 2003.

———. "Make Your Company a Talent Factory." *Harvard Business Review* 85, no. 6 (June 2007): 68–77.

Schmitt, N., J.K. Ford, and D.M. Stults. "Changes in Self-Perceived Ability as a Function of Performance in an Assessment Center." *Journal of Occupational Psychology* 59 (1986): 327–335.

Sims, H.P., and C.C. Manz. "Modeling Influences on Employee Behavior." *Personnel Journal* (January 1982): 45–51.

Young, D., and N. Dixon. *Helping Leaders Take Effective Action*. Greensboro, NC: Center for Creative Leadership, 1996.

25

Pursuing Authentic Leadership Development

Bruce J. Avolio

Introduction

My focus on understanding what constitutes exemplary leadership has followed many paths over the last two decades, but in aggregate it seems as though this journey may be best described as representing a reverse telescope effect. Like many in the field of leadership, I concentrated a lot of my early attention on what the leader was like, what the leader did, and how the leader performed. So, inside my telescopic view there was clearly one image that loomed large, and it covered most of the visual space. Only after a number of years of reflection did it become obvious to me that we also needed to pull back and look at the larger global context to see exactly where we were in explaining what constituted the range and depth of "good" leadership.

My overriding mission in writing this paper is to offer an integrative summary of my developmental journey toward laying the groundwork for examining what I believe is the next challenging frontier for both the science and practice of leadership—defining what constitutes genuine leadership development. In pursuing this focus, I hope to promote a partnership among scholars and practitioners to work together in exploring what remains one of the most important frontiers in both the practice and science of leadership. This would involve scientist-practitioners like me working with what I would call the future leaders and managers in our organizations—*practitioner-scientists*. A practitioner-scientist doesn't necessarily participate in scientific work per se; rather, he or she simply knows the discipline it takes to conclude that a finding is "evidence based."

A practical reason for promoting a true collaborative between scientists and practitioners at this point in human history is simple. We are on the precipice of a "war for leadership talent" perhaps unrivaled in human history. As the world population expands, as well as the number of governments and businesses, how will we develop the best leadership required to promote a sustainable world? Hopefully, not the way we are currently developing leaders in most organizations, which is typically accidental, by luck and happenstance. No one in their right mind would use a new prescription drug if it were produced using the current processes that masquerade as leadership development programs.

The Time Is Propitious for Change

One beneficial outcome of the globalization of our planet has been the clear sense that, like any organization, town, city, region, or country, the resources in this world are finite. Whenever there are finite resources, the quality of one's leadership and management matter even more. I would contend that if the quality of leadership matters more, then so does its development. Unfortunately, one of the least researched areas in the science of leadership is in fact the science of leadership development. Only recently has there been any serious attention given in the leadership literature to putting forth a model of leadership development. Indeed, readers of this chapter might be surprised to know that there is not even a theory of leader self-awareness. I say surprised, because what training or educational program on leadership has not focused on enhancing a leader's self-awareness? All of the leadership development interventions I have known focus in one way or the other on enhancing leader self-awareness, absent any well-developed and, more important, tested theory. I view this omission as a huge opportunity for creating and validating what we have called authentic leadership development models and methods, described in more detail below.

The Origin of My Interest in Leadership

My early interest in leadership began with the most heroic, or what has been called charismatic leadership (Bass, 1985; Avolio and Gibbons, 1988). Charismatic leaders were described as those who could energize followers through their use of symbols, images, stories, and rhetoric to perform at extraordinary levels. They were leaders who typically stood for some cause, had a vision of a better future, and were oftentimes willing to sacrifice everything to prove to their followers how committed they were to achieving the vision.

For me, such charismatic leadership was in the center of the telescope, and there was little else that fit into that narrow field of vision. This focus lasted for a short while until my colleagues and I started turning our attention to exploring what constituted transformational leadership, which built directly on Jim Burns's authoritative work (Burns, 1978). Burns described transforming leaders as being charismatic, inspiring, morally uplifting, and focused on developing followers into leaders. In fact, the signature difference between a transforming leader and one described as charismatic was the focus on developing or transforming followers into leaders (Avolio, 1999).

There were two critical points discussed in Jim Burns's book *Leadership* that really intrigued me. The first was his focus on leaders who were described as morally uplifting. The second was his focus on "transforming" leadership, by which he meant leaders who purposely set out to develop their followers into leaders. Since reading his work, I have seen that Burns was not alone in his focus on leaders transforming followers into leaders. Indeed, one of the best management scholars of the twentieth century, Mary Parker Follett, wrote in her 1924 book *The Creative Experience* the following with regard to uplifting leadership: "Leadership is not defined by the exercise of power but by the capacity to increase the sense of power among those led. The most essential work of the leader is to create more leaders." If you adopt this goal as the high-impact point of your focus on leadership, how does that change the way one depicts and develops leaders? This was the question that I began to focus on, which ultimately expanded my telescopic view of leadership to include development.

One of the advantages of adopting Burns's two criteria for transforming leadership was that they provided greater clarity for what constituted "good" leadership. Certainly there have been many leaders throughout history who are labeled charismatic who had as their goal morally uplifting others, including such leaders as Nelson Mandela. Moreover, these same leaders thought long and hard on how best to develop their current generation of followers into the next generation of exemplary leaders. Yet, equally charismatic leaders throughout history have also done just the opposite, such as Joseph Stalin or Idi Amin. These charismatic leaders typically set out to advantage one group by destroying all others, which would certainly not pass Burns's morally uplifting test. Moreover, their goal was to eliminate any followers who might have had any inclination to lead, because they posed a threat to their authority. This sort of pattern was captured in a top U.S. military officer's comment about the current state of leadership in Iraq. This officer indicated that unlike the United States, the potential founding fathers/leaders of a future Iraqi democracy were probably all dead. During his years of dictatorship, Saddam Hussein did one thing very effectively: he eliminated all internal opposition.

It was clear from the outset of our work on transformational leadership that the transformational leader, compared with what became known as a personalized charismatic, was wired differently, and that wiring was both heritable as well as laid over the course of one's life span (Avolio, 2005; Avolio and Luthans, 2006). Personalized charismatic leaders were equally inspiring, and perhaps even visionary, yet their focus was on accumulating power, controlling their followers and key stakeholders, and, whenever necessary, wielding power for their own gain as opposed to the larger group's or society's benefits. This distinction between the "good" and "bad" charismatic leader triggered a long line of research that has empirically shown that transformational leadership positively engages individuals at all levels of just about every type of organization, ranging from R&D scientists to New Zealand police officers, to enhance performance potential and outcomes at individual, dyadic, group, organizational, and even community levels (Bass and Riggio, 2006). Indeed, a recent meta-analysis of this literature, which used a technique to quantitatively summarize research findings and represented at least the fourth meta-analysis on the same topic, concluded that transformational leadership was positively related to a broad range of positive individual and organizational outcomes (Judge and Piccolo, 2004).

Early on in my career, as a trained life-span psychologist, I became familiar with the work of Kohlberg (1984) and Kegan (1994) on the issues of life-span personality and moral development. This work became the foundation for exploring why transformational leaders were more morally centered and uplifting than other leaders. Using Kegan's (1994) terminology, we might ask, What is the level of perspective-taking capacity required of a leader to support that leader's belief in the importance of developing followers into leaders? Kegan argues that individuals who exhibit a lower level of perspective-taking capacity are typically stuck in the "What's in it for me?" phase of development. Their decisions and judgments are guided totally by self-interest, which makes it difficult, if not impossible, for them to invest any time whatsoever in developing their followers into leaders. Why would such leaders ever be willing to be more vulnerable to the change that is required when enabling followers to step up and lead? It was my work with Tracy Gibbons, an OD consultant with the Digital Equipment Company, that helped focus my interest on linking Kegan's idea of moral perspective-taking capacity with good leadership. Specifically, leaders who have a higher moral perspective can weigh the benefits to themselves and others in judging what might be the best overall course to pursue. This is not the case for someone at the lowest level of moral perspective-taking capacity. In 1986, Tracy and I began collaborating on a project to determine whether transformational leaders described as being the "good charismatic" type, inspiring, stimulating, and developmentally oriented, were at a higher level of moral development than transactional leaders, which her dissertation results confirmed (Avolio and Gibbons, 1988).

As is often the case in most scientific fields, Kuhnert and Lewis (1987) were working at the same time on exploring these linkages, which culminated in their publishing a revised theory of transformational leadership. Their work nicely paralleled what we were discovering in our work at Digital. I could see very clearly that the distinction concerning moral perspective-taking capacity and its importance to defining what is at the core of transforming leadership would become the Holy Grail for research on transformational leadership and subsequently its development. I started telling managers, whenever given the opportunity, that the Holy Grail of leadership was establishing and developing the moral center in leaders, and of course in those they led.

In a number of training workshops held around the globe, I used to do an exercise in which participants would work individually and then in small teams to design a delegation task for a high-potential colleague.

Unbeknownst to the groups, I took Kohlberg's and Kegan's work, and instead of presenting to these teams a stage or level of moral perspective taking, I relabeled the stages with names such as Sam. I purposely chose names that could be a male or female (e.g., Samuel or Samantha) and told the teams it could refer to either a male or a female.

Repeatedly, these teams would develop elaborate plans to "control" the development of the "morally challenged" character, while delegating based on trust and very few external controls to the highest morally developed character. It didn't matter at all which culture I was in or the level of management—the results were the same. I would then ask the workshop group who was the normative character they typically saw advancing to the top of their organization, and invariably the answer was "the least morally developed." This discussion always reminded me of Steven Kerr's classic organizational behavior article entitled "On the Folly of Rewarding A While Hoping for B." Could we promote people we inherently and justifiably didn't trust? We promoted them into leadership positions quite simply because they were outstanding individual producers with a record of tearing up the performance charts. Yet, as I have seen countless times before, being a great individual performer does not necessarily make one a good leader. Indeed, I am convinced that the rapid growth in coaching consultancy services is in part due to a significant failure in our leadership development system.

The problem of the individual performance paradox was brought into clear focus for me during a presentation given by Bill George, former CEO of Medtronics and well-known author writing on what constitutes "authentic" leadership. An authentic leader is someone who is very self-aware, has a clear moral center, is transparent, and is a fair or balanced decision maker. Bill said that in college he had repeatedly run for the top leadership role in his fraternity and lost. Finally, after several losses, a friend of his came up to him and said that he would never win the election if he kept running based on his desire to win for himself. This was not an election for Bill, this was for the leadership position of the fraternity, and to win it, he had to show he really cared about others. Bill did eventually win the presidency. He also went on to become one of the most successful U.S. CEOs in the history of business on anyone's performance dashboard and did so setting the highest ethical standards for business. Today, Bill George is at Harvard teaching MBAs about what it means to be an authentic leader in a classroom that, I would guess, given the level of competition required to get a seat in Harvard's Business School, has its fair share of individual performers who desperately want to be the next fraternity or sorority president, so to speak (George, 2003).

At the same time I was exploring these linkages between leadership and moral capacity, I also noticed in the survey data we were collecting on transformational leadership that in most organizations, as you move up levels, the mean values for the transformational scales increased (Bass and Avolio, 1990). This seemed rather paradoxical to me, in that we appear to promote individual performers, but somehow they end up being transformational. I entertained several reasons for this contradiction between my data and field observations. First, as individuals ascend and gain life experience and wisdom, they can develop from an individual performer who is more likely to see the world in terms of what is only best for him or her to someone who is morally uplifting and focused on transforming followers into leaders.

Second, there was potentially a flaw in the measurement of transformational leadership. Specifically, what appeared to be transformational was indeed not. I recall this observation leading to a lengthy conversation with Bernie Bass, a world-renowned scholar on leadership and a close colleague of mine. In that conversation, dating back to the early 1990s, we discussed whether there was an authentic transformational leader and one who was inauthentic, or what he and Paul Steidlmeier later labeled "pseudo" in their 1999 publication (Bass and Steidlmeier, 1999). The pseudo-transformational leader looked like the transformational leader but was not genuine; he or she was able to display transformational qualities and actions, but did not have the moral basis for being transformational. These leaders were great at managing the impression of being transformational, but unfortunately, the shadow was not matched with substance.

The third option represented a combination of my two explanations above. Certainly, there were a number of Bill Georges out there who had seen the light, and developed with the help of others into authentic transformational leaders. And certainly there were those leaders who learned very well how to feign this good form of leadership without really being the type of morally uplifting leader that Burns had described. This third option was a reasonable one for me, as there were countless cases of fallen leaders around the turn of the century who appeared to be very successful and yet in a few years left their organizations in ruins. Many reports of these leaders' followers described how surprised some of them were by the type of leader the individual turned out to be in the end, which, by the way, was not transformational.

As I have progressed in my career, I have learned that one provides many of the stepping stones to advance the science and practice of one's work. Yet, without serendipity, where would some of the truly great discoveries in science be? And as serendipity would have it, I came across this quote by Starbuck (1994) while writing this paper: "A random event does not merely affect a single period; it becomes part of the foundation for future periods and its consequences may accumulate over time until they dominate the behavior of the causal process." I have learned to appreciate the random events and the contribution that serendipity plays in one's life-stream development. Indeed, I have wondered to what extent great leadership is in part creating the conditions for serendipity to occur and reoccur, because planning for such trigger events seems beyond the reach of most leaders and followers. In the spirit of serendipity, I will leave this as a "maybe."

The Roots of Genuine Development

As I became more intrigued with the work on moral perspective taking, my interest in leadership development began to take shape in terms of focusing on what was made and what was born. My inclination and beliefs centered on leadership being more made than born, but I frequently encountered the opposite opinion in workshops. When I asked participants to put a percentage value on how much they thought leadership was born versus made, frequently a majority of the workshop placed more points on the born rather than the made explanation. I always found this interesting in that their organizations were paying to have them developed as leaders, but many in the workshop had what has been called an "entity" versus "incremental" perspective toward development (Dweck, 1986, 1999; Dweck and Leggett, 1988). The *entity* perspective views such things as personality and leadership as being fixed at a certain point in one's life stream. Conversely, the *incremental* perspective views development as being more elastic and modifiable over the life course.

What is perhaps most interesting is that the research on these different perspectives has concluded that one can easily influence someone to have more of an entity versus incremental perspective if his or her views are not fixed. This was an important trigger moment for me, in that I thought any leadership developer would be at a distinct disadvantage to the extent that the learners believed things were fixed. I quickly embraced and joined the incremental party, but it took several years to figure out how to best prime would-be leaders to think incremental. I will discuss our strategy for doing so later in this chapter.

In 1986, Tichy and Devanna wrote a ground-breaking text on transformational leadership. A year earlier, Bernie Bass (1985) had produced his main thesis on transformational and what he called transactional leadership. Transactional leadership was based on the exchange or economic theories of human behavior, whereby people are motivated to perform based on the return or rewards received. In their work, Tichy and Devanna placed more emphasis on the leadership at the tops of organizations, suggesting that transformational leadership should reside in strategic leadership levels. Although Bass argued that one could find more evidence for transformational leadership at the tops of organizations, he also believed that it could occur at all levels in varying degree.

Subsequent work by Bass, Waldman, Avolio, and Bebb (1987) demonstrated that there was indeed what they referred to as a "cascading" or "falling dominoes" effect with respect to transformational leadership and that if it appeared at the top of an organization, it was likely evidenced at subsequent levels. The falling dominoes effect was attributed to a number of potential explanations, including transforming leaders developing followers into leaders, as well as selecting such leaders as followers, or both. My inclination was more in line with Bass's work, and agreed that transformational leadership could occur at all levels of an organization.

In the late 1980s, I began work with the Canadian correctional services to test whether transformational leadership could be developed in a field experiment with first-line supervisors comparing our training to situational leadership. The target leaders were supervisors working in the correctional services who ran workshops, contracts, and departments. The followers were the inmates, who completed leadership surveys rating their supervisors' transformational and transactional leadership, which my colleague Bernie Bass and I started referring to as falling along what we called a "full range" of leadership. By *full range* we meant a continuum of leadership that was at the highest point of the range described as very proactive, inspiring, and idealized, while at the lowest point was described as reactive, avoidant, or laissez-faire.

The top of the full range represented, in our minds, the most active and effective leadership, which we were now referring to as transformational. Within the transformational range we included what we began referring to as the four I's of transformational leadership: individualized consideration, intellectual stimulation, inspirational, and idealized influence. We chose the term *idealized* to convey to those using the model that we were specifically not referring to "idolized" leaders, but rather to leaders who had set high ideals, values, and ethical standards. This helped us differentiate transformational leadership from the "bad" charismatic leaders, who certainly liked to be idolized rather than idealized.

The individualized consideration style represented the type of leadership that focused on each individual as being unique, whereby the leader assumed responsibility for developing his or her followers to their full potential, and ultimately to be leaders themselves, as Burns had described. The intellectual stimulation style was not the leader being smart, but rather developing followers who could come up with the best ideas and solutions. The inspirational motivation constituted the visionary and positive energy associated with transformational leadership.

In the middle of the full-range model we included the transactional leadership styles. In the more effective range, we referred to the constructive forms of transactional leadership, which entailed setting goals and objectives and providing feedback, recognition, and rewards for one's followers to achieve expected performance. Slightly lower on the full range and less effective was the more corrective transactional style that represented leadership that focused on finding what might go wrong, or did go wrong, and correcting it. At the very bottom of the full range, and the least effective style, was passive-avoidant leadership. This type of leader just waited and waited before taking any action whether things were going right or wrong. Regarding this lowest end of the range, many of our colleagues suggested that we should drop the passive-avoidant style, arguing it didn't really represent leadership. We thought about dropping it, but decided to keep it in the range because it represented in large part what we would counsel leaders not to do, or to do as little as possible.

From the late 1980s onward, we used the full-range model as an organizing framework for developing leadership. Our typical focus in training programs was to help leaders first understand that they could exhibit the entire range of leadership styles or behaviors prior to providing them with ratings feedback from supervisors, peers, and followers. Next, we would focus on helping them increase the more active and proactive end of the full range, which of course would reduce the amount of time they were investing in simply looking for mistakes in others. I should add that even at this early point in the full-range model's development, we had substantial evidence that supported the idea that by developing transformational and constructive transactional leadership styles one could expect a greater, positive impact on follower motivation and performance (Avolio, 1999).

Returning to the Canadian correctional services, when I arrived at Dorchester Prison near Halifax, Canada, I was given a tour of the facility to familiarize myself with the working environment—think Alcatraz with a bad attitude. During the tour we stopped in a machine shop where there was a wall of inmates with their backs to us holding sharp tools. In the middle of the pack was a supervisor named Sam (just a coincidence), who was instructing them on his six-week career development program. Sam was pointing to the wall where he had placed the type of metal products they could make after week 1 and, if they stuck with him, by week 6 of his program. He indicated that if you could produce that shiny metal product by week 6, you would be making more than most professionals, adding "and then we would not have to see each other again." Dorchester was at that time a high-security correctional center, so the fellows with tools behind Sam were very dangerous. I marveled at Sam's confidence and his clarity and simplicity in relating to these inmates and learned over time of his compassion to treat each inmate as a unique individual.

After the workshop ended, I met with Sam to discuss what I would be doing over the next several days. He was very interested in our work on leadership development and thought it would be very worthwhile—he was clearly an incrementalist. As I reflect back on Sam, he was unfailingly humble, genuine, compassionate, ethical, inspiring to a large cadre of inmates, and willing to challenge the core assumption that most inmates end up failing to do—that there is no better life than crime. Sam was a transformational leader in every sense, and more important, he was authentic. I found out later that Sam had the highest productivity rates in his shop, the lowest absenteeism of inmates failing to come to work, and one of the lowest recidivism rates. He not only fit the styles and behaviors of a constructive transactional and transformational leader, he had the results to prove it! Although I was basing my assumptions on conjecture, I believed the Sams of this world were not born to be transformational, but rather developed that perspective and ability over time.

The results of the work we did in the Canadian prison ended up in Paul Crookall's (1989) dissertation, where he showed not only that the intervention we had designed improved the transformational leadership style of participants but also had affected the performance, absenteeism, and turnover rates of their units. In the Canadian correctional services, inmates can choose to stay in their cells and can leave a job voluntarily. On all of these metrics, the trained experimental group had outperformed the group that had gone through situational leadership training. Situational leadership was a very popular model and program at that time, in which managers were taught to be more or less considerate and task-oriented depending on the demands of the situation and the level of maturity of their followers. And then serendipity struck again! A social worker approached Paul with case notes on inmates in the correctional services who were in our experimental groups. The notes were a record of the inmates' behavior. When we went back and carefully analyzed the notes, we found that the inmates in the transformational leadership condition were acting more positively and more proactively, and were demonstrating what has been called better "organizational citizenship behavior." In these completely independently collected notes, we were finding evidence for the incremental versus entity perspective.

As the work on transformational leadership expanded, we found ourselves doing presentations and workshops around the globe. In the mid to late 1990s, we began work in Israel with a number of colleagues interested in assessing and developing transformational leadership and ultimately the high end of the full range of leadership. In one particular project, we worked with the Israel Defense Forces (IDF) to develop what would become one of the purest field experiments ever conducted on whether leadership can be developed (see Dvir, Eden, Avolio, and Shamir, 2002). In this study, we designed several days of training on transformational leadership that we deployed with a randomly assigned group of platoon commanders taking their platoons through basic training. The other randomly assigned group would go through the existing program, which was also focused on transformational leadership but in our view had drifted from the core model, in that it had become over time more eclectic and clinical. The instructors, who largely spoke Hebrew, as well as participants in the IDF, were each randomly assigned to the two training conditions. My role was to train the instructors in English with a lot of help from my Israeli collaborators.

Over the course of this experimental program, we demonstrated significant change in transformational leadership, paralleling the results in the correctional services. These changes, as in the previous case, were in the eyes of the followers via ratings we collected on their platoon commander's leadership style. We also saw changes in followers' attitudes and performance months out from training. Again, we had provided evidence to support an incremental versus entity perspective toward development at the higher end of the full range of leadership.

When we dug into what might have influenced the training impact, we could see that the feedback these young commanders received on their leadership through the Multifactor Leadership Questionnaire (Avolio, Bass, Walumbwa, and Zhu, 2004), which contained behavioral items that measured our full range of leadership styles—both transformational and transactional leadership—and their discussions with coaches in the workshop had been a profound trigger event for their development. They simply had not received any sort of prior feedback on their leadership, especially from peers and followers. In addition, prior to the onset of our training program, we obtained short videos of commanders sitting inside their tents discussing after their first day what it was like to take over a platoon. These platoon commanders reflected on their anxiety, confidence (or lack thereof), what they expected to occur, how they prepared, and what they did when they walked out and became the commander of their unit, oftentimes being only a couple of years older than the other soldiers in their units. We used these tapes in our program, and all of the instructors concluded that "bringing the future to the present" for these young commanders had been a very powerful tool in developing leadership—and, by the way, their conclusions were evidence based.

The Inevitable Born Versus Made Question

Evidence was now accumulating from the work of other colleagues that one could develop transactional and transformational leadership (see Barling, Weber, and Kelloway, 1996; Day and O'Connor, 2003). My attention started to shift to a research initiative that Rich Arvey had begun at the University of Minnesota on examining the heritability of job satisfaction. Using a longitudinal database of identical and fraternal twins, called the Minnesota Twins database, Arvey and his colleagues had shown that a good percentage of one's job satisfaction was heritable. He and I then met at a national conference and began to discuss how to use the twins database to investigate the born versus made issue in leadership. The research being conducted using twin pairs is based on the assumption that identical twin pairs have 100 percent identical genes, whereas fraternal twins have about 50 percent overlap. Knowing whether the twins are identical or fraternal allows you to estimate and control for heritability while examining how much environmental experience then contributes to each twin's leadership emergence and development over the course of his or her career (Avolio, Rotundo, and Walumbwa, in press; Arvey, Zhang, Avolio, and Krueger, 2007).

Our research with twins has focused primarily on examining whether the twin pairs emerged or did not emerge in leadership roles throughout their careers. We felt that being in a leadership role in high school, college, one's community, and at work provided us with the most objective assessment of leadership. Over a series of studies, we have found, for both men and women, that approximately 30 percent of leadership emergence was heritable, whereas 70 percent was due to environmental events. Indeed, the heritability of leadership was far less than what other researchers had reported with respect to intelligence and personality. This set of empirical data provided the basis for arguing more stridently for the incremental approach to leadership development. It also provided me, personally, with an evidence-based response to the question of whether leaders are born or made. My answer was now "yes."

Developmental Readiness

Returning to my earlier comments, many come to leadership training events because they have been asked to come for development. Others come with a desire and a theory of leadership in their minds that supports the idea that leadership indeed can be developed. As we discovered these different starting points for our interventions, it suggested that we needed to get a better understanding of the developmental readiness of participants in order to meet each individual at his or her starting point for development. Moreover, part of the role in developing leadership is to enhance the individual's readiness, so as to prepare him or her to engage at a level that will move the individual toward more effective leadership (Avolio and Wernsing, 2007).

Sean Hannah, a former doctoral candidate who came to the Global Leadership Institute at the University of Nebraska to receive his PhD and who now is the director of the Army's Center for the Professional Military Ethic located at the U.S. West Point Military Academy, became interested in the area of development readiness early on in his doctoral work. West Pointers say that when you have four years to develop the next generation of your nation's leaders, you have to make every minute count. Anyone who has been affiliated with West Point has learned quickly that the hardest thing to ask for as an outsider is some time with the cadets. Literally, their entire day, every day, is scheduled with academics, sports, and military training, so being able to "accelerate" leadership development seemed appealing to both us and West Point leaders.

In Sean's dissertation he focused on what he called agentic leadership, which was built on a long line of research and theory developed by Albert Bandura called social learning theory (Bandura, 1997). Bandura's core work over the last forty years has focused on a construct he labeled "efficacy." By *efficacy*, Bandura meant the probability in one's head that you could be successful at a task. Bandura viewed all human beings as potential agents of change and argued that to enact change, human beings must feel efficacious or confident. Bandura has described the concept of efficacy as being "statelike," meaning that it was more elastic than, say, traits and therefore could be developed. Bandura and his colleagues have shown repeatedly that one's level of efficacy predicts performance (see Stajkovic and Luthans, 1998), and that efficacy is also something that can be developed.

We were somewhat surprised, at the start of Sean's work on developmental readiness, that there was very little research on efficacy that had been applied to the field of leadership (Hannah, 2006). We felt that if one could develop leaders' efficacy for such things as having confidence in their thinking, decision making, actions, and behaviors, then positive leadership development could be accelerated. This work on leader efficacy motivated us to explore such constructs as an individual's motivation to lead, motivation to learn, and motivation to develop.

In one of now several longitudinal field investigations completed at the West Point military academy, we have consistently shown that the concepts that make up developmental readiness do predict, over several months' time and longer, how well the target leader (cadet) learns to lead and to perform in leadership roles. For example, we measured at time 1 target leaders' ability to think about how they think, which is called meta-cognitive ability, as well as their learning goal orientation (whether they were prevention- or promotion-oriented, with promotion being more positive about engaging in learning), and how clear an understanding they had of themselves (referred to in the cognitive literature as "self-concept clarity"). All three of these concepts can be considered components of developmental readiness, and all three predicted the individual's level of agentic leadership at multiple time periods, as well as the individual's motivation to lead and, in subsequent research, his or her performance. Over nearly an entire academic year, we were able to show how developmental readiness predicted the confidence to lead, as well as motivation and actual performance. These results were pivotal to examining how we might accelerate leadership development by examining each and every individual's level of readiness, perhaps in the same way that Sam had intuitively done with his inmates.

Authentic Leadership Development

A lot of the pieces were falling into place in terms of my ultimate goal of determining what constituted *genuine* leadership development. We had evidence that leaders were more made than born. We also had preliminary evidence that we could intervene with relatively short interventions that were targeted to specific leadership styles and could effect a change in styles, attitudes, and performance. What we were perhaps missing was a general understanding of what others had tried and seen to be successful in developing leadership. This led to a three-year (and still ongoing) effort to examine the entire history of leadership development work in the academic literature to determine what had "caused" leadership to change. I have highlighted the word *caused* because we were only interested in examining interventions that had tried to change leadership either by developing it or through other means. This was a pure test of evidence-based development.

After a year of reviewing the leadership intervention literature with a large group of doctoral candidates and a postdoctoral supervisor working on this project, we were able to come up with 201 studies that had examined whether leadership could be systematically altered. Only about one third of these studies actually set out to develop leadership, whereas the rest focused on manipulating it through role plays, scripts, or some other experimental means. Our search of the literature convinced me that the science of leadership development was at best in its infancy, since it represented an extremely small percentage of the work that had been done on leadership.

Interested readers can go to Reichard and Avolio (2005) for what was called a meta-analysis of this literature. A meta-analysis is a commonly used quantitative procedure that one can employ to systematically assess trends in the literature. Very simply, you can use this procedure to aggregate study findings, such that the study becomes your subject or focal point, so to speak. In our case, we were interested in aggregating whether an attempt at changing leadership made a difference, so we examined, for example, whether an experimental training versus control condition made leaders more transformational. What we found provided further support for our initiative to build a base for the science of evidence-based leadership development.

Overall, the interventions we examined in aggregate proved to have a positive effect on changing leadership. If estimated as a probability, those in the experimental groups could be assigned a 70 percent success rate, versus, say, 30 percent for the comparison groups. If 50/50 represents random results for the intervention effects, then we were finding a moderately strong effect for these interventions, including those focused on development. Our findings also showed that some theories had more of an impact on such things as changing attitudes, behavior, and performance. For example, theories that were primarily based on examining behaviors such as whether the leader was shown to initiate structure or consideration did in fact have a stronger and causal impact on behavioral change, whereas theories such as transformational leadership that focused beyond simply changing behaviors to changing emotions and ways of thinking had more of an impact on the way participants thought and reacted emotionally.

Taking the Next Big Steps

What I have attempted to provide thus far is the foundational logic for studying what constituted authentic leadership and its development. Yet, like development itself, some of the next steps were triggered in part by serendipity. For example, I recall receiving the results from a poll we had conducted with the U.S. working adult population, where we found that less than 20 percent of Americans would agree or strongly agree with the statement that "their organizational leaders say exactly what they mean" (Avolio, 2005). This figure kept returning in my thoughts, and eventually in all of my presentations on leadership. Recently, in a similar national panel study, we found the figure was 17 percent.

Around the time of the first poll, I attended a conference at the Kravitz Institute in California on leadership. A colleague from one of the most distinguished training centers on leadership had just finished her presentation. She was talking about leadership development, but I felt her talk had fallen short on describing the evidence for positively developing leadership in the groups she had referred to in her presentation. I waited until the end of the questioning period to ask her whether her organization had solid proof that it had ever developed one leader. She responded that a colleague in "another department" was supposedly working on addressing that issue. I will leave readers to make your own interpretations of her response, but her rapidly coloring rosy cheeks suggested to me that one of the most pre-eminent centers for leadership development had no evidence to substantiate that it had developed even one leader.

In combination with the poll results, I was extremely energized to make a difference in evolving the science and practice of leadership development. As serendipity would have it, my colleague Fred Luthans at the University of Nebraska was also beginning a whole new area of work on what he had labeled "positive organizational behavior," or simply POB (Luthans, 2002). Fred's focus was on examining those models and methods that would positively affect how people behave and perform in organizations. Yet, at first glance, the logic for combining his work and mine into what we would refer to as authentic leadership development may not be so obvious, so let me explain some of the core connections.

As I noted earlier, the work we did on heritability was to establish that more was open to development in terms of leadership then previously considered. One of Fred's early POB interests was in an area he referred to as "psychological capital," or Psycap. Fred was interested in identifying positive constructs that could be used ultimately to enhance the human condition at work, which is part of the foundation for the field of organizational behavior.

We began our collaboration by examining four constructs that had been researched in the clinical psychology literature but rarely applied or examined in work contexts. These constructs were optimism, hope, resiliency, and efficacy. Fred had toyed with the idea of exploring emotional intelligence, but he ruled it out because it did not meet his criteria for inclusion in this line of research. Specifically, we were interested in investigating positive psychological constructs that had a strong theoretical base, a validated measure to assess the construct, and were states or what we called "statelike." The four components above met those criteria and were included in the initial cluster of constructs that we began to investigate. From the very start, we did not rule out the addition of other positive constructs, and today we are currently exploring how we might include constructs such as ownership, wisdom, and courage in the published Psycap inventory (see Luthans, Avolio, and Youseff, 2007).

Two key points of integration for our work focused on constructs that were state or statelike and had placed an emphasis on positivity. A state or statelike construct by definition is something one can develop or change. The focus on these positive constructs paralleled to some degree my earlier work on transformational leadership, which included all four Psycap constructs, but not directly, as we now envisioned. Moreover, by focusing on positive constructs, we were suggesting a different approach to leadership development. Specifically, most leadership development interventions have traditionally been based on a deficit reduction model. For example, after receiving feedback on a manager's leadership style, we might point to her inability to listen to others, and then make recommendations on how to change and improve her listening capabilities. The alternative approach might start with what this manager is really good at and then use those capabilities to enhance her listening skills. For instance, she may have great analytical skills or future perspective-taking capacity, and by first focusing on how she listens to others in those areas of strength, we might then help accelerate her leadership development.

Fred and I both agreed that we were not in any way negating the deficit approach to development, but rather felt we were complementing it with a more specific focus on these four positive constructs. This line of thinking also led to an "aha!" moment for both of us, in which we reasoned that perhaps leadership development was triggered by both positive and negative moments. Traditionally in the leadership literature, most authors focused on major life events that were negative, such as dramatic losses, life-threatening diseases that the leader had survived, or some cataclysmic event that ultimately shaped leadership development. Again, our position did not negate this possibility; we simply felt that in other instances leadership development could be, let's say, less painful.

The idea of trigger moments took us to an extreme place, where we were suggesting that leadership development might actually occur in moments, not hours, days, weeks, or months. In fact, we were saying that the start of "genuine" leadership development could be a trigger that motivated the individual to reflect and learn from the event, which ultimately could result in enhanced leadership potential. Supporting our notion of triggers, parallel work on jolts by our colleagues in the positive organizational scholarship group at Michigan reinforced the idea of an events-driven strategy to leadership development. Where we differed in our focus, perhaps, was in terms of the length and magnitude of these events.

After we published our first paper in which we merged our work on authentic leadership development (see Luthans and Avolio, 2003), we started to build a research program to study both authentic leadership and Psycap. Working in overlapping research teams and in parallel, we built and constructed validated survey measures of authentic leadership (Walumbwa, Avolio, Gardner, Wernsing, and Peterson, 2008) and Psycap (Luthans, Avolio, Avey, and Norman, 2007). The work that went into developing and validating these respective measures demonstrated that the constructs in each were different from similar constructs already published in these respective literatures. For example, the constructs comprising authentic leadership, which included self-awareness, balanced processing, moral perspective, and transparency, were shown to be positively related to measures of ethical and transformational leadership, but were also sufficiently independent. Similarly, the measure of Psycap correlated with measures of positivity and personality, but was sufficiently different as to warrant evidence for being separate or independent.

What we reported in both published studies cited above showed that our new measures, which were now based on revised and more refined theories (see Avolio and Gardner, 2005; Gardner, Avolio, Luthans, May, and Walumbwa, 2005; and Luthans et al., 2007), not only predicted a wide array of performance outcomes, but did so by augmenting the more established measures of leadership. In other words, if our measures had not provided evidence for incrementally predicting performance, then why would anyone choose to use them in any practical setting? We had to establish that they were different, which we did.

There are several points worth noting about the models that underlie each of these measures that hopefully provide a more solid basis for further discussion below about authentic leadership development. First, each model is designed to represent what can be referred to as multiple levels of analysis. In the case of authentic leadership, that means we would include the follower in the development process, because an authentic follower just may be the trigger for authentic leadership development of the leader. Moreover, we include the organizational climate in which these interactions are embedded, oftentimes referring to that climate as representing a positive and ethical climate, which transparently promotes growth and development.

Second, we see development patterns as being less linear and more cyclical, in which a follower's Psycap can enhance a leader's, and the leader's in turn can enhance the follower's, the follower's team, and at some point the positive climate that emerges. We suggest that most development likely does not follow in simple lock-step fashion, and that a trigger can promote nonlinear as well as linear growth.

Third, the initial focus we have taken on trigger events led us to explore what we have labeled as "micro-interventions" for leadership development. For instance, we might focus on how to enhance the level of transparency that is exhibited between leaders and followers as the main focus for a developmental intervention. Taking this focus, one could develop online materials, stories, cases, and measurement tools that, when reviewed, trigger a particular action. Of course, these triggers can be delivered face to face, or even through follow-ups after a face-to-face program using mobile technology such as cell phones, which we have labeled "booster events." These booster events are designed to be short triggers lasting, at most, minutes rather than hours. They are designed to prime individuals to continue reflecting on and also working on changing these states we call authentic leadership and positive psychological capital.

We have been working over the last several years on deploying these micro-interventions with particular emphasis on Psycap and, more recently, self-awareness. As we had suspected, we can not only promote changes in individual leader's Psycap scores who have gone through these micro-interventions, but also we are showing that these statelike changes can positively affect human motivation and performance. Paralleling the lean operational strategy for enhancing organizational performance that is being taught around the globe, we have also adopted the idea that "less leadership development is potentially more leadership development" (see Luthans, Avey, Avolio, Norman, and Combs, 2006).

Along the lines of supporting the use of micro-interventions, I routinely ask leadership developers around the globe what is the one thing they do above all else that triggers the most positive development in leadership. At first, many are taken aback by the question, and after some reflection they usually don't know. I have asked this question at our most prestigious institutions of learning, which say they focus on leadership development, and have received the same response or lack thereof.

Why is this question important? I am not suggesting there is one key trigger to developing leadership. However, I am confident that if you don't know what your high-impact point for developing leadership is, you are likely not very lean in your thinking, nor are you likely to be focusing on accelerating leadership development. My main purpose in asking this question of myself and others is to bring a sense of discipline to our work on accelerating authentic leadership development, and you can interpret "discipline" as also representing science and being evidence based.

Envisioning the Future of Genuine Leadership Development

As the war for leadership talent looms on the horizon, the time for investing in genuine leadership development has never been more propitious. To some extent, I believe we will experience a sort of "back to the future" effect in the field of leadership development. Prior to the advent of corporate training centers, coaches, and leadership trainers, much of what passed as leadership development occurred in context. Of course, there were many institutions that focused on leadership development out of context, such as West Point, but even there, one would find that the context was never too far away in terms of the focus on leadership development. For example, at our military academies, many of the faculty and instructors are full-time military officers. In using this cadre of individuals, the military is sending a clear signal of bringing the context right into the academic center, where cadets can work with and role model "real officers."

As I attempt to look out over the next fifty years, I envision us getting a much better balance between learning and application. In the near term, embedding leadership development in context, where we can enhance development as well as performance in parallel, will be the "program" of choice, I suspect. Indeed, if organizations continue to move to being knowledge-based learning centers, then why would we not expect leadership development to occur *in* the organization versus outside the organization? The outsourcing of leadership development for the latter half of the twentieth century was likely due in part to the fact that organizations were made and rewarded to produce, not necessarily to learn and to develop their employees and future leaders.

As we move toward embedding leadership development in context at all levels of organizations, we can also expect to see more attention to what I would call the "return on development investment" (RODI). To the degree that developing followers into leaders is defined as a job requirement, the time allocated for doing so and the success of the effort will no doubt be measured and quantified. Indeed, the calculation of RODI will likely fuel even more investment in embedded leadership development. Why? We have already accumulated evidence showing that even very short micro training interventions lasting less than one day can return over 200 percent on one's investment in terms of impact on performance. By estimating the total costs for actually conducting leadership development, and the lost opportunity costs for individuals being in training, we have found that even modestly effective training can provide huge dividends in what business executives would certainly label "hard metrics." In fact, as far as a future trend, I envision that we will develop a more exacting science of human capital appreciation by far than exists today. For equipment, organizational leaders are encouraged to depreciate the value over time, whereas for human capital, we may just have to do the reverse—especially as it applies to authentic leadership development.

The opportunity for estimating RODI corresponds with the surge in interest that I am witnessing in estimating human capital, psychological capital, and well-being as leading indicators of how individuals, groups, and organizations will perform. For example, a number of organizations are examining how to evaluate well-being in order to assess a company's or country's overall "health" to complement more traditional economic indicators in predicting future performance. The work in these areas by behavioral economists and organizational behaviorists will likely fuel more strategic investments in authentic leadership development across the career span. Why? If we can measure it and show how one's developmental proficiency predicts performance, organizations will invest in this human stock value.

Another trend I expect to see in the future regarding leadership development will likely parallel what has been emerging in the area of language development in many preschool curricula. Specifically, the earlier we can intervene to develop a positive mind-set regarding leadership development, the less remedial work will need to be done later in the life stream. Indeed, I am optimistic that we will see more and more attention in primary and secondary education that focuses on how to best develop leadership, and that will include followership. Already one would be hard pressed to find a college or university in the United States that does not mention leadership development as a goal in its values or mission statement. Of course, most of these institutions are not yet genuinely developing or measuring how well they achieve positive leadership development impact, but mentioning the desire in the mission and values statement highlights its growing importance in education. I believe we will see more emphasis earlier in the life stream on leadership development.

We are also now seeing a shift in the telescopic lens from just focusing on leaders to focusing more on followers and the context in which leadership is enacted. Clearly, more attention in the future will be placed on developing exemplary followership as an antecedent to developing effective leadership. Discussing leading up, sideways, diagonally, and down will become more the norm than the exception in our educational institutions. This is not to say that leaders will not loom large in our telescopes even fifty years from now. They will. Yet, we are moving to more of a balance between the heroic models of charismatic leadership and the models that recognize that leadership is a much more dynamic and complex process that encapsulates the full development of individuals as they engage in complex, adaptive challenges (Marion and Uhl-Bien, 2001).

As genuine leadership development occurs more and more in context, the type of training that occurs external to one's organization will also change. Teaching leaders and followers to process and reflect, as opposed to developing a particular style or behavior, will become more the norm than the exception. In addition, I would envision entire programs focusing on development around one profoundly important construct. For example, in a two-year running project in health care, we have focused specifically on developing an understanding of one construct that we label "psychological ownership." This root construct underlies much of what human beings have engaged in conflict over throughout human history. It has also been the root construct underlying some of the greatest accomplishments in human history, where members of teams, research labs, foundations, and even governments have taken ownership for pursuing a mission or cause.

In this health care project, we have used ownership as the organizing principle for all of the work we do in this particular organization on leadership. The basic question we ask is the following: How do you lead and follow to promote a positive sense of ownership in interactions with each other, followers, patients, and other important stakeholders? This question focuses on how one develops in others a sense of identification, belonging, accountability, and confidence to act in one's best interests as well as the organization's best interests. It is amazing how clarifying one profoundly important question can be for designing a rigorous evidence-based leadership development initiative. Indeed, we can now show empirical linkages between levels of psychological ownership and health care performance, which motivated us even further to develop leadership that develops ownership.

I believe the leadership development field is now on the right course toward identifying simpler and more profound formulas for what constitutes optimal leadership development. Paralleling other sciences, less will be more as the basis for the science and practice of leadership. One might now ask, In what ways? As information technology becomes more agile and mobile, we will be able to embed learning even more effectively in context. In a recent conversation that I had with six top executives from some of the most innovative companies on Earth, each spoke about the importance of follow-up to the success of any leadership development intervention. One of the CEOs in the room remarked that we roll out these great programs and, time after time, fail in our follow-up, leaving a lot of potential returns sitting on the table. We invest huge amounts of human and capital resources and then let the intervention die from its own inertia.

As I suggested above, if we can tie in RODI, we will be able to get executives tracking how well the leadership development initiative is returning on the investment. The checking of human stock, like we do financial stock, will become more of a daily activity as we connect human development with capital development. This checking provides some of the grist for follow-up that can be supported by micro-interventions deployed via technology. For instance, we should be able to customize, as Amazon does with our preferences for books, the sorts of follow-up triggers that would work for Bob more than Sally. In many instances today, we still provide leadership development as Henry Ford advocated: you can have a model T in any color you want as long as it's black. Certainly, over the next fifty years, there will be no reason whatsoever why we can't enable leadership development in context through highly mobile technology that enhances each leader's, follower's, and organization's leadership development.

At the same time that we will be able to follow learners into their respective performance context, we also will be able to pull them out into what will still be called "virtual" but in fifty years may be difficult to discern from, say, the feelings one gets when embedded at the workplace. If you compare the Edwin Link flight simulator used to train World War II pilots to what we use today, it is not hard to envision how "real" virtual simulations will become. Today, pilots can be recertified for flying certain planes by simply passing the simulator tests because of the extremely high fidelity of the flight simulators. By the way, Ed Link started with a wooden box that a pilot would sit in as Link manipulated it by hand with levers, tossing the pilot to and fro to simulate turbulence. I believe we will see the same rapid advances in fidelity of leadership development simulations that will become the norm in fifty years, perhaps not unlike what was depicted in the popular film *The Matrix*.

Readers might be surprised to discover that some of the simulators that the U.S. military is already using today, not fifty years from now, show the enormous potential for accelerating leadership development through high-fidelity simulations. If we can project onto the battlefield what looks like a set of tanks, but in reality is a hologram, how far-fetched is developing virtual worlds such as Second Life that place leaders, followers, their teams, and their organizations in high-fidelity simulations?

The last area I will cover in the future is without a doubt the most controversial. This area deals with the biological revolution that is upon us. In fifty years, researchers will likely look back on our twins research as being very crude in its estimate of heritability. As we continue to discover more about the human genome and brain research, what might be the impact of this knowledge on what we discover in terms of genuine leadership development? Like biofeedback was to the therapies of the 1980s, functional magnetic resonance imaging may be to the next twenty years of human leadership development. Being able to see where one's brain processes information or ignores it, and even training oneself to be more disciplined in how that occurs using feedback mechanisms from this technology, may be a very profitable strategy for accelerating leadership development (Galvin, Waldman, and Balthazard, 2008). For example, we know that individuals rely on what are called implicit theories in terms of making quick judgments and decisions (Lord and Brown, 2004). Our implicit theory is sort of the story or script we carry around in our head that helps us to explain how people behave and, in terms of our focus here, what attributes characterize good and bad leaders. In some instances, these implicit theories function as stereotypes that result in overgeneralizations and incorrect attributions. In others, the rapid processing that is associated with implicit theories may advantage a leader embedded in a rapidly changing and dangerous context, if properly trained.

In terms of biogenetics, the more we learn regarding how to prevent illnesses and sustain health and well-being, the better able our leaders will be to lead more effectively. For the last hundred years, positive energy has been correlated with leadership emergence (Bass, 1990). People who feel well will have more positive energy to perform and sustain performance over time. Imagine how many leaders throughout history were suffering from chronic diseases and the impact such diseases may have had on their judgment. What if those diseases could have been treated, or at least minimized in their impact? Sustaining leaders' health for longer periods in the life span may allow us to take greater advantage of their wisdom and the upper reaches of their development. To the degree that wisdom is developed, we can expect better use of it the longer we sustain a healthy life among leaders and followers.

Today leadership research is primarily conducted by psychologists, sociologists, historians, management theorists, political scientists, educators, ethicists, philosophers, and anthropologists. I have no doubt that over the next fifty years critical additions to the leadership research team will involve engineers, biologists, geneticists, and chemists. A more holistic approach to human development is on the horizon, and leadership development has traditionally trailed only a short distance behind the science of human development.

Concluding Comments

If one were setting sail from Europe to discover the New World, and land was still in sight, this in my view would be analogous to the journey we have begun in order to discover what constitutes genuine leadership development. Land is still in sight, but the vast ocean before us clearly calls for a great new adventure. And like those early navigators, the better able we are to develop our maps and navigational tools, the more likely we will end up where we intended to in the new world. Thus, I encourage us all to reflect on our respective journeys to discover what constitutes the very essence of good leadership, and to work over the next hundred years to discover the best ways to accelerate its development. Indeed, I have little doubt that the speakers who step up to the stage at the 200th celebration of the Harvard Business School celebration will have a lot to say about what we actually mean by genuine leadership development.

References

Arvey, R.D., Z. Zhang, B.J. Avolio, and R. Kruger. "Understanding the Developmental and Genetic Determinants of Leadership Among Females." *Journal of Applied Psychology* 92 (2007): 693–706.

Avolio, B.J. *Full Range Leadership: Building the Vital Forces in Organizations.* Thousand Oaks, CA: Sage Publications, 1999.

———. *Leadership Development in Balance: Made/Born.* Mahwah, NJ: Lawrence Erlbaum, 2005.

Avolio, B.J., B.M. Bass, F.O. Walumbwa, and W. Zhu. *Manual for the Multifactor Leadership Questionnaire.* Palo Alto, CA: Mindgarden, 2004.

Avolio, B.J., and W.L. Gardner. "Authentic Leadership Development: Getting to the Root of Positive Forms of Leadership." *Leadership Quarterly* 16 (2005): 315–338.

Avolio, B.J., and T. Gibbons. "Developing Transformational Leaders: A Life-Span Approach." In *Charismatic Leadership: The Elusive Factor in Organizational Effectiveness,* edited by J. Conger and R. Kanungo, 276–308. San-Francisco: Jossey-Bass, 1988.

Avolio, B.J., and F. Luthans. *High Impact Leader: Moments Matter in Authentic Leadership Development.* New York: McGraw-Hill, 2006.

Avolio, B.J., M. Rotundo, and F.O. Walumbwa. "Early Life Experiences and Environmental Factors as Determinants of Leadership Emergence: The Role of Parental Influence and Rule Breaking Behavior." *The Leadership Quarterly,* in press.

Avolio, B.J., and T.S. Wernsing. "Practicing Authentic Leadership." In *Positive Psychology: Exploring the Best in People,* edited by S.J. Lopez. Westport, CT: Greenwood Publishing Company, 2007.

Bandura, A. *Self-Efficacy: The Exercise of Control.* New York: Freeman, 1997.

Barling J., T. Weber, and E.K. Kelloway. "Effects of Transformational Leadership Training on Attitudinal and Financial Outcomes: A Field Experiment." *Journal of Applied Psychology* 81 (1996): 827–832.

Bass, B.M. *Leadership and Performance Beyond Expectations.* New York: The Free Press, 1985.

Bass, B.M. *Bass & Stogdill Handbook of Leadership.* New York: The Free Press, 1990.

Bass, B.M., and B.J. Avolio. "Training and Development of Transformational Leadership: Looking to 1992 and Beyond." *Journal of European Industrial Training* 14, no. 5 (1990): 21–27.

Bass, B.M., and R.E. Riggio. *Transformational Leadership.* 2nd ed. Mahwah, NJ: Lawrence Erlbaum, 2006.

Bass, B.M., and P. Steidlmeier. "Ethics Character and Authentic Transformational Leadership." *Leadership Quarterly* 10 (1999): 181–217.

Bass, B.M., D.A. Waldman, B.J. Avolio, and M. Bebb. "Transformational Leaders: The Falling Dominoes Effect." *Group and Organization Studies* 12, no. 1 (1987): 73–87.

Burns, J.M. *Leadership.* New York: The Free Press, 1978.

Crookall, P. "Management of Inmate Workers: A Field Test of Transformational and Situational Leadership." Unpublished Ph.D. diss., University of Western Ontario, 1989.

Day, D.V., and P.M.G. O'Connor. "Leadership Development: Understanding the Process." In *The Future of Leadership Development*, edited by S.E. Murphy and R.E. Riggio, 11–28. Mahwah, NJ: Lawrence Erlbaum, 2003.

Dvir, T., E. Eden, B.J. Avolio, and B. Shamir. "Impact of Transformational Leadership Training on Follower Development and Performance: A Field Experiment." *Academy of Management Journal* 45 (2002): 735–744.

Dweck, C.S. "Motivational Processes Affecting Learning." *American Psychologist* 41, no. 10 (1986): 1040–1048.

———. *Self-Theories: Their Role in Motivation, Personality, and Development.* Philadelphia: Psychology Press, 1999.

Dweck, C.S., and E.L. Leggett. "A Social-Cognitive Approach to Motivation and Personality." *Psychological Review* 95 (1988): 256–273.

Follet, Mary Parker. *The Creative Experience.* New York: Longmans, Green, 1924.

Galvin, B., D.A. Waldman, and P. Balthazard. "Narcissism and Communication: Uncovering the Etiology of Transformational Leadership." Unpublished manuscript, Arizona State University, 2008.

Gardner, W.L., B.J. Avolio, F. Luthans, D.R. May, and F.O. Walumbwa. "Can You See the Real Me? A Self-Based Model of Authentic Leader and Follower Development." *Leadership Quarterly* 16 (2005): 343–372.

George, B. *Authentic Leadership: Rediscovering the Secrets to Creating Lasting Value.* San Francisco: Jossey-Bass, 2003.

Hannah, S.T. *Agentic Leadership Efficacy: Test of a new construct and model for development and performance.* Unpublished doctoral dissertation. University of Nebraska-Lincoln, 2006.

Judge, T.A., and R.F. Piccolo. "Transformational and Transactional Leadership: A Meta-analytic Test of Their Relative Validity." *Journal of Applied Psychology* 89 (2004): 755–768.

Kegan, R. *In Over Our Heads: The Mental Demands of Modern Life*. Cambridge, MA: Harvard University Press, 1994.

Kerr, S. "On the folly of rewarding A, while hoping for B." *Academy of Management Journal*, 18 (1975): 769–783.

Kohlberg, L. *The Psychology of Moral Development*. New York: Harper & Row, 1984.

Kuhnert, K.W., and P. Lewis. "Transactional and Transformational Leadership: A Constructive/Developmental Analysis." *Academy of Management Review* 12 (1987): 648–657.

Lord, R.G., and D.J. Brown. *Leadership Processes and Follower Self-Identity*. Mahwah, NJ: Erlbaum, 2004.

Luthans, F. "The Need for and Meaning of Positive Organizational Behavior." *Journal of Organizational Behavior* 23 (2002): 695–706.

Luthans, F., J.B. Avey, B.J. Avolio, S. Norman, and G.M. Combs. "Psychological Capital Development: A Micro Intervention." *Journal of Organizational Behavior* 27 (2006): 387–393.

Luthans, F., Avolio, B.J., Avey, J.B., & Norman, S.M. "Positive psychological capital: Measurement and relationship with performance and satisfaction." *Personnel Psychology*, 60 (2007): 541–572.

Luthans, F., and B.J. Avolio. "Authentic Leadership: A Positive Developmental Approach." In *Positive Organizational Scholarship*, edited by K.S. Cameron, J.E. Dutton, and R.E. Quinn, 241–258. San Francisco: Berrett-Koehler Publishers, 2003.

Luthans, F.L., B.J. Avolio, and C. Youseff. *Psychological Capital: Developing the Human Capital Edge*. Oxford: Oxford University Press, 2007.

Marion, R., and M. Uhl-Bien. "Leadership in Complex Organizations." *Leadership Quarterly* 12 (2001): 389–418.

Reichard, J., and B.J. Avolio. "Where Are We? The Status of Leadership Intervention Research: A Meta-analytic Summary." In *Authentic Leadership Theory and Practice: Origins, Effects and Development*, edited by W.L. Gardner, B.J. Avolio, and F.O. Walumbwa, 203–226. Amsterdam: Elsevier Press, 2005.

Stajkovic, A., and F. Luthans. "Self-Efficacy and Work-Related Performance: A Meta-analysis." *Psychological Bulletin* 44 (1998): 580–590.

Starbuck, W.H. "On Behalf of Naiveté." In *Evolutionary Dynamics of Organizations*, edited by J.A.C. Baum and J.V. Singh, 205–220. New York: Oxford University Press, 1994.

Tichy, N., and M.A. Devanna. *Transformational Leadership*. New York: Wiley, 1986.

Walumbwa, F.O., B.J. Avolio, W.L. Gardner, T.S. Wernsing, and S.J. Peterson. "Authentic Leadership: Development and Validation of a Theory-Based Measure." *Journal of Management* 34 (2008): 89–126.

26

ADULT DEVELOPMENT AND ORGANIZATIONAL LEADERSHIP

Robert Kegan and Lisa Lahey

Whole Cloth, Inc., is a retail clothing company with operations in the United States, Europe, and Asia. Over the last several years, CEO Thomas Schmidt has been grooming Peter Hayes, a high-potential subordinate whom Thomas has admired for his general intelligence, technical knowledge of their business, and people skills. Fourteen months ago Thomas promoted Peter to a platform presidency within the company, putting him in charge of an internationally distributed high-end clothing line for teen girls.

Things are not going well for either of them. Although Peter continues to be insightful in his observations and inferences, he is charged now with developing an overall strategy for his own business, and he seems somehow unable to get enough distance on a number of promising separate ideas to integrate them into a compelling whole. At the same time, for all his continuing ease and comfort with people and their feelings, he is now called upon to make tough personnel decisions, set limits on others' access to him and his counsel, and work out his own conflicting loyalties with a

Author note: This chapter is adapted from chapter 1 of R. Kegan and L.L. Lahey, *Immunity to Change: How to Overcome It and Unlock Potential in Yourself and Your Organization* (Boston: Harvard Business School Press, 2009).

set of former peers who have now become subordinates. He is failing on all of these fronts, and seems not even to realize how he is complicating things by his unwillingness to hold the underperformers accountable, his inability to say no to demands on his time, and his ambivalence about making the platform presidents his new reference group within the company.

Thomas, for his part, is struggling with challenges of his own. Developing an overall strategy—and regulating his relationships in service of it—has been his hallmark since arriving at Whole Cloth, and the company has prospered because of it. But significant changes both in international supply and domestic demand now suggest that persisting in his signature strategy may put the company on a declining path. Thomas has not been blind to these changes nor avoided responding to them, but his responses amount to strategy-preserving tactical fixes rather than a dramatic rethinking of the strategy itself. "If I've learned anything in this business," he has said more than once, "it is this: if what you know how to do is make coats and dresses, then you should stick to making coats and dresses. We are not immune to the cycles of the bigger economy. We don't have to change ships; we just need to ride out the storm." Meanwhile, the ship is taking on a lot of water.

What will distinguish your leadership from others' in the years ahead? We believe it will be your ability to develop yourself, your people, and your teams. Throughout the world—and this is as true in the United States and Europe as it is in China and India—*human capability* will be the critical variable in the new century. But leaders who seek to win a war for talent by conceiving of capability as a *fixed resource* to be found "out there" put themselves and their organizations at a serious disadvantage.

In contrast, leaders who ask themselves, "What can I do to make my setting the most fertile ground in the world for the *growth* of talent?" will put themselves in the best position to succeed. These leaders will understand that in order to deliver on their biggest aspirations—to take advantage of new opportunities or meet new challenges—their people and they themselves must all grow into their own future possibilities. These leaders will know what makes that more possible—and what prevents it.

We have spent a generation now studying the growth of mental complexity in adulthood. We think what we have learned may help you to better understand yourself and those who work with you and for you. In gaining that awareness, you will begin to see a new frontier of human capabilities, the place where tomorrow's most successful leaders will focus their leadership attention.

The New View of Age and Mental Complexity

We begin by identifying a widespread misconception about the potential trajectory of mental development across the lifespan. When we began our work, the accepted picture of mental development was akin to the picture of physical development—your growth was thought fundamentally to end by your twenties. If, thirty years ago, you were to have placed "age" on one axis and "mental complexity" on another and asked the experts in the field to draw the graph as they understood it, they would have produced something similar to figure 26-1: an upward sloping line until the twenties and a flat line thereafter. And they would have drawn it with confidence.

When we began reporting the results of our research in the 1980s, suggesting that some (though not all) adults seemed to undergo qualitative advances in their mental complexity akin to earlier, well-documented quantum leaps from early childhood to later childhood and from later childhood to adolescence, our brain-researcher colleagues sitting next to us on distinguished panels would smile with polite disdain. "You might think you can infer this from your longitudinal interviews," they would say, "but hard science doesn't have to make inferences. We're looking at

FIGURE 26-1

Age and mental complexity: The view thirty years ago

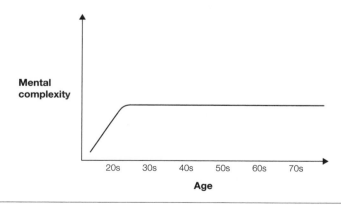

the real thing. The brain simply doesn't undergo any significant change in capacity after late adolescence. Sorry." Of course, these "hard scientists" would grant that older people are often wiser or more capable than younger people, but this they attributed to the benefits of experience, a consequence of learning how to get more out of the same mental equipment rather than any qualitative advances or upgrades to the equipment itself.

Thirty years later? Whoops! It turns out everybody was making inferences, even the brain scientists who thought they were looking at "the thing itself." The hard scientists have better instruments today, and the brain doesn't look to them the way it did thirty years ago. Today they talk about neural plasticity and the phenomenal capacities of the brain to keep adapting throughout life.

If we were to draw the graph showing age and mental complexity today? On the basis of thirty years of longitudinal research by our colleagues and us, and as a result of thoroughly analyzing the transcripts of hundreds of people, interviewed at several-year intervals, the graph would look like figure 26-2.

Two things are evident from this graph:

- If you have a large enough sample size, you can detect a mildly upward-sloping curve. That is, looking at a population as a whole, mental complexity tends to increase with age, throughout adulthood, at least until old age; thus, the story of mental complexity is certainly *not* a story that ends in our twenties.

FIGURE 26-2

Age and mental complexity: The revised view today

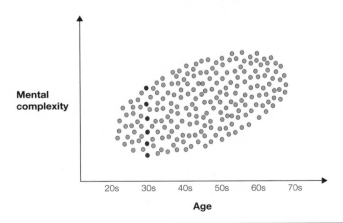

- There is considerable variation within any age. For example, six people in their thirties (the bold dots) could all be at different places in their level of mental complexity, and some could be *more* complex than a person in his or her forties.

If we were to draw a quick picture of what we have learned about the individual trajectory of mental development in adulthood, it might look something like figure 26-3. This picture suggests several different elements:

- There are qualitatively different, discernibly distinct levels (the "plateaus"); that is, the demarcations between levels of mental complexity are not arbitrary. Each level represents a quite different way of knowing the world.

- Development does not unfold continuously; there are periods of stability and periods of change. When a new plateau is reached, we tend to stay on that level for a considerable period of time (although within-system elaborations and extensions can certainly occur).

- The intervals between transformations to new levels—"time on a plateau"—get longer and longer.

- The line gets thinner, representing fewer and fewer people at the higher plateaus.

But what do these different levels of mental complexity in adulthood actually look like? Can we say something about what a more

FIGURE 26-3

The trajectory of mental development in adulthood

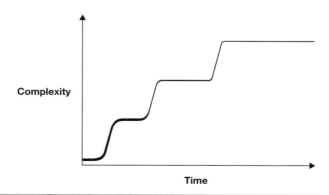

complex level can see or do that a less complex level cannot? Indeed, we can now say a great deal about these levels. Mental complexity and its evolution is not about how smart you are in the ordinary sense of the word. It is not about how high your IQ is. It is not about developing more and more abstract, abstruse apprehensions of the world, as if "most complex" means finally being able to understand a physicist's blackboard filled with complex equations.

Three Plateaus in Adult Mental Complexity

Let's begin with a quick overview of three qualitatively different plateaus in mental complexity we see among adults, as suggested in figure 26-4 and table 26-1. These three adult meaning systems—the socialized mind, self-authoring mind, and self-transforming mind—make sense of the world, and operate within it, in profoundly different ways. We can see how this shows up at work by focusing on any significant aspect of organizational life and seeing how the very same phenomenon—for example, information flow—takes on a completely different character when viewed through the lens of each perspective.

FIGURE 26-4

Three plateaus in adult mental development

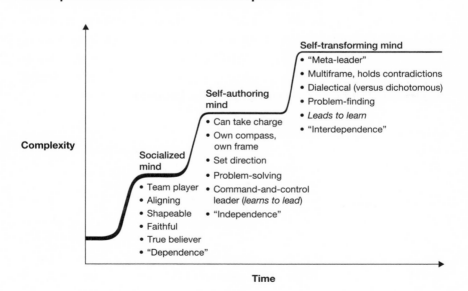

TABLE 26-1

Adult meaning systems

The socialized mind

- We are shaped by the definitions and expectations of our personal environment.

- Our self coheres by its alignment with or loyalty to that with which it identifies.

- This can express itself primarily in our relationships with people or with ideas and beliefs, or both.

The self-authoring mind

- We are able to step back enough from the social environment to generate an internal "seat of judgment" or personal authority, which evaluates and makes choices about external expectations.

- Our self coheres by its alignment with its own belief system, ideology, or personal code; by its ability to self-direct, take stands, set limits, create, and regulate its boundaries on behalf of its own voice.

The self-transforming mind

- We can step back from and reflect on the limits of our own ideology or personal author-ity; see that any one system or self-organization is in some way partial or incomplete; be friendlier toward contradiction and oppositeness; seek to hold onto multiple systems rather than projecting all but one onto the other.

- Our self coheres through its ability to distinguish internal consistency from wholeness or completeness; its alignment with the dialectic rather than either pole.

The way information does or does not flow through an organiza-tion—what people "send," to whom they send it, how they receive or attend to what flows to them—is an obviously crucial feature of how any system works. Experts on organizational culture, organizational behavior, or organizational change often address this subject with a sophisticated sense of how systems affect individual behavior, but with an astonishingly naive sense of how powerful a factor is the level of mental complexity with which the individual views that culture or change initiative.

Socialized Mind

Having a socialized mind dramatically influences both the sending and receiving aspects of information flow at work. If this is the level of men-tal complexity with which I view the world, then—like Peter Hayes of Whole Cloth, Inc.—what I think to send will be strongly influenced by what I believe others want to hear. You may be familiar with the classic groupthink studies, which show team members withholding crucial information from collective decision processes because (it is later learned in follow-up research) "although I knew the plan had almost no chance of succeeding, I saw that the leader wanted our support."

Some of these groupthink studies were originally done in Asian cultures, where withholding team members talked about "saving face" of leaders and not subjecting them to shame, even at the price of setting the company on a losing path. The studies were often presented as if they were uncovering a particularly cultural phenomenon. Similarly, Stanley Milgram's famous obedience-to-authority research was originally undertaken to fathom the mentality of "the good German," and what it was about the German culture that could enable otherwise decent, nonsadistic people to carry out orders to exterminate millions of Jews and Poles.[1] But Milgram, in practice runs of his data-gathering method, was surprised to find "good Germans" all over Main Street, U.S.A., and although we think of sensitivity to shame as a particular feature of Asian culture, the research of Irving Janis and Paul t'Hart has made it clear that groupthink is as robust a phenomenon in Texas and Toronto as it is in Tokyo and Taiwan.[2] It is a phenomenon that owes its origin not to culture, but to complexity of mind.

The socialized mind also strongly influences how information is *received* and *attended to*. When maintaining alignment with important others and valued "surrounds" is crucial to the coherence of one's very being, as it is for Peter, the socialized mind is highly sensitive to, and influenced by, what it picks up. And what it picks up often runs far beyond the explicit message. It may well include the results of highly invested attention to imagined subtexts that may have more impact on the receiver than the intended message. This is often astonishing and dismaying to leaders who cannot understand how subordinates could possibly have "made *that* sense out of *this*" communication, but because the receiver's signal-to-noise detector may be highly distorted, the actual information that comes through may have only a distant relationship to the sender's intention.

Self-Authoring Mind

Let's contrast all this with the self-authoring mind. If I view the world from this level of mental complexity, as does CEO Thomas Schmidt, what I "send" is more likely to be a function of what I deem others need to hear to best further the agenda or mission of my design. Consciously or unconsciously, I have a direction, an agenda, a stance, a strategy, an analysis of what is needed, and a prior context from which my communication arises. My direction or plan may be an excellent one, or it may be riddled with blind spots. I may be masterful or inept at recruiting others to invest themselves in this direction. These matters implicate other aspects of the self. But mental complexity strongly influences whether my information sending is oriented toward getting behind the wheel in order to drive (the self-authoring mind) or getting myself included in the car so I can be driven (the socialized mind).

We can see a similar mind-set operating in "receiving" as well. The self-authoring mind creates a filter for what it will allow to come through. It places a priority on receiving the information it has sought. Next in importance is information whose relevance to the individual's plan, stance, or frame is immediately clear. Information the person hasn't asked for, and which does not have obvious relevance to his or her own design for action, has a much tougher time making it through the filter.

It is easy to see how all of this could describe an admirable capacity for focus, for distinguishing the important from the urgent, for making the best use of one's limited time by having a means to cut through the unending and ever-mounting claims on one's attention. This speaks to the way the self-authoring mind is an advance over the socialized mind. But this same description may also be a recipe for disaster if one's plan or stance is flawed in some way, if it leaves out some crucial element of the equation not appreciated by the filter, or if, as in Thomas's case, the world changes in such a way that a once-good frame becomes an antiquated one.

Self-Transforming Mind

In contrast, the self-transforming mind also has a filter, but is not fused with it and is not identical to it. The self-transforming mind can stand back from its own filter and look *at* it, not just *through* it. And why would it do so? Because the self-transforming mind both values and *is wary about* any one stance, analysis, or agenda. It is mindful that, powerful though a given design might be, any design almost inevitably leaves something out. It is aware that it lives in time and that the world is in motion, and what might have made sense today may not make as much sense tomorrow.

Therefore, when sending communications, people with self-transforming minds are not only advancing their agenda and design. They are also making space for the modification or expansion of their agenda or design. Like those with self-authoring minds, what they send may include inquiries and requests for information. But rather than inquiring only *within* the frame of their design (seeking information that will advance their agenda), they are also inquiring about the design itself. They are seeking information that may lead them or their team to enhance, refine, or alter the original design or make it more inclusive. Information sending is not just on behalf of driving; it is also on behalf of remaking the map or resetting the direction.

Similarly, the way the self-transforming mind receives information includes the advantages of the self-authoring mind's filter, but is not a prisoner of it. People at this level of mental complexity can still focus, select, and drive when they feel they have a good map. But they place a higher priority on information that may also alert them to the limits of their current design or frame. They value their filter and its ability to separate the wheat from the chaff, but they know it can also screen out "the golden chaff," the unasked-for, the anomaly, the apparently inconsequential that may be just what is needed to turn the design on its head and bring it to the next level of quality.

Those with self-transforming minds are more likely to have the chance even to consider such information, because people are more likely to send it to them. Why is this? Because those with self-transforming minds not only attend to information once it gets to their door; they also realize their behavior can have a big effect, *upstream*, on whether people decide to approach the door. Others are not left guessing whether to send a potentially "off-mission" communication they judge to be important. They send it because people with self-transforming minds have found ways to let them know such information will be welcomed.

Mental Complexity and Performance

These descriptions, focusing on just a single important element of organizational life—information flow—should begin to make the different levels of mental complexity a little clearer. They also suggest a value proposition for mental complexity. Each successive level of mental complexity is formally higher than the preceding one because it can perform the mental functions of the prior level as well as additional functions. But the discussion of how information flow is conceived and handled also suggests that these formal mental properties translate into real actions with real consequences for organizational behavior and work competence. The implication is that a higher level of mental complexity outperforms a lower level.

Is this just a hypothesis, albeit with some plausible face validity, or has it actually been tested and systematically demonstrated? There are now a number of studies correlating measures of mental complexity with independent assessments of work competence or performance. We will consider these results in greater depth later, but for now let's just take a peek at what these studies show.

Keith Eigel assessed the level of mental complexity of twenty-one CEOs of large, successful companies, each company an industry leader with average gross revenue of over $5 billion.[3] (He used a ninety-minute interview assessment measure that we and our colleagues developed. The Subject-Object Interview, described in the box entitled "How Do We Assess Level of Mental Complexity?" has been used all over the world, across all sectors, over the last twenty years. It discriminates developmental movement between, and within, the levels of mental complexity with high degrees of interrater reliability.) Using separate performance assessments, Eigel also evaluated the CEOs' effectiveness in terms of the ability to

- Challenge existing processes

- Inspire a shared vision

- Manage conflict

- Solve problems

- Delegate

- Empower

- Build relationships

In addition, for comparison, Eigel did similar assessments in each of the same companies, interviewing promising middle managers nominated by their respective CEOs. Figure 26-5 summarizes his findings.

How Do We Assess Level of Mental Complexity?

Our assessment tool is a ninety-minute interview we call the Subject-Object Interview, so named because the complexity of a mind-set is a function of the way it distinguishes the thoughts and feelings we have (i.e., can look at, can take *as object*) from the thoughts and feelings that "have us" (i.e., we are run by them, are *subject to* them). Each different level of mind-set complexity differently draws the line between what is subject and what is object. Greater complexity means being able to *look at* more (take more *as object*). The blind spot (what is *subject*) becomes smaller and smaller. The assessment instrument has proven to be quite subtle: it can identify, with high degrees of interrater reliability, fully five different transitional places between any two mind-sets.

The interview begins by handing the subject ten index cards, upon which are written the following cues:

1. Angry

2. Anxious, nervous

3. Success

4. Strong stand, conviction

5. Sad

6. Torn

7. Moved, touched

8. Lost something, farewells

9. Change

10. Important

In the first fifteen minutes, we ask the interviewee to make notes on each card in response to questions of the following form: "If you were to think of some times, over the last few days or weeks, when you found yourself feeling really mad or angry about something [or nervous, scared or anxious, etc.], jot down what comes to mind."

A highly exploratory interview then proceeds in which the interviewee tells us the *whats* (what made him or her feel angry, successful, etc.) and we probe to learn the *whys* (why would that make him or her feel angry or successful; just what is at stake?). We chose these prompts because earlier research showed them to be highly eliciting of what is at stake for people given the way they construct reality. A trained interviewer can probe such material to learn the underlying principle of what the person can see and not see (the blind spot).

The interviews are transcribed and analyzed according to a uniform process. Thousands of these interviews have now been conducted with people all over the world, of all ages and all walks of life. Most people find the interview a highly engaging experience.

Source: L. Lahey, E. Souvaine, R. Kegan, et al., *A Guide to the Subject-Object Interview: Its Administration and Analysis* (Cambridge, MA: The Subject-Object Research Group, Harvard University Graduate School of Education, 1988).

Several results stand out. The first one is the clearly discernible upward slope, signifying that increased mental complexity and work competence, assessed on a number of dimensions, are correlated. So not only is it possible to reach higher planes of mental complexity, but such growth correlates with effectiveness, for both CEOs and middle managers. This finding has been replicated in a variety of fine-grained studies of small numbers of leaders, assessed on particular competencies.[4] Taken together, the cumulative data speak anew to the problem

FIGURE 26-5

Eigel results

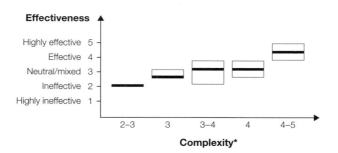

		Socializing		Self-authoring		
CEO →	0	0	0	17	4	n = 21
MM →	1	2	7	10	1	n = 21

Source: K. Eigel, 1998 doctoral thesis, University of Georgia.
* 3 = Socializing mind; 4 = Self-authoring mind; 5 = Self-transforming mind

of complexity: we begin to see how being at a given level of mental complexity can make a "complex world" more or less manageable.

We can also take a more sweeping view of the same issue by considering the new demands on leaders and their subordinates in the faster, flatter, more interconnected world in which we live. Take another look at figure 26-4, the chart of the various plateaus in adult mental complexity.

Now let's consider what was asked, and is now being asked, of subordinates, such as Peter Hayes at Whole Cloth, Inc. In the world in which we *used to* live, it was enough in most cases if people were good team players, pulled their weight, were loyal to the company or organization where they worked, and could be counted on to follow conscientiously the directions and signals of their boss. In other words, the socialized mind would be perfectly adequate to handle the nature of yesterday's demands upon subordinates.

And today? Nathaniel Branden writes:

In the past two or three decades, extraordinary developments have occurred in the American and global economies. The United States has shifted from a manufacturing society to an information society. We have witnessed the transition from physical labor to mind work as the dominant employee activity. We now live in a global economy characterized by rapid change, accelerating scientific and technological breakthroughs, and an unprecedented level of competitiveness. These developments create demand for higher levels of education and training than were required of previous generations. Everyone acquainted with business culture knows this. What is not understood is that these developments also create new demands on our psychological resources. Specifically, these developments ask for a greater capacity for innovation, self-management, personal responsibility, and self-direction. This is not just asked at the top, it is asked at every level of a business enterprise, from senior management to first-line supervisors and even to entry-level personnel . . . Today, organizations need not only an unprecedentedly higher level of knowledge and skill among all those who participate but also a higher level of independence, self-reliance, self-trust, and the capacity to exercise initiative.[5]

What is Branden—and many others who write about what we are now looking for from our workforce—really saying, as it relates to level of mental complexity? He is saying, without realizing it, that it used to be sufficient for workers to be at the level of the socialized mind, but today we need workers who are at the level of the self-authoring mind. In effect, we are calling upon workers to understand themselves and their world at a qualitatively higher level of mental complexity.

And what is the picture if we look not at subordinates but at bosses and leaders, like Thomas Schmidt? Organizational theorist Chris Argyris raises similar issues about the ever-growing insufficiency of traditional conceptions of managerial and leadership effectiveness that still dominate our thinking today. There may have been a day when it was enough for leaders to develop worthy goals and sensible norms, cultivate alignment around them, and work "to keep organizational performance within the range specified—all the while exercising the strength of character to advocate for one's position and hold one's ground in the face of opposition."[6] Skillful as such managers may be, their abilities will no longer suffice in a world that calls for leaders who can not only run but also reconstitute their organizations—its norms, missions, and culture—in an increasingly fast-changing environment. For example, a company that chooses to transform itself from a low-cost standardized-products organization to a mass customizer or a provider of organization-wide solutions will need to develop a whole new set of individual and team capabilities.

Argyris and Schon described the challenges of a similar organizational transition thirty years ago:

> This, in turn, requires that members of the corporation adopt new approaches to marketing, managing, and advertising; that they become accustomed to a much shorter product life cycle and to a more rapid cycle of changes in their pattern of activities; that they, in fact, change the very image of the business they are in. And these requirements for change come into conflict with another sort of corporate norm, one that requires predictability in the management of corporate affairs . . . A process of change initiated with an eye to effectiveness under existing norms turns out to yield a conflict in the norms themselves.[7]

For more than a generation, Argyris (and those who have been influenced by him) has unwittingly been calling for a new capacity of mind. This new mind would have the ability not just to *author* a view of how the organization should run and have the courage to stand steadfastly within it, but also to step outside *its own* ideology or framework; such a mind can observe its limitations or defects and *reauthor* a more comprehensive view—which it will also hold with sufficient tentativeness that its limitations can be discovered as well. In other words, the kind of learner Argyris rightly looks for in the leader of today may need to be a person who is making meaning with a *self-transforming* mind.

Thus, we are asking more and more workers, like Peter, who could once perform their work successfully with socialized minds—good soldiers—to shift to self-authoring minds. And we are asking more and more leaders, like Thomas, who could once lead successfully with self-authoring minds—sure and certain captains—to develop self-transforming minds. In short, we are asking for a quantum shift in individual mental complexity across the board.

So how big *is* the gap between what we now expect of people's minds and what they are actually like? Are we expecting something that is too big a reach? After all, if the world has gotten more complex over the last half century, then perhaps the world has become a better incubator of mental complexity as well, and the supply of mental complexity has risen with the demand.

We now have two sophisticated, reliable, and widely used measures for assessing mental complexity along the lines we are talking about here. (This is something quite different, obviously, from IQ testing, which has only the most modest correlation with mental complexity; you can have an above-average IQ, say 125, and be at any of the three plateaus.) These are the Subject-Object Interview (SOI) we introduced earlier and Loevinger's Sentence Completion Test (SCT).[8] Two large meta-analyses of studies using one or the other of these measures have now been performed, with several hundred participants in each study. Figure 26-6 presents a quick summary of results.

Two observations stand out from the data in figure 26-6:

- Both studies, each done with completely different samples, arrive at the same finding—that in a majority of respondents, mental complexity is not as complex as the self-authoring mind (in fact, in each study exactly 58 percent are not at this level)—and since both studies are skewed toward middle-class, college-educated

FIGURE 26-6

Study results

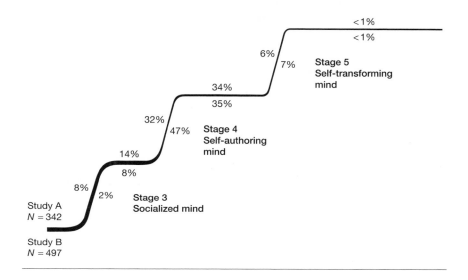

professionals, the actual percentage in the general population is likely even higher.

- The percentage of people *beyond* the plateau of the self-authoring mind is quite small.

These data suggest that the gap between what we now expect of people's minds (including our own minds) and what our minds are actually like is quite large. We expect most workers to be self-authoring, but most are not. We expect most leaders to be more complex than self-authoring, and very few are.

We can see these same macro trends confirmed at the micro level if we return for a moment to the Eigel study (have another look at figure 26-5). Note here that only about half of the "promising middle managers" are self-authoring (and those who are do better than those who are not), and only four of the twenty-one CEOs from industry-leading companies are beyond self-authoring (and those who are do better than those who are not).

Our colleague and friend Ronald Heifetz makes an important distinction that helps us summarize the central points we have made so far. Heifetz distinguishes between two kinds of change challenges, those he calls "technical" and others he calls "adaptive."[9] Technical changes are not necessarily easy, nor are their results necessarily unimportant or insignificant. Learning how to remove an inflamed appendix or how to land an airplane with a stuck nose wheel are examples of technical challenges, and their accomplishment is certainly important to the patient on the surgeon's table or the nervous passengers contemplating a crash landing.

They are nonetheless "technical" from Heifetz's point of view because the skill sets necessary to perform these complicated behaviors are well known. The routines and processes by which we might help an intern or novice pilot become an accomplished practitioner are well practiced and proven. While it is entirely possible that an intern or a pilot in training will become qualitatively more complex over years of training, such mental growth is beyond the scope of his or her technical training. Novice surgeons, for example, become sufficiently skilled surgeons without anyone worrying about their adult development or mental growth.

However, many, if not most, of the change challenges you face today and will face tomorrow—such as those Peter and Thomas are facing—require something more than incorporating new technical skills into your current mind-set. These are the "adaptive challenges," and they can only be met by transforming mind-sets—yours and your subordinates—by advancing to more sophisticated levels of mental development.

Heifetz says the biggest error leaders make is their attempt to apply technical means to solving adaptive challenges. In other words, we may be unable to bring about the changes we want because we are misdiagnosing our aspiration as technical, when in reality it is an adaptive challenge. The implication is that we must find *adaptive* (nontechnical) means of supporting ourselves and others to meet adaptive challenges.

Distinguishing adaptive challenges from technical ones again brings our attention back from the "problem" to the "person having the problem." We've said that "complexity" is really a story about the relationship between the complex demands and arrangements of the world and our own complexity of mind. When we look at this relationship, we discover a gap: our own mental complexity lags behind the complexity of the world's demands. We are in over our heads.

Is it possible that the field of "leadership development" has overattended to *leadership* and underattended to *development*? An endless stream of books declares one or another characteristic crucial to leadership success, and then sets out to help you master it. The various attributes called for in a leader make claims on cognitive, emotional, and interpersonal regulation. Meanwhile, the underlying "operating system" itself—which *sets the terms* on mastery; which shapes our thinking, feeling, and social relating—goes unaddressed. Just imagine how much more powerful the work of *leadership development* would be if it were anchored in what we now know about fostering the development of the meaning-making self in adulthood.[10]

Notes

1. S. Milgram, *Obedience to Authority* (New York: Harper & Row, 1974).

2. I. Janis, *Groupthink* (Boston: Houghton Mifflin, 1982); P. t'Hart, *Groupthink in Government* (Baltimore, MD: Johns Hopkins University Press, 1990).

3. K. Eigel, "Leader Effectiveness: A Constructive-Developmental View and Investigation," PhD diss., University of Georgia, 1998.

4. Bartone compared level of mental complexity and leadership performance rankings among graduating West Point cadets and found a significant positive correlation. (P. Bartone et al., "Psychological Development and Leader Performance in West Point Cadets," paper presented at AERA, Seattle, April 2001.) Benay assessed the mental complexity of eight leaders in a midsized food distribution company and found the same upward-sloping relationship with a multifactor leadership measure assessing "transformational leadership abilities." (P. Benay, "Social-Cognitive Development and Transformational Leadership: A Case Study," PhD diss., University of Massachusetts, 1997.) Bushe and Gibb studied sixty-four consultants and found that their level of mental complexity was strongly and significantly associated with peer ratings for consulting competence via a seventy-seven-item instrument tested for reliability and validity. (G.R. Bushe and B.W. Gibb, "Predicting Organization Development Consulting Competence from the Myers-Briggs Type Indicator and Stage of Ego Development," *Journal of Applied Behavioral Science* 26 [1990]: 337–357.)

5. N. Branden, *The Six Pillars of self-Esteem* (New York: Bantam, 1995), 22–23.

6. C. Argyris and D. Schön, *Organizational Learning* (Reading, MA: Addison-Wesley, 1978), 21.

7. Ibid.

8. J. Loevinger and R. Wessler, *Measuring Ego Development* (San Francisco: Jossey-Bass, 1970).

9. R. Heifetz, *Leadership Without Easy Answers* (Cambridge, MA: Harvard University Press, 1998).

10. See, for example, R. Kegan and L. Lahey, *Immunity to Change: How to Overcome It and Unlock Potential in Yourself and Your Organization* (Boston: Harvard Business School Press, 2009).

INDEX

ABN AMRO, 578
abusive behavior, and leadership failure, 199–200
Academy of Management Journal (AMJ), 119, 120, 126–132, 141, 146–154
accommodation, 111
action, in social movements, 553–556
action learning development initiatives, 733–736
activist leadership teams, 479–480
Administrative Science Quarterly (ASQ), 119, 120, 126–132, 141, 146–154
adult development, 769–787
   leadership development programs and, 717
   mental complexity and performance in, 778–787
   new view of age and mental capacity and, 771–774
   plateaus of adult mental complexity and, 774–787
   self-authoring mind and, 776–777
   self-transforming mind and, 777–778
   socialized mind and, 775–776
   Subject-Object Interview (SOI) and, 779, 780–781, 784
Aghion, P., 241, 244
agile software development, 621–622
alignment teams, 488
Allen, George, 321
AlliedSignal, 276
Alumni Workshop (for alumni of New CEO Workshop), Harvard Business School, 468
ambiguity, in a leader's behavior, 163

Amelio, William, 519
Ancona, D., 481, 491–492
anticipation, 214
Argyris, C., 783, 784
Army, U.S., 723
Arvey, Rich, 751
assimilation, 111
Asymmetric Society, The (Coleman), 96
authenticity, 285–287
authentic leadership development, 739–766
   development readiness and, 752–754
   leadership born versus made question in, 747–748, 751–752
   moral capacity and, 743–745
   practitioner-scientists developed in, 740
   transformational leaders and, 742–743, 745, 747–751
authority
   ambiguity in a leader's behavior and, 163
   CEO leadership and, 462
   delegation of, 243–244
   leadership teams and, 491–495
   voluntary association leaders and, 529
   Weberian approach to, 225, 314
autonomous leadership, 338, 350, 366
Avolio, B.J., 172, 338, 755
Axelrod, Robert, 268–269, 278

Bacon, Francis, 319
Baldwin, Neil, 618
Bales, Robert F., 67
Banco Real, 578, 587, 590

Bandura, Albert, 753
Bank of America, 577
Barbosa, Fabio, 578, 590
Barnard, Chester, 16, 29, 65, 69, 71–72, 93, 97, 109, 232, 475, 476, 510
Baron, J.N., 169
Barrett, Colleen, 277
Bass, Bernard M., 11, 68, 119, 120, 121, 125, 338, 745, 747
Bazerman, Max, 512
Bear Stearns, 507–509, 511, 521
Beckman, C., 231
behavioral flexibility, 162–163
behavioral theories of leadership, 122–123, 125, 142
behaviors of leaders
    impact on the organization and, 32
    leadership theories based on, 125
    top management teams and, 478
Bendix, Reinhard, 225, 229–231
Bennis, Warren G., 9, 11, 22, 66, 265–266, 270, 274, 281, 286, 287–288, 412
Berg, D.N., 497, 498
Berson, Y., 172, 338
Bertrand, M., 32
Biggart, Nicole W., 231
bin Laden, Osama, 309, 315–316, 318
Bion, Wilfred, 493
bipolar disorder, 203
Black, Konrad, 245
Blanchard, Kenneth, 710
Block, Peter, 622–623, 631
blueprint concept, in leading organizations, 169
Boal, K.B., 162
boards of directors
    CEO leadership and, 245–246, 437–438
    decision making and, 515–516
Boeing, 516–517, 521
Bossidy, Larry, 276
Brand, Stewart, 632–633
Branden, Nathaniel, 782–783
Bray, D., 682–683
Bresnen, Michael J., 92–93
Brickley, James A., 278–279, 280, 285
brokerage advantage, 234–235
Brown, John Seely, 617, 718
Brown, Tim, 615

Brueggemann, Walter, 530, 531
Bruner, Jerome, 534
Building 20 (MIT), 633, 643
bullying, 316, 326
bureaucratic leadership, 348–349, 366, 369
Burke, Jim, 425
Burns, James MacGregor, 305, 317, 741–742
Burr, Donald, 139
Burt, Ronald, 34, 42, 57, 234–235
Burton, Dianne M., 231
Bush, George W., 317
business history, 298–300
Business Leadership (Metcalf), 292
business process redesign (BPR), 662, 667
Business Roundtable, 516
business schools
    educational goals of, 4
    gap between purpose and practice in, 4–6
    women in, 378
Butler, Timothy, 630

Caldwell, Philip, 312
campaigns, in social movements, 557–558
Campbell, Sherlock R., 83
Carli, Linda, 389
Carnegie, Andrew, 291, 292, 293, 316
Carnegie Institute of Technology, 292
Carpenter, Kenneth, 293
Carter, Jimmy, 463
Carter, Larry, 514
cascading initiatives, 730–731
case method, Harvard Business School, 298
Catalyst, 385, 388
Catmull, Ed, 613, 615–616, 621
cause-effect models, 113
Cayne, James, 308
Cemex, 581, 583, 584, 592, 602, 605
Center for Work-Life Policy, 383, 389
CEO leadership
    board of directors and, 245–246, 437–438
    communication by, 454–455

CEO leadership (*continued*)
  constraints and firm performance
    and, 28–32
  contingent opportunities view of,
    27–28, 33–58
  empirical studies of, 31–32
  evolution of corporation and,
    434–435A
  expectations of change and, 441–442
  functions of, 436
  impact on organization of, 27
  indirect influence and, 443–450
  industries and impact of, 39–55
  information gathering and, 455–456
  legitimacy of, 461–466
  limits of power of, 438–439
  limits of time and, 442–443
  obtaining information and, 439
  opportunities and external task
    environment and, 33–36, 53–54
  personal agenda of, 452–453
  as personification of company,
    440–441
  presence used by, 451
  resource availability and, 37–38,
    53–54
  role in organization and, 433–470
  scope of job and, 437
  studies of, 434
  symbolism leveraged by, 459–460
  time horizon and, 441
  unpredictability and, 442–443
  variations across industries in, 33–36,
    50–53
  visibility of, 440
Chambers, John, 514
Chandler, Alfred D., Jr., 14, 292, 293,
  296–300, 301, 434–435
change, 527–561
  action mobilization in, 553–556
  background of leaders in, 529–531
  building relationships and, 531–533
  CEO leadership and, 441–442
  corporate performance and, 224
  facilitating, 210–217
  leaders and, 205–210
  need for leadership to lead in, 527–528
  social movements and, 527, 528–529,
    550–561

strategy in, 545–552
  telling the story (public narrative) in,
    533–545
  transitional space and, 213–214
Change Masters, The (Kanter), 505–596
change process, and leadership
    theories, 125
character, 286
Charan, Ram, 659, 701
charisma
  international companies and, 586–587
  social movements and, 539
charismatic authority, 225, 314
charismatic influence, 417–418,
    423, 426
charismatic leadership, 70–71, 125, 233,
    741–742
Chávez, César, 530, 550–551
Cheney, Dick, 316–317
Child, John, 29, 640
Children's Safe Drinking Water
    (CSDW), 585
Chohung Bank, 590–591, 603–604
circulation of elites, 228–229
Cisco Systems, 513–514
Citigroup, 572
Civil Rights movement, 552
claims making, 553
clarification, 209
Clark, Burton R., 75–76
Clinton, Hillary, 377, 378–379
coaching
  leadership development using, 713,
    718, 720, 723, 727, 734
  for leadership team members,
    499–500
  for work-group members, 166–167
Coase, Ronald, 239, 322
Cockburn, Alistair, 621–622
co-design process, in innovation,
    617–620
Cohen, Michael D., 8–9, 66
Cole, Arthur, 293, 294
Coleman, James S., 11, 96
collaboration, 426, 553
collective cognition, 341
Collins, Jim, 275, 276, 284
commitment, 276–278, 282, 287,
    622–623

communication
    decisions of leaders and, 421
    economic approaches to leadership
        and, 246–247, 252, 258–260,
        281–285
    effective leadership with, 242
    power and, 314–315
    symbolic, 421
    two-way aspect of, 242, 259–260,
        284–285
Communications Equipment industry,
    CEO leadership in, 34–36, 35*t*,
    36*t*, 38
Community (Block), 622, 631
competence, 40, 228, 379, 386–387,
    393, 423, 426, 462, 467
complexity, and international
    companies, 574, 575, 576–579
concept of leadership, 107–116
    conditions and, 113–116
    context of leadership and, 111–113
    criteria of leadership success and,
        108–109
    domain of leadership and, 107–108
    functions of leadership and,
        109–111
Conference Board, 434
conflict avoidance, 199
conflict triangle, 207–209
confrontation, 208
conscience collective, 80
consistency, of a leader's behavior, 163,
    171–173
constraints, in contingent opportunities
    view, 27–28, 33–55
constructive narcissism, 194–195
Construrama, 584
consultative teams, 488
context of leadership, 111–113
contingency theory of leadership,
    411–428
    activities of leadership in, 419–421
    context and, 111–112
    contingent variables in, 416-
    definition of leadership in, 413–414
    expectations of followers in, 422
    international differences across a
        company and, 423–425
    leaders and followers in, 417–419

    organizational complexity and,
        422–423
    organization behavior (OB)
        approaches and, 123–124, 142,
        143–144, 411–413
    task to be accomplished and, 425–427
    value of, 414–416
contingent opportunities view of CEO
    leadership, 27–28, 33–58
    matrix view of, 38–39, 39
    opportunities and external task
        environment and, 33–36, 53–54
    resource availability and, 37–38, 53–54
    study of industries in, 39–55
    variations across industries in, 33–36,
        50–53
control rights, 241, 244
conviction, 255
coordinating teams, 488
coordination, 250–251
cooperation, in work groups, 167–168
core conflictual relationship themes
    (CCRT), 190–191
corporate citizenship, and international
    companies, 584–586
creative agility, 618
creative abrasion, 617–618
Creative Experience (Follett), 619, 741
creativity, conditions for, 114
Crocker, Jennifer, 398
Crookall, Paul, 750
cross-cultural research, 140
cultural context, 335–371
    GLOBE dimensions for measuring,
        344–354
    implicit leadership theory and,
        340–343
    national culture and, 339–340
    organizational culture and, 338
    research on, 354–371
culturally endorsed implicit leadership
    theory (CLT), 336–337, 341,
    342, 368
culture of an organization
    international differences across a
        company and, 423–425
    leader's efforts to change the
        organization and, 31
    as a leadership tool, 170–171

cumulative theory-building, 142–144
cyclothymia, 203

David and Goliath story, 546–547
Davis, G.F., 143
Davis-Blake, Allison, 67
Day, D.V., 342
debt, and impact of CEO leadership,
    37–38
decision making, 507–522
    Boeing example of, 516–518
    Enron example of, 515–516
    importance of leadership to, 510–511
    inner and outer circles of advisers
        and, 513–514
    investment banking crisis example of,
        507–509
    Lenovo's acquisition of IBM as
        example of, 518–520
    Mount Everest expedition example
        of, 520–521
    role of boards of directors in, 515–516
    70 percent solution in, 514
    underpreparation and, 512–513
decision-making teams, 488–489
decisiveness, of a leader's behavior, 163
definitions of leadership
    contingency theory of leadership and,
        413–414
    organizational theory and, 8–9
    organization behavior (OB) literature
        on, 121
defensive behavior, 207–208
delegation of authority, 243–244
Department of Commerce Survey of
    Current Business, 42
design process, in innovation, 617–620
Devanna, Mary Anne, 68, 747
development programs. *See* leadership
    development programs
diagnostic activity of leadership,
    161–162
Dimon, James, 418, 508, 511
discretion, and impact of managers, 33
diversity
    international companies and, 598–599
    programs to encourage, 76, 272–273
Division of Labour, The (Durkheim), 80

Dobbin, Frank, 76, 77
domain of leadership, 107–108
Donofrio, Nick, 591
Dotlich, D., 701
Dowd, Maureen, 378
Drotter, S., 659
Drucker, Peter, 29, 630
Duguid, P., 718
Dunlap, Al, 326
Durkheim, Émile, 11, 58, 69, 70,
    80, 232

Eagly, Alice, 389
Early Leaders initiative, Simon
    Graduate School of Business
    (University of Rochester), 272–273
Eastman, George, 316
eBay, 509
Eccles, Robert G., 92
ecology, organizational, 9
economic perspective, 265–289
economists, perspectives of, 239–263
Eckert, Bob, 265
Edison, Thomas, 615, 618, 621
Edmondson, A., 485, 497
education for leadership.
    See leadership development
    programs
Egorov, G., 261
Eigel, Keith, 779, 785
Eisenhower, Dwight, 309–310
Eisner, Michael, 325
Eller College of Management
    (University of Arizona), 271–272
emotional intelligence, 161–162,
    287, 711
empowering others, and effective
    leadership, 242, 252, 260–262
Emrich, C.G., 341
encouragement, 213–214
enrollment, 274–276
Enron, 143, 509, 515
equal opportunity programs, 76
Erhard, Werner, 278–279, 280, 285
Evans, Philip, 322
example, and commitment, 277
exchange constraints, 34–35, 36, 39,
    41–42, 44–45, 53, 57

execution, and effective leadership, 242, 252, 258
executive education programs, 205–206. *See also* leadership development programs
experience, 679–705
  developing leadership and, 680–681
  focus on transition and, 702–704
  future research agenda for, 704–705
  identifying developmental experiences, 687
  identifying potential in, 688–690
  increasing the odds for learning from, 695–700
  leadership programs based in, 681–682
  research on core elements of, 682–687
  right experience at the right time in, 692–695

face-saving leadership, 351, 366–367
fairness, 463
FedEx, 725
feminine style of leadership, 323–324
Ferreira, D., 250, 252
Fiedler, Frederick E., 124, 412
Financial Times, 322
Finkelstein, S., 28, 33, 37, 42, 51, 53, 57, 67
Fiorina, Carly, 325, 377, 378
firm, economic theory of, 239–240
First Chicago, 418
Fischer, David Hackett, 299, 300
Fisher, Colin, 115–116
flexibility, behavioral, 162–163
Florida, Richard, 617–618
Follett, Mary Parker, 619, 620, 639–640, 741
Ford, Henry, 312, 764
Ford Motor Company, 312
founding blueprints, 169
Freeman, Douglass Southall, 299–300
Freeman, Jo, 30, 559
Freud, Anna, 200
Freud, Sigmund, 187, 191
Friebel, G., 261
Friedman, Thomas, 319

functions of leadership, 109–111, 475–476
Functions of the Executive, The (Barnard), 71–72, 232, 475, 510
Fuqua/Coach K Center of Leadership and Ethics, 266
Fuqua School of Business (Duke University), 266

Gallup polls, 377
Gamson, Bill, 536
Gandhi, Indira, 379
Gantt, Henry L., 292
Gardner, Howard, 121, 614
Gardner, John, 421
Gates, Bill, 270
Geletkanycz, M.A., 339
gender differences, 382–383, 386, 389
gender diversity, 389–390, 400–401, 403
gender egalitarianism, 347–348, 354, 361, 366, 368
gender roles, changes in, 377–378
gender stereotypes, 323–325, 379, 384–385, 388, 397
General Electric (GE), 245, 510, 572, 693, 712, 725
generational aspect of leadership, 295–296
generational envy, 203–204
George, Bill, 285, 744–745
Gersick, Connie, 557
Gerstner, C.R., 342
Gerstner, Louis, Jr., 719–720
Gervais, S., 252
Ghosn, Carlos, 680
Gibbons, Tracy, 743
Gibson, Rowan, 634
Gillette, 603
globalization, 20, 140, 269, 318–319, 324, 569–570, 571, 574–575, 576, 577–578, 587–588, 592, 596–597, 606, 740
Global Leadership and Organizational Behavior Effectiveness (GLOBE) database, 143–144, 336–337, 338, 341–348, 350–358, 368, 369, 370
Goebbels, Joseph, 310
Goel, A., 262

Goffman, Erving, 600
Goldstein, I., 252
Goleman, Daniel, 326
Gore & Associates, 631–632
Gould, Stephen Jay, 556
graduate business schools
    educational goals of, 4
    gap between purpose and practice in,
        4–6
grammar, as indicator of meaningful
    action, 86–91, 92
grammatical metaphor, 89–90
Gramsci, Antonio, 308
Grange, 528
Granovetter, Mark, 532
Greater Boston Interfaith Organization
    (GBIO), 532–533
"Great Man" theories of leadership, 122
Grossman, S.J., 239, 241, 243
groups. *See also* teams; work groups
    leadership education in, 711.
        See also leadership development
        programs
Grove, Andy, 200, 300

Haass, Richard, 312
Hackman, J. Richard, 67, 97, 479, 481,
    482, 555, 673
Hall, R.J., 162, 658, 667
Halliday, M.A.K., 84, 87–90
Hambrick, D.C., 28, 33, 37, 42, 51, 53,
    57, 67, 478
Hamilton, Gary G., 231
Hannah, Sean, 753
Hannan, M.T., 30, 169
Hansen, Morten, 629
hard power, 307, 309, 314–318
Harris, E., 338
Hart, O., 239, 241, 243
Hart, Paul t', 776
Harvard Business Review, 119
Harvard Business School, 293
    Alumni Workshop at, 468
    case method used at, 298
    "Leadership: Advancing an
        Intellectual Discipline" colloquium
        at, 6
    mission statement of, 4

New CEO Workshop at, 433–434,
    468–469
Harvard Research Center in
    Entrepreneurial History, 291–292,
    301
    Chandler at, 296–300
    Redlich at, 292–296
Hayek, Friedrich A., 270, 275
Hegel, Georg W.F., 79
Heifetz, Ronald, 311, 704–705, 785–786
Heineman, Ben, 572
Hennessy, T.J., Jr., 338
Hermalin, B., 248–249, 252, 277,
    278, 288
Hershey, Paul, 710
Hesburgh, Theodore, 269
Hesselbein, Frances, 286
Hewlett-Packard, 588
hierarchical organization
    consistency of leader's behavior
        across, 172–173
    paradox of leadership and position
        in, 164
    power and networks and, 321–322
    sociological approaches to leadership
        and, 236
high-growth industries, impact of CEO
    leadership in, 36–37
Highsmith, Jim, 621–622
Hill, L.A., 661
Hillary, Edmund, 520, 521
Hill-Popper, M., 119–120, 126, 132,
    141, 159, 624
Himalayan Committee, 520–521
historians, perspectives of, 291–301
History of American Business Leaders
    (Redlich), 293, 295, 300
Hitler, Adolf, 193, 310, 313, 317
Hobbes, Thomas, 624
Hollenbeck, George, 721
Hollinger International, 245
Homans, George C., 71
Howard, A., 682–683
How Buildings Learn (Brand), 632–633
Huising, R., 662, 663, 665, 666, 667
humane leadership, 351–352, 356, 367
Hume, David, 317
Hunt, John, 520–521
hypomania, 203

Iacocca, Lee, 312
Ibarra, Herminia, 395, 397, 667
IBM, 509, 577, 580, 581, 582, 583,
    601–602, 603, 605, 624–625
  corporate citizenship and, 584–586
  Gerstner and competency model at,
    719–720
  globalization and integrative work by,
    588–589, 589–594, 595
  Lenovo's acquisition of, 518–520
  Watson's power at, 316
idealizing transference, 196, 197–198
identification of members with groups,
    164–166
identification-with-the aggressor
    syndrome, 200
identity-based leaders, 657–674
  identity change in role transitions
    and, 660–662
  leader development and, 662–673
  meaning of identity in, 659
  studies on, 657–658
  transitions to leadership roles in,
    659–660
identity development
  in international companies, 602–604
  of women leaders, 391–392, 394, 395
IDEO, 615, 618
Immelt, Jeff, 317
implicit leadership theory (ILT), 336,
    340–343, 344
imposter feelings, 202
*Improving Organizational Effectiveness
    Through Transformational Leadership*
    (Bass), 11
incomplete contracts, 240–241
indirect influence, of CEOs, 443–450
industrial leadership, 229–230
Industrial Leadership (Gantt), 292
influence, 309, 414, 417–418
information revolution, 321–322
information-sharing teams, 488
Infosys, 592
Inner Circle, The (Useem), 231
inner circle theory, 231
innovation, 611–646
  co-design process in, 617–620
  community building as foundation
    for, 620–624

creative agility and, 618
creative abrasion and, 617–618
facing realities of, 614–620
future research agenda in, 639–646
integrative problem solving and,
    618–620
leaders and, 20, 626–634
leading from behind in, 635–639
Pixar example of, 613, 615–616
teams in, 616–617
Innovation to the Core (Skarzynski and
    Gibson), 634
institutional approach, in study of
    leadership, 232–233, 236
institutional theory, and meaning of
    leadership, 75–78, 144–145
integrative complexity, 162
integrative problem solving, 618–620
integrity, 242–243, 252, 255–256, 258,
    278–281, 285, 463–464
intentional model of organizing,
    169–170
internalization, 214, 215
internally competitive leadership,
    353–354, 367–368, 369
international companies, 569–608
  complexity and, 574, 575, 576–579
  common identity in, 602–604
  corporate citizenship and, 584–586
  diversity and, 574, 575
  globalization and national and local
    connections in, 580–584
  global trends and, 569–572
  iconic stories used by, 585–586
  integrative work and, 587–596
  organizational challenges for leaders
    of, 573–576
  purpose and values transmission in,
    579–580
  social capital used by, 594–596
  transparency and, 574
  uncertainty and, 574, 575
interventions, in leadership programs,
    215–217
iron law of oligarchy, 229
isolation from reality, and leadership
    failure, 198–199
Israel Defense Forces (IDF),
    750–751

J.P. Morgan Chase, 507, 508
Janis, Irving, 776
Jaques, E., 441
Jang, Sujin, 116
Jensen, Michael C., 30, 273, 274,
    278–279, 280, 282, 283, 285, 286
Jobs, Steve, 316, 615
Johnson & Johnson, 425
Jones, Jim, 310, 316
*Journal of Leadership and Organization
    Studies*, 132
Jung, D.I., 338
Junior Achievement, 292

Kahneman, Daniel, 521
kaizen, 247
Kanter, Rosabeth Moss, 569,
    595–596, 639
Kaplan, S., 251
Katzenbach, J.R., 476
Kegan, R., 742, 743, 744
Kellerman, Barbara, 305
Kennedy, J.K., Jr., 342
Kennedy, John F., 270, 417–418, 509
Kerr, Steven, 744
Khurana, Rakesh, 119–120, 126, 132,
    141, 159, 233, 418, 577, 586, 624
Kilts, Jim, 603
King, Martin Luther, Jr., 270, 530, 544
Kohlberg, L., 742, 744
Kotter, John P., 9, 11, 29, 68, 412,
    413, 453
Kouzes, James, 714
Kozlowski, Dennis, 143
Kramer, Roderick, 325, 465
Krishnan, V.R., 339–340
Krzyzewski, Mike, 266
Kuhnert, K.W., 743
Kunda, Gideon, 91

Lafley, A.G., 579
language of individuals
    as indicator of meaning in
        organization, 82–86
    political correctness in work groups
        and, 168–169
Lawler, Edward E., 415

Lawrence-Lightfoot, Sara, 641
Lay, Kenneth, 143
leader development. *See* leadership
    development programs
Leader Behavior Description
    Questionnaire (LBDQ), 123
Leader-Member Exchange theory
    (LMX), 125
Leaders (Bennis and Nanus), 286
Leadership (Burns), 305
"Leadership: Advancing an Intellectual
    Discipline" colloquium, Harvard
    Business School, 6
*Leadership and Performance Beyond
    Expectations* (Bass), 11, 68
Leadership Conference on Civil Rights,
    552
leadership development programs,
    709–737
    action learning development initia-
        tives in, 733–736
    advantages of interventions in,
        215–217
    authentic leadership development
        approach in, 739–740, 755–766
    changing leaders and, 205
    critical role of, 709–710
    customized programs for companies
        developed in, 712–713
    decision making and, 521–522
    development readiness and, 752–754
    economic incentives in, 712
    gap between purpose and practice in,
        4–6
    historical overview of early work in,
        710–713
    identification of the focal issue of
        participants in, 211–213
    identity-based leaders and, 662–673
    individual skill development in,
        715–722
    internalization and, 214–215
    leadership born versus made question
        in, 747–748, 751–752
    leadership teams and, 480
    moral capacity and, 743–745
    participation selection for, 211
    practitioner-scientists developed
        in, 740

leadership development programs
(*continued*)
  socializing leadership vision and
    values initiatives in, 722–727
  social movements and, 559–561
  strategic leadership initiatives in,
    727–733
  transformational leaders and,
    742–743, 745, 747–751
  transitional space in, 213–214
  typology of formal development
    approaches in, 715–736
leadership education. *See* leadership
  development programs
Leadership Factor, The (Kotter), 68
Leadership in Administration (Selznick),
  232
Leadership Quarterly, 132
Leadership Research Network, 5
leadership teams, 475–503
  activist leadership teams and,
    479–480
  agenda for, 497
  authority dynamics on, 491–495
  couching for, 499–500
  definition of, 477–478
  design of, 481–485
  essential competencies of executive
    and, 501–503
  features of, 480–495
  functions of leaders and, 475–476
  leaders of, 492, 495–501
  membership issues for, 485–489,
    497–498
  norms for, 498–499
  overloaded work of, 489–491
  purpose of, 484–485, 503
  as social systems, 502
  studies of, 478–480
  top management teams and, 478–479
  underperformance by, 476
Leadership Without Easy Answers
  (Heifetz), 705
leading by example, 248–250
Least Preferred Coworker (LPC)
  Scale, 124
Lee, Robert E., 509
legal-rational authority, 225, 314
legitimacy, of CEO leadership, 461–466

Lencioni, P., 476
Lenovo, 518–520, 521, 580
Leviathan (Hobbes), 624
Levinson, D.J., 671
Lévy, Maurice, 600
Lewin, K., 123
Lewis, P., 743
Likert, Rensis, 412
Lincoln, Abraham, 266, 277, 326
linguistics, and indicators of meaningful
  action, 84–85
Link, Edwin, 764
Linux, 643
Lippitt, R., 123
Loevinger, J., 784
Lord, Robert G., 340, 341, 342, 391,
  658, 667
Lukes, Steven, 306
Luthans, Fred, 756–757

Machiavelli, Niccoló, 317
Machiavellianism, 316–317
Magner, N.R., 339
Mahoney, T.A., 32
Maimonides, Moses, 537
Major, John, 316
Majumdar, S., 250, 261
Management and the Worker
  (Lawler), 415
Mandela, Nelson, 266, 635, 742
manic-depression, 203
Mann, Thomas, 227–228
March, James G., 8–9, 66, 141, 306
Marchand, Roland, 77
Marchioro, C.A., 162
Marcus, George, 534–535
Margolis, Joshua D., 75
Marine Corps' Officer Candidates
  School, 514
Marquis, C., 143
Marshall School of Business (University
  of Southern California), 271
Martin, Roger, 619–620
Maskin, Eric, 112
Mason, P.A., 478
Matthiessen, Christian M.I.M., 84
Mayo, Elton, 71, 125
McCall, Morgan, Jr., 721

McCauley, C., 682
McClelland, David, 326
McDonald, Bob, 579
McGahan, A.M., 40, 43
McGrath, Joseph, 475, 476
McGregor, Douglas, 412
McKinsey & Company, 425, 434
McNamara, Robert, 325
meaning of leadership, 65–100
  charismatic leadership and, 70–71
  common purpose for organization
    established by, 71–73
  criticisms of pursuing inquiries on,
    65–67
  decoupling the joint focus on
    leadership and, 74–78
  definition of meaningful action and,
    78–81
  grammatical indicators of, 86–91
  institutional theory of organizations
    on, 75–78, 232
  language of individuals as indicator
    of, 82–86
  meaning-making capacity of leaders
    and, 69–74
  operationalizing meaningful action in
    organizations and, 81–92
  organization theory on, 65–70
  scope of leadership activities and,
    92–97
  strong culture concept and, 91–92
Meat Products industry, CEO leader-
    ship in, 34–36, 35t, 36t, 38
mechanism design theory, 112
Meckling, William H., 30, 273
Mehra, P., 339–340
Meir, Golda, 379
member identification in groups,
    164–166
mental life triangle, 206–207
Merkel, Angela, 379
Metcalf, Henry C., 292
Meyer, John W., 77–78, 93–94
Michels, Robert, 228, 229
micro-interventions for leadership
    development, 760
micromanagement, 201
Milgram, Stanley, 776
Mills, C. Wright, 231, 233

minority members, in work groups,
    167–168
Mintzberg, Henry, 456, 681
Mirabeau, Comte de, 312
mirroring transference, 196–197
MIT, 633, 643
*Molding of American Banking, Men and
    Ideas, The* (Redlich), 293
Monte Cristo complex, 195
mood disorders, 203
Morgridge, John, 514
Morris, C.G., 482
Mosca, Gaetano, 233
motivation, of women leaders, 398–399
motivational interviewing, 209, 213, 216
motivational need systems, 188–190
Mount Everest expedition, 520–521
Mugabe, Robert, 193, 325
Mukand, S., 250, 261
Multifactor Leadership
    Questionnaire, 751
Myerson, R., 262

Nadler, D., 481, 491–492
Nanus, Burt, 269, 270, 274, 281, 286,
    287–288
narcissism, 193–196, 205, 465
national culture, 336, 339–340
Naval Academy, 299
neo-Marxist approach, 225, 233–234,
    235–236
Nestlé, 572
networks, and power, 318–325
Neustadt, Richard, 309, 456
New CEO Workshop (Harvard
    Business School), 433–434,
    468–469
New York Times Magazine, 388
Nicholson, N., 682
Noel, J., 659
Nohria, Nitin, 92, 125, 511, 630–631
Norgay, Tenzing, 520, 521
norms
  leadership teams and, 498–499
  work groups and, 167–169
Noyce, Robert, 300, 316
NRA, 528
Nucor, 276

Nussbaum, Martha, 534
Nye, Joseph S., Jr., 112

Obama, Barack, 533, 541, 542–543, 543–544, 545, 562–564
O'Connor, James F., 8, 11, 28, 31, 32, 49, 66, 224
O'Connell, M.K., 342
O'Connell, M.S., 342
Offerman, L.R., 342
Ogbonna, E., 338
Ohmae, Kenichi, 572
Oldham, Greg R., 97
Omron, 579–580, 585, 603
On Demand Community, 584
opportunities, and impact of CEO leadership, 33–36, 41–42, 53–54
Opposable Mind, The (Martin), 619–620
organizational context, for women leaders, 400–403
organizational culture, 336, 338
organizational ecology, 9
organizational theory, 8–9, 65–69
Organizational Weapon, The (Selznick), 82
organization behavior (OB), 7–10, 119–154
  behavioral theories of leadership in, 122–123
  contingency theories of leadership and, 123–124, 411–413
  cumulative theory-building approaches in, 142–144
  definition of leadership in, 121
  empirical research on leadership reported in, 126–140, 146–154
  institutional theory and, 144–145
  leadership theories in, 121–126
  psychological perspective of leadership traits in, 122
Organization Man, The (Whyte), 96
Organization Science (OS), 126–127, 146–154
overconfidence, 252, 255, 262

Palmer, D., 133–134
Palmisano, Samuel J., 322, 335–336, 577, 580, 581, 588, 589–590, 591, 593, 624–625

paradox of leadership, 163–164
paranoia, 200–201
Pareto, Vilfredo, 228–229
Parks, Rosa, 277
Parsons, Richard, 242, 255, 260
Parsons, Talcott, 232
path-goal theory of leadership, 124
Patten, Chris, 316
Paulson, Henry, Jr., 507–509, 511
Pelosi, Nancy, 377, 556
Pennebaker, James W., 83
People Express, 139
people orientation, in behavioral theories of leadership, 123
performance of organization
  changes of leadership and, 224
  contingent opportunities view of CEO leadership and, 27–28, 33–55
  definition of leadership and, 121
  impact of leadership on, 10–12, 172–173
  meaning of leadership linked to, 74–75, 77
  organizational theory on leaders and, 8–9, 65–67
  scope of leadership activities and, 92–97
  top management teams and, 477–478
personal authority, 225
personification of company, and CEOs, 440–441
Peterson, M.F., 339
Petriglieri, Jennifer, 395, 397
Pfeffer, Jeffrey, 32, 53, 67, 133
Pickett, George, 509
Pixar Animation Studio, 613, 615–616, 621, 643
Platt, Lewis, 516
Podolny, Joel, 108, 119–120, 126, 132, 141, 159, 577, 624
political correctness, and work groups, 168–169
political intelligence, 325
political skills, and power, 325–327
politics, women in, 378–379
Porter, Michael E., 43, 511
positional power, 417
positive organizational behavior (POB), 756–757
Posner, Barry, 714

power, 305–327
  contingency theory of leadership and,
    417–419
  definition of, 306–307
  followers and, 310–313
  mixture of hard and soft power,
    314–318
  networks and, 318–325
  paradox of leadership and, 164
  political skills and, 325–327
  soft power concept and, 307–310
Powerchex, 280
Power (Lukes), 306
Power Elite, The (Mills), 233
practitioner-scientists, 740
Prahalad, C.K., 642
primal leadership model, 161
principal-agent paradigm of the firm, 240
prisoner's dilemma, 267–269, 278, 279,
    286–287
Procter & Gamble (P&G), 579, 585,
    590, 598, 602, 603, 605
property-rights theory of the firm, 241,
    243–244
Protestant Ethic, The (Weber), 82
psychoanalysis, 186–188
psychodynamics of leadership, 192–198
  emotional pulse of followers and, 193
  narcissism and, 193–196
  transference and, 196–198
psychological capital (Psycap), 756–757,
    758, 759
psychological perspectives, 159–174
  behavioral flexibility and, 162–163
  coaching work group members and,
    166–167
  consistent signaling by leader and,
    171–173
  cooperation in work groups and,
    167–168
  culture as a leadership tool and,
    170–171
  diagnostic activity and, 161–162
  emotional intelligence and, 161–162
  group norms and, 167
  intentional model of organizing and,
    169–170
  leading organizations and, 169–173
  member identification with work
    groups and, 164–166

  paradox of leadership and, 163–164
  political correctness in, 168–169
  trait theories of leadership and, 122
Publicis Groupe, 571, 572, 600
public narrative, in social movements,
    533–545
purpose of an organization
  executive's role in establishing, 71–73
  institutional approach to leadership
    and, 232
  international companies and
    communicating, 579–580
  leadership teams and, 484–485, 503
purposive social systems, 107–108
Putnam, Robert, 532

Quelch, John, 323

Rahim, M.A., 339
Raith, M., 261
reactive narcissism, 194, 195–196
Reagan, Ronald, 417–418
Redlich, Fritz, 14, 292–296, 297,
    300, 301
reframing, 213
rehearsal, 214
Reichard, J., 755
relational bases of leadership, 125
relationship building, and change in
    social movements, 531–533
relationship triangle, 209–210
research on leadership
  lack of, 3–4
  organizational theory and, 8–10
  organization behavior (OB) approach
    in, 126–140
  sociological approaches to, 223–236
  state of, 6–7
resoluteness, 255
resources
  impact of CEO leadership and
    availability of, 37–38, 41–42, 53–54
  power and possession of, 307
return on development investment
    (RODI), 760–761, 763
Rezende, M., 250, 252
Rice, Condoleeza, 377
Rickover, Hyman, 316

Rittel, Horst, 640
Roberto, M., 485, 497
Roberts, Kevin, 600
Roethlisberger, Fritz J., 71
roles of leadership
  organizational theory on, 8–10
  paradox of leadership and, 164
  translating institutional context
    and, 145
Roosevelt, Franklin Delano, 312, 509
Roosevelt, Theodore, 277
Rosch, E., 340
Rotemberg, J.J., 29, 246–247, 249,
  284–285
Rousseau, Jean-Jacques, 79–80
Rowan, Brian, 77–78, 93–94
Roy, William G., 77
Rumelt, Richard P., 43, 299
Russo, J. Edward, 512

Saatchi & Saatchi, 600
Sakuta, Hisao, 579–580
Salancik, G.R., 32
Saloner, G., 29, 246–247, 249,
  284–285
Santander, 578
Sawyer, Keith, 614–615
Schein, E.H., 169–170, 338
Schein, Virginia, 384
Schendel, Dan, 299
Scherr, Allan, 274, 282, 283
Schmalensee, R., 43
Schmidt, Ronald M., 276
Schmidt, Warren H., 411
Schoar, A., 32
Schön, D., 783
Schumpeter, Joseph, 292, 294, 295
Schwartz, Alan, 507, 508, 509
Schwartz, S.H., 339
Schweitzer, Albert, 277
scientific management, 292
scripts, and personal behavior, 188,
  190–191
Scully, Gerald, 279–280
secondary gain concept, 208
self-authoring mind, 776–777
self-governing teams, 481
self-monitoring, 161, 162

self-sacrificial leadership, 337, 352–353,
  367, 368
self-transforming mind, 777–778
Selznick, Philip, 8, 16, 65, 69, 73, 75,
  77, 80–81, 232
sensitivity training, 711
Sentence Completion Test (SCT), 784
70 percent solution, in decision
  making, 514
sexism, 377, 385–386
Shaw, J.B., 341, 342
Shils, Edward, 70–71
Shinseki, Eric, 308
Shinhan Bank, 572, 590–591, 603–604
Shipton, Eric, 520
Shoemaker, Paul, 512
Sierra Club, 528, 555, 560–561
Silverstein, Michael, 84
Simmel, Georg, 234
Simon, H.A., 239
Simon Graduate School of Business,
  University of Rochester, 272–273
Sitkin, Sam, 558
Situational Leadership Model, 161, 710
Six Sigma, 574
Skarzynski, Peter, 634
Skilling, Jeffrey, 143
slack resources, and impact of CEO
  leadership, 37–38
Slater, Philip E., 67
Sloan School of Management (MIT),
  4–5
Smith, Adam, 267, 275, 315
Smith, Clifford W., Jr., 278–279,
  280, 285
Smith, John F., Jr., 680
Smith, P.B., 339
social capital, and international
  companies, 594–596
Social Contract and Discourses, The
  (Rousseau), 79–80
social identity theory, 164–165
social intelligence, 325–326
socialized mind, 775–776
social learning theory, 753
social movements, 527–561
  action mobilization in, 553–556
  background of leaders in, 529–531
  building relationships and, 531–533

social movements (*continued*)
campaigns in, 557–558
description of, 527–529
need for leadership to lead in, 527–528
strategy in, 545–552
structuring, 550–561
telling the story in, 533–545
social networks, 9, 225, 234–235, 236
Social Psychology of Organizing, The (Weick), 621
Social Science Research Network, 5
social systems, teams as, 502
sociological approaches to study of leadership, 223–236
institutional approach in, 232–233
main school of thought in, 225
neo-Marxist approach in, 233–234
number of articles published using, 223
relationship between leaders and led in, 224–225
social networks and, 234–235
Weberian approach in, 225–231
soft power, 307–310, 314–318
Song, Fenghua, 245
Sonin, K., 261
Speer, Albert, 310
Stalin, Joseph, 193, 742
Stanford Graduate School of Business, 4
Starbuck, W.H, 746
status-conscious leadership, 346–348, 361–366, 369
status of leaders, 164, 387–388
Steidlmeier, Paul, 745
Stewart, Martha, 143, 316
Stewart, Rosemary, 681
Stogdill, Ralph M., 66
storytelling, 212, 533–545
strategic leadership development initiatives, 727–733
strategy, in social movements, 545–552
Strategy and Structure (Chandler), 297–299, 300
Strauss, A.L., 671
strong culture concept, 91–92
Structural Holes (Burt), 234–235
Subject-Object Interview (SOI), 779, 780–781, 784

success
cooperation in work groups and, 168
defining criteria for, 108–109
leader's commitment to, 163
successors, reactions to appointing, 203–204
Suicide (Durkheim), 80
Summitt, Pat, 266
Supercorp (Kanter), 569
Survey of Current Business, Department of Commerce, 42
symbolic communication, 421
symbolism, and CEO leadership, 459–460

Tannenbaum, Robert, 411
task orientation, in behavioral theories of leadership, 122–123
Taussig, Frank, 292
Taylor, Charles, 541
Taylor, Frederick W., 292
Team Diagnostic Survey (TDS), 479, 481
team leaders
critical tasks for, 164
leadership teams and, 492, 495–501
leading by example by, 248–250
team player, leader as, 251
teams. *See also* leadership teams; work groups
coaching members in, 166–167
cooperation in, 167–168
group identification in, 164–166
group norms in, 167–169
innovation and, 616–617
political correctness in, 168–169
psychological perspectives on leading, 164–169
as social systems, 502
Teece, David, 299
Temirkanov, Yuri, 114–115
Terkel, Studs, 84–86
Thakor, A., 262
Thakor, Anjan, 245
Thatcher, Margaret, 199, 316, 325, 379
Theory of Economic Development, The (Schumpeter), 292, 295
Theory of Moral Sentiments (Smith), 315
Thomas, A.B., 27, 32, 33

Thyssen, August, 300
Tichy, Noel M., 68, 747
Tirole, J., 241, 244
Tocqueville, Alexis de, 559
Tonnies, Ferdinand, 11, 69
top management teams, 477, 478–479.
  See also leadership teams
Total Quality Management, 574
Toyota, 247–248, 322, 686
traditional authority, 225, 314
training in leadership. *See* leadership
  development programs
trait theories of leadership, 122,
  125, 142
transactional leadership, 125
transaction economics, 112
transference, 196–198, 210
Transformational Leader, The (Tichy and
  Devanna), 68
transformational leadership, 125, 384,
  742–743, 745, 748–752
Triandis, H.C, 343
trust, and CEO leadership, 462–463
Tuck School of Business (Dartmouth), 4
Tucker, Robert C., 305
Turner, V., 669
two-way communication, 242, 259–260,
  284–285
Tyo, 143

unconscious processes, 191
United Nations, 583
United Parcel Service (UPS), 421
U.S. Army, 723
U.S. Department of Commerce Survey
  of Current Business, 42
U.S. Naval Academy, 299
U.S. West Point Military Academy,
  753–754
Useem, Michael, 231, 233

values of organization
  consistency of leader's behavior
    regarding, 171–172
  leadership development programs
    using, 722–727
  significance to members of, 76–77

Van den Steen, E., 252
Van Gennep, A., 664, 666
Van Maanen, John, 91
Vedantam, Shankar, 379
Venn diagrams, 319
Visible Hand, The (Chandler), 293
vision
  commitment to, 278
  communication of, 282
  economic approaches to, 253–254,
    258, 269–274
  as element of effective leadership, 242
  impact of CEO leadership and, 29–30
  organizational architecture of,
    273–274
  sources of, 270–274
voluntary associations, 529
Vroom, Victor H., 160, 411–412
Vygotsky, L.S., 671

W.L. Gore & Associates, 631–632
Wageman, Ruth, 110, 555,
  560–561, 673
Walder, Andrew G., 231
Waldroop, James, 630
Walsh, James P., 75
Washington, George, 313
Watkins, M., 485, 497
Watson, Thomas J., 316
Wealth of Nations, The (Smith), 267, 275
Weber, Klaus, 75
Weber, Max, 7–8, 13, 65, 69–70, 71, 72,
  73, 77, 79, 81–82, 225, 229, 314,
  417, 418, 573
Weberian approach, 225–231, 235–236
Weick, K., 142, 145
Weick, Karl, 621
Weiner, N., 31–32
Welch, Jack, 245, 510
West, M., 682
West Point Military Academy, 753–754
White, R.K., 123
Whithead, C.J., 162
Whitman, Margaret, 509
Whyte, William H., 96
Williamson, O.E., 239
Wilson, James Q., 529
Winfrey, Oprah, 143

Winnicott, D.W., 669
Wirtz, P.W., 342
Wolf, Bob, 322
women leaders, 377–403
  agenda for future research on,
    394–403
  attitudinal barriers to, 384–388
  challenge for, 392–394
  consequences of lack of, 388–390
  diversity and, 389–390, 400–401, 403
  egalitarianism and, 347–348, 354,
    361, 366, 368
  gender differences and, 382–383,
    386, 389
  identity and skills development by,
    391–392, 395
  increasing prominence of, 377
  organizational context and, 400–403
  motivation of, 398–399
  role changes and, 377–378
  power and networks and, 323–325
  stereotypes and, 323–325, 379,
    384–385, 388, 397
  structural barriers to, 380–384
Work and Authority in Industry (Bendix),
  229–230

work groups. *See also* teams
  coaching members in, 166–167
  cooperation in, 167–168
  group identification in, 164–166
  group norms in, 167–169
  political correctness in, 168–169
  psychological perspectives on leading,
    164–169
Working (Terkel), 84–86
Workman, J.W., 162
World Values Survey, 355
Wriston, Walter, 572

Xerox PARC, 617

Yetton, Philip W., 411–412
Yukl, Gary, 141, 510

Zaffron, Steve, 278–279, 280, 285
Zaleznik, Abraham, 412, 413
Zelizer, Viviana A., 79
Zimmerman, Jerold L., 278–279,
  280, 285

About the Contributors

Bharat Anand is a professor in the Strategy Unit at Harvard Business School, where he teaches corporate strategy. He received an AB in economics, magna cum laude, from Harvard University and his PhD in economics from Princeton University, where he was also nominated to the Princeton Society of Fellows. Professor Anand's research is in applied and empirical industrial organization, and corporate strategy, and he is currently examining competition in information goods markets, with a primary focus on media and entertainment. His research focuses on two central strategic challenges that firms face in these markets: the challenge of "getting noticed" among the increasing clutter of alternatives that are widely available to consumers, and the challenge that firms face in "getting paid" for what they produce, since property rights over inputs and outputs are often difficult to establish in these markets.

Bruce J. Avolio, PhD, is the Marion B. Ingersoll Professor of Management and Executive Director, Foster Center for Leadership, at the University of Washington. Avolio has published five books and more than one hundred articles on leadership. His books include *Transformational and Charismatic Leadership: The Road Ahead* (Elsevier Science, 2002), *Full Leadership Development: Building the Vital Forces in Organizations* (Sage Publications, 1999), and *Developing Potential Across a Full Range of Leadership: Cases on Transactional and Transformational Leadership* (Lawrence Erlbaum Associates, 2000). His newest books are *Leadership Development in Balance: Made/Born* (Lawrence Erlbaum Associates, 2005) and *Authentic Leadership Development: Moments Matter* (McGraw-Hill, 2005).

Marya L. Besharov is Assistant Professor of Organizational Behavior at Cornell School of Industrial Labor Relations. She attained her PhD in organizational behavior at Harvard University in 2008.

Patrick Bolton is the David Zalaznick Professor of Business at Columbia Business School. He joined Columbia Business School in July 2005. He received his PhD from the London School of Economics in 1986 and holds a BA in economics from the University of Cambridge and a BA in political science from the Institut d'Études Politiques de Paris. He began his career as an assistant professor at the University of California, Berkeley and then moved to Harvard University, joining their economics department from 1987 to 1989. He was Chargé de Recherche at the C.N.R.S. Laboratoire d' Econométrie de L' École Polytechnique from 1989 to 1991, Cassel Professor of Money and Banking at the London School of Economics from 1991 to 1994, Chargé de Cours Associé at the Institut d'Études Européennes de l'Université Libre de Bruxelles from 1994 to 1998, and John H. Scully '66 Professor of Finance and Economics at Princeton University from 1998 to 2005. His research and areas of interest are in contract theory and contracting issues in corporate finance and industrial organization. A central focus of his work is on the allocation of control and decision rights to contracting parties when long-term contracts are incomplete. This issue is relevant in many different contracting areas, including the firm's choice of optimal debt structure, corporate governance and the firm's optimal ownership structure, vertical integration, and constitution design. He recently published his first book, *Contract Theory*, with Mathias Dewatripont and has coedited a second book, *Credit Markets for the Poor*, with Howard Rosenthal.

Greg Brandeau is the Senior Vice President of Technology at Pixar Animation Studios in Emeryville, California.

Markus K. Brunnermeier is the Edwards S. Sanford Professor at Princeton University. He is a member of the Department of Economics and affiliated with Princeton's Bendheim Center for Finance and the International Economics Section. He is also a research associate at CEPR, NBER, and CESifo, and an academic consultant to the Federal Reserve Bank of New York. He was awarded his PhD by the London

School of Economics (LSE), where he was also affiliated with its Financial Markets Group. He is a Sloan Research Fellow, an associate editor of the *Journal of Finance* and the *Review of Financial Studies*, and on the editorial board of the *Journal of Financial Intermediation*. His research spans economics and finance. He is primarily interested in studying financial crises and significant mispricings resulting from institutional frictions, strategic considerations, and behavioral trading. His work shows that a bubble can emerge and persist, since rational sophisticated traders prefer to ride it rather than attack it. His research also explains why liquidity dries up when it is needed most and has important implications for risk management. His research on belief distortions proposes a shift away from the rational expectations paradigm towards "optimal expectations."

Jennifer A. Chatman is Paul J. Cortese Distinguished Professor of Management, Haas School of Business, Affiliated Faculty of the Institute of Personality and Social Research, University of California, Berkeley. She holds a PhD in business administration from the University of California, Berkeley.

Jay A. Conger is the Henry Kravis Research Professor of Leadership Studies at Claremont McKenna College. He is also Senior Research Scientist at the Center for Effective Organizations at the University of Southern California in Los Angeles and visiting professor of Organizational Behavior at the London Business School. He is a prolific writer, having written or cowritten more than ninety articles and twelve books. Conger has two new books in progress, on best practices in leadership and CEO leadership. His most recent book is *The Practice of Leadership*.

Rich DeJordy is a PhD candidate at Boston College in organizational studies. His primary research interest is in institutional, network, and identity-based mechanisms of conformity in and of organizations and he has applied institutional theory and social identity theory in his research. Under that umbrella, his dissertation focuses on how agency is used to preserve and stabilize institutions that have come under threat. Empirically based on the creation of the Securities and Exchange Commission, his work uses grounded theory to examine the mechanisms used by agents attempting to restore stability to the stock market in the wake of the crash of 1929. His other research interests include leadership, social networks, and innovative applications of research methodologies.

Peter W. Dorfman is Professor and Department Head of the Department of Management at New Mexico State University. Dorfman's research interests span both the human resources management and organizational behavior fields. His articles on leadership, cross-cultural management, and employee discrimination have appeared in the *Journal of Applied Psychology, Academy of Management Journal, Academy of Management Review, Journal of Management,* and *Advances in International Comparative Management,* among others. He is currently investigating the impact of cultural influences on managerial behavior and leadership styles. In addition, he is an expert witness and consultant in employee discrimination and sexual harassment cases.

Robin J. Ely is Professor of Organizational Behavior at Harvard Business School. She investigates how organizations can better manage their race and gender relations while at the same time increasing their effectiveness. Her research in this area focuses on organizational change, group dynamics, learning, conflict, power, and social identity. Ely also teaches in Harvard's Executive Education programs, the IWF Leadership Foundation Fellow Program, and the Women's Leadership Forum. She has published numerous articles on these topics in books and journals and lectures both in the United States and abroad to academics and practitioners alike. She is currently launching a study of senior women's experiences of power and authority in professional service firms. For the past several years, Ely has maintained an active faculty affiliation at the Center for Gender in Organizations, Simmons Graduate School of Management, in Boston. Ely is a member of the Academy of Management and an Associate Editor of *Administrative Science Quarterly.*

Elisabet Engellau is Adjunct Clinical Professor of Management at INSEAD (Fontainebleau/Singapore). As Program Director at INSEAD's Global Leadership Center, she focuses on leadership development and coaching in executive programs. In addition, she regularly serves as visiting faculty at the Center for Creative Leadership, and the Stockholm School of Economics. She has been an affiliate professor at McGill University, Faculty of Management, and a teaching fellow at Harvard University and at Concordia University, Montreal. She has also produced and directed a number of films for management education and has recently been involved in developing two new feedback instruments. She is the coauthor (with Manfred Kets de Vries) of "Doing an Alexander: Lessons on Leadership by a Master Conqueror" (2004).

Walter A. Friedman (PhD, Columbia University) is a Research Fellow at Harvard Business School. He also serves as coeditor of *Business History Review*. He specializes in business, labor, and economic history. His book *Birth of a Salesman: The Transformation of Selling in America* (Harvard University Press, 2004) traced the history of selling from the days of peddlers and traveling drummers to the development of modern, professional sales forces. He is currently writing a history of economic forecasting agencies in the United States. He was formerly a Newcomen Post-Doctoral Fellow in Business History and a Trustee of the Business History Conference.

Marshall Ganz is a lecturer in Public Policy at Harvard Kennedy School. He entered Harvard College in the fall of 1960. In 1964, a year before graduating, he left to volunteer as a civil rights organizer in Mississippi. In 1965, he joined César Chávez and the United Farm Workers; over the next sixteen years he gained experience in union, community, issue, and political organizing and became the Union's Director of Organizing. During the 1980s, he worked with grassroots groups to develop effective organizing programs, designing innovative voter mobilization strategies for local, state, and national electoral campaigns. In 1991, in order to deepen his intellectual understanding of his work, he returned to Harvard College and, after a twenty-eight-year leave of absence, completed his undergraduate degree in history and government. He was awarded an MPA by the Kennedy School in 1993 and completed his PhD in sociology in 2000. He teaches, researches, and writes on leadership, organization, and strategy in social movements, civic associations, and politics.

Mary Ann Glynn is a Fellow of the Winston Center for Leadership and Ethics and the Joseph F. Cotter Professor of Organizational Studies at Boston College. She received her BA from Fordham University, her MA from Rider University, her MBA from Long Island University, and her PhD from Columbia University. Professor Glynn has taught PhD students at Yale University, Emory University, and the University of Michigan. By courtesy, she also serves as a professor of sociology. Her research interests are at the intersection of micro-level cognitive processes (such as learning, creativity, and intelligence) and cultural influences (social norms, institutional arrangements, and status affiliations) on identity, symbolism, and organizational leadership. Her research has been published in many leading journals, including the *Academy of Management Journal, Academy of Management Review, Organization Science, Strategic Management Journal, Journal of Applied Psychology, Journal of Management Studies, Journal of Marketing*, and *Poetics: International Journal of Empirical Research on Art, Media, and Literature*, as well as numerous edited books.

Mauro F. Guillén is Dr. Felix Zandman Professor in International Management; Professor of Management and Sociology, and Director, Joseph H. Lauder Institute for Management and International Studies at the Wharton School. His research interests include multinational and comparative management; and the sociology of organizations. He is the author of *The Rise of Spanish Multinationals* (Cambridge University Press, 2005) and *The Limits of Convergence: Globalization and Organizational Change in Argentina, South Korea, and Spain* (Princeton University Press, 2001), as well as numerous articles.

Laura Guillén Ramo is a postdoctoral fellow at INSEAD in Spain.

J. Richard Hackman is the Edgar Pierce Professor of Social and Organizational Psychology at Harvard University. He received his undergraduate degree in mathematics from MacMurray College in 1962 and his doctorate in social psychology from the University of Illinois in 1966. He taught at Yale until 1986, when he moved to Harvard. Hackman conducts research on a variety of topics in social and organizational psychology, including team dynamics and performance, social influences on individual behavior, and the design and leadership of self-managing groups and organizations. He is on the editorial board of several professional journals, and has consulted to a variety of organizations on issues having to do with work design, leadership, and team effectiveness. He has published numerous articles and seven books, the most recent being *Leading Teams: Setting the Stage for Great Performances*. Hackman was awarded the Sixth Annual AIR Creative Talent Award in the field of "Measurement and Evaluation: Individual and Group Behavior," the Distinguished Scientific Contribution Award of the American Psychological Association's division on industrial and organizational psychology, and both the Distinguished Educator Award and the Distinguished Scholar Award of the Academy of Management. In 2004, *Leading Teams* won the Academy of Management's Terry Award for the most outstanding management book of the year.

Paul J. Hanges is the Director of Graduate Studies and Associate Chair of the Department of Psychology at the University of Maryland. He is also a coprincipal investigator of the Global Leader and Organizational Behavior Effectiveness (GLOBE) research project. This multiyear, multination project seeks to determine the relationship between leadership traits and organizational and societal culture. Currently, Hanges is on the editorial board of the *Leadership Quarterly* and *Journal of Applied Psychology*.

Linda A. Hill is the Wallace Brett Donham Professor of Business Administration and the faculty chair of the Leadership Initiative at Harvard Business School. She is the author of *Becoming a Manager: How New Managers Master the Challenges of Leadership* (2nd edition). She is also author of the course modules *Managing Your Career*, *Managing Teams*, and *Power and Influence* and of the award-winning multimedia management development programs *High Performance Management*, *Coaching*, and *Managing for Performance*. Hill is currently working on three projects: becoming a boss in the twenty-first-century context; leadership in emerging markets; and leadership for innovation.

Jon Paul Howell is Professor Emeritus at New Mexico State University. He has published the leadership textbook *Understanding Behaviors for Effective Leadership* as well as book chapters and articles in various management journals. He has received several awards for his research and is a member of the Global Leadership and Organizational Behavior Effectiveness project. His primary research interests are leadership and followership, leadership across cultures, and substitutes for leadership.

Herminia Ibarra is the Cora Chaired Professor in Leadership and Learning at INSEAD, faculty director of the INSEAD Leadership Initiative, and a member of the INSEAD Board. She received her MA and PhD from Yale University, where she was a National Science Fellow. Prior to joining INSEAD in 2002 she served on the Harvard Business School faculty for thirteen years. A native of Cuba, Professor Ibarra is an expert on professional and leadership development. Her book *Working Identity: Unconventional Strategies for Reinventing Your Career* (Harvard Business School Press, 2003) documents how people reinvent themselves at work. Her numerous articles on innovation, networking, career development, women's careers, and professional identity are published in leading journals including the *Harvard Business Review*, *Administrative Science Quarterly*, *Academy of Management Review*, *Academy of Management Journal*, and *Organization Science*. Ibarra directs The Leadership Transition, an executive program designed for managers moving into broader leadership roles, and Women Leading Change in Global Business, INSEAD's first program for executive women.

Mansour Javidan is Dean of Research and Garvin Distinguished Professor at the Thunderbird School of Global Management. His research interests include cross-cultural issues, global leadership, mergers and acquisitions, strategic management, and international management.

Rosabeth Moss Kanter holds the Ernest L. Arbuckle Professorship at Harvard Business School, where she specializes in strategy, innovation, and leadership for change. Her strategic and practical insights have guided leaders of large and small organizations worldwide for over twenty-five years, through teaching, writing, and direct consultation to major corporations and governments. The former editor of *Harvard Business Review* (1989–1992), Professor Kanter has been named to lists of the "50 most powerful women in the world" (*Times of London*), and the "50 most influential business thinkers in the world" (Accenture and Thinkers 50 research). In 2001, she received the Academy of Management's Distinguished Career Award for her scholarly contributions to management knowledge, and in 2002 was named "Intelligent Community Visionary of the Year" by the World Teleport Association. Kanter is the author or coauthor of seventeen books, which have been translated into seventeen languages. Her recent book, *Confidence: How*

Winning Streaks and Losing Streaks Begin and End (a *New York Times* business and #1 *BusinessWeek* bestseller), describes the culture and dynamics of high-performance organizations as compared with those in decline, and shows how to lead turnarounds, whether in businesses, hospitals, schools, sports teams, community organizations, or countries. She chairs a Harvard University group creating an innovative initiative on advanced leadership, to help successful leaders at the top of their professions apply their skills to addressing challenging national and global problems.

Robert Kegan is the William and Miriam Meehan Professor in Adult Learning and Professional Development at Harvard Graduate School of Education. He holds the Educational Chair at the Institute for Management and Leadership in Education and is Codirector of the Change Leadership Group. Kegan is a psychologist who teaches, researches, writes, and consults about adult development, adult learning, and professional development. His work explores the possibility and necessity of ongoing psychological transformation in adulthood; the fit between adult capacities and the hidden demands of modern life; and the evolution of consciousness in adulthood and its implications for supporting adult learning, professional development, and adult education. Kegan, a licensed clinical psychologist and practicing therapist, lectures widely to professional and lay audiences, and consults in the area of professional development.

Jessica A. Kennedy is a PhD candidate at the Haas School of Business, University of California, Berkeley.

Manfred Kets de Vries is a Clinical Professor of Leadership Development who holds the Raoul de Vitry d'Avaucourt Chair of Leadership Development at INSEAD. He is the Director of INSEAD's Global Leadership Centre (IGLC), the Program Director of INSEAD's top management seminar, "The Challenge of Leadership: Creating Reflective Leaders," and of the programs "Consulting and Coaching for Change: Creating Reflective Change Agents" and "Leadership for Creativity: Insights to Expand the Limits of Organizational Performance." Kets de Vries has also held professorships at McGill University's École des Hautes Études Commerciales in Montreal and the Harvard Business School in Boston and has lectured at management institutions around the world. He is a founding member of the International Society for the Psychoanalytic Study of Organizations. The *Financial Times*, *Le Capital*, *Wirtschaftswoche*, and the *Economist* have judged Kets de Vries one of world's leading thinkers on leadership. He is the author, coauthor, or editor of more than thirty books and has published over three hundred scientific papers as chapters in books or as articles. Kets de Vries is also the first non-American recipient of the International Leadership Award for "his contributions to the classroom and the boardroom" by the International Leadership Association (ILA).

Lisa Lahey is Research Director of the Change Leadership Group at the Graduate School of Education, Harvard University.

Jay Lorsch is the Louis Kirstein Professor of Human Relations at the Harvard Business School. He is the author of over a dozen books, the most recent of which are *Back to the Drawing Board: Designing Boards for a Complex World* (with Colin B. Carter, 2003), *Aligning the Stars: How to Succeed When Professionals Drive Results* (with Thomas J. Tierney, 2002), and *Pawns or Potentates: The Reality of America's Corporate Boards* (1989). *Organization and Environment* (with Paul R. Lawrence) won the Academy of Management's Best Management Book of the Year Award and the James A. Hamilton Book Award of the College of Hospital Administrators in 1969. He is currently Chairman of the Harvard Business School Global Corporate Governance Initiative and Faculty Chairman of the Executive Education Corporate Governance Series.

Morgan W. McCall Jr., is Professor of Management and Organization at Marshall School of Business, University of Southern California.

Joseph S. Nye Jr., University Distinguished Service Professor, is also the Sultan of Oman Professor of International Relations and former Dean of the Kennedy School. He received his bachelor's degree, summa cum laude, from Princeton University, did postgraduate work at Oxford University on a Rhodes Scholarship, and earned a PhD in political science from Harvard. He has served as Assistant Secretary of Defense for International Security Affairs, Chair of the National Intelligence Council, and Deputy Undersecretary of State for Security Assistance, Science, and Technology. In 2004, he published *Soft Power: The Means* *to Success in World Politics*; *Understanding International Conflict* (5th edition); and *The Power Game: A Washington Novel.*

Joel M. Podolny is the former Dean of the Yale School of Management. On 2009 he assumed the position of Vice President and Dean of Apple Inc.'s new venture, Apple University. Prior to his arrival at Yale, he was Professor and Director of Research at Harvard Business School, where he taught courses in business strategy, organizational behavior, and global management. Podolny was also a faculty member at Stanford Graduate School of Business for eleven years; he held the position of Senior Associate Dean during the latter part of his Stanford tenure. Podolny has developed a sociological theory of market competition based on status dynamics. To do so, he has examined a variety of industries including venture capital, semiconductors, and investment banking. Podolny has also conducted research on the role of social networks in mobility and information transfer within organizations. He is the author of *Status Signals: A Sociological Study of Market Competition* and coauthor (with Garth Saloner and Andrea Shepard) of the textbook *Strategic Management.* Podolny earned his AB, magna cum laude, AM, and PhD degrees from Harvard University.

Michael E. Porter is the Bishop William Lawrence University Professor at Harvard Business School and a leading authority on competitive strategy; the competitiveness and economic development of nations, states, and regions; and the application of competitive principles to social problems such as health care, the environment, and corporate responsibility. Porter is generally recognized as the father of the modern strategy field, and has been identified in a variety of rankings and surveys as the world's most influential thinker on management and competitiveness. In 2001, Harvard Business School and Harvard University jointly created the Institute for Strategy and Competitiveness, dedicated to furthering Professor Porter's work. He is the author of eighteen books and over 125 articles.

Deborah L. Rhode is Ernest W. McFarland Professor of Law at Stanford Law School, she is also one of the nation's leading scholars in the fields of legal ethics and gender, law, and public policy. An author of twenty books, including *Women and Leadership* and *Moral Leadership*, she is the most frequently cited scholar in legal ethics. She is the director of the Stanford Center on the Legal Profession. Rhode is the former president of the Association of American Law Schools, the former chair of the American Bar Association's Commission on Women in the Profession, the founder and former Director of Stanford's Center on Ethics, and the former Director of the Michelle R. Clayman Institute for Gender Research at Stanford.

Scott Snook is an Associate Professor at the Harvard Business School and serves on the faculty of the Program for Leadership Development in HBS executive education. He graduated with honors from West Point and was commissioned in the U.S. Army Corps of Engineers, where he served in various command and staff positions for over twenty-two years, earning the rank of Colonel before retiring in 2002. Among his military decorations are the Legion of Merit, Bronze Star, Purple Heart, and Master Parachutist badge. He has an MBA from Harvard Business School, where he graduated with high distinction as a Baker Scholar. Snook earned his PhD in organizational behavior from Harvard University, winning the Sage-Louis Pondy Best Dissertation Award from the Academy of Management for his study of the friendly fire shootdown in Northern Iraq. Until July of 2002, Colonel Snook served as an Academy Professor in the Behavioral Sciences and Leadership Department at the United States Military Academy. He also directed West Point's Center for Leadership and Organizations Research as well as its joint Master's Program in Leader Development. Snook's book *Friendly Fire* was selected by the Academy of Management to receive the 2002 Terry Award. He has also coauthored *Practical Intelligence in Everyday Life*, a book that explores the role of "common sense" in leadership.

Emily Stecker is a research assistant at Harvard Business School.

Maurizio Travaglini is the founder and CEO of Architects of Group Genius in Milan, Italy.

Michael Useem is the William and Jacalyn Egan Professor and Director of the Center for Leadership and Change Management at Wharton School, University of Pennsylvania. His research focuses on leadership, decision making, and governance; and corporate change and restructuring. He is the author of numerous articles. His most recent book is *The Go Point: When It's Time to Decide* (Crown Business, 2006).

Laura Veldkamp is Associate Professor of Economics at the Stern School of Business, New York University. Professor Veldkamp earned a BA in applied mathematics and economics from Northwestern University and a PhD in economic analysis and policy from Stanford Graduate School of Business. Professor Veldkamp's research focuses on how individuals, investors, and firms get their information, how that information affects the decisions they make, and how those decisions affect the macroeconomy and asset prices. Her work spans macroeconomics, monetary economics, international finance, microeconomic theory, and asset pricing. Professor Veldkamp has published articles in the *American Economic Review*, *Journal of Finance*, *Review of Economic Studies*, *Journal of Economic Theory*, and *Journal of Monetary Economics*.

Ruth Wageman is Associate Professor of Business Administration at Dartmouth University. Her teaching, consulting, and research focus on leadership and team effectiveness. Her current research interests include the uses and misuses of power in teams, the influence of task and reward system designs on team effectiveness, and effective team coaching.

Noam Wasserman is Associate Professor at Harvard Business School, where he teaches a second-year MBA elective, "Founders' Dilemmas: Money and Power in Entrepreneurial Ventures." The course is based on his research over the last decade into the tough early choices that founders face that have important long-term implications for them and their ventures. He is one of three members of the core faculty of the Kauffman Foundation's Global Scholars program, and has delivered numerous keynote addresses to meetings of the Young Presidents Organization (YPO) and various entrepreneurship conferences. Wasserman received his PhD in organizational behavior (with concentrations in sociology and microeconomics) from Harvard University in 2002, and received an MBA (with high distinction) from Harvard Business School in 1999, graduating as a Baker Scholar. He received a BSE, magna cum laude, in computer science and engineering from the

School of Engineering at the University of Pennsylvania, and a BS, magna cum laude, in corporate finance and strategic management from the Wharton School at the University of Pennsylvania.

Mark A. Zupan is the Dean of the Simon School of Business at the University of Rochester as well as Professor of Economics and Public Policy. Before assuming these positions in 2004, Zupan served as Dean and Professor of Economics at the University of Arizona's Eller College of Management from 1997 to 2003, where he organized several successful fundraisers and improved community outreach. Before teaching at Eller College, Zupan taught at the University of South Carolina's Marshall School of Business, where he also served as Associate Dean of the masters program. Zupan was a teaching fellow in Harvard's Department of Economics while pursuing his doctoral studies at MIT. Zupan is the coauthor of *Microeconomic Theory and Applications* with Edgar K. Browning and *Microeconomic Cases and Applications* with T.W. Gillian and A.M. Marino. Zupan is also the author of several scholarly articles featured in leading publications including the *American Economic Review*, *Journal of Law and Economics*, *Rand Journal of Economics*, *Public Choice*, and *Journal of Regulatory Economics*.

About the Editors

Rakesh Khurana is the Marvin Bower Professor of Leadership Development at the Harvard Business School. He teaches a doctoral seminar on Management and Markets and The Board of Directors and Corporate Governance in the MBA program. Professor Khurana received his BS from Cornell University and his AM in Sociology and PhD in Organization Behavior from Harvard University. Prior to attending graduate school, he worked as a founding member of Cambridge Technology Partners in sales and marketing. His most recent book, *From Higher Aims to Hired Hands: The Social Transformation of American Business Schools and the Unfulfilled Promise of Management as a Profession* (2007: Princeton University Press), chronicles the evolution of management as a profession, with particular focus on the institutional development of the MBA. Khurana's work argues that without a recommitment to the professionalization project, business schools risk devolving into narrow vocational schools and serving largely as a credentialing system, ultimately weakening the legitimacy of MBA programs and contributing to a business culture that garners low trust and low legitimacy in society. *From Higher Aims to Hired Hands* received the American Sociological Association's Max Weber Book Award in 2008 for most outstanding contribution to scholarship in the past two years. The book was also the winner of the Association of American Publishers' 2007 Best Professional/Scholarly Publishing Book in Business, Finance, and Management.

Nitin Nohria is Richard P. Chapman Professor of Business Administration at Harvard Business School. His research centers on human motivation, leadership, and corporate transformation and sustainable performance. Coauthor of more than ten books, his most recent, *Paths to Power: How Insiders and Outsiders Shaped American Business Leadership* (with Anthony Mayo and Laura Singleton), chronicles how leaders from different backgrounds rose to power in American business. This is a companion book to *In Their Time* (with Anthony Mayo), which draws lessons from some of the greatest American business leaders of the twentieth century. His other books include: *What Really Works: The 4+2 Formula for Sustained Business Success* (with William Joyce and Bruce Roberson), a systematic large-scale study of management practices that truly differentiate business winners; *Changing Fortunes: Remaking the Industrial Corporation* (with Davis Dyer and Frederick Dalzell),which examines the decline of industrial firms in the last quarter of the twentieth century and discusses what can be learned from this experience; *Driven: How Human Nature Shapes Our Choices* (with Paul Lawrence), which explores four basic drives that shape human motivation and choice; *Master Passions: Emotion, Narrative, and the Development of Culture* (with Mihnea Moldoveanu), a discussion of how the passions shape not only our individual lives but our social and organizational culture as well; and *The Arc of Ambition: Defining the Leadership Journey* (with James Champy), which examines the role of ambition in the making of great achievers. He is also the author of over seventy-five journal articles, book chapters, cases, working papers, and notes.